John Palmer, Robert Henry Codrington

A dictionary of the language of Mota

With a short grammar and index

John Palmer, Robert Henry Codrington

A dictionary of the language of Mota
With a short grammar and index

ISBN/EAN: 9783744723275

Printed in Europe, USA, Canada, Australia, Japan

Cover: Foto ©Paul-Georg Meister /pixelio.de

More available books at **www.hansebooks.com**

A DICTIONARY

OF THE

LANGUAGE OF MOTA,

SUGARLOAF ISLAND. BANKS' ISLANDS.

BY

REV. R. H. CODRINGTON, D.D.

LATE OF THE MELANESIAN MISSION,

AND

VEN. J. PALMER, B.D.

ARCHDEACON OF SOUTHERN MELANESIA.

WITH A SHORT GRAMMAR AND INDEX.

SOCIETY FOR PROMOTING CHRISTIAN KNOWLEDGE,
LONDON : NORTHUMBERLAND AVENUE, W.C.
1896.

PREFACE.

The language of Mota is spoken as their native tongue by some eight hundred people, and has never probably been spoken in a past generation by more than a thousand. It derives its only importance from its having become, by circumstances rather than by choice, the language used as a common medium of communication in the Melanesian Mission. Being used in translations, in the oral teaching given to natives of many widely distant islands, and in the inter-communication of those so taught which has now continued for thirty years, it has become, next to the language of Fiji, the most generally known of the Melanesian tongues. It has certainly merits of its own; it is phonologically free from the difficulties which beset some of the languages of the same and of neighbouring groups; and it is full, precise and flexible enough for use in teaching and in translations. A Mota Dictionary may be taken as exhibiting a specimen of the group of languages to which it belongs; and should be followed by Dictionaries or ample Vocabularies of the languages of the principal islands in which the Melanesian Mission is at work.

Mota, Sugarloaf I., is one of the Banks' Group, which lies to the north of the New Hebrides. The Mota language is closely connected with the other languages and dialects of the Banks' Islands, and of the northernmost islands of the New Hebrides. These belong to a well-defined group of Melanesian languages; and these again are members of the great family of Oceanic Languages spoken throughout the island world, which stretches from the coasts of Africa and Asia to the most Eastern groups of Polynesia. In this wide expanse Madagascar and Formosa are included, but Australia and, in the main, New Guinea are left out.

The Languages of the Ocean Family fall naturally into place in four principal geographical areas: Indonesia, Micronesia, Melanesia, and Polynesia. These are found to form convenient philological divisions.

1. The Indonesian Group includes the language of Madagascar with those of the Malay Archipelago; the principal members of it are Malagasy, Malay, the various languages of the Philippine Islands, Sumatra, Java, Borneo, Celebes, and of the islands eastwards towards New Guinea.

2. The Micronesian Group takes in the Caroline Islands, the Pellew, Marshall, and Gilbert Islands.

3. The Melanesian languages are those spoken by the present inhabitants of the great chain of islands which extends from the East of New Guinea to New Caledonia, including Fiji.

4. The Polynesian languages of the Eastern Pacific are well known as those of Samoa, Tonga, Hawaii, and the Maori of New Zealand.

Upon a general view of these very numerous and widespread tongues, Mr. Sidney Ray has advanced four propositions: 1. The Vocabulary throughout shews evidence of a common origin. 2. The differences which appear in the grammar are modifications of the same method rather than differences of structure. 3. The principal constructive particles are the same. 4. The languages are in various stages of condition, of which the latest is that of the Polynesian.

With reference to the Mota language in particular two points may be touched with advantage. Mr. Ray has observed that comparison of two or more lists of words brought together from very distant parts of the area occupied by the Oceanic Languages seldom fails to shew agreement; and this by no means only in the names of things which commerce would carry with it. He selects among others three words, representing the English 'leaf,' 'fish-hook,' 'fathom.' Beginning with the Malagasy and ending with the Mota forms, these words may be thus arranged—Leaf: Malagasy, *ravina*, Malay, *dawun*, Philippine, *dahon*, Micronesia, *ra*, New Hebrides, *rau*, Polynesian, *rau*, Mota, *naui*. Hook: Malagasy, *havitra*, Malay, *kawit*, Philippine, *kait*, Micronesia, *kaj*, New Hebrides, *ngau*, Mota, *gau*. Fathom: Malagasy, *refy*, Malay, *depa*, Sumatra, *dopa*, Celebes, *refa*, Philippine, *dopa*, New Guinea, *rof*, Mota, *rova*. Words that can in this way be traced across vast distances of ocean are often the names of insignificant objects, as will be seen in the examples given in the Dictionary. The abundant illustration, given by Professor Kern, of the Fiji language by the languages of the Malay Archipelago and Madagascar shews in a striking and incontrovertible manner the large stock of words common in various forms to the most widely distant members of the Family.

In the second place a few words are needed to make clear the relation between the Polynesian and the Melanesian groups of languages. It is certain that many words are common to both, and it is certain also that there are among Melanesians colonies or settlements of Polynesian people of pure Polynesian speech. In Mota, in particular, there are many words which are evidently the same with those that answer to them in Samoa. To the question whether generally the Melanesian vocabularies have borrowed the words common to them and to the Polynesian from the Eastern Polynesian islands, an affirmative answer is hardly likely now to be given. It was natural that missionaries, for example, who found in New Guinea what they had left in Samoa, should be disposed to think so; but it is impossible to hold such an opinion when it is known that these words, common to Polynesia and Melanesia, are common also, in very large measure, to Micronesia and Indonesia; and further, that these common words have, as a rule, a fuller form in Melanesian than in Polynesian languages. If the question be narrowed to the comparison of Mota and Samoa one example will suffice, the interrogative 'what.' To follow the series in which, geographically, the Indonesian *apa, aha,* pass to New Guinea *saha, tava, daha,* and Melanesian *sava, hava, taha, safa, cava,* and to the Polynesian *aha, aa, a,* leaves no doubt that the Mota *sava* and the Samoan *a* are the same word; but no one can believe that Mota borrowed *sava* from Samoa. When Vocabulary is left for Grammar, the respective uses of the suffixed personal pronouns indicating possession in Melanesian and Polynesian languages point plainly in the same direction.

No attempt has been made in this Dictionary to bring together all the words from cognate tongues which may be taken to be parallel to the Mota forms. It has been my aim to produce illustrative examples which may suffice to shew the connexion of the Mota language with the others. If in comparison with a Mota word examples can be brought from the three great divisions of the Ocean Family outside the limits of the Melanesian groups, and some for further illustration from within those limits, enough has been done to carry out this purpose. In this I have been particularly indebted to Mr. Ray for the assistance he has kindly afforded me.*

The vocabulary of this Dictionary by no means exhausts the stock of words belonging to the language; there are certainly very many which we have not learnt; and we cannot hope that all we give are correctly interpreted. The language is a living one, and is free to use its own resources of prefixes and suffixes, for enlarging the vocabulary now furnished. Everything presented to the eye, every action, has its proper name in native use appropriated to it; and these words intercourse with Europeans tends rather to diminish than to increase in number.

The examples which are given with some words are almost all written or dictated by natives. A keen interest was taken by those with whom the vocabulary was last revised, and their help has been much missed in the compilation of the Dictionary in England.

No English-Mota Dictionary is given; but an Index is added to facilitate reference to the Mota words. The student of language will probably be content with this, and to those who wish to speak the language it is no gain to have more. The first care of one who desires to use the language should be lest any Mota word should be taken to be the equivalent of the English word which it appears to represent. To avoid 'dog' Mota is the great thing. It is probable that some corruption of a native language is inevitable in Mission work, in which the language must be used before it is known; and no great harm is done. But great mischief is done when a native language is weakened and impoverished for teaching and translating by the use of an incorrect and narrow vocabulary. It is not only that the usefully effective richness of the native vocabulary is lost, but with it is lost, too probably, some of the activity of the native mind, for natives will follow their teachers.

* Mr. Ray has selected the following words as good examples of the wide extension of a common vocabulary. Aka, asu, av; Gana, gau, gil, gima; Iga, ima; Lan, lano, lava, lisa, lum, lumuta; Manu, mana, maran, mata, matagtag, mate, matur, maur; Nana, namu, nat, naui; Pepe, pul, pun, putoi; Qon; Ronotag, rova; Sus; Tae, tali, tano, tanu, tani, tas, tir, toliu, totou, tou, tul, tun; Ulo, ului, uma, ura, utoi, uwa; Vanua, var, vat, vatiu, vava, vavine, vitu; Wose.

The same danger besets the learner in the matter of the sounds of native language. These are, almost as a matter of course, represented by Roman letters. It is natural that the European should assume that these have in the native tongue the same value that they have in his own; an Englishman, for example, tends to pronounce g, t, p, v, in Mota as in English. Thus the danger everywhere is that the true native language will perish in words and sounds, and that a new and inferior form of speech will supplant the true original in the mouths of the natives themselves.

R. H. C.

Chichester, March 1896.

REFERENCES TO PLACES AND LANGUAGES.

Ar. Araga, Pentecost or Whitsuntide, New Hebrides.
Bat. Batak, Sumatra; Bks. I. Banks' Islands; Bis. Bisaya, Philippine Islands.
Cel. Celebes.
D.Y. Duke of York Island; Dy., Day. Dayak, Borneo.
Esp. Sto. Espiritu Santo, New Hebrides.
Fij. Fiji Islands; Fl. Florida, Solomon Islands.
Gil. Gilolo; Gilb. Gilbert Islands, Micronesia.
Hawn. Hawaii, Sandwich Islands.
Jav. Java.
Kerep. Kerepunu, New Guinea.
Lak. Lakona, Banks' Islands; Lep. Lepers' Island, New Hebrides; Lif. Lifu, Loyalty Islands.
Macas. Macassar, Celebes; Mae. Maewo, Aurora Island, New Hebrides; Mal. Malay; Mala. Malanta, Solomon Islands; Malag. Malagasy, Madagascar; Mao. Maori of New Zealand; Marsh. Marshall Islands, Micronesia; Mel. Melanesian; Merl. Meralava, Banks' Islands; Motu, New Guinea; Mtl. Motlav, Banks' Islands.
N.B. New Britain, Bismarck Archipelago; N.G. New Guinea; N. Georgia, Solomon Islands; N.H. New Hebrides.
O.J. Old Javanese.
Paumotu, Low Archipelago; Pent. Pentecost, New Hebrides; Phil. Philippines; Pol. Polynesian; Pon. Ponape, Caroline Islands.
Sam. Samoa; San Cr. San Cristoval, Solomon Islands; Sta Cr. Sta Cruz; Sta M. Sta Maria, Gaua, Banks' Islands; Savu Island near Timor; Ses. Sesake, Three Hills, New Hebrides; Sol. Solomon Islands.
Tag. Tagala, Philippine Islands; Tong. Tonga, Friendly Islands.
Ul. Ulawa, Contrariété Island, Solomon Islands.
V.L. Vanua Lava, Banks' Islands.
Yap, Caroline Islands.

ABBREVIATIONS.

act. active; adj. adjective; adv. adverb; art. article.
conj. conjunction; constr. constructed; comp. compounded.
def. definite, definitive; dem. demonstrative; determ. determinative.
ex. excl. exclamation; excl. exclusive.
fem. feminine.
incl. inclusive; indef. indefinite; inf. infinitive; intens. intensitive; interj. interjection; interr. interrogative; imper. imperative; impers. impersonal.
(k) marks a noun as taking suffixed pronouns, k, ma, na. See Nouns 1.
M. a word of Maligo, of one dialect of Mota; met. metaphorical; metath. metathesis.
n. noun; n. v. neuter verb; neg. negative; neut. neuter.
part. particle; pers. person; pers. art. personal article; pl. plural; poss. possessive; pr. pronoun; pref. prefix; prep. preposition; prov. proverbial.
redupl. reduplication.
sing. singular; suff. suffix.
term. termination; tr. transitive.
V. a word of Veverau, of one dialect of Mota; v. verb; v. n. verbal noun; v. p. verbal particle; voc. vocative.

SHORT GRAMMAR.

I. ALPHABET. Letters of the Roman Alphabet are used to represent the sounds of the native speech; but it may be said that few letters represent precisely the same sound in Mota and in English. The language is printed in the main for the use of native people, and for the sake of simplicity a single letter is used where diacritical marks would be required to exhibit differences with exactness; as e.g. in the vowels and in the consonants q, r. No letters are used arbitrarily; the letter is used as representing the sound in the native language which answers in a general way to that which is commonly represented by that letter; as e.g. t, p, and v are not equivalent to English t, p, and v, and g is far from the hard English g; yet the dental, labial, and guttural character is common. In one case only is an italic letter in common use among the Roman type; *n* is printed for ng, which represents a variation of n. In writing, dots are added above the n; and when, as in this Dictionary, Mota words are printed in italics, the change is shown by a Roman n.

Aspirates are unknown.

Vowels; a, e, i, o, u, with their proper sound. There is a longer and shorter a, e, i. A broad a, as in *gap*, may be taken for a short o; but is to the native without question a. So also a sound of o may be taken for u, as in the English 'pull,' in a close syllable, e.g. in tol *toa*, a fowl's egg; but in *toliu*, where the syllable of the same word is not closed, it is plainly o; and a native will rarely, if ever, doubt.

Diphthongs are ae, ai, ao, au; clearly distinct, as in *gae, gai, gao, gau*.

Consonants are k, g; t; p, v, w; q; m, *m*, n, *n*; r, l; s. Of these k, w, m, n, s, have the English sound.

1. The sound of hard g is never heard; the letter is used for a guttural trill, sometimes hardly heard (and so answering to the 'break' in Samoan), sometimes almost k, sometimes nearly r. Thus when the language was first written *tagai* was *takai* or *tarai*, *gate* was *ate*.

2. t is never the English dental, but has a blunter sound.

3. The Mota labials are less explosive than the English; v approaches b; p approaches v. A syllable is closed with w; *gaw* is distinct from *gau*.

4. q represents a compound sound in which k, p, w, are present, sometimes the guttural sometimes the labial predominating.

5. The guttural nasal ng, as in 'sing,' is represented by *n*; the sound of ng in 'finger' is unknown. There are two forms of the labial nasal m, one more nasal represented by *m*. The latter is certain in the words in which it occurs, natives never hesitate or differ. It closes a syllable as in *nom* for *noma*. It is not marked by an italic in ordinary use, but it is so important to observe it (as comparative words will shew) that it is marked in the Dictionary in all cases where it is known.

6. The trills are sharper than in English; there are two sounds of r. This, r, cannot be sounded after n without an intervening d, or after l without d or u; e.g. *munra* is pronounced *mundra*, *pulrua* as *puldrua* or *pulurua*; but d is not written.

II. PARTS OF SPEECH. It is convenient to divide words according to the commonly received arrangement as Parts of Speech; but it must be understood that a word may be according to its use almost any one of these Parts, noun, adjective, verb, adverb, exclamation. But there are words which by their form shew themselves to be nouns or verbs, such as nouns with the terminations *i*, *ui*, *va*, and verbs with transitive suffixes. Nevertheless such a noun when used with a verbal particle is a verb, and such a verb with an article is a noun; the name of an object and the name of an action have each a grammatical form and usage.

III. ARTICLES.
These are Demonstrative, *o, na*; Personal, *i*.

1. *Demonstrative.* There is no difference in meaning between *o* and *na*, but in use; both are to be translated by 'a,' 'an,' 'the,' in English; but there is no strict correspondence between these and 'a,' since there is in them no meaning of number. If one thing is particularly meant, *tuwale*, 'one,' must be used.

(a) These Articles are definite; so when the notion is quite general none is used; *rave iga*, catch fish.

(b) As a demonstrative, *o* is used with the names of places.

(c) *Na* is used always and only before nouns to which personal pronouns are suffixed with possessive sense; *o panei* a hand, *napanena* his hand. The practice of writing the Article in one word with the noun has become established, though not reasonable.

2. *Personal.* The Article *i* is used with personal names, male and female, native and foreign; but is not used of necessity.

(a) This *i* applied to a word makes it at once a proper name; it also personifies the notion conveyed by the word; *qaratu* a flying fox, *i Qaratu* a name; *gale* to deceive, *i gale* the deceiver.

(b) The feminine form *iro* is made by the addition of *ro*, which by itself marks a name as feminine. Mota names only, or those common to the neighbouring islands, take the sign *ro*.

(c) Plural forms are, masculine *ira*, feminine *iraro;* but these not with personal names.

(d) Personal names being taken from names of things, the words *gene*, thing, *sava*, what, stand in the place of names not remembered or not, for some reason, to be mentioned. Thus *i gene, iro gene, i sava, iro sava* means the person, male or female, whose name is such and such a thing.

IV. NOUNS.

Common Nouns fall into two groups, according as, 1, they take, or do not take, a suffixed pronoun with possessive sense; and, 2, as they have or have not a termination shewing them to be Nouns.

1. This division of nouns is properly exhaustive, and is most important to observe.

(a) One class of nouns takes the pronoun of the possessor in the suffixed form, *k, ma, na;* see Personal Pronouns (b); being the names of parts, members, equipments, possessions, which stand in close and constant relation to the possessor. It is not always easy to perceive the ground of the distinction; *na usuna* his bow, *non a wose* his paddle.

When the pronoun is suffixed the Article *na* is used. These Nouns are marked in the Dictionary with (k).

(b) The remaining Nouns are used with the Possessives, *no, mo, ga, ma;* see Possessives.

2. Nouns which have a termination shewing them to be Nouns substantive are, (a) Verbal Nouns, or (b) Independent Nouns. Those which have no special form as Nouns require no notice.

(a) Verbal Nouns are formed from Verbs by the terminations *a, ia, ga, ra, va; mate,* to die, *matea,* death; *nonom,* to think, *nonomia,* thought; *vano,* to go, *vanoga,* going; *toga,* to abide, *togara,* way of life; *mule,* to go, *muleva,* going. These different forms of termination have no difference of signification in themselves; though there are examples where a verb takes two terminations and the nouns differ in meaning; see *toga.*

(b) Independent Nouns. The terminations *i, iu* or *ui,* and in a few cases *e,* shew the nouns to which they are suffixed to be without dependence, in thought or grammar, upon things or persons, or upon the names, to which they may otherwise belong or stand in relation. Thus in *namatana,* his eye, (*na* article, *na* suffixed pronoun), *mata,* eye, is thought and spoken of in relation to a person; but an eye, independent of such relation, is *matai, mata-i;* so *na-pane-na,* his hand, *panei;* a pig's head, *qut qoe;* a head generally, *qatui.*

These independent forms, naturally, do not appear in a noun which forms the first part of a compound.

Nouns which appear in independent form, with these terminations, generally belong to the class 1 (a), which take a suffixed pronoun.

3. *Construct form of Nouns.* Two Nouns are often coupled together with a possessive relation. In the cases in which the first

of the two is one which has no special substantival termination there is no change; where there can be an independent termination, *i, iu, ui*, there is no cause in this composition for its occurrence; but where the word ends in *a* this vowel in words so constructed is lightened to *e*. Thus *mata* the true form, *matai* in independent form, *mate tanun* a man's eye; *nonomia* a verbal substantive, *nonomie tanun*, man's thought; *sinaga*, a word with no special form, *sinage tanun*, man's food.

The same construct form is rarely used where there is no possessive relation; *moe gene*, a chief thing.

There is here an appearance of inflexion, but no true inflexion.

4. *Prefixes to Nouns*. There are two instrumental prefixes, *i* 4. and *ga* 3. with which verbs become substantives; *ras* to bale, *iras* a baler; *pulut* to stick, *gapulut* glue. The latter, *ga*, is also prefixed to words other than verbs, but rarely.

5. *Number*. The Noun itself has no number. If there be no sign of plurality it must not be thought that the word is in the singular number; if particularly meant to be singular *tuwale*, one, must be added.

The Plural of Nouns is marked by Reduplication, (see below), by (a) a plural sign, and by (b) a prefix.

(a) The sign in common use is nan; *ima*, house, *ima nan* houses. This is by no means the equivalent of the English plural in s; there must be a considerable number definitely in view to make the use appropriate. The collective noun *taure* is rarely used.

(b) The Prefixes *ra, re*, are used when persons are spoken of in regard to age and relationship; *re* of the class, *ra* of certain persons; *o retamtamai* the fathers as a class in the village; *ratamak* my fathers, uncles, etc.

The Personal Pronoun shews the same *ra* in the 3rd Person Plural. In the expression *ira ta Mota*, the Mota people, *ira* may be called a Pronoun; but *ira* before a person's name signifies that person and those with him; *i Qarat*, as above, *ira Qarat*, Qarat and his company; and here *ira* is the plural Personal Article.

6. There is no *Gender*; the adjectives *mereata, tavine,* or *vavine*, are added when the word does not itself shew sex.

7. *Reduplication*. Either (1) the whole word is reduplicated; *vat-vat* stones; or (2) the first syllable; *nanatiu* children; or (3) the first syllable closed by the succeeding consonant; *ranranoi* legs. The effect of Reduplication is to express number and size; with the closed syllable (3) rather intensity and exaggeration; *gate ranranona!* what legs he has!

Reduplication in the name of a plant signifies that it is wild or useless; *matig, metigtig; qeta, qetaqeta*.

V. PRONOUNS.

1. *Personal Pronouns* are in two distinct forms; (a) those which are used as the subject or object of a Verb; (b) those which are suffixed to Nouns substantive.

(a) Singular. 1. *inau, nau, na*.
2. *iniko, ko, ka*.
3. *ineia, neia, ni, a*.
Plural. 1. inclusive, *inina, nina*.
exclusive, *ikamam, kamam*.
2. *ikamiu, kamiu, kam*.
3. *ineira, neira, ira, ra*.
Dual. 1. inclusive, *inarua, narua, inara, nara*.
exclusive, *ikarua, karua, ikara, kara*.
2. *ikamurua, kamurua, kamrua, kamra*.
3. *irarua, rarua, irara, rara*.
Trial. 1. inclusive, *inatol, natol*.
exclusive, *ikatol, katol*.
2. *ikamtol, kamtol*.
3. *iratol, ratol*.

The Inclusive 1st person plural includes the speaker with those spoken to, the Exclusive excludes him.

(1) In the Singular and Plural, *na, ka, ni, kam*, are always the subject, never the object of a Verb.

(2) *a*, 3rd singular, and *ra*, 3rd plural, are always the object, never simply the subject of a Verb, and are governed by Prepositions as by Verbs. It may be said that *ra* is a plural personal Demonstrative, and so finds place with Personal Articles and Pronouns, as well as a prefix to plural Nouns; Nouns 5. b. Thus when *ra* is prefixed to *ta*, as in *ra ta Mota*, the Mota people, it is rather the plural personal demonstrative *ra* with *ta* used as a Noun, than *ra* the Pronoun.

(3) In direct indicative sentences *na, ni, kam*, are used as subject, but hardly *ka*. In indirect, potential, optative, subjunctive sentences, *na, ni, ka*, are used, not *nau, neia, ko*.

(4) The 2nd and 3rd singular, and 3rd plural, *ko, a, ra*, are written as suffixes; and after a consonant *i*, or *u*, is introduced; *iloko, iloa, ilora; vus keluko, ni me vus kelua, vusira; ilo* to see, *vus* to strike, *kel*, back.

(5) It is plain that the Dual and Trial are in fact the Plural with the numerals *rua* two, *tol* three, suffixed; *rua* being shortened to *ra*.

(6) The stems appear to be, Sing. *au, ko, a;* Plural *na = ta, am, mi, ra*.

(7) The Dual or Trial must be used when two or three persons are in view; never the Plural. The Trial is used also, less exactly, when more than three, but not many more, are meant.

(8) The Dual is used in speaking to a single person when connected by marriage with the speaker. It is used also when one speaks to another of an action with which both are concerned, though but one is active; *nara te vanogag iniko*, I will convey you; *va ma, nara te wurvagiko*, come here, I will put you to rights.

(9) Except when a person is spoken of, *a* hardly becomes the object of a Verb; *gaganag lnea ma*, point him, her, out to me; *ko*

qe rasuar o qeta lue ma, if you find taro pull (it) up. The same is the case with 3rd plural *ra*.

(b) Pronouns suffixed to Nouns.
Singular. 1. *k, ku*. 2. *ma, m*. 3. *na, n*.
Plural. 1. incl. *nina*, excl. *mam*. 2. *miu*. 3. *ra, r*.

(1) Of these the Singular only is a distinct Pronoun.
(2) These are suffixed to the particular Class of Nouns; see Nouns 1. (a); above described.
(3) The 3rd sing. *n*, as distinct from *na*, points to some particular person; *ape kikin o tanun* by a man's side, *ape kiki ima* beside a house; *o tete we tako ape sus tavine* an infant hangs at a woman's breast, but *ape susun ravevena* at its mother's.
(4) In the Exclusive 1st and 3rd Dual and Trial, *n* is introduced before the suffixed Pronoun; *napanenkara, napanenkatol*, hands of us two, or three; *napanenrara, napanenratol*, of them two, three; but in the 3rd person not always so.
(5) After *k* is often added the syllable *sa*; *napaneksa* my hand; which cannot be explained.

2. *Demonstrative Pronouns.*
Iloke, loke, this; *ilone, lone*, that; *ike*, this, *ine*, that.
Of these *ine* and *ike* can be used with the articles *o* and *i*, as if Nouns; but in *tamaike, tamaine*, like this, like that, are seen to be Pronouns.
To all these the Demonstratives *nake, nane*, are often added; *ke* being a demonstrative particle pointing near, and *ne* farther away.
The plural *ragai* is also a demonstrative Pronoun; often, with the personal Article, *iragai*, those. Dual *iragera, ragera*; Trial *iragetol, ragetol*.

3. *Interrogative Pronouns.*
The Nouns *sei, sava*, with Personal Articles make *isei* who? singular, *irasei* who? plural; *irosei* who? of a woman, *irarosei* of women; with the demonstrative Article *o sava* what?
(a) *Sei* represents the name, not the person himself; *isei?* really asks what is that person's name? To ask a name is not *o sava nasasana?* what is his name, but *isei nasasana?*
(b) *Sava* is shewn a Noun by the question *nasarama?* your what? of a part of the body or a relative. Person's names being names of things, the Personal Article with *sava* asks a person's name; *i sava?* who? *iro sava?* who? of a woman.
Sava becomes *sa*; *o sa?* what?

4. *Indefinite Pronouns.*
The Nouns *sei* and *sava* also make Indefinite Pronouns; *isei, irasei* some one, some persons, *o sava* some, any, thing.
A word which is also a numeral, *tea*, is also an indefinite Pronoun, some, any.
The distributive *val* expresses 'each.'
There are no Relative Pronouns; care must be taken lest an Indefinite be used as Relative.

VI. POSSESSIVES.

These are Nouns taking the suffixed Personal Pronouns, and used with Nouns that do not take Pronouns suffixed (see Nouns 1.) to express the possessive relation. The meaning of the Possessive Noun is 'a thing belonging.'

The Possessives are *no, mo, ga, ma*.

(a) The difference between *no* and *mo* is that *no* means a thing that has come into possession from without, while *mo* is that which belongs because of the action of the possessor, a person's because it is his doing; *anoma, tama apeniko, we van ma; amoma, tama ko me ge*. This distinction is important.

(b) A closer relation is signified by *ga*, very often of food, but by no means with an original connexion with eating; *gak o qatia* an arrow to shoot me with; *gan o wena* rain got for him by a charm.

(c) *ma* is of things drunk or chewed for the juice.

(d) To all of these *a* 4. is very commonly prefixed.

(e) Any of these Possessives with Article and suffixed Pronoun, in form a pure substantive, answers to 'mine,' 'thine,' 'his,' 'hers,' etc.; *nanok, nagana*, etc. Similarly with the Interrogative; *nanonsei iloke? nanok;* Whose is this? Mine.

VII. ADJECTIVES.

1. Words which are qualifying terms are commonly used in the form of Verbs; but some can be used without Verbal particles, following the qualified word; *ima mantagai,* small house, *tanun liwoa* big man. Nouns when used to qualify follow simply; *ima vat,* stone house.

2. Some words are marked as Adjectives by special terminations; these are—

ga; often formed from Nouns, *wuwuai* dust, *wuwuaga* dusty. Sometimes the ending is *iga; mamasaiga* dry.

ra; as in *ligligira* fluid, from *ligiu*.

ta; as *mamanigata* ulcerous, from *maniga*.

More rare are *sa* and *la*.

3. *Adjectival Prefixes.* The prefixes *ma* and *ta* are common in words which can fairly be called Adjectives; *taniniga* straight, *matoltol* thick; and these are the same which are applied to Verbs; see Verbs.

4. *Comparison.* Degrees of comparison are shewn by Prepositions and Adverbs; *we poa nan* bigger; *we poa aneane* very big, biggest. A positive statement implies a comparison; *iloke we wia* this is the best; *iloke we wia, ilone we tatas,* this is good, that is bad, i. e. this is better than that.

See also *matai* 2. good, *mala* 2. ill, *mano, vara* 6. rather, *tur* 3. very, and *sokorai, parasiu, matig* 3., *mere, man* 3.

VIII. VERBS.

Almost any word, an Exclamation, an Adverb, is used as a Verb with Verbal Particles prefixed ; but some words are naturally Verbs, as being names of actions not things.

Verbal Particles come before the Verb, written separate from it. They are 1. Temporal, 2. Modal.

1. *Temporal Particles; we, me, te, ti.*

(a) There is no strict sense of time in *we*, only so far as that the action is not regarded as past or future. The time, if necessary in a narrative, having been marked by *me*, past, or *te*, future, is carried on with *we*.

(b) Past time is marked by *me;* with the addition of the Adverb *vetu* to signify a completed action. But *me* is used of the future already realized as if past.

(c) The Future is given by *te*. This is used in narration of things past, but future at the time when the action narrated took place. Time is not in view when *te* is used of things regarded as sure to happen. The adverb *anaisa* is used to give a decided future.

(d) *Ti* is a particle of continuity, succession, and so commonly used in narration. It has no strictly temporal force.

2. *Modal Particles; qe, ta.*

These are conditional, potential, optative, subjunctive ; *ta* having rather a potential and optative character.

3. There is another Particle *ti* used with Verbs, but not such a Verbal Particle as the preceding. It follows the Verb. This, if the word be one, has three uses. (a) It throws back the time, so as to make a pluperfect. (b) It gives a sense of incompleteness to the action described. (c) It mitigates the directness or harshness of a request or command. See *ti* 2, 3, 4, 5.

4. Verbs are used without Verbal Particles, (1) in the Imperative, (2) in a subjoined clause, (3) in the Negative, and (4) after certain adverbs.

(1) In the *Imperative* the simple Verb is enough ; but it is common to use the Pronouns *na, ka, ni, nina, nara, karu*. After *kamam* the preposition *a* is introduced. For the 2nd person in the Dual, *ura, wura,* in the Trial *tol,* in the Plural *tur,* precede the verb.

A Negative Imperative is made by the use of *pea* 1, a verb in form and meaning, to be not or nothing ; so *ni pea,* let it not be, and *ura pea, tol pea, tur pea,* do not you two, or you three, or you.

(2) In stories, *kakakae,* also the 3rd pronoun is used without a verbal particle ; *neira totoga, tawan ni uwa.*

(3) In a Negative sentence with *gate, tete,* though verbal particles appear to be wanting, there is no doubt that *ga* and *te* are such particles, and that the negative force resides in the final *te.* The conditional optative particles *qe, ta,* also precede *tete.*

(4) There is no verbal particle after *qara, qale, kere, teve.*

5. *Suffixes to Verbs.*

There are certain terminations which, when suffixed to neuter verbs or verbs active in a general way, make them definitely transitive, or determine the action upon some object. These transitive, definitive, determinative, terminations are 1. Consonantal, 2. Syllabic.

The *Consonantal* g, t, v, r, s, n, ñ, are suffixed to verbs ending in a vowel; e.g. *manag, mavat, sorav, kokor, kokos, raun, tiqan.*

The *Syllabic* suffixes are *ag, gag, tag, vag, rag, sag, mag,* mag, *lag, nag,* nag; e.g. *taliag, vanogag, altag, sirvag, matarag, muraesag, saromag, anumag, gasolag, tigonag, lilnag.*

A second termination *vag* is distinct from these; the separable *vag*, which may be suffixed to the verb or separated from it, and may always be translated by 'with'; *neira me matevag o vuru* they died with, or of, a cough; *iragai me mate veta nan vag o vuru* those who have already died in numbers with a cough.

Two adverbs are written as suffixes; *vitag* because *i* is dropped, as *toavtag* for *toa vitag*, and *reag* by habit only.

6. *Prefixes to Verbs.*

These are Caustive, Reciprocal, of Condition, and of Spontaneity.

The *Causative* is *va*, sometimes *vaga*. It may be affixed to almost any verb, but it is common to use *na, ge,* make, with the same sense. From Causative *va* the verb *va* to go, used as auxiliary, must be distinguished.

The *Reciprocal* is *var*. This sometimes (compare Fiji *vei*) does not convey reciprocal but combined action; *o reremera we var-rara-rao* children crying all at once.

The prefixes of *Condition, ma, ta,* are those mentioned under the head of Adjectives, and make of verbs something like participles; *sare* to tear, *masare* torn; *wosa* 2. to burst, *tawosa* burst. To these may be added *sa* 2.

Prefixes of *Spontaneity* are *tava, tav, tapa,* and less common *tama, tawa.*

7. *Impersonal Verbs.*

There are some Verbs which are regularly used without a Nominative, *vivtig, rakut, vule, tama.*

8. *Reflective Verbs.*

The Adverb *kel,* back, describes a reflected action; *ni me ge mate kelua,* he killed himself.

9. *Voice.*

The Verb names the action or condition without regard to Voice as Active or Passive; *neira me taur paso o ima* they have built the house; *o ima me taur veta* the house is built.

10. *Reduplication.*

Verbs, like Nouns, are reduplicated in three ways; by (1) repetition of the first syllable, (2) of the first syllable closed by the succeeding consonant, (3) of the whole word; e.g. *pute,* to sit, *pupute, putpute, putepute.* The force of (1) is generally continuance, of (2) intensification, of (3) repetition. Each form admits of repetition; *o aka me salesalesale sasasale* the canoe drifted and drifted and drifted on.

IX. ADVERBS.
Place and *Time* are generally conceived as the same. The native mind has place constantly in view, and by Adverbs and Particles, such as *ke, ne, ma, at,* continually directs the action.

Words which serve as Adverbs are some of them Nouns with Prepositions, as *vea, avea,* where; *naisa, anaisa,* when. Past time is shewn by *na* before *naisa, nora, qarig, risa.*

The *Negative tagai* is a Noun.

X. PREPOSITIONS.
These may be divided into Simple and Compound.

1. *Simple.* Some are certainly Nouns, *pe, ma, me, lo,* which though used simply are commonly used in compound form.

Locative; a, pe, lo.
Motion; to, i, sur, goro ; from, *nan.*
Dative; mu, mun.
Instrumental; mun, nia.
Relation; ta, men, ma, pe.

The locative *a,* at, is often used where in English 'from' would be used, the place in the native mind being that at which the motion starts ; *ni me van ma avea? a Mota,* where did he come from? from Mota.

Goro adheres to the Verb, not, like other Prepositions, to the Noun it governs.

Nan, nia, like the English 'from,' 'with,' can come at the end of a sentence.

Ta in ordinary use refers to the place to which a person or thing belongs ; *o tanun ta Mota, o varae ta Mota,* man or speech of Mota ; *we vava ta Mota* speak Mota ; *o ta Mota* a Mota person. The word is no doubt originally a Noun. It is sometimes used, as in other languages, as a Preposition of simple reference, but only in compound expressions, as *lesles-ta-gasuwe, pun-ta-ligas.*

2. *Compound.* These are Nouns, (some of which are in use also as simple Prepositions) compounded with simple Prepositions. From *pe; ape, ipe, tape;* from *ma, me; ama, ame, ima, ime, tama, tame;* from *lo; alo, ilo, talo.*

Of which it should be observed that they are shewn to be Nouns by (1) the use of a Preposition before them; (2) by their taking sometimes a suffixed Pronoun, as *apena,* as commonly in neighbouring tongues ; (3) by the absence of the Article after them. By my side is *ape kikik,* not *ape na kikik* ; in his garden cannot be *alo na tuqena* but *alo tuqena.* The construction of *pe kikik* and *lo tuqena* is that of two nouns in possessive relation. But it is admissible to say *ape nanok siopa, ape nagak sinaga,* where the possessive nouns have the article ; *nanok, nagak* being explanatory of the character of *siopa* and *sinaga.* When *ape, alo,* are used as Adverbs the Article is naturally in place.

Many words, consisting of Nouns with simple Prepositions, are taken as Compound Prepositions; rather because they are translated by English Prepositions; *vunai* the upper side, *avune* above; *lalanai* the under side, *alalane* under. Thus also with other Prepositions, *ivune, tavune, ilalane, talalane;* and, with the Noun *vatitnai, alovatitne, ilovatitne, talovatitne*. In these instances the Noun is one which has a construct form; but it is the same with words like *vawo* and *lele*, the upper and inner parts, making *avawo, ivawo, tavawo, alele, ilele, talele*. Other words, though translated by an English Preposition, retain the form of Noun and Preposition; *a pan pei* beside the water, *a tavala pei* beyond the water, *panei, tavalai*. These Nouns also serve as Prepositions themselves; *vune, vawo, lele, ima; pan pei, tavala pei*.

XI. Conjunctions.

Copulative *wa, pa*. Adversative *pa, nava*. Connective *nan*. Disjunctive *si*. Conditional *si*. Illative *si*.

A mark of quotation is *wa*. The same sound *wa* is also 'lest.' 'Until' is *gai*. To express cause the noun *manigiu* is used.

Where the Conjunction 'and' is used in English, the Noun *ta* 4. is often employed, almost entirely where persons are in view.

XII. Numerals.

The numeral system is imperfectly decimal; all numbers above ten are expressed in tens, but the series of independent numerals reaches only to five, the digits of the first hand. For the second hand there is a prefix of *lavea*.

1. *Cardinals.*

1 *tuwale.*	6 *laveatea.*
2 *rua.*	7 *lavearua.*
3 *tol, tolu.*	8 *laveatol.*
4 *vat.*	9 *laveavat.*
5 *tavelima.*	10 *sanavul.*

To *rua, tol, vat,* and sometimes to *tuwale,* the Verbal Particle *ni* is prefixed. All may appear in the form of Verbs, with the various Verbal Particles.

For the units above tens the Noun *numei* is used; twelve, *sanavul tuwale o numei nirua*.

A hundred is *melnol;* the sum above the hundred *avaviu;* thus a hundred and thirty-two, *melnol vatuwale, o avaviu sanavul tol, o numei nirua*. A thousand is *tar*.

2. *Ordinals.*

The Cardinals with substantival termination form Ordinals; the second, third and fourth taking the multiplicative *vaga,* or *va,* instead of *ni,* and *a* being dropped from *lavea*.

1st	6th *laveteai.*
2nd *varuei, vagaruei.*	7th *laveruai.*
3rd *vatoliu, vagatoliu.*	8th *lavetoliu.*
4th *vavatiu, vagavatiu.*	9th *lavevatiu.*
5th *tavelimai, vagatavelimai.*	10th *sanavuliu.*

There is no Ordinal in the first place; *moai* is first; hundredth is *melnolanai*.

In numbers above tens and hundreds the Ordinal goes with the *numei* or *avariu* which comes last; *sanavul rua o numei varuei*, twenty-second; *melnol vagarua o avaviu varuei*, two hundred and second; *melnol vatuwale o avaviu sanavul rua o numei varuei* hundred and twenty-second.

3. *Multiplicatives* are formed with the Causative *vaga, va*: *vagatuwale, vatuwale* once, *vagasanavul* ten times.

4. *Descriptive Prefixes* precede Numerals when certain objects are counted; *pul* 9, *sage* 4, *sogo* 3, *tur* or *tira* 2, *taqa* 3, *tal* 5, *sorako, pepe* 3, *rowo* 4, *raka* 3; for the meaning of which see the Dictionary.

The word *visa*, how many? so many, is treated as a Numeral; *ni visa, raga visa, pul visa*.

XIII. DIALECTS.

The language tends to divide into two dialects, the one resembling the language of Motalava, the other that of Meralava. In the ring of settlements which lies between the cliffs and peak of Mota the division is most clearly marked between Maligo and Veverau. To the Veverau people the speech of Maligo sounds 'thin,' as that of Motalava; to the Maligo people that of Veverau sounds 'thick,' as that of Meralava. The two dialects, which are confused in the language in literary use, are distinguished in the Dictionary by V. and M. The use of *i* and *u*, *g* and *w*, respectively, is characteristic. In Veverau *g* at the end of a word is sounded *i*, *mantai* for *mantag;* and thus the transitive suffix *g* of Verbs becomes *i*, a cause of some confusion, as *rusai* for *rusag*, *sokoi* for *sokog*. There is also a certain difference in Vocabulary; from which the Maligo people call the Veverau people, and those who speak like them, *ira we nao;* and these call the others *ira we tak*.

XIV. *UN* WORDS.

Those who are connected by marriage cannot use words or parts of words which are the names or parts of names of those so connected with them. There are therefore certain words which take the place of those which in most common usage have to be avoided. To use these words is to *vava viro, galiga* or *un;* in the Dictionary they are marked as '*un* words.'

MOTA DICTIONARY

A.

A, 1. pers. pr. 3. sing. suffixed as object to v. and prep.; him, her, it.

A, 2. simple prep., locative; at; before inf. v. to; before 1st, 2nd pl. imper. as "are to"; in idiomatic use, from; *ma avea? ma a Mota*, where from? from Mota; *me masu a vune tangae*, fell from off a tree; *me ilo o aka a matenua*, saw a ship from the cliff. Used before the names of places, *Arao, a Rao*. Forms compound prep. *avune*, on, &c.

A, 3. v. to dash, fly swiftly; *o tika ti a.*

A, 4. pref. to (1) some verbs and (2) some nouns, without meaning. (1) *anig, avut*; perhaps in this v. p. of Anaiteum, &c. (2) *anok, aavik, aimak, atuqek*; perhaps art. of Fiji, &c.

A, 5. term. of verbal n.; *galea, matea.*

A, 6. interj. in combination, *are! awo!* &c.

Aavi, (k) *av*, fire, with *a* 4; *aavinsei?* whose fire? *aavik*, mine.

Ae, 1. adv. without meeting anything; *ilo ae*, fail to see; *sike ae*, seek in vain; *ni me van ae inau alo imak; masu ae*, fall clear.
2. v. *ae kalo*, climb without obstacle; *o lan ni ae ni ae*, may the wind blow without harming anything.

Ag, tr. term. of v.

Aga, 1. (k) poss. n., *a* 4. and *ga* 1.

Aga, 2. excl. no! not finished! *aga! gale toga.*

Agavig, [*a* 2.] far off; *gavig*.

Ai, [*a* 3.] rush, dash, of wind, or *tika*; probably *ag* M.

Aia, 1. adv. [*a* 2.] there; see *ia* 3.
2. excl. of assent, that's it! that's right!

Aka, (k) canoe; *aka paspasau*, with plank sides. Fiji, *waqa*; Mao. *waka*; Sam. *va'a*; Bouru, *waga, waa*; Amboyna, *haka*; Ponape, *wa*.

A canoe is hewn out, *we tara o aka*; in shaping the hull, *turiai*, the tree trunk is cut with sideways strokes, *ari*, on the outside, and hollowed inside with straight strokes, *pari*. The two ends are shaped alike, the hollow part under the bows or stern being the *qanqanai*; the upper part of each end being decked with a *taqava*. Upon the hull is built, *pasau*, the bulwarks of plank, *irav*, *me tara mun o lakae, we was-was lue mun o nurnuriaka*, shaped (in old times) with the shell adze and bored at the edge with a shell; these holes in the planks and trunk are *matewas*, and *we vil o irav ape turiai mun o gapn ape matewas*, a lashing of sinnet passes through them. A staging of rods of hibiscus covers the two ends upon the bulwarks, *we las o qeaqea varu*. At the two extremities of the hull double horns, *tikataso*, of *gasur*, are made fast, to work the steering paddle, *turwose*, in, which is tied in place with the *ga-ta-wose*. The outrigger, *sama*, is connected with the canoe by three yokes, *iwatia*, the ends of which are made fast, *vil*, to pegs, of nira wood, the *pisvatoto*, driven into the outrigger. The free ends of the two outer yokes, *iwatia mot*, pass under the stages, *qeaqea*, and are made fast to the bulwarks, *we vil ape irav*; the free end of the middle yoke is not tied fast, *we risa gap*. The outrigger is thought always to be on the left of the canoe, the open side of which is the *gatae*; the outrigger has its corresponding *gatae*.

The sail, *epa*, is carried by two spars; the longer the mast, *turgae*, the shorter the boom, *pane*; these altogether make the *gapan*. The forked butt, *kere turgae*, of the mast rests on the middle yoke, *iwatia*, is not made fast, *we pute gap gate rot*; the forked butt of the boom, *kere pane*, lies in the same way on the *kere turgae*. The mast is supported by shrouds, *tal*, made fast to the middle of the mast; three brought down to the end of the middle *iwatia*, carried under and wound to the *pisvatoto*, and three to the base of each outer *iwatia mot*; these are the *tan-gae*. The boom is set to the open side of the canoe, *o pane te risa ape gatae*, leaning over; it is supported by two *tal-pane*, each fastened to the *iwatia mot* where it projects from the *irav*.

The sail, *epa*, is made of mats woven by women, *me vau mun gavine gae*, and sewn together by men with a needle of tree fern wood, or a ray's sting, and hibiscus fibre, *o mereata we susur mun o gavaru, mun o qatia o qasai apena, si o togo rar*. It is laced, *ritata*, to the *turgae* and *pane* with a small line; all is hoisted together, *we tape o epa*, and when not in use is folded with the lines attached. The leech of the sail above is the *qat-matalawa*, the belly the *toqai*, the part in the angle below the *keretotovoi*.

Al, 1. v. to move; *alial*, move from place to place; *al piro*, go quickly out of sight; *al sea*, change place. Sam. Ponape, *alu*; Java, *alik*, move.

altag, to go about in charge of.

Al, 2. n. a climbing arad, *alu*.

Alan, to make a speech, harangue. Mao. *karanga*; Sam. *'alaga*.

Alalan**ana**, adv. beneath; *a* 2. *lalanai*; *na* 3.

Alalan**e**, [*a* 2.] under; *lalanai* constr.

Ale, v. to put yam or *tomago* into cocoa-nut sauce which has been used for *toape*.

Aleale, a mountain shrub.

Aleg, to sing with a loud voice; *aleleg,* as a man on a hill sings to be heard below; *aleg matmateas,* to sing on return from dunning a man, so that he may hear.

Alele, [*a* 2.] inside, only used of a house.

Alena, [*a* 4.] bounty, bountiful, bountifully; *lena*.

Aliaga, [*ga* 5.] prickly with fine spicules, like *tou, togo, au*; powdered as with spray dried on; sticky with *garusa*.

Alial, go about; *al* 1.

Alig, to carry, as a bird food in its beak.

Alivaw, [*a* 2.] in the open; *livawu,* a Mosina V.L. word.

Alo, 1. compound prep. in, on; [*a* 2., *lo*]; cannot be followed by the art. *na* before governed n. See Grammar.

2. adv. while, as; *alo ilone,* while, as that was going on, then.

Alo, 3. to steer with the stroke paddle, without a steering paddle, *turwose; alo goro,* to change the paddle to the other side for steering. Sam. *alo,* to paddle; Motu N.G. *kalo,* N.B. *walu;* Lifu, *galu,* to paddle.

Alo, 4. v. stem of *alov, alovag*; probably Sam. *alo,* to fan.

Alo ilone, compound adv. while, then.

Alolona, compound adv. therein; *loloi*.

Alomasalepei, measure of length; from breastbone to finger-end.

Alotne, *alo tine,* in the midst of.

Alov, [*alo* 4.] to obtain *mana* from a *vui; we alov nan o vui, wa tama o vui we managia*.

Alova, interj. really! is it so? *lora*.

Alovag, [*alo* 4.] beckon to, invite, greet, by signs.

Alovatitnai, [*alo* 1.] comp. adv. in the midst, *vatitnai*.

Alovatitne, comp. prep. in the midst of, amid.

Alpiro, [*al* 1.] to move so quickly as to cheat the sight, *piro*.

Alqon, a swallow; always on the move [*al* 1.] till night, *qon*.

Altag, [*al* 1.] of movement directed to an object [*tag* 2.], go in charge, look after; *ni we gopa, isei gate altagia;* followed by *goro,* to go about looking after with a view to protection; thence in new use to shepherd.

Alu, a climbing arad, monstera; *alu* also in Ysabel; called *no-al* from its leaves.

Am, to nibble with the lips, not teeth; *tama we amiam o nai nan o vai; am ilo,* taste with lips; *am nolonolo,* to swallow food unchewed.

Ama, 1. [*a* 4.] (k) poss. n. *ma* 1.; of a thing to drink or suck.

Ama, 2. [*a* 2.] comp. prep. *ma* 2.; (1) with; used only with suffixed 3rd pers. pr. *amaia* with him or her; *amaira,* with them; and 2nd sing. *amaiko,* with thee. (2) by force of *a* 2. from, from with. (3) *amaia,* a man's wife, the woman with him; *nan amaia wa,* then said his wife. (4) also used in place of poss. *o gasal amaiko, amaia,* your, his, knife.

Amam, to deceive.

Amaran, [*a* 2.] to-morrow, at light, *maran*.

Ame, [*a* 2.] comp. prep. see *me.*

Amen, with suff. pr. *n* 2.; with, and by idiom under *a* 2. from, him, her; so also, *amenkamam,* with us, excl. *amen kara, rara, kamiu, kamurua, katol, kamtol, ratol,* with us two, them two, you two, us three, you three, them three. See *me.*

Amenau, with, from, me; *o qoe amenau,* my pig.

Amenina, with, from, us, incl.

Amenara, with, from, us two, incl.

Amenarua, with, from, us two, incl.

Amenatol, with, from, us three, incl.

Amenra, with, from, them, *ra* 1.

Amera, with, from, them, *ra* 1.

Amo, (k) (*a* 4.) poss. n. mo; something of one's own doing.

Amoa, [*a* 2.] before, first; m*oai.*

An, same as *ane* 2.

Ana, [*a* 2.] pref. in adverbs of time, giving sense of past time; as in Pol.

Anai, (k) one belonging to person, family, place; perhaps Mal. *anak;* Malag. *zanaka;* Macassar, Bugis, *ana. o tanun anai,* a man of the place, not a visitor; *o tanun anak,* a man of mine; *anan vanua,* the man of the place, the fighting man, *tanun vavakae.* The termination in m*elnolanai, paspasoanai, vunvunanai,* is the same word.

Ananora, adv. yesterday.

Ananaisa, adv. when? in past time, thereafter.

Anapup, [*a* 2.] at the further end of the house, *pup; na* probably the article.

Anaqarig, [*a* 2. *na* 5.] to-day, when of past time, lately.

Anarisa, [*a* 2. *na* 5.] adv. the day before yesterday; *anarisa siwo,* the day before that.

Anatano, [*a* 2. *na* 1.] on the ground, *tano,* below.

Ane, 1. to surpass.

Ane, 2. to press, stamp, in; *me ane o lot gita!* the *nai* is pressed into the *lot,* it is finished.

maaneane, trampled, as a wet place.

Aneane, [*ane* 1.] adv. much, very, exceedingly.

Anian, [*an*] met. to be urgent, pressing; as in forbidding.

Anig, [*a* 4.] to build a nest, *nig.*

Anika, ex. indeed!

Ano, (k) [*a* 4.] poss. n. *no,* something belonging.

Anor, 1. [*a* 4.] to stir up to ill-feeling, excitement; *nor.*

Anor, 2. poss. with suff. pr. *r* 2. their.

Anqis, [*an*] met. one upon whom refusal or prohibition makes no impression; *qis.*

Anu, 1. n. a sedge with cutting edges. 2. met. of annoyance, irritation, hatred; *anuanu,* to feel annoyance; *lolounu,* ill-feeling.

anumag, tr. v. annoy, irritate, worry.

Anus, 1. v. to spit. 2. n. spittle. 3. n. the lungs. Sam. *anu;* Motu N.G., *kanudi.*

An, same as *ani* below.

Ana, to shoot up; *o sul vetal we ana lue nan o tano,* a banana sucker springs out of the ground. Malag. *anga,* lifted up.

Anaisa, [*a* 2.] adv. when? in the future, hereafter; n*aisa.*

Ananora, [*ano*] becoming yellow, as a white thing sinking in the sea. *ra* 4.

Ani, *anian, anani,* to loom large

on the horizon; as the full moon rising; as a full loaded canoe goes out of sight, *me anani ran lo! me sogon tul*, how big she looms, laden enough to sink her.

maaniani, met. of dizziness, *o nagoi ti maaniani.*

Anis, impers. v. probably tr. *ani;* suit, please; *me anisia ape mawmawui*, work came handy to him, he liked work.

Ano, 1. n. turmeric, Fij. *cago;* Sam. *ago;* Ponape, *ong.*
2. v. to be yellow; *o vula ti ano*, the moon is turning yellow towards setting; *o maran ti ano*, the morning dawns yellow.

anoano, adj. yellow in colour.

Ape, 1. comp. prep. [*a* 2.], see *pe;* of relation and place; at, by, for, in reference to, about, because of; no article after it before the object; *ni we tigotigo ape ranona*, he uses a stick for his leg.
The same as if adv. because, *ni we tigotigo ape na ranona me malate ti*, he uses a stick because his leg was broken.

Ape, 2. constr. *apei.*

Ape, 3. v. to be quiet, subdued, to come quietly; *naapena tama we rono, ti ape ma*, he seems in low spirits he comes so quietly; *loloape*, submissively.

apes, v. tr. to jeer at, so as to make *ape* 3.

Apeape, adv. [*ape* 3.] quietly, submissively.

Apei, (k) constr. *ape*, something within a man which is the seat of feeling; *o apei we mas*, this sinks, falls, when one is tired; *na we mule mun o apei we sov gese*, I go with confidence; *naapek we maragai,* this within me trembles, I am shy.
From the constr. *ape* the following words:—*apegalo*, shame, ashamed, *galo; apekiria*, the feeling of shrinking, with awe, *kiria; apemaragai*, sby, shyness, shame, *maragai; apemot*, fatigue, weary, *mot* 2.; *apemulemule*, with spirit refreshed, *mule* 2.; *aperig*, humble, meek, without presumption, *rig* 2.; *aperono*, listlessness, inert, *rono; apesov*, confidence, with mind at rest, *sov.*

Apen, a form of *ape* 1. which shows *pe* n.; used before a personal n. or pr. *Ko me kakakae apensei? apen Qat? Apen irara qa tana Ro Lei.* About whom are you telling a story? about Qat? Yes, about him and Ro Lei.

Apena, 1. *ape* 1. with suff. pr. *na*, showing *pe* n.; with regard to it, at it, beside it, about it. 2. in use as adv. there; *o sinaga tea apena? apena gina*, is there any food? There is.

Apera, with regard to persons, *ape* 1. *ra* 1.; conf. *apena.*

Apes, [*ape* 3.] as above; *isei qe masu o sul we apesia*, when any one falls people jeer at him, he feels small, *loloape.*

Apesa, [*ape* 1.] what for, why? *sa* for *sava.*

Apula, (k) [*a* 4.] poss. n. a property, *pulai.*

Aqaga, white; *ayaga les*, white like the underside of leaves.

Aqarig, [*a* 2.] to-day, soon; *qarig.*

Aqit, [*a* 2.] far off, *qit.*

Aqo, 1. to wash the face and head. Fl. *apo*, to wash.

Aqo, 2. to break off the soft end of a yam in digging it; *me gil,* *we nonom si me qeresa veta, we gisir, we are nan o tano; nara gate qeresa, ti aqo,* the digging is done, you think that the end of the yam is clear, you push your fingers under and raise it from the earth; but it was not clear at the tip, it breaks short off.

Aqou, excl. of astonishment; *aqou! gate patau we lin lana ti,* oh! what heaps of bread-fruit lying about!

Ar, 1. n. currents in the sea between Mota and Gaua; *ar Gaua,* carries to Gaua; *ar lama* and *ar matalo,* carries away to sea; same as *gar* 5. N.B. *al.;* Motu N.G., *aru;* Mal. *arus,* current.

Ar, 2. v. 1. to pull to pieces, strip; *ar o ima,* pull a house to pieces; *ar o tou,* strip the leaves off sugar-cane; when a tusked pig is killed they *ar* him; a man's own son, *ti ar navarana,* pulls at his heart, because he thinks so anxiously about him. 2. neuter, to come to pieces; *o parou me ar,* the male blossom of the pandanus has fallen apart; met. see *parou.*

Ara, 1. v. 1. to drive away, chase, follow up. 2. keep off.

Ara, 2. interj. addressed to a person, *ara! pa o sa?*

Ararovag, adv. lengthways; *arovag; tano ararovag,* place into which a thing is put end on.

Aras, [*a* 2.] adv. afar; *rasu;* makes superlative.

Are, interj. expressing pain, grief.

Areare, n. loud crying; adv. loud; probably *are!*

Arelau, 1. n. a lizard, tachydroma, on the beach, *lau.*

Arelau, 2. a pain in the back caused by staying on the beach, *lau.*

Aresag, to scoff at, make game of, annoy.

Aresaro, to ask a thing back.

Ari, to cut with sideways strokes in shaping the outside of a canoe. N.B. *arik,* split.

Arike, admire, covet, desiderate, repine as when another succeeds, or when one has missed a shot; with *ape* prep.

Aris, to choose the best; probably *ar* 2. determ.; the thing *ti aris ineia,* therefore he chooses it.

Arisa, [*a* 2.] adv. the day after to-morrow; *risa* 2.; *arisa siwo,* the day after that; *arisa talavano.*

Arivtag, [*a* 2.] adv. near, nearly; *rivtag.*

Aro, a tree of which bows are made.

Aromea, a fish.

Aron, to do again and again, as a crowd begging.

Arosa, hoarse; *nalinansei ti arosa.* Jav. *garok,* hoarse.

Arovag, to insert, put in lengthways, end on; *o tano ararovag,* the opening above the doorway through which the lashing of the door is inserted. *a tano-ararovag,* adv. end on.

Artow, a tree.

Aru, the casuarina tree; has a sacred character; hence, *tano aruaru,* a sacred place with *aru* trees, and the cry in *varowog* of *rawo aru! aru lama,* branching coral, gorgonia.

Arupata, very big; *gate tanun we arupata.* Motu N.G. *bada,* large.

Arvau, a kind of pandanus.

As, 1. v. to pierce, stab, prick. Sam. *ati.*

As, 2. n. smoke, *asu.*

As, 3. n. a convolvulus, ipomœa, *ga-as.*

As, 4. n. (k) a song; the suff. pr. shows the person about whom the song is made; *Tursal me tara Lelena ti; naasin L. nake, natowon T.*, Tursal made a song about Lelena; it is Lelena's song, Tursal's composition. Malag. *antsa,* singing.

Asa, to rub; so to wash with rubbing.

   asag, determ. to rub something.

   asan, intens. to rub hard, rub into shreds; *asan o tapia,* rub the platter clean.

   asania, adj. *o lan asania,* a strong wind that rubs leaves, &c. together and shreds them.

Asasor, begin to turn colour, *asor.*

Asasura, smoky, *asu; ra* 4.

Asau, [*a* 2.] adv. far off, afar, aloof.

   asauna, a distant object, as fruit at end of branch, a man aloof from crowd.

Ase, [*a* 4.] to separate, take apart; *kamam me ase masao,* we took the space of time by itself, *i. e.* between squalls, to cross.

   aseg, divide in portions, separate and allot.

   aserag, to separate; *asease wut,* to search for lice, separating the curls of hair.

Asiasi, v. to roll up *loko* in *toape* in lengths.

Askov, to dive as a bird for fish; met. of one who has boasted and been killed, *ni we ge askov ineia.*

Aso, v. not to meet, miss, of points and ends; *tarauso,* to slip out of place or joint, *tara; taliaso,* to go round without meeting or touching; *rariaso,* to fail to meet, the one thing the other; as when a joint is dislocated the bones each fail to meet the other, *rar.*

Asoa, to produce abundantly, of a garden.

Ason, [*a* 4.] to deceive, *son.*

Asor, [*a* 4.] to turn colour in getting ripe, *sor;* said only of bread-fruit.

Asosomag, [*a* 4.] to pack tight, *soso.*

Aspul, adj. dark, of a cloud; like smoke of *pul.*

Astega, adj. very black.

Asu, 1. n. smoke. Mao. *au;* Sam. N.G., Tagal, *asu;* Mal. *asap.* 2. v. to smoke as fire, to go up as smoke.

Asuasu, said of a canoe running swiftly, *o aka we asuasu sage salilina,* runs up ashore in smoking surf.

Asui, *o asui we tatano,* smoke so thick in a house that nothing can be seen; said also of fat, sleek pig.

Asur, excl. truly! same as *sur, tasur,* used at Tasmate.

At, adv. of direction from the speaker, outward, forward. Pol. Mel. *atu.*

   at aia, thither.

Ata, male; as in *mereata, mara ata.*

Atai, (k) the soul; properly something distinct from the man with which he thought himself peculiarly connected, in which his personality reflected; it might be snake or stone; not a thing in which he thought his soul was contained. Not new in the met.

sense of soul. Mao. *ata*, a reflected image; Sam. *ata*, shadow; Motu N.G. *vata*, ghost.

Atalia, adv. about, *tal.*

Atana, to become encrusted with a peculiar enamel.

atanavag, *o lasa ti atanavag o gea,* the drinking cup gets enamelled with the kava.

Ate, 1. to turn the face, direct the look. *ate kalo,* look up; *ate kelkel,* look about; *ate lan,* turn the face upwards as to heaven, *lan*; *ate lilin,* turn the head on one side; *ate lue,* turn the face over the shoulder; *ate ris,* turn the face another way; *ate sinorua,* talk with heads together, *sino*; *ate ratut,* look with the head straight up; *ate wot,* look with the head rising out of something; *ate wutui,* look out with the head only appearing; *atevtag,* turn the face away and leave, *vitag*; *ate tivtag nan,* turn from with rejection; *ate qolilin,* to hold the head on one side. Tanna N.H. *ate teling,* turn the ear.

Ate, 2. to visit, go and see; *ate palu,* see under *ateate.*

atev, to visit; *vaater,* visit after *goto.*

Ateate, the visiting with presents of one who makes a *kole,* when he ceases to *goto*; the proper day, *o tur qon ateate,* or *tur ateate,* is the eve of the *kole*; but on the day before is a private view, *ate palu.*

Atenoroa, [ate 1.] to sit quiet; met. like a *roa,* a turret univalve that goes very slowly.

Atu, 1. adv. outwards, forwards, *at.*

Atu, 2. to give single strokes in drumming while the other performer is using both drumsticks; met. of an ovenful of food, some cooked, some not.

Au, 1. n. the bamboo; *au kalan,* a striped variety; *au malum,* with softer substance; *au qalis,* with small leaves; *au rat,* large strong kind.

au non Qat, a scallop shell.

Au, 2. v. to step, move on the feet; *au getget,* to hop; *au ninit,* go lightly, stealthily; *au palatag,* go at random; *au qalo masal,* go with long steps; *au qalo vaon,* with short steps, met. from lengths of bamboo, *qalo au; au saksakerewaka,* with hasty careless steps; *au taniniga,* go straight on; *au tegteg,* go on tiptoe; *au ralago,* run; *au ragorgor,* with quick steps; *au patpat,* take very short steps; *au sasawuara,* to pass by.

Ausag, to fail in paying debts; shirk, put off payment.

Autegteg, [au 2.] go on tiptoe.

Av, 1. n. fire; Pol. *ahi, afi*; Mal. *api*; Malag. *afo*; met. as in *ruavsis,* excessive.

2. a place, step, in the *suqe.*

Av, 3. n. a climbing plant, *ga-av.*

Av, 4. v. to strike flakes, shape by so striking; *we av o mavin, o wetov,* strike flakes of obsidian, glass-bottle. N.B. *ap.*

Av, 5. v. to pile, as stones for a fence, to fence; *we av goro o qoe,* fence against a pig with stones lightly piled; *we av o wona,* make a fish-fence, *av goro iga.* Malag. *arosa,* heap; Motu N.G. *ahu,* to fence.

avaviu, what is piled; see below.

avtag, to throw in a heap.

Ava, 1. v. to miss the mark, make

a mistake, go wrong; *mate ara*, appear to die but revive.

Ava, 2. n. a small stone amulet, long, black, and thin.

Ava, 3. n. a mesh; *o ava ape gape we poa; o gene ape malosar tuwale apena ape gape we poa, o ava we sasarita yese.*

Avarea, [*a* 2.] adv. outside the house, in the *rarea*.

Avaviu, [*av* 5.] in numeration the sum above the hundreds; 103, *melnol tuwale o avariu nitol*; 130, *o avaviu sanavul tol*.

Avawo, adv. [*a* 2.] above, upon, *vawo*.

Avawosus, a measure of length; *we rova avawo sus*, a fathom measured from right breast, *sus*, to fingers of left hand.

Ave, v. guide, direct, steer; *we ave o nam alo qarana nan o tano*, move carefully a yam in digging it.

averag, to draw.

Avea, [*a* 2.] adv. 1. where? *vea* 1. 2. which, whether, in choice, *avea ko we maros?* which do you like; *tam avea*, how.

Aveave, a tree, in V.L.

Averag, to draw down the bough of a tree; probably *ave*.

Avi, (k) fire, *av* 1.; see *aavi*.

Avirik, the first stage in the *suqe; avrig*.

Avkete, to squat with one knee up.

Avlasolaso, adv. insecurely, so as to slip; *taur avlasolaso*, without good hold, as a thing too short to grasp well, or slippery like a fish.

Avlava, [*av* 1.] the fire outside the *gamal*; the position of one not yet in the *suqe; lava*.

Avnag, to carry in the arm, on or under, *vinai*.

Avne-wis, adv. standing on one leg, as an owl, *wis*, stands with the other tucked up under his wing, *avnag*.

Avrig, the lowest, or one of the lowest, ranks in the *suqe*, the little fire.

Avtag, 1. to wave, toss as a branch; wave the arm, throwing it up, as in dances; toss out the hook in fishing; to throw underhand.

2. [*av* 4.] to put in a heap one thing on another, as yams ready for planting.

Avtag, 3. to do the first part of a mat, *epa; we qeteg vauvau, we tig*; see *vinit* 1.

Avtagataga, one of the lower ranks, fires, in the *suqe*.

Avtapug, a fire, rank, in the *suqe*; of all ranks; *tapug*.

Avtogo, to make compensation; *ni me avtogo mun o qoe*, he has given a pig in payment for some one killed.

Avu, 1. to borrow.

Avu, 2. v. 1. to come out, as a secret or piece of news; *o gagas qaranis ti avu lue nan*, the steam comes out of the oven. 2. impers. to come as a habit; *gate avu tiqa munia, qara les ti*, he has not yet got into the way of it, he has only just been admitted. 3. tr. v. to let out, as a secret, or news.

avut, as below.

Avuai, (k) fluff, tomentum on plants, scales on butterflies' wings; *o avuai me sara nan napanena*.

avuaga, fluffy, downy, dusty; met. misty, indistinct.

Avunana, [*a* 2.] adv. above; n. on him, her, it; *vunai*.

Avune, [*a* 2.] 1. adv. on; *ni me mas avune tangae*, he fell from a tree. 2. n. *vunai*, in constr. with prep.

Avut, 1. [*u* 4.] take up, move, *vut*; *avut raka*, take up and transplant.

Avut, 2. [*avu* 2.] 1. tr. cause to move, attract, as by a charm; *o sor me avutia*, the *sor* has attracted him; a man has made a charm by rubbing *sor*, the crowd influenced by the charm are attracted to the feast. 2. the people thus attracted, *we avut*, go all together.

Avut, 3. when three men are at a drum the middle one is said to *avut*, the two outer to *pala*; *qatavuvut*, the drumstick.

Awa, ex. in lamentation, sad surprise.

Awatega, adj. clean.

Awisiga, [*a* 4.] budding into leaf, *wisiu*; to come into leaf.

Awo, 1. cry of pain or grief; thence 2. v. to cry out in pain or grief.
   awo*n*, to exclaim loudly at.
   awosag, to cry with pain.
   awoawo, to shout.

Awo, 2. to entice, as an eel from its hole with a bait, or a sick man out of his house with promise of something nice.

Awo*n*, 1. [*awo* 1.] as above.

Awo*n*, 2. to steam over the fire and straighten, as a reed.

Awosa, [*u* 4.] to cleanse, beating with the hand, *wosa*, as a dirty mat in salt-water, or beating out dry dirt.

E.

E, 1. exclamation, of surprise, denial, disapproval, calling a person's attention; many compounds:—
   ea! of fear, deprecation.
   ei! of refusal.
   eke! of surprise.
   eo! of disapproval.
   eqa! eqe! eqei! of astonishment.
   e! si—, doubt, disavowing; don't know!
   e we! surprise.
   e wun! of doubtful assent, *wun*.

E, 2. expletive added to *ti*; *mantagai ti e*, yet a little.

Eleele, adj. high, lofty.

Epa, (k) constr. *epe*. 1. mat, piece of matting. *epa pepepe*, mat in which infants are carried, *pepe*. 2. sail of matting, *o epa me vau mun garine gae*, woven by women; *o mereata ti susur*, sewn by men, *mun o gavaru*; *mun o qatiu o qasai apena*, with a tree-fern needle.

Ere, a kind of pandanus; the leaves, *no-ere*, used for the ridge thatching of houses.

Es, esu, live, life; be in health; *esu kel*, recover health.

esuva, life, living, saving, safety.

esuvag, live with, by.

Ete, to turn up the face, for *ate*; *soeteete*.

G.

This letter represents a guttural trill, never the hard *g*. In V. it is commonly replaced by *w*, and at the end of a word is sounded as *i*.

G, tr. suffix to v.

Ga, 1. poss. n. (k) of close relation, generally of food; *gak o qatia*, arrow to shoot me with; *nagak namatama*, an expression of endearment; as *gak taema*, of admiration. Fl. *ga*; Fij. *ke*; D.Y. Marsh. *a*; N.G. Aroma, *ga*; Kerep. *a*.

Ga, 2. constr. *gae;* common in names of plants and trees with fibrous bark.

Ga, 3. pref. of instrument or condition.

Ga, 4. v. p. as in neg. *gate*. V.L. *ga, ge, ga;* Lep. *ga;* Sta. C. Lif. Mao. *ka;* Ul. *a;* used in songs, charms, &c. *Na ga van, na we ret row mini Lul mame=nau we van, we ret rowo.*

Ga, 5. adj. term. as in Ar. Lep. Mae. Bks. I. generally *ga, g;* Sol. I. generally *ga, ha, 'a;* Fij. Sam. *a;* Motu N.G. *ka.*

Ga, 6. term. of verbal n.

Gaal, [*ga* 2.] creeping arad, *alu.*

Gaas, [*ga* 2.] 1. ipomœa, *as.* 2. met. sinew, tendon.
 gaasgona, ipomœa bona nox.

Gaav, [*ga* 2.] creeper, *av.*

Gae, constr. *ga.* 1. creeper, trailing plant. 2. fibre, string made from it. 3. tie, bond. 4. bunch of banana or pandanus fruit. Fij. *wa.*
 met. *o gae ni kalo taniniga,* speaking of the rightful heir of a property, *isei o tag gan o utag;* the vine runs straight.

Gaei, (k) bunch of banana or pandanus fruit.

Gaela, [*gae*] stringy, tough.

Gaereere, [*ga* 3. *ere*] contracted, thin-waisted, like orange-leaf or wasp.

Gag, v. suff. Fij. *kaka;* Marsh. *kake.*

Gaga, n. v. crack.
 gagagi, tr. break skin, wound.

Gagaega, [*ga* 5.] sticky.

Gagaganor, [*nor*] wantonly mischievous, of bad disposition.

Gagagao, 1. [*gagao*] writhe, move in water by arms, legs, tentacles.

Gagagao, 2. [*gao*] adv. smoothly; *vil gagagao,* serve evenly with sinnet.

Gagaleg, [*gale*] practise upon with charms so as to attract or repel.

Gagalig, ascend, of smoke in small volume from unseen fire, *o asu me gagalig kalo.*

Gagaliwo, the handle of a *gete.*

Gagalo, [*galo* 2.] weak, helpless.

Gagamail, shake the head; *na-qatik te gagamail vitag,* I shall reject by shaking my head.

Gagan, [*gan* 1.] to work upon the skin so as to impress a mark, make a sore; *me gagan tawasis,* has broken the skin.

Gaganag, to show, tell.

Gaganarag, [*gana*] eat to excess, confusedly.

Gaganor, [*nor*] mischievous.

Gagao, 1. throw about arms, legs, tentacles, so to swim, of men, nautilus, cuttle-fish, &c. Sam. *'a' au,* swim.

Gagao, 2. stiff, straight; *o pisui tuwale we gagao;* flat, *o ima we taqa gagao,* a house with a flatter gable than common; *o malo we rasa gagao;* compare *vat-gao.*

Gagapiag, to dun, demand tenaciously; see next word.

Gagapiaga, [*ga* 3. *piai, ga* 5.] tenacious, glutinous, like cooked sago.

Gagapior, shrug, back away in refusal, restive.

Gagaqor, [*ga* 2. *qor.*] disturbed, of the stomach.

Gagar, [*gar*] 1. to rake, scrape. 2. a rake. 3. to threaten.

Gagara, to itch.

Gagarag, [*gara* 1.] to scrape away; *o gagarag lepa,* a scraper.

Gagarakae, [*gara* 2.] urgent, urgently.

Gagaramamasa, [*gara* 2.] go without food, fast.

Gagaramea, [*gara* 2.] to draw out the tongue.

Gagarat, the itch, to have the itch.

Gagareaga, getting light in colour, of a bread-fruit mature.

Gagaro, clutch, tear at.

Gagaroro, [*ga* 3.] coming with loud noise, *roro* 1.

Gagas, 1. rise in particles, as dust, spray, steam. 2. annoy, pain.
 gagasiu, what rises in particles, *gagas tano*, dust; *gagas pei*, steam; *gagas nawo*, spray.

Gagasir, diligent, diligently.

Gagasoag, impers. v. with *goro*, to be fit to do anything, *neira gate gagasoag gorora lai*, they could do nothing, from fatigue.

Gagasuwe, a mollusc, chiton.

Gagata, to scratch.

Gagatpoapoa, [*gat*] stutter, as if chewing the words.

Gagauwa, sea-woodlouse.

Gagavu, thick, muddy, cloudy, of water.
 gagavug, to make thick, as scent in the air.

Gagin-mot, [*ga* 3. *gin*] said of strong, successful men; one who grips and holds.

Gai, 1. demons. pr. see *ragai*; only used as sing. in voc. *gai*, you fellow!
 2. interj. giving emphasis.

Gai, 3. conj. till, until.

Gala, qualifying prefix.

Galamas, [*ga* 3.] beating, thrashing; the sound of it.

Galao, (k) left hand, left-handed.

Galaqar, [*ga* 3. *laqa*] a stone or other object from which *mana* springs out.

Galaqot, [*ga* 3. *laqot*] in a large bundle, as arrows; *pul galaqot*, take a large handful.

Galava, 1. [*ga* 3. *lava.*] long lasting, everlasting. 2. [*ga* 2.] a long creeper. 3. a kind of *qauro*.

Galaveai, a swine-fish.

Galavetanun, a small man.

Galaviv, [*viv* 2.] whistle, sound as wind blowing round a point, voice close to the ear, wind in a hole.

Gale, deceive, trick, lie.
 galea, (k) deceiving, deceit, being deceived; *na galeana*, what deceived him.
 galeg, practise upon, as with charms, so as to deceive.
 galesag, succeed in deceiving one.
 galeva, deception, trickery, temptation.
 gale ilo, try, tempt.

Galean, adv. for a time, awhile.

Galesag; see *gale*.

Galete, [*ga* 3. *lete*] shrink with a curl, as *wosoisoi*, green wood, underdone food.
 gagalete, adv. with ends curving in; *ti kalokalo gagalete*, of geometer caterpillar.

Galeul, give money on first pregnancy.

Galeva; see *gale*.

Galewora, adv. for a short time, after a short interval.

Galgalamemea, ruddy, reddish.

Galgalelan, a toy, windmill of palm frondlets.

Galgalematika, a blue star-fish put on bananas to keep away *matika*.

Galgaluanara, [*nara*] blush, flushing.

Galo, 1. v. to roll fibre on the thigh into twine. Fl. *galo*, a line. *galo wetwet qoe*, to roll with one strand over another.

Galo, 2. feeble, depressed.

Galoi, to endeavour; *galoi lai*,

persevere and succeed; *galoi matila*, fail in endeavour.

Galolo, tr. v. to turn round and round, revolve.

galoloag, adv. with a twist; *malawo galoloag*, grow tall and twisted.

Galoma, M. to roll fibre on the thigh into twine; *galoma galao*, to twist, roll to the left; *galoma matua*, to the right.

galomtag, rub with rolling motion, twist in preparing fibre; *savsavula galomtag*, wash the hands rubbing the knuckles in the palm.

Galtag, adv. for a while; *la galtag*, to lend.

Galwonia, said of a fire burnt to red coals; *me gan matanona*.

Gamal, (k) club-house of *suqe*, or of a single high rank; *gamal wemeteloa*.

Gamalmalaqauro, [*ga* 2.] creeper of wild *qauro*.

Gamanin, [*ga* 2.] yellow-wood tree.

Gamao, [*ga* 3.] swift, as a falling star, of a vessel.

Gamas, [*ga* 2.] a tree.

Gamasig, [*ga* 3.] thing given to *masig* with.

Gamataninnin, a soft creeper, no good fibre.

Gamataviro, [*gau*] fish-hook made of *nug ota*, prickle of sago palm.

Gamau, an acacia.

Gamemes, [*ga* 3.] what makes the eye *memes*, red, inflamed.

Gameto, [*ga* 2.] a creeper.

Gamgamera, [*ga* 3. *mera*] reddish, rusty-coloured.

Gamo, v. to sail, make a sailing voyage; *gamo peperua*, *gamo rupe*, of two canoes sailing together.

gamova, sailing, a sailing voyage.

gamovag, [*vag* 2.] sail with.

Gan, 1. V. to eat food. Fl. *yani*; Lif. *xen=gen*; N.B. *an.*; Mal. *makan*; N.G. *kani*, *ani*.

Gan, 2. V.M. to eat as an ulcer or sore, spread as fire.

Gan, 3. to swim by the movement of the body; of fish, eels.

Gan, 4. n. a kind of ant, the bite painful; its nest is *ime gan*.

Gana, M. to eat food. Fij. *kana*; Malag. *hanina*.

ganagana, n. M. *gangan* V. an eating, meal, feast.

ganavag, [*vag* 2.] eat with something as an accompaniment.

gana gogona, of one who still eats the *av tapug*, does not yet *gana popolotag*; *gana-isis*, to eat with expression of disgust, *rara we gana isisia*, at him; *gana mate* [*mate* 2.] eat and finish; *gana matea*, eat the death meals and feasts; *gana popolotag*, eat ordinary food when the days of *gana tapug* are expired; *gana pulul*, eat, giving all present a share; as if many are eating and one is apart, they say, *tagai, nina gana pulul*, Not so, let us, all of us, eat together; *gana qatmatea*, to eat the *tapug* without payment after a death, allowed to children, see *gana tapug*; *gana sal*, to miss an oven in eating the *tapug*, and so gain a step in the *suqe*; *gana sapur*, to eat careless of the quality of food, eat bad food; *gana sei nin*, to make a feast when the enclosure, *nin*, for the *qat* is removed; *gana simpei*, to sip water as one eats, eat and drink together as in sickness; *gana sinere* [*sinerei*] to eat sparingly while others eat largely; *gana sopun*, to eat all up; *gana tapug*, the ceremonial eating by which one is admitted to a rank in the *suqe*; *gana tavaltuwale*, to eat with others without contributing a share of food; *gana tulag*, to make a farewell feast for a person, *gana tulagia*; *gana vare tamate*, said of an angry man; *gana vasigtag*, loathe eating with a person, *kamrua me gana vasigtagia* could not eat with him in sight, *nan wa lulua*; *gana vasvag*, to eat, picking off the good bits and throwing away the bad; *gana vasvas*, the same; *gana vilerag*, to eat delicately, choice bits; *gana voro*, to make a feast after a deliverance, *gana vovo gak*; *gana vule ima*, to eat for the first time in a new house; *gana wonot*, to choke in eating; *gana wonwono*, to eat a step in *suqe*, and so set oneself right after anything one has been ashamed of; *gana wora*, eat and do little work.

Ganae, small, dwarfed.

Ganagana, n. a feast, meal; *ganagana liwoa*, a big feast; *ganagana matea, tapug, tulag, voro*, see *gana*.

Ganaman, [*ga* 2.] a tree.

Ganamera, 1. n. *o gene o natmera te wota ma ni we toga alolona*, placenta, after-birth. 2. v. to be occupied about childbirth.

Ganarawe,*un* word for *tapera wol*.

Ganaro, [*ga* 2.] the neck-rope worn as a sign of *naro*.

Ganase, a fish, mullet. Mao. *kanae*; Fij. *kanace*.

Ganawasia, a tree.

Ganawono, [*ga* 3.] 1. n. distress, sorrow. 2. adv. wantonly, carelessly.

Ganene, [*ga* 3. *nenei*] 1. a beetle. 2. a yam eaten by *ganene*.

Ganere, [*ga* 3. *nere*] something very nice; *ti nere*, breaks short *alo vakama*, in your mouth.

Gangan, V. n. and v. same as *ganagana* with its compounds.

Ganganira, [*gan* 2., *ra* 4.] scarred, as a tree often chopped, or leg marked by sores.

Ganganor, [*nor*] n. adj. intensified *ganor*, malice, ill-feeling, so a desire to do mischief, evil disposition; thence wickedness, sin, wickedly, sinfully, in recent use.

Ganganpewu, warty growth like a *pewu*.

Ganialo, anything sweet.

Ganig, [*nig*] to separate the useful from useless part of a vine, nip out the fibre.

Ganir, [*ga* 2.] 1. the fibre of *nir* of which sinnet is made. 2. adv. exactly, in following a pattern.

Ganlue, [*gan* 2.] a sore in the sole of the foot which eats through.

Gan-mata-nona, [*gan* 2.] burn clear; of a fire newly lighted when the air draws through the openings, *matai*, in the fuel.

Gan-mule, n. one who eats much and quickly, as birds do just before dark when the *paka* fruit is ripe, eating and going off.

Ganor, [*nor*] malevolent disposition, malice.

Gan-rowo, 1. a kind of ant [*gan.* 4.] that leaps.

Gan-rowo, 2. [*gan* 1.] scarcity of food.

Gan-rowo, 3. to eat for the first time in a house; *ganrowo ima*.

Gansar, [*gan* 2.] burn furiously.
 gansarqov, *gansarnor*, burn quickly as a fire of soft wood.
 gansar popo, burn strongly as fire of solid fuel; see *popo*.

Gansasa, [*sasa* 2.] to approach, collide.

Gansewsew, tale-bearing, *tama si ni we ganagana, ni we ronotag isei ilone we rara apensei, ni we mule we gaganag nunia*.

Gantavalaima, [*gan* 4.] a stinking ant.

Gantawela, [*gan* 2.] an open sore, not deep.

Gantaweraga, [*gan* 2.] of a fire burning to ashes, *taweraga*.

Gantawtawilis, [*gan* 1.] of a fish such as *sauma* feeding at a reef, rolls, *wil*, on the waves, but keeps on eating.

Gantul, [*gan* 3.] of fishes sinking, *tul*, as they swim.

Gantutut, [*gan* 2.] to burn out to an end, as a log, or wick.

Ganua, [*ga* 2.] a creeper, used to poison fish.

Ganue, west wind, *o ganue ti tur ma sage alo Gaua; ganue mate*, as it dies away over Gaua; *ganue qoe, ti tur alo maea, o Meralava sage wa o Gaua siwo ma, pa alo ratitnai*, blows from the open sea between Star I. and Sta. Maria; *ganue siwo, ti tur ma alo Nus Paut*, blows from Vanua Lava over Qakea.

Ganvataleag, to take food one from another; *ko we la nagak, na we la nayama*.

Ganvun, [*gan* 2.] consume to the end, *vun*.

Ganwora, [*gan* 1.] eat to burst.

Ganwot, [*gan* 3.] of fishes coming to the surface, *wot*, as they swim.

Ganwune, [*gan* 1. *wune*] a jocular saying, *ko me ganwune inau alo sava?* how did you come to think of me? see *wune*.

Gao, 1. to spread from point to point; *ratgao*, stone continuous, in bed. 2. to burn, of fire, active and neuter. 1. *gao talaray*, spread as a secret carelessly let out. 2. *gao searag*, of fire that spreads from the middle to the outside fuel; *gao serlawalawa*, burn with flame; *gao taweraga*, burn down into embers, *taweris*.

Gaosa, pass across on branches from one tree to another.

Gap, 1. adv. with no particular thought, purpose, or effect, merely, only.
 2. *gap!* interj. be quick!

Gapa, 1. food, such as is secretly given to women.

Gapa, 2. a bat. Sam. '*apa*.

Gapagapa, 1. swallow, Collocalia uropygialis. 2. the cross-shaped mark on the *qat*. 3. harpoon iron. The two latter from the shape of the bird.

Gapaka, [*ga* 2.] bowstring, generally made from fibre of *paka*.

Gapakasamali, prov. a wet bowstring, bad shooting.

Gapakapulpul, prov. of one who does not tell of or notice a wrong; like a sticky bowstring which an arrow does not quickly leave.

Gapalag, to do, act, work.
 gagapalag, n. 1. actions.
 2. assistant, minister, officer; in recent use.

Gapalao, [*ga* 2.] 1. tendons, which tetanus, *palao*, affects.
 2. veins.

Gapane, 1. the sail of a canoe, also *gapan*. 2. *gapan ta Roua*, the middle ribs, of a pig.

Gapatun, [*ga* 3.] thing to pelt with; said in ridicule of a large heavy fishing-line.

Gape, 1. n. a net, *we tia o gape*; various nets, *gape saosao, gape taqataqa, gape tultul*.

Gape, 2. v. to break or tear apart with both hands; *gape sare*, tear apart; *gape wora*, break apart; *gape sansan*, tear to pieces, as a dog a fowl; *gape sau*, break up a door by lifting.

  gapeag, met. to annoy, distract, as when a man thinks of what he has to pay for *suqe; ti gapeagia ape som*.

Gapgaperue, [*yapa* 2.] a bat, small.

Gapilwana, 1. to flash like lightning; *wan*, in Gaua red summer lightning. 2. n. *un* for lightning. 3. a flower.

Gaplei, n. opening, mouth, of a wound or ulcer.

Gaplot, [*gap* 2.] adv. quickly, soon; v. to be quick; it is said to be met. from the quick motion in making *lot*.

Gapmatava, [*gap* 1.] the early morning time generally.

Gaprono, an ornamental girdle which women *kole*; native money (Fl. *rono*) is platted into it; the word may probably be *ga* 2. *pe, rono*.

Gapul, [*ga* 3.] union, bond of union; *gapulpul*.

Gapulut, [*ga* 3.] 1. earth used between the stones in building a *wona*, see *tanopulut*. 2. glue made of *totoe patau*, used in making *tamate*. 3. in new use, glue, paint.

Gapun, a kind of crab.

Gapur**pur**, [*ga* 3.] the fencing at the bottom of the doorway of a house.

Gaqale, [*ga* 3.] very crooked, of a stick, road, life; see *qale*.

  gaqalesag, to deal crookedly with.

  gaqaleva, witchcraft, harmful magic.

Gaqatmot, [*ga* 3.] something very bitter to eat or drink.

Gaqir, [*ga* 2.] a creeper used for tying thatch; *puto* or *uto yaqir* is very strong.

Gaqisan, [*ga* 3.] something oppressive, that weighs down, *qisan*.

Gaqoag, twist; *gaqoagmot*, break with twisting motion.

Gaqoas, [*ga* 3.] bandage, leaves, cocoa-nut husk, to tie round, *qoas goro*, a sore foot.

Gaqonamate, the line strung through the meshes of the *gape saosao* next to the bow.

Gaqora, 1. [*ga* 3.] something causing unevenness; *qora*. 2. a fish, silurus.

Gaqot, [*ga* 3.] a swelling in which matter gathers in a lump, *qote*, and will not burst.

Gar, 1. same as *gara* 1. thence to scrape.

Gar, 2. same as *gara* 4. poss.

Gar, 3. v. M. to chop, cut down.

Gar, 4. a cockle; *vingar*, cockle-shell, used to cut yam vines, and to scrape out meat of cocoa-nut.

Gar, 5. same as *ar* 1. current, *ar Gaua, ar lama*.

Gar, 6. same as *garu; garmotmot*.

Gara, 1. to bring together so as fit or press evenly upon something opposite, as teeth upon teeth in eating and speaking; so to eat, bite, speak; *me gara ara*, made a mistake in speaking; neuter, to fit close to.

garagara, v. to clench the teeth ; *garagara ninin*, in pain ; *garagara mamasa*, going without food, shutting jaws upon nothing.

garat, v. to bring things close together.

garav, to bring, press, close.

garavag, go with shut mouth ; *garavag o rarae*, go with a message in the mouth.

Gara, 2. to come apart ; reverse of *gara* 1.; *tagaragara*; *garawora*.

Gara, 3. v. spread, swarm, like *un*; catch and spread like fire ; *gara-ava*, of fire, where not meant to burn. Motu N.G. *kara*.

Gara, 4. 3rd plural of poss. *ga* 1.

Gara-ava, 1. [*gara* 1.] make a mistake in speaking, be wrong in what one has said.

2. [*gara* 3.] of fire ; *o av me gara-ava ape qatia*, the fire spread and caught a tree-fern which was not intended to be burnt.

Garake, n. fat of meat ; see *tutup*.

Garalate, [*gara* 1.] 1. v. to leave off words half spoken.

2. adv. *mawui garalate*, in planting a garden to leave off work half done.

3. v. to bite in pieces, *gara latelate*.

Garamal, [*gar* 4.] a bivalve, cockle.

Garamama, soft, of wind and speech.

Garamata, of the first fish or crustacean caught in a new net or pot, *me garamata nivisa?* how many were caught ?

Garameai, [*ga* 2.] (k) tongue ; *mea* is probably tongue, as in San Cr. Mala. N. Georgia ; Fij. *yame*; D.Y. *karame*.

Garameav, flame, tongue of fire.

Garamis, [*ga* 3.] 1. something to smear, *ramis*. 2. v. to take a little to eat, just enough to *ramis* with.

garamisa, bitter in taste, like *ramiai*.

Garamos, [*gara* 1.] to close lips firmly ; *garamomos*, to close the lips as when a man lifts a heavy weight.

Gara-nit-late, to eat biting short off.

Garanoman, [*ga* 2.] the loop of the bowstring at the lower end of bow, *kereus*, as *nagoqasa* at *qat us*; from likeness to bird's foot.

Garaorior, [*gara* 1.] to make a noise in eating, or in grinding the teeth in sleep ; *ori*, to creak.

Garaoror, the same.

Garapig, [*gara* 1., *pig*] to eat vegetable with animal food ; *we pig mun o qoe*.

Garapul, to shut the jaws closely, *pul*; *garapul goro*, to swallow, gulp down.

Garapupsag, to blow, puff out, *pupsag*, through closed teeth, as in rejecting food.

Gararua, [*gara* 1.] said of two persons who are always together, or of things that go in pairs.

Garaqa, new.

garaqai, (k) n. from *garaqa*, the first thing, doing ; what is new to a person ; *o tau ilone ni qara toga garaqana*, that year he made his first stay.

Garaqosa, [*gar* 4.] a kind of cockle.

Garasawsaw, [*gara* 1.] to eat a thing hot, steaming, *sawu*.

Garasilsil, [*gara* 1.] close, shut, so as to darken, *sil*.

c

Garat, [*gara* 1.] to bring things to meet, as firebrands end to end keep the fire in; thence of fire remaining but hidden, as on the hill *Garat* on Sta. Maria, where the volcanic fires remain; see *ragarat*; *yarat qalo*, said of thick darkness settling down, *o siliga ti garat qalo.*

Garata, (k) fragment of food, &c. used as medium for a charm; so the charm thus brought to work. It is the *garata* of the subject who is to be affected by the charm, *garatausei.* To prepare a *garatu* is to *woro garata.*
  garata lalai, a man thin in the ribs by reason of a *garata* charm; *garata tapilta*, one with shrivelled stomach; *garata toqatoqa*, one with stomach swelled.

Garatai, (k) fragment, remnant. *Isei o garata tapilta me map nagaratana iake?* What man whose belly will be pinched for it has left a fragment of his food here? Mal. *krat.*

Garatapug, [*gara* 1.] same as *ganatapug.*

Garataqai, take the first bite.

Garatigiu, (k) a row, things or persons in a line.
  garatig tano, row of holes dug for planting yams.

Garaug, M. *garauw*, V. 1. to blow, *ug*, through closed lips. 2. met. to urge.

Garauwav, to blow the fire with the mouth.
  gagarauwav, n. [*ga* 3.] bellows, new word.

Garav, [*gara* 1.] to climb a cocoa-nut tree badly, pressing body and knees against the trunk, to swarm up.

Garavag; see *gara* 1.

Garavalor, to eat [*gara* 1.] mixing, *lor*, one food with another.

Garavis, [*ga* 3.] anything that will *ravis* a man; said of wind blowing hard; *tano garavis*, at the edge of a cliff.

Garavrag, to eat, *gara* 1., with mouth too full, so that the food bursts, *vura*, out.

Garavura, n. v. said of *loko* in which almonds, *nai*, are imbedded; when the *loko* is bitten the almonds burst through.
  garavurag, tr. v. see *garavrag.*

Garawisota, said of black hair with red tips.

Garawora, [*gara* 2.] split, as when two parts which have been close together part asunder; *e. g.* the cotyledons of a growing bean.

Garawotora, to bite a stone or other hard substance, *wotorai*, in food.

Garegare, a small fish.

Garenaw, tasty, as salt, *nawo*, in food.

Garenren, burnt in cooking, as *toape* without enough water.

Garere, [*ga* 3.] a narrow channel through which the tide ebbs and flows; *rere* 2.

Garerea, [*ga* 3.] place of strong current, *rere*, tide-rip.

Garete, [*ga* 2.] kind of pandanus.

Gareve, [*ga* 3.] adj. very long; n. a long thing; *rere.*

Gargara, [*gara* 1.] redupl. to close mouth, teeth; *gargara mamasa*, go without food, fast; *gargara ninin*, clench hard the teeth in pain.

Gargarat, [*gagara*] to bite, burn, the tongue or throat, as underdone *qeta.*

Gargareano, a yellow *garegare* fish.

Gargarewolgesa, kind of *garegare* fish.

Gargarial, roots of the *alu*; *gariu*.

Gargaroa, a sunburnt fruit very good and sweet.

Gargartintin, small yams good to roast, *tin*; *gariu*.

Gariawasa, [*wasa*] waste, empty, where there is space.

Garisa, a creeping fern, ligodium, much used as a tie, *gae*, in building, thatching.

Garitata, [*ga* 2.] the lacing, *ritata*, of a sail.

Garitgae, small rootlets met in digging yam-holes.

Gariu, (k) a root; *gar tauwe*, base of mountain or hill. Mal. *akar*.

Garmotmot, [*gar* 6.] squalls of rain coming in succession, *motmot*, on the sea; *garu* 2.

Garo, 1. n. the hard ground under the soil; adj. hard; see *tinegaro, matagaro*.

Garo, 2. v. to stretch the arm bending it; *kamam me gagagaro o taqagaro*, we scooped up a little muddy water.

garovag, to throw the arms round something.

Garogaro, 1. white with scratching, as the body of one who has the itch. 2. a scratched place. Sunda *garo*, scratch.

Garotrot, n. tie, bond; *rot*.

Garov, 1. the hard inner fibrous part, *gae*, of the rachis of cocoa palm-leaf; *garov qatiu*, the scalp.
2. a kind of yam.

Garovag, to throw the arms round, *garo*, and clasp to the breast, embrace a person, gather into both arms.

Gartaga, a kind of cockle.

Gartanasul, a fire-stick, brand.

Gartaweris, black embers, charcoal; *o av me gao tagea o lito pa me gartaweris vires*, the wood has all burnt away, there is nothing but charcoal.

Gartuka, name first given to iron, as if pieces of the base of the sky; *gariu*.

Garu, 1. to advance by motion of legs and arms, so to wade and swim, of men. Mal. *arung*, wade. *ti garu ma qaurouro*, he comes helping himself with his hands weak with hunger.
2. to sweep on as a rain shower, or current.
tamate garugaru, a waterspout.

garuvag, swim or wade with.

Garugaru, from same word, reckless; *ge garugaru viteg*, squander recklessly.

Garululu, advancing ripples before the wind on the sea, a catspaw; see *lulu*.

Garurus, [*ga* 2.] a running line; see *rurus*; said of one who talks at great length, *ni me la o garurus*.

Garusa, salt spray settled on leaves, &c.

Garusaro, 1. a way of taking fish; men wade, *garu*, and drive fish into a space enclosed by roughly-woven cocoa-nut fronds; the fish try to enter, *saro*, but are driven back by the spikes, *sinai*, of the frondlets, and they are shot.
2. met. of a smart person, who does things with little labour.

Garuturgoro, a way of taking fish; men wade, *garu*, and drive fish into a hollow rock or pool and stand to prevent escape, *turgoro*, till the tide goes out; they then poison them, *vun*.

Garuvag; see *garu*.
Garuwe, a flattened crab; *garuwe ta Panoi*, one kind of such crab.
Garviteg, recklessly; see *garugaru*; *vava garviteg*, speak without due respect.
Garwetav, [*garuwe*] a skin disease.
Gas, 1. to rise in particles, stem of *gagas*.
Gas, 2. adj. sharp: probably *as* 1.
Gasakalo, [*ga* 3.] a man who hangs things safely up, does not let them fall; *sakalo, sakau*.
Gasal, [*ga* 3.] an instrument to cut, *sal*, with; probably a new word for a knife; the bamboo strips in former use not being fit to *sal*.
Gasala, persons whose children have intermarried, as if on the same road, *sala*.
Gasalosalo, [*ga* 3.] a thing laid endlong, *salo*.
Gasalsal, [*ga* 2.] a line used as a snare or fishing-line, *sal*.
Gasasao, [*ga* 2.] the neck-rope of one who is *naro*.
Gasavai, V. [*ga* 3. *sava*] how; *gasavai nia*, by what means.
Gasei, M. [*ga* 3. *sei*] how; *gasei nia*, by what means; see *sei* 4.
Gasene, [*ga* 3.] very sharp, said of adze or knife that cuts rapidly; *sene* 2.
Gasesega, [*ga* 2.] a kind of *qauro*.
Gasgasowag, a kind of yam.
Gasgastapatara, a kind of yam.
Gasiosio, rainbow, perhaps because curved like a *sio*.
Gaslag, 1. to stick things, knives, &c., between the layers of thatch inside; probably *gasolag* below.
Gaslag, 2. to range the cut pieces of yam on the hills for planting.

Gaso, 1. n. a rafter. Mao. *kaho*; Mal. *kasau*; Fij. *kaso*, cross beams in canoe.
met. *o pisui o gaso*, dirty fingers, as rafters black with smoke; *gaso mot*, rafters consisting of a pair of bamboos crossing at the ridge-pole; not as is usual one long bamboo bent, *ruqa*, to make a pair; *gaso name*, a rafter broken and hanging.
2. v. to put on the rafters of a house; *me gaso qet qara luluqa*, when the rafters have all been put on, begin to tie on the purlins.
Gasolag, to stuff one thing within another, between others.
Gasoma, M. to husk cocoa-nuts with a stick.
Gasomag, same as *gasolag*.
Gasor, a tree; *vinsorsor*.
Gasovag, same as *gasolag*.
Gasuga, a tree bearing edible nuts.
Gasur, a tree from the wood of which the *tikataso* is made; an euphorbia.
Gasurlan, met. *isei qe leqaleqa lan ineia o gasurlan*.
Gasusuliav, [*ga* 3.] name given to a yam badly cooked, burnt outside, raw within.
Gasusumatig, [*ga* 2.] a creeping plant.
Gasuware, [*ga* 3.] 1. n. one who is always sending others about, *suware*. 2. v. to hurry people.
Gasuwe, 1. a rat. Varying forms in Banks' Islands, New Hebrides, Solomon Islands, show the stem to be *suwe*. Fij. *kucuve*.
gasuwe ta Roua, a rat of smaller species.
2. a mollusc, the woodcock shellfish.

3. a kind of *qauro*.

Gasuwetavtav, a heap thrown up by a rat outside its hole.

Gat, to chew; perhaps common Pol. *kati*, *'ati*, *aki*.

Gatae, the free side of canoe where the outrigger is not; *gatae sama*, the side of outrigger towards the canoe; *par gatae*, to paddle between the canoe and the outrigger; see *par*. Fij. *kata*.

Gatakul, [*ga* 3.] said of one who holds fast to, *takul*, his property; *gatakul qoe*, *gatakul turag*, a close-fisted man.

Gataqava, [*ga* 2.] a creeper, not good to tie with.

Gataqes, a tree.

Gatasig, [*ga* 3.] salt water to *tasig* with; *un* word for *nawo*.

Gatava, the shutter, door, of a house; used all over Mota, as *matetipatipag* is in parts; it is made of lengths of the rachis of sago palm, *lape ota*, run through, *sus*, with a stick. *Gatava*, a district in Mota.

Gatavag, to look about on all sides; *sale gatavag*, hover as a hawk does looking for prey; met. of a man walking and looking.

Gatavanoro, [*ga* 2.] a creeper, used to *malov* enemies; *ti gat o gatavanoro*, *ti pupus*, *ti malov neira*.

Gatawose, the rudder-band, *gae*; observe prep. *ta*, of, belonging to, the paddle *wose*.

Gate, neg. used with verbs; being *ga* 4. with the neg. part. *te* 2.; *gate!* is used as excl. *gate tanun gai!* Oh what a man! Isn't he a man! as the neg. *taho* in Fl.

Gatig, stiff, of the jaws; *napalasana me gatig o qon nitol*, he could not move his jaw for three days; *ga* 3. *tiga*.

Gatipa, [*ga* 3.] a stake, rammed into the ground, *tipa*, for a fence, or to keep back, *vin goro*, earth.

Gato, v. 1. to speak. 2. talk another language, *ni we gato rua*, he speaks two languages, interprets. 3. talk nonsense in sickness, *ni me gato veta*, he has become delirious. 4. *gato goro*, to forbid. 5. *n*. a foreign tongue.

gato linalina, to speak in an improper way to or of a *sogoi*; see *un* 2. *qaliga*.

gato val tanun, to speak to one man after another, it may be in different languages.

Gatogo, [*ga* 2.] a creeper.

Gatogoi, [*ga* 2. *togoi*] the backbone; a range of hills.

Gatoso, a sparoid fish.

Gatou, the hermit crab; N.B. *katu*.

Gatowos, [*ga* 2.] cord to flog with, *towos*, lash of whip.

Gatowtowos, [*ga* 3.] whip, including handle; probably new.

Gatpoapoa, [*gat*] speak as if with mouth full, indistinctly, stammer with nervousness.

Gaturgae, [*ga* 2.] a fishing-line of *gaav* well made.

Gaturtur, [*ga* 3.] a tree that stands, *tur*, fixed below highwater to bathe from, or in villages to hang *wowosa* on.

Gatutuag, [*ga* 2.] a small wild gourd.

Gatuwa, [*ga* 2.] a creeper used to poison, *vun*, fish with.

Gatuwale, *gatwale*, [*ga* 2.] a creeper without branches, all in one, *tuwale*.

Gau, a fish-hook. N.G. *gahu*, *kau*, *igau*. Malag. *havitra*.

Gaua, the island of Sta. Maria; particularly the part called by the people *Gog.*

Gaun, sinnet of cocoa-nut fibre. met. *o tur gaun,* a good strong worker.

Gauna, east wind, *ape mate loa,* over Merlav.

Gauramolaso, a strong man who snatches things from others.

Gaus, [*ga* 2.] bow-string.

Gav, 1. see *gavu.* 2. to crumble in hands, to work up earth with fingers; *gavir.*

Gava, to flap the wings, fly with flapping wings; *gava vatoga,* hover. Mao. *kapa;* Tong. *kaba;* Mal. *kapak.*

  gavag, 1. to carry flying; *o tagere qara gavag raru,* whereupon the fantail carried the two of them as she flew. 2. met. to carry away captive.

  gavarag, of many birds flying together.

Gavaru, [*ga* 2.] 1. fibre of the hibiscus tiliaceus, *varu,* used for stringing money, sewing sails, *epa,* &c.
2. *ul gavaru,* fine flowing hair, like *gavaru.*

Gavarur, [*ga* 2.] the great bean vine common on the beach.

Gave, 1. v. to snatch away, claw; *gave late,* to break; *gavelike,* take quickly off the covering of the oven; *gave sau,* snatch and take away; met. be beforehand.
2. *n.* a crab; so named from its claws. Esp. Sto. *gave,* arm; N.G. Motu, *gave,* tentacles of octopus.

The following are some of the species called *gave;—gave gapun, gave kakeuwa,* tortoise crab, *gave keremino, gave lumuta,* porcupine crab, *gave mara, gave mawoa, gare nam,* spotted crab, *gave naras,* swimming crab, *gave nerenere,* a little crab which when taken up cries, *nerenere,* and froth, *moromorosa,* is seen in its eyes; *gave qeteypapaluk, gave rowo, gave sasaqoe, gave suasua, gave surut, gave takor, gave tapia, gave vat.*

gave nerenere, met. a child ready to cry.

Gavetaga, sticky to the teeth, like bread-fruit.

Gavetal, a bunch of bananas; *gae* 4.

Gavetlamalama, [*ga* 3.] drumsticks used at the ends of a drum, to start the tune, *vet,* and beat, *lama.* Gaua word.

Gavet-tultul, [*ga* 3.] drumsticks used in the midst of the drum, to begin, *tul.*

Gavgagaga, a kind of *gaviga.*

Gavganaretamate, a kind of *gaviga.*

Gavgavmot, one who runs so quickly, as away from a fight, that the wind from his body, *gavgavuna,* is felt.

Gavgavtun; see *gavtun.*

Gavgavui, (k) the wind of a moving body; *gavug.*

Gavig, far away; *me gargavig veta gina!* a long way off already; *roro gavig,* very deep; *agavig.*

Gaviga, the Malay apple, eugenia malaccensis; *malmala gaviga,* wild uneatable kind.

Gavilvilqat, [*ga* 2.] an ornamental band tied round the head.

Gavine—or Gavne-gae, a fibre-producing pandanus of which mats, &c., are made.

Gavir, [*yav*] squeeze, wring, with the hands.

gavir nina, grasp, making the

fingers meet; *gavir tagu,* grasp an object too large for the fingers to meet round it; *gavir tavarasu,* to let fall unperceived from the grasp.

gavirtag, squeeze, grasp, some definite object.

Gavivis, [*ga* 2.] 1. a line wound round, *vivis.*
2. met. a man who withholds what he has.

Gavivsa, [*ga* 2.] the long strip of hibiscus bark wound round, *vis,* the dried bread-fruit, *kor.*

Gavtun, 1. to broil, *tun,* something small, fish, &c., as *laqan.*
2. Thence, since a little smoke rises from the cooking, *gavgavtun* is used to describe a column of smoke; *o as ilone, irasei te gavtun ti?* there is a smoke going up, who are cooking some morsel? *o as we poa ti gavtun kalo,* a great smoke ascending straight up.

Gavu, to make payment for a man killed.

Gavug, winnow as with a fan.

Gavun, hide, deceive; conf. *tavun;* stem, *vun;* Mal. *buni.*

Gavut, [*ga* 3. *vut*] the stomach; of a fowl the gizzard.

Gaw, gawu, take up in handful.

Gawele, [*ga* 2.] the creeping mimosa that produces "crab's-eyes," abrus precatorius; the seed *wowele.*

Gawismea, [*ga* 2.] a kind of *qauro.*

Gawo, 1. to exaggerate.
  gawotag, to exaggerate something, or to some one.

Gawo, 2. to twist.
  gawoag, twist, contort; *gawoag mot,* break by twisting; *gawoag savrag,* shake, wrench, oneself clear of.

Gawola, [*ga* 2.] the creeping palm, calamus, rattan, *wola.*

Gawolawolas, [*ga* 2.] the fine line or fibre with which the hook is made fast, *wolas,* to the fishing-line.

Gawolowolo, [*ga* 3.] the main purlin of a house, which rests crosswise, *wolowolo,* on the *pete.*

Gawono, [*ga* 3.] same as *ganawono; manig gawono,* heedlessly, with culpable carelessness.

Gawu, to take a handful, in handfuls. Motu N.G. *kahu.*
  gawrag, take a big handful, as many small yams at once.

Gawug, gawuw, V. a mound where there are graves, therefore sacred, *rono.*

Gawur, [*ga* 3.] dirt; see *wuwur.*

Ge, M. to do, make; *ge ilo,* to try; *gevtag = gevitag,* to do away with; *ge wora,* n. a trifle.

gege, molest, punish.

gen, determinative from *ge,* as *nag* from *na.*

Gea, piper methysticum; *kava* of Polynesia; *mak o gea.*

Geara, a fence, to fence; *geara goro,* fence against, round; *ara.*
  geara mun, fence of sticks or stones laid horizontally between pairs of upright stakes, which are tied together above the top rail or log, the *sagere toa; geara nor o tulgona; geara pala,* upright stakes wattled, *we tutgag qara pala; geara pul,* a close fence; *geara renegag,* single stakes fastened by two horizontal bamboos at the top, *we tutgag tuwatuwale, we laq, qara tatal mun o gae; geara qatqoe, o masavi we poapoa we maluelue.*

Gega, an amaranthus.

Gegasoma, M. the stick to husk cocoa-nuts with, *gasoma.*

Gegesa, a tradescantia with bright blue flowers and bright green leaves; see *gesagesaga*.

Gege usurgae, to treat one's *usur* with liberty allowed to the connexion; *ineia usurik, nau we mule we gaw o orooro we map avune qatuna*, he is my father's sister's husband, I go and take up a handful of dust and put it on his head.

Gegona, a tree.

Ge-ilo, try, tempt.

Ge-lanalana, [*lana*] stir up, turn up, to fight or dance.

Gele, underdone, raw.

Gen, determinative of *ge*; *gen o sava inia?* how can it be done? effect what thereby?

Gene, a thing. With personal art. *i, iro*, a person; the word *gene* standing for the name, not the person; *iro gene*, a woman whose name is not at the moment remembered, or it is not well to mention; the woman is not called a thing. In the same way *gene* is used as v. *ni me gene qa*, he did whatever you call it; *na me gene ti—nanagok me mulemule wawaliog*, I was—I don't know how to express it—my face went round and round. Similar use with *anu, hanu*, Mal. Malag. Java, Dayak, &c., Sol. Islands, N. H.

Ge-ne-tas, [*ne* dem.] of a bad place to go along; *o matesala we genetas*, the path is bad; *a pan qarana me genetas*, it is slippery walking by the ravine; see *tasgala*.

Ge-risris, [*ris*] met. disturb, annoy.

Gesagesaga, [*gegesa*] bright blue, or bright green.

Gese, 1. a term of plurality, including all in question, and excluding all else; never properly with a singular; translated all or only; *kamam ta Mota gese iake*, we are all Mota people here, we are Mota people only; *kamam we gana o kumara vires gese*, we eat only sweet potatoes. The same word *geh* in Motlav, *ges* in Merlav, is the plural sign. Fij. *kece, kecega*, all, every.

2. v. to keep apart, eat alone, not giving to others; Sam. *'ese*.

Geseqora, trunk-fish, ostracion.

Gesesala, [*gese* 2.] one who walks by himself.

Gesevuvun, [*gese* 2.] one who eats secretly, stealthily.

Get, 1. to rise, stand, stiffly; *get raka*, make a brisk start.

2. to hop; *get raka*, of a ball bounding, *getget*, hopping.

Gete, a woven basket. Mao. *kete*; Sam. *'ete*.

Getget, [*get*] adv. hopping; *pute getget*, sit on the heels; *au getget*.

Getgetenai, a kind of yam.

Ge-tigatiga, [*tiga*] to set up on end; met. stir up to fight or dance, keep people to it.

Gevtag, put away, reject; *ge vitag*.

Gewora, 1. n. a trifle; *matewol o gewora*, die for a little fault.

2. v. *ge wora*, to separate, sunder.

Gig, a balanus.

Gigilrag, [*gil*] intens. form, to dig much, many; *we gil o qatag nam tuwale, we gigilrag we qoqo*, if the tubers attached to one yam vine are dug you say *gil*, if those belonging to many are dug you say *gilgilrag*.

Giginpis, [*gin-pis*] fix the toes in

the ground; *tano gigínpis*, place for taking off in a jump.

Gil, 1. to dig. Mao. *keri*; Sam. *'eli*; Fij. *kili*; N.B. *kir, kire*; Mal. *gali*.

gigilrag, as above.

gilgil, of heavy rain that digs the ground.

giliag, dig deep, and fix. 2. to move by entreaty.

Gilala, to know, understand.

gilaglala, n. understanding.

Gilulsir-sur, to dig, *gil*, down, *sur*, to the end, *ul*, of a long yam.

Gima, the bear's-paw clam; Fl. *gime* the giant clam; Mal. Tagala, *kima*; Batak, Malag. *hima*.

Gin, to pinch with fingers or toes, nip; *gin* mot, pinch off clean. Mao. *kini*; Sam. *'ini*; Ponape *kini*.

ginit, V. to pinch, nip off.

ginita, M. the same. Met. to persist. Fij. *kinita*.

gintag, clench fingers or toes, grip the ground with toes.

Gina, expletive, emphatic.

Ginginigau, 1. to stroll. N.B. *kinkinit*. 2. a game.

Ginginpilage, [*gin*] to trip on the toes, as a *pilage* runs.

Ginpis, [*gin*] to pinch the ground with the toes, *pisui*, for a firm foothold; so *tano giginpis* above.

Gintag, [*gin*] to stand one's ground in fighting, so, to be brave; *gintag goro*, make a firm stand against an enemy; see above; *gintag lea*, to tell a story out.

Gior, creak, as a tree or mast.

Gir, 1. to clear away, in a quantity; *gir o wotano*, clear away weeds; *gir tuwus*, remove ashes from hearth.

Gir, 2. to rouse; *gir goroko, gigir goro*, rouse yourself; *gir rasosor*, stir up to quicker action; see *wir*.

Gir, 3. to be in abundance; *o lalais ti girgir goro neira*, they are all over sweat.

Gir, 4. *we gir sarusaru*, of a yam vine without tubers, *we gil o nam, o wiai tagai apena*.

Gira, unripe, uncooked.

Gire, pandanus odoratissimus, female tree; *vun gire*, the fruit-cluster; *wo gire*, the single fruit. Motu N.G. *geregere*; possibly Mao. *kiekie*.

Giregire, the tropic or boatswain bird, Phaethon æthereus.

Girei, to buy or sell, money passing; *un* word for *som*.

Girgiroro, a man good for nothing but to clear away rubbish, *orooro; gir* 1.

Gis, 1. v. to be employed, busy about; *gis valgoro*, make oneself busy, be actively employed everywhere; chiefly seen in composition.

Gis, 2. thrust, poke, with finger; *gisgoro*, to stop with fingers, so to choke; *gis goro matepei*, stop the source of water with the finger; met. cut off a chance.

gisir, thrust finger into, thence throttle, choke; *we gisir o qeres nam*, thrust the finger under the end of a yam in digging, so as to raise without breaking.

1. *gismamate*, to get ready beforehand, prepare overnight, *mate* 2.

gismana, one who deals in *mana*, magic, a wizard, thence a doctor.

gismantag, one who is accomplished, able.

gismataka, to rise up in excitement, mataka; kamam me gis mataka nol ape neia, we nonom si ni te mate.

gisqiqlon, do secretly, hide.

gisraka, make a start; raka.

gisvalgoro, to be active all round, able to do anything.

2. gisgagalo, hold feebly, with weak fingers, gagalo; tama isei we taur o sava mantagai pa we mavatia.

gisgoro, stop with finger.

giskov, stretch fingers before a light of pul, to shade it; met. to interfere and stop a quarrel.

giswenar, to put fingers into something soft; giswera, the same.

Gisgis, gisigisi, a game.

Gita, expletive, as gina.

Goa, remove the core, uloi, and seeds of bread-fruit in making kor, with matesipa.

Goana, ropy, like cobweb, or stale flesh.

Goar, a fish.

Goara, abide, stay; in company, not alone.

Gogae, stay constantly, reside.

Gogo, 1, shrink, shrivel; o tanun we gopa ti inar, ti gogo, ti wawae, a sick man dwindles, shrivels, has nothing in him; often with mirmir. N.B. kogo. 2. n. a thing that has been plump now shrivelled, a weasened pig.

Gogoi, come quickly, arrive.

Gogolo, 1. [golo 1.] to shake, tremble, with cold or fear.
2. to fear, be afraid.
gogoloiga, fearful, trembling.

Gogololava, a thing that greatly terrifies.

Gogona, 1. [gona] bitter, acrid; o valai tama te gona apena, the mouth is constricted. Sam. 'o'ona. met. bad; tau gogona, bad season for planting; tangae we gogona, a tree that sheds its leaves.
2. close, unapproachable, as haunt of ghost.

Gogoparag, [gopa] to be sick in numbers at once.

Gogor, a flowering shrub, eranthemum.

Gogorag, [gora] to gather together, act. and neut. flow together in crowd or mass.

gogorag ninin o tuqei, gather, clear away, weeds, and make a garden neat, ninin. gogorag pata ilo lia, pour as surf or tide into a hollow rock. gogorag qon, go in a body, as travellers, till night. gogorag sur o pulua, scrape the dirt down the back; met. to do a man a pleasant service. gogorag ralis, n. the name of the little finger, the grass-gatherer, in clearing gardens.

Gogoroi, withhold, refuse.

Gol, use angry language; ni me gol amenau, he scolded me. N.B. kolot.

Gole, neut. v. turn on axis, revolve; gole goro, turn round towards; gole ris, turn backwards. Fl. kolili; Mal. kuliling, guling.

goleag, tr. to turn round; ti goleagia, he turns himself.

Goleav, a V.L. tree.

Golgolgapelia, a fish.

Golgoloaga, said of very ripe fruit.

Golgolomea, [goloi] a red-tailed fish.

Golgolonoota, the eaves of a house; goloi.

Golo, 1, to tremble; redupl. gogolo, gologolo. Malag. horohoro.

Golo, 2. to fade, wither, said also of sick persons.

Golo, 3. to thicken, curdle, as

scum or blood ; *o suora ti golo, o nara ti golo.*

Gologolo, 1. v. to tremble, quiver. 2. n. a toy, windmill made of undeveloped frondlets of palm, same as *galgalelan*.

Goloi, (k) tail ; *golgolo-epa*, skirt of mat ; *golgolonoota*, eaves of a house, edge of thatch.

Golokete, with tail erect, *kete;* said of a bird.

Golokut, a game ; children string *nai* and come into the village singing, others chase them.

Goloman, a young sprout from the ground.

Golonur, the last man of a party.

Golopita, a white-tailed fish.

Goloqet, to cut short a sow's tail so as to make her prolific.

Golowanara, a scorpion, its tail forked, *wanara*.

Goltogoa, a fish.

Gom, to hold liquid in the mouth, *gomgom*. Malag. *hombona*, Motu N. G. *he-gomogomo*.

Gomal, used in stories for *gamal*.

Gomo, twist up, tear as in anger ; *we gomo naulura*.

Gona, entangled, intricate, so difficult ; to be engaged, occupied. *gona ta Roua*, a slip-knot, *vagae maslag; vanua gona*, a district occupied by enemy or *tamate*, so that it is closed ; *mule gona ma*, of the enemy coming to close the country ; *van gona*, V. *va gona*, M. the same ; also to go in danger ; *vagona* [*va* 3.] to tie in a knot.

gonatag, to secure as by tying ; *me gonatag goro o tavine mun o som*, a small sum of money has been paid to secure the arrangement for a marriage.

Gonagona, [*gona*] 1. to be in a difficulty, as a man who has eaten in the wrong place in the *suqe*. 2. a button, a new use.

Gongonesava, [*gona*] occupations, business, *o sava sin gona apena*, something to engage him ; *o retavine tagai nor o gongonesava tam o mereatu ape garata*, women have nothing to do with *garata* charms as men have.

Gono, a conical basket used for taking small fish at Gaua, filled with coral and set in narrow channel in a reef ; the fish hunted into it and taken up.

Gonogono, shaped like a *gono*, hollow with a mouth ; of dish or bowl.

Gopa, to be sick, ill. Sam. *'opa*, weak.

gogoparag, to be sick in numbers together.

gopavag, to be sick with ; *we gopavag o vur*, ill with a cough.

Gopae, 1. sickness ; *gopae solorag*, endemic sickness. 2. a sick person.

Gopgop, ornamental scar by burning with pith of a tree.

Goqo, bubble, boil, ferment, effervesce.

goqovag, to bubble with, ferment with.

Gor, to rasp, scrape ; of a pig *gate sirvag me gor wia*, after being killed not shaved, only scraped ; to scrape out the meat of *vusa*, young cocoa-nut, with the bracts, or top of shell.

Gora, 1. v. sweep, away or together, push away or together, advance or retire ; *o nawo me gora savrag o nai nan o lot*, the surf swept the almonds off the pudding ; *gora savrag gai o av nan o tangae iane* *rowo*, push away (with a stick) the fire from that tree there; *o sul te gora vavtig ma*, the crowd is coming along in a body; *te gora lue at*, is clearing out.

gogorag, as above.

goras, scrape out, grate, the hard meat of cocoa-nut with *vin-gar*. Fij. *kora*.

Gora, 2. a rich man.

Gora, 3. n. a stunted person, does not grow up.

Gorai, [*gora*] what is brought together.

gore savasava wealth, acquired property.

Goragora, n. a rich man, who has scraped together.

Goras, see *gora*.

gorasiam, to nibble the cocoa-nut meat as one scrapes it out.

Gorasmule, said of a rich man.

Gorgor, n. a cocoa-nut with enough meat to be scraped out after drinking; see *matig*.

Gorgoriav, to blow sparks of fire on a person.

Gorgorogae, [*goro* 3.] said of a runaway from a fight, he cuts *goro*, the creepers, *gae*, in his haste to escape.

Gorgortepie, a children's game.

Goriam, [*gor*] to clear out the soft meat of drinking cocoa-nut and nibble it.

Goro, 1. prep. of motion towards, around, against. *geara goro o tuqei*, fence round a garden; *geara goro a qoe*, fence against pigs, to keep them in or out; *saru goroko mun o siopa*, clothe yourself over with a garment; *pute goro*, sit over to take care of, or over against; *ilo goro*, look out for, or against, after; *mule goroa*, go after him; *gana goro*, to eat so as to stop hunger, *ima goro marou* drink to stop thirst; *kurkur goro*, eat to correspond, to prevent waste, see *mamamas*; *ni me vava, wa nau qara rave goro siwo*, he told the story and I wrote it down after him; *na we varus goroko iniko we savai? nau we maros we ronotag goro ko*, to ask for an answer, hear in answer, about you. This prep. follows closely on the verb, does not admit an adverb between it and object.

Goro, 2. v. to cut, cut round, formerly with a shell; *goro late*, cut short off, as a line, twig; *goro savrag*, cut away with a shell.

gorotag, to cut a quantity of things; *gorotag o toape*, cut a number of edible hibiscus plants off.

gorogoro, the cutting off the yam vines, with a shell, before digging them up; in new use, harvest.

goronana, to impress a circular wound or mark.

Goro, 3. to embrace, with *goro* 1. prep.

gorovag, to hold in crook of elbow, to embrace round the neck.

Goro, 4. v. to pass over, of sound, probably same as *goro* 1.; *goro mot*, the sound ceases.

gorot, pass over and strike, of sound; *o sawai, o rorovia, ti gorot*, the noise of distant dance, shout, comes over and strikes our ears.

Gorog, to give magic power; *ni me gorog napanena*, he drank some very bitter decoction to give force to his hand, so that he should shoot and kill.

Gorogoro, 1. n. [*goro* 2.] the cutting of yam vines.
Gorogoro, 2. v. [*goro* 4.] dissension arising with noise.
Gorogoro, 3. n. shouting, uproar, of dissension ; *o gorogoro me goro mot,* the noise of disputation ceased.
Gorogoro, 4. v. to throw arms round the neck.
Gorogoro, 5. a fish, chætodon.
Goronana, [*goro* 2.] to make circular cut or mark by pressure, as a *taqas* will ; see *nana.*
Goron, to stick to work.
Gorot, [*goro* 4.] strike as sound from distance.
Gorotag, 1. to squeeze and roll grated cocoa-nut in the *tapia* dish so as to soften it.
Gorotag, 2. [*goro* 2.] to cut in quantity.
Gorotano, v. of a hurricane or very strong wind ; *o lan we gorotano.*
Gorotoqa, a scented *gega,* amaranthus.
Gorotou, a shell, chiton.
Gorov, same as *goron.*
Gorovag, [*goro* 3.] hold in crook of elbow, hug round the neck.
Gorovalesigo, [*goro* 2.] to cut the end of a round stick on both sides so as to bring it to a wedge ; like a kingfisher's beak.
Goso, 1. v. to job a spike, thence to husk a cocoa-nut with a pointed stick. *goso o iga,* to spear a big fish ; *goso taqesgag,* to husk, leaving a strip to carry by ; *goso mate o qoe,* stab and kill a pig.
igoso, the stick used to husk with.
gosoma, M. same as *goso* 1. V.; but *mule goso ma o matig,* go, husk, bring me cocoa-nuts.

Goso, 2. talk injuriously ; *line gosogoso,* slander.
gosorag, accuse falsely, slander a person.
Got, 1. to prod, dig in with point, cut with point of knife. *got wora,* sunder with point ; *we got o vare qeta,* cut the head of caladium ; to run in, penetrate, as thorn or pointed stone. N.B. *koto.*
igot, the pointed wooden knife used to divide *lot* with.
vagotgot, to hurt the back as a burden with points or knobs.
gotgot, *sir gotgot,* to cut pieces out of a yam by careless scraping.
Goto, to keep inside the house or *gamal* so many days after taking step in *suqe,* entrance into *salagoro,* childbirth, giving or receiving wounds, with a particular diet, *tete gana popolotag.* When a man is shot, his friends *we goto amaia o qon tavelima,* stay indoors with him five days, faring as he does. Fij. *koto.*
Gov, a man full of sores.
Govgov, 1. to dazzle, quiver, of light ; *o loa ti sar govgov namatak,* the sun shines dazzling on my eyes ; *namatak me sar govgov apena,* my eyes were dazzled.
2. to bicker with the fingers, crooking them and shaking them in derision or cursing.

I.

I, 1. personal article ; making a noun into a proper name, and a verb into a descriptive name. *qaratu,* a flying fox ; *i Qaratu,* a man's name ; *gale,* to deceive; *i gale,* deceiver ; applied to personal names, native and foreign, and prefixed at pleasure to all pers. pr. Corresponds to Pol. and Sol. I. *a ;* Malag. *i.*

ira, pl. the companions of some one, the people of.

iro, fem. with *ro ;* used with native names only.

I, 2. has pronominal sense in *ike, ine,* &c.

I, 3. prep. to, with sense of motion towards ; *i siwo,* westwards, *i rowo,* eastwards, in the west, east ; *ilo* 3. *ilolona.*

I, 4. instrumental prefix; *iras,* baler; *ilano,* roller, from verbs, *ras, lano.* Very common in Fiji, but written with art. not noun ; *ai lago* in Fiji, *o ilano* in Mota. Motu N.G. *kokoa,* to nail, *ikoko,* a nail.

I, 5. pref. without meaning; *itagai, ituwale.*

I, 6. exclamation ; 1. of excitement, as in *mago.* 2. of refusal.

I, 7. euphonic ; *maros-i-ava* for *maros ava, qatiaka* for *qat aka.*

Ia, 1. pers. pr. 3. sing.; *pa ia, ni me rowo gis reta apena,* but this man here, he has already been at work at it ; *ineia.*

2. adv. here ; as when a thing looked for is found, *ia !* here it is.

iake, this, here, *ke* demons.
iane, that, there, *ne* demons.

Ia, 3. pers. pr. 3. sing. ; suffixed to v. and prep., probably *i* 7. ; see *a* 1.

Ia, 4. exclamation.

Iake, 1. dem. pr. this, these ; *iake nan,* these many ; *iake nake,* this here. 2. adv. here, now ; *iake nake,* here, now ; *iake at,* hence ; *iake at nake,* henceforward.

Iane, 1. dem. pr. that, those ; *iane nan,* those many ; *iane nane,* that, those, there. 2. adv. there, then ; with *nane.*

Ie, exclamation, of self-satisfaction, I know that !

Iga, a fish. Mal. *ikan;* Mao. Pol. *ika* ; Sam. *i'a* ; Marsh, *iek;* Mafoor, *ijen.*

Many fish are named after leaves of plants ; *iga no-nat, iga no-taqava, iga no-raru,* cobbler fish, *iga no-viloq.*

iga non, or *pulan,* Qat, red firefish, pterois ; *iga tole,* kingfish.

I gene, iro gene [*i* 1.] stands for the name of man or woman which is not remembered or is not mentioned ; *gene,* thing, is that the name of which is a common noun, and with *i* becomes a proper name ; see *gene ;* so *ira gene, irogene.*

Igoso, [*i* 4.] stick to husk, *goso,* cocoa-nuts with, to stab with.

Igot, [*i* 4.] knife to cut, *got,* pudding with ; *te got, te sura mun o igot, we sapalo,* cut the pudding, slide the knife under the slice, *suei,* and take it up, carry it with both hands to the mouth.

Ikamam, pers. pr. 1. pl. excl. we, us.

Ikamiu, pers. pr. 2. pl. you.

Ikamra, pers. pr. dual 2. you two.

Ikamtol, pers. pr. trial 2. you three.

Ikamurua, ikamrua, pers. pr. dual 2. you two.

Ikara, pers. pr. dual 1. excl. we, us, two.

Ikarua, pers. pr. dual 1. excl. we, us, two.

Ikatol, pers. pr. trial 1. excl. we, us, three.

Ikau, [*i* 4.] forked bamboo, to twitch off *nai*, &c., with; *kau*.

Ike, [*i* 2.] 1. demons. pr. this, these; persons or things; with article, *i* and *o ike*. 2. adv. of place; *na qale totoga ran nake ike*, I have always lived here; dem. particle *ke*.

Il, 1. M. to smear, paint, the face.

Il, 2. M. to loose, *ul* V.

Ilalanana, [*i* 3.] under it; adv. underneath; with motion.

Ilalane, [*i* 3.] under with motion; *lalanai* constr.

Ilano, [*i* 4.] roller for dragging canoes; Fij. *ilago*.

Ilele, [*i* 3.] into, of house only; *lele*.

Ilina, M. 1. n. (k) a head-rest or pillow. 2. v. to rest the head.

Ilo, 1. v. to see, know; after another verb often to try; *ge ilo*, try to do, see if one can do. Sam. *ilo*, see.
ilo goro, look after, take care of, overlook; *ilo mana*, view with favour; *ilo maturtur*, see as with closed eyes, *matur;* *ilo nagoi*, remember a person, as if seeing his face; *ilo raka*, choose from among others; *ilo sur ano*, prefer, from liking; *mule ma, ilo sur anoma*, come here, choose which you like; *ilo tanun we ilo tamate*, as in the dark, is it man or ghost? *ilo vaglala*, see plainly; *ilo valaqat*, to see an object flat against the land, not standing out from it; *ilo varirgala*, see without recognizing in a crowd; *ilo wolowolo*, look askance at, with envy.
ilova, v. n. seeing, sight.
2. adv. at all; in a neg. sentence; *ni gate ronotag ilo*, he did not hear at all.

Ilo, 3. prep. [*i* 3.] into; *lo;* *tur risa sur sivo ilo tanomiu*, go and lie down in your places.

Ilogoro, n. a caretaker, overseer; probably new use.

Iloilo, n. a vision.

Iloilonagoi, n. a memorial of one absent or dead, whereby his face is seen.

Iloke, [*i* 2.] 1. pr. demons. this, these; cannot take the article. 2. adv. here, now. see *lo, ke*.

Ilokenake, 1. pro., this; 2. adv. now, *iloke at nake*, henceforth; *nan ilokenake*, the same; *iloke raka nake*, from this time forward.

Ilolona, [*i* 3.] into the inside of it; into; *loloi*.

Ilone, [*i* 2.] dem. pro. that, those; no article; *lo, ne; ilone nane*, that, emphatically.

Iloneia, that, those, at distance; *ia* 1.

Ilova, v. n. of *ilo*, seeing, sight.

Ima, 1. n. a house. Mal. *rumah;* Motu N.G., D.Y., *ruma;* San Cr. *ruma, rima;* Mala *luma, nima;* Bouru, Amboyna, &c. *luma;* Java, Ceram, Lakona, Bks. I. *uma, uma;* Gilolo, Anaiteum, *um;* Pent. *ima;* Merlav, V. L. *im;* Saddle I. *em;* V.L. Pak, *en;* Sta. Cr. *ma;* Nengone, *'ma*.
kule ima; the outside of the roof; *ima vanogag soko*, rubbish-heap, not house; *ime gan*, the tuber of the *lalaso* in which the ant *gan* is always found.
When a house is built, 1. *sirvag*, level the site; 2. *towo*, measure it out; 3. *woso leqaleqa mun o wote tangae me taso*, mark the points by pegs; 4. *map o tur-*

sana, set the two main posts with forked tops in their places ; 5. *salo o qatsuna*, lay the ridge-pole horizontally in the forks of the *tursana ;* 6. *tara paparis, giliag ape paparis, qara map*, cut slabs, *irav*, for the low side walls, dig deep for them and place them ; 7. fix stakes, *puton*, to stiffen them, along the top of which two bamboos run tied, *we laq*, to the stakes ; 8. fix *pete we wanara*, the side posts, forked at the top, the four at the corners, *sigrai*, being large ; 9. lay on these the *ga-wolowolo*, the plates, which at the outer corners make the *sisi ima* ; 10. *gaso*, put on rafters, bamboos bent, *me ruqa*, in the middle, lying over the *qatsuna*, lashed, *vil*, to the *gawolowolo*, the ends tied to the bamboo at the *paparis ;* 11. *luluqa*, tie on the purlins, *varat*, the projecting ends of which are *sipala*.

The front, *matai*, and the back, *pup*, of the house is filled in, *turatura*, with perpendicular bamboos. The doorway, *mateima*, is not placed in the middle of this screen, so as to avoid the *tursana*, unless it be far enough away; it is formed of stout bamboos, and over the lintel, *qatmateima*, is a hole similarly made, *tano ararovag*, through which the cord is passed to tie the shutter when the door is fastened. The shutter, *gatava, matetipatipag*, is made of *lape ota*, sago stalks, run through, *sus*, with a stick, and when used is thrust down, *tipag*, between the two parts of the *tiqanal*, the rails over which entrance, *kalo, rowo, pata*, is made. Below the *tiqanal* the doorway is filled up with *gapurpur* of bamboos ; and the whole *mateima we vin goro* is protected by logs.

For thatching see *tuwur*.

Ima, 2. v. M. to drink.

imarag, *rag* intens. to drink often.

Imal, a tree with which fences are made ; the wood soft, the leaves eaten; *imal pita*, light-coloured; *imal qoe*, large kind.

Ime, [*i* 3.] comp. prep. *me;* as *ame;* with a person, after motion to him ; *nau we maros si katol iragetol imenau*, I desire that we, I and those three that come to me to be with me.

Inagtawasvar, a kind of yam.

Inara, pers. pr. dual 1. incl. we, us, two.

Inarua, pers. pr. dual 1. incl. we, us, two.

Inatol, pers. pr. trial 1. incl. we, us, three.

Inau, pers. pr. sing. I, me.

Ine, [*i* 2.] demons. pro. that, those, of things and persons ; with article *i* and *o ine ; ne*.

Inegen, ex. there ! so ! *kamam te vet si inegen! si aia!*

Ineia, pers. pr. sing. 3. he, him, she, her, it ; *ineia!* that's it.

Ineira, pers. pr. plu. 3. they, them.

Inia, V. thereby; *nag savai inia; kamam qara wol o sava inia;* see *nia*.

Iniko, pers. pr. sing. 2. thou, thee.

Inina, pers. pr. pl. 1. incl. we, us.

In, M. a bunch, of cocoa-nuts, or *nai ;* see *vun*.

Invaw, a kind of yam.

Io, ex. here it is ! of satisfaction.

Ioe, ex. of fear.

Ipala, [*i* 4.] tongs, cleft stick with which to *pala* hot stones.
Ipe, [*i* 3.] comp. prep. locative, with motion; beside, at; *pe.*
Ir, shrug the shoulder, shrink; so to be unwilling, unfriendly to approach; a disobedient wife *ti irir nan rasoana;* see *tapeir.*
  irvitag, shrug away from, refuse friendly intercourse with.
Ira, 1. pers. pr. pl. 3. suffixed to v. and prep.; never subject.
Ira, 2. [*i* 1.] pers. art. pl. the people, companions, of; *ira ta* Mota, the Mota people; *ira Qat,* Qat's companions, Qat and his party; *ira we nao,* those who say *na;* *ira we tak,* those who say *tak,* the people of two sides of Mota, whose dialects are characterized by those words; *ira gene,* the persons, whose names are not mentioned.
Iragai, dem. pr. pl. 3. those definite persons; *ragai.*
Iragera, dem. pr. dual 3. those two.
Iragetol, dem. pr. trial 3. those three.
Iraka, [*i* 6.] 1. ex. up! excitement; *raka.* 2. v. to rise up in excitement.
Irara, pers. pr. dual 3. they, them, two; *rara.*
Iraro, pers. art. [*i* 1.] fem. pl. the women.
Irarosei, 1. interr. pr. what women? 2. indef. pr. some women; *sei.*
Irarua, pers. pr. dual 3. they, them, two; *rarua.*
Iras, 1. [*i* 4.] a baler; *ras* 3.
Iras, 2. [*i* 3.] adv. afar, to a distance with motion; *ras* 1.
Irasei, 1. interr. pr. pl. who? whom? 2. indef. pr. pl. whosoever, those soever, some people.
Iratol, pers. pr. trial 3. they, them, three; the three.
Irav, board, slab of wood, in canoe and house.
Iri, 1. same as *ir.*
Iri, 2. to ask privately; *matairi, o tavine qe paere pata.*
Iro, per. art. fem. see *i* 1.; *iro gene,* the woman, whose name, *gene* the thing the name of which is hers, is not mentioned; *iro sava,* what's her name?
Iroiv, no; a V.L. word, but used in Mota.
Irosei, 1. interr. pr. fem. sing. who? whom? 2. indef. pr. fem. sing. some one woman.
Irvaltanun, to refuse every man.
Irvitag, *ir* above; refuse agreement with, obedience, consent to.
Is, 1. ex. of disgust.
Is, 2. to make a hissing noise as a sign of disgust, refusal; *is nan,* reject an imputation or suggestion. Malag. *isy!* excl. *isitra,* reject with contempt. *isvitay,* to reject and leave.
Is, 3. 1. to take off from a peg or hook, unhitch; *is reag o epa,* unhitch a sail and move it away; *is vitag,* take something off, leaving something. 2. to remove, as by cutting, what hangs, as a bunch of fruit.
  tavais, to come off, as from a peg or hook, come unhitched.
Isa, 1. M. v. to chew a juicy thing, sugar-cane, pandanus fruit.
Isa, 2. n. a bitter thing, such as bad *wo-us;* *o liwoi te manon apena,* sets the teeth on edge.
Isar, [*i* 4.] a stick to pierce, stab, with; a pointed stick for

D

stabbing pigs at a feast, pointed staff to walk with; a spear.

Isei, 1. interr. pr. sing. who? whom? 2. indef. pr. some one. *isei* is not properly who? but what is his name? *isei nasasana*, what is his name? *i* pers. art.; so *irosei, irasei, irarosei*. See *sei*.

Isvitag, 1. [*is* 2.] reject and leave with disgust; *vitag*.

Isvitag, 2. [*is* 3.] take off, from peg or hook, leaving something behind.

Ita, M. 1. a nosegay of scented leaves, fruit, &c. 2. plant used for the purpose.

Itagai, [*i* 5.] 1. nothing. 2. no; *tagai*.

Ituwale, [*i* 5.] one, single; *tuwale*.

Ivawo, [*i* 3.] upon, with motion.

Ivea, [*i* 3.] whither; *rea*.

Ivsale, fly as an unbalanced arrow.

Ivuna- (k) [*i* 3.] comp. prep. with *runai;* on, with motion; *ivunak*, on me, *ivunana*, on him, upon it.

Ivunana, to heaven, the region above.

Ivune, [*i* 3.] comp. prep. with constr. *runai*, on, upon, with motion.

Iwa, 1. n. the collar-bone. 2. v. to carry over the shoulder on a stick, *qatiiwa*, with burden on both ends.

Iwasasa, to carry, two men with *qatiiwa* on their shoulders and the burden between them; *sasa*.

Iwasola, ground plate of *pugoro*.

Iwatia, 1. [*i* 4.] the yoke connecting the outrigger with the canoe; *iwatia mot*, the free end over the canoe; *watia*. 2. a yam.

K.

K, pers. pr. sing. 1. suffixed to some nouns; my; same as *ku;* common throughout Pol. and Mel. and in Malaysia.

Ka, pers. pr. sing. 2. thou; always the subject, never object of v.

Kae, to speak, talk; *kakae, kakakae*, talk, tell a story.

Kaekae, 1. to begin to talk, as a child.

Kaekae, 2. n. the cry of a *matika*, a rail, porphyrio.

Kaesa, to persist after reproof; *ko we rava mun o tanun ape savasava gate mona; ti mule ma ti ge mulan*.

Kaka, 1. v. to stretch out the arm so as to lay hold. Mal. *kakap*. 2. a generous man.

Kakae, 1. 1. v. to talk; 2. n. talk. *kakae lea*, form with which a story begins.

Kakae, 2. n. *un* word for *nam*, yam.

Kakakae, 1. v. to talk, tell a story; 2. n. a story.

Kakalatoga, confusedly, not according to pattern; *me rus kakalatoga o pul*, the pattern of the tattooing was wrong; thence of bad writing.

Kakamarga, light yellow colour; *o tanun we wenewene, si tapanaiga, tama o vetal we memea*, a clear light or yellow complexioned man, like a ripe banana.

Kakamor, to scrape together with fingers spread out.

Kakarau, [*kaka*] to climb like a bat, hanging on by the hands.

Kakareti, heartily, of laughing.

Kakarmag, [*karu*] to scratch, making a hole; *o qaratu ti* *kakarmag ape patun*, a flying fox is scratching a hole in the bread-fruit.

Kakatariga, *o tanun we siriga, tete rara munsei, gate wia*.

Kakau, [*kau*] to visit constantly; *ni we kakau ragae ma*, he is always coming and hooking himself on.

Kakawa, a pinna shell.

Kakeuwa, a mollusc in sand, white, crablike.

Kal, to stir round and round, mix stirring; to rub with circular motion, as a painful leg with a finger.

   kalmag, make up line into a hank.

Kala, a lizard, blue; *nona kala*, adv. head downwards.

Kalakala, stale taste.

Kalan, striped, chequered.

Kalato, 1. a nettle tree. Fij. *salato*. N.B. *kalang*.

Kalato, 2. a mollusc, frog shell.

Kalit, to tease, annoy, as by importunity.

Kalmag, [*kal*] to wind line into a hank and tie towards the end.

Kalmatag, to bundle together, crumple up, in lengths.

Kalo, 1. adv. up, upwards; *kalo sage*; adv. of time, *kalo sage ran ma*, from long ago up to the present time.

   2. v. 1. to go up, climb up; *ni me kalo sage ma*, he climbed up inland to us. 2. to enter a house, over the *tiqanal*.

   kalovag, come up, climb, with.

Kalo, 3. v. to crawl, creep; *kalo naveravera*, crawl slowly; *o mataqa ti kalo naveravera*, a poisonous land mollusc crawls like a vera.

Kalo, 4. v. to take up a fish which has been hooked, with the hand; a large fish or a flying-fish.

Kalokalo, 1. [*kalo* 1.] 1. adj. steep; 2. n. a steep place.

Kalokalo, 2. [*kalo* 2.] *un* word for *maligo*, cloud.

Kalokalo, 3. a tree.

Kalovag, 1.[*kalo* 2.] climb, ascend, with. 2. [*kalo* 3.] crawl with.

Kaltaqataqa, to stoop, *taqa*, in entering the doorway.

Kaltatau, to bend the back in going through a doorway, or in pain.

Kaltavutug, to bend the back going under a heavy burden.

Kam, pers. pr. pl. 2. you; only as subject of v.

Kamam, pers. pr. pl. 1. excl. we, us.

Kamiu, pers. pr. pl. 2. you.

Kamra, same as *kamrua*, you two.

Kamrua, pers. pr. dual 2., you two.

Kamtol, pers. pr. trial 2., you three.

Kamurua, same as *kamrua*, you two.

Kaova, an egret, herodias; *kaova pita*, white egret.

Kar, to scratch. Same as *karu*.

   karmag, tr. determ. to scratch through.

Kara, 1. pers. pr. dual 1. excl. we, us, two.

Kara, 2. n. a forked arrow, with four or six prongs, made of *qatia* or *nira*, to shoot fish with.

Kara, 3. v. to stick flowers in a curve over the ears, the hair being felted into pads there, and combed up above.

Karia, dracœna.

Karu, v. to scratch. Mao. *raku*; Sam. *la'u*; Jav. Mal. *garut*.

   kakarumag, to scratch a hole.

Karua, pers. pr. dual 1. excl. we, us, two.

Karui, (k) tentacles of cephalopods; *o wirita ti towtowola mun na karkaruna*, the octopus rolls itself along with its tentacles; feelers, antennæ, of butterflies, moths, beetles, &c.; strings of bags to carry by, *ape sa we siplag o tana mun o karu tana*, why hang up a bag by the strings? *karkaru gea*, the small stringy roots of piper methysticum.

Karwae, a pig; *un* word for *qoe*.

Kas, to damage, do injury, violence, to, provoke; *ape sa ni we kaskas gap tamaike*, why is he so wantonly mischievous, quarrelsome? *ni me kas nau*, he ill-treated me.

  kasiva, violent. injurious conduct, quarrelling.

Kasavui, (k) *kasavui*, 1. the knot whence shoots of a plant proceed. 2. the shoots from a knot, sprouts from a stock, as on the edible caladium *qeta*.

Kasiana, a kind of tomago; Valuwa name, *kasan*.

Kasiva, [*kas*] v. n. disturbance, a row.

Kat, to persist, in asking, denying, arguing. Malag. *hanta*.

Kata, to stick, cleave; with *ape*.

Katmaran, [*kat*] one who solicits till morning; a word not to be used.

Katol, pers. pr. trial 1. excl., we, us, three.

Kau, to catch hold, as with a claw. Malag. *kaotra*. *wolakaukau*, the calamus with hooks.

  kaula, M. 1. v. to claw off; 2. n. the stick to *kaula* with.

kaut, to catch hold and pluck, twitch; as with *ikau*, and to call attention.

ikau, [*i* 4.] the cleft bamboo used to twitch off almonds, bread-fruit, &c.; *o au o valai apena, we kau o nai, o patau, o wotaga nia*.

Kavakava, a fish.

Ke, 1. ex. of astonishment.
  2. to cry *ke! ni me ke apena*, he cried out in wonder at it.

Ke, 3. dem. particle, of direction and place, here, this way; suffixed to many demons. pronouns and adverbs of time and place, *iloke nake*; introduced as directive, *iake ke wa!* here, this way! in enumerating things as if before the eyes, *o qoe ke, o rawe ke, o toa ke.*

Kearag, to remove, take away from.

Kei, ex. stronger than *ke!*

Keke, to spread out the arms, of a bird the wings; *me keke wora o qarqar nania ti rowolue*, came out parting the screen with his hands.

  kekerag, tr. determ. to stretch the arms for a certain effect; in opening a (European) door, in measuring, not a full fathom; to stretch the arms apart and cast away; *kekerag mot*, to throw the arms apart and break what is in the hands.

Kekeasag, to throw the shoulders apart.

Kekeluag, [*kel*] crooked, winding.

Kekerag, see *keke*, to stretch out the arms, or wings.

Kekete, 1. adj. high; 2. v. to rise up.

Kel, 1. adv. back, backwards; again; with v. gives a reflec-

tive sense, *nan we rereg kel nau*, I condemn myself.
kelkel, backwards and forwards, about; *tiratira kelkel*, stand in place after place.
2. v. to go or come back, return. Malag. *helihely*.
keluag, turn back.
keluva, v. n. return, returning; *we tak o keluva*, start on a return journey.
kelvag, return with.
Kele, to put the finger in a hole. Mal. *kele*.
Keleag, to turn the eyes round in looking at any one, look out of the corner of the eyes.
Keleva, to give money, pay a fine, for crossing the legs of certain relatives, such as *vere vus rawe*, or on returning home.
Kelkeluag, crooked, irregular.
Kelmatemate, [*mate* 2.] to go and sleep at a place so as to be ready for a start the next morning.
Kelo, adj. barren, of living things.
Keluag, adv. turning again; *o qoe ti war keluag*, the boar's tusks are making their second round.
Keluva, [*kel*] returning, return journey.
Kelvag, to return with.
Kere, 1. n. 1. the thick or butt end, thence a club. 2. bottom.
Kere, 2. adv. equivalent to *teve*, just, only, nothing but that; *na kere tut wia neia*, I only just hit him with my fist; see *teve* 2. Motlav, Merl. Gaua, *kere, ker*, neg.
Kereai, (k) [*kere*] a little at the bottom.
Kereag, to wipe utterly away.
Kerei, (k) 1. the thick end, butt, of something long; 2. the bottom where there is depth.

kereaka, the stern part of a canoe.
keregapurpur, the lower part of that which bars, *pur*, the doorway.
kerepei, the lower part and mouth of a stream.
kererara, the latter part of the winter season; *rara*.
keresala, one who is last of the company on the road; *sala*.
keremino, the bottom of a pool on the reef, *mino*, or of the sea near the shore.
kerepue, the bottom of a bamboo water-carrier; met. a rank in the *suqe*.
kerequloi, or *qiloi*, the lower part of the abdomen below the navel.
Proverbial expressions; *o kerei me malue* the bottom has a hole in it, *na kerena me malue* there is a hole in the bottom of it, the matter has been patched up incompletely, it is still open; *o kere qoe, o kere som, gate wono*, the bottom of the pig, or money, is not patched soundly up, *i. e.* what was at the bottom of the question, about pig or money, has not been thoroughly settled.
Keremainiin, a large bag of money.
Keresovin, said of a man who squats in fear ready to jump up, as if on the end, *kerei*, of his posteriors.
Kerevag, to turn the head, look round moving the head. Malag. *herika. kerevag nona malau*, to look round with eyes only moving, without turning the head; as the *malau* does lest it should attract attention by moving.
Kergalgalaput, 1. n. the notch

in the butt of an arrow. 2. v. to shoot an arrow into the notch of one shot before.

Kerkerevalerai, a number of various objects, bewildering *valerai*.

Kerkersanavul, a kind of yam with many ends, *kerei*, of the tuber.

Kertaworag, almonds at the bottom of the *pugoro*, chest, lying at the bottom, *kerei*, of the side pieces, *taworag*.

Kertotovoi, the lower part, *kerei*, of a sail in the angle between the mast and the boom.

Kesa, n. quarrel, disturbance, v. to fight, quarrel ; *kesaraka*, raise a disturbance.

kesava, v. n. fighting, quarrelling, a riot.

Kesakesa siwo tano, one who is always moving about, never resting, always disturbing the ground under his feet.

Kete, high, raised up ; commonly *ketekete*.

kekete, v. to rise up.

Kik, to draw aside or back, shrink, turning the elbow up, as in dread ; as from mother-in-law.

kiksag, in *vakiksag*, go by the side of.

Kikina, 1. adj. dreadful, awful, makes one *kik*.
2. v. to draw back in dread, as from *qaliga*.

Kikiu, (k) a side ; *ape kikik*, *pe kiksak*, beside me. Malag. *kiko*, elbow.

Kilau, 1. v. to turn the back, turn the head back ; *kilau ris*, turn round.
2. adv. with the back turned ; *pute kilau*, sit turning the back ; *vara kilau*, step, stamp, kick, with the back turned. Fij. *kilavaka* ; Malag. *hilana*.

Kilokilom, to tease, bother.

Kilmata, to roll the eyes and lift the eyebrows, making a sign ; *rova kilmata*, to measure a length with the right hand on the collar-bone, turning the eyes round to observe the length.

Kilsai, (k) the outer part of the eyebrow.

kilse matai, the eyebrow.

Kio, a whale.

Kiogale, met. said of one who persuades others to do something dangerous or troublesome and withdraws himself ; the whale plays a trick, *gale*, on fish, *nina vano salilina*, let's go ashore ; they go and are caught, he remains in the sea.

Kir, to snap off, asunder, neuter ; from this *sakir*.

Kiria, to shrink as in pain or shyness ; *ape kiria*, shy.

Kiskislag, to annoy mischievously ; *toga kiskislag*, behaving badly.

Kita, fierce, bad-tempered, wild ; *we kita nan*, to be unmanageable by.

Ko, 1. pers. pr. sing. 2. ; thou, thee.
2. pers. pr. sing. 2., suffixed to verb and prep., thee.

Koa, to be unsteady ; whence *takoakoa*.

Koalag, to take and keep what does not belong to one ; with *goro* of the person to whom the wrong is done ; *e. g.* if a man takes by force another's inheritance.

Koe, to pull backwards and forwards, loosen, and pull out ; the proper term for pulling sugar-cane, *koe tou*.

koesag, to loosen by shaking.

makoekoe, loose and shaky.

Koko, 1. tr. v. to keep close, contract; carry water in hands or leaf; *koko kalo*, take up a soft thing in both hands, keeping it from falling abroad; *koko goro*, protect as with the hand enclosing; neuter, of an ulcer getting smaller as it heals, *o nir ti kokoko.* Malag. *hohota.*

kokomag, to keep something carefully; careful, trustworthy.

kokor, to enclose, hold carefully with both hands; keep carefully, faithfully; *o tavine ti kokor o natmera nol mun napanena.*

kokos, to enclose, prevent from escaping, as fish in a net, fowls by the people catching them.

kokot, to enclose in narrow limits, contract.

kokota, 1. adj. narrow, confined. 2. n. a narrow canoe.

Koko, 2. to cluck, make the cry of fowls; *kokoko.*

Kokok, n. a fowl of the introduced kind; probably from the English word cock.

Kokolovuga, [*koko* 1.] overhung, covered close; *o ranua we kokolovuga* with clouds, *o mot we kokolovuga* with trees overhead.

Kokomag, tr. determ. *koko* 1. keep carefully; faithful.

Kokomatag, [*koko* 1.] look carefully after, *matag.*

Kokopei, adv. in such a way as to hold water, *koko pei; o mala ti salesale kokopei,* a hawk soars so steadily that water would not spill from its wings; *o epa we kokopei,* a sail not well set will hold water in the bulge.

Kokor, 1. tr. v. *koko* 1. hold, enclose carefully; *ni ramo leas reug kokor magarosa inau nan o ike nan*, may he have pity and rescue and preserve.

Kokor, 2. *un* word for *artapug.*

Kokorako, to crow as a cock, *koko* 2.

Kokoroma, to hold the arms over the breast, to fold the wings.

Kokoromag, to crackle as broken twigs or bones; to crash as falling trees.

Kokorou, [*koko* 1.] to cross the arms over the breast, as in cold; of a bird to close the wings, *we pute kokorou.*

Kokos, tr. determ. *koko* 1. to enclose.

Kokot, tr. determ. *koko* 1. to narrow, confine.

Kokota, [*ta* 6.] narrow, confined; *koko* 1.

Kole, v. to make a feast with a view to some particular thing or circumstance.

kole gamal, when a new *gamal* is built, or part added; *kole ima,* a new house; *kole liwantamate,* the figure of a dead person; *kole nereqoe,* for the right of wearing a pig's tail in the hair; *kole nule,* for a carved wooden image; *kole sarlano,* for wearing the *lano* hat; *kole sewere,* for a stone to remain in the *marana; kole valvalai,* for a house with ornamented ends to its purlins; *kole rat,* for a stone placed as a memorial of the feast; *kole wetapup,* for the right to wear a lace of feathers; *kole varowoi* completed, *me kole veta, me ukeg veta.*

Kolekole, a feast made as above.

Kolo, to contract, be contracted.

kolot, to press together, crush

with the hands, to stop the mouth of a pig with the hands.

Koloi, (k) a hole, probably *kolo*.

Kolkoloi, a small contracted thing, *kolo;* an abortive cocoa-nut.

Kom, to keep food in the mouth, in the cheek. Malag. *homoka.*

Komara, a creeping plant with large hooked thorns.

Komas, a tree.

Kome, to break off with a twist, wring off; *te kome o run nai, te kome late o nol tangae.*

Komkom, 1. n. something kept in the mouth. v. redupl. *kom.* 2. a small *make,* Tahitian chestnut.

Komtaqola, to put food into a mouth already full; *kom.*

Kor, 1. n. v. to become dry, with heat or time. 2. n. 1. a cocoa-nut in its last condition before it falls from the tree. 2. a bread-fruit artificially dried, *tin, tun;* also *tin kor; te teve, te goa, te wilwil goro, te rasayer alo av, te ris, paso nan me manoga qet, pa te lano.* 3. a dry tree, *kor gara garo* old but green.

Kor, 3. adj. clear, of the sky and sea; the clear sky behind seen between clouds, *tuka kor;* the open sea clear of islands, *lama kor.*

Kora, 1. shrunk, wasted, as the eye in sickness, or cocoa-nut with little meat. 2. n. a narrow canoe.

Kora, 3. v. to break, or cut short, branches, in clearing for a garden.

koran, tr. determ. to break a branch downwards at its base on the trunk.

Korave, to draw aside, *rave.*
korave lea, take credit for what some one else has done, say that another's work is one's own.

Kore, the trunk of a tree used as a drum, hollowed from a longitudinal slit, the lip of which is struck.

Kos, to do damage to, assault.
kos lea, break peace; *apesa ko we kos moma o lea ivunak?* why do you want to quarrel with me?

Kota, to talk, chatter; commonly *kotakota.*

Koto, 1. tr. v. to nip; *koto mot* nip short off, as money, or *no mata* leaves. 2. term used in *suqe* or *kole; me koto val neira mun o som,* money was broken off for every one of them. 2. n. v. to snap; *koto mot,* to snap suddenly short like a brittle stick; *ti malate malarowo.*

Kou, to keep secret, property or information; *te kou rorono o som.*

Kov, 1. tr. v. to obscure; *kov goro pul,* put earth on the torch of gum to make the light dim; so *giskor.* 2. n. v. to be obscure, dim, *talkov; o loa ti sar kovkov namatana,* the sun dazzles his eyes so that things are obscure to him. Distinguish from *gorgov.*

Ku, pers. pr. sing. 1. suffixed to nouns; same as *k;* my.

Kukulmatag, to crumple, bundle up.

Kukurag, [*kur*] to eat fruit in abundance, such as *rai.*

Kukurwota, [*kur*] to bite a fruit and come upon, *wota,* a stone or hard seed.

Kula, n. 1. a hump, bent back; 2. a humpbacked person.

Kulai, (k) 1. the humped or rounded part; so, of a man or animal, the back. 2. in secondary sense, the hinder part, behind; *ape kulak*, behind me.
1. *kule ima*, the roof of a house, outside, never the back of a house; *kule panei*, the back of the hand; *kule gave*, the carapace of a crab, thence met. the instep of the foot; *kule aka*, the bottom of a vessel.
2. *kule qon*, the next day after.
Kulum, to handle a thing till it is spoilt, as a child does a banana.
Kur, to eat hard food, as fruit, things uncooked; to gnaw as dogs do bones; always used of eating men.
kur matika, met. to eat things raw, as the rail; *manoga kur matika*, said of underdone food, cooked for a *matika's* eating, raw; *kur qulo*, one who eats fruit before it is ripe.
kukurag, to eat in abundance, *rag* 2. intens.
Kurakura, a shell used as a trumpet.
Kurut, a dog; there were no dogs in the Banks' Islands, but the name given them is no doubt connected with Sta. Cr. *kuli*; Fij. *koli*; Maori, *kuri*.

L.

La, M. to give or take, with *at* or *ma* respectively; *la o tavaliu*, to take one's side.
lav, tr. determ. take.
Laeolo, a tree with handsome flowers, a cassia.
Lag, 1. to marry, to be married; *i lag* the bridegroom, *iro lag* the bride; *lag valtanun*, one constantly changing her husband.
Lag, 2. tr. suffix to v.
Lagalaga, a fruit tree.
Lagau, to pass, cross over; of impediment rather than space. *o lagau tauwe*, met. a tall man, can step over a mountain.
lagaus, tr. determ. to cross over from tree to tree.
Laget, to climb a cocoa-nut tree with feet against the trunk, *we veresag mun o ranoi.*
Lago, 1. v. to step, stretch the legs; *te lago avune wot tangae,* steps across from the top of one tree to another. Fij. *lako*; San. Cr. *rago*; Day. *laku*; Bat. *laho*; Tag. *lakar*; Motu N.G. *lao*.
valago, to run.
Lago, 2. cylindrical large basket of flattened bamboo to hold yams, &c.
La goro, [*la*] to make preliminary payment for securing the purchase of pig, or engagement of wife.
Lagota, giant; of man or pig.
Lagsar, a tree.
Lai, 1. v. to be able, succeed. Gaua *lai*, to strike; *me lai,* it has been successfully done.
2. adv. after a verb "can"; *te nina lai at,* can get there.
3. adv. at all.
Lailai, adj. said of small things, persons; *i gene we lailai*; but not as in Fiji, small in a general use.
Lais, v. to beat, as heavy rain; to speak in loud angry tone; from Gaua, rather than Mota, *lai.*
Laka, 1. to kick up the heels, as in dancing; 2. to dance.

lakalaka, 1. v. to rejoice, dance. 2. n. a dance, a merry-making.

malakalaka, joyful, happy, rejoicing.

Lakalaka pule loa, one who lives comfortably in a worn-out house in fine weather; prov.; as if rejoicing in his having sunshine.

Laka pule masu, one who rejoices in present abundance, *masu*, without thinking of the future.

Lakae, adze made of clam shell, tridacna.

Lakitiu, a small quantity, a small bundle, as of *toape*, that can be carried in the hand.

Lak, hard.

Laklak, v. to crackle as biscuit in the mouth, or a light hard thing when tapped.

Laklak ta Vava, a trap of pointed bamboo in a hole, set against thieves.

Lakona, a part of Sta. Maria; Lakon.

Lakosa, disturbed, tossed, of sea, mind, feelings.

Laku, to fasten with horizontal sticks or bamboos, laid along and bound round; *we laku mun o au*; same as *laq*.

Lala, 1. n. v. to come open, *lala wora*; *tavalala*.

Lala, 2. to burn clear and hot. **lalav,** tr. to scorch.

Lala, 3. 1. univalve, top-shell. 2. bracelet made of it. N.B. *lala*, the same.

Lalai, (k) rib, side.

Lalais, sweat, perspire, perspiration.

Lalak, a bush bearing a round fruit.

Lalakete, [*la-kete*] to be victorious, successful, get the upper hand; *lalakete nan ra taralalea;* to be victorious over the enemy, *nan o ragalo*, in the battle.

Lalakorekore, the drumming noise of an insect in hollow tree; *kore*.

Lalaktera, [*lak*] hard, as earth, &c.; adv. hard.

Lalala goro, to talk down.

Lalalano, to keep things in order in house or cultivations, go properly about business; *lanol*.

Lalalnara; see *lalanara*.

Lalamanolnol, the short ribs; *lalai, nol*.

Lalamarag, [*lama* 3.] to beat down in quantities, as children do *nai*.

Lalamas, beat, redupl.

Lalamera, child-bearing; *tano lalamera,* time of; *la*, mera.

Lalanag, [*lana*] to raise the hand, arm.

Lalanai, (k) the underpart or side; *alalane, alalanana,* also *lalane, lalanana,* under, underneath.

lalanaviga, adj. with an underside.

Lalanara, [*lanar*] cloying sweet; *we pun lalanara,* smells sweet, but hurts the nose between the eyes.

Lalanaviga, adj. having an underside, *lalanai;* as a stone lying apparently firm, but it is unsteady, *magmagoa*, you know it is *lalanaviga*, has an underside that can be got at, *qara gil, we wil savrag;* or as a recess, deep horizontally under a rock.

Lalanitiga, adj. all in a sweat; *o ranua we lalanitigaray o tutunsay*.

Lalaparpar, to dash about, as fowl, fish; *o gasuwe ti lala-*

parpar alo pugoro, when a fire is lighted underneath to kill it.

Lalapeag, springy, as long elastic pole.

Lalaptape, to sing away from the tune; see *tape siwo*.

Lalasiaga, adj. full to repletion; *o togai ti lalasiaga*.

Lalaso, a kind of half-wild yam, with tubers on the vine.

Lalateag, to move away from an object it is desired one should approach; as a child from its mat not wanting to lie down.

Lalaus, stretch out, up; redupl. *laus*; a damaged tree recovering *ti lalaus*; *ineia tama o turgae qa, qara lalalaus sage*, of a sick man, he is shaky like a mast just set up, before the stays are tight.

Lalav, [*lala* 2.] 1. tr. to send out a blast, burn, scorch. 2. neuter, to be hot, burnt; *natarapena ti lalar*, his body is scorched.

Lalaviu, (k) n. the blast of heat from fire, sun; *lalavi av, lalav loa*.

Lalaviai, *lalaviag*, steep, precipitous; *ti lalav aia*.

Lalaviu, [*lalav*] 1. the blast of heat. 2. the blast of a swift passing body, as a falling rock; *tagai, na me ronotag gap nalalavina*, it did not touch me, I only felt the wind of it as it went by.

Lalawora, [*lala* 1.] burst and come open.

Laloloi, whet to appetite; *ko we ima o gene we gogona, ko we malinsala*.

Lama, 1. the open sea. Marsh. *lama*; Kerepunu N.G. *lama*, salt, sea.

lama kor, the clear sea between islands, *kor* 3.

lama marmararan, clear sea.

lama punmao, the unvisited, mouldy, sea.

lama sasa, deep water close on shore.

lama ranameag, empty sea without islands.

Lama, 2. adj. vast; probably same word; *rui lama!* said of one much grown; *vui*.

lamlamaga, very large.

Lama, 3. to beat, strike, with a drawing motion.

lamarag, tr. intens. beat in quantities, *lalamarag*.

lamas, tr. def. to strike something, with drawing stroke.

lamasag, tr. def. to beat upon.

Lamanawo, the tail of a fish; *ti lamalama o nawo*.

Lamansia, to work for nothing, *ape tuqensei*, look after for nothing, *ape pulansei o som; la manasia*.

Lamas, [*lama* 3.] to strike with drawing strokes; as an arrow that strikes with the side as it passes; as a branch drawn back strikes in flying back; as in adzing off smooth the sides of a canoe; as in striking the brush in painting; thence in new use to paint.

Lamasag, to beat upon, give stripes upon; *lama* 3.
o mera ti lamasag, day breaks, the streaks of dawn beat upon the sky.

lamasag noronoro, a month in which the wind beats and rattles the dry reeds.

lamasag pue nawo, to break a bamboo water-carrier of salt water on a sow's back; a charm to promote birth of pigs.

Lamasasa, the sea at the end of deep water.

Lamlamasag kere, a very strong man.

Lamlamaga, [lama 2.] very large, immense.

Lamlamalou, a greedy man who eats anything ripe or unripe, as if he beat the trees in the lou.

Lano, 1. v. to go about.

Lano, 2. n. 1. hat worn in a certain rank; 2. rank, oven, in suqe.

Lan, 1. n. (k) wind; *nalanina*, his wind to sail with; *gan o lan*, wind worked by charms against him.
  2. adv. upwards, heavenwards; *ate lan*, to turn the face, look upwards.
  lan mamata, a wind that blows all night; met. a man who wakes all night.
  lan sere, steady strong wind, trade-wind.
  lan tale va! cry in hurricane, tale.
  lan ta Panoi, whirlwind.
  lan ta wo-rara, N. wind in winter, shakes off the *rara*.
  lan vus, a hurricane.
  Names of winds; *Ganue, Gauna, Masalava, Nualiu, Togalau*.
  3. met. a lazy man; *iniko lan!* Mal. *langit;* Malag. *lanitra;* Mao. *rangi;* Sam. *lagi;* Pol. generally, the sky; Mortlock, *lan*, sky; Ponape, *lon*, cloud; Fij. *lagi*, the heavens or atmosphere; N.H. *lani*, wind; Fij. *cagi*, wind and atmosphere; Motu N.G. *la'i*, wind; Sol. I. San Cr. *rani*, rain; Fl. *lani gabu*, the iris on surf or rainbow, rain of blood.

Lana, to lift up, turn up, so as to show the underside, as the edge of a mat, the sole of foot, leaf from the end.
  lanag, tr. determ. in *lalanag* redupl. to lift up the arm. Sam. *laga;* Fij. *laya*.

Lanai, the underside, *lalanai;* same word as *lana*.

Lanalana, [lana] 1. to shave the edge of the hair.
  2. turn up on end; *o tangae we vile lanalana*, the leaves of trees above a cliff are turned up as the wind blows on its face.

Lanameme, [lana] the lowest purlin of a roof.

Lanar, to cloy, as certain strong-tasted over-sweet food; when one has eaten such *me lanarnau, me paso*, can't eat more.
  lalanara, adj. cloying, over-sweet.

Lanavag, to stop a hole in thatch with a sago leaf; probably turning up, *lana*, the thatch to insert it.

Lanlan, 1. to use effort, *we lanlan goro matila*, try in vain.

Lanlan, 2. [lan] (k) the wind of swiftly passing object; *na lanlanina apena*.

Lanlananau, to sleep sound with eyes open, eyeballs turned back, *lana;* when the man wakes, *namatana we wil, gate lik*.

Lano, 1. the bluebottle fly. Mao. *ngaro, rango;* Sam. *lago;* Pol. *rango;* Fij. *lago;* N.H. commonly *lano, lan;* Anaiteum, *lag;* Sol. I. *lano, rano, thano;* Mal. *langau;* Sangir, *lango;* Motu N.G. *lao;* Mefoor, *ran*.

Lano, 2. to place horizontally across in order, as wood for the fire; *we lano o varu ape kor*, hibiscus rods laid in order for drying bread-fruit on,

*we lano kor qara laqai goro.
te lano o pugoro*, construct a food-chest.
3. to lay rollers for drawing canoes.
4. met. 1. *lano goro*, to take the place of another, as in speaking; 2. to arrange in lending money for repayment, with *goro*; A lends 10 hanks of money to B., he *we lano goro* A. by lending him at the same time four hanks.
Mao. *rango*, roller for canoes; Sam. *lago*, prop for canoes; common Pol. in these senses; Fij. *lagona*, to put pieces of wood under anything.
la*n*on, tr. to arrange bread-fruit, &c. on *qat lano* for drying, &c.
ila*n*o, a roller for canoes. Fij. *ilago*.
Lanolano, a fish.
Lan**on**, [*lano* 2.] to arrange make kernels, or bread-fruit, for drying.
Lapa, to flap; *sis-lapa*.
Lapalapa, with flapping motion; *o toa ti wosa lapalapa napanina*, a fowl flaps his wings.
Lapai, (k) the rachis of a palm-frond, tree-fern frond, banana or caladium leaf. Sam. *lapalapa*.
Lapasag, to serve with food; probably *lapa*.
Laplapesoraka, quickly and badly.
Laq, to strengthen a single row of stakes with horizontal bamboos along the top, which are bound round, *tatal*, with a running line; same as *laku*.
Laqa, to spring up, spring back, fly up, as a spring or anything elastic, flip up or back; *laqa i wora*, to [split, burst

asunder, fly apart as a stone on the fire; *laqa sare*, to be rent, split; *rara laqa*, to speak clear again, the voice returning after hoarseness, *me soso ti pa me laqa kel*; of a vessel not observed springing up suddenly into view, *o aka me laqa wia vano*. See *ralaqat*.
laqar, tr. to spring back upon; as a spring-trap on rat, &c.; *o vanua ti laqaria*, the place strikes him with delight, its pleasantness, beauty, spring upon him as he first sees it; impers. *me laqar nau*, I was struck with dizziness.
laqarag, 1. to spring back, recover, as a bent bough, or bow; *laqlaqarag*, elastic. 2. to flip off in springing.
Laqai, (k) the blade, flat, broad and thin, part, as blade of paddle *laqe wose*, tail of eel (not of fish) *laqe marea*.
Laqan, to wrap food in leaves and cook on embers.
laqan ranranai, to cook in the same way with fewer leaves so that it is more like broiling, *ranai*.
Laqar, to spring upon; see *laqa*.
Laqarag, 1. recover with elasticity. 2. flip off; *laqa*.
Laqasare, to tear, split asunder; neuter.
Laqe, 1. a creeping plant of which a crimson dye is made.
Laqe, 2. v. to spread and join. *laqelaqe* in *nara laqelaqe, sis laqelaqe*.
laqea, spreading out, and so sinking down.
Laqei, same as *laqai*.
Laqetaga, small as a bundle; *laqan*.
Laqlaqea, flattened, flatten down;

o tano me vutvut kalo ti pa me laqlaqea siwo, the earth has stood in heaps but has been flattened down, after rain; when in cutting a canoe a part projects too much *te tara laqlaqea siwo* adze it down.

Laqlaqe-maligo, [*laqe* 2.] connected clouds, spreading to touch.

Laqlaqe-vanua, a town or village made up of connected parts.

Laqot, to hold in a large bunch or bundle; *galaqot*.

Laqotiu, a bundle or bunch, large.

Lareag, [*la*] to take away, leaving some behind; *reag*; subtract.

Las, 1. live coral, of the branching kinds; *las tur*, large kinds.

Las, 2. to lay in rows, set side by side; *we las o qeaqea mun o var*, make the stage in a canoe by laying rods of hibiscus side by side; *we las o togo* for a screen, set reeds side by side; *las no gae* make the mats of leaves for *qaranis* fastening on one after the other by thrusting in the stalks.

Las, 3. a tree.

Lasa, a drinking cup; *vinlasa*, one made of cocoa-nut shell; *lasa tangae* cut out of wood, as for *gea*.

Laslasorawe, a small tree with curious fruit, rare.

Laso, a *rawe* pig.

Lasoi, (k) the male members. 2. a big boar pig. Mao. *raho*, testicle; Sam. *laho*, scrotum; Macassar, *laso*, penis.

Las-no-gae, [*las* 2.] n. mat of leaves for closing the native oven.

Late, 1. v. to break, snap; *te late savrag o sine noota*, to break and pull off the midrib of sago frondlet. 2. adv. in broken bits, breaking short; *tira late*, stop short in walking; see *luqe late, wola late; vus lutelate*, beat to bits.

lateg, tr. to break; particularly of the reeds on which yams are trained; *we viawo, we qeteg taur, we la kalo o tuei avune togo, qara lateg;* when the vine has reached the end of the reed, the reed is broken so as to bend and meet another set upright to take the runner, this and others in succession are so broken, till the vine is full-grown, then *ruqa*.

lateg qatremeat, to break and bend the reed high up.

lateg ranomara, to break and bend the reed near the ground, like a dove's leg.

malate, broken.

Lateqalo, the sound of the breakings of twigs, &c.; *qalo*.

Latlataga, bottle-shaped, narrow above, bulging below, like some yams, and *toqe nai; naqatuna ti gaereere, naturiana we sasarita; talatlat*.

Lau, the seaside as opposed to the inland, the beach as approached from the land. Mal. *laut*.

Laulau, long, at length; *vereg laulau*, to stretch the head out far in spying at something.

Laus, [*us* 6.] to give, put, forward, up, out.

Lav, [*la*] to take, receive; *o tarine te lav natuna*, a woman has a child.

Lava, 1. n. a large sea-urchin, echinus; *maru lava*, its spines.

Lava, 2. adj. great, large. Mao. *raha*, wide; San Cr. *raha*, great; Marsh. *lap*, large; Malag. *lara*, long; Mal. *lapang*.

Lave, the prefix to numerals between five and ten, *i. e.* the digits of the second hand; in cardinals *a* is added, making *larea*. N.B. *lap-tikai*, 6; *lavurua*, 7.

  laveatea, six; *lareteai*, sixth.

  lavearua, seven; *laveruai*, seventh.

  laveatol, eight; *lavetoliu*, eighth.

  laveavat, nine; *lareratiu*, ninth.

Laviao, to eat greedily and ask for more.

Laviulo, to make its appearance, of the male flower, *uloi*, of the bread-fruit, *o uloi ti lariulo*.

Lavlavat, 1. tr. v. to hurry, bustle up with fear, as when a *tamate* chases a man, *ti lavlavat neia*; 2. impers. v. *me lavlavat neira*, they were in a hurry because of their fright; 3. adv. in a hurry and fright, *kamiu me tavaraka lavlavat apesa?*

Lavlaviae, steep, precipitous.

Lavparan, to oil a bow; *ran* is ram.

Lawa, 1. to blaze, flame; 2. to be of a blazing, brilliant, red colour.

  lawalawa, adj. 1. blazing red; 2. met. in exaggeration.

  lawatura, crimson, like a *wetapup*.

  lawlawaga, burning red; *napalasana we lawlawaga*, his cheek is burning with a blush.

Lawe, a blenny fish; of many species, e.g. *lawe-matu-memea*, a red-eyed blenny, *lawe patau, lawe puputa, lawe qatgayarat, lawe qatu kura, lawe talo sama, lawe ta malai* lives in pools, *lawe taqa, taqasagau, lawe we win*; the calf of the leg, *toqelawe*, from its form.

Lawesus, an abscess or boil; called after a species of *lawe*, which is eaten as a cure.

Lawu, a fish.

Le, give, take, same as *la*; *le ris*, change.

Lea, M. word, report, law; same as V. *leo*, which see.

  lea lol, stupidity, indifference, refusing to attend; *lol*.

  lea sorsororo, rumour; *sororo*.

  lea ta matesala, news picked up on the road.

  lea tatas, bad news.

  tavala lea, the one or other side in the question, enemy.

  lea vargol, quarrel.

Leas, 1. v. to take the place of, put in place of, change; 2. adv. instead of, in change.

Leasag, [*lea*] to argue or contend against a statement or order, contradict, disobey.

  leleleasag, to be contentious.

Leasmera, a child adopted to take the place of one dead.

Leg, to hang up; *manleg*.

Legao, to pass over; same as *lagau*.

Lego, last of all; always with *nia*; *tawur, tagir, lego nia*, last of all, behind.

Leilei, an oyster; *vin leilei* oyster shell.

Lekir, to beat, dash with violence; *o makaru me wota ti we rowo mun o gae, te lekir ti*, a flying-fish when caught leaps with the line dashing itself on the surface; *rowo leklekir*, leap and stamp.

leklekir, adv. violently, strongly.

Lele, 1. a flat-fish, sole; see *lelenawo*.

Lele, 2. n. 1. the inside of a building ; so with prep. *a, i,* comp. prep. *alele, ilele ima,* in, into the house.
2. without *a* or *i,* itself prep., *lele ima,* in the house, indoors.

Lelenawo, V. to swim on the surf-board. Motu N.G. *lele,* swim, of fish.

Lelena, v. to stray ; adv. astray.

Lelep, to cover and protect from dirt, as leaves *lelep goro tarowo* in eating keep food off the ashes, *we lelep avune vat* are laid over the stones to keep the food clean in the oven ; the leaf so used *nolelep.*

Lelera, to be possessed as by a *tamat lelera,* be delirious ; *lera.*

Leles, v. to succeed, be heir.

Lelesiu, (k) successor, heir, to position, property.

Lelete, to warp ; to draw in the back as in avoiding an arrow ; *lete.*

Leleva, to leave a track ; see next word.

Lelevai, (k) a track shown on grass, bushes, &c. of one who has passed, not footprints on the ground.

Lelvetur, said of one who goes about not settling or sitting, with traces, *lelevai,* of standing, *tur,* only.

Lelvotur, said of a village in excitement, anxiety, in expectation of a fight ; *votur.*

Lemes, the point of an arrow.

Lena, 1. a woman's dance ; *we ras o lena.*

Lena, 2. to be indistinct, bewildering ; as in *valenai, valenalena, alena.*

Lenas, (k) brilliancy, dazzling splendour, as of sun, moon, *gaviga* in full bloom, &c. ; *lena.*

Leo, V. same as *lea* M. word, report, law. In N.H. Lep. Pent. Mae. speech ; Mao. *reo ;* Sam. *leo.*

Lepa, 1. n. dirt of the ground, mud, dirt generally ; 2. adj. dirty. Bugotu, *dhepa,* ground.

lepaga, *lepalepaga,* adj. dirty.

lepava, v. n. dirtiness, filth.

lepavag, to be dirty with, defiled by.

Leplep, an unripe *make,* Tahitian chestnut.

Lepmatua, said of *tanun gate poa mantag, te toga solsol amen o tarine, ti gopa.*

Leqa, 1. 1. v. to dig a trench to carry water, lead water in a trench ; 2. n. a lead.

Leqa, 2. v. to fly before, dash away from ; *o reremera te leqa o tamate ; leqa nawo,* on a surf-board ; *leqa lan,* fly before a gale.

valeqas, to put to hasty flight.

Leqaleqa, adv. loosely, temporarily ; *rot leqaleqa,* to bind loosely round fence or purlin ; *woso leqaleqa o wote tangae me taso,* hammer in pegs to mark the points of the ground-plan for a house.

Leqleq, same as *leplep,* a *make* not full-grown or ripe.

Lera, 1. to wander, go astray. 2. to talk deliriously.

lerava, v. n. wandering, error, delirium.

leravag, to wander with, be delirious in.

Les, 1. v. to become a member of a *tamate* society, be initiated ; *gate avu tiqa munia, qara les ti ; we les o tamate, o qat.*

Les, 2. v. to turn over, act. or neut. ; roll, fold, up.

les ris, turn inside out ; *aqaga les*, very white.
3. adj. blunt, with edge turned ; of metal tools.
malesles, ready to turn over, unsteady, drunk.
matalesles, full so that the liquid curls over the vessel's brim ; *we ura matalesles*.
Lesles-ta-gasuwe, head over heels.
Leso, a kind of ficus elastica, Moreton Bay fig.
Lesu, see *les*, with derivatives.
Lete, fo curve in or out, protrude like elbow of a branch, curl, warp ; *nusletelete*, protrude the lips ; *lelete*, above ; *galete*, *tatagalete*, shrink with a curl.
Levegao, to cross over, pass over, a space ; *sua levegao*, paddle over from shore to shore.
Lia, 1. (k) hollow in or under a rock, cave, den ; *lie peserag*, a shallow cave. Mal. *liyang*; Mao. *rua*; Sam. *lua*, pit, hole ; Malag. *luaka*, hole.
Lia, 2. v. in the words below.
Liamule, to shoot a man of one's own party in a fight ; *me liamule ineia*.
Liawora, to come through to land, as a canoe.
Ligiu, (k) moisture, juice, sap, gravy, liquid contained.
ligligira, fluid, juicy.
Lig-sinaga, food of a juicy unsubstantial kind, fruit, &c.
Lig-telepue, honey ; new word.
Lignamele, the shell-collecting phorus, univalve.
Ligo, 1. to tie with the end of a line, as when tying up a pig ; to hang by the neck, strangle. met. to engage, promise ; N.G. *rigo, ligo, rio*.
2. conceive in the womb.
ligog, (1.) to make an engagement for, promise ; *me ligog o qon*, the day is fixed, as for a feast.
ligovag, (2.) be conceived with.
Ligomate, 1. to hang to death ; *o tavine qara ligomate kelua*, thereupon the woman hanged herself.
Ligomate, 2. a tree.
Ligorea, a hollow between two knobs or prominences, as the narrow part of a kite, *rea*, between the body and the tail.
Ligotapug, the appointed day for taking the *suqe*.
Ligowol, to hang, strangle oneself for some one's sake ; *wol*, in compensation ; see *matewol*.
Lik, to open with unfolding motion, as the eye, hand, to lift up from one end as a leaf ; *we like o mona iga, we la kalo o takelei si a la munsei, we lik*. When you open a wrapper in which fish has been cooked you *like*, when you lift up a piece of fish by the end to give it to somebody you *lik*.
Like, 1. to open by turning back a cover, as an oven by taking off *roqo*. 2. particularly to open the oven.
like weswes, to open *mona* or *um* after delay.
liketag, determ. to lift up turning over ; *liketag risris*, turning over one way and another as in searching.
Lil, 1. to spread, as in laying a mat, a bird opening its wings, to peel drawing off the skin, thus (1.) in opening, and also (2.) in covering with corresponding motion ; *o manu ti lil lue, ti lil kel, napanena*, a bird opens, shuts, its wings ;

E

te lil lue, te lil kel o vilog, open and shut an umbrella ; *te lil goro o tano mun o epa*, spread over the ground with a mat. So (3.) water spread abroad, or a crowd *te lil warwar ma*.

liliv, tr. determ. to cover over with spreading motion.

lil*n*ag, tr. to spread out over, cover over spreading.

Lil, 2. to haul up the *wele* of a sail when the wind falls.

Lil, 3. to go aside, fall away from ; *na me vivir pa me lil*, I threw a stone, but it missed, went nowhere near.

adv. *lilil, valil.*

Lilgon, 1. v. to set a snare on ground or in tree, *we lil o gae sin gona* ; 2. n. the snare so set.

Liliake, a tree.

Liliava, [*lil* 3.] to stagger from weakness, falling away from the path ; *ava* 1.

Lilikiaga, adj. disobedient, word used in scolding.

Lilil, 1. adv. [*lil* 3.] astray, not rightly ; *nom lilil*, think wrongly, be in error ; *ni we toga lilil, ni gate toga mantag amen tamana*.

2. v. [*lil* 1.] redupl. to peel.

Lilipa, to be irregularly scattered ; *we matur lilipa*, when sleeping in disorder, not in *tano-epa*.

Liliv, [*lil* 1.] 1. to cover over with something that spreads, as water, earth, a crowd ; *o malau ti liliv goro natolina*, the brush turkey, megapod, spreads earth over its eggs ; *o sul ti liliv warwar ma*, the crowd spreads hither over the ground. 2. n. *liliv pei*, a flood of water.

liliv maleka, met. to take yams, &c., from a place where some one has been before so as to be undiscovered ; as if traces, *malekai*, covered over.

Lilivit, sore, as hands made sore with work.

Liliwei, one not full grown.

Lilmalo, [*lil* 1.] said of a strong wind, blows up a *malo*.

Lil*n*ag, [*lil* 1.] tr. to cover over by spreading something above.

Lilpataru, to lie down together, *o tangae me lilpataru qet*.

Lilwora, said of a garden used by two persons ; *o tuqei tuwale ; isei o tavaliu, isei o tavaliu*.

Lima, *un* word for *panei*, hand ; also the stem of the numeral *tavelima*, five. As "hand" or "five" it is common throughout the Ocean languages ; Mao. *ringa*, hand ; *rima*, five ; see *tavelima*.

Lin, 1. to incline, lean ; *lin o qoroi*, incline the ear, *tarapei*, the body ; *linwia*, lie down only. 2. to pour gently. Mao. *ringi* ; Sam. *ligi*, to pour.

lin*r*ag, intens. of 2. to pour abundantly.

lin sur natapana, met. has come safe through, has inclined his surf-board to the shore.

linlin, adv. bending over, thence, of a tree, abundantly.

Lina, to be out of sight.

lin*a*rag, tr. determ. to hide.

Linai, (k) sound, voice, taste, way of life, manner.

linai o galamas, sound as of beating.

linai o mala, clear voice as of a hawk.

linai we manesenese, clear pleasant voice.

linai masmasawora, when a poor man calls another poor.

linai we mate, a mild temper.
linai we nunumrag, resonant bass voice.
linai we qega, voice failing with hoarseness.
linai we sesere, a rasping sound.
linai we wora garviteg, speaking without respect.
linai o worile, an endless talker, *gate rulerulea; worile.*
line gosogoso, constr. slander.
line maran, lazy disposition.
line woramata, deceptive wailing as for death.
Linalala, one who speaks openly and cheerfully.
Linalava, much speaking.
Linalina, [*lina*] adv. heedlessly; *we ilo linalina*, to see without recognizing; *gato linalina*, to speak in an improper way to a *sogoi*; *toga linalina*, to behave like a bully caring for no one.
Linamenamena, to refuse to help one who has given help; with *goro*.
Linarag, [*lina*] to hide, act. and neut.
linarag non we vula, partially hide; *we vula*, as in Gaua.
Linasapur, [*linai*] to speak evil of, *sapur*, use bad language.
Lineline, bungling, ignorant; *taqel lineline*, said of one who misunderstands, does the wrong thing.
Lineroa, adj. *o matig we lineroa*, a cocoa-nut so far advanced that when shaken the sound, *linai*, of the water is heard.
Line-tamate, the noise made to represent the voice of the ghosts, by the members of the *tamate* 3.
Lineul, one with a ready flow of speech, *id*.

Lini, numeral, seven in counting *tika*.
Linlin, adv. plentifully, *o tangae we uwa linlin*, a tree bears so much fruit as to lean, *lin* 1.
Linkor, a shrub.
Linrag, [*lin*] to pour profusely; met. to produce abundant offspring, *tam o mala qe vasus we qoqo we linrag o natqoe* pours forth her progeny.
Linwia, [*lin* 1.] to sleep without eating, nothing besides leaning over to sleep; *wia*.
Lipe, to prise with lever, move with something introduced underneath.
liperag, tr. determ. to prise a thing off; *lipe savrag*, to throw off, flip off, with toe, finger, stick.
Lipe nun, of a thing falling with heavy sound, *nuniu*, as if it lifted the ground.
Lipotag, to start a false or idle story.
Lisa, a nit, pupa of louse. Mao. *riha*; Sam. *lia*; Jav. Bat. Tag. *lisa*.
Lislawe, a shrub growing on beach, also *weslawe*.
Lispuna, a yam rotting in the ground and smelling, *puna*.
Lito, firewood.
Livit, to make sore, as hands by work.
Livun, 1. to bury. 2. to burrow.
Liw, same as *liwu*, water.
Liwantamate, the figure of a dead person set up to *kole*.
Liwat, to be full to the brim, as water in a *qilosiu ti ura liwat*.
liwatvag, to be filled, full, with.
Liwo, 1. n. a bracelet of pig's tusk, *liwoi*.
Liwo, 2. to pour out; *liwoliwo goro*, to pour over.

liworag, intens. to pour out quickly.

Liwoa, great, large, important; *liwoliwoa,* redupl.

Liwoi, tooth, pincer of crab, spider, &c.
By change with n Mao. *niho;* Sam. *nifo;* Malag. *nify;* San Cr. *riho, lifo;* Fl. *livo;* Malanta, *niho* and *livo.*

Liwolava, the large right claw of *naer,* birgus latro.

Liwomanon, of teeth aching or set on edge, as after eating many oranges or an *isa, o liwoi te manon apena.*

Liwomarae, the teeth showing in laughing, *marae,* one who shows his teeth as if smiling.

Liwomaran, full day, noon; *liwoa; tine liwomaran,* the point of noon.

Liwoninara, a tree, a red *kalato.*

Liwonira, showing the teeth in laughter or death.

Liwopas, one who has lost his teeth, *me paso.*

Liworag, [*liwo* 2.] intens. to pour out quickly, completely.

Liwosaru, [*liwo* 2.] to pour and sweep away with what is poured out.

Liwosis, adv. not being able to shut mouth as in laughter, *marae liwosis; o liwoi ti sis.*

Liwosurata, high noon, *surata; tine liwosurata,* the point of noon; *liwoa.*

Liwotapit, a person who has to be often spoken to; *o liwoi te tapit ape we vava vagaqoqo munia.*

Liwu, *un* word for *pei;* Gaua for water.

Liwun, to count on the fingers, same as *luwun.*

Lo, 1. n. what is inward, and thence place; as in *iloke,* &c. 2. prep. in, at; as in comp. prep. *alo, ilo, talo;* in names of places, *Lo Sepere, alo Make,* at the *sepere, make,* tree. 3. adv. there, in rare use; *me anani ran lo?* of a canoe; *naapek lo we marmaragai.*
See the redupl. *loloi.* That *lo* in use as prep. whether simple or comp. remains a noun is shown by the absence of the article after it. See Grammar.

Loa, the sun; probably the same word with *alo* of Lak. Pent. as in Salibabo, Celebes: possibly same as *aho* of Lep. and Sol. and so *aho,* Mao.
loa ta Varono; prov. of a sunny place, like *Varono* on the beach of Veveran.
loa-vil, constant sunshine, drought, as if the sun were bound, *vil,* with charms to shine.

Loaroro, the left claw of the *naeru,* birgus latro, which holds till the sun sinks, *roro.*

Loas, to flog with small rod or cord.

Loasag, adv. worrying, as pigs *nit loasag,* bite and worry a newcomer.

Loav, blacken by fire, as *nai* in *pugoro.*

Log, to call, give name to.
loglue, new word, ecclesia, church.
logwia, new word, praise, bless.

Loke, [*lo*] pron. this; adv. here; *iloke.*

Lokean, 1. to spoil, make badly. 2. adv. badly.

Loki, a creeping plant, used in making *toto,* so-called poisoned arrows.

Loko, 1. a pudding of grated yam; *we rasa o nam, ti lolorag, we savur o nai, we luqeg, o loko nane.* 2. to make a pudding by grating yam, cocoa-nut, almonds.

Lol, blunt, stupid.
 loliga, blunt.

Loliwao, a dance, named from the cry.

Lolo, 1. to spread as a creeper or vine; met. *me lolo goro natoqana*, of the feelings, mind, obscured, impenetrable by light.
 lolovag, tr. spread thick.

Lolo, 2. n. a liberal man.

Lolo, 3. constr. of *loloi;* see compound words.

Loloae, [*loloi, ae*] 1. without interruption, obstacle; *matur loloae*, sleep sound, undisturbed by dreams, &c.
 2. a bad man or thing.

Loloanu, [*loloi, anu*] hatred, loathing, irritated, met. from the cutting sedge, *o anu we salsal*.

Lolog, v. to be all of one, to be nothing but; *o vanua me lolog punai nia*, the place was all one smell with it, was nothing but smell; adv. all, nothing but; *lolog pei vires*, nothing but water; *lolog qatqat tavine*, all a pack, nothing but a pack, of women.

Lologagara, anger, irritation; angry, irritated, as if a man's *loloi* were scratched, *gagara*.

Lologona, of ill-feeling, malicious; *o loloi we gona*.

Lologoro, [*lolo* 1.] to grow over as a vine; grown over, impervious, densely obstructed.

Loloi, (k) [*lo*] 1. the inner part. 2. a hollow. 3. the inward part of man, heart, affections.
 1. The prep. *a, i, ta*, with the construct form *lolo* and the suffixed pers. pron. *k, ma, na*, &c. make up words written in one, *alolona, ilolona, talolona*, within it, into it, belonging to the inward part of it, and so on.
 2. *o loloi apena*, there is an inner part to it, there is a hollow in it, it is hollow; *o loloi tagai*, it is solid.
 3. Compounds of *lolo* with adj. or noun, describing affection, disposition, character, are very numerous, and are therefore placed as they come.

Lololera, [*loloi*] error, erroneous, wandering, in mind; *lera*.

Lololiga, [*lol*] adj. blunt.

Lololo, [*lolo* 1.] spread as creeper, &c.; said also of fire, *av lololo!* spread fire! said to make the fire burn off the stuff in preparing a garden.

Lololoa, [*loloi*] one engaged in making sunshine and fasting.

Lololop, tall, of a man or tree.

Lolomagarosa, [*loloi*] a merciful pitiful, disposition.

Lolomalumlum, [*loloi*] softhearted, of an easy, mild, temper; gently.

Lolomanana, [*loloi*] longing, as a pregnant woman, who fancies food.

Lolomaran, [*loloi*] enlightened, *maran*, within; intelligent, understanding; *ko me vatogo lolomaran nau*, you educated me, taught me till I became enlightened.

Lolomatartoga, [*loloi*] of pure character, guileless, clear and clean, *matartoga*.

Lolomawunwun, [*loloi*] of a feeling of sickness.

Lolonun, [*loloi*] true in heart, disposition.

Lolomomogo, [*loloi*] reverent, *momogo*.

Lolomot, [*loloi*] generous, decided

good feeling ; *nalolok ti mot suria;* mot.

Lolona, [*lona*] to gather and abound ; *o ninisa ti lolona alo valama*, the saliva gathers in your mouth ; *o Mota we sea nan amoa, o varae mon God me lolona aia*, the word has spread abundantly.

lolonar, 1. to spread throughout, be plentiful, as at once, not gradually ; *o mas lolonar*, a great and general abundance of fruit ; *we mena lolonar*, fruit ripe in quantities all together ; *o gopae me lolonar*, there was great general sickness.

Lolonar, 2. [*loloi*] thinking less of a person than formerly ; *nar* 1.

Lolopepewu, [*loloi*] humble, *pepewu*.

Lolopewupewu, [*loloi*] tired of food, loathing it as a sick person; *pewu*.

Loloqon, [*loloi*] 1. ignorant, stupid, unenlightened, contrary to *lolomaran* as *qon* to *maran* ; adv. in a stupid way.
2. to forget ; *na tete loloqon lai*, I shall never forget, *na tete loloqon naniko*, I shall not forget you. In both senses the parts are separated; *nalolona we qon*, he is ignorant ; *nalolok tete qon laiko*, I shall never forget you.

Loloqorag, [*loloi*] said of one who rejects nothing, nothing is bad to him.

Lolos, to roll up, envelope, in a covering.

lolosiu, a thing enveloped ; *lolos vetal*, a bunch of banana fruit wrapped in leaves to protect it from birds.

Lolosa, to writhe, wallow.

Lolosarsaramot, [*loloi*] exceedingly angry.

Lolosuwasuwa, [*loloi*] loathing, feeling of repulsion; *suwa*.

Lolotape, [*loloi*] kind, loving ; *tape*.

Lolotitin, M. [*loloi*] eager, hot, *titin*, about a thing.

Lolototoepe, [*loloi*] upright in character ; *totoepe*.

Lolotutun, V. same as *lolotitin*.

Lolovag, [*lolo* 1.] to spread out, act. and neut. in a thickness, as mash of yam in making *loko, te lolovag o nam mun o panei;* when two or three sleep on one *epa*, they *lolovag*.

Lolovaruarua, [*loloi*] doubtful, hesitating, as of two minds ; *rua*.

Lolovatawasai, [*loloi*] open, freeminded; *tawasa*.

Lolovil, [*loloi*] liberal ; met. as *ima vil*, a well-built house.

Lolowena, [*loloi*] one engaged in rain-making, eats nothing.

Lolowia, [*loloi*] good-hearted, kindly; *wia*.

Lolowo, to flame, flare, of fire.
lolowosag, intens. *we lolowosag alo toqana*, of a man in a flaming rage.

Lolowono, [*loloi*] sorry, sorrow, straitened feeling ; *wono*.

Lolroworowo, bad food which makes one feel sick ; *o loloi te roworowo*.

Loltamate, a freehanded person.

Lone, [*lo* 1.] same as *ilone*, that, there, then.

Lon, to cover with leaves, &c., *lon goro*, met. to disguise a failure or fault, as if covering over a broken place.

Lona, to flow, trickle ; *o ninisa ti lonalona*, a mouth watering ; see *lolona*.

Lonlonai, [*lona*] *lonlone maran*

the time before dawn, about 3 a.m.
Lonos, to begin to rise, of the tide, *qara lonlonos kalo ti;* probably from same origin with preceding word.
Lope, a shrub.
  loplopega, watery, like *lope*, of unripe fruit.
Loplopgormetil, *reremera we qoqo, tete ranan qet lai.*
Lopsag, afflicted, miserable.
Lopusar, a fish.
Loqo, to bulge out, project in a lump; *nawareana ti loqo,* he has a bulging forehead; *sig loqo,* to swell after a blow; *tansag, we loqoloqo,* lay the mat evenly, it is unevenly laid.
Loquga, swelling, as a thriving plant; *o wotiu ti loqloquga,* when about to bear fruit; probably *qulo,* by metathesis of syllables.
Lor, to mix, mingle, be mixed, variegated.
  loriag, tr. to mix together, mingle.
  lorlor, adv. confusedly, mixed.
Lortogove, a kind of yam.
Los, to play the fool in a dance.
  loslos, the dance in which some play the fool.
Losalosa, to stay about in a place.
Lot, 1. v. to mash bread-fruit. 2. n. a mash of bread-fruit; done in a *tapia* with a *vat-ge-lot,* pestle; *ti qusa mun o vatgelot, ti veasag mun o vin matig, ti lin o matig, ti sura mun o igot, we sapalo—o lot patau.*
Lou, garden ground.
Louae, one who has no garden.
Lov, to eat fruit from the rind.
Lova, 1. v. to be stiff; *napanek we lova,* my hand is stiff; *pan-lova,* a stiff hand.

Lova, 2. n. a thing lent by father's sister, or father's brother to *lakaluka* with and make a show in a *kolekole;* the nephew returns it with money; see *sirsir lovana.*
Lova, 3. adv. by-the-bye, recurring to something that should have been mentioned; yes! true! or introducing a suggestion; same word as *alova,* to-be-sure.
Love, same as *lova* 3.
Lovelove, quickly; *o aka we tiu lovelove ma.*
Lovi, numeral used in playing *tika,* three.
Lovlov, feeling of illness; *naapek we lovlov,* I am out of sorts.
Low, the chequered swine-fish.
Lua, to put out of the mouth, spew, vomit. Malag. *loa;* Fiji, *lua;* Day. *malua;* Tagala, *lua,* saliva.
  luag, tr. determ. to vomit out, put out of the mouth, *ineira we gat o gea, we luag,* they chew the *kava* root, put it out of their mouths. Mal. *luat;* Mao. *ruaki.*
  lulua, to vomit, be sick; *luluai, luluava.*
Luata, a fish.
Lue, 1. adv. out, through; *vava lue,* speak out.
  2. v. to pull out, up; *we lue o qeta,* to pull *taro; lue salsal,* to pull out at intervals, as every other plant in a row.
  maluelue, in holes.
Lugun, to count on the fingers, *luwun.*
Luk, 1. to bend at an angle, as arm or leg. 2. to squat with bended knees; *ko me rowo rereg ma, we luk pata kel,* you rose up to look in and squat down again to hide.

lukluk, adj. bent, cramped as legs; *tarauok me lukluk,* my foot is asleep.

malukluk, bent, bending.

lukun, tr. to bend at an angle. N.B. *likun,* bend.

Luka, v. in *taraluka.*

Lul, 1. n. a fair person, albino; generally used of a female; a white pig; a ripe but pale *gaviga.*

Lul, 2. v. to be abundant, numerous, increase in number. **lulug,** tr. in *valulug.*

Lul, 3. v. to ripple, cause a ripple; a flaw of wind on the sea *ti lulu ma;* when a breeze ruffles a calm sea *ti lul goro o taro;* a shoal of fish on the surface *ti lul.*

lul wo-ganase, the disturbance made by a shoal of *ganase* pursued by a shark, crowding together and leaping; thence, met. the shouting and leaping of dancers at the end of the dance, *qara map o sawai.*

Lulei, to suck a second time; *we lulei o same gire.*

Lulganase, same as above, *lul wo ganase.*

Lulmule, n. [*lul* 3.] the wind chops round after a heavy blow, and blows softly, *ilone o lulmule.*

Lulu, same as *lul.*

Lulua, [*lua*] to vomit. **luluai,** n. (k) vomit. **luluava,** sickness, vomiting.

Lulul, [*lul* 3.] redupl. *o lan we lulul goro taro,* wind breaks up the calm, by raising ripples.

Lulum, beautiful, of persons, places, things.

Luluqa, to put on the purlins, *raral,* of a house; *me gaso qet qara luluqa.*

Lulus, to close over, cover over, as a wound or sore as it heals; with *goro; te ge lulus wonowono goro kel lai o gaplei.*

Lum, 1. n. an edible seaweed growing on rocks.

Lum, 2. v. to shoot with many arrows, in fighting at close quarters.

Lumagapuei, a boy just growing up.

Lumagav, a youth, young man. *lumagav leqalequ,* a boy not quite a youth. *lumagav mena,* with a beard; *lumagav puen,* beardless. *lumagav tur rorono,* one who goes by himself.

Lumlum, a pudding of grated almond cooked in the oven; soft, see *malumlum.*

Lumuta, moss. Sam. *limu;* Mao. *rimu,* seaweed, moss; Macassar, *lumu,* moss; Mal. *lumut,* moss.

lumtaga, i. e. *lumutaga,* covered with moss.

Luna, same as *lina,* to be out of sight.

lunavag, to hide, as under the edge of a mat.

Luqai, to cover in the ovenful of food, *qaranis,* with mats of leaves, *roqo; te luqai goro o um mun o nogae; te luqai goro o matemaro nan wa sawu ae,* cover over the hole through which water is poured into the oven, lest steam should escape.

Luqaluqa, to play at cooking, covering in the oven, *luqai.*

Luqe, to fold, bend; *luqe goro,* to fold over so as to hide; met. to keep concealed.

luqe late, to turn down, or up, and fold over, so as to shorten.

luqeg, tr. determ. to fold over; *we rasa o nam, ti lolovag, we* *sawar o nai*, *we luqeg*, grate yam, spread it out flat, sprinkle grated almonds, fold it over, in making *loko*.

luqeag, to bend over or fold forcibly; beat or stamp, so as to bend out of shape, *varaluqeag*.

maluqeluqe, folded, bent.

Lusa, a small solitary flying fox, lives in the interior of banyans, *lolo paka*.

Lusalusa, the same.

Luto, dumb, a dumb person.

Luve, grated cocoa-nut that has been squeezed for *woro*, food for pigs; *o same matig me garir ti*; at Gaua, *nuve*.

Luvun, V. same as M. *liwun*; cover, as waves wash over and bury a canoe.

Luwai, a district of Mota.

Luwai-av, one of the lower ranks in the *suqe*.

Luwun, V. same at *liwun* and *lugun*, a Gaua word, to count on the fingers; refers to the movement of the fingers in counting, *lukan*; an *un* word.

M. *M*.

The nasal m, printed *m*, and in writing marked with dots above the letter, is not separated from the common m in the vocabulary, but is marked in all words in which it is known to occur. When the Mota word is in italic letters this *mala m*, as it is called, is in Roman type. The distinction between the sounds of m and *m* is very important.

M, pers. pron. sing. 2. suffixed to possessives, *nom*, *mom*, *gam*, *mam*, *pulam*, for *ma*; of thee.

Ma, 1. poss. n. used of things to drink, and such as are chewed for the juice; *mak o pei* water for me to drink, *mam o tou* sugar-cane for you to chew, *man o gire* pandanus fruit for him to suck; also of a vessel to drink out of, *mak o lasa*. Fij. *me*.

Ma, 2. prep. of relation, in fact a noun; with simple prep. *a*, *ta*, becomes comp. prep. *ama*, *tama*. See *me* 2. It is properly used only with regard to persons, and therefore with pers. pron., *amaia*, *tamaia*, *amaiko*, *tamaiko*, *amaira*, *tamaira*; in simple form, *maiko*, *maia*, *maira*. The sense of *ma* is that of simple relation; with *a* 2., which see, it becomes with, from; *ni we toga amaiko*, he stays with you; *ilone na me lav ma ti amaia*, that which I had from him.

Ma, 3. adv. hither, this way. Common through the Ocean languages as *mai*; taken for prep. and v. Must be sometimes translated by English prep. "from," but is never prep.; *ko me mule ma area?* where have you come from? *ma Gaua*, from Gaua. Time is signified as space, *alo tuara tan run ma*, from last year up to the present time. In messages and letters the point towards which the hitherward motion is directed is that at which the letter or message is delivered.

Ma, *ma*, 4. prefix of condition, making what appear to be participles, as *malate* broken, *late* break, and adjectives not formed from verbs, as *mavinrin*. This prefix is very common in Melanesia; in Pol. as Sam. *maligi* from *ligi*; Mao. *mahore* from *hore*; a "large class of adjectives in Malag. beginning with *ma* or *m*." Richardson; common in adj. of Malay Archipelago.

Ma, 5. pers. pron. sing. 2. suffixed to nouns; of thee; with poss. n. shortened to *m*. See Grammar.

Maaeae, adj. light in weight.

Maaleale, adj. hanging and loosely moving, as a child's head in *epa pepepe*.

Maaneane, adj. [*ane*] soft, beaten or trodden soft.

Maanian, [*aniani*] adj. dizzy.

Maaniani, the same; *o nagoi te maaniani ape mate nua*, one gets dizzy at the edge of a cliff; of the face, not the person.

Maari, [*ar*] emptied, despoiled; of a house from which money, &c., has all been spent.

Maave, 1. adj. very tall; *salo maave*; redupl. *maaveave*.
2. n. a tall man or tree.

Maaviu, a heavy dull sound.

Maavuavu, [*ma* 4.] adj. [*avu* 2.] looking small in distance.

Maea, n. the open, the air, space; adj. open, spacious.

Maekeeke, adj. light, as some wood.

Maele, [*eleele*] elevated, lofty.

Maeto, black volcanic stone, *o vat maeto*; from the dark colour. Malag. *mainty*; Salibabo, *maitu*; Ses. Lep. *maeto*; Fl. *meto*, dirty: see *meto*.

Mag, tr. suffix to v. Fij. *maka*; Motu, *mai*.

Mag, tr. suff. to v.

Magaegae, [*ma* 4., *gae*] 1. tough, stringy; *o tangae we magaegae te koran, tete malate gaplot,* you will have to break off a branch of such a tree by pulling it downwards, it will not be readily broken in two.
2. tough, tenacious, like well-cooked *lot patau*; you can draw it out in strings.

Magalgal, adj. of the feeling of the skin when tickled, as by something crawling over it.

Magan, n. a small insect that lives under mats, and bites.

Maganrowolue, adj. said of a badly woven mat with holes, the *magan* can come out.

Magapei, [*ma* 4., *gape* 1.] n. what can be broken in the hands; said of a weak bow.

Magargar, [*ma* 4.] loosened, as the *iwatia* of a canoe by use; it moves itself *garu*.

Magarosa, 1. adj. 1. pitying, compassionate, kindhearted.
2. pitiable, to be sympathized with, poor, as an object of compassion.
3. v. to pity, sympathize with.
4. n. pity, compassion.
ma 2. of condition; *sa* 3. adj. termination; *garo* probably *aro* in Fl. *arovi*.

Magarugaru, [*garu*] rough, of waves; *magargar*.

Magasa, a tree, an *ita*, with yellow flowers growing on the branches.

Magasagasa, a shrub.

Magasei, 1. (k) same as *magesei*.
2. a solitary man.

Magatea, 1. an old woman, one past early middle age.
2. a fish, gurnard, scorpœna.
3. the cocoon of a certain moth, like housebuilder.
4. an ant-lion.

Magav, 1. painful; *rono magav*, to suffer pain; a Gaua word; *un* word.

2. v. impers. *me magavua*, it pained him.

Magavgav, [*gav*] soft, comminuted, as if worked with the hands.

Magavui, an old feeble person.

Magege, one who makes much of a little trouble, as of a sore or weight.

Mageregere, weak.

Magesei, (k) 1. a solitary, self alone; in form a noun, only to be translated as if adj. or adverb, alone; *inau magesek*, I alone; *ni we toga mayesena aia*, he stays there by himself, alone. Though *magasei* is used the word is *ma 4, gese;* conf. Fl. *hege*, by metathesis, Bugotu, *gehe;* Nguna, *siki;* in each case, *heyegu, gehegu, sikigu*, I alone, my self alone.
2. a solitary man.

Magetget, [*get*] conspicuous, standing out to view; *o aka we tira magetget;* also *maget*.

Magingin, [*gin*] 1. as when a man with itch warms himself or scratches it is pleasant to him.
2. met. of the sea in a nice condition for paddling, *o lama we magingin, o lan we lul apena, gate rep.*

Magirit, [*gir*] tickle.

Magisgis, [*gis*] soft to touch, yielding, can run finger into it.

Mago, a dance.

Magoa, shaking; from *goa*, unknown.
  magmagoa, shaky, vibrating.
  magoagoa, shaky, with continuance.

Magolgol, tremulous: *naqatuna, napanena, we magolgol.*

Magologolo, [*golo*] tremulous, shaking.

Magoqogoqo, [*goqo*] like a bubble, puffed up, hollow; of a boil.

Magoqolava, large and light, like a big bubble, *goqo;* said of a bundle, big with little in it.

Magorgor, soft, squeezable.

Magoro, a serpula which pierces the foot when trodden on, and smashes; *qagala puto magoro, mate magoro*, varieties of hibiscus.

Magoto, 1. a grass, panax, springing up as summer approaches.
2. the summer season, after the erythrina, *rara*, has shed its leaves; *magoto qaro*, the early season, when the grass is fresh; *magoto rano*, later, when the grass is withered.

Magovgov, [*gov*] quivering, as the air with heat.

Magovagova, bending, giving; as the side of a boat when struck by surf; elastic.

Magun, M. moving with creeping crawling motion; as a child moves under a mat; as the stomach rises in nausea; *naqatima ti magungun*, you feel a creeping in your hair; *mawunwun* V.

Magupegupe, weak.

Mai, a sea-snake, haunting the beach and rocks.
  mai tiratira, valeleas, the *mai* that stands on end, or is brilliantly variegated, the snake that changes into man or woman.

Mai-sale, the sea-snake floating with its head erect, met. of a man who goes peering about.

Mai-tamate, the figure of a *mai* in a *salagoro*.

Maia, [*ma 2.*] with him, her, it; *amaia*.

Maiko, with thee; *amaiko*.
Maira, with them; *amaira*.
Maimaitagai, a child which takes again what is taken from it; as a *mai* thrown into the sea comes back.
Mait, to crowd close together; *o sul we qoqo we vug*.
Mak, [*ma* 1.] something for me to drink.
Makala, adv. in the way of pattern; *ilo makala*, take example by, copy.
Makaliu, (k) model, pattern, example; *makala*.
makaliva, likeness, fashion, pattern.
Makarag, to give up, part with, have done with; *we makarag o nonomia*, dismiss a thought; *me makaragia*, parted with a companion; *we makarag o tautaur o tue nam*, give over training yam vines.
Makaru, flying-fish; several species.
makaru maswurep, short thick fish.
makaru paumea, with red wings, a gurnard.
makaru paragoro, a small kind.
makaru rowlava, a very large one.
Make, the Tahitian chestnut; inocarpus edulis. Tahiti, *mate*.
Makei, 1. v. to add, in number or quantity.
2. adv. besides, over and above.
Makeru, to lean head on hand; *pute makeru*, to sit leaning head on hand as poor people without food.
Makik, decreased but still much; *qale purat pa gate qoqo aneane*.
Makira, neap; *rue makira, meat makira*, high and low tide at neap.

Makmakalas-taro, said of one who thinks it easy to do what he sees another do, and fails, *o makmakalas taro me ge neia; makala*.
Makmakevat, [*makei*] to heap up, in large quantity.
Mako, 1. to make a garland.
2. to put leaves on money as a garland for one entering, or rising in, the *suqe; neira we mako munia*.
makomako, a garland; wreath; *we soso o makomako* in the *suqe*, when the friends of the candidate lay leaves on the money in a basket; *we sese makomako*, when they pull apart the garland and distribute the money.
makosag, tr. 1. to decorate with garland; 2. to make a fine show.
Makoekoe, [*koe*] loose, as a thing which can be moved backwards and forwards, with fixed base, and so be pulled out.
Makomkom, [*kom*] soft, as mealy yam, giving a good mouthful.
Makurkur, [*kur*] underdone, so that one must *kur* the food.
Mal, 1. adj. red, of eyes red with crying, or diving.
Mal, 2. n. 1. a young cocoa-nut, *malu*.
2. a *gaviga*, not sweet, as a *malu* is not sweet enough to drink.
Mala, 1. 1. a hawk, kite, osprey.
2. a toy kite in shape of *mala; we vino o rea apena*.
3. met. one who runs quickly as a *mala* flies; *o mala lova!*
Mala, 2. 1. adj. ill, bad; *o mala tanun*, bad character; but often only in depreciation, poor; hence 2. pref. of depreciation, ill; *malagagapalag*,

ill-doing; often distinguishes wild from cultivated plants, *malatou, malmalagiviga.*
*M*ala, 3. a sow.
Malagagapalag, [*mala* 2.] ill-doer, ill-doing.
Malagene, [*mala* 2.] a bad thing, misfortune.
Malagesa, [*mala* 2., *gesa*] pale in colour; *loa malagesa,* sunshine between showers.
malagesai, green unripe breadfruit.
Malagisiaga, clammy like cold food.
*M*algolago, [*ma* 4.] loose, not fitting closely.
*M*alai, 1. (k) something inside a man that jumps when he is startled; *na malak me rowo,* I was startled.
Malai, 2. a bad thing; *mala* 2. Sam. *mala.*
Malai, 3. v. to make payment or present after an offence. *I Sogoiv me malai mun Sigagrawe ape rasoana.*
Malakalaka, [*laka*] 1. rejoice. 2. adv. with pleasure.
Malakegaviga, light in complexion but not very light; *gate pita aneane.*
Malakenuma, a small fish.
Malakoukou, [*mala* 2.] a place overgrown, overcast; *kou; alo malakoukou,* under the shade of other trees; a damp place where sun never shines; overcast with clouds.
*M*alakurvat, a gardenia shrub.
Malalolou, [*mala* 2.] too much shaded over; *lolo.*
*M*alamala, 1. a girl.
tano-malamala, (1.) girl-hood.
Malamala, 2.[*mala* 2.]redupl.bad.
tano-malamala, (2.) bad ground, where things won't grow well.

Malamalaqauro, a wild *qauro,* no good.
*M*alan, a fish, cottus; *te qis o malan,* with the palm and bent fingers.
malan momo, malan goe, kinds, the latter large.
Malanisiaga, [*mala* 2.] dirty, as hands with food; mildewed; *nis* 1.
Malanonomia, an ill thought, bad design.
Malana, [*ma* 4.] raised up, *lana; o mot malana,* bush clear underneath, with no undergrowth.
Malanalana, uplifted, lifting; *me wena ti pa o maligo we malanalana,* it has rained but the clouds have lifted; *ti malanalana,* sky is lifting, won't rain.
Malanenenene, [*mala* 2.] damp, wet, *nene,* altogether.
Malao, a tree.
Malaor, a tree.
Malaova, [*mala* 2.] 1. a poor, thin, egret, *ova.*
2. met. a thin person, emaciated with hunger or sickness.
Malapao, a beetle.
Malapopo, [*mala* 2.] unsound, not solid, *popo.*
Malapusa, slow in movement.
Malaqauro, a kind of wild yam, *qauro,* with tendrils.
Malaqei, [*ma* 4.] flat and thin like the blade, *laqei,* of a paddle.
Malaqo, 1. a white spot, spotted; a spotted pig.
2. a fighting arrow made white with *vin nornai.*
Malaqona, a kind of pigeon, *qona.*
Malaqon, [*mala* 4.] evil day, *qon.*
Malaqorevereve, a long whitened fighting arrow; *reve.*

Malarowo, 1. sudden alarm. 2. startled; *o malai ti rowo-rowo*.

Malas, 1. n. food not eaten the day it is cooked; *malasiu*. 2. adj. adv. the next day's. 3. v. to go sour.

Malasina, an acacia, with gum; *o walie malasina*, the lumps of *malasina*-gum.

Malasiu, const. *malas*; 1. food not eaten when cooked, so cold; *o malas qoe*. 2. food distributed and taken away at feasts.

Malaso, n. cold. Fl. *malaho*.

Malasomsoma, [mala 3.] met. a greedy eater, gobbles like a sow.

Malasorovia, [mala 3.] a sow that snortles; met. a man that eats his food with noises in his throat.

Malate, [ma 4., *late*] broken, bent by breaking.
  malatei, (k) a piece broken off, a length broken or cut off; the broken part, place which shows the break.
  malatelate, broken to pieces.
  malate somotag, confusedly broken, like waves, branches of trees; *malate valqei, va luqeg*, breaking and bending down another; *malate vasusmag goro*, breaking so as to fall flat above another; *o tangae me masu amoa, tuara ti mas valaqatia*.

Malatou, [mala 3.] 1. large grass, something like sugar-cane, *tou*, which grows in neglected ground. 2. garden ground overgrown, fallow.

Malau, a megapodius; brush turkey; in Celebes, *maleo*.
  malau gil rorono, one that digs the hole for its eggs silently; *malau uloulo*, one that cries out; used proverbially.

Malau-gan-Qat, 1. a yellow creeping thing that rolls itself into a ball when a *malau* scratches near it, in Gaua. 2. sulphur such as is found in the solfataras in V.L., and at Lakona.

Malau-kilakilau, met. one who wishes for anything he has rejected; see *kerevag nona malau*.

Malauligogsala, 1. a kind of *malau* which has no settled place for sleeping. 2. met. a man whose habit is to sleep about away from home.

Malav, to speak with a lisp.

Malaweaga, adj. very many; *o un we malaweaga*.

Malawereta, of a flock, crowd, shoal.

Malawesaga, [mala 3.] moist, clammy.

Malawo, 1. tall, long; so 2. weak.
  malawo galoloag, to grow tall and spirally twisted, of a tree.
  malawo piplotag, to grow tall and crooked.
  malawo sasalovega, tall without bulk, said of a tall, weak man.
  malawo sou, said of caladium which has grown again after being mature; *o qeta qe rano ti, o noliu ti natiu, qe wena ti ge kel o naui*.
  malawo ratvat, to grow as a tree with short intervals between the branches; *vatiu*.
  malawo-av, fire flaming high.
  malawoi, (k) 1. the tall part; *o tangae, o ulusui ti toletole sage, na malawona nane*; *na-malawon o tanun*, a man's growing tall, his tallness. 2. a thing still lengthening, half-

grown; a fish, *gate poa mantay;* a tree half grown; met. *kamiu me sol goro o malawona,* you have cut down its growing part before the time, have been too quick about a thing.

Malawonog, [*malo* 3., *wono*] a damp close place, in forest.

Malawonon, same as *malawonog.*

Malawosal, the name of the middle finger, as rising long, *malawo,* above, *sal,* the rest.

Malea, tasteless, of no effect; *pei malea,* sweet water as opposed to *tor; ge malea,* to make of no effect, disregard.

malean, modified, softened to taste, either better or worse according to habit or use; *pei malean,* brackish water; distasteful as when one is tired of a thing.

Maleatovlau, brackish water, as in a *tov a lau.*

*M*aleg, a blight-bird, silver-eye, zosterops.

Malekai, (k.) 1. the sole of the foot, the foot.
2. a footprint, track.

Malekenana, dirty, befouled, as if with traces of *nana,* pus.

Maleko, scale on yams.

Malele, nearly ripe.

Malemalewa, a tree, limp *malewa.*

Malesles, malesulesu, [*ma* 4.] bending over, *lesu;* unsteady in gait; intoxicated; *o gea neira we ima we vus malesles o apei.*

*M*alete, clear, open, of eyes, sky. *ma*malete, clean and flourishing, of a garden.

Malewa, strengthless, as soft wood trees, bananas, &c.; weak from want of food, feeble, faint.

Malgotur, see *maligo tur.*

Maliemao, M. same as *maluemao* V.

Maligo, a cloud.
maligo takau, a cloud hanging, *takau,* on a hill; said also of two clouds connecting.
maligo tur, the clouds of night, abiding, *tur; we vene goro gap o malgo-tur alo qon,* when there is war they shoot abroad into the dark on the chance of frightening the enemy.
maligo vat, a cloud coming up slowly without rain, a mass of cloud.

Maligo, a part of Mota of which the speech, characterized by the use of *i* rather than *u,* is thought by the neighbouring people of Veverau to be thin, *marinvin.*

Maligoligo, [*ma* 4.] fat, well-grown.

Maliklik, said of few persons in a large house; *lik.*

Malin, a kind of yam.

Malinsala, n. hunger, adj. hungry, v. to be hungry; *inau o malinsala,* I am hungry.

Maliqo, to come or go, with *ma* and *kel,* in a crowd.

Malisalisa, [*ma* 4.] 1. moving like *lisa,* wriggling; *o ulo we malisalisa,* maggots alive in meat.
2. said of grated cocoa-nut in the mouth, moves in little bits, gritty.

*M*alisiu, (k) a remnant; *malis gavneyae,* material left over after finishing an *epa;* small tubers left in digging yams; food remaining.

Maliu, swelling of testicle.

Malkeke, bad.

Malmalagaviga, [*mala* 3.] wild eugenia, *gaviga.*

Malmalai, a man of no consequence, who has to pay respect, and *malai* 3. if he fails.

Malmalakastaro, see *makmakalastaro*, metathesis of syllables

Malmalamamaua, a useless *mamaua* tree.

Malmalapuaka, a kind of bulrush growing in wet places, *puaka*.

Malmalapeg, hanging down; *malulpeg*.

Malmalaqatman, a bird, - in native belief the female *qatman*.

Malmalaqauro, wild uneatable *qauro*.

Malmalaviv, slight beginnings of pain.

Malmalawerita, a kind of starfish.

Malmalawotaga, 1. wild *wotaga*. 2. swellings on the skin when cold is caught; *o malmalawotaga we na sei*.

Malmaluga, smooth, soft, like the body of an infant.

Malmaluima, a verandah; *malu* 2., *ima*.

Malnai, (k) the sloping side of hill or cliff; *malne nua*.

Malnoa, broken with valleys; *ta ilo tauwe, pa o qarana aia, we vet was we malnoa*.

Malo, 1. a sunken rock where the sea breaks.

Malo, 2. a tree; probably a mulberry.

Malo, 3. the girdle of leaves and flowers used by *tamate*; the Pol. breech cloth *maro, malo*; Fij. *malo*, N.B. *mal*, mulberry, broussonetia, out of which *malo*, native cloth, is made.

Maloaloa, drowsy, sleepy; *namatak we maloaloa*.

Maloke, by metathesis for *maleko*.

Malol, [*ma* 4., *lol*] 1. indistinct, of speech; *o vavara malol*. 2. one who does not listen, disobedient.

Maloloa, hungry.

Malope, to hang, bend, down, overhang.

malopelope, of money, hanging, long.

Malopegaro, the plaited cocoanut fronds that cover the ridge of a house.

Maloplop, 1. soft, compressible. 2. dull, of sound.

Malosalosa, weak, tired; *naapena we malosalosa*, after play or running.

Malosaru, a dress, *malo*, woven and highly ornamented, put on over the head *saru*, and worn at *kokekole*, &c.

Malot, [*ma* 4., *lot*] bruised, mashed, as a ripe fruit that has fallen on a root; *malotlot*, all in a mash as a beaten man's body.

Maloulou, with few inhabitants, of a village; as if it were *lou*.

Malov, 1. an erythrina tree with strong-smelling leaves. 2. v. to charm people with *malov* or other leaves; either to attract them or keep them off; when enemies are coming, *isei te gat o gatavanoro, te pupus, te malov neira*; by chewing and puffing out the smell, or burning and puffing out the smoke.

Malqei, a folded piece, bale of folded stuff; *maluqe*.

Malqolue, come out in a crowd, *maliqo lue*.

Malrurus, the charmed *malu* which causes *rurus*.

Malsagilo, another name for *malo-saru; malo sagilo*.

Malsalis, for *malisalisa*.

Malu, 1. a young green cocoa-nut, the shell just formed, the fluid not yet drinkable, much used in charms.
  mal-garata, a *malu* made *mana* to give effect to *garata* charm.
  mal-lumagar, one used to *oloolo* for a young man that he may be attractive.
  mal-maniga, used to *oloolo* that a man might effect a charm to bring *maniga*, sores.
  mal-qatrirtig, for making the charm that causes head-ache.
  mal-rurus, as above.
  mal-sinaga, used to *oloolo* so that food may abound.
  mal-suqe, for success in rising in *suqe*.
  mal-usu, one made *mana* and drunk so that a man's bow might shoot straight.

Malu, 2. to shade, shade; generally in redupl. Fij. Sam. *malu*; Mao. *maru*.

Malu, 3. soft, appears in next word. Sam. *malu*; Pol. *maru*.

Maluape, [*malu* 3.] dispirited, feeble; no strength in *apei*.

Malue, [*ma* 4.] having a hole through, *lue*; burst, come open; to burst.
  maluelue, in holes, full of holes.

Maluemao, V. very much torn; *mao* 3.; *maorowolue*.

Maluk, [*ma* 4.] bent inwards, a crook inwards, *luk*; opposite to *sigrai*.
  maluk panei, the inner bend of the elbow; *alo* *maluk panei*, a measure of length, see *rova*.
  maluk pisui, the inner crook of the knuckles.
  maluk ranoi, the inner bend of the knee.
  malukluk, 1. bending, with crooked arms or legs; *sus malukluk*, crouch with bended knees.
  2. asleep, as foot or leg, because bent.

Malulpeg, bending, curved downwards; see *malupelupe*.

Malumalu, 1. v. to shade; *malumalu goro*, overshadow. n. shade, not shadow.

Malumalu, 2. of waves rising high above a canoe; *o rep ti malumalu goro aka*.

Malumlum, soft, gentle. Fij. *malumu*; Sol. Ids. *marumurumu*, *malumu*; D.Y. *galom*; Ceram, *mulumu*; Mysol, *rum*; Macassar, *lumu*; Mal. *lâmah*; Malag. *lemy*.

Malumuaga, patient, *we gagapalag malumlum*; *rono malumuaga*, be patient.

Malupelupe, bending, as a branch heavy with fruit; *malumalupe*, another reduplication, whence *malulpeg*.

Maluqaluqa, [*ma* 4.] creased; *luqa*, probably *luqe*.

Maluqe, [*ma* 4., *luqe*] folded, in folds.
  maluqeluqe, in many folds.
  malqei, a folded bundle or bale; *maluqei*.

Maluqegaro, a water weed.

Malurav, dusk of evening; *malu* 2., *ravrav*.

Maluveluve, broken.

Mam, 1. pers. pron. 1. plur. excl. suffixed to nouns; of us.

Mam, 2. poss. n. *ma* 1. with suff. pers. pr. sing. 2.; thine to drink.

Mama, 1. father; in addressing him; also in speaking of him, less properly; *o mama inau*, my father, for *tamak*; perhaps a recent use. Motu N.G. *mama*.
  2. to call father; *isei we mama*

F

inau? who is calling "father!" to me?

Mama, 3. to make a small sound, rustle like leaves in the breeze; *mamama,* noise of wind or rain; *mamama rutrut,* to talk low.

Mama, 4. thine to drink; *ma* 1., suff. *ma* 5.

Mamagela, 1. to look after, care for; *isei te mamagela kara?* 2. *un* word for *maros.*

Mamagerig, to get smaller and smaller; *rig.*

Mamagese, childless, desolate; *magesei.*

Mamakei, to wonder; *mamakei ape,* to wonder at, admire; perhaps from *kei!* excl. of wonder. *tano mamakei,* object of wonder, admiration.

Mamalau, a tree.

Mamaleas, to take another man to call father, *mama,* when the mother marries again; conf. *tupleas.*

Mamalete, clean, flourishing, of a garden; *malete.*

Mamaligota, overcast with cloud, *maligo;* dull as evening without sun; *ta* 6.

Mamalraga, [*malu* 2.] shaded, shady; *o vanua me mamalraga veta, o loa me tul.*

Mamalu, to bind on the cross bamboo' purlin at foot of rafters, *gaso;* beginning to thatch at the eaves; *we rot o au wa o togo ape papuris;* see *tuwur.*

Mamalue, shade; *o malumalu;* shady.

Mamaluga, [*malu* 2.] shady.

Mamama, to sound lightly as wind or rain; *mama* 3.

Mamamas, adv. falling; *kamiu te kurkur mamamas, nau te kurkur goro alo tano,* while you are eating in the tree, and making the fruit fall, I will eat what falls, upon the ground.

Mamanei, adv. in small pieces; *wota mamanei o lito; manei.*

Mamanigata, afflicted with ulcers, sores, *maniga.*

Mama-oraora, to show delight with inarticulate sounds, *mama,* as child at return of its father; to frisk, *oraora,* and *mama,* as a pig when its owner comes, or when it sees food.

Mamaota, a tree.

Mamaova, to gape, yawn.

Mamarir, adj. cold. Wahai, *maririr.*

Mamarisa, smarting, to smart; biting in taste.

Mamarog, to desire eagerly, want, ask for; *ni me mamarog o rusa mun i gene.*

Mamaroi, the same; also *mamaron.*

Mamaru, [*maru*] docile, manageable, tame; *mamar qulo,* said of a young girl taken as a wife, early broken in; *me mamar veta mun rasoana.*

Mamasa, 1. dry, bare, unoccupied.
2. adv. gratis, without payment or reward.
mamasaiga, dry, very dry.

Mamasa, a tree.

Mamasarewo, a tree.

Mamasua, a disease, *o rigariga.*

Mamasug, [*masu*] to let go, loose, let fall.
mamasug vitag, let alone, forbear.
mamasug o apei, naapensei we mamasug, to set the mind at ease, to have the mind at ease, as when pain ceases or lessens.

Mamasur, to sound faint in the distance, as a tree falling; *o tangae we mama sur.*

Mamata, 1. v. to have the eyes, *matai*, open, be awake, watch ; *mamata goro*, keep watch over ; *mamata varleas*, keep watch in turns.
2. n. a fresh-water fish with big eyes.

Mamataiga, flourishing.

Mamatuaga, [*matua*] full grown, of trees ; wood hardened.

Mamaua, a tree.

Mamaureure. playful, as child with father.

Man, 1. a bird, beetle, *manu*.
2. prefix signifying love for something, as a bird or beetle, *man*, loves certain trees and plants.

Man, 3. a place at the bottom of the sea where *ganase* eat the sand and all is *gagavu*, turbid.

Mana, 1. an invisible spiritual force or influence ; a very common Ocean word.
2. v. to influence, work upon, with *mana* ; to have *mana*.
3. to poison, as certain fish when eaten.
4. a charm, sung with *mana*, to pass it.

Mana, 5. to moisten and so soften ; to become soft when moistened, *me tuk mot o kor, paso nan me mana*.

Mana, 6. *ilo mana*, to regard with favour. Bugotu, *mugnahagi*. Mao. *manako*.

Manag, convey *mana* to, make to be *mana*, influence with *mana*, a charm ; *te sur o as o mana, ti va ma, we managia ma*.

Manamnam, [*nam*] bruised, beaten ; *vus manamnam*.

Manara, 1. [ma 4.] ground hot with springs, as on V.L. and Tauwe Garat ; *ape manara we tutun, alau we vamamarir*.

Manara, 2. said by some for *menaro*.

Manarag, to describe accurately; *we manarag o vavae*, speak accurately.

Manaranara, [*ma* 4.] bloody; *nara*.

Manaras, [*ma* 4., *naras*] 1. hurt with bloodshed. 2. hurt ; *ge manaras*, to hurt.

Manariu, fallen decayed trunk of tree ; may be sound within.

Manarnar, [*nar*] soft ; of food overcooked, *ko we gana pa we nolo ran*, wants no mastication.

Manasnas, [*nas*] pointed.

Manatuatu, a pigeon, same as *mantap*.

Manawenawe, soft, as food overcooked.

Manawo, of fair complexion, used of male rather than female ; perhaps from *nawo*.

Maneepa, [*manei*] a short small mat.

Manei, a small thing or quantity ; *o mane sava*, bit of something. **mamanei**, adv. to bits ; *manmanenei*.

Manepurapura, bits of crushed yam, *pura*.

Manerei, small bit, fragment.

Manereqauro, an ulcer ; *o maniga ape vutui vires, tete vava lue apena ;* said in ridicule ; *o natmera navutena we maniga, ineia o manere qauro*.

Manesenese, high and clear, of the voice ; clearly heard, as wind and waves in the distance.

Mangaela, one who lingers ; *gaela*.

Mangawono, i. e. *manig gawono*, with no cause but heedlessness ; *mangawono qa !* a piece of heedless folly.

Mangege, [*man* 2.] one who will do what is forbidden.

Mangevus, one who runs into danger.

Mangorgor, one who is fond of *gorgor*, cocoa-nut.

Mania, papaw, carica papaya; corrupted from mammy apple; though of recent introduction there are named, *tur mania*, the common papaw; *mania malagesa* fruit green when ripe; *maniaqoe*, kind with large fruit; *mania parou*, the male plant.

Manig, to dive; *manig goro*, dive after.

Maniga, M. 1. ulcer, sore. 2. charm to produce ulcers.
maniga tiutiu, an irregular breaking out; *we gan popolotag o turie tanun*.
manigata, ulcerous, *mamanigata*, full of sores; *ta* 6.

Manigiu, cause, reason, purpose, means; *o manig gale* with purpose of deceiving, by means of deceit.

Manile, [*ma* 4.] chipped, with a bit knocked out; *o wowo apena*; as an adze; *nile*.
manilenile, chipped along the edge, with little notches, *o wowo tagai; manlenle*.

Manimonimo, [*ma* 4.] still water near the shore; *o rue we rue aneane pa o nawo itagai*.

Maniniag, to go about unobserved; *maniniag rorono*.

Maninin, [*ma* 4.] smooth, *ninin*; slippery, *tete taur lai*; *ko we taur o garake napanema ti maninin apena*.

Manin, to tap with a slight noise; *wena manin*, light rain making a dripping noise.

Manirin, [*nir*] to make known the whereabouts of a man to his enemy, betray.

Manirnir, [*na* 4.] bald in patches, the scalp shows through, *nir lue; qat manirnir*.

Maniu, M. (k) nose, beak; *namanina*; not of a pig.

Mankalkalmalau, a creeping thing, *manu*, like a woodlouse, that rolls itself into a ball when a *malau* scratches near; the *malau* mixes it up, *kal*, in the dirt and it escapes.

Mankukukur, [*man* 3.] one who loves to eat fruit, &c., *kur*.

Manlago, a beetle, *manu*, frequenting the yam *lago*.

Manlau, one in the habit of going to the beach; *man* 2.; *nau gate manlau mulan*, I used to be fond of the beach, can't go now.

Manleg, to hang up empty; *ni we manleg o tapera; tapera manleg*, bag with nothing in it.

Manlenle, notched with small notches; *manilenile*.

Manligo, a crowd of bats hanging together, *ligo*.

Manlol, a bird, lalage Banksiana.

Manlope, a beetle, *manu*, frequenting the *lope* shrub.

Manlorgarata, [*man* 3.] one who is always mixing, *lor*, things for *garata* charms.

Manman, to itch in the palm of hand or sole of foot, a sign that some one is coming.

Manmanenei, [*manei*] adv. in very little bits; *sipa* or *teve manmanenei*.

Manmanlul, a V.L. bird.

Man-manole, a bird, riphidura.

Manmanolea, v. to make little of a law, *mano*; much the same as *tamtames goro lea*.

Manmanonine, [*mano*] a small kind of cowry shell, *nine*.

Manmanosom, [*mano*] very small fine *som* used as ornament.
Manmantomago, a kind of *tomago*.
Manmanu, inferior, common, same as *purepurei*.
Manmava, 1. a cold in the head; *o manui we mava*, heavy nose; *namanik we mava*, I have a cold.
Manmava, 2. a shrub.
Manmemea, a red bird.
Manmonmo, same as *manimonimo*.
Manmout, a *wirita* with broken tentacles; *ut* 1.
Man-ninninnoota, a beetle in the thatch.
Man-*n*orisa, [*maniu*] dirty nose; *nor*.
Man-*n*ornor, nose with a cold, *nor*.
Mano, adverb of depreciation to n. adj. v.; just, a little, rather, not very; *pa mano inau*, but (take) only just me; *nan mano i pulsalanina ti qa tuwale*, there is still one of our friends, poor fellow, missing; *o mano tuaniu*, some, none so many.
Manoa, [*ma* 4.] small, fine; *noa*.
    manoanoa, in fine particles, to little bits; *pura manoanoa*, smash very small.
Manoai, (k) the soft place in infants' heads; *we maworwor*.
Manoga, [*ma* 4.] cooked, well done; *manoga sisgarov*, outside cooked; *manoga kur matika*, underdone; from *noga* 2. to bruise; Motu N.G. *manoka*, soft.
    manoganoga, bruised, squashed, as *qero* fungus when handled.
Manole, a bird.
Manon, set on edge as teeth; also *manoni*.

Manono, [*ma* 4.] sunk away, as when earth falls into a pit, or a hollowed wave shows a rock; a sunken place.
Manonoata, [*manoa*] finely crushed, powdered, powdery; like flour, or flower of *magoto*.
Manonenone, [*ma*] rattling, sounding, when shaken, as milk in cocoa-nut; *noneray*.
Manora, [*ma* 4.] splashing so as to sound, *nora*; as water into which something falls.
    manoranora, of water beaten flatly with the hand, makes lapping sound.
Manornor, singing out of time.
Manoronoro, [*ma* 4., *noro*] rattling.
Manounou, mispronunciation of *malonlou*, one who remains alone in the *vanua*.
Manove, [*ma* 4.] broken through with holes; *nove*.
Manpalpal, [*man* 3.] given to stealing, a thief; *palu*.
Manpuasa, a bird that eats *puasa*.
Manqasa, [*maniu*] a man with a nose flattened at the end; *qasai*.
Manqeqe, flat-nosed; *qea*.
Manras, a scratching bird.
Manroe, like a large caterpillar; *o pulai*, people like to have one.
Mansa*n*, one who eats till all is done; met. from *matika*, a bird that destroys, *san*.
Manseneuwa, said of a torn net, or of a house full of holes.
Mansinaga, [*man* 3.] a glutton.
Mansom, [*man* 3.] fond of money.
Mantag, properly, perfectly, well.
Mantagai, small; a little; *mantagai ti e*, within a little.
Mantanara, a small flying fox.
Mantap, a small green dove; met. a quick runner.

Mantapmele, a kind of *mantap*.
Mantavusrawe, a bird; *ta* 1.; *mylagra*.
Mantikeke, small.
Mantilele, small.
Man-toape, the beetle that feeds on *toape*.
Man-toganae, the frigate bird, man-of-war hawk; appears in *togalau* wind; stays, *toga*, on the *Vat ganae*.
Man-tut, a V.L. pigeon that cries *tut*.
Manu, 1. bird, flying creature, beetle, bat. The common Ocean word in Pol. Mel. and Malay Archipelago.
2. the bird or beetle which for food or other reason attaches itself to a tree or plant is the *manu* of it; e.g. *manlope*; thence the prefix *man*, before vowels *manu*, meaning fond of, given to.
Manu, 3. thunder; *o manu we vara*, when lightning strikes.
Manu, 4. a particular beetle, black, in trees; eaten.
Manua, orphan.
Manuarar, a beetle which strips, *ar*, the bark of trees to get at the juices; met. a pertinacious man.
Manuepa, [*manu* 2.] one who loves his sleeping mat.
Manuga, V. same as *maniga*, ulcer, sore. Sam. *manu'a*; N.B. *manua*.
Manuganuga, [*ma* 4.] weak with sickness, not able to hold things tight from weakness.
Manui, V. nose, beak.
Manuima, [*manu* 2.] fond of drinking.
Manulenule, [*ma* 4.] cut in figures, carved, *nule*; said of *kor* eaten by *susmawo*.
Manumaro, one who eats and is never satisfied; *manu* 2., *maro*.
Manun, sheltered, shaded, a damp close place in the bush.
Manur, heavy, principal, important, successful; *napanena we manur*, he is a good hand at shooting, fishing; *manursala*, at Tasmate a main road, elsewhere a cross road; *manur tangae*, a heavy log cast up on shore; *panmanur*, one who is a good hand at shooting, fishing; having *mana* for it.
Manurlama, dark blue; *lama*.
Manursala, cross road, at Tasmate high road.
Manuvutvalis, small green V.L. parrot.
Manvas, [*man* 3.] one who pretends not to have what he really has; *we vas goro*.
Manvetvet, a memorial.
Manvus, [*man* 3.] one who loves to beat and kill.
Manwara, [*man* 1.] an owl, *wis*; from its cry.
Manwotmele, same as *mantapmele*, a dove that sits on the top of the cycas, *wot* mele.
Manwowono, a child who grubs in the dirt.
Man, 1. v. to wipe.
manmanpul, sponge.
2. n. dry husk of cocoa-nut; used to *man* with.
manman, a thing to wipe with.
Mana, 1. n. an opening with lips, mouth.
2. v. to open, gape. Mal. *manga*; O.J. *mangang*.
manamana, keep opening and shutting a mouth.
manmanai, fold of flesh.
manarag, to make known by speech.
manasag, to declare.
Mao. *mangai*, mouth; Pol. Fij.

maga, mouth, orifice with lips ; Fl. *mana*, mouth.

Manalu, things eaten raw, fruit generally ; *wo manalu*.

Manamana, 1. to work the gills as a fish ; *o iga ti manamana mun na wanwanana*.

Manamana, 2. waste ; *ge manamana*, to waste.

Manana, sickly, as some fruits in smell when ripe, as the smell of fish to woman lying in ; *lolo manana*, longing as of a woman in pregnancy for something to eat, of a man who longs to kill another.

manamanana, sickly in smell.

Manana, [*ma* 4.] conspicuous, striking the sight, *nana ;* as a person seen for the first time strikes as good-looking ; as a bright flower shines out.

Manara, dirt on an unwashed child.

Manarag, [*mana*] tr. to make known by speech.

Manarai, 1. (k) money.

Manarai, 2. waste ; *manamana* 2.

Manariu, [*nar*] something marked by biting, nibbled.

Manarnar, [*ma* 4.] sickly smell of fish or swamp ; probably *manar* tr. of *mana* in *manana*.

Manaro, a tree.

manaronaro, like the bark of *manaro*, rough ; *vinit manaronaro* of yam.

Manaroi, (k) gums of the teeth ; palate.

Manas, to be obedient, diligent.

manasia, work, what is done in obedience ; conf. *mawui*.

meremanas, obedient, working properly, diligent.

Manasag, [*mana*] to make known, declare.

Manasia, what is done in obedience, work.

Manaunau, [*ma* 4., *nau*] said of over-cooked food.

Manenenene, [*ma* 4., *nene*] damp, sticky.

Manirnir, [*nir* 1.] contracted, wincing, of the face.

Manitnit, [*ma* 4.] drawn in, *nit*, with feeling, as the face ; *o nagoi we manitnit*.

Manman, 1. n. [*man*] a thing to wipe with ; in recent use towel.

Manman, 2. dark, invisible ; *matamanman*.

Manmanai, (k) [*mana*] the folds of flesh between the arm and the breast.

Manmanaroi, (k) gums, palate.

Manmanaroolo, a swelling in the palate.

Manmanpul, sponge ; used to wipe, *man*, in tattooing, *vus o pul*.

Manoinoi, toothless ; *manono*.

Manolnol, [*ma* 4.] cropped, as a plant the top of which has been broken ; *nol*.

Manono, [*ma* 4.] toothless, like an old worn-out, *nono*, hatchet.

Manreag, to wipe away ; from something that remains.

Manurnur, [*ma* 4.] wrinkled, of men or fruit ; e. g. a melon gathered and left in the sun.

Mao, 1. mildew, mould ; to be mouldy.

Mao, 2. to stick in an opening too narrow to go through.

Mao, 3, a shooting star, meteor ; *o mao ti pepeperoworowo*, a meteor leaves a trail of light.

Maoi, (k) dry remains of bird, rat, &c., the flesh gone, the shape remaining ; *o mao gasuwe* ; met. a lean person.

Maoloolo, watery, as a yam ; *ta rasa o nam iloke o pei we qoqo, we maoloolo*.

Maoraora, [*ma* 4.] playful ; *ora-ora.*

*M***aorowolue,** torn in shreds ; as if falling stars, *mao*, were seen through ; same as *maluemao.*

Maovaova, [*maoi*] all skin and bones ; empty, of *tana* or *pugoro.*

Map, 1. to put, place, set ; of a blow, or arrow, to hit, *me map alo panena.*

we map o qon, to appoint a day.

2. to leave off ; *map late,* to do a part and leave off at a certain place ; *map o sawai,* finish a *sawai* on the drum.

na gate map sur ilo nan o roroi gate wia me gege inau ti, cannot get clear of the ill report.

Mapitu, [*ma* 4.] roll, move rolling ; conf. *tapitu ; o sariu me mapit nan o wuei,* the stalk has come out of the fruit, as that rolled over.

mapitvag, to roll with, give way with ; *o vat me mapitvagia.*

Maploa, a tree, with smooth scented leaves and bark.

*M***apsag,** 1. to breathe ; draw in and send out breath; *mapsag kalo,* to take a deep breath ; *o uwa, o ririgo, we mapsag kalo o nawo,* turtles, porpoises, throw up spray with their breathing.

2. reflective, to take rest, breathe oneself ; *sin mapsagia ;* also simply *mapsag,* to take rest. Mao. *mapu.*

*m***apsagiu,** (k) breath, breathing.

Maqirqir, [*ma* 4.] soft, penetrable.

Maqisqis, [*ma* 4.] soft like *qis* 1. mashed food ; of hair, food.

Maqoqo, without strength, as soft-wood trees.

Maqusa, [*ma* 4.] bruised, crushed ; *o tanqae me koran gate mulate,* as a tree that has been bent down and crushed, *qusa,* not broken off.

Mar, 1. [*ma* 1.] same as *mara* 1. theirs to drink.

Mar, 2. to sink down, subside, shrink, dwindle, of water, wind, swelling, sick persons ; also *maru.*

mamar, tame, submiss.

Mar, 3. const. *mariu,* claw.

Mara, 1. poss. n. of drink, &c. *ma* 1., with suff. *ra* 3.; theirs to drink or chew.

Mara, 2. a dove.

mara ata, a large kind, in native notion male, *ata.*

mara sala, a dove that runs in the path ; *sala.*

mara tano, a ground dove, *tano.*

Marae, to laugh, smile.

marae pipin to laugh with the mouth shut, *we pipin goro.*

*m***araesag,** tr. determ. to laugh at someone.

maraeva, laughing, laughter.

Maraeko, a mollusc, chiton.

Maraesag, [*marae*] to laugh one down, determ.

Maraeva, v. subs. laughing, laughter.

Maragai, to tremble, quiver ; *na apek we maragai,* I am shy, ashamed, my *apei* within me trembles; *matamaragai,* sleepiness, eye quivers.

Marakei, a kind of yam.

Marama, the world ; *i. e.* the Banks' Islands with nearest neighbouring islands and the surrounding sea. Fl. *maramana.*

Maran, 1. n. light, daylight, morning, day ; v. to be light. Malag. *maraina ;* N.B. *malana ;* Pon. *marain.*

2. to-morrow's light, the mor-

row; *a maran*, to-morrow; *tarala maran*, next morning; *matur, mamata, maran*, sleep, wake, till morning, sleep, wake, all night.
3. time, season ; *maran gopae*, a time of sickness ; *maran malinsala*, time of hunger, famine; *maran mawmawui*, the season of working gardens ; *maran rarrarea*, the season when food is scarce ; *maran sosoyot, suar*, fruitful season.

Marana, a place where the monuments of a great man's rank are assembled ; *o wona ne, o mele ne, o gamal ne, welamaragai ne, nule ne, vat ne.* In recent use adopted for kingdom.

maranaga, one who has a *marana*, had attained high rank and influence ; in recent use a king.

Mara*n*, idle, lazy, of man ; infertile, of ground ; *.tano maran*, useless ground ; probably *ma* 4. and *raniu*.

mara*n*ra*n*, bare, treeless ; *raraniu* 2.

marantag, tr. determ. to be lazy with reference to something ; *ape sava kamiu we marantag o kor?* why are you lazy about drying bread-fruit ? *i. e.* when you ought to be making *kor; we maran nan o kor*.

Mara*n*orano, one who has no food.

Maraoneone, white sand, *one*, seen on sea bottom.

Maraowoowo, to be quite black and ripe, *maras*.

Marapun, 1. to cook ma*k*e in the oven, *qaranis*, after roasting.

Marapun, 2. *un* word for *vatu*, stone.

Maraqaraqa, a shrub with orange-coloured fruit ; *we vagalo oraoru mun o wo-maraqaraqa*.

Mararara, transparent, translucent. Fl. *marara*, light.

Maras, dark purple, black ; said of the ripe *nai*.

maras-galegora, to be black and cheat the pottle ; of *nai* which ripen but have no kernel.

Marasama, a tree.

ura marasam, a sea crayfish named after the tree.

Maratano, a ground dove ; met. a short person.

Maratata, a fish.

Maraui, (k) a man or woman's mother's brother ; the nearest of kin in native system.

Marav, [*ma* 4., *rav*] v. to be dim, misty ; n. dimness, mist, fog ; *marav goro*, to come over in a mist.

maravrav, dim, misty.

Maravrig, 1. name of a hill in V.L. 2. adv. very far off.

Marawa, 1. a spider. Fij. *lawa*, net, *virita-lawalawa*, cobweb ; Mal. *lawalawa*, spider ; Bisaya, *lawa*, cobweb.

marawa matawonowono, a black spider.

marawa salagoro, yellow ; *marawa taviro*, one that runs behind its web when alarmed: *marawa tavun*, trap-door spider ; *marawa ratvat*, one that weaves a cross in the midst of its web, *we vauvau; o marawa ti tia o talau,.* spins its web.

2. *Marawa a Vui*, who acted like a spider.

marawatavun, hidden, out of sight, as *Marawa* hid himself.

pismarawa, from Marawa's fingers, iron nails.

Marea, an eel. N.B. *maleo*, sea-eel.
  marea laqlaqar, a forked-tailed thing, not an eel, said to be in holes in salt-water, and deadly; springs suddenly up, *laqa; ta taqa ape qoe, naniniana ta qe apena, te mate*, pigs die if touched by its shadow; it is also called a *puasa* though not a *puasa*.
  mareaqoe, a large kind of eel.
Mareanusa, a district, village, of Mota.
Mareaqoe, 1. a kind of yam; 2. a large *qeta*.
Marekereke, [ma 4.] confident, eager, well-pleased with oneself; *reke*.
Maremare, 1. adj. hard, strong; difficult.
  2. adv. very, sufficiently; *gate purat maremare*, not very many; *neira me vug maremare ma*, they came in good numbers.
Marerere, [ma 4.] tender, as when one draws back, *rere*, when touched with pain.
Maresaresa, [ma 4.] thin, shrunken; of men.
Marete, a sea slug.
Maretret, [ma 4.] slender.
Margav, a crab's claw used as a whistle; *mariu, gave*.
Marina, the Mota name of Espiritu Santo.
Marinorino, [ma 4., *rino*] shaky, quaking.
Marir, 1. cold, damp; *mamarir*.
Marir, 2. [ma 4.] shaking like an earthquake, *rir*.
  marir nua, *mariri nua*, 1. the sound of heavy surf in the hollow of a cliff; 2. met. thunder without lightning.
Maris, one who can't climb; *maris gana tano* belonging to the ground, *o tanun gate vegregi wia*.
Marisarisa, [ma 4.] thin.
Mariu, 1. (k) M. claw; *mar naer*, claw of birgus latro used as a whistle; spine of sea-urchin.
Mariu, 2. [ma 4.] leaning over about to fall; moved from its place, *riu*; as a tree.
  mariuriu, bending over as a tree heavy with fruit.
Markom, a myrtaceous tree, metrosideros.
Marmaranrua, said of a night in which the moon rises after dark, a double day; *maran rua*.
Marmararan, bright, brightness of light; *maran; lama marmararan*, clear sea.
Marmaroa, a distant noise, as of wind.
Marmaroi, [*maroi*] a little, quantity to starve on; *me map gama sinaga? tagai, o marmaroi ti*, has your food been put for you? no, just a famine allowance.
Marmarosepa, a skin disease; white.
Marmarsaga, [ga 5.] calm, calming down; *mar*.
Marmarwirta, an uneatable sort of octopus; *maroi*.
Maro, famine, scarcity of food.
  maroi, a famine bit of food.
Maroa, 1. to advance; *o wena ti maroa ma iane*.
  2. to sit with legs stretched out.
  maroaroa, 1. with extended legs.
Maroaroa, 2. worked loose, stretched with use, as *qeaqea* of a canoe.
Maroasag, tr. determ. to work for a person; see *vanmaroasag*.
Maroeroe, very large in person; *natarapena we poa aneane*.
Maroi, [*maro*] a bit of food, such

as may be had in famine; ironically, *o maroi gai!* when in abundance one is given short commons; *marmaroi.*

Maronowonowono, a slight scarcity of food.

Maroparopa, [*ma* 4.] thin like a *make; ropa* 2.

Maroporopo, [*ma* 4.] thin, lean.

Maroprop, [*ma* 4.] damp; of a place.

Maroroa, with legs extended; *maroa* 2.

Marororo, [*ma* 4.] soft, swampy, where one sinks in, *roro.*

Maros, to like, desire, wish for, want; *maros ran,* to stand in need of; *maros nerei,* in recent usage, to hope. Probably a root *maro,* with *s* tr. term.; *mamarog.*

marosiva, liking, wishing, desire.

Marosvanoga, a fish.

Marotoroto, [*ma* 4.] that can be easily eaten or gnawed through, *roto;* of soft wood.

Marou, thirst, thirsty; *inau o marou,* I am thirsty. Marsh. *maru.*

Maru, to sink, subside, shrink, dwindle; *mar; o lan me vus ti qara* maru; *o tanun qe gopa ti mar; naqauk me riga ti pa gate maru tiqa.*

mamaru, subdued, tame.

Marui, V. (k) the spine of an echinus, *maru lara;* tip of the claw of a *naeru* used as a whistle, *maru naer;* not of a crab; *mariu* 1.

Maruqa, [*ma* 4.] bent, not broken off or cut off; *ruqa.*

Marur, *nau we tawe sei, ni gate wono lai, o marur avunana.*

Marurqena, in a stooping position; *pute marurqena.*

Marurur, fleshy; said of the flesh of big man or pig.

Marusa, [*maru*] subside, as a wave in a calm does not break against a rock, *te marusa gap ti.*

Marutrut, [*ma* 4.] indistinct, as distant voices, *rut; we vara marutrut.*

Maruwe, to plant something else in a hole from which a yam of two seasons, *siworag,* has been dug.

Mas, 1. v. to fall; n. abundance of fruit; see *masu.*

Mas, 2. unskilful, unsuccessful; as in fishing, shooting; opposite to *manur.*

Masa, a fish.

Masaeva, leisure, opportunity.

Masag, ague.

Masal, [*ma* 4., *sal* 2.] at some distance apart; with some interval; *pute masal,* sit with sufficient room between; in sewing, *o masal we tatas, we raon we wia,* close stitching best; *qalo masal,* of bamboo with joints, *qaloi,* far apart; met. *au qalo masal,* walk with long strides.

Masalava, a wind; *ti tur ma siwo alo Nus Nualava,* blows over the high mountain of V.L.

Masale, 1. [*ma* 4.] 1. adrift, *sale* 3.; *natoqak we masale,* my heart fails me; 2. to run short, fail; *isei tuwale gate masale nan, gate vule isei,* not one failed to be present, not one got tired of the work; *tete masale lai* when a great quantity; *valmasale,* short of everything.

Masale, 2. same as *masal; riv masale,* plant apart.

Masale, 3. channel; *masalepei; sale,* to flow.

Masaleaga, very light; such as can float, *sale.*

Masalepei, 1. water-course; 2.

the hollow down the breast, and that down the back.
alo masalepei, a measure of length ; see *rova*.

Masaletano, the space between two rows of yams.

Masalsal, redupl. *masal*, with frequent intervals, with spaces between ; *pute masalsal*, sit without crowding.

Masanara, the channel between V.L. and Qakea ; *manara*.

Masaneg, 1. to hang or be hitched up in a crotch or angle, as a bunch of bananas in a tree. 2. met. to linger ; *saneg*.

Masansan, [*ma* 4.] torn, spoilt ; *san* ; as banana leaves blown in strips, hair blown into disorder ; *nago masansan*, the face injured by wind and spray.

Masao, length of a *noota* atap in thatching ; space between the rafters, *gaso*, in a roof.

Masaoi, space, of place or time ; place, time ; const. form in some compounds *maso*.

Masara, poor, needy.

Masare, [*ma* 4.] torn, *sare*.
  masaresare, in strips ; as a palm frond, or deeply-divided leaf.
  masarei, a shred, rag.

Masarusaru, [*ma* 4.] 1. ashamed; 2. to dissuade from an enterprise, to cool down anger.

Masasa, narrow cleft between rocks, on land or in sea.

Masausau, poor, weak, without food.

Masega,

Masekeseke, [*ma* 4.] in good spirits, joyful, cheerful ; *masekeseke kel*, recover health and spirits.

Maserere, banana leaves made *mana* with fire and rubbed on the arms before fighting, for strength and valour.

Masevaseva, [*ma* 4., *seva*] faint with emptiness.

Masgaqora, loosely enveloped, as small things in large leaf ; *masigiu*.

Masig, to present a man with something, *no mele, qatia, karia, liwo*, when he has distinguished himself, e. g. in dancing, *we masagia mun o qatia* ; or when a man comes back home with some rarity and exhibits it. The man who receives the present, *gamasig*, has to *ul o masig*, make return with money.

Masigiu, a little ; small quantity.

Masil, to warm oneself in sun, or before fire ; bask.

Masile, 1. an amulet of coral stone, *sile* 1., by wearing which one can avoid arrows ; *vene masile*; 2. one who escapes an arrow.

Masilesile, [*ma* 4.] fat with *sile* 3., of a pig.

Masinai, a small shelter ; *masine lia*, a shallow cave; *masne mot*, the space under a small clump of trees.

Masipe, [*ma* 4., *sipe*] removed, stript off.

Masisgala, [*ma* 4.] slippery, as a dry and smooth tree-trunk or rock, or wet ground ; to slip.

Masisiu, (k) the straight hair of the temples.

Maskara, [*ma* 4.] willing, industrious, cheerful ; probably *maseke*.

Maslag, [*mas*] 1. to tie with a single loop, as the end of a line of *som* is made fast. 2. adv. with a loop which can run, or with a running bow; *vagae maslag*.

maslailai, (*i* for *g*) a man wrongly accused or punished *te rono maslailai wora*; probably as if the fault were not fixed upon him.

Maslepalepa, a time of great abundance, *mas*, when fruits fall in the dirt.

Masmaliwrere, a children's game; they come into the *wnua* singing, with strings of *nai*; others chase them, and if they catch them take away the *nai*.

Masmasawora, utterly destitute and poor; *mamasa, wora* 3.

Masnelia, a shallow *lia*, cave; *masinai*.

Masnemot, place under a few trees; *masinai*.

Maso, constr. of *masaoi* in *masomot, masorowolue*.

Masoe, a disc, therefore a planet as opposed to *vitu*; particularly the planet of morning and evening. Malag. *maso*, eye, *maso andro*, sun; Espir. Sto. *maso*, sun; Sesake, *masoe*, Ambrym, *moho*, Lakon, *maha*, V.L. *mase*, star.

Masokesoke, loose, slack.

Masoko, [ma 4.] place where rubbish, ordure, is thrown up, *soko*; a dungheap; rubbish, refuse; euph. excrement *tae, we savrag o masoko*.

Masomaran, the morning planet; *qagala masomaran*, an hibiscus.

Masomot, a forest, wooded place; *masaoi, mot*.

Mason, hiccough; *son*.
  masonson, sob, same as *masorsor*.

Masopsop, sleek, fat.

Masorowolue, strait, passage, between two islands; *o masaoi te rowolue lai aia*.

Masorsor, [ma 4. *sor* 1.] sob, sobbing.

Masovsov, compare *rasosor*, hasten; *me masorsov gese kamam*.

Mastag, stubborn, intractable; *we mastag nan*, to be stubbornly disobedient to.

Mastav, swine-fish.

Masu, 1. to fall; *mas*.
  2. n. abundance of fruit, falling, time of abundance.
  masuva, v. subs. fall, falling.
  masuvag, to fall with.
  tavamasu, to fall of itself.

Masug, 1. [*masu*] to loose; *mamasug*.
  masugsug, slack; *togtogoa gate masugsug*.

Masug, 2. to move in a mass as maggots.

Masul, to run out as a line from a loop; *mas, ul*.

Masur, [*ma* 4., *sur*] easy, at rest, in mind.

Masuva, [*masu*] a fall, falling.

Masuvag, to fall with.

Maswurep, a short big kind of flying fish.

Mata, 1. a snake; Fij. Sam. *gata*, by change of *m* and *n*.

Mata, 2. a heliconium, same as *vao*; *no-mata, nos-mata, wismata*.

Mata, 3. a place where are springs of water; as on V.L.

Mata, 4. 1. n. the stem of *matai* 1. 2. v. stem of *matag*.

Mataaraara, to stare, not making out what is seen.

Matag, tr. stem *mata* 4.; to eye a thing, look hard at.
  matag goro 1. look out after, take care of, watch over. 2. a watcher.
  matag kelkeluag, look out all round.
  matag raka, choose out, observe and take.
  matag risris, gaze hither and thither.

Mataga, *un* word for *taro,* calm.
  matagataga, [*ma* 4.] quite still, of water; us if enclosed, *tagataga.*
Matagaraqa, [*mata* 4.] first-born; *garaqa.*
Matagarere, [*mata* 4.] one who cannot see distinctly in the light, such as an albino; sees things as if in rapid motion; *garere.*
Matagaro, [*mata* 4.] hard-hearted, unmerciful; *garo.*
Matagesegese, [*mata* 4.] selfish, with an eye to self alone; *magesei.*
Matagiragira, [*mata* 4.] new, fresh, *gira;* said of bow, &c.
Matagis, [*mata* 4.] a knowing person, skilful; *gis* 1.
  matagisgis, to take care of, watch.
Matagtag, M. to fear; rare but true Mota word.
Matagut, M. tr. determ. of *matag* in *matagtag,* to be afraid of.
  Common in Sol. Ids. *mataku, matagu,* also in N. Hebrides. Mao. *mataku;* Sam. *mata'u;* Mal. *takut;* Malag. *tahotra* n.; Pon. *majak.*
Matai, 1. (k) 1. an opening, eye; source of water; front.
  2. cover for an opening, lid.
  3. edge, point.
  Very common in Ocean tongues, often "face." Mal. *mata;* Mao. *mata,* eye, edge; Dyak, *maten,* eye; Formosa, *macha,* eye; Tagal, *mata;* Macassar, *mata,* point, source, mesh; D.Y. *mata,* eye and face; N.B. *mata,* eye; San Crist. Mala. *ma,* face; Sol. Ids., N. Hebr., Bks. Ids. *mata;* Pon. *maja;* Marsh. *mej;* Gilbert I. *mata.*
  matu 4. in compound words often means no more than thing, person.
  matai o vula; prov. big eyes, moon-eyed.
Matai, 2. good, prefixed to the n. qualified.
  3. (k) a good thing, excellence; *matai vires,* something very choice; *namatana!* the goodness of it, how excellent! Tahiti, Hawaii, *maitai, maikai.*
Mataigene, [*maitai* 2.] a good thing.
Matairiiri, [*mata* 4.] a woman who makes advances; *iriiri.*
Mataka, 1. a tree.
Mataka, 2. to get excited, rise in excitement.
Matakalava, willing, eager; with alacrity; *gate* matakalava, not think much about doing something.
Matakaukau, [*mata* 4.] a big strong man; can *kau.*
Matakeaga, [*ma* 4.] very light, of no importance; next word.
Mataketake, [*ma* 4.] light, of no importance; *take; nom mataketake,* think lightly of; *o vanua we mataketake* when a person of influence is away.
Matakorkor, [*mata* 4., *kor* 3.] one who does nothing but look idly about; *we tira matakorkor.*
Matalaulau, [*matai* 3.] the bone point of an arrow too long; *laulau.*
Matalesles, [*matai* 3.] full to overflowing, the fluid curling over, *lesu,* the brim; *ura matalesles.*
Matalo, *ar matalo,* the current that carries out to sea between Mota and Gaua.
Mataloaga, light, easily carried.
Mataloav, [*mata* 4.] smoked *nai* very black and light; *loav.*
Matalotalo, exceedingly light.

Matalue, [*mata* 4.] the first strong shoot of the yam that comes up, *lue*.

Matamal, 1. a sea-spider.
2. sore with the sea, of the eyes, *matai*; *taro matamal*, a dead calm, which makes the eyes sore; *mal*, the young cocoa-nut with bitter fluid.

Matamanman, [*matai*] indistinct sight; *manman*; *o qon, o matamanman, nipea mule kelkel*.

Matamaragai, sleepy, sleepiness; *o matai we maragai*.

Matamemea, redness of eyes.

Matamot, singularly; *turwia matamot*, singularly excellent; *mata*, to see, *mot*, cease; *i. e.* will not see the like.

Matamotmot, stingy, as if the action or feeling of liberality were broken short.

Matanaunau, stingy; *nau* used for poisoning fish.

Matanena, [*mata* 4.] blind; *nena*.

Mataniarova, [*mata* 4.] pitiable; *aro* in *magarosa*.

Matanisiaga, stingy; see next word.

Matanistuvag, [*mata* 4.] stingy of money, *tuvag*; *nis* used in poisoning fish; conf. *matanaunau*.

Matanoneav, a garden which has been burnt off for planting.

Matanoto, stingy; *noto*, poisonous leaf, as above.

Matanur, [*mata* 4.] careful, diligent; *nur*.

Mataotao, [*ma* 4.] quieted down, as a quarrel.

Matapalpal, 1. to see a thing done and take away the pattern or way of doing it; as if the eye stole, *palu*.
2. if another looks at a man rubbing fire, *sososo av*, and it goes out, the looking steals the fire.

Matapaparau, looking to a distance; *paparau*.

Mataparparu, [*mata* 4.] twinkling like a star; *peruperu*.

Matapei, blind; *o matai ti pei* 2.

Mataperu, eye blinking; *o matai ti peruperu*.

Matapiroi, remnant; of a family; or of bananas, small suckers left.

Matapiropiro, [*matai* 1.] distracting the sight with sudden appearance and disappearance; one who distracts the sight, *we mule kelkel vagae goro nanagoma*; *piro*.

Matapui, (k) spontaneity, doing by oneself; corresponding in form to *magesei*; *ni me ge matapuna*, he did it by himself, spontaneously; *we toga matapuna*, he is his own master; *napugak matapuk*, all my own fault.

Matapulea, [*mata* 4.] without seeing; as if *pulei* in the eye; *we log matapulea*, call a person's name without seeing him; *rasogo matapulea*, to count without tokens, in recent use to repeat by heart; generally, in the dark.

Matapulepule, as *matapulea*, dark, without full sight, as if an opaque spot in the eye; *pulei*.

Matapurei, [*mata* 4.] ignorant; *purei*.

Mataqa, 1. a poisonous mollusc that sticks on rocks or stones; *mataqa we gogona* on *toape*.

Mataqa, 2. a wound or sore; *mate mataqa*, opening of wound.

Mataqai, (k) 1. a wound or sore with reference to the person

affected ; *mataqe qatia*, wound of arrow.
2. a man with a wound or sore.
3. a bread-fruit with a wounded part.

mataqaga, 1. adj. with wounds, sores.
2. a bread-fruit with a wound.

Mataqale*n*a, [*mata* 4.] confused, bewildered, in sight ; *qalena ; me ge mataqalena inau, me mataqalena inau*, I forget, memory confused.

Mataqalera, confused, bothered ; *me mataqalera inau*, I can't remember.

Mataqea, a stone hatchet ; *matai* 3., *qea*, flat.

Mataqelaqela, [*mata* 4.] bewildering in the eyes ; *qela ; tar mataqelaqela*, numerous beyond counting ; *mateqel*, Gaua, blind.

Mataqeropatau, a sea anemone.

Mataqet, [*mata* 4.] a fruit quite ripe, *qet ; e. g.* a cocoa-nut just fallen, no shoot, *vara*, as yet ; *o patau o mataqet, o sariu me mapit nan o wuei.*

Mataqetaqe, [*ma* 4.] ill-formed ; *o wovtei we mataqetaqe.*

Mataqurega, [*mata* 4.] ignorant, ignorance ; *qurega.*

Matarag, tr. *mata* 4., to behold, look at.

Mataratara, [*ma* 4.] peaked, sharpened by illness ; of the face, as if cut, *tara.*

Matarav, [*mata* 4.] of the evening, *ravrav ; un matarav*, the *palolo* that comes at evening, *we sau kalo alo ravrav.*

Mataroro*n*o, [*mata* 4.] a fish that looks at the bait without taking it, keeps quiet, *rorono.*

Mataro*n*ro*n*oas, one who can't bear, *rono*, smoke, *as*, in his eyes, *matai.*

Matarowo, [*mata* 4.] 1. to eye with desire to get. 2. one who asks for what he sees ; as, in both cases, a child who sees food being eaten ; his eyes *rowo* to the food.

Matarowoparpar, the chips that fly off, *rowo*, in cutting, *par*, a canoe.

Matartoga, clear ; *ma* 4., *ga* 5.

Matasaraav, [*mata* 4.] dazzling of the eyes ; going from light into the dark ; *o matasaraav te ge ko.*

Matasiliga, [*mata* 4.] darkling ; *van matasiliga*, to go in darkness without fire.

Matasisia, [*mata* 4.] eye with matter, *sisia*, in it.

Matatira, with eyes fixed ; *tira.*

Matatoatoa, with eyes moving, *toa*, as an albino's.

Matatowo, [*mata* 4.] for the first time ; *totowo.*

Matava, morning, generally ; the stages of advance are, 1. *o lonlone maran ;* 2. *o maran ti teve ;* 3. *o maran ti anoano ;* 4. *o mera ti lamasag ;* 5. *maran tawasawasa.*

matava qonqon, dark of morning.

matava rowo, next morning ; in narration.

toto matava, early morning.

Matavgae, the betel pepper ; *no-matavgae*, betel leaf ; an infusion of betel leaves in *lig matig* is drunk for cough.

Matavilerag, to choose out the best of a number.

Matavir, [*mata* 4.] stingy ; like water poisoned for fish, *me vir o gene we gogona alolona ; matanaunau*, &c.

Matavires, [*matai* 3.] precious ; *matai vires*, only good.

Matavulavula, [*mata* 4.] a white fresh-water fish with big eyes, that burrows in the mud; *ti livun alo one*; moon eyes.

Matavuravurasa, with projecting eyes; *o matai we vura lue; sa* 3.

Matavuvur, [*mata* 4.] crumbling; *vur* as in *savur*.

Matawasawasa, [*mata* 4.] name of a large striped crawfish; *ura*.

Matawasia, a creeping plant; *usur ga-matawasia*, to tell a long story.

Matawawaliog, n. a fatiguing thing; makes the eyes go round with faintness.

Matawenewene, 1. luminous fungus, luminous objects in the sea; white eye.

Matawenewene, 2. [*mata* 4.] uncoloured; *loko matawenewene*, without *toape* in it.

Matawereav, [*mata* 4.] live ember; *werei, av*.

Matawiawia, [*mata* 4.] a single possession, therefore valued; *wia; ituwale amenau, o matawiawia*.

Matawolowolo, 1. to look askance with envy, to envy; 2. envy; the eyes, *matai*, across, *wolowolo*.

Matawonowono, one not initiated into a *tamate* society; his eyes yet closed, *wono*.

Mataworiu, [*mata* 4.] a single disk of shell money; *woriu*.

Matawovat, hard-eyed, hardhearted; eyes like stones.

Matawtaw, V. to fear, be afraid; *matagtag*.

Matawura, a lizard, gecko, with projecting eyes; *wura*.

Matawut, 1. a fish; berycida.

Matawut, 2. V. tr. of *matawu = matagu*, to fear; be afraid of; *me matawutia*, or *matagutia*, feared him.

Matawutiana, terrible; *matawut* 2.

Mate, 1. to die, faint and appear to die. Common throughout the Ocean; Malag. *maty*; Mal. *mati*; Pol. *mate*; N.B. *mat*; Formosa, *matis*; Anaiteum, *mas*; Kerepunu N.G. *mae*; Marsh. *mij*.

matea, death, dying.

matevag, die with, die of.

Mate, 2. ready, complete; *matemate, taurmate*; probably Fl. *mate* in *uto mate*, perfectly good; Motu N.G. *matemate*; N.B. *mat*; Pon. *maj*, intensive.

Mate, 3. negative with verb; V.L. word; strong expression, *na mate taka ineia*, I won't do what he wishes.

Mate, 4. constr. of *matai*.

Matea, (k) v. s. [*mate*] dying, death; *matea tultulvat*, slow death.

Mateav, 1. [*mate* 4.] mouth of an oven, *um*, in *gamal*; 2. the various ovens belonging to the ranks in *suqe*; 3. opening through which a fire is blown.

Mate-ava, swoon and revive; *ni me mate ava vagarua veta*.

Mateawot, a fit; *o matea tama ti wot ma suria*.

Mateawota, an accident, sudden death; *wota*.

Mategae, [*matai* 1.] a gift, pig or money, to help a man to eat his *suqe*; his wife, and her father, the chief givers.

Mategas, a bat's bone instrument to tattoo with; the *matai* edge is *gas* sharp.

Mategasilasila, money given to *sila* with; *ga* 3.

Mategawoso, the stick, hammered, *woso*, into the ground, to which a pig is tied in a *kolekole*.

G

Mategeara, [*matai* 1.] the opening in a fence; gateway.

Mategerave, the pointed stick used in rubbing for fire; *matai* 3.

Mategareve, the same.

Mategorgor, 1. bracts at the base of a *vusa*, used to scrape out, *gor*, the meat. 2. the bit of shell knocked off to drink the *vusa*, and used to *gor* with.

Mateima, the opening, *matai*, of a house, doorway; *we tipag goro o mateima* in shutting a door. The *mateima* is a space unfilled in the *turatura*, with sides and lintel of large bamboos; above the lintel, *qat-mateima*, is the *tano araroray* for fastening the door; the lower part of the doorway, *lalane mateima* is closed with bamboos, *gapurpur;* above which is the *tiqanal* of two horizontal bamboos, between which the door, *gatava* or *ma-tetipatipag*, is thrust; the *la-lane mateima* is protected with logs, *we vin goro*.

Matekaova, an egret's eye; met. *o loa ti sar matekaova*, the sun shines through a narrow opening in clouds; *ti teve mate-kaova*, a narrow slit in clouds appears.

Matekolekole, kind of *kolekole*, *val mate kolekole*, every kind.

Matelama, the edge, *matai*, of the sea.

Matelan, the eye of the wind; *wasiwis goro matelan*, beat in the wind's eye.

Matelinai, principal, characteristic, ways of life or manners, *linai; matai*, source.

Mateloa, eye of the sun, East; *lan ape mateloa*, East wind.

Matelul, albino's eye; met. bluish, *o pei tama o matelul*, water with bluish opaque colour.

Matemagoro, a variety of hibiscus.

Matemaro, the hole, *matai*, left at the top of the ovenful of food, *qaranis*, to pour water, *tirui*, into, then stopped; *te luqai goro o matemaro nan wa sawu ae*.

Matemate, 1. die in numbers, or successively; redupl. *mate* 1. 2. deadly; *pei matemate*, poison, in recent use.

Matemate, 3. ready, prepared; redupl. *mate* 2.

Matemate, 4. v. to eye with desire; *o tavine we matemate siria*, admires him.

Matemawu, [*matai* 2.] one who does things very well; *mawu*.

Matemele, [*matai* 2.] a cycas, *mele*, carried in a *kolekole* and planted by a *wona*, or planted before the door of a *gamal*, *ape tapug*.

Matemule, to faint, die and come to.

Matenania, a stunted pig or tree.

Matenua, edge, brow, *matai*, of cliff.

Matepei, spring, source of water; mouth of well.

Matepurpur, *un* word for door; cover, *matai*, that blocks the way, *pur goro*.

Mateqatia, peg, *matai*, of treefern; two used to wind a hank of money, *siga som*.

Mateqavaqava, a covering, *matai*, of something buried, such as money under a *tapas*.

Mateqiroqiroso, a stopper of bottle; *te qiroso goro o mate wetov nia*.

Mateqoe, 1. [*matai* 2.] a stone amulet, good for pigs.

2. one who chooses a fine pig to buy.

Mateqolor, a short bit of money, *qolor*.

Materemama, fathers, *remama*, are dead ; *i. e.* a child's father and uncles are dead and a *sogoi* takes their place.

Materetere, [*ma* 4.] clear after rain ; *tere*.

Materewu, [*matai* 1.] the open face of a rain-pit, *rewu*.

Materir, the side opening, *matai*, in a *gamal* to each *sarctapug; rir* 2.

Materiv-garaqa, the first plantings, of *norao, toape*, &c.

Matesala, road, path; the trodden line, *matai*, of the road, *sala*.

Matesalemara, a path made and used by a dove, *mara*, in the bush.

Matesasarnopalako, [*mata* 4.] one who has no food or property ; *napulana tagai ran, ni we sasar gap wun o nopalako.*

Matesinaga, stingy about food.

Matesipa, [*matai* 1.] a pointed turtle-shell knife used to pare and slice, *sipa.*

Matesirvanoga, very lame, will die on the way ; *mate* 1.

Matesivura, a phorus shell.

Matesoa, [*matai* 2.] skilful workman in using *soa* 2. for images.

Matetamate, the two hollows in small of the back, like eyes.

Matetavine, lascivious.

Matetawatawa, a source, *matai*, of water on the face of a cliff ; *o pei ti tawatawa lue aia.*

Matetipatipag, the cover, *matai*, with which the doorway of a house is closed, *tipag*, shutter, door; *we tipag goro o mateima mun o matetipatipag;* it is made of layers of *lape ota*, rachis of sago palm, run through, *sis*, with a stick ; see *tipag.*

Matetul, to die right out, not *matemule; tul* 1.

Mateugug, M. blow-hole on shore ; *matai* 1., *ug.*

Matevag, die with, of, by.

Matevarawu, a point of land, *o nus vat we reve, o tano oloolo we tuai.*

Matevat, [*matai* 2.] a precious stone, such as concretion in clam-shell ; distinct from *matai vat*, a good stone.

Mateveteve, [*ma* 4.] 1. clear, of sky in the morning, *o maran me teve; o nago tuka we mateveteve, we wia.*

2. sharp, small of countenance, clear cut, *teve;* admired ; *o nago tanun we mateveteve, we lulum.*

Matevinparpar, chips, with an edge, *matai*, made in chopping, *par*, a canoe into shape.

Matevtag, to die and leave ; *mate vitag.*

Matevui, (k) natural disposition, kind, condition ; of uncertain derivation.

Matevura, a source, *matai*, whence water wells, *vura*, forth, a spring.

Matevuravura, redupl. head of spring.

Matevwona, to pay at once for building a *wona.*

Matewanara, divided source.

Matewarwarir, a hole, *matai* 1., made by boring, *warir.*

Matewas, the holes, *matai* . 1., bored, *was*, for sewing on the *irav* to the body of a canoe.

Matewol, to die in compensation, *wol*, on behalf of one, to redeem his fault.

matewol gana to run into danger for one's food.

matewol linana, of one who falsely accuses himself and dies for his saying, *linai*.

matewol o ge wora, to run into danger, give away one's life, for a trifle.

Matewona, [*matai* 1.] the face of a *wona* platform.

Matewonowono, numb, without feeling, asleep as a foot; *mate* 1., *wono*.

Mateworara, [*matai* 1.] the midst of the winter season, *rara*; *savsavur mateworara*, shower in the *rara*.

Mateworuru, in small quantity; *worurnai*; *woro mateworuru*, pour sauce on dried breadfruit, *kor*.

Matia, sneeze; *matia revereve gama sulate*, said when one's *usur* sneezes.

Matieg, M. same as *matueg*, as *tieg* is *tueg*.

Matig, 1. the cocoa-nut palm; the nut.

The names of the nut in successive stages from the bud *wovan, wopanas, roiroi*, are 1. *matmategapun*, 2. *sutarara*, 3. *malu*, 4. *garake qarat*, 5. *vusa gorgor*, 6. *vusa*, 7. *vusa maremare*, 8. *vusa sisis*, 9. *pulutgar*, 10. *pepega*, 11. *pane uwa*, 12, *kor*. When the nut has fallen *o noliu ti sigag kalo* the shoot starts, the *qoqoe vara*; the first two fronds entire *turvara*, then the *saragete* with divided frondlets.

2. good, as applied to food; *matig wia*.

3. big, in exaggeration; *matig aka*, a canoe with few on board; *matig linai*, big talk about a small matter; *matig mona*, small thing in big wrapper; *matig roqoroqoi*, a little man with big head of hair; *matig-sava*, one who owns much; *matig toqai*, big belly and small body; *matig ununtai*, a little man very hairy; *matig wanwanai*, loud-voiced; *na matig manuna*, his big nose. Compare *mateg* pl. sign in V.L.

Matigtig, 1. white of egg; 2. fat or marrow in head of fish or pig; from likeness to meat of *matig*.

Matika, a rail, porphyrio; *matika rasag tano*, one that never flies; *matika sale*, one that skims with outstretched wings; one species with different habits; met. *tama o matika rasag tano* 1. slowly; 2. met. said of one who can't climb a tree; *tama o matika sale*, quickly.

Matikotiko, [*ma* 4.] disturbed, troubled.

Matila, adv. in vain.

Matir, M. to sleep; see *matur*; shut the eyes.

matiriva, sleeping, sleep, sleepiness.

matirvag, sleep with, because of. *matir lanlananau* sleep lightly, *we ronronotag o sava*.

matir matarav to go to sleep in the evening, before night.

matir nornor to dislike one's bed, want to change.

matir wora sleep without eating when food is to be had, so to fast; but also when there is no choice; *wora*.

Matiriva, M. v. n. sleeping, sleep, sleepiness.

Matirvag, M. to sleep with, on account of; *ni we matirvag matana* he is asleep in the morning after a sleepless night, because of his eyes.

Mativetive, [*ma* 4.] peaked, sharp, of the face; *nuy matiretive*; met. from *tive*, chisel shell.

Matkasale, *matika sale*, above; met. a tall thin man.

Matmatantas, a sea snake, *mata, tas* 1.; in native belief a land *mata* goes into the sea and becomes a *matmatantas*.

Matmate, [*matai* 1.] desire, with lust; *matmate tavine*.

Matmateas, *aley matmateas*, to sing a song on returning from dunning a debtor that he may hear.

Matmategapun, the cocoa-nut just set; like the eye of the *gapun* crab.

Matmatelea, one for whom a *kole* is made; *ti vamot*.

Matmatir, 1. *nona mala*, steady sleep, like a hawk soaring. 2. *nona uwa*, like a turtle fast asleep on the surface.

Matmetir, unfeeling, pitiless, one who does not help the sick or troubled; shuts his eyes, *matir*.

Matoatoa, [*ma* 4.] loose in socket, shaky, weak.

Matoketoke, [*ma* 4.] 1. champing; *toke*. 2. met. *o vanua te matoketoke ti*, the place full of all the noises of festivity.

Matoltol, [*ma* 4.] 1. thick, thick-skinned, callous, 2. of speech, broad, thick. Mao. Pol. *matorutoru, matoru, makoru,* thick; Pon. *mejul*; Marsh. *mejil*.

Matranoman, the loop of the bowstring at the *kere us*, bottom.

Matua, 1. full-grown, ripe; *tamatua*.
  matuaga, full-grown; *mamatuaga*.
2. the right hand; adj. belonging to the right hand; adv. at the right hand, *tira matua*. Mao. *matua, katua*; Fij. *matua*, ripe; Sikayana, *matua*, old. O.J. Bat. *matuwa*; Malag. *matoa*; Day. *batua*; N.B. *matuka*. The stem *tua*, in *tuai*; Mal. Jav. *tuwa*.

Matualate, ripe before the time.

Matuav, doze, slumber.

Matueg, to incline, lean; *matueg avine*, lean upon, rest upon, met. trust in; *tue; tama isei we tigo, pa ni qe matueg lava ivune qat-tigo, pa ti malate*.

Matuerav, afternoon.

Matugtug, [*ma* 4.] slack as a line; *tug, tamatug*.

Matultul, slow, to walk slow, sing slow.

Matur, V. to close the eyes, have the eyes shut, sleep. Jav. *turu*; Mal. *tidor*; Malag. *tory*.
  maturiva, sleeping, sleep, sleepiness.
  maturvag, sleep with, because of.
  matur loloae, to be sunk in sleep, unconscious.
  matur qatwono, sound, unbroken.
  matur qoqoara, sleep with noises, snoring, &c.
  matur tapesopeso, uneasily, leaning not lying.
  matur taqa, sleep heavily.
  matur taragiate, to sleep on the back.
  matur wora, sleep only, without food; either with purpose of fasting or from necessity.

Maturav, a tree.

Matureture, [*ma* 4.] shaky, easily shaken in upper part; *ture*.

Maturiva, v. n. sleeping, sleepiness, sleep; *matur*.

Maturu, same as *matur*.

Maturvag, 1. to sleep with, or because of. 2. *maturvag no ranorano; maturvag mera*, said of the full moon which rises when children go to sleep.

Mau, dusty mould on damp things, and inside bad *kor*; distinct from *mao* 1.

Maua, a village in Mota.

Mauai, (k) long feathers in cock's tail, projections, horns on the head of crawfish, plumelike shoots of trees; *o maue gire ape ulusui retret*, the outermost tips of the branches of a pandanus; see *mauwai*.

Mauareve, tall, long drawn out, like *mauai; reve*.

Mauau, a sharp point, as of a bone arrow-head.

Mauka, to get well, begin to recover from sickness; euphemism for opening of bowels; *pei mauka, vamauka*.

Maukeg, to let go, allow; *ukeg*.

Maul, linger, delay; for a long time.

Mauliu, M. (k) 1. slough of snake, lizard, insect. 2. met. memorial, thing remaining to recall the former owner or maker; probably *ma* 4. *ul* 3. to cast the skin.

Maului, V. (k) same as *mauliu*.

Maumau, 1. to stifle; 2. to choke, be stifled; *maumau wora*, to be drowned simply.

Maumaugun, M. to move uneasily, stir, as a child sleeping under an *epa* stirs it, as a chick in the egg; see *mawun*.

Maur, to live, remain alive; *pei maur*, water of a spring; *tamaur*, a living man; *maur!* cry to a child that sneezes; *maur! e! tatagoragora mae!* Pon. *maur;* Marsh. *mour;* Motu, N.G.; *mauri*.

Mausa, 1. white sand hardened into a crust, found in *lia;* 2. met. white, *ul mausa*, gray hair.

mausausa, gray-headed; said of *nat manwara*, owlet.

Maute, a district of Mota.

Mautouto, [*ma* 4.] light so as to float high on the water, as a canoe; *uto* 1.

Mautut, [*ma* 4.] broken, chopped, in short bits; *ut* 1.

Mauun, [*ma* 4.] all in holes, worn out; *un* 4.

Mauwai, (k) better form of *mauai; mauwe gaus*, the end of a bowstring hanging loose; *mauwe gavaru*, the loose end of a string of money.

Mav, to be tedious, tire one.

Mava, 1. heavy, important; *o ranua we mava*, when a person of authority is there. 2. to weigh, neuter. Sam. *mamafa;* Mao. *taumaha*.

mavat, tr. to be heavy upon, weigh down. Sam. *mafati*.

Mavana, a sage, ocymum; an *ita*.

Mavea, adv. whence, whencesoever; *ma* 3., *vea* 1.

Mavin, obsidian.

Mavinraga, very thin, *mavinvin*.

Mavinvin, [*ma* 4.] thin; of speech, sharp, opposite to *matoltol; viniu*.

Mavtalulum, sleepy in morning; *o tanun qe mamata maran, alo me rivtag o maran namatana we maragai*.

Mavut, [*ma* 4.] taken up by the roots; *vut* 1.

Mavutvut, [*ma* 4.] humped, *vut* 2., as with a load heaped on the back.

Maw, same as *mawu;* one who does things well.

Mawaka, [*ma* 4.] broken, having openings; *waka*.
Mawea, crippled in the legs.
  maweawea, weakened through age or wear.
Mawerewere, [*ma* 4.] still, as beach in a calm.
Maweruweru, weak in knees, hands, wrists.
Mawes, [*ma* 4.] having pain in hip-joint as from walking; *wes, tawes*.
Mawia, [*ma* 4.] finish, complete; *mawia!* that will do! well enough! *wia*.
Mawiga, *un* word for moon.
Mawmawui, to act in obedience, work; *mawui; we mawui goro sei si a mawmawui suria*; conf. *manas*.
  mawmawuitag, tr. determ., work for a person; one who works for another.
Mawmawun, V. same as *mawunwun*.
Mawo, 1. v. to heal, heal over, as a wound. Fij. *mavo*; Sam. *mafu*; Mao. *mahu*.
Mawo, 2. n. food for the dead, laid on or hung over the grave; also money so placed.
Mawoa, a kind of crab.
Mawonotaqava, a woman of loose life, goes into *no-taqava* bushes.
Mawora, [*ma* 4.] broken, come apart; *wora*.
  maworawora, broken to pieces, all to pieces.
  maworavag, to be broken with, or because of, come apart with.
Maworosaga, [*ma* 4.] crumbly, dry, in the mouth; *woros*.
Maworwor, soft, giving way to pressure; like a cooked banana.
Mawota, [*ma* 4.] accidental, an accident; *wota*.

Mawotai, [*mawo*] one who has recovered from an arrow-wound; probably *mawotag* tr. determ.
Mawowo, 1. to sink in, as earth. 2. a sunken depression in the ground; *ma* 4. *wowo*.
Mawrawura, *mawurawura*.
Mawsapur, a bad workman; *mawu, sapur*.
Mawu, one who does work well, an artificer.
  mawutag, tr. determ. to work something well.
Mawua, a kind of crab.
Mawui, 1. to nod the head in assent; *qatmawui*; 2. to consent, obey; 3. thence, conf. *manas*, to work.
  mawmawui, to work.
  mawui garalate 1. to half consent; 2. to leave work half undone.
  mawui kurutqoe, to give half consent, half dog, half pig; said on one side of Mota recently.
  mawui nonomotmot, to pluck things to eat in uncultivated ground; *naui, mot*.
  mawui sakerewaka, to work quickly.
  mawui saragao, to work with open gardens, with no bush between.
Mawun, V. same as *magun*, to stir, move gently.
  mawunwun, moving as a waking child under its mat, as a chick in the egg; *naapensei ti mawunwun* when he feels sick; *naqatuma ti mawunwun* when you feel a creeping in your hair; *o toqai ti mawunwun*, stomach rising with nausea.
Mawunwun, very dry; *tawunwun*.

Mawurawura, [*ma* 4.] weak in the heels, which project, *wura*.

*M*a**wutag,** [*mawu*] tr. to do a thing well.

Mawuwu, to twitch in sleep, making noises, as infants do; *o tanun we poa we matur qoqoara, pa o reremera was we mawuwu;* cognate with *mawun*.

Me, 1. v. p. of past time; sometimes in anticipation; see Grammar.

Me, 2. prep. of relation, in fact a noun; with simple prep. *a, i, ta,* becomes compound prep. *ame, ime, tame.* It is used properly only with regard to persons, or living things regarded as persons, and so with pers. pron. *menan, meniko, menina, mera.* In these, and the compound forms *amenan,* &c., *me* appears as prep. of relation, with, and by the idiom of these languages, from. The form *me* is rarely used unless followed by *n* in the pronoun; but M. *mera,* with them, and *me kamin o qoe?* have you a pig? See *men*.

Mea, 1. red earth, used as pigment. 2. a red pig.

memea, red.

meameaga, red; *tano meameaga,* with *mea* in it.

Meamea, a fish, red.

Meara, thin, with shrunken legs.

Meat, ebb, low tide; *nol meat,* fringing reef.

meat kuleloa, ebb after sunset, follows the sun.

meat makira, low neap tide.

meat matara, a morning ebb.

meat rakaraka, ebb tide at the spring tides.

meat rar, an evening ebb.

meat siliga, low tide on a dark night.

meat tavalaloa, ebb at sunset.

meat tawakewake, dead low tide, at spring tides.

meat topa, low tide soon turning.

meat tur mamalete, very low tide.

meat vula, low tide on moonlight night.

Mei, soothe, say what will please; *meimei*.

Mel, to refuse, disobey.

*M*e**le,** 1. cycas; having something of a sacred character; hence *vawo* mele; see *varowog*.

mele *matamemea,* one kind of cycas.

o mele *iniko,* a kind of curse.

2. a rank in the *suqe;* the man who has the rank.

Meles, a fish.

Melmel, clear, smooth; *melumelu; we ninin aneane, o sava gate toga goro.*

Melmelo, keeping aloof; *melmelo lea,* the disposition to keep aloof.

Melmeloga, said of a man whose bow is not suited to him, *gate taramia.*

Melnol, a hundred; a whole mele frond counted; the practice having been to count days with a cycas frond, pinching down the frondlets on one side after the other.

melnolanai, hundredth; *anai.*

Melomelo, same as *melumelu.*

Melumelu, clear and open, smooth; *o tuka ti melumelu* when without clouds.

Melwotrow, a cycas in sacred place; said in anger, *varowog;* mele *wota rowo.*

Meme, 1. bladder. 2. urine, to

pass urine. Fiji, Sol. Ids. and commonly Pol. *mimi*. 3. *saru meme*, to pour out in a curve.

Memea, red ; met. exaggerating quality, *vasasa we memea*, amazing wonder, perhaps passing slang.

Memelraga, clearly shining like polished metal ; *melmel*.

Memerusag, *meromero*.

Memes, red as the eye from smoke ; *mes* 1.

Memesmata, a mantis which emits a liquid very harmful to the eyes, *matai; memes*.

Men, 1. prep. V. same as *me*, 2. probably n. *me* with *n* suff. pron. ; with, from ; making comp. prep. *amen, imen, tamen; men kara qoe*, pigs belonging to us two. May be *men nau, men nina*, as well as *menau, menina;* and *menra* as well as *mera;* but cannot be used with 3. sing. pers. pron.

Men, 2. to dress with oil ; as a wound, as a bow with *lig nai*, or the skin after bathing in salt water.

Mena, ripe, full-grown ; *o mot mena*, where disused gardens have become occupied by full-grown bush ; original meaning probably yellow.

Menaro, skilful, clever.

Menas, hard timber ; *o tangae tama kamam we la a Qakea ape ima tataro, ilone o menas;* probably *mena* tr.

Menmen, 1. smooth in skin ; *men* 2. ; 2. *we menmen o us mun o nai*.

Menmenaga, faded, of leaves ; *mena*.

menmenen-no-tangae, faded leaves ; *mena*.

Menra, *men.* 1. *ra* suff. 3. pl. pers. pron. with them, with the.

Meno, redness, reddish ; as overcooked fish, &c.

menmenora, reddish inside, like *loko me taru*, food recooked.

Mera, 1. a child ; pl. *reremera*. Motu N.G. *mero;* Kerep. *melo*.

2. when a party are poisoning fish they will not mention the name of any one, but call him *mera*, lest the fish should die in a *lia*, not in the open.

Mera, 3. red light in the sky, of morning or evening ; *o mera ti lamasag* at dawn. Mal. *merah;* San Crist., *meramera*, red.

Mera, 4. a fish.

Merakoukou, a two-headed lizard-like pattern of tattoo, and other ornament.

Meralava, Star I. the big, as opposed to Merig the little, boy.

Meramavule, a dead child not buried, but hidden away.

Meramera, a child, boy; *mera* 1.

Meramera vagarua, second childhood.

Meramerasa, [*mera* 3.] reddish, yellow ; as rotten yam.

Meraqulo, 1. newly born child. 2. female recently delivered.

Meratape, a beloved child ; generally dear ; *tape*.

Mere, prefixed to n. and v. signifying abundant possession ; *merei*.

Mereata, [*merei, ata*] 1. male child. 2. male ; applied to pigs, birds, &c. ; in plural, *rereata, merei* being dropped. *qeta* mereata, a very large esculent caladium.

Meregale, 1. one who has abundance of guile, deceit. 2. v. to love, try, to deceive, test, tempt.

meregalea, temptation, deceit.

meregaleva, temptation, deceivableness.

Merei, 1. (k) constr. me*re*, a child, with reference to the parent.

me*r*merei, (k) the children belonging to the house ; a man's own children, brother's and sister's children who live with him, and adopted children.

Merei, 2. constr. *mere*, dry food without sauce ; *we gan merei*, to eat without anything on the food such as *woro matig; mere toape*, hibiscus leaves without sauce or salt.

Meremanas, [*merei* 1.] diligent, obedient ; *manas*.

Merepulai, rich in possessions, *pulai*.

Meresom, rich in money, *som*.

Meresavasava, possessed of all sorts of things, rich.

Meretan, a *tamate* club ; named probably after a bird.

Meretoape, hibiscus leaves without sauce or salt, as above *merei* 2.

Merig, St. Clare. The small me*ra*, opposed to Me*ralava*.

Meris, *un* word for *gave*, crab.

Mero, sulk, be angry; *ni me mero kamam*, he was sulky, angry, with us.

Meru, bending, bent.

Mervakavaka, a strong person ; mer as me*rei* 1., *vaka*.

Mes, 1. red, a meaning which appears in *mes* 2. *memes, mesmes;* perhaps Boero *miha*.
  2. a red parrot, trichoglossus Massena.
  3. parrot-fish, scarus.

Mesmes, reddish-brown, colour of dying leaves ; *ul mesmes* light reddish hair ; *mes* 1.

Mesqoloqolo, kind of parrot-fish, *mes* 3.

Mesvaume, great talking.

Metektek, a party bathing hold each other by the hands and float singing.

Metigtig, a wild palm, with red fruit ; *matig*.

Metmetektek, same as *matikotiko*.

Meto, small black mole on skin ; *maeto*.

Mewmewu, feel disgust ; *ualalok ti mewmewu apena*.

Mewu, moisture of light rain, dew.

Milos, to whistle by drawing the under lip under the upper teeth and drawing in breath; as in going up hill.

Mimir, to shrivel ; *mirmir gogo* of a pricked bladder, of fruits, and of old men.

Mino, 1. to eat in little bits, slowly, as a delicacy; a slow eater.

Mino, 2. a pool on the reef.

Mirmir, to shrivel ; *mimir*.

Mit, to bring close together ; same as *nit; salmit*.

Miu, pers. pron. pl. 2. suffixed to nouns; appearing also in *kamiu;* of you.

Mo, 1. (k) poss. n. a thing belonging to because proceeding from oneself, of one's doing ; often with *a* 4. prefixed ; mo*k* my, of my doing, mo*ma* thy, of thy doing, &c. *anoma tama apeniko, we van ma; amoma tama ko me ge; o sinaga tagai amonina, we wol gese,* we have no food of our own growing, have to buy all. A singular use, *na we kakakae* mo*ma*, I tell you a story for your information, *ka gaganag* mo*k ma*.

Mo, 2. a clump, grove, patch of trees, plants ; only as constructed with the name of the trees, mo-mol, &c.

Moai, constr. moe, 1. first, foremost, principal ; moai nan, before ; 2. to be first; moai goro, to take the lead of, be leader, manager.
   constr. moe ; o moe tanun, principal person.
   Perhaps Pol. mua ; Aniwa, moa.

Moegene, first, principal, best, thing.

Moemera, the first-born child ; mera.

Moesala, [moai] the first of a party on the road, sala.

Mogir, M. same as mowur V.

Mok, poss. mo 1. with suff. pron.; so with the other suff. pron.

Moko, an albino.

Mol, native orange, moli.

Molemole, 1. to cool oneself in a breeze ; 2. un word for lan wind ; we rug luelue rowo ilau si a molemole.

Moli, native orange ; Sam. Fij. Sol. I. moli.

Molo, to tremble.

Molore, the small garfish.

Momŏ, 1. red pipe-coral, tubipore ; pipe-coral stone.

Momo, 2. a small pool on the reef.

Momogo, to feel awe, to be in awe of something, somebody.

Momol, [mo 2.] a clump or grove of oranges, mol.

Momoleag, to blow softly in the trees ; o lan we momoleag; molemole.

Momoloiga, trembling ; molo.

Momoro, groan, roar, make noises in sleep.

Momorosiga, muddy; mormor.

Momos, firm, close ; mos 1.

Mon, 1. to mend, a house, sail, &c.

Mon, 2. poss. mo 1. with suff. 3. pers. pron.

Mona, 1. poss. mo 1. with suff. 3. pers. pron.

Mona, 2. v. to wrap, conceal. n. a bundle, a wrap, e.g. of fish in leaves.

Monamona, redupl. mona, of many wraps, bundles.

Monatama, left-handed, difficult; tama 2.; eo ! pa o monatama ? is it difficult ?

Monmon, to mend a hole, patch ; net, fence, &c. mon 1.

Monog, to keep secret.

Monon, to go away from, be lost ; from same stem with monog.

Mor, 1. obstinate, disobedient.

Mor, 2. stem of mormor, mormoriga.

Mor, 3. poss. mo, 3. pers. pron. pl. suff.

Mormor, 1. mud.
  momorosiga, muddy.

Mormor, 2. in number together ; vamormor.
  mormoriga, adj. of many things together, as a densely packed crowd, shoal of fish, swarm of bees.

Morosai, (k) constr. morose, scum.
  moromorosa, foam.

Mos, 1. close, firm ; momos, garamos.

Mos, 2. constr. mosiu.
  mosmos, an old worn-out canoe, tapera, &c.

Mosiu, old, worn out ; constr. mos; mos siopa, worn-out clothes.

Mosmos, a worn-out canoe, me mosiu reta.

Mot, 1. n. bush, uncleared ground, land grown over with trees. v. to grow over, be grown over ; mot goro, grow thick over cleared ground.

m*ot mena*, old clearing grown over with big trees.

maso mot, uncultivated region; *masaoi* motmot, forest.

Mot, 2. v. to cut, break, stop, short off; adv. short, short off.

nalolok me m*ot*, I am settled in my feelings. *vet* m*ot*, to speak decisively, once for all; *nonom mot*, to make up one's mind, agree, think and bring thought to an end; *paso mot*, finish completely.

motmot, redupl. see below.

A common Ocean word. Pol. *motu*.

Mota, the island, *a* Mota.

Motalava, part of Saddle I. Motlav; big Mota.

Motarig, Mota as distinguished from Motalava, little Mota.

Motangae, [m*o* 2.] a clump of trees, grove.

Motar, [m*oai*] title of rank in women's *suqe*.

Motmena, wood of old trees.

Motmot, 1. forest; m*ot* 1.

Motmot, 2. adj. broken short in places, separate; adv. from time to time; m*ot* 2.

2. to leave off from time to time, stop now and then, here and there.

3. to break over and over again.

Motmot-wora, a careless, easy, giver; *we tenegag ape gae we* motmot.

Motogo, a clump of reeds.

Motogol, a kind of palm with small nuts; V.L.

Motor, a tall man.

Motu, same as *mot*.

Mou, adv. thoroughly, utterly; *kor mou, mena mou*.

moumoura, adj. complete, quite.

Movetal, [m*o* 2.] clump of bananas.

Mowur, V. one who does things slowly.

Mu, prep. stem of *mun*; originally n.; takes suffixed pron. in *mura, murara*, and, with less certainty, in *munau, munina*.

Muimuira, very wet, as firewood.

Mula*n*, again, moreover.

Mule, 1. V. come, go; *mule tak*, carry.

muleva, coming, going, journey, motion.

mulevag, come, go, with.

Mule, 2. to refresh, restore in sickness.

Mulegona, hostile movement, the enemy come or go to make the opponents' country *gona*; *o tavalalea we mulemule gona ma; kamam me mulegona goro veta;* the enemy come hither to molest us; we had already invaded.

Mulemule, [*mule* 2.] refreshment, damp, moist; *ge mulemule o apei*, refresh the mind and spirits; *ape mulemule*, with spirit refreshed.

mulemulei, (k) the giving of good things for the comfort and refreshment of the sick.

Muleqleq, a firefly.

Muleva, [*mule*] v. n. constr. *muleve*, going, coming, movement, journey.

Mulevag, [*mule*] to go, come, with.

Mum, 1. to make indistinct hum; *ni gate vava we mum gap*.

Mum, 2. a shallow circular pool or reef.

Mumeiatag, shake from unseen cause; when a pig is running among bushes *o mot ti mumeiatag*.

Mumumuara, a children's game.

Mumuritiga, [*mur* 1.] to groan in lifting a weight.

Mun, 1. [*mu*] prep. *mu*, with suff. *n.* 1. dative, to, for ; *ka vet mun natuk was nalolok nol mun kamrua*, tell my son that all my heart is with, for, you two. Peculiar use before n. without art., *ni me ramoa mun natuna*, he adopted him for, to be, his son; a construction of two nouns in apposition.
2. Instrumental, with, by. 3. Accompaniment, with.
There is a further use in which *mun* is transferred from an apparently instrumental use to a dative ; *o aro, o tangae te tara mun o us*, a tree out of which a bow is made, which is chopped into shape for a bow.

Mun, 2. See *geara mun*.

Muna, 1. to throw bait to entice fish ; *we muna o iga*.

Muna, 3. to be stale ; *o iga we muna*, fish kept too long before cooking.

Munata, traces of people who have been sitting and throwing things about ; *muna* 1.

Munqoro, excessive, excessively; *visarag munqoro o lito*, break up firewood with vehement blows ; *pei munqoro*, make *woro* sauce with an excessive quantity of water ; *we toga alo lama munqoro*, to make an excessively long voyage.

Munrag, smash ; when a rotten piece of wood falls and smashes into bits *ti munragia;* so, met. of a man ; the stem probably *mun* 2.

munmunrag, adv. in same sense.

Mur, 1. to groan, utter a hoarse cry.

Mur, 2. a suckling pig.

Mura, *mu* prep., 3. pers. pl. pron. to, for, with, them.

Muragai, *mu* prep. *ragai*, to, for, with, those persons.

Murara, *mu* prep. *rara*, to, for, with, those two.

Murasei, *mu* prep. *rasei*, to, for, with, themsoever, to whom ?

Murmur, redupl. *mur* 1. groan ; of a pig to make a roaring cry.

Murmuriga, adj. swarming, like *un*, palolo viridis.

Murmuritiga, to groan in lifting a weight ; *mur* 1.

Murmurut, [*mur* 1.] of a child beginning to fret.

Muroga, term of abuse.

Muromurosa, foam of the sea.

Murumur, a fish, berycida.

Mut, maimed in foot or hand. Pol. *mutu;* Fij. *mudu;* Mal. O. Jav. *putus;* Jav. *motjok*.

N.

N, 1. suff. to v. ; *rau*, to thrust in the hand as into a bag ; *raun*, to thrust in the hand and take something.

N, 2. pers. pron. sing. 3. suffixed to a class of nouns, generally before a following n. ; and referring to some individual ; same as *na* 3.

Na, 1. art. used almost always with a n. to which pers. pron. is suffixed ; and then written, without reason, in one word with the n.; *o panei*, a hand ; *napanena*, his hand ; a, the. Rarely used when no suffix ; *a na tano, a na pup, rowoag na maea*. The common art. in cognate tongues ; Malag. *ny*.

Na, 2. pers. pron. sing. 1. when subject of v. ; always in indirect, subjunctive, optative, potential, sentences, but also in indicative ; I, let me.

Na, 3. pers. pron. sing. 3. suffixed to a class of nouns, and to one prep., originally n., *ape, apena;* translated his, her, its. In Pol. suffixed only to so-called possessive pronouns ; in Mel. almost universal, as, *n, na, ne, de, gna.* Malay, *ña;* Malag. *ny;* Marshall, *n.*

Na, 4. V. to do, make ; frequent as *da, dau,* in Bks. I. and N. H.

Na, 5. sign of past in adv. of time ; *anaqarig, anarisa.* Sam. *ana.*

Na, 6. a demonstrative particle ; *nake, nane.*

Nae, to be still ; *nae toga,* keep quiet, silent.

naenae, keep quiet, silent.

Naenaeai, constr. *naenae,* particle, little bit; *naenae tangae,* minute bit of wood.

Naeru, the robber crab, birgus latro, *naer;* the left claw *loaroro,* the right *liwolava;* the pincers *maru-naer* are used as whistles. Fij. *lairo.*

Nag, 1. V. determinative of *na* 4.; *nag savai?* do it in what way ? might appear to be *na gasavai* (*na* 4), but M. equivalent is *gen o sara nia.*

Nag, 2. trans. suff. to v. Sam. *nai;* Fate, *naki;* Anaiteum, *naig;* Maewo, *nagi.*

Nagmativetive, [*nagoi*] peaked-faced, in illness ; *mativetive.*

Naga, eight in counting *tika.*

Nagoaromea, a fish ; *aromea.*

Nagoi, (k) constr. *nago,* face, front, cutting edge.
nagoi we mataratara, face sharpened in illness, *tara; nagoi o paltara,* face shaped like a *paltara,* hatchet-faced ; *nagoi we terterei,* face thinned by illness, *teve; nagoi o wutmata,* short-faced.

Nagnagoi, good-looking.

Nagnagolan**sere**, appearance of a steady stiff trade wind, *lan sere.*

Nagnagomatea, one who will run into danger, do what will bring death, goes in the face of death.

Nagnagomit, distressed countenance ; *mit* for *nit.*

Nagolagia, wedding ; *lag.*

Nagomala, swine-fish, labrus.

Nagomasan**sa**n, weatherbeaten countenance ; *masansan.*

Nagomate, of quiet countenance, abashed ; *mate.*

Nagomaur, of bold countenance ; *maur,* opposed to *mate* in word before.

Nagomawora, a bad headache ; the face split, *mawora.*

Nagoqasa, same as *nagotamaragai; qasa.*

Nagoqatetega, a face like a white ants' nest, *qatete.*

Nagorara, the season when winter begins, the *rara* flowers ; the beginning, face, of it.

Nagororon**o**, silent, quiet, the face unmoved ; *rorono.*

Nagosag, tr. determ. *nago* stem of *nagoi,* to oppose, stand in the way of; *lareag o gene nan iloke we nagosag loa* take away those things that keep out the sunshine; *pute siwo, ape sava we nagosag loa?* sit down, why do you stand in the light ?

Nagosala, the foremost party of a company on the road as they come out into a village.

Nagosasarur, looking serious after laughter or smiles ; *o nagoi ti sasarur.*

Nagotailil, one whose head shakes in palsy ; who looks about in fear.

Nagotamaragai, the knot of the bow-string at the top of the bow, *ape qat-us*, shaped like the face of a *wetamaragai* image.

Nagowono, M. said by some for *nawono*.

Nake, pron. adv. this, here, now; *na* demons. *ke*.

Nakeiloke, this, here, now.

Nakeloke, this, here, now.

Nal, to walk slowly, stroll, in a round.
  nal goro, to make a round for something.

Nalia, to move continually, stir.

Nalial, a weak person.

Naliog, to whirl round, as a sling; *nal*.

Nalnal, 1. an amomum with fine bunches of flowers.

Nalnal, 2. redupl. *nal*, to go continually about.

Nalnalia, to keep moving, stirring, as men in a crowd; as a sail flapping from side to side; *nalia*.

Nalnalwora, idle, doing nothing but stroll about; *nal, wora* 3.

Nam, 1. the yam; dioscorea. N.H. *nam, dam, dem, rem*; Jabim N.G. *ami*.
  namuga, yam-like.

Nam, 2. mosquito, *namu*.

Nam, 3. v. to beat hard; *namu*.
  namsag, determ. to beat small.
  manamnam, beaten to bits.

Nam, 4. v. to touch with the tongue, taste; *nami*; Hawaii, *namunamu*; Ponape, *nominom*; *nam ilo*, to taste and see what it is.
  namis, tr. taste, touch with the tongue.

Namala, name of a stone in V.L.

Namalag, 1. to toss, as a stone, without force; to be tossed or thrown about, as a gate in the wind.

Namalag, 2. to do exactly; *ko me namalag*; adv. exactly, *neira me gamo namalag ma*, they sailed exactly to this place.

Name, to hang, neuter, to depend.
  namei, a hanging part.
  nameag, in *vanameag*.
  namera, hanging.
  nameae, to hang without touching; met. to be helpless, without resource.
  name nunuale, to hang on end of branch or top of tree bending with the weight.
  name womatig, to hang in a bunch like cocoa-nuts, said of *qaratu*, flying foxes.

Namei, a hanging bit, as of money-string, short bit over.

Nameme, weak; *o tanun nameme*.

Namera, [*name*] hanging; *o qaratu we namera*.

Nametwale, a single fruit, hanging alone, *name tuwale*.

Namgae, a kind of yam.

Namis, [*nam* 4.] to put the tongue to something so as to taste or lick it up; *we namis o liy iga nan o qat pisui*.
  namis tarave, to try whether a fruit is ripe; *tarave*.

Namisa, bitter, acid; said of native orange, or quinine.

Namnamuga, [*nam* 1.] yam-like, of good food not stringy.

Namo, a lagoon within a reef; Sam. *namo*.

Nam-pulan Taroroae, a kind of yam.

Namsag, [*nam* 3.] to beat small.

Namtultul, a kind of yam.

Namu, [*nam* 2.] a mosquito. Mel. Pol. very common. Mal. *ñamok*; N.G. *namo, nemo*.

Namuano, a kind of yam.

Nan, 1. prep. from, therefrom;

generally of motion from, and met. than, lest; *iloke we poa nan tasina*, he is bigger than his brother; *we gilala nan o tuara*, knows more than the other; *ilo goro nan wa masu*, take care lest you fall.

Used at the end of a sentence referring back to a noun that has come before; *naimak ilone nau me rowolue nan*, my house that I came out from.

In such a phrase as *maran nan*, see *marantag*, the meaning of motion away from is clear; *ape sava kamiu we maran nan o kor?* why are you so lazy as to leave the work of drying bread-fruit?

Nan, 2. same as *nane*.

Nan, 3. n. one who talks about one thing.

Nan, 4. v. *nan goro*, an abscess which has broken and subsided swells again.

Nana, pus, matter. Mal. *nanah*; Malag. *nana*; Ponape, *nana*.

Nanae, stale, watery, as scraped yam when left; *nana*.

Nanalnara, [*nal*] to go about without thought of harm as a *qilowar*; not kept in restraint; in good or bad sense; *nara* 3.

Nanamatea, [*na* 4.] a bull-roarer, used after death, *matea*, and as a toy.

Naname, a tree.

Nananam, redupl. *nam* 4. to lick, taste.

Nanara, a tree.

Nanare, echo.

Nangasuwe, anything quite small; *we log o natmera we mantagai, si o sava nan we manmantagai*.

Nanora, n. yesterday; *a-nanora*, on that day; *na* 5., *nora* 2.

Nan, a narrative conjunction, now, then; can follow *wa, pa*.

Nana, to draw out, act. and neut.; of people on a journey, *we sir we nana*.

Nanana, striped, as a kind of sugar-cane; *nana*.

Nannan, an elevated position, as where Veverau is; a Luwai word.

Nannanai, (k) const. e. the fat chops of pigs, cock's wattles, the under part of the bows of a canoe, *qatu aka*.

Nao, Maligo people call the Veverau *ira we nao*, from their use of *na* 4.

Nara, 1. pers. pron. dual 1. inclusive, we, us, two.

Nara, 2. constr. e. blood, bleed. Mal. *narah*; Malag. *ra*; Fiji, *dra*; Gao Ysabel, *dadara*; Motu, N. G. *rara*.

naras, tr. to make bleed.

manaranara, bloody.

naralaqelaqe, a disease of females.

nara we sosogoro, said of an obstinate man who will not listen.

Naraga, [*nara* 2.] nutmeg.

Naraqulo, first menses; *ape tarine vulaqulo*.

Naras, [*nara* 2.] tr. determ. to bring blood, make bleed; to prick, cut, so as to bring blood.

Nare, to wait, expect. Motu N.G. *nari*.

Nari, an edible fruit, *wo ta Luwai*.

Narisa, adv. of time, the day before yesterday; *na* 5., *risa* 2.

Narnaraga, [*nara* 2., *ga* 5.] gory, like congealed blood.

Naro, 1. to eat certain inferior food, or abstain from certain good food, as a sign of mourning for husband, wife, father, mother, child; *we naro nan o nam*. 2. a widow, or widower.

naro qiloiwar to *naro*, and remain unmarried.

Naru, to rot, be rotten.

Narua, pers. pron. dual 1. incl. we, us, two.

Nase, to crackle, rustle as leaves in wind.

Nasenase, rustle, crackle; *vara nasenase*, tread so as to make a crackling noise.

tanasenase, rustling, crackling.

Nasnaseparau, a long drought; prolonged, *parau*, till things get dry and rattle, *nase*.

Naspuna, term of abuse.

Nat, 1. fruit-tree, *natu*.

Nat, 2. constr. of *natiu*; small.

Natiu, 1. M. (k) constr. *nat, nati*. 1. a small thing, or quantity. 2. a child, young of anything. 2. *un* word for *vatu*, stone.

Natgae, a young boar pig.

Natgaegae, 1. young pigs born in the thicket, *gaegae*, not in the *rarea*; 2. met. bastards, *me wota vanameag*; 3. met. name called in reproach when children throw food about, misconduct themselves.

Natgapa, a bat's young one; met. child father unknown.

Natgavarur, pigling found alone in the bush; *tama si o gae ilone me vasusia*, the great bean vine on the beach.

Natmera, a little child, *mera*.

Natmot, child of the bush, *mot* 1.; met. bastard, ill-bred.

Natnawono, one who makes barefaced excuses; *nawono*.

Natnerenere, a whimpering child.

Natpugasal, a child neglected at home, a friend takes him over, *sal*, and feeds him, *puga*.

Natpurei, said of one who disregards propriety, walks over food, does not respect age or rank; *purei*.

Natqaratu, young flying-fox; met. a noisy impudent child, *gate ronotay isei we vara munia*.

Natvanua, a small island.

Natol, pers. pron. 1. trial, incl. we, us, three.

Natu, a fruit-tree.

Natui, V. (k) constr. *natu, nat*; 1. a small thing or quantity, little one. 2. a child, young of anything. N.G. *natu*; D.Y. *nat*.

natui rasras, a very little.

Nau, 1. pers. pron. 1. sing. I, me.

Nau, 2. a creeping plant with bitter poisonous juice; *o gae we pusa te vun o iga nia*; met. *ronronotay pune nau*, said when one man goes to a village where another has died, as one fish after another.

naunau, the same.

naunauga, bitter, like *naunau*.

matanaunau, stingy.

Naui, (k) const. *no*; a leaf, primary meaning flake. Mal. *daun*; Jav. *ron*; Malag. *ravina*; Pol. *rau, lau*; Fij. *drau*; Nengone, *ru*; Sta. Cr. *len*; D.Y. *dono*; N.G. *rau, lau, au*.

naunaui, leaves in quantity, *naunauna*, its leaves.

Naunau, a creeping plant, bitter, poisonous, *nau* 2.

naunauga, bitter.

Nav, mucus of nose; *sursurun nav*.

nav maroto, a child with dirty nose.

Nava, conj. but; adversative.

Navaisa, the talus of a cliff, slope between cliff and beach.

Naveravera, adv. like a *veravera*; *o mataqa ti kalo naveravera*.

Nawewe, a kind of yam.

Nawnawoga, [*nawo*] adj. salt; of food with too much salt.

H

Nawo, salt-water, salt; surf; v. *me nawo goro yese o tursao*.
nawo nun, surf coming in long line, *ti malate vagaegae*.
nawo taso, high surf, coming inland; *o nun nawo ta lau ti woso-woso o nua nan ape nawo taso*.

Nawono, [*nago-wono* M. *nawo-wono* V.] careless, barefaced, without due cause, wantonly.
tira nawono, stand unabashed.
vus nawono, wanton homicide, murder.

Nawowono, V. said by some for *nawono*; *si tama nanagona we wono*.

Ne, demonst. particle, pointing to what is distant; suffixed in *ine, nane, ilone;* often repeated in a list of nouns; see *marana; o matesala we ge ne tas*, the path, that way, over there, is slippery; *o tano tul ne loa, tano rowo ne loa*, the place, there, where sun rises, sets; combined with *wa* expletive, *ne wa* refers to time or fact; *gate nomtup ne wa*, did not believe that, or then.

Negneg, 1. v. a point in the initiation into the *suqe*, when all put *nai* to the mouth and at a word *negneg*, eat together.

Negneg, 2. adv. with bended knees; *rowo negneg*, jump about with knees bent, like birds, in *mago*.

Neia, pers. pron. sing. 3. he, him, she, her, it.

Neira, pers. pron. pl. 3. they, them.

Nene, 1. to gather, have a gathering, of matter.

Nene, 2. to knock, tap.
nenes, to crackle, with the noise of *nene*.

Nenei, (k.) const. *nene*, neck, neck of land.

Nenemea, [*nene* 1.] a pustule gathering, red, *mea*.

Nenene, redupl. *nene* 2. to tap as a bamboo drum, *vatgeuro*.

Nenenweru, [*nenei*] small, like the neck of a *weru*; *teve nenenweru*, cut small.

Nenenag, [*nene*] to shake off.

Nenes, tr. *nene* 2. to crackle.

Nenevalete, to knock, *nene*, and change, *valete*, in the game of *ninenine*.

Nenewono, sore throat, when the neck, *nenei*, is constricted, *wono*.

Nen, same as *nene*.

Nena, blind; *matanena*.

Nene, to knock; shake; *iro Puget te nene wora o pue ape qatima*, Puget will break her bamboo water-carrier by knocking it on your head; *we nene o pel*, ring a bell.
nenenag, tr. determ. to shake off, knocking backwards and forwards.

Nenenenepis, to flip, shake the fingers, in wonder or admiration.

Nere, 1. to pinch, break, off, as leaves of *toape, nomata*. 2. *nere o som*, break money-string, break off a short length. 3. a part of the *wol tapug* of the *suqe*.
nere vasesei, to pay back money without interest.
neren, tr. to break off.

Nerei, 1. to conceive a child. 2. to wait, wait for.

Neremot, sweet; *we nere mot alo valama*, the taste breaks off agreeably.

Neren, tr. *nere*, to break off; *te neren gap o nomata* if caught in the rain.

Netenete, firm, close.

Nev, adv. firmly, lastingly; *pute*

nev, to sit right down; *toga nev*, abide, remain.

Nevag-tap, the sleeping round a corpse, watch.

Newanewa, veritable, *mas newanewa*; *mas 2*.

Ni, 1. pers. pron. sing. 3. he, she, it; always the subject; always in subjoined clause, in potential, optative sentences; used also in indicative.

Ni, 2. v. p. with numerals; also in stories, *kakakae*; *o wena ni wena*, the rain rained. Mtl. *n*—with shifting vowel.

Nia, prep. thereby, with, withal; always comes after the noun or verb; *me vusia mun o kere*; *iloke ni me vusia ti nia*, this is what he struck him with. Some few verbs always take *nia*, e.g. *ris, lego*; *o torou te ris rupe nia*, a caterpillar changes into a butterfly. Instrumental prep. *ni* in Merlav, Gaua; genitive prep. in many languages. Fl. *nia*, with, used also after *liliu*, to change.

Nig, 1. v. to build a nest; n. constr. of *nigiu*.

Nig, 2. to strip, split, as with the nail separating inner and outer parts of vine for fibre; *te nig savrag o viniu nan o uto gaqir*, strip off the rind from the inner fibrous part of *gaqir*; *te nig savrag o utoi nau o au*, to strip off with the nail the softer fibrous part leaving the cutting edge of bamboo. met. *nig o apei*, to flinch; *me nig naapena*.

nig tavala rua au, or *takela rua* proverb, to make a cutting edge on both sides of the bamboo knife; said of one who carries tales to both sides,

telling what each says of the other.

Nigiu, (k) constr. *nig*; a nest, of a bird, and pig.

Niiv, *un* for *tagai*, no. V.L. word.

Nile, to break, crack; *we nile o som, o wut*.

ninletag, break food small; *niniletag*.

Nim, 1. to touch with the lips, sip, taste, kiss.

2. tide beginning to rise *ti nim kalo*; as if the first movements were like those of lips, lapping.

nim sasar, fish taking and tearing bait.

nimis, tr. determ. take a taste of.

ninim, sip, taste.

Nima, to be wet, damp.

Nimiu, constr. *nim*; oil, grease, liquid fat; *nim nai*, oil of almonds.

Nimis, tr. determ. *nim*, take a taste of, sip of.

Nimsai, (k) constr. *e*; slime, slimy track, as of snail.

Nimtoto, smooth, as sea in calm, water-worn stones.

Nin, 1. v. to enclose, partition off; *nin goro*, part off a chamber with a fence.

n. (k) constr. *nini*; an enclosure, as for the *qat*, a chamber in a house; both the enclosing fence and the space enclosed; to set up the enclosing fence *we woso o nin*.

ninin, tr. to put a fence round. Mal. *dinding*; Makas. *rinring*; Malag. *rindrina*.

Nin, 2. to be smooth, level.

niniaga, smooth.

Nina, 1. pers. pron. pl. incl. we, us.

2. pers. pron. pl. 1. incl. suffixed to n. and v.

Niniaga, [*nin* 2.] smooth, as tree

or man smooth in bark and skin; clear; so of the skin stretched and shining smooth; *o wosa ti riga, ti loqo, ti niniaga, ti mulue.*

Niniai, (k) shadow, reflection; with defined figure.

Ninile, break in small bits; *nile*.

Ninim, redupl. *nim*, to taste, sip, kiss.

Ninin, [*nin* 2.] adj. smooth.

Nininwena,

Nininsa, redupl. *ninisa*, saliva.

Ninin, tr. determ. *nin* 1. put fence round, enclose, for protection or restraint; *we ninin goro o uwa* to prevent its escape; *we ninin goro o tangae qara riv ti* to shade and shelter it.

Ninisa, saliva, water of the mouth not *anus*; *o ninisa, o nininsa, ti lolonar, ti lolona*, the mouth waters; probably *nis = nus* in *anus*.

ninisaga, watery, slimy.

Ninit, on tiptoe; *au ninit*.

Niniu, a small red ant.

Ninlana, to lie in confusion, abundance; *aqou! gate patau we ninlana ti.*

Ninletag, tr. determ. redupl. *nile*, to break small; to break off and give a small portion of food to each person; *tama alo we wata qa a Qakea*, when food is scarce.

Ninmis, *nimis* redupl. *ninmis qalo*, taste a bit.

Ninroa, [*nin* 2.] smooth, glassy, like surface of calm water.

Ninsaga, [*ninisa*] like the water of the mouth, said of badly cooked *toape*.

Ninwas, to spirt, scatter, as water when a stone is thrown into it, or mud under the feet.

Nin, same as *nini*; sometimes as *nina*; *nin wora*, rap with fingers and open.

Nina, 1. to reach, arrive; *varnina*, meet.

Nina, 2. to collect money from many persons for *suqe*; *nina o som*.

Nina, 3, to knock, hit.

ninag, tr. to beat upon, ram down, distress, startle; to break, *me ninag late napunena*.

ninaninag, adv. bumping up and down; *valago ninaninag*, to run in jumps, or as one carrying another on his back.

Nine, a flat cowry, ovulum; *wonine*, the shell.

Ninenine, a game played with *nine* shells, spinning them with the finger so as to run and knock, *nene*.

Nini, to rattle, tap, rap; in recent use to ring.

Ninira, a sea-urchin, small echinus.

Ninmot, [*nina*] to stop, break off journey.

Ninnin, to go to place after place; *we ninnin taso* not *kelkel*.

Ninov, a tree.

Nipea, let it be not, *ni pea*, let it not be, don't; *pea* 1.

Nir, 1. to make known what is concealed, divulge.

manirin, to betray.

manirnir, showing through.

nir qatrawe, after a *kolekole* a *rawe* is killed, then there is *tap* for five days; on the fifth day the *qat-rawe* is set up over *mate gamal*, and a man gets up a tree and proclaims that the *tap* is over; they then beat drums.

Nir, 2. money given, *vene*, in *suqe*. *nir tamate som*, the money, *nir*, kept and full measure given in return.

Nir, 3. to chop; *nir lue*, chop a hole through.

Nir, 4. the fibrous spathe of a cocoa-nut frond, used to strain sago.

Nirua, [*ni* 2.] two.

Niruarua, two by two, by twos, two at a time.

Nis, 1. a plant used in poisoning food; met. a stingy man; to be stingy.
2. to delay eating food, out of stinginess.

nisiaga in *matanisiaga*.

Nis, 3. to sing a song in a low voice.

Nisqalo, smooth.

Nit, to tie, connect; of land shutting in the sea, *o vanua we nit goro o lama*.
nit saratuwale linai, to conspire.

Nitol, [*ni* 2.] three.

Nitoltol, by threes, three at a time.

Niuniura, [*ra* 4.] adj. ragged; *o gae we galoma o samsamui apena*.

Nivat, [*ni* 2.] four.

Nivatvat, by fours, four at a time.

Niwa, a man who is fond of meat, birds, fish.

Niwiai, roe of fish.

No, 1. (k) poss. n. with general notion of appertaining, of what is possessed; *anoma tama apeniko, we van ma*, a thing with you that comes to you; *amoma tama ko me ge.*
Banks' Ids. generally *no*; Fij. *no*; N. H. northern Ids. *no*; Sol. Ids. *no, nu, ni*; Mao. Pol. *no* called prep. but *nona* his.

No, 2. const. *naui*, leaf; but often part of the name of a tree.

no-aeae, 1. name of a fern. 2. anything very light; *ae*.

no-arvau, broad leaves of the *arvau*, pinned, *vino*, to make *suova*.

no-ere, leaf of a small pandanus, used in covering in, *vus*, the ridge of a house.

no-ganagana, a leaf to eat off, laid down to place food on.

no-gae, leaves made into *roqo*, mats to cover in the oven; *te luqai goro o um mun o nogae. las nogae* the leaf mat woven together by the stalks.

nolaslas, the leaf mats, *roqo*, for covering the oven, woven, *las* 3., when new and light.

nolelep, a leaf laid down to keep food clean; *te lelep goro o tarowo nia*.

nomae, a tree.

nomaaeae, very light leaf; met. anything light; *maaeae*.

nomalu, a tree, aralia.

nomata, leaf of heliconium; a wrap in cooking.

nomatavgae, leaf of betel pepper; drunk in *lig matig* for cough, makes it *mamarisa*.

noota, 1. leaf of sago palm, *ota*;
2. the atap, leaf made up for thatch.

noqalata, a banana leaf dead and dry.

norara, 1. leaf of erythrina, which decays to a skeleton.
2. met. a very thin man.

nosalite, the leaf of *salite*, catappa terminalis.

nosaqsaqat, a leaf to guard the fingers; *saqat*.

nosin, cocoa-nut fronds used as torches for taking fish, *te sin o iga nia*.

nosurere, leaf of a shrub used in closing in the ridge of a house.

notagai, no leaves, *tagai*; 1. a tree that has shed its leaves;
2. met. a poor man.

notangae, 1. leaf of tree. 2. *un* for *no-mele*.

noto, 1. leaf of the excævaria agallocha; 2. the tree itself, used in preparing *toto* arrows; 3. met. a stingy man.

novao, leaf of heliconium, same as *mata* 2.

novau, leaf of a pandanus, *vau*.

nononawo, lapping waves.

Noa, minute, fragmentary, in *manoa, manoanoa*.

Noaliu, a wind, over Motalava, *vawo vat*.

Noarag, to catch a fish at once on throwing the line.

Noasu, 1. smoke rising from a fire which has not yet burnt clear. 2. the smell of smoke in food or water. Probably *no* 2., *asu*, flakes of smoke.

Noga, 1. to come near, stay near, be at hand.

Noga, 2. to bruise, soften.
  manoga, well cooked, soft.
  m a n o g a n o g a, crushed, squashed.

Nol, whole, the whole, all collectively; *nolo nol* swallow whole, *sugsug nol* wash the whole body. Banks' Ids., *dol, del;* Maewo, *dolu, odulu;* Lepers' I. *doloegi;* Fl. Bugotu, *udolu;* Nengone, *nodei*.

Nolava, coarse, made with large leaves, *no* 2., *lara;* of mats.

Nolo, to swallow.
  nolo masur o anus, one who has had a dangerous voyage with his heart in his mouth, when he nears the shore *qara nolo masur o anus* swallows down the *qat anus* and is at ease.
  nolo rerereg, to stretch out the neck in swallowing; *isei we nolo o sinaya ti ge tole nanenena*.
  tano-nolonolo, the gullet, swallow.

Nom, 1. same as *noma*, poss. thy.

Nom, 2. to think, have in mind.

nom goro kel, to have the mind in restraint.

nomkel, to call to mind, remember, neuter; *nomkel ape*, remember, transitive.

nomleas, change the mind, thought; repent.

nomlilil, to err in thought, misapprehend, misbelieve.

nomliwoa, to think highly of.

nommataketake, to think lightly of.

nommava, have respect for.

nom mot, 1. to make up the mind, be resolute; *nom mot matila*, to fail in making up the mind, irresolute.

nommot, 2. to break off thought, cease to think; *kamam gate nom mot tiqa apeniko*.

nom nerei, think of something waiting for it to come; a new word for hope.

nom nurnur, to think carefully.

nompepewu, think lowly, humbly.

nompurei, with little thought, heedless.

nomqerqeret, to be incredulous.

nomrekereke, to be set up in conceit, self-confident.

nomris, to change direction of thought, repent.

nomruarua, 1. to be in two minds. 2. think of two things at once.

nomsuar, think and find, recollect.

nomtitin, tutun, to be anxious, eager.

nomtup, bring thought to a point, cease to have doubt, believe, be careful; *ko gate nomnomtup?* don't you mind what you are about? see *nonomtup*.

nomvaglala, be quite certain.
nomvano, think much of, *ape sara, apensei*.
nomvaruarua, be in two minds, hesitate, doubt.
nomvitag, think no more of, forgive debt or fault; *nipea nomvitag inau*, don't forget me.
nomwune, to have a thought come into one's mind; *wune;* occur to one to think; *ko qara nom wune inau*, this is the first time you have thought of me.
Noma, poss. n. *no* 1. suff. *ma* 5. thy.
Nomala, abundantly, in profusion.
Nomam, poss. n. *no* 1. suff. *mam* 1. pl. excl. our.
Nomanoa, [*no* 2.] made of fine leaf; *manoa;* of a mat.
Nomatag, 1. to catch fish in abundance. 2. to cover with *nomata* after pouring water into an oven.
Non, 1. v. to smear.
Non, 2. poss. *no* 1. suffix *n*, pers. pr. sing. 3. his, her, its; often to be translated 'of'; same as *nona* 1.
Nona, 1. poss. *no* 1. suff. *na* pers. pr. sing. 3. his, her, its; of.
Nona, 2. v. to clatter, make a clattering noise.
Nona-kala, head downwards, like a *kala* lizard; *nona* 1; *ni me siwo nona kala*, he climbed down head downwards.
Nonina, poss. *no* 1. pl. 1. incl. our.
Nono, a small beetle that comes on decaying fruit.
Nononawo, [*no* 2.] little lapping waves; leaves, flakes, of seawater.
Nonom, redupl. *nom* 2. to think.
nonomia, thought.

Nonomotmot, [*no* 2.] cropping off leaves; *mawui nonomotmot*, to plant without proper preparation, as if just cropping off leaves to make room; *mot* 2.
Nonomtup, redupl. regard; *nipea nonomtup o qeteg tangae, rave maremare*, never mind the stumps, pull hard.
Nonon, to anoint, smear.
Non, 1. plaited cocoa-nut fronds hung as a screen.
2. coarsely plaited mat of cocoa-nut fronds; *tape non*, a small one.
non pit, a mat, *non*, with the rachis picked off, *pit*, used to *vear goro tano*, under an *epa*.
non tamate, a *non* plaited on one side.
None, to shake.
nonerag, to shake up, holding in the hands.
Nonos, begin to rise, of the tide, *nonos kalo*.
Nonpitpit, a fish.
Nonpurei, mispronunciation of *nompurei;* good Mota.
Nopitu, a certain *vui*.
Noqalata, dry leaf of banana.
Noqetaqeta, dieffenbachia.
Nor, 1. poss. n. *no* 1. same as *nora*, their.
Nor, 2. v. to have ill-feeling, grudge, bear malice; *anor*.
ganor, n. ill-feeling, grudge, malicious action.
gaganor, same in habit.
ganganor, same in strong character; wickedness.
Nora, 1. poss. n. *no* 1. pl. 3. their.
Nora, 2. yesterday; Fl. *nola;* always with *na* 5., *nanora*.
Nora, 3. to rattle, make short sharp noise; *o line vat-geuro; vat-nora*, length of bamboo.
nora-vanona, rattle and clatter; many things together.

Norara, 1. poss. *no* 1. dual 3. of the two, their.
Norara, 2. leaf *no* 2. of *rara*, erythrina; see above.
Nore, to make a noise; *nore goro,* disturb by noise.
  norenore, noise, as of surf.
Noriu, const. *nor,* thin inner skin in almond, *nai ;* same as *pesiu.*
Nornor, redupl. *nor* 2. bear grudge, entertain ill-feeling
Noro, to tap, sound by tapping, rattle.
  noronoro, make rattling noise; *o pei ti sale noronoro,* when it runs into a tank.
  wonoronoro, a rattle, a toy.
  qat-noronoro, the bamboo used in *vara qat,* which one man holds and taps, *noro.*
  noron, tr. determ. to rattle something; *vanvanoron-sur,* rattle bones.
Nosa, to gasp; *qale nosa* is still gasping, almost dead, at the last gasp.
Nosalite, 1. leaf of *salite,* catappa.
Nosalite, 2. a fish.
Nosiu, constr. *nos;* a young curled leaf, in vernation, as of banana, heliconium.
  nosmata, young curled leaf of *mata,* also *nos-nomata;* met. a man not easily provoked, *tete lologagara tete golgol.*
Notao, a fish.
Noto, tree, excævaria agallocha; *toto;* met. a stingy man.
Nov, complete; *me nov,* it is quite finished.
Nove, to break a hole through; *i David me nove nawarean i gene nan qa.*
Novnau, a fish, holocanthus.
Nowo, to gather up weeds, grass, &c.; *wura nowo valis nan o qeta,* you two clear the grass from the taro; *iragai we nowonowo alo tuqei,* they are weeding in the garden.
Nowoa, *un* word for *vagalo,* fight.
Nowonowono, 1. an entire leaf, as of cocoa-nut palm before the frondlets divide, small, early; 2. met. *maro nawonowono,* a slight scarcity of food.
Nua, 1. a cliff.
Nua, 2. a creeping plant, used to poison fish ;' *ganua.*
Nua, 3. v. move along.
  nuarevereve, come in continual succession; *reve.*
Nug, 1. M. n. spikes inside the base of the rachis of a sago frond; used as pins for *noota;* same as *nuw. nug ras,* a comb made of sago *nug.*
  o nug alo vutena, said of one always moving about, can't sit down.
Nug, 2. M. v. to come or go; *nug kel,* return; *nug retret,* to finish a part and give up.
  nugnug ret, to take short spells; *ret* at the edge.
Nule, 1. v. to deceive, mislead.
Nule, 2. n. a carved image of Nule at the door of a house, set up after *kolekole.*
Numa, a fish, blenny.
  malake numa, a small fish in a *qilo.*
Numeg, 1. to nibble at a bait.
  2. to twitch, as at the beginning of tetanus, *palao.*
Numei, n. the unit in numbers above the tens; *o numei nivisa?* what is the unit above the ten? *o numei we qoqo,* a large number above ten; *o varuzi numei,* the twelfth.
Nun, 1. to shed leaves, to be shed as leaves; met. of one who carries nothing.
  nun saru, to pour down as shed leaves.

Nun, 2. to go, to take first steps in walking, of infants ; *ni me nun veta,* he has begun to go. *nun aeae,* to go for a thing and fail ; *ae.*

Nun, 3. true, truth. *we nun,* yes.

Nunlagolago, [*nun* 1.] to be loose on arm or body, as armlet, girdle.

Nunrearea, [*nun* 2.] to go straggling along.

Nunrevereve, [*nun* 2.] extending at length ; as fish laid out in a long line ; *reve.*

Nunua, to change colour ; *o sav ti nunua* when it turns yellow.

Nunuai, (k) the mental impression of sound or force, rather than actual impression, but taken to be real. The same word with *niniai;* see *nununuara.*

Nunuale, bending; *name nunuale.*

Nunug, M. [*nug*] to tell out, to come, get, as information; *roro, gaganag, tapare ma.*

Nunume, a tree.

Nununuara, faint in sound ; *vava nununuara,* to speak so that only the *nunuai* of the words is heard, a faint impression of the meaning.

Nununrag, [*nun*] to be resonant.

Nunur, 1. to throw bait to entice fish ; so that when people are eating fish that they will not give to children, as unwholesome, they say *we gana nunur.*
2. to soak into ; when *toape, imal,* &c., are put into a *mona* with *pig,* the *ligui ti nunur ilo toape.*
3. to talk of many things to a man *we nunuria.*

nunurvag, to stain, defile.

Nunuuwa, to go early in the morning.

Nunuw, V. same as *nunug; nununuwa* ask him.

Nunuwou, a fish.

Nunvag, bring in quantity ; perhaps *nun* 2.

Nun, to make a resounding noise, as thunder, surf.

nuniu, constr. *nun* ; a heavy sound as of thunder, surf.

nununrag, tr. to resound, as a bass voice, to strike the ear with resonance.

nununununrag of the distant cry of a bird.

Nuna, to seek, look out for, a loan, or a purchaser for something to sell ; *tama isei we la ma o sava si a tuvag pa we nuna apena ; si qe tete wol we nuna matila.*

Nunpurei, mispronunciation of *nompurei ;* but good Mota, *we toga nunpurei ;* see *nonpurei.*

Nunrag, tr. *nun,* to resound, be resonant upon.

Nunus, only, nothing but, continuously ; *nunus vagvagalo* nothing but fighting ; *ti qe nunus vigo,* goes on playing though he be called away.

Nur, to dig, as a hole, to make a hole.

Nuravag, 1. to carry up, as a high tide carries a log ashore.
2. to remember a thing not paid for.

Nurenure, without noise or movement, of crowd and calm ; *gate magmagoa, we one rorono.*

Nurnur, adv. carefully, thoroughly ; probably *nur.*

Nurnuriaka, a spindle shell, the columella used for boring holes in canoe building ; *nur, aka.*

Nurpanoi, a tree.

Nuru, a boar pig.

Nurug, to be cunning, cunningly ;

redupl. *nunurug, nurnurug;* see *nurnur.*

Nuruw, V. same as *nurug.*

Nuw, 1. V. the spike in rachis of palm; same as *nug.*

nuwras, comb made of palm spikes.

Nuw, 2. V. to move, come rather than go; *nuw kel* return, *o nonomia te nuw kel* thought returns upon itself in consideration, self-examination; same as *nug.*

nunuw, same as *nunug.*

N.

This letter represents ng, as in "singer." In manuscript it is marked with dots above; in Roman print an italic *n* is used; in Italic print a Roman n.

N, transitive suffix to verbs; *tiqa* to let fly an arrow; *tiqan* to shoot and hit. Fij. *ga;* Fl. *ni.*

Na, to notch, whence *nar, nana,* &c.

Nae, to whine or cry; *vanae.*

Nag, tr. determ. suff. to verbs; *lilnag* from *lil.*

Nai, 1. V. same suff. as *nag.*

Nai, 2. mispronunciation of *nan;* wrong but established.

Nai, 3. canarium, tree and nut, almond-like, much used in cooking; constr. *ne.*

ne'*kor,* dried nut; *ne nig,* flat-sided nut; *ne qaro,* fresh nuts, not dried; *ne tao,* straight-shaped nut; *ne tawatawa,* nut that opens easily, *we wesar ti tawa, we nit ti tawa.*

4. good, of food; *nai wia,* good as *nai.*

nainai, wild, uneatable canarium.

Naisa, n. time when; with prep. *a, anaisa,* when, in future, hereafter, thereafter; with sign of past *na* 5., *ananaisa* when? in the past, beforetime. Fl. *niha;* N.H. *naha, naiha, nasa;* Fij. *enaica.*

Nala, to be out of breath, pant, to be tired.

Nalnaloa, straight, not properly curly, of hair; *ul tatas.*

Nalo, to eat without proper accompaniment; meat, fish, without vegetable food, vegetable without animal relish; *we nalo wia,* opposite of *pig,* same as *gana vatuga.*

Naloag, to mumble food and swallow slowly, as a *liwopas* does.

Nanoi, the dividing partitions in the knots of reeds, bamboos, &c., *nano togo, au.*

Nanololo, a full-grown cocoa-nut with only milk, no meat; *o matig o ligiu apena, pa o wiai tagai, gate tatas.*

Nanonano, to eat in pregnancy things not common food.

Nanora, indistinct of speech, stuttering.

Nan, 1. plural sign with nouns; by no means used always when plurality is meant; 2. follows verbs, adverbs, with sense of plurality; *na me nina nan alo vanua nan iake,* I have come to these islands; many comings, many islands; *na gate mule aras nan,* I don't go to places far off.

Nana, 1. to come forth into sight, become manifest; *nana lue.*

nanarag, tr. to make conspicuous.

Nana, 2. redupl. *na;* to chew small and soft, as mothers do food for infants ; to bite small, as ants do earth for their nests.

nanar, tr. to nibble a thing, leaving marks of teeth, as bats do fruit.

nanasag, tr. 1. feed with chewed food. 2. met. teach, first easy teachings.

Nanarag, 1. [*nana* 1.] to make itself conspicuous, as a thing white, bright; *ti nanaragia, ti nanarag luea.*

Nanarag, 2. [*nara*] to come to after fainting, recover from illness, come to oneself; *nanaray kel.*

Nanaraiga, colour between red and yellow, bright, conspicuous; *nana* 1.

Nanariu, refuse, nibbled, food; *nanar qaratu; nariu.*

Nanasag, [*nana* 1.] to teach, first early instruction; met. from the chewed first food of infants.

Nanau, redupl. *nau;* to eat vegetable food only.

Nar, 1. tr. *na;* to notch, tooth, indent; *we nar o nule,* the image *nule* is shaped with notches; *o sur qarat me nar,* a bat's bone serrated, the instrument for tattooing; *o kere we nar, o isar we nar,* club or spear with notches, and so projecting points or edges ; *we nar valiliug,* barbed like Solomon I. spears.
2. to mark with the teeth in biting, nibbling.
nanar, to nibble, bite small, mark with the teeth.
nariu, bits of stick; *nanariu,* bitten refuse.

Nara, 1. spider shell, strombus.

Nara, 2. same as *nala ; nanenensei we tantan we nara apena.*

Nara, 3. to go about; used at Gaua if not at Mota.

narag, tr. determ. to go about with a thing for sale, to hawk about.

Nariu, [*nar*] constr. *nar;* small dry sticks, used for fires ; such as fall when birds, flying foxes, are feeding.

Narnarqasapule, one who brings small sticks for firewood is so called in ridicule ; the *qasapule* makes its nest of small twigs, *narnariu.*

Nau, to gnaw, champ, bite. Mao. *ngau;* Sam. *gau.*
nau qeqen, to eat with closed lips.
nau wosowoso, to champ, make a noise with the jaws in eating.

Ne, constr. *nai*, canarium ; *ne kor, ne nig, ne qaro, ne tao, ne tawatawa*, various kinds.

Nene, damp ; *malanenenene.*

Nennenelau, [*nene*] faint, exhausted with exposure on the beach ; a man has been *alau*, he comes up exhausted, wants food saying he is *nennenelau.*

Nene, to mutter ill words against a man ; *we gol pata amensei we nene o tanun ilone;* to consult secretly about an injury to be done.

Nenekor, to talk secretly about a man with a view to his destruction, *we nenekorua ; kor.*

Nenene, redupl. *nene*, to be moist, bursting with juice, said of *gire* fruit just fit to suck.

Neneresiga, stunted, not able to grow; man or tree.

Nere, 1. a point, same as *nusui,* snout ; point of land, *we rono, o tamate we vugvug aia.*
nere mot, a point of forest land.
nereqoe, pig's snout, *kolekole nereqoe.*

Nere, 2. to whine, squeak, cry like an infant, like some birds.
  nat nerenere, a small whining infant ; nernerewora, always crying ; nere ta Qakea, to cry for a short time ; nernere qatgasuwe, said to a child to tease and frighten it.
Neremot, projecting point, nere, of bush, mot.
Nereqoe, a kolekole named from a pig's snout.
Nernewel, a tree like the nai, canarium ; a canoe made of it.
Nernerewora, one who readily cries, nere.
Nin, clench.
Ninin, clench close ; gargara ninin, clench close the teeth, in pain or rage.
Ninisa, to grin.
Nir, 1. to screw up the face, drawing in breath ; in pain, apprehension, dislike ; thence
  nir goro 1. to wince, with such expression of face. 2. to warn with such a sign ; na gate mule nir goro wun, I did not go carefully.
  manirnir, puckered up with pain, apprehension ; of the face.
Nir, 2. to creak, squeak ; same word perhaps as nere 2.
  nirnir, to creak as trees in the wind, as a rope ; to make a querulous whining like a sick person.
  nirit, tr. determ. to whine, cry, to or for.
Nira, 1. a hard wooded shrub, used for pisvatoto, kara, qatigsar.
Nira, 2. to gape ; of the mouth, of a wogire, pandanus fruit, opening when ripe.
Nirit, tr. determ. nir, to cry, whine after a person or thing ; to worry one for something desired.
Nis, mispronunciation of gis, as vanis for vagis.
Nit, to bite.
  nit o karia, a charm.
Noa, extinct, dead, of fire.
Noi, to hold out a snake, or some such thing, to frighten people.
Nol, to crop short, break off the top.
  nonolrag, break off many tops.
  noliu, the top shoot of a plant.
  manol, bent down.
Nolmatig, a grub in trees, white, with legs, eaten.
Nolmeat, the fringing reef about low water, meat.
Nono, blunt, without cutting edge ; o parapara we tuai, o mosiu, we nono.
Nonolrag, tr. nol, to gather many tops of toape, &c.
Nonono, to wander at large.
Nonotaga, [nota] finely separated ; as well combed hair, sav with fine small leaves.
Nor, mucus of nose.
  norisa, full of mucus.
Nora, grunt, snort, snore.
  nora taragiate, snore lying on the back.
Norae, a sacred place ; we rono, o tamate aia, tete mule lai alo ravrav.
Norag, to warn against doing wrong, or rebuke for going to do wrong ; one will varowog and norag goro. Probably nora tr. determ. making a deterrent or warning noise.
Norasere, a fish.
Norata, thrush in children ; makes them nora.
Norisa, [nor] full of mucus.
Noriu, (k) constr. nor, nori. A flat space within an angle.

nori-ima, the space at the apex of a gable, under eaves.
nornoriu, redupl. nornor ima as nori ima; nornor manui, qoroi, triangular base of nose between nostrils, base of ear.
nornor parou, the triangular space below the nose on the upper lip.
nornor qoe, qarat, noses of pigs, bats, which have not manui.
nornoriu retret, an outside angle; ret.
Nornormalekas, a fish.
Nornorparou, see noriu.
Nornortag, [nora] to mumble food with snorting.
Norogao, to play and shout, as noisy children in tinesara.
Notonoto, broken, of teeth, liwo notonoto; also said of children's teeth when changing.
Norov, to rebuke, forbid; norov goro.
Nota, fine, small, finely separated, leaves or hair.
nonotaga, finely separated.
Nusa, blunt; vanusag.
Nusiu, M. nusui V. (k) constr. nus; snout, a man's two lips projecting together, a point of land.
tavala nusui, a lip, upper or nether.
Fij. gusu; Pol. ngutu, gutu, nuku; Motu N.G. udu.
Nuskor, black lip; like a kor dried bread-fruit; in ridicule.
Nusletelete, [lete] to shoot out the lip, in scorn, muttering.
Nus-sere, quarrelsome; sere.
Nustup, to hate; from sign of hatred, projected lips.

O.

O, 1. exclam. doubt, hesitation.
oo, refusal, prohibition.
O, 2. article, demonst. a, the; pl. as well as singular.
Oet, a bird, in Gaua and V.L.
Olo, 1. to turn up at the end, turn down and then turn up, as the branch of a tree; to turn up so as to overlap.
2. to come ashore, of a canoe, its bow turning upwards to the beach; olo sisirvag, to shave, sirvag, a rock in coming ashore. D.Y. olo.
3. to get wrong in a song, not keeping together, so that one singer overlaps another.
olovag, 1. tr. lean over upon; taqa olovay.
olovag, 2. separable vag, to come ashore with, land with.
ololovag, M. to come through surf on the tapa, surf-board.
Oloolo, 1. v. 1. to make an offering, of money and gea, to a man B. who has a stone, or other object, with which a vui is connected; we oloolo mun i gene (B.) we gilala o vat, mun o som wa o gea, ape vat. The bringer of the offering A. does not oloolo to the vui, but to the man B.
v. 2. to put the offering of money and gea upon the stone on behalf of A. the bringer of the offering. B. we oloolo avune vat ape A. He B. does not oloolo to the vui, but on the stone. The offerer A. may himself oloolo, i. e. put or throw down money on a sacred stone or place, we oloolo ape vat; so a young fellow will oloolo ape lumagav for himself, or to another for him, with a view to good looks, favour, &c.
n. 1. the offering; 2. the man who receives and presents the offering.
tano-oloolo, the stone, tree-

stump, spot, on which the offering, *oloolo*, is made ; *qarani oloolo*, a hollow place which is *tano-oloolo*. In recent use *oloolo* stands for sacrifice and sacrificer ; *tano-oloolo* for altar.

Oloolo, 2. a fish.

Ona, to kindle, keep alight, neuter.

One, 1. to lie wide and open ; *o lama we one goro* the sea lies wide between to separate, *we one rorono* in a calm.
one wora, lie waste and be useless ; *namatak we one wora*, my eyes fail me.

One, 2. sand ; *one tano*, dusty earth.
oneone, a sandy beach.
ononega, mealy, of a yam.
Mao. *one*, sand, beach ; *oneone*, earth. Pol. *oneone*, *one*, sand, earth.

Opa, Lepers' I. *Omba*.

Ora, to keep under control ; with *goro*; to restrain, keep off ; *ora goro kel*, be temperate.

Oraora, to play, sport.

Ori, to creak, make creaking sound ; *oriori* of the sound of wind.

Oroi, const. *oro;* rubbish ; decayed or useless parts, appurtenances.
oroima, ruins of a house, rubbish of a house.
oronawo, light stuff carried up by the surf ; *oropei*, rubbish carried by water.
oroutag, the useless wild things in the *utag*, trees, shrubs, herbs, not planted or cultivated.
orovalis, straw.
orooro, rubbish, in water or on land.
ororoga, full of rubbish, water or surf carrying *orooro*.

Orosaga, abundant, all about, many, in a depreciating way ; *o reremera we orosaga, na gate gilala si isei me ge*, there are such a lot of children about, I don't know if one of them has done it.

Orotou, something edible growing on stones on reef.

Ota, the sago palm, sagus.
ota lava, the large species, the starch of which is prepared for eating; *ota nan*, the smaller species, the leaves of which, *no-ota*, are used for thatch. In preparing sago the trunk of the palm is split and the pith chopped small with a *qaia*. The pith is strained in woven dishes with water, *we sene alo tapera*, over a shallow hole in the ground surrounded by stones and covered with the *viro ota*, the fibrous plexus at the base of the leaves ; the *piai*, starch, stays on this and the water runs through.

Otakaova, a mussel.

Ova, egret, same as *kaova* ; *mala-ova*,

Ovi, a tree.

Oviovi, the name of a *tamate* society ; *sare-oviov*.

Oviovira, [ra 4.] flat roofed ; *o ima we taqa gagau; o qatima gate eleele*.

Owo, to have a white mark on the skin ; *nawareana we owo*.

P.

Pa, conj. but, and.
Paere, beg, ask for.
Pagigiu, (k) constr. *pagig*, side, flank.
Pagoa, shark. Gilb. Ids. *bakoa* ;

Marsh. *bako*; Ponap. *poko*; Fl. *bagea*, N.G. *paowa*.
pagoa mea, said of ill cooked bread-fruit, because red, *o gatogo pagoa we memea*.

Pagpagoai, 1. dorsal fin of a fish, like that of *pagoa*, also anal fin. 2. met. a very thin man, *gate tur tanun pagpagoai vires*.

Pagpagaloa, same as *gapagapa*.

Paito, a shed, temporary lodge in a garden. Sam. *paito*, a cooking-house.

Paka, banyan, ficus; various species, *paka mea*, *paka ronovagalo*, *paka vat*.

Pakalava, an European vessel: uncertain origin; perhaps a form of *aka* canoe.

Pakapaka, fornication, adultery; properly refers to the money that passes.

Pakasagoi, (k) the under shell of crab and turtle.

Pakasoai, (k) same as *pakasagoi*.

Pakul, to sit in a crouching attitude.

Pal, same as *palu*.

Pala, 1. to double, set stick against stick, set across, wattle, fasten between two sticks, take up with, between, two sticks; in recent use to cut with scissors; *pala goro*, fasten with cross sticks.

palag, M. *palai* V. tr. to wattle sticks, to set across.

palat, tr. to fasten between sticks, one on either side; to take between sticks.

palaga, crossing obliquely.

palapala, redupl. to move crossing one the other.

palala, redupl. divide in two.

ipala, *i* 4., tongs.

Pala, 2. to be double, as two kernels in a nut.

Pala, 3. to curl singly; when only one tusk of a pig curls, *ti pala*.

Pala, 4. to beat the drum at the ends; when three are drumming the two outside *pala*.

Pala ta Vava, to strangle a man by pressing a stick across his throat.

Palag, M. palai V. to set one thing obliquely across another, to wattle sticks; *palag goro*, to cross obliquely one over the other, as the legs; *palai late*, to break by catching between things crossing, as when one catches a stick between the legs and breaks it.

Palaga, [*pala*] adj. crossing obliquely.

Palagarua, divided and the two parts crossing; said of a tree.

Palako, a tree with edible leaves; a certain *mana* attaches to it; *palako* logs smeared with *mea* are carried in feasts.

Palakomot, a fish.

Palala, redupl. *pala*, to divide in two.

Palao, spasm of tetanus, twitching, a convulsion which draws the sinews, *gapalao*; *o palao ti ramoa*, he has tetanus; *o palao me rare aneanea*, he had strong convulsions; *palao malum*, tetanus without convulsions, but with great pain.

Palaotiu, *palaot mala*, extremely thin.

Palapala, redupl. *pala*, in recent use, 1. to cut with scissors. 2. scissors.

Palaqatiaka, to be double, as kernels in a nut, with the shape of the head of a canoe, *qati-aka*; *o wotaga si o salite qe pala, o takelei we wono wa we mavinvin*.

Palasa, the jawbone of a pig kept as a memorial of a feast.

Palasai, (k) constr. *e.* the cheek; of a canoe, *me gape wora qet o palase aka nan neira.*

Palasapugapuga, a great talker; *napalasana we pugapuga.*

Palasvala, the flat stones laid round the rim of the oven, *um;* the *palase vala.*

Palat, tr. *pala,* to keep upright between supports at the two ends; as firewood built up between supporting stakes.

Palatai, a scattered heap of stones; same as *polotai.*

papalatag, confusedly.

Palatakura, to take up, *pala,* a hot stone with *ipala,* and replace it on food put into the oven; *takura.*

Palatanilen, to put hot stones on *loko,* with *ipala; we palatanilen goro loko.*

Palawai, (k) the inside of the thigh.

Palawana, one who gobbles, *we gana vagorgor.*

Pale, 1. n. handle.

Palega, [*pale*] turned inwards; of a leg a little turned upon the other.

Palegetava, [*pala*] door, shutter; *gatava.*

Palil, [*lil*] to go round the sides and meet; as in adzing the inner sides of a canoe; as the wings of a fighting party make a circuit and draw to the main body; *we uma palil* when the main party working clear the middle of the garden while two or three work round the edge.

palil tal goro, one makes a circuit to meet others from whom he has separated.

Paloloi, (k) something broad and thin; flat-fish, braid.

Palpal, redupl. *pal, palu;* to steal; a thief; *palpal takir soko* a thief of family property; *natima tipal kel napulamrua.*

Palpalag, [*palag*] to be twisted one across another; as the legs of a man who stumbles as he runs.

Palpalatai, redupl. *palatai; palpalate vat,* a natural heap of stones.

Palpalaus, two bows, *us,* shooting exactly together, *pala* like double kernels.

Paltara, a wooden chopper, *tara,* in the shape of a shell adze, for cutting bread-fruit.

Palu, 1. to do secretly, out of sight; adv. secretly, out of sight.

2. to steal; a thief; adv. stealthily.

papalrag, to steal many things.

3. *un* word for *matika,* a bird that steals.

Pan, 1. constr. *paniu.* 2. prep. beside; *panei, paniu; a pan vanua* alongside the village; *we nina napanvanuana* came alongside his village, to the side of it.

Panava, conj. adversative, *pa, nava,* nevertheless, but.

Pane, 1. an armlet.

2. boom of canoe, between which and mast lies the sail.

Panei, (k) constr. *pane; pane tanun* hand and arm, *pane manu* wing, *pane iga* pectoral fin; *pane qoe* shoulder. Same word as *paniu.*

When the hand is spoken of in connexion with food, when food is in the hand or on the hand, the poss. *ga* 1. is added between the noun *pane* and the suffixed pronoun; *napanegak, napanegama,* my hand, thine, and so on ; *panei o gana vere manmanu* said of one who eats with dirty hands, *manmanu*.

paneg, v. tr. to carry across the shoulder with a string. N.H. *bane* is used for wing of bird and shoulder of pig; German N.G. *ban* hand.

Paneg, tr. from *pane*, suff. *g*, to carry over the shoulder with a string ; *tana panpaneg* a satchel.

Panegaegae, a long-armed man ; *gaegae* creepers.

Panegaro, one who spoils tools ; *ti gagar o parapara, ti tatas qet ;* met. from *garo* hard clay.

Panegisgisir, one who is always using charms, *talamatai, garata*.

Panelalav, one whose hand is hot, *lalar*, to kill with charms; *we map o talamatai te qalo sei* tam *o ar*.

Panelusa, a bat's wing ; *lusa ;* met. one outside the *suqe*.

Panemataketake, light-handed.

Panemaran, an idle hand ; *ni gate mawmawui*.

Panematea, dead hand in shooting; *we vene, we mate gaplot*.

Panepane, an armlet.

Paneqote, big hands and arms, short and thick ; *qote*.

Panesasakariga, a thief ; a mischievous hand.

Panesasasaga, a thief.

Panesigo, kingfisher's wing, the blue flame in fire.

Panesila, boom of canoe ; *sila*.

Panesiwo, a disease, a swelling of hand and arm ; the arm is held down, *siwo*, that the swelling may go away downwards.

Panetitin, M. hot-handed, one who has shot and killed ; *titin*.

Paneuwa, turtle-fin, name of a cocoa-nut at one stage of ripeness : see *matig*.

Pangaegae, [*paniu*] same as *panegaegae*.

Panisvenevene, one who has been killed by an arrow.

Paniu, (k) constr. *pani, pan ;* same as *panei*.

Panlepa, [*paniu*] dirty hand ; *gana panlepa* to eat without washing the hands.

Panlova, stiff hand ; *napanik we lova*.

Panmalmalaviviv, hand beginning to be painful ; *malaviviv*.

Panmanur, hand with *mana* in it, *manur ;* one who is able or skilful in shooting, fishing, &c.

Panmasorsor, a hand that makes one groan ; one who has a painful hand ; *masorsor*.

Panmea, a species of flying-fish, with red fins.

Panoi, Hades; the abode of the dead.

Panpan, 1. the side of a valley ; *qat-panpan* the hill beside a valley ; *pan* 1.
2. adv. beside, redupl. *pan* 2.

Panpanlau, 1. the sea-shore ; 2. by the shore ; *lau*.

Panpuna, one who shoots and kills ; *napanena ti puna apena*.

Pansasar, one who shoots and misses ; *sasar*.

Pansasara, the same as *pansasar*, a bad shot.

Pantagarir, wing, *panei*, of the *tagarir ;* met. good hard firewood, so called from its colour.

Pantaniga, straight hand, *taniniga*, one who shoots straight.

Pantatatano, meddlesome, said of a child handling things in the house ; *panei, tano*.

Pantawa, a hand with cracked

I

skin, *tawa*; one who has split the skin of his hand with work.

Pantutun, V. same as *panetitin*; *paniu, tutun*.

Panito, the bamboo filling in of the gable of a house, inside; *ape panito* in the corner inside a house near the *panito*; *panito ima* the space in the corner.

pantolava, the broader *panito*; *pantorig*, the smaller; the door not being in the middle of the front of the house.

Papalak, a shrub, met. of a man, thin, bony.

Papalaota, very thin, such as a sow with many pigs; like a door made of sago, *pala ota*.

Papalatag, M. in confusion like a heap of stones, confusedly; *palatai*.

Papalrag, [*palu*] to steal often, many things; *palpal vagae*.

Papansag, tr. v. from *pan* 2., to go aside to; a boy wants to go with people his father tells him not to follow, when his father is not looking *ni we papansag sur ragai*.

Paparau, 1. long, extended; *mapsag paparau* take a long breath. 2. to stretch out, lengthen, neuter.

Paparis, [*parisiu*] the low wall, generally of boards, *irav*, which forms the sides of a house or *gamal* under the eaves; see *ima*.

Papatau, a shrub.

Papatuaga, [*patuai*] thin.

Papatun, to shelter, grow over; as large banyans, *paka*, shelter a village in a hurricane.

Par, to cut the inside of a canoe; *pari* 1.

Para, 1. sideways, turning aside.

wena para, rain that misses a place and falls elsewhere.

Para, 2. full grown; *o toape we para* fit to pull.

paraga, strong, full grown, abundant; of leaves, hair.

Paragoro, a small kind of flying-fish.

Paramake, a shrub, kind of *sav*.

Paran, *lav paran* to take off the string and oil the bow; *ran* same as *ram*.

Parapara, [*para*] 1. sideways, beside, sloping; *mule parapara* go slanting off; *tira parapara* stand sideways off; *Ureparapara*, the island with slopes.

2. in recent use an axe, hatchet, with the blade set sideways, unlike the adze.

Parasiu, constr. *paras*, a thing of inferior sort; *paras qoe* poor sort of pig, *paras tanun* inferior person, *paras toto* bad arrow, *paras tuqei* poor garden.

Parau, long; *paparau*; Fij. *balavu*.

paraus, to protract; protracted, long but with the end in view or at hand.

Parewarewa, vagabond; *tama isei gate toga ape kikin tamana, ni we toga parewarewa nan tamana*.

Pargatae, to paddle with short strokes between the canoe and the outrigger; as if cutting, *par*, the *gatae* of the *sama*.

Pari, 1. to cut with straight strokes, in shaping the inside of a canoe.

Pari, 2. the women's belt.

Parira, a district of Mota.

Paririu, the temple of the head; *qaririu*.

Parisiu, M. side, *paparis*.

paris tuqei the side of a garden; *paris vanua* the side, skirt, of a village.

Paroto, *un* word for *matig*.

Parou, 1. a tree with male flowers; particularly the male pandanus, of which *gire* is female. 2. the male flower, as of pandanus.

o parou me ar, meaning *o nawo me malate*; it was not right to say *nawo* at sea, and on nearing land and seeing surf they *rava viro*, the male flower has fallen apart.

Parpar, redupl. *par*, cut the inside of canoe with straight strokes.

Parparat, to shoot at a mark, in a party.

Parparus-matai, eyelashes; *parusiu*.

Paru, same as *peru* in *peruperu*.

Parugiu, nothing whatever; *parug sinaga* no food at all.

Parusiu, V. same as *parisiu*.

Pas, a kind of yam; *pasiu*.

Pasau, to join to wood, as to add boards to body of canoe, to helve an adze; in recent use to build a wooden house.

aka paspasau a canoe with *irav* joined to body; *paspasau* in recent use, carpenter.

Pasiu, (k) const. *pasi*, *pas*; smoothness, attractive smoothness of person; *napasina me qalo inau*; *pas nai*; in songs equivalent to beauty, as in the Bishop's song, *nirman sororo ma napasi nago*ma, *napasigar manu*ma.

pasiga, smooth.

Paso, 1. to finish, complete. 2. to be finished, come to an end, gone by; *paso!* enough, all over.

3. adv. of time, after that; *o aka me kel paso ma*, after that the vessel has come back.

pasopaso, adv. completely, in conclusion.

Paspasiga, [*pasiu*] smooth dark and shining, from comparison with *pas nai*.

Paspasoanai, [*paso*] 1. a last one, *anai*, last of a series; 2. adj. last; constr. *ane*, *paspasoane qon* the last day.

Pasraveg, to take all one by one; *paso*, *rave*.

Pat, to eat with the eye-teeth, *patiu*, gnaw with the side teeth; *pat wolowolo* eat with the side teeth and the head on one side, like a cat.

patiu, the upper tusk of a pig.

Pata, adv. in, inwardly, secretly.

patarag, tr. v. to look into at, peer into.

Patau, bread-fruit, artocarpus; many varieties; to gather a bread-fruit *qes patau*.

Patipati, [*pat*] to eat a cocoa-nut without scraping the meat, biting it out of the shell with the upper side teeth, *patiu*.

Patiu, [*pat*] 1. the upper tusk in a boar, knocked out to let the lower tusk grow long. 2. the corresponding teeth in man; eye-teeth, upper side teeth; not however properly *patiu*. Fij. *bati*.

Patomava, heavy bread-fruit, one who can't run or climb.

Patomesmes, variety of *patau*, bread-fruit, reddish in colour. *mes* 1.

Patpatara vavae, *o tanun ti vava we sea, neia te vava we sea*.

Patu, to thatch close, keep the *noota* reeds close together; *si qe patu we susur mun o qatia*.

Patua, thin and flat like *patuai*, applied to legs.

Patuai, (k) the thin buttresses of some trees, m*ake*, *salite*; *patue ranoi* thin flat leg.

Patun, to pelt with stones, sticks, &c.

Paut, *pautu*, a grasshopper, locust.

Pawa, a fish, serranus.

Pawou, empty, desolate, same as *wou*.

Pawura, a tree; *pawura mes* a variety, *mes* 1.

Pawurai, (k) constr. e. 1. the projecting bone of the ankle; 2. the projecting part of a pig's jawbone, whence the tusk *ti war lue*, curls forth.

Pe, noun used as prep.; with *a, i, ta*, compound prep., *ape, ipe, tape*; of relation to place, or cause; at, by, in reference to. The use of suffixed pron. in *apena, a pe na*, shows plainly the noun; as also the same suff. pron. *n* in *pen, apen*. The same character of the word is shown by the absence of the article before the noun which follows: *ape nagok*, not *ape nanagok*, before my face. See Grammar.

Pea, 1. nought, be not, come to nothing; *ni pea*, let it not be; *me pea*, it has come to nothing, *na me pea ran*, I am good for nothing. In neg. imper. or dehortatory verbs *nipea* goes with sing. and plural; but with 2d pers. plural *turpea*, with 2d dual *urapea*, with 2d trial, *tol pea*. Sam. *pea 'oe*, to quiet a child.

Pea, 2. n. bait, and v., to entice by a bait.

 peapea, the tinder used when fire is got by rubbing, *soso*, to entice the fire to the firewood.

 peas, tr. to entice with bait, tame with feeding; n. a tamed creature, pet.

 peas mateav, kindling for a fire, to entice it.

Pego, name given to bread-fruit *tarala garana* M.

Pei, 1. fresh water, fluid, liquor, grease; a pool, or stream. N.G. *bei, vei*.

2. to mix water, pour, add, water; *we pei o gea*, a man takes water into his mouth when he chews, *gat*, the kava, he adds more after he has squeezed out the juice.

3. to pour water, salt or fresh, into the oven, *um*, for *qaranis*.

4. salt-water in canoes; *ras o pei*, bale out water.

5. medicine, from the practice of charming water for healing drink.

6. blindness in *matapei, namatanu me pei*.

peis, tr. v. to pour water on. The word *pei* is almost restricted to Banks' Ids.

pei lava, river, probably recent.

pei mana, water that has been charmed, medicine.

peimatemate, poison, recent use.

pei nom o mule, water from a sacred stone used for sickness or wound; *te ge mulemule* 2.

pei tup, water running sharply; *o wena ti poa, pa o pei ti tup apena, ti sale maremare*.

Peipei, redupl. *pei* 2., to pour water on to the grated cocoanut, *goras*, so as to *woro*, squeeze out the juice.

Peis, tr. *pei*, to pour water on grated cocoa-nut, or into *qaranis*.

Peka, solitude, same as *pupuel*.

Pekepeke, same as *peka*.

Pekil, a tree.

Pelagolago, [*lago*] a bridge, contrivance for passing over streams in V.L.; *we rowoay o yawola nirua; we vara o tuara, we taktakau ape tuara,* two rattans are stretched across above the bed of the stream, men cross over walking on the lower, holding on by the hands to the upper.

Pelu, crooked, curved round; to bend round or crooked; *o matesala we pelupelu,* a path is crooked, bends; *we ave tataga pelu o vini uwa,* to bend round tortoise-shell following a curve, or crooked line. Sam. *mapelu;* Fij. *beluka.*

Penen, something good; *o gene we wia; o vara ta uta.*

Pepe, 1. v. to carry a child on the back or astride on the hip; with or without a carrying scarf *epa pepepe;* on the hip *pepe avnag,* where if too young to sit, *taqa,* the child is supported by an *epa.*

Pepe, 2. a yellow butterfly.
 pepega, yellow.

Pepe, 3. fish, chætodon, cobblerfish.
 Common word for butterfly. Banks' I. N.H. Sol. I. Fij. *pepe, pep, bebe, uleulebe, bebeula;* Mao. *pepepe;* Pol. *pepe, bebe;* Motu N.G. *kaubebe;* Amboyna, *pepeul.*

Pepega, [*pepe* 2.] yellow; name of a cocoa-nut as its husk gets yellow.

Pepegasuwe, a small centipede, luminous at night when touched.

Pepekalo, to take up and carry a child; *pepe* 1.

Pepemotar, a kind of chætodon; *pepe* 3.

Pepemurumur, kind of chætodon fish; *pepe* 3.

Pepenovar, chætodon fish; *pepe* 3.

Pepeqaratu, kind of chætodon fish; *pepe* 3.

Pepeqoe, a large yellow butterfly; *pepe* 2.

Pepepemera, bruise on the back, *tama we pepe o natmera;* sore, bruised; *pepe* 1.

Peperag, to stretch the arms; same as *kekerag.*

Pepero, a tree.

Peperoworowo, 1. to fly up, flare, flash, of sparks and flames. 2. to flash and leave a trail of light like a meteor, mao. 3. a flying spark or flame; like flying butterfly; *pepe* 2, *rowo* 2.

Pepersag, to wriggle away; met. shirk, be unwilling.

Peperua, two together like butterflies; *pepe* 2; *gamo peperua,* two canoes sailing together, their sails like butterflies; see *visa.*

Pepeso, 1. pilot fish. 2. remora. 3. met. one who follows another about, sticks to him; importunate.

Pepetano, a small centipede in the ground.

Pepeure, a shrub.

Pepewu, low, humble, small; *lolo pepewu* with no appetite or desire; *vava pepewu apensei* to disparage a person.

Pera, a man startles another by pushing his knee and cries *pera!*

Perete, a very level fence; Gaua word.

Perir, crooked, leaning on one side; same as *parapara.*
 perperir, adv. contrarily; *tiu perperir* said of one who is told to do one thing and does another.

Perosa, a shrub.

Peru, brilliant, shining; *mataperu*.
peruperu, with shining surface, of whatever colour.

Pes, 1. persuade, urge; probably same as next word.

Pes, 2. to peel the *pesiu* skin from the *nai* almond.

Pesag,

Pesenag, to lean up against, so to be supported, to be hitched into and held up.

Peserai-rag, shallow; *o lia peserai, peserag*, shallow cave.

Peserig, to put the door horizontally across the doorway; *te peserig goro o mateima mun o gatava*.

Pesiu, thin covering or film; such as the inner skin of the kernel of *nai* and *wotaya*, the involucre of flowers, any thin covering, wrapper, in plants; *pesgaav* the sheath of the unopened flower of the creeper *gaav*.

Pespes, *pes* 2., with *goro*, *pespes goro* to peel almonds, &c.

Peso, to lean over; *tapesopeso*.

Pete, the side post of a house which carries the *wolowolo*, plate.

Peten, 1. to approach, come close to. 2. adv. near, close to.

Petepete, fornication, adultery; refers to money passing; differs from *pakupaka* in being occasional.

Petpeten, something said which the person concerned does not hear; *lea petpeten*.

Pewu, a wild species of yam; *pewu qoe*, a large kind; the *pewu* is sometimes planted.

Piai, (k) coagulated vegetable sap; such as sap of bananas when cut; the sap of the pith of sago; *te tara o ota, te wora o turiai, te toto o utoi; tavala maran o piai apena*, cut down the sago palm, split the trunk, chop the pith, next morning there is the *piai*. Sam. Tahiti, *pia*, arrowroot. Mao. *pia*, sap exuded.

Pig, v. 1. to eat food with the proper accompaniment, meat or fish with vegetable food, vegetable with meat, *te pig mun o qoe, o nam*; if *toape* only and no yam, *o pig tagai*. 2. to put food for *pig* into the oven.

n. *pig, pigpig*, the food, animal or vegetable eaten in accompaniment; also *pigiu*.

3. *pig pei, pigpig pei*, 1. to eat dried bread-fruit, *kor*, dipping it in water. 2. met. to mix languages together.

pig tou, to eat cocoa-nut and *nai* together.

pigiu, (k) food to *pig; na pigin katol*.

Piglagolago, see *pelagolago*.

Pigtangae, *o tungae we risa we log si o pigtangae*.

Pilage, 1. a bird, rail. 2. met. a swift runner.

pilage parvuv, name given to a man whose head is bald in patches; *vuv*.

pilage ret, a canoe whose bows and stern rise in a curve.

Pilei, (k) constr. *e*; tip, pointed end; *we nile o pile som* in making money.

Pilolo, 1. to curl round and round, revolve; *o sasa ti rowo pilolo*, the leaf of a croton shoots with a curl; a dry leaf *ti pilolo*; to skim revolving as a flat stone or *nai* shell does when thrown.

2. to throw flat stones, which revolve, play ducks and drakes, on the surface of the sea.

3. A small preparation of *loko*.

Pilosag, to writhe, contort; *o sinaga we gogona we ge pilpilosag o toqai; pilo*, stem of *pilolo*.

Pilpilita, puckered, crumpled in plaits; *rave teterag o siopa, we pilpilita*.

Pilu, curled; *tapera pilu*.
   pilug, curled; *o golo pilug*, curly-tailed pig.

Pinai, shell; *pine talai*, shell of the giant clam.

Pio, the child of a brother is so called by brother or sister of the father.

Pip, 1. to stick to; one who sticks to another; *o pip, ni we kata amaia*.

Pip, 2. to bend; *pip letelete*, to draw in the back, as in dodging an arrow, or as a child when beaten.

Pipilosag, redupl. *pilosag*.

Pipilotag, contort, contorted; *tangae we malawo piplotag*, a tree twisted as it grew up; stem *pilo*.

Pipio, a very young infant; *pio*.

Pipin, to close, press, upon; *nau pipin*, to work the jaws with the mouth shut; *o qava me pipin mate i Kas*, a guava pressed down and killed.

Pipis, redupl. *pis*; 1. to twist up; 2. a twist, something twisted up; *pipis loko, nai, wotaga, qauro*, food cooked in a twist of leaves.
   pipisiag, adj. twisted, closely curled.

Pirgov, a lily, crinum.

Pirin, help, assist; *i pirinik*, my helper.
   piriniva, helping, assistance.

Pirnora, worn down on one side; said of a *tapera*.

Piro, swift in motion; to be indistinct from quickness of motion; *ni me piro mot*, got quickly out of sight; *ilo piro qalo*, to get a sight of a swiftly moving object, as a bird; *al piro, matapiropiro*.

Piroro, deep, far off; so as to be indistinct; *piro*.

Piroroag, to twist round and round in making yarn; not the same as *galo*.

Pirpir, a tree.

Pisara, a fish.

Pisarsar, a fish.

Pisiag, twist; stem *pis*.

Pisig, a stay at home.

Pisiu, M. (k) constr. *pis*; finger, toe, leg of insect or crustacean, being hard not soft.

piskorkor, one who plants what withers, *kor*.

pislava, the thumb.

pismalmalowo, long fingers.

pismaran, one who plants what dies; *maran* in Valuga means *kor*; *piskorkor*.

pismaremare, nail of finger or toe.

pismarawa, iron nail; recent use, from the fingers of Marawa the spider *vui*.

pis-tavasvas, the skin beside the nails torn by work; *tavasvas*.

Pispisig, to stay in one house, attend to, care for, one person, as in looking after sick people.

Pispisu, a *qauro* wild yam.

Pisu, a shell-fish; *pis ta Meralava* Venus' ear, haliotis.

Pisua, finger; *pisua lava*, thumb; *pisua rig*, little finger; a form of *pisui*.

Pisui, V. (k) constr. *pisu*, same as *pisiu*.

Pisumot, food so sweet that one licks his fingers after it; *mot* as in *neremot*.

Pisvatoto, pegs driven into the outrigger, *sama,* of a canoe, to which the *iwatia* are tied.

Pit, to take up or off with the tips of the fingers, pick, pluck ; *pit o nai, o gire, nan o vun* pick off from the bunch; divide, pluck apart, with fingers, as *loko, non;* see *pit* mot, *pit ul.*

Pita, fair in complexion, of men ; light-coloured, white, of birds, *kaova, weru, pita.*

Pitanonor, same as *penen.*

Pitiniu, (k) constr. *pitin*; midway between stem and end of branch ; *ilone alo pitinui.*

Pitmot, to pick quickly one by one ; so swiftly passing out of sight ; *sis pitmot,* point to what is going out of sight; *van pit mot,* come or go quickly.

Pitpitgavara, very sweet, plucks at the *ga* 2. *vara* 4.

Pitu, to move rolling ; *mapitu, tapitu.*

Pitul, to pick loose, as from a stalk; *we pitul o nai nan o sari vun.*

Piwa, a mollusc on rocks on the beach.

Poa, large, great ; to grow big, grow up.
  poava, bigness ; growing up.
  poavag, be big with ; grow up with.

Poarag, to carry, drive, as a strong wind or tide *te poarag o aka.*

Pogo, stem of *tapogopogo.*

Poi, to daub, smudge as a face with smut ; *te poi goro loko mun o nai; ape sava ko we poi nanagok mun o vain sinaga?*

Polotai, a natural heap of stones, same as *palatai.*
  polote vat, same as *palpalate vat.*

polote ima, met. scraps of food got together in the house, *we vivile gap alele ima.*

popolotag, in confusion, disorderly.

Polopolo, a small basket.

Polpolano, to tie a belt, *rotig,* higher up than the *tano rotrotig,* the waist.

Pona, dumb, imperfect in speech.

Popo, solid, as a tree with no pith, gives a ringing sound when struck.
  gansar popo, steady burning, of fire ; *taro popo,* solid calm.

Popoi, rotten, as tree, canoe.

Popolotag, adv. confusedly, out of order ; *polotai.*

Poporo, to seize, appropriate.

Poposia, a game, stroking the face.

Popot, a fish ; *popot* make.

Pora 1. to coil a line, simply round and round.

Pora 2. a rough basket, pottle, a plaited cocoa-nut frond put round fruit ; *te saru goro o vetal mun o pora nan o matika.* Mao. *porapora;* Sam. *pola;* Fij. *bola.*

Poro, to joke, talk lightly, chaff ; *poroporo.*
  porosag, tr. determ. make jokes at, mock at, laugh at.

Pos, *un* word for *salite.*

Puaka, boggy ground, mud.

Puapuaga, [*ga* 5.] bruised ; *vus puapuaga* beat and bruise ; stem *pua.*

Puasa, 1. a black lizard, iguana. 2. the same with *marea laqlaqar,* a *puasa* with forked tail that kills pigs. San. Cr. *huasa* crocodile, which is Mal. *buaya,* and Mota *via,* which see.

Puav, to give a sudden shock, startle.

Pue 1. bamboo water-carrier. N.B. *pu* a bamboo.

Pue 2. to surround with a view to capture.
Puel, solitary, deserted.
Puepei, very cold ; as a *pue* of cold water.
Puepuei, (k) the throat, gullet.
Puepuemera, to dandle a child, *mera*.
Pug 1. n. (k) a debt, fault. The pron. suff. when the debt is due by the person, *napugnk* my debt that I owe ; the debt owing to a creditor is his *mo;* *mok pug* the debt due to me, the origin of which is with me. ·
   tag pug, a creditor, also *tag mon pug*.
   v. to owe a debt : *nau we pug ape neia*, I am in debt on his account ; to bear blame.
Pug 2. a fish that cries *pug!* when taken, trigger-fish, balistes ; *pug gov* one species.
Puga, to feed and bring up, *tokos.* **pugas**, tr. to bring one up, supply food to.
Pugai, (k) fault ; same word with *pug* 1., but no recent differentiation.
Pugapuga, to be tired in the joints ; *naranok we pugapuga.*
Pugas, [*puga*] to bring up with food ; to tame by feeding ; peas.
Puget, bird's-nest fern, asplenium nidus avis.
   iro *Puget*, a female *vui, me pute goro o matesale marama ;* iro *Puget te nene wora o pue ape qatima*, said to one who lingers, or whose ear is not bored.
Pugete, adj. one who shows off, impudent, noisy ; *te qaraqara gese, tete apemaragai, te uloulo alo vanua.*
Pugiu, M. (k) hip-joint ; *napugi-*
pugik we motmot, tired in the hips ; same as *pugui* V.
Pugnarunaru, to owe and not pay ; a bad debt ; *pug* 1. *naru.*
Pugoro, a chest on legs, *tura*, to keep *kor* and *nai* in ; to construct a food-chest *we lano o pugoro.*
Pugsila, a lump on the buttock; *o pugiu we sila.*
Pugu, same as *pug* 1.
Pugupugui, V. (k) hip-joints ; *napugupuguk me mot ran*, hip-joints tired; same as *pugiu* M.
Pugvalvalenai, a trigger fish, balistes ; *pug* 2.
Pukai, to bind one stick to another to make it longer.
Pul 1. gum of trees, particularly of canarium, *nai.*
   2. torch of canarium gum.
   3. tattoo, done with *pul nai;* *te vus o pul.*
   4. birdlime, to catch birds with birdlime ; *we pul o manu mun o totoe gasur.*
   5. to stick, active and neuter ; *pulgoro.*
   6. v. to be friend with, to combine ; *pul ape*, have share in, have in common ; n. a friend ; see *pul-gale, pul mot, pul tatas, pul wora.*
   pulpul, adv. together, on friendly terms.
   pulut, v. tr. to make to stick ; *gapulut.*
Pul 7. v. to hold many things in the hand at once ; *te pul o qatia we qoqo ; pul galaqot.* n. a handful ; *o pul qeta.*
pulun, tr. determ. grasp and carry.
Pul 8. to curl and meet as pigs' tusks ; *o qoe we pul*, a well-tusked boar.
Pul 9. prefix with numbers of

persons; *pul visa?* how many men; *pul tol*, three men; *ni me gaganag ma si pulvisa, si pul vat*, he told me how many there were of them, that there were four men.
From common original meaning to be sticky, sticky stuff, stick together. Java, *pulut*, gum; Sam. *pulu*.

Pula 1. v. to deceive in jest; to deceive in a jesting way.
vava pula, to speak ironically.
pulasag, tr. deceive, trick, someone.
pulapula, n. deceiving, deception, with pleasant manner.

Pula 2. adj. pleasant, delightful, good-looking.

Pulai, (k) constr. *e*; property, a piece of property, chattel, having reference to something of more consequence than what would be represented by poss. n. *no*; the use is that of poss. n.; *a* 4. sometimes prefixed, *apulak*. Mtly. *blege*; V.L. *pele, polo*; Sta. Ma. *bula*; N.H. *bula, pila*.

Pulagao, one always working; *wopulagao*.

Pulala, a rack for *pue*, &c., in *gamal*.

Pulan, to arrange wood on or for a fire; same as *lano*; *pulan o av*, make up a fire.

Pulapula, 1. v. to trick; to ask for a thing when one has it, *ni me pulapula inau*, he made me think he had not what he asked for.
2. n. trickery; *pulapula ta Vanua Lava*, ironical praise of other's by depreciation of one's own property.

Pulasag, tr. determ. *pula*, to deceive, trick, someone; *vava pulasag lea*, to ask for a thing one has as if he had it not.

Pulawono, deceitful filling up, *pula* 1., *wono*; as when a tree falls across a path.

Pule, 1. a very dark cowry shell. 2. opaque white spot over the iris or pupil of the eye; *o pule me rowo*; *matapulepule*. Sam. *pule*, a cowry, white. Pon. *pwili*, cowry.

Pulei, (k) the pupil of the eye.

Pulemot, wild, no one's property, *pulai, mot*.

Puletogo, a kind of yam.

Pulewowut, a kind of cowry, *pule*.

Pulgalaqot, [*pul* 7.] to hold things in a bundle together in the hand, as arrows; *laqotiu*.

Pulgale [*pul* 6.] to be false friend.

Pulgoro, [*pul* 5.] to fasten with *pul*, gum, &c., stop an opening, caulk a crack in canoe.

Puliva, a climbing ficus; *pulva*.

Pulnovar, a dove; *no-varu*.

Pulpul 1. n. a burr, that sticks, *pul* 5.

Pulpul 2. adv. together; v. to combine, be friends together.

Pulpul 3. [*pul* 9.] redupl. so many persons at a time; *we mule pulpulrua*, go two and two.

Pulqatia, [*pul* 7.] a bundle of arrows, *qatia*.

Pulsakasaka, [*pul* 7.] a bundle of *qeta*, caladium, or growing cocoa-nuts, tied with the leaves standing up, *saka*.

Pulsala, 1. a friend, comrade; 2. wife or husband; one who has a common path, *pul* 6. *sala*.

Pulsama, [*pul* 5. *samai*] filthy, sticky, as with refuse.

Pulsamegire, [*pul* 6.] crabs crowd upon a sucked pandanus fruit, *same gire*; met. of many people claiming shares in one man's property.

Pultatas, [*pul* 6.] an ill friend ; to be associates in what is bad.

Pultuwale, [*pul*. 6.] to unite, associate ; live in harmony ; n. unity, harmony.

Pulu, same as *pul*. Mal. *pulut;* N.B. *pulit;* Pon. *pwil*.

Pulua, n. dirt, filth ; adj. dirty, filthy ; *gogorag sur o pulua*.

Pului, to take fish by torchlight, *pul* 2. ; probably tr. *pulug. un* word for *sin o iga*.

Pulul, 1. to have in common property ; *o tanun pul tol si pulvat te pulul ape qoe tuwale*. 2. adv. in common, equally ; *ni me vile pulul ti mun kamam;* uncertain whether *pul, ul*.

Pulun, [*pul* 7.] tr. to grasp several things together and carry ; *pupupulun*, to carry a good number.

Pulut, [*pul* 5.] tr. to make to stick, make sticky; n. sticking stuff ; in recent use glue ; *tano pulut*, tenacious earth ; *gapulut*. Sam. *puluti*.

Pulutgar, a cocoa-nut getting ripe ; the meat sticks to the scraper, *ti pulut o gar*.

Pulva, *pulira;* the leaves cooked and eaten.

Pulvara, a bundle of growing cocoa-nuts ; *pul* 7., *vara* 4.

Pulvisa, [*pul* 9.] how many, so many, men ; *visa*.

Pulwora, [*pul* 6.] to break off friendship ; *wora*.

Pun, 1. to dash out by hand or foot, rub out, as fire or anything written on a slate ; *pun mate gai!* put it out with your foot ; *pun reag*, dash it away. N.B. *punu*. 2. met. to satisfy, said of food ; *me pun neia*, he can eat no more.

Pun, 3. V. same as *puna*, to smell, active and neuter, stink ; *o garatu we pun o maligo*, flying foxes smell the clouds of coming rain ; *pun ilo*, try the smell.

puniu, V. (k) constr. *pun*, n. smell, scent.

pupupun, to snuff by way of kissing.

punpun, generally of pleasant smells.

Malag. *fofona;* Fij. *bona;* Motu N.G. *bona*.

Puna, M. same as *pun*, to smell, active, neuter, stink ; *me puna veta*, has stunk, in decay.

punai, M. (k) constr. *e;* smell, scent.

punapuna, generally of pleasant smell, by no means always.

puna gagavug, to smell with a thick, abundant, diffused, scent ; *we puna mantag*.

puna ilo, try the smell, try by the smell, smell and see.

puna talota, a bad smell from a man, *ni gate sugsug vagae*.

Punai, n. (k) constr. *e;* smell, scent, stink ; *puna*.

pune-qalqalosur, the smell of a thing that has been dead a long time, skeleton.

pune sagsage-ta-marama, all the sweet smells of the world ; said of quantities of flowers, scented leaves, *ita; sageai*.

Puniu, (k) constr. *pun;* n. smell, scent, stink ; *pun* 3.

Punmao, mildew, mould, *mao* 1., primarily of the smell of it, *puniu*.

lama punmao, unfrequented sea.

Punpun, 1. redupl. *pun* 3., generally of pleasant smells. 2. to snuff in the native way of kissing.

Puntalatlat, smell of stagnant water, where *talatlat* are.

Puntaligas, [*pun* 3.] n. smell of the liquor, *ligiu*, of fire; *i. e.* of the moisture carried up by the smoke of wood fire; v. to smell of that moisture; *ta* 1.

Punui, a district of Mota.

Puna, 1. a tree cricket, cicada; *o puna ti sorosoro.*

Puna, 2. madrepore coral; *vat puna*, madrepore stone. Sam. *puga*, coral.

Punalot, a shrub.

Punaro, a dark man.

Pup, 1. n. the further end of a house, end of a *pugoro; ana-pup,* at the end; *pupu ima.*

Pup, 2. v. to hold firmly; *o gae we pup;* adv. firmly; *vagae pup,* tie a knot that will hold, not run, *maslag; rave pup,* pull the knot firm, draw tight.

Pup, 3. to puff; *pupu;* see *pupus.*

pupsag, tr. determ. to puff out from the mouth, water, chewed leaves, the *mana* belonging to the leaves; *te pupsag lue o gea me gat veta.*

pupus, tr. to puff forth.

Pup-we-ulosa, said to a wounded man who has joined a fight without cause; *ulosa,* referring to his death.

Pupua, grandparents call grandchildren, and *vice versâ.* Fl. *kukua;* Motu N.G. *bubu.*

Pupuel, when or where no one is about, solitude, solitary; *alo pupuel; we pupuel; nau we toga pupuel magesek;* redupl. *puel.*

Pupun, [*pun* 3.] redupl. to snuff at, in the native way of kissing an infant.

Pupupur, [*pur*] to throw sticks and rubbish outside a garden, along the fence.

Pupus, tr. *pup* 3., to puff out from the mouth; as in charms water, leaves, &c. See *malov; o kio ti pupus kalo o nawo.* Mao *puhi;* Pol *pupuhi;* Mal. *ambusi.*

Papusa, the soap tree.

Puputa, dark, dirty; at Luwai black, at Maligo and Parira dirty.

Putputmake, a fish.

Puputrag, [*put*] to abuse, insult, in quarrelling and fighting, with stamping.

Pur, to stop by an obstruction, set something in the way.

pur goro, to shut the door: *a Mota nol we pur goro mun o gatava.*

pur wono, to close completely with an obstacle.

pur o kerei, met. to stop the beginning of a race, to cut off a retreat.

pupur goro, to stop, *e. g.* a path, by throwing down or placing branches, sticks, &c.

pupupur, to throw sticks and rubbish from a garden outside the fence, as a protection.

purug, tr. to cover over, as swelling covers a wound; *rave purug.* Mao. *puru;* Fij. *bulu.*

Pura, 1. v. to smash with a blow; *pura ut,* crush with heavy blow.

purarag, smash in quantities.

Pura, 2. n. elephantiasis.

Purat, plenty, many, much, enough.

Purei, 1. adj. inferior, common; *nat-purei,* one who makes a mess of things in the *gamal.*

Purei, 2. adv. for all that, but yet; when a person does what he does not like to do; *o wena—pa na te van purei*, it is raining, but still I will go; *na te tiravag purei*, I will take the blame.

Purepurei, adj. common, not distinguished by skill, or rank in *suqe*.

Purere, to dip in oil or sauce, as *lot* in *lig nai*, *toape* in *lig matig* in the *noganagana*.

purereag, determ. to dip or turn over *toape* in cocoa-nut sauce.

Purgetava, the last behind; should shut the door, *pur gatava*.

Puria, tufa stone.

Purisa, 1. a tree. 2. scab on a *maniga*, same as *purusa* V.

Purug, tr. *pur*; in *ravepurug* swell and cover.

Purus, to break wind; *purus qoe*, puff in contempt.

Purusa, V. blood and matter hardened on a *maniga*, scab; same as *purisa* 2. *te wilit nan*.

purpurusa, rotten, of wood; met. of a man, scabby.

Pusa, 1. to finish off the thatch on ridge of house; *gate pusa goro tiqa o qati ima;* see housebuilding under *ima*.

Pusa, 2. n. the down of birds. v. to stick white down of birds in the hair.

Puso, to exaggerate, in joke, to excite wonder.

Put, to stamp on the ground; 1. in anger, 2. in singing.
1. *putput*, *pupuput*, redupl. to stamp by way of showing and encouraging valour, defy, challenge; *put goro o tavalalea*, defy enemies; *put mun o tavalalea*, encourage friends.

puputrag, intens. redupl. make demonstrations of anger and hatred by stamping and gesticulating; *rowoputput*, to jump about stamping in defiance.
2. to lead off a song, *put raka*, a single singer starting with a stamp, the party joining in.

Pute, to sit; *pute goro*, to sit over against, to guard, watch over, ambush.

pute getget, to sit on the heels; *pute nev*, to sit down on the ground; *pute wotwot*, to sit ready to rise.

putepute, sit repeatedly; *pupute*, *pupupute*, continue sitting; *putpute*, sit closely.

puteg, to make to sit, place; *vaputeg*, *vapteg*.

putei, seat, of the person.

Puteg, tr. *pute*, to seat, make to sit, set, place.

Putegoro, to sit over against, in watching, guarding, in ambush.

Putei, (k) the part that sits, seat of the person.

Pute-kilau, to sit with the back turned.

Pute-magoro, a rotten treestump appears to stand solid, *pute*, when touched it falls to pieces like a *magoro*.

Pute-maken, to sit hungry.

Pute-nitnit-pisui, to sit biting the fingers; met. not knowing what to do.

Puteputetoa, a yam.

Pute-sage-naro, to sit mourning and fasting; *ni gate mule kelkel*, *o qon sanavul ni qara sagesage*.

Pute-sino-maro, to sit silent, in hunger; *sino*.

Pute-sinov, [*sino*] to sit with face on the ground.

Pute-sonorag, to sit with legs stretched out.
Pute-sovasova, to sit panting.
Pute-talasag, [*tala*] to sit for a short time without noticing anything, and then go.
Pute-taroamate, to sit still, like a *taroa*.
Pute-tawalag, to sit with a child, or anything, between the legs.
Pute-tawurpea, to sit with back turned.
Pute-tigawun, to sit with the chin, *wuniu,* propped, *tiga,* on knees.
Putewora, to sit apart, not joining in work.
Puti, [*put* 1.] *mun napuputina,* with his strength.
Putirua, [*put* 2.] two together; *sawai putirua.*
Putoa, 1. adj. curdled, like cooked cocoa-nut milk. 2. adv. dully; *o av we gao putoa,* the wood does not burn well, clogs in black embers.
Putoi, (k) something that stands up round; navel; inner substance of a rod or withe; pistil of flowers.
puto gaqir, the inner *gae* of the *qir,* when the rind is stripped off.
puto lakae, concretion in a clam shell.
putolawalawa, a big, conspicuous navel.
qagala puto magoro, a variety of hibiscus, the pistil like a *magoro* mollusc.
putomera, a mollusc, magilus; child's navel.
puto nawo, standing stone in surf; *puto one,* standing on the sandy beach.
Mao. *pito,* navel, end; Pol. *pito, piko, bito;* Macass. *potji;* Malag. *poitra;* Mal. *pusa;* Pon. *puja.*
Puton, stakes fixed in pairs to stiffen the *paparis;* a bamboo running above tied to *puton* the *salegasuwe.*
Putona, a large black fish.
Putputualan, [*put*] to challenge with loud insult and defiance; *alan.*
Putvanua, one who stirs up to fight and shows his valour, *put,* at home, *alo vanua.*

Q.

Represents a compound of *kpw*.

Qa, 1. excl. explanatory. 2. expletive, moderating the expression, *si qa ilo!* just look; *na qa vava ilo ti,* let me just go and see; *si qa toga rorono,* do be quiet.
Qae, 1. a simple person; with kindly meaning.
Qae, 2. to crackle, a crackling noise.
Qaeqae, the cry of the m*atika.*
Qagala, flowering hibiscus of many varieties; *masomaran, putomagoro, qatman, sogosanavul, uwalava, vusrawe,* &c.
Qagare, 1. a fish, urchin fish.
Qagare, 2. a yam.
Qagav, to handle soft stuff, as *toape.*
Qage, 1. a duck.
Qage, 2. a lily, crinum.
Qageqage, to tie a white band round arm or neck.
Qages, lame; *qages tavaltuwale,* lame on one leg; *qages nirua,* lame on both legs.
Qagqagei, a tree.
Qaia, 1. v. to chop up sago pith. 2. n. the instrument with

which sago pith is chopped up; *o au me vatojo mun o tangae we vanara, we qaia nia.*

3. adv. quickly; *ravrave qaia,* from the rapid motion in chopping.

Qaiareve, long, tall; of man, tree, line, &c. *reve.*

Qakea, an islet close to V.L., frequented by Mota people.

Qalag, to begin a *tapanau* with the first crossing of the leaves, *qalag gona.*

Qalata, dead or dry leaf of banana; *no-qalata.*

Qale, 1. adv. still, yet.

Qale, 2. n. 1. a stick with a crook. 2. a club foot, club-footed. 3. to get with a crook; *ni me la o tangae o qale, me qale sur o wot gariga,* she took a hooked stick, and hooked down the end of a branch.

qaleag, in *qaqaleag.*

Qaleasa, not nice, tasteless, mawkish; *gate wia alo valai, we ronotag pe taqalsai.*

Qaleleag, to stir and mix *toape,* &c., in cocoa-nut sauce.

Qalena, [*lena*] lost to sense, to sight; to forget; *we qalena, we loloqon gaplot o sava; mataqalena; namamatevuna we qalena,* one of whom you would not think it; he says he will take a thing, you think he does not mean it, but he takes it.

Qaleqale, [*qale* 3.] to get with a crook.

Qalevaru, [*qale* 2.] barked branch of hibiscus, *varu,* with cocoanuts, &c., stuck on it.

Qalgai, (k) relative by marriage; *qaliga.*

Qaliga, (k) 1. relative by marriage. 2. to use words made necessary by that relation, to *un.*

Qaligiu, (k) pricking hairs or filaments, as on sugar-cane and some annelids; *qaligi suslelo.*

qaligiaga, covered with pricking hairs, as *tou, suslelo.*

Qalik, small lizards, some dark, some blue with white tail.

Qalnag, [*qalu*] to coil, roll together.

qalnagiu, (k) a coil or roll; bolt of canvas, piece of calico.

Qalo, 1. v. to strike, hit the mark, succeed.

qalo manman, to hit, but with the side of the arrow, so as to *man wia,* wipe, not strike; *qalo nev,* to hit plump, with an arrow; *qalo savsav,* to hit so as to make the feathers fly, *gate qalo mantag we sav vires ului; qalo sisvinvin,* to hit and graze the skin.

adv. with success; *vivir qalo,* to throw and hit, succeed in hitting; *nina qalo,* to reach completely, come right up to.

Qalo, 2. sound or noise; *qalo lea,* message, news; *qalo sava,* sound of something; *o qalo sa? o qalo us, o gaus we toqal;* see also *qaloi* 2.

Qalo, 3. constr. *qaloi.*

Qaloi, 1. (k) 1. the knot in reeds, bamboos, canes, &c. 2. the length between two knots. 3. joints, knuckles; *qalo pisui,* the knuckles outside; *qalo surui,* the knots of joints.

qalo au, a length of bamboo, *qalogaav,* length of *gaav* creeper.

qalo masal, with long space between *qaloi,* of bamboo, reed, &c., *qalo vaon* with short spaces; so 1. *au qalo masal, au qalo vaon* of bamboo; *au* 1. and 2. met. *au qalo masal*, to take long strides in walking; *au qalo vaon*, to take short steps; *au* 2.

Qaloi, 2. [*qalo* 2.] sound, report; *ko we nonom si o tamatetiqa ti toqal aneane, was te qaloqalo gese ran? wa gate qalo lai mun o isar wa mun o qatia, ape o qaloi tagai?* does a gun hit if it makes a noise? and can't you hit with a spear or arrow because it has no report?

Qalon, to open the knots of a bamboo; *vat qalon*, a water-carrier with the knot entire at one end, the knot at the mouth pierced, and the diaphragms throughout knocked open; *vat wot*.

Qalqal, *un* word for *marea* or *qaratu*.

Qalqalelau, a briar.

Qalqalopanei, (k) knuckle-bones, *qaloi*, of the hand.

Qalqalosuriu, (k) joints, knots, of the bones of limbs; *qalqalosur*, a skeleton, remains of dead thing when flesh is dried up, and the *qaloi* are conspicuous.

Qalu, to coil, coil in loops.

   qaluag, tr. to coil; *qaqaluag*, coil like a snake.

   qalunag, *qalnag*, tr. determ. to coil a line.

   qalunag late o tal, to loop back the end of a line too long for the purpose.

   qalnagiu, a coil, a roll; bolt of canvas, piece of calico.

Qalus, *un* word for *nam*, yam.

Qan, constr. *qaniu*, a short person or thing.

Qanerei, [*qan*] end, short ending; at Gatava.

Qanitonito, a short person.

Qaniu, (k) constr. *qan*; 1. the side parts of the end of a house below the eaves, beneath the apex of the gable; *qanqaniima; qanqanilia*, overhanging cave. 2. an obtusely formed space or thing.

Qanoriu, [*qan*] a short thing, tree, speech.

Qantotou, [*qan*] 1. anything that does not grow well, is stunted. 2. one whose beard grows before he is tall; *totou*.

Qanusa, blunt, obtuse; *vanusa*.

Qanusai, a blunt adze or other tool.

Qaora, one who makes friends with anyone and everyone.

Qaqa, wizened, dry and hard; of trees and shrubs too old to bear fruit or flower well.

Qaqae, [*qae* 1.] foolish, a fool; to be delirious.

Qaqaete, [*qaqa*] stunted, not of full size.

Qaqagae, [*qaqa*] a tree branched near the ground.

Qaqaleag, [*qale* 2.] crooked, of a tree.

Qaqaluag, [*qalu*] coiled like a snake or eel.

Qaqaro, foolish, talking nonsense; *qoqoaru*.

Qaqaqaroa tanoma, talking about what one knows nothing of.

Qaqatag, to speak against, same as *vavavag*.

Qara, 1. adv. then or now for the first time; upon this, upon that, then, next; no v. p. used; *nau qara ilogoro mok reremera*.

Qara, 2. v. 1. to cry out loudly, scream; in rudeness, insolence, or in play, rejoicing. *te qaraqara gese, tete apemaragai*, see *pugete; o qara*, a loud impudent woman. 2. to be playful; to rejoice.

qaraqara, n. crying out with joy, rejoicing.
Qarana, (k) a hole, grave, gully, valley; *qaraniu*.
Qaranis, v. to cook in a native oven; n. an ovenful of food; *qaraniu*.
qaranis worwor, food cooked and nothing to eat with it; *o pig tagai ape sinaga*.
Qaraniu, (k) a hole, grave; *qaran vat*, a hole in a rock, *qaran tumate*, a grave.
qarani oloolo, a place to offer, *oloolo,* in, not always a hole; *qaran som,* a place of offering for money; *qaran suqe,* a place of offering for success in *suqe,* also *suqe* oven.
Qarapuna, a disease.
Qarasiu, (k) a hole, orifice; *qaras ninira*.
Qaratu, flying fox.
Qarau, a large cavity with small opening; *o aka we qarau;* v. to eat out the inside of a fruit as a bird or rat does.
Qarig, [*rig* 2.] now, to-day; *aqarig, anaqarig*.
Qaririu, the part of the head above the ear.
Qaro, raw, uncooked, green, unripe; of men in green old age, *qale qaro*.
qaro gagalete, curled by shrinking and not seasoned, as wood.
Qarorovega, with a deep hollow and raised margin; *o manuga we qaroroveya; roro* 2.
Qarqar, same as *qaruqaru*.
Qaru, two, in *tika* numerals.
Qaruga, without a leading shoot; *o tangae we qarqaruga*.
Qaruqaru, a screen of cocoa-nut fronds in a *gamal;* *me keke wora o qarqar*.
Qasa, 1. one, in *tika* numerals.
Qasa, 2. bald; a bald person; a certain *tamate* 3.; *qasa lapematig,* bald as the *lapai* of a cocoa-nut palm, quite hairless.
Qasai, (k) top of head, mountain, stone; rounded, enlarged, part at top, head of pin, &c., thick end of a wedge; *te sususur mun o qatia, o qasai apena; qase um,* the top of the *qarunis* into which the water is poured; *te tivui alo qase um; vawo qasqasana,* on the top of it, a hill.
rowoqasqasevat, to go on stepping stones.
qasqasaga, having a flat rounded top.
Qasamenas, [*qasai*] to talk tête-à-tête.
Qasapule, a dove.
Qasavara, a very strong *Vui* in the story of Qat; ironically used to a weak man doing heavy work.
Qasis, to rub in the closed left hand with the right forefinger boring round, to work leaves small by so rubbing; *we qasis o notangae, we savur goro o mala, wa kita,* rub leaves and scatter them over a sow with young to quiet her; same word with *qesis*.
Qasqasaga, [*ga* 5.] having a *qasai* not a *torai,* said of a cock with little comb.
Qat, 1. a *Vui,* chief figure in stories.
Qat, 2. a secret society with a peculiar dance; the dance of the *qat* society, *we vara o qat; qatu* 2.
Qat, 3. a knob, knob-stick, thick stick.
 4. constr. of *qatiu;* rather root of that word.
 5. v. to club, bring thick together; *neira me qat nalinara,*

K

they agreed together, combined in a plot.
6. prefix in composition, meaning something thick, often a stick used for some purpose, sometimes person or thing.

Qatag, 1. a bunch of leaves tied with *mana* charm, an amulet to keep off arrows, &c., in fighting; *qatagiu*.
2. one who has such an amulet, *we taur o qatag notangae*, is therefore a bold fighter, leader, champion; *o tanasama amaia, o qatag notangae; tete qalo laia alo vagalo, o vavakae nane*.

Qataga, same as *qatag* 2.; *masile*.

Qatagiav, a low rank in the *suqe*.

Qatagiu, constr. *qatag*, a bunch, hank.
qatag som, a hank of money consisting of ten double strings, *tal sanavul*.

Qatagpanei, (k) shoulder, the *qatagiu* of the arm.

Qatanus, [*qat* 4.] the head of the lungs, *anus*, thought to rise in the throat; *we nolo masur o qat anus*.

Qataqata, adv. in a mass, bunch, *qatagiu*; *we gora qataqata*, every one goes.

Qatavuvut, [*qat* 6.] drum-sticks used in the middle of a drum; *avuvut*.

Qatete, the nest of the white ant, *vanoa*.
qatetega, *ga* 5. like a white ant's nest; *o nagoi qatetega*, a short face, not admired.

Qatgagarat, [*qat* 6.] a person with the itch.

Qatgalgaleg, [*qat* 6.] a practiser with charms.

Qatgamemes, [*qat* 6.] one who refuses to pay debts; *gamemes*.

Qatgatowos, [*qat* 6.] a whip stick.

Qatgaus, [*qat* 4.] a charm; *takolo* shells, leaves, tied on the upper end of the bowstring, *ga-us*, to secure the death of one shot with the bow.

Qatgavivis, [*qat* 6.] close-fisted, one who won't part with what he has; *qe ilo snar nonsei, tete la lue lai*.

Qatgelot, [*qat* 3.] stick used as a pestle in making *lot*.

Qatgetapul, [*qat* 3.] stick to *tapul*, throw end over end.

Qatgeuro, a bamboo used to tap upon, for dancing.

Qatgoragora, [*qat* 6.] long stick used by women in turning over the rubbish in preparing gardens.

Qatia, 1. tree fern. 2. arrow-head, needle, of tree-fern wood. 3. an arrow.

Qatiaka, [*qat* 4.] the head, prow, of a canoe.

Qatianago, to pitch as a vessel in a wind.

Qatianoi, a bitter thing to eat or drink, *o sinaga we gogona si o pei*.

Qatianus, [*qat* 4.] the head of the lungs, same as *qatanus*.

Qatiauwa, a banana or cocoa-nut with all the leaves cut off, leaving the central shoot only; *qatiuwa*.

Qatigsar, [*qat* 6.] forked arrow with four prongs for shooting flying fox and fish; *we vene nia*.

Qatiima, [*qat* 4.] the top of a house along the ridge; *we vus o qatiima*, when the ridge is thatched.

Qatiiwa, [*qat* 6.] stick used to *iwa*, carry a burden at both ends over the shoulder.

Qatilina, M. [*qat* 3.] (k) log used as a pillow; *ilina*.

Qatiqati, to lie, deceive.
Qatiu, M. (k) constr. *qat;* head, in primary meaning a knob; common in varying forms in Banks' Ids., as *qat, qotu, qitegi, qi'iyi, qujugi.* N.H. *bwau, botu, qatu, qatugi;* Sol. Ids. *pa'u, ba'u, butu.*
Qatiutag, [*qat* 4.] the head of the cultivated ground, the upper end, nearest to the mountain.
Qatiuwa, [*qat* 4.] turtle's head, standing up like it; *o vetal ti rowo qatiuwa*, when the fruit-stalk first appears, *ti sigag qatiuwa*, when e. g. the leaves having been torn off by the wind the new leaf-shoot stands up by itself; *rur qatiuwa.*
Qatkara, a shell-fish; winkle.
Qatkere, [*qat* 3.] a thick club, knob-stick.
Qatkorkor, [*qat* 6.] a man without heirs, without sister or sister's children; as if a head of *toape* withered, *kor*, from which no leaves can be gathered.
Qatkura, a fish.
Qatlamalama, [*qat* 6.] drumsticks.
Qatlano, [*qat* 6.] sticks to dry *kor* bread-fruit on; *te lano avune um.*
Qatlanon, [*qat* 6.] sticks arranged, *lanon*, over the fire for drying bread-fruit, *kor.*
Qatlava, a petrel, *man qarana*, with big head.
Qatleasag, [*qat* 6.] disputatious, disobedient; *leasag.*
Qatmaaroaro, [*qat* 6.] one who stays by himself, *gate pulpul.*
Qatmaluveluve, [*qat* 4.] broken head; *ta rus wora naqatinsei, was ni me qatmaluveluve.*
Qatman, 1. a red-headed honeyeater, male; cock bird of *tasis.* 2. met. *ko te qatman qarig*, you will have your head broken to-day, red with blood.
Qatmanirnir, [*qat* 4.] a head of hair thin or bald in patches; *manirnir.*
Qatmaragai, a fish.
Qatmaremare, hard-head, met. one who won't hear.
Qatmatalava, [*qat* 4.] the leech of a sail between the *turgae* and the *pane.*
Qatmatau, solid, thick, big.
Qatmate, 1. [*qat* 4.] dead top; *gana qatmate o nam*, to eat up yams leaving nothing to plant. 2. a man without child or successor; *qatkorkor.*
Qatmateima, [*qat* 4.] the lintel of a door; part above the door in which is the *tano ararovag.*
Qatmategetava, same as *qatmateima;* Saddle I. word.
Qatmawui, [*qat* 4.] to make sign of assent, *mawui*, with the head, nod in recognition, acknowledgment.
Qatmona, [*qat* 6.] bundle of *toto* arrows wrapped in *nir matig*, carried to supply combatants.
Qatnoronoro, [*qat* 6.] a little drum made of a length of bamboo; *ti noronoro*, rattles.
Qatmotmot, [*qat* 4.] a short head of hair; *mot.*
Qatnornor, a fish.
Qatpalapala, [*qat* 6.] drum-sticks used by those who *pala* at the ends of the drum.
Qatpalpalai, [*qat* 6.] drum-sticks, used in pairs, *palai.*
Qatpanei, [*qat* 4.] the shoulder, head of arm.
Qatpanpan, [*qat* 4.] upper part, upper slope, of side of valley, *panpan.*
Qatpaparau, [*qat* 4.] *un* word for *lano* 2.

Qatparapara, [*qat* 4.] head carried sideways, *parapara,* turned aside.

Qatperir, [*qat* 4.] head turned aside; *perir.*

Qatpisui, [*qat* 4.] tip of finger or toe.

Qatpulpul, [*qat* 6.] one who is close companion, friend; *we pul vagae.*

Qatqaratu, a fish.

Qatraverave, [*qat.* 6.] 1. a fishing-rod, *te raverave iga nia.* 2. in recent use, pen or pencil.

Qatremeat, [*qat* 4.] the edge of low tide, *meat;* met. *lateg qatremeat.*

Qatsaksakvotur, [*qat* 4.] hair on end, *saka,* as with fright; *votur;* also *qatsakavotur.*

Qatsareia, [*qat* 4.] ragged head, stript of leaves, *sare;* said of *toape.*

Qatsasagatur, [*qat* 6.] something at which the hair stands on end with fright; *sasagatur.*

Qatsasasa, [*qat* 6.] stick for carrying a burden between two men.

Qatsinaga, [*qat* 3.] *un* word for *wowosa.*

Qatsinov, [*qat* 4.] head bent forward, as if to *sinov.*

Qatsuna, [*qat* 6.] the ridge-pole of a house.

Qat-tagiaka, [*qat* 4.] the chief owner of a canoe, captain.

Qat-taltal, [*qat* 6.] the stick used to carry, *reverag,* a basket, *gete,* on the back by its strings, *tal.*

Qat-tamate, [*qat* 4.] a dead man's head; met. one who takes no care for others.

Qat-tiatia, [*qat* 6.] steel-yard, balance to weigh with; a new word; *tiutia.*

Qat-tiatiag, [*qat* 6.] trap, to *tiatiag* with.

Qat-tigatiga, [*qat* 6.] a gag, a short stick tied on end in a pig's mouth; *tiga.*

Qat-tigo, [*qat* 6.] a walking-stick, to support the steps, *tigo.*

Qat-tomago, part of the head of a crawfish near the *mauai;* like the head of a *tomago.*

Qat-towotowo, [*qat* 6.] a rod to measure with; for money or thatch, a reed; *towo.*

Qat-towotowos, [*qat* 6.] a stick to flog with, *towos.*

Qatuluna, (k) pillow; V.

Qatvanua, [*qat* 6.] all the country at once, all the place; *ni me valago qatvanua si a taso goro kamam,* he ran across all the country to meet us.

Qatvanisnis, [*qat* 6.] something mysterious; *we qatvanisnis, we vava vagae ape gene o tanun gate gilala apena,* men whisper together, no one knows what about; *vanis* same as *vagis.*

Qatvisarag, [*qat* 6.] one who works well, acts with force, *visarag,* shifts for himself.

Qatvuv, [*qat* 4.] head with hair cut very short; *vuv.*

Qatwirtamot, the great toe with the skin broken, and sore, *o manuga apena; qat wirita,* head of octopus.

Qatwolowolo, [*qat* 4.] the head full face; *wolowolo* not *parapara.*

Qatwono, [*qat* 6.] heavy, dull, obstinate; thick-headed; *we matur qatwono,* sleep heavily; superlative adverb; *wono.*

Qatwosowoso, [*qat* 6.] stick used to hammer in a fence; in recent use, hammer.

Qatwowe, cry in swimming or in paddling by night, the word being sung.

Qatwut, [*qat* 4.] lousy head, *wut.*

Qatoqato, short ; same as *qatutui.*

Qatqat, [*qat* 4.] 1. a head of *toape* with only short leaves left, inferior quality ; *mule gin o qatqat.*
rotqatqat, a bundle of small *toape* leaves ; met. a poor head of hair, *o qatiu o rotqatqat.*
2. a lot of poor things, a poor lot ; *loglog qatqat tavine,* nothing but a lot of women.

Qatqatmemea, [*qat* 4.] head reddened as a distinction in a *kolekole,* same as *urai non Qat.*

Qatu, 1. a fish.

Qatu, 2. a heliconium, from which probably *qatu* 3. is named.

Qatu, 3. the secret society *qat* 2.; and its dance.

Qatua, short.
qatuai, a short thing or person.

Qatualito, a short man, tree, line ; probably met. from log of firewood, *lito.*

Qatuate, to put out the head, *qatui,* and look, *ate.*

Qatui, V. (k) constr. *qatu, qat;* same as *qatiu.*

Qatutui, constr. *qatut,* adj. in form n. ; short ; *qatut som,* a short string of money ; *qatut tanun,* a short man.

Qatuuwa, V. same as *qatiuwa.*

Qaui, (k) 1. knee ; *o qaui we vile rua,* knock-kneed.
2. a turn in a song ; *ape sa we sur narnare o tuan qau as?* be behind at the turn.

Qaunalovlov, [*nalo*] to swallow without chewing, as *lot.*

Qauqaumatika, 1. crooked kneed like a *matika.* 2. with a kink, in a line, like *qau matika.*

Qauro, a yam that grows wild, but is sometimes planted ; *qauro latelate, qauro vusa,* varieties.

Qauro-uro, time of scarcity when *qauro* is eaten.

Qautogo, said of anything stuck full of arrows.

Qava, to cover over, as a hole with a stone, leaving hollow space, as in covering with a basket or box turned over.

Qe, 1. excl. surprise, admiration.

Qe, 2. v. p. conditional, potential.

Qea, a stage for stores, platform on piles ; to construct a stage or platform, *we las o qea;* Sol. Id. *bwea.*

qearag, tr. v. to make level like a *qea.*

qeasag, tr. v. to press down, flatten.

qean, tr. v. to flatten.

qeaqea, stage in canoes.

taqeaqea, level, flat.

Qean, [*qea*] tr. v. to flatten ; *qean taqai,* begin to level down and smooth the inside of a canoe which has been chopped hollow, *pari.*

Qeaqea, the deck or stage of rods of *varu* or bamboo which covers the ends of the upper *irav* part of a canoe, *aka paspasau.*

Qearag, [*qea*] to press down and make smooth and flat, as in making *lot patau.*

Qeasag, [*qea*] to flatten down with force, crush down ; *qeasag wora,* to flatten and crush apart ; *qeasag gagagao,* to go along, crushing down the overgrowth with legs and arms, *gagao,* as a man in an overgrown path.

Qega, 1. to be empty of liquid when the liquid has gone ; *o wetov me qega,* there is nothing left in the bottle. 2.

to be gone, exhausted, of liquid; *o pei me qega nan o pue*, the water is all gone from the bamboo water-carrier; *tur sarsavula gega o pue nawo nan*, empty all the salt-water carrying bamboos with washing your hands. 3. met. to come to nothing, nothing left; *o linai me qega*, no voice left.

Qei, excl. astonishment.
Qel, see *qelu*.
Qela, invisible, bewildering sight; *mataqelaqela*.
Qele, adv. still, yet; said by some for *qale* 1.; not dialectic.
Qelse, out of tune, said of a *vigo*, panpipes, with improper intervals, or of a man who cannot sing right; probably *qelu*.
Qelu, 1. to be crooked over in a loop, but not enough to meet; a stick with such a crook; probably same as *pelu*.
2. club-footed, with the foot turned over; club-fingered.
3. v. active, to bend over in a crook, as softened turtle-shell.
Qeqe, to squeeze, press. Mao. *pepe*.
 qeqen, tr. to press down, not evenly; to squeeze; *we qeqen o womol; nau qeqen*, chew with mouth shut.
 qeqet, tr. to press down gently and evenly.
Qeren, to press down; same as *qeret*; tr. *qere*.
Qeresa, to clear the end of a yam in digging it; see *aqo* 2.
Qerestomago, a trochus shell; like *qeres tomago*.
Qeresai, (k) the lower soft end of a yam; *qeresa*.
Qeresiu, (k) constr. *qeres*, the lower end of a yam which is soft, still growing, when the yam is dug.
Qeret, tr. *qere*; to press, push; *o vigo qerqeret*, harmonium, because the fingers *qeret* to produce the sound; *na we kakalo, we qeret mun o panei*, I crawl, resting on my hands.
 qerqeret, adv. depressed, *nom qerqeret*, to be downcast, doubtful.
Qero, 1. n. 1. fungus, mushroom. 2. inner fat of pigs, in shape like fungus, conglomerated; *qeroqoe*.
2. v. to conglomerate; *o sul we qero ma*, congregates in groups.
 qeroqero, a rounded cloud, fleecy.
Qerovlug, a yam; *qero ta Valuga*.
Qes, to twist off, as in gathering bread-fruit; *qes patau*.
Qesa, to lodge, as a *tika* in a tree or elsewhere.
Qesis, same as *qasis*, to rub small in the hand as is done with hot bitter leaves after a man has been shot; these are eaten or rubbed on the bow to inflame the wound; *ti qesis alo panena, ti gana, ti nononon nausuna nia*.
Qet, to be complete, completed; finished; to come or go all; adv. completely. Mao. *peti*. *sua qet*, to paddle only, without sailing.
Qeta, 1. caladium esculentum; taro; *qeta mereata*, very large. 2. name of a yam.
Qetaqeta, wild *qeta*; *no-qetaqeta*, dieffenbachia.
Qete, to begin; stem of following words.
 qetei, (k) a thing which is truly one's own, beginning with one; *naqetena, na tur mona*.

qeteg, to begin, act. neut., to begin to be, become.
qetegiu, (k) beginning, stem, root-stock, origin.
Qetegmatig, a kind of yam; like cocoa-nut stem.
Qetegqatia, stem of tree-fern; met. a very dark man.
Qetegvanua, (k) 1. place of family or birth. 2. one belonging to a place by family or birth.
Qetegwono, large, round, squat in figure; *o qetegiu we wono.*
Qetqetmanu, a word whistled for concealment, not spoken; as the *qatman* whistles; *wosgalegale.*
Qet-tamate, a yam; for *qat.*
Qiare, a fish, thorn-tail, seasurgeon.
Qil, to bargain, arrange, make a bargain with or about; *we qil o tanun,* hire a man, *we rava amoa apena; ira ta Roua we qil o iya mun o nam,* the Roua people exchange fish for yams, by bargain; *me qil inau ti apena,* according to an arrangement made with me. Probably same word with *wol.*
Qilin, to shake from below; as a rope, or torch.
qilin lawalawa, to shake a torch till it flames.
qilin rave, a way of catching, *rave,* flying foxes; men below shake, *qilin,* torches of *nomatig,* the *qaratu* fly out in confusion and are knocked down.
Qilo, a pool of salt-water.
qilog, tr. to make a pool.
Qiloi, (k) the part below the navel, same as *quloi.*
Qilosiu, hollow in stone or tree in which water lodges; *qilos vat, qilos tangae.*

Qilowar, an unmarried person; generally young; *naro qilowar,* one remaining unmarried in mourning.
Qilqilog, [*qilo*] to make a vessel of *no-mata, no-via,* by supporting it round with sticks and stones to hold water; sometimes pronounced *qilqilon.*
Qiqiare, a tree.
Qiqilo, mangrove.
Qiqlon, same as *qilqilog; gis qiqlon,* to do something secretly, so that it should not come out.
Qir, 1. a creeping plant; *gaqir.*
Qir, 2. v. to be close together; *vaqirqir.* Mao. *piri;* Pol. *pili;* Motu N.G. *hebiri;* Mal. *ambiri.*
Qiroso, to close with stopper; *qiroso goro mate wetov mun o mateqiroqiroso.*
Qis, 1. n. mash, pap; for pigs, food mixed with *luve;* for infants, dried bread-fruit, *kor,* chewed and cooked in *laqan;* softened food; v. to make the *qis,* for infants or pigs; *maqisqis.*
Qis, 2. to bend the hand with stiffened fingers so as to catch something against a corner; *we qisqis o malan;* to squeeze with the hand so bending.
Qisa, to press, crush.
Qisan, tr. to press upon, heavily down.
qisanwono, n. heavy sorrow, distress.
Qismera, one on whom abortion has been produced by squeezing, *qis,* with the hand; *mera* l.
Qisoso, stuffed; *o linai we qisoso,* voice is gone because throat stuffed up; *soso.*
Qit, to fan, to shake so as to fan

and make burn brightly; *we qit o nomatig*, lifting up and shaking the torch so that it may be seen far off; *aqit*.

Qoa, to take things without asking; *ui me qoa gap*.

Qoas, to bind on, roll round with, a thick band; *te qoaqoas goro ranoi mun o vin man*, protect a sore on the sole of the foot by tying on cocoa-nut husk.

Qoe, 1. a pig, male pig, barrow pig; any kind of quadruped. Common Mel. *qo, bo, po, pui*; Mal. *babi*. 2. v. to act like a pig, make a mess; *me qoe avunama*. 3. adj. large; *mania qoe, marea qoe, taqale qoe*.

Qoga, a tree; has a certain sacred character; *rawo qoga*; see *varowog*.

Qogorai, (k) constr. e. the knot at the base of a branch; v. to come out like a knot; *o wote tangae ti qogorai lue ma*.

Qogotiu, a dwarf.

Qolago, a barrel; new word, the old word *lago*.

Qoleqole, tangled, of hair in small thin tufts or ringlets.

Qolilin, on one side; *ate qolilin*.

Qolo, 1. a fish.

Qolo, 2. lying close together. 3. double as kernels of *nai*, *make*, *qolo rua*; *qolovisa*, so many close together.

qolon, tr. to make lie close together; *te qolon o kor we tuk*, to put stones on dried breadfruit in soak so as to keep them down; same as *takura*.

Qolor, money, *som*.

Qoloviovio, a fish.

Qolovisa, how many? so many, lying together.

Qolqolega, curly in ringlets, of hair; *qoleqole*.

Qolul, one who invents stories, boasts of things not true.

Qomate, 1. dead pig, corresponding to *tamate* 1., a pig killed at a feast.

Qomate, 2. a tree.

Qomulemule, the name of a man who used to bring a small yam to the common oven, *qaranis*; anyone so doing is called *Qomulemule*.

Qona, a pigeon.

qona rena, a green pigeon; *qona tauwe*, mountain pigeon, *we logo* with a lump on its forehead; *qona wotuenai*, a small pigeon which sits on the tips of *nai* branches.

Qonag, [*qona*] to be shy, jealous; *qonag goro*, shy of, jealous of; *vaqonqonag*, apprehend danger.

Qonaqona, a tree.

Qonaronotoga, to blow heavily in squalls with intervals of calm: *o lan ti qonaronotoga*.

Qonasagerua, two pigeons sitting together, *sage* 1.; name of a hill in V.L.

Qon, night, darkness, to be dark; in regard to time, day, time, season; *qon silsil*, dark time of night; *tineqon*, midnight. Common throughout the Ocean; Jav. *bungi*; Marshall, *bung*; D.Y. *bung*; Sol. Ids. *boni*; N.H. *boni, poni, pong, ping*; Bks. Ids. *qon, qen*; Fij. *bogi*; Motu N.G. *boi*; Pol. *po*; Ponape, *bong*.

Qonlau, a sea-lion.

Qonove, a fish.

Qonqon, 1. very dark; *matava qonqon*, the morning while still dark; *qon*.

Qonqon, 2. the sound of the cry of the pilage; *ti murmur, nalinana o qonqon mur*.

Qonut, a short stumpy man.
Qoqo, 1. many, to be many.
Qoqo, 2. to set, of fruit, to bud of flowers.
   qoqoi, the bud of flowers, first setting, showing of fruit.
Qoqoaru, unintelligible noises; *matur qoqoaru*, to groan and talk in sleep.
Qoqoleag, curled in little ringlets; *qoleqole*.
Qoqorosiga, [*qoroi*] having first show of leaf-shoots; *ti qorqorosiga, rigrig te sasalit*.
Qoqotave, [*qoqo* 2.] set but undeveloped, of fruit.
Qoqovara, the shoot, *qoqoi*, of the growing cocoa-nut, *vara*.
Qor, to turn round and round.
   qoriag, tr. stir round, whirl.
Qora, 1. a coil of line, or of money.
Qora, 2. to back water with the paddle.
Qorarau, thick-headed, dull, does not attend; *qatwono*.
Qore, to dream, dream of a person or thing.
   qore mot, to dream a man to death by means of a magic stone.
   qoreqore, a dream.
Qoriag, [*qor*] to whirl about, as surf; *qoriag risris*, whirl and turn over and over.
Qoro, to throw down something heavy; *munqoro*.
   qoron, tr. to beat upon, be heavy on.
   qoro lito, to throw down firewood, *alo panito*, in the corner of the house.
Qoroi, (k) ear, not the orifice but the outer part; pectoral fin of a fish; shooting leaves of caladium; young bud; tendril, of plants; knot on the back of a bow, *qoro us*.

Common Bks. Ids., northern N.H.; Celebes, *boronga*; N.H. *qero, qerogi*, shows *qoroi* same as *qero*.
Qorosa, adj. eared, with points, projections.
Qorogatagata, noise, noisy.
Qoron, tr. *qoro*, in *so-qoron*; *kamiu me qoron mun o lan, o rep, o wena*, having come through a storm.
Qorosa, with projecting *qoroi*; *ragae qorosa*, to finish off with a knot; *sa* 3.
Qorowiswis, whizzing sound in the ear, as after a sharp report.
Qorowiuwiu, singing in the ears, *wiu*, from fatigue; *tama we vivtig o muleva*.
Qorowono, deaf; *naqorona we wono*.
Qorowonwon-te-mel, extremely deaf; *melmel*.
Qorqoroi, (k) redupl. *qoroi*; shell of the ears; tendrils of plants; not climbing tendrils.
Qorqorolava, big ears; rank in *suqe*; a *tamate* 2. image representing the rank, carried about in *kolekole*, set up in *gamal*.
Qorqoron-ta-rur, one who does not notice reproof; *tama si naqorqorona me rur*, as if his ears had been cropped. *rur* 1.
Qorqorosa, adj. with *qoroi* projections; 1. as a plant gemming for leaf, not yet budding, *qoqo* 2.; 2. with the leaf showing at the tip of the leaf-shoot as in *sasa*, crotons; 3. as a pimply nose.
Qortanaro, ears of Tanaro; the fruit of *tawan* not quite ripe.
Qos, to exaggerate, boast; same as *pos*.
Qosai, an imperfect, worthless thing; *qose patau*, a breadfruit not yet fit for food.

Qoso, same as *qos*.

Qosorooro, poor; nothing but *orooro*; worthless, *qosai*, rubbish, *orooro*.

Qosus, very short.

Qotaptara, one who is self-confident, thinks he can do something difficult, such as cutting out a canoe, and fails; called *i Qotaptara*, after a man of that character and name.

Qote, anything lumpy in form; *surun qote*.

qotela, adj. lumpy, thick; *na qoronsei ti qotela, we poa*, when it swells.

Qotoga, one who stays at home; a pig, *qoe*, that stays about, *toga*, the place.

Qou, excl. of astonishment. *qou vasaleag*, to drive away with a cry *qou!* as a thief.

Qulo, young, fresh, succulent.

quloi, (k) something young, fresh.

quloga, adj. fresh, young.

Quloi, 1. [*qulo*] something young and fresh; a newly born child, a young plant.

Quloi, 2. V. same as *qiloi* M.; *kere quloi*, lower part of abdomen.

Qulolava, large while young; *wota qulolava*.

Quloquloga, [*qulo*] strong growing, fresh-looking, of a child; free growing, lush, of plants.

Qure, ignorant, unskilled, foolish; opposed to *menaro*.

qurega, [*qa* 5.] n. ignorance, foolishness.

Qus, to have the mouth full, cheeks distended with food.

Qusa, V. same as M. *qisa*, to press down, pound, crush; *te qusa o patau mun o ratgelot*, in making *lot*; *we qusa o qatiima, qara paso*, the last thing done in thatching the ridge of a house, otherwise *vus*.

R.

R, 1. pers. pron. pl. 3. suffixed to poss. n.; *nor, mor, gar;* same as *ra* 3.; of them.

R, 2. tr. suffix to v.; *koko, kokor*.

Ra, 1. sign of plural, with regard to persons only, often with pers. art. *i*; *ra tamak, ira tatasik, ra ta Motalava*; also, the persons with, the company of, a person named, *ira* Bishop, the Bishop's people, he and those with him. See *ira*.)

2. pers. pron. pl. 3.; after v. and prep.; same as *ra* 1.; makes part of *ineira*; never subject of v.; never properly represents inanimate things; them.

3. the same in the series of pron. suffixed to n.; *napanera* their hands; of them.

Ra, 4. adjectival termination; n. *ligiu* fluid, adj. *ligligira* fluid.

Ra, 5. term. of verbal nouns; *toga* to abide, *togara* way of life.

Rae, M. a fruit tree; V. *rau*.

Rag, verbal suffix. 1. trans. determ. 2. intens. particularly of number.

Ragai, [*ra* 1., *gai* 2.] 1. demonstr. pr. pl. 3. those persons; 2. [*gai* 3.] pl. vocative, you!

Ragera, [*ra* 1., *gai* 2., *rua*] 1. demons. pr. dual 3. they two, them two, those two; 2. [*gai* 3.] voc. you two!

Ragetol, [*ra* 1., *gai* 2., *tol*] 1. demonstr. pr. trial, 3. they three, them three, those three; 2. [*gai* 3.] voc. you three!;

may refer to more than three, if no great number.

Ragragai, a tree that branches near the ground; bush.

Rait, to fit tight, to be firm when tied or bound.

Rak, a fish.

Raka, 1. adv. 1. up, of direction upwards; *raka rowo* in direction, *raka sage* high up, in place, and superlative, highly; see *iraka, gisraka, tavaraka*. 2. for the first time, in the first place; *ti ligo raka o rawe* he begins by tying up a pig of that kind.
2. v. to lift up, take up, get up.
    rakasag, tr. determ. turn up.
3. descriptive prefix with numerals when strokes, blows, are numbered; *me towosia; raka visa? raka vat;* he was flogged; with how many strokes? four; represents the raising of the arm to strike.
4. v. to increase the quantity of money given for *tamate* or *suqe; te rene mun o som, te sar kel; ta tete tira, te raka mon o som.*

Raka-ava, [*raka* 2.] to take up the wrong thing, and leave what ought to have been taken; *ava* 1.

Raka non ro Sommaimai, proverbial saying when one does what a woman of that name did, goes for a fire-stick and takes the fire away.

Rakaqau, to fall over a tree, &c. in the wood; *qaui*.

Rakaraka, 1. adv. redupl. *raka* up; *ravinir rakaraka* to pull up, e. g. bananas closely planted, so as to make room; *meat rakaraka* ebb at spring tides.

Rakaraka, 2. n. a single arrow.

Raka-reag, to take up away from something left behind.

Rakasag, [*raka* 2.] to turn over cut stuff that it may dry; a stage in preparing gardens, *we unia, we rakasag, we tara, we sin, we nur*.

Rakavisa, [*raka* 3.] how many strokes.

Rakavtag, to take up from other things; *raka* 2. *vitag*.

Raketea, a piece of higher ground, a hillock.

Rakut, impers. v. to pain one severely; *rono rarakut*, suffer severe pain.

Ram, 1. a crab, crawfish, with *rameai*, eggs.
    rame, v. to cover with eggs; *o rameai ti rame o gatou*.
    rameai, (k) the eggs of crawfish, crabs, &c.

Ram, 2. to anoint with *ramiai; ram vires nagoi*.
    ramiai, the liquor of a cocoa-nut that has begun to grow, *vara* forming in it; not drinkable, *o nene ti arosa niu*.
    ramis, to roughen the throat, be astringent, like *ramie vara; garamis*.

Ramo, to draw, drag; to adopt a child; the proper term for pulling a bunch of bananas, *we ramo o vetal*.
    we ramo nan o sus, to wean a child.
    o aka we ramo kel, when it turns back on its course.
    ramos, tr. to draw.
    ramova, drawing, adoption.

Ramoparu, to shine; *peruperu*.

Ramos, to draw towards one, pull together; *ti ramramos o notantangue; ramo*.

Ran, adv. entirely, thoroughly, throughout; with notion of distance, *ran ma* all the time hitherto from a certain period, always up to the present.

Ranai, to roast or bake over embers, without a wrapper; *laqan ranranai*, bake on embers in thin wrapper. Sam. *lagilagi*.

Raniu, hard ground; *raran tangae*.

Rano, 1. constr. of *ranoi*.

Rano, 2. to become dry, dried up, in course of nature; to die out, as fire.

Ranoal, [*rano* 1., *al* 1.] vagabond, going about on foot.

Ranoi, (k) leg and foot, of men and animals. Malag. *ranjo*.

Ranoqaloqalo, pettitoes of a pig; *ranoi*, *qaloi*.

Ranolelete, legs [*ranoi*] stiff with standing; *lete*.

Ranomara, dove's leg; *lateg ranomara*, to bend the reeds on which yam vines are trained, with a break near the ground, making a short part as of a leg below; *lateg*.

Ranorano, shrub, acalypha; many varieties.

Ranovanovano, vagabond, always going about, afoot; *ranoi*, *vano*.

Ranrania, [*raniu* 2.] a tree bare of leaves.

Rap, V. 1. to climb. *ti rap avune tangae ti tara na wotwotina.* 2. met., of disease, to increase upon. *o gopae me rap avunansei, me rap kalo ma, me rap lue ma, me rapia, paso nan me sola sur.* 3. to rise as land when rapidly approached; *we sua susua, si rara ilo ma o tauwe we lava we sage raprap goro rara ma.*

raptag, tr. determ. climb upon, climb for a person; see *vegatag*.

Rapa, to make even, so avenge, revenge; *te rapa munsei apensei*, revenge upon the injurer the wrongs of the injured; *te rapa apenau*, avenge me, take revenge for me; *te rapa munia*, execute revenge upon him; *we rapa gak o qoe*, make even in counting in *tika*.

rapat, tr. revenge; *ilokenake na we rapat nau*.

Rapai, to support by a prop, strengthen by support.

Raprapit, to be disagreeable to one; *ni me valago raprapit neia*.

Raptag, V. [*rap*] 1. to climb to a thing, for a person. 2. met. do again and again; *rara me raptag ragatar*, two men quarrelled, were separated, but went at it again and again.

Rapus, to wash, lave, as water does a rock; probably tr. *rap*.

Rara, 1. pers. pr. dual 3. they, them, two.

Rara, 2. v. to dry before a fire. Pol. *rara, lala*; Motu N.G. *raraia*; Macas. *rarang*.

Rara, 3. n. 1. erythrina, coral tree. 2. the season in which the *rara* flowers, winter. Sam. *laulala*.

rara tano, a creeping erythrina.

Raramo, delay long drawn out, *ramo*; *ni me ge mun nau we raramo*, he vexed me with delay.

Raran, v. 1. dazzle by reflection; *o one ti raran o matai*. 2. be reflected, of light, colour; *me raran, o lama qara memea apena*, there was a red reflection on the sea. Fl. *rarana*, reflection of colour.

raraniu, (k) 1. reflection of light or colour; *raran one* in

*rar*an 1. above ; *raran rat* in *raran* 2.
Raraniu, 2. hard dry ground ; *raran tangae*, ground hard near roots of trees; *raniu;* perhaps *rara* 2.
Rarao, to weep, cry ; referring to the noise.
  raraog, tr. cry with regard to something; see *var-raraog.*
Rararau, [*rau*] to go grubbing for *sese,* &c. on the reef, or for land crabs, *gave,* in the bush.
Rarav, an erythrina that grows tall and straight.
Raravea, shortness of food ; *maran raravea,* hungry time ; *masu raravea,* short crops of fruit.
Raro, [*ra* 1.] fem. pl. prefix to names and designations ; see *ro.*
Rarua, pers. pr. dual 3. they, them, two ; *ra* 1.
Ras, 1. far ; *aras,* afar ; very ; same as *rasu* 1.
Ras, 2. v. to approach, *rasu* 2.
Ras, 3. v. to rub, scrape, scratch ; same as *rasa.*
  iras, a baler.
  ras o pei, scrape up, bale out, water from a canoe.
  ras o lena, perform a woman's dance, scraping the ground with the feet.
Rasa, to scrape, scratch, rub, with straight motions backwards and forwards ; so, to sharpen by rubbing backwards and forwards on a stone.
  rasa gagao, to wear level ; *o malo me rasa gagao,* a rock washed by the sea.
  rasag, tr. to rub, scrape, sharpen by rubbing ; *vatrasag,* whetstone.
Rasalele, a fish like a sole, said to be scraped thin ; *lele.*

Rasgaruwe, to make yam holes too near ; as the *garuwe* crabs scratch, *ras,* their holes in the sand.
Raso, to bale out ; *me raso o mino,* the pool is baled out.
Rasoai, [*ra* 1.] husband or wife ; *soai.*
Rasqoqo, to rise above the ground as a yam does which has been planted in a shallow hole, as it rises *o nam we ras o tano.*
Rasras, 1. a dance which women *ras* 3. ; *o lena.*
Rasras, 2. adv. exceedingly ; *natiu rasras* very small ; is said to be from *ras* 3., not *ras* 1.
Rasu, 1. 1. far, *arasu,* afar ; same as *ras* 1. ; *ma rasu,* from far. 2. met. superlative, *we wia resu,* exceedingly good.
Rasu, 2. to come near, arrive, with *ma* hither. Maewo *rasu* come or go.
Rasun, scatter, sprinkle, as with water.
Rata, level ground, plain. Mal. Jav. Dy. *rata;* Malag. *ratana;* Tagal. *datig.*
Rato, to rebake *sinaga* that has been cooked before ; *ruto o malas.*
  raton, tr. cook over again ; *varaton.*
Ratol, [*ra* 1.] pers. pron. trial 3. they three, them three ; used also for more than three, if not many.
Rau, 1. n. V. a fruit tree ; M. *rae.*
Rau, 2. v. to put in the hand, as into a bag.
  raun, tr. to put the hand in and take something ; *raun lue,* take out of a bag, *e.g.* with the hand; *raraun loloi* said of *gea,* when one who has eaten his fill, drinks *gea* and is hungry

again ; *o gea o raraun toge tanun*.
Rararau, to search with the hand in holes on reef or in bush.
Raurau, a yam.
Rav, dusk, stem of *marav, ravrav*, &c.
Rava, 1. an aroid, *tacca pinnatifolia*, of which native arrowroot is made.
Rava, 2. a yam.
Ravarava, a pipe-fish.
Rave, 1. to draw, pull ; active.
rave loas, to drag and flog.
rave pup, to draw a knot tight; *rave ul*, to draw out a slipknot.
rave sansan, to spoil by drawing, as a canoe often drawn down into the sea.
rave saru, to drop or lose things in pulling away what they rest upon.
rave totomot, to draw quickly away ; from drawing away fingers lest they should be chopped off ; *toto, mot*.
rave wora, to draw apart.
rave o vetal, to pull a bunch of bananas.
2. to draw out fish, to catch fish, to fish ; with a line.
rave nunuuwa, to go very early fishing.
3. to put out new leaves ; *o tangae me kor, o wena we poa, ti rave nanaunauna apena*.
4. to draw a line, a figure ; in recent use to write.
5. neut. to draw, be drawn ; *rave wora*, to draw apart ; of pain, *rave gingin, rave mar siwo;* to withdraw.
rave purug, to swell and cover over the wound, as a *tano qatia* an arrow wound.
raveg, tr. drag a person or thing.

raveag, tr. to draw through ; to withdraw, neut. ; *raveag rorono* to withdraw without speaking.
raveag, adv. through : *raveaglue*, through and out, right through.
ravraveag, adv. striped.
Ravegingin, [*rave* 5.] of deepseated pain that pricks, catches, *gin*.
Ravenoro, to pull and knock at the door ; *noro*.
Raverua, 1. to be drawn together by two strings, as a bag.
Raverua, 2. the season when yams are planted ; scarcity of food.
Raveve, (k) [*ra* 1.] mother ; in pl. form sing. meaning.
Ravis, to make thin, of the person ; food continually the same *te ravisiko* ; see *garavis*.
Ravrav, evening, the dusk of evening.
ravrav mataruarua, dusk.
Ravraveag, [*rave* 4.] striped.
Ravravelulua, [*rave* 5.] to have a feeling of sickness, *lulua*.
Ravravenosin, 1. to pull cocoanut fronds to burn in night fishing, *no-sin*. 2. met. to fly into the bush in a fright.
Ravraveqaia, long waiting ; when one party waits long for the other side in a game at night, they say this.
Ravravetoa, [*rave* 5.] twitching, in the beginning of tetanus.
Ravravtapera, game, trying who shall clean up the dish first ; *we ganagana oraora* ; *Inina ravrav tapera !*
Raw, to sing in a low voice ; *raw maran*, sing all night as in a *gamal* ; *rawraw, rawn*.
Rawarawa, long slip or slide ; *sis rawarawa*.

Rawe, an hermaphrodite pig, female.
rawe toketoke, one that grunts, *ti toke ape mala*.
rawe wosowoso, one that champs its teeth, behaves like a boar.

Rawea, thin, of man or animal.

Rawu, same as *raw; rawu maran*.

Re, sign of plural, like *ra* 1.; makes no part of pronouns; applied only to persons with regard to age and relationship, when the whole class of such persons is spoken of; such terms of relationship with *re* do not take the suffixed pronouns; *o retatasiu* the set of brothers, *ratatasik* my brothers; redupl *rere*.
relumagav, rerelumagav, the young men; *remama*, fathers and uncles on father's side; *reremera*, boys, and boy; *rereatu*, men folk; *retamai, retamtamai*, fathers, men of the father's generation; *retasiu, retatasiu*, brothers, or sisters; *retavine*, women folk; *retaunu*, strangers in the place; *retutuai*, brothers, or sisters; *revananoi*, sister's children, *revavine* V. women folk; *reveve*, mothers.
With these terms the article *o*, or personal art. *ira*, are both used; *o rereata, ira rereata*.

Rea, 1. a barren open patch, on recent volcanic vent; one only at Mota on shoulder of the hill, *vawo rea; ne re* on Saddle I.

Rea, 2. a kite, of sago fronds; *we rino o noota apena*. 3. anything light like a kite.

Reag, 1. adv. away from something; with motion away from something, leaving something behind; *la reag*, take away from something to be left. 2. v. to move, advance; *reag poa*, increase.

Reatuqei, [*rea* 1.] a number of gardens all in one open space.

Reg, 1. to put out the head: *rereg, vareg*.

Reg, 2. to wilt over fire; also *rei*.

Reke, stem of *marekereke; nom rekereke*.

Rekiu, a fish.

Remama, the fathers, set, class, of fathers in a village; *iragai o nanat remama*, those whose fathers are alive, not orphans.

Remarema, small; *wota remarema*, born small and not growing.

Remrem, small; *wena remrem*, small rain.

Ren, appliances, weapons, tools; *renren*.

Rena, 1. a fish, from its colour, see *rerena*.
2. a parrot.

Renas, a green and yellow parrot; trichoglossus palmarum; from its colour; *rerena*.

Rene, (k) burden, load, cargo; *narenena o tapera*.
rene sogonia, large, various, freight.
rene tulagia, another person's load; *o rene monsei we sea, ko te la ma*.

Reniu, a small thing or person; *ren tanun*, a little lean man.

Rep, waves, tide rip; *o rep ti towtowola*, waves roll along; also *repu*. Sam. *lepu*.
rep qatgasuwe, waves with pointed tops, like rats' heads, in a tide rip.

Repes, *un* word for *pug*, debt.

Rere, 1. see *rerere*, to tremble. Mao. *rere*.

Rere, 2. set of sea, current; Mao. *rere.*
rere aka, the wake of a canoe.
rerevag, tr. determ. to carry in a current.
Rerea, 1. [*rere*] small stream running through the reef at low tide; *te tarina o gape ape kere rerea.*
Rerea, 2. the shoulder of the hill; where *rea* 1. is.
Rereata, the male persons, plural of *mereata* in usage, but *re; ata* male.
Rereg, 1. to stretch out the head and neck, as in looking out for something; *nolo rerereg.*
rereg taaloalo, to stretch forward and peer; *rerereg laulau,* the same; *reg* 1.
Rereg, 2. to wilt a leaf over the fire to make it soft; *reg* 2.
Rerei, V. same as *rereg* 2.
Rereke, [*reke*] to dodge an arrow by drawing up shoulders and drawing down the head.
Rerelumagav, the youths of a place.
Reremera, boys, *re,* mera; but also a boy, plural in form, singular in meaning; see *raveve.*
Rerena, the yolk of an egg; from yellow colour; Sam. *lega.*
Rereosa, slender.
Rerere, to tremble, shake, with fear; redupl. *rere* 1.
vara rerere, stagger; *sur-rere,* quaking of bones, fear.
tarerere, unsteady.
Reret, to reach out, stretch out the arm after something.
valago rereret, run to catch, touch.
Rerevag, to carry away, make to drift, of wind and tide; to drift; *rere* 2. Sam. *lelea.*
Rerevanvanoi, the set of mothers' brothers whom children in a village look to.
Rereve, to fish for flying-fish; probably *rave* 2.
Rereveag, [*reve*] to go a long way round.
Resa, 1. variegated in stripes of colour; *o resa,* a pig red and black in stripes.
2. a fish, bodian, pristipoma.
Retamai, the set of fathers in a place; *o retamtamai; re.*
Ret, at the edge, extremity; *nugnug ret.*
tano retret, to touch at the extreme edge; *o maue gire ape ulusui retret,* the *mauai* of the pandanus are at the ends of the branches all round the tree.
Retawu, strangers visiting or resident in a place.
Reug, a bird, in V.L.
Reve, 1. long, extended, to be drawn out; *mauareve,* of a tree with long tips to the branches.
o lama we reve nan ilo vanua, the sea runs in places into the land; *o vanua we reve rowo ilo lama,* the land runs out into the sea; *we reve goro,* stretches out so as to hide another point.
reve ae motmot, when trees, rocks, &c., are drawn out in rapid succession as a canoe passes swiftly by; *nua reve, nunrevereve.*
2. used in songs for *rave;* being the same word.
Revo, a kind of yam.
Reworewo, a variety of ficus, banyan.
Rewu, 1. a hole dug at the foot of a cocoa-nut tree to catch water; the water caught; *materewu,* the opening, well,

of *rewu*. 2. *un* word for *pei*, water.

Rewurewu, a bad ulcerated sore.

Rig, 1. v. to carry on the shoulder.

Rig, 2. adj. small; in rare use; *Motariy, pisnariy, qariy, tuqeriy, vanua rig;* adv. *rigrig.* Mao. *riki;* Pol. *liki li'i;* D.Y. *lik;* Sol. Ids. *ri'i;* Marsh. *lik.*

Riga, 1. to rule, exercise authority; *riga goro*, rule over.

Riga, 2. to swell.

rigariga, n. a swelling.

Rigot, to satisfy spite, ill-feeling; *me rigot iniko, nok o gene me tatas*, you are satisfied now that my things are spoiled; as when a woman in jealousy destroys, spoils, what belongs to her husband.

Rigrig, adj. [*rig* 2.] presently, in a little; *rigrig ti*, after a bit; when of past time, but lately.

Rina, five in *tika* counting.

Rino, to shake, be shaken.

rino*v*, tr. to shake, as earthquake or loud noise.

marino*rino*, shaken, disturbed.

Rip, 1. to grow big, be big, sound; *rip lava*, grow to size, *rip kel*, recover soundness; 2. adv. entirely; *we nima rip*, to be wet all over.

Rir, 1. v. to quake; n. an earthquake.

Mao. *ruru*, Pol. *lu, ru*.

Rir, 2. to pass close by, as one vessel passes another; to come close up to, crowd.

varirir, to crowd.

Rirqetegmake, [*rir* 1.] a spider with small body and long legs, not a *marawa*, which when approached vibrates so as to be invisible.

Rir-togo, a cry in earthquakes.

Ririgo, a porpoise; *o ririgo ti towtowola* swims.

Ririnitiga, to grunt when lifting something heavy; *ririnitiga goro*, to groan under a burden.

Ririrwatia, [*rir* 2.] to carry a great number of things over the shoulder; *watia.*

Ririsa, [*risa*] to turn from side to side while lying.

Ririv, [*riv* 2.] to sup up, sip up, suck through a tube.

Rirvag, to carry to leeward.

Ris, 1. v. to change, turn, be changed; *neira te ris ape sava?* why should they change for the better?

2. *ris nia*, to turn into.

3. adv. in another direction; *tira ris*, stand and turn round, turn course in walking; of a canoe, to stand on different course.

ris maran, to turn from side to side in anxiety all night; *ni me ris maran apena.*

Risa, 1. v. to lie down; *risa punpun*, to lie long sick.

risavag, lie down with, because of.

Risa, 2. n. the second day, past or future; *arisa* on the day after to-morrow; *anarisa* on the day before yesterday. Mal. *lusa;* Fl. *valiha.*

Risavag, to lie down with, be laid up with; *risa* separable *vag; ni we risavag naranona*, he is laid up with his leg.

Risris, [*ris*] 1. v. move about, change position, *risris goro* change place with regard to something, as of bread-fruit to the fire.

2. adv. turning away; *ni me na risris nan*, he rejected it in anger.

Ritata, 1. to lace, as a sail to the mast and boom; *te ritata o*

L

epa ape turgue wa o pane, mun o ritata. 2. the cord used for lacing.

Riu, move the feet or legs; *nipea we riu kelkel,* don't shuffle your feet.

riug, tr. to move away the legs or feet; *riug iniko!* take your legs out of the way; to move legs out of the way of a passer-by; *nipea riuriug kelkel,* don't shuffle your feet.

mariuriu, shifting.

Riv, 1. to plant; see *rivu.*
riv rowo, the time of scarcity after yams are planted.
rivriv naru, to plant so many yams as to let them rot undug; met. a man rich in food.

Riv, 2. to suck through a tube, sup up; *ririv.*

Rivriv, 1. [*riv* 1.] a planting: *rivriv lele tagai,* planting with no taking; met. a man idle about planting.
rivriv puleuwa, 1. a very small garden, in ridicule. 2. after eating a turtle it was not safe to plant immediately in one's garden; a man planted a few things in a very small patch made for the purpose, as the turtle's property, *pule uwa,* then went on to his garden.

Rivriv, 2. a fan; *te gavug isei nia.*

Rivtag, 1. to approach, come near. 2. adv. near, *arivtag.*

Rivu, to plant, same as *riv.*
rivuag, tr. determ. *rivuag suqe,* to plant for *suqe.*

Ro, sign of name being feminine, with or without *i* 1. sing. and pl. *iro, iraro, raro.* Only used when the name is a Mota word.

Roa, 1. n. a small univalve, turris.

Roa, 2. v. to tie round; *roa goro,* to stay, strengthen by splicing, fishing; *o tangae ta mavut, te vatira kalo, qara rowoag o gae apena, we roa;* when a tree falls with earth on its roots, set it up, and stay it with a vine; *we sagaro o pagigi aku me mosiu ti, we map o tangae avunana, we was lue o aka, qara vil tuwale; we roa;* remove the rotten piece, cover with a sound piece of wood, bore holes and lash together.

roan, tr. to tie round the neck, carry round the neck; *ni we roan o tana som; wo-roaroan,* an ornament so worn.

Roiroi, bud of the cocoa-nut flower.

Roma, to taste or smell rank, putrid; to have bad after-taste in the throat.

Rono, 1. heavy, listless, inert; *naapena we rono, gate* masekeseke, he is out of sorts, *tama tete sau kalo lai naapena.*
ronorono, *we mara ronorono,* very heavy.

Rono, 2. n. not in use, but stem of following words.
ronoga, adj. having reputation of wealth, famous.
ronronotar, all sorts of things, all things; *tar.*

Rono, 1. n. a fish, the thresher.

Rono, 2. adj. 1. sacred, unapproachable, with inherent sanctity, not *tapu;* awful, portentous.
2. n. something mysterious, portentous; *o rono alo vanua; o rono we kuriko.*
ronova, sanctity.

Rono, 3. to feel, hear, smell, taste, apprehend by senses; be patient of, be in a passive state; *nipea ronorono nalinara,* don't listen to what they say.

ro*no*tag, tr. determ. hear, taste, smell, feel, something.
ro*no*vag, tr. determ. feel, &c. something.
Mao. *rongo*; Sam. *logo*; Pol. *rongo*, *lono*, *roo*; Sol. Islands, *rono*, *ronovi*; N. H. *rono*, *dono*; Fij. *rogo*; Java, *rungu*; Pon. *ron*; Gilb. *ono*.
Obs.; in most of these hearing is the sense signified; and the further meaning is present of "report" and "news," which is unknown in Mota.
rono leasag, suffering contentious treatment.
rono magav, to suffer pain; see *magav*.
rono malapusa, long-suffering, slow to resent.
rono malamuaga, to be patient under pain.
rono maud, to endure with patience, suffer long.
rono puna, or *pun*, to have the sense of smelling, discover by smell.
rono rua, to have two tastes.
rono ririg, to brace oneself up for endurance, be patient under suffering.
rono vivtig, to suffer pain.
Ronoa, a fish.
Ronorav, a *sawai* on the evening before a *kolekole*.
Ronoro*no*, redupl. *rono*, listen to, hear.
Ronorua, to have two tastes; *o pei we ronorua*, half fresh, half salt.
Ro*no*tag, tr. *rono* 3., perceive by sense, hear, feel, taste, smell.
ro*no*tagiva, v. n. hearing, feeling, tasting, smelling.
Ronova, [*rono* 2.] v. n. sanctity, holiness.
Ro*no*vag, tr. [*rono* 3.] to feel, suffer.

Ro*no*viga, [*rono* 3.] dull, inactive, with pain; *o qoe we roronoviga*, a pig stands, stares, suffers something.
Ronronotag, redupl. *tano ronronotag*, the seat of hearing, and other senses; *ronronotag pune nau* met. see *nau*.
Ronro*no*tau, to bear every other year, *tau*, as some cocoa-nuts.
Ronro*n*velil, inattentive; *we rono valil*.
Ropa, 1. to have heavy leafage, of a tree; to have much hair, of a man; *o paka we ropa, o aru tagai.*
Ropa, 2. same as m*a*ke; whence *maroparopa*, thin.
Rope, to flap; waves *rorope* as they fall and break; the belly of a thin pig *ti roperope*, flaps about as it walks; *o epa ti roperope ape taro, ti roperope goro lan.*
Ropesrawe, a woman who had many children; whence *ira nanatin Ro Pesrawe*, a proverbial saying, very many.
Roqo, 1. n. old leaf-mat added in covering in the oven, *qaranis*. 2. v. to cover, *luqai*, with old leaf mats; *te roqo goro o qaranis mun o roqo*. 3. to have a rough head of hair like an old leaf-mat; *sage roqoroqo*, to sit, as a bird, with ruffled feathers and outspread wings.
roqoi, 1. a thing cast away like an old leaf-mat, worthless, *o roqo iga, roqo qoe*, fish, pig, only fit to be thrown away, and also, thrown away; *tama o roqo nogae*, met. of one whose death has not been honoured with a feast.
2. (k) rough large head of hair like a *roqo*.

roqroqoi, (k) redupl. *matig roqroqoi,* a little man with large rough head of hair, a bird all feathers ; *matig* 3.

roqoroqo, adv. all rough, of hair, feathers.

Roro, 1. to spread as sound, travel as news ; *roro at go,* spread out, *roro ma* arrive, as a report or news.

roroi, n. sound travelling, report, news.

Roro, 2. v. 1. to sink down, be low, be deep ; also to be sunk down and so shallow; *o qarana we roro,* a pit is deep; *o pei me roro alo qarana,* the water in the pit has become shallow. 2. adj. deep, low, shallow.

roro gavig torotoro, very deep ; *me gavgavig veta gina.*

roro pistoa, shallow, of water only up to fowls' toes.

rorovag, go down with, sink with.

Roroi, 1. [*roro* 1.] (k) sound, report, of something ; *o roro lama,* the sound of the sea ; *narorona,* report concerning him ; *roro vanua,* news of the place.

Roroi, 2. [*roro* 2.] depth ; *roro lama,* deep of the sea.

Roromtag, to kiss in a native fashion ; to nuzzle into the face or body ; *te pupun mun o manui, te roromtag mun o nusui.*

Rorono, to be silent, quiet, still ; *te rorono goro o toretore,* to keep silence for a speech.

roronoa, silence, a respectful silence kept after a speech, *tama we momogo,* with hum of assent.

Roronoviga, [*rono* 3.] with a look of pain, distress ; *ronoviga.*

Roroqon, a small *um,* fire place as under a *pugoro,* food chest; *gate qaranis we poa.*

Roropei, 1. [*roroi* 1.] sound of unseen water.

Roropei, 2. a dragon-fly.

3. one quickly grown tall, lanky, like a dragon-fly.

Roros, to utter sounds of joy or grief ; *te roros ape sinaga si we wia ;* probably *roro* 1.

rorosvag, to make sound because of ; *te rorosvag o virtig,* to groan with pain.

Rorot, to carry, holding on the bosom with the arms.

Rorotnana, to tie, *rot,* in the middle, *tinai,* of two things ; in the midst of two things far apart.

Rorotov, to eat till one is tired ; *ko we gana we vuleko.*

Rorov, [*rov*] to shout, clamour, cry.

rorovia, shouting, clamour.

Rorovag, [*roro* 2.] to sink, go down with.

Rorou, a tree.

Rosag, to smash, hurt by a blow or fall ; *ni me masu vawo tanyae ! me rosag nasuvana ? navarana nan qa !* what did he hurt by a fall from a tree ? he broke his ribs.

rosarosag, to be too heavy to run, will break himself to pieces.

Rot, to tie, bind things or parts of things together ; *rot leqaleqa,* to bind for a time with running lines ; *te rot o tanun, tete rot lai o qoe, te ligo wia,* a man is bound by tying his limbs together, *we rot ;* a pig is tied up by the end of a line, *we ligo.*

rotig, tr. to gird.

rotiu, a bundle of things tied together.

rotiva, binding, tying.

Rotasiu, Sister, a woman so calls her sister in place of her name, *ro* making *tasiu* into a name.

Rotava, sandstone, coral stone, on the shore, soft.

Rotig, [*rot*] 1. v. to gird round, as the body; as a tree in measuring its girth.
2. n. (k) a girdle; *narotigik me roro*, my girdle has gone under; met. I am deep sunk in misfortune.

Rotiu, [*rot*] a bundle of things tied together; *o rot toape* of hibiscus leaves; *o rot no matig te sin nia*, cocoa-nut fronds bound into a torch.

Rotiva, [*rot*] verbal n. binding together.

Roto, to gnaw like a rat; *rotoroto*; *marotoroto*.

Rot-qatmona, to tie a bundle, or package, at the top, as a *qatmona* is tied.

Rotqatqat, [*rotiu*] a bundle of the small leaves of the top, *qatqat*, of *toape*; met. *naqatina o rotqatqat*, he has a thin head of hair.

Rot-vatnam, to tie in places.

Rou, to decorate the hair with flowers, &c.; *rou naqatuma*.

Roua, a reef island in the Banks' group.

Rov, 1. to shout; *o sul we rov goro*; *rorov*; root *ro, rovo* 1.
2. to sound like dashing water; *tete rovrov* to dash through water with a roaring sound as a fish or vessel, *tama o siriv* like a waterfall.

Rova, 1. to stretch out the arm, stretch out at arm's-length; *ni me rova o kere sin vusira*.
2. to measure with the stretch of the arms; 3. a fathom. Mao. *roha* to stretch the arms;
Motu N.G. *doha*; Mefor N.G. *rof*; Bat. *dopa*; Malag. *refy*.

rova alo masalepei, measure from the breast-bone, *masalepei*, to fingers of outstretched arm.

we atelue alo we rova, from the outstretched left hand to the right held upon the shoulder, where the face turns, *ate lue*, to meet it.

rova avawo sus, from right breast to left hand.

rova keke, with an arm not fully stretched, *keke*.

rova kilmata, from the outstretched left hand to the right collar-bone to which the eyes look down.

rova togtogoa, with both arms fully outstretched. The measures *alo maluk*, *alo vivnai* are not *rova*.

Rowo, 1. adv. 1. of direction according to locality; up. 2. in regard to time, forward; *me matava rowo*, next morning came; *alo tuara tau rowo*, next coming year.
2. v. 1. to spring, leap, move quickly up forward, rise, grow. 2. of birds and flying-fish, to fly. The many compounds are given separately. Motu N.G. *roho*, to fly.
3. to come in as gain, go out as loss; of money.
4. descriptive term in counting creeping plants, *gae*.

rowoag, to draw out at length.

rowog, make to fly.

rowov, advance upon; startle.

rowovag, spring, fly, rise, with.

rowovag, to serve.

varowog, send off flying, &c.

Rowo, 5. a fish; also *rowou*, which leaps; bonito.

Rowo-aeae, to leap and miss; of a yam when the vine grows forward and finds no reed to cling to.

Rowo-gaegaei, to grow with no tubers on the vine, *gae*, as some have; of the *qauro* wild yam.

Rowogis, to be active in service, be quick about some piece of work; *pa ia, ni me rowogis veta apena; gis.*

Rowolagau, to leap, pass, over; see *lagau*.

Rowolatelate, to break with jumping; leap, &c. and come to bits.

Rowolava, [*rowo* 3.] to come in with much interest, of money; to turn to much gain.

Rowolue, to go, come, out, issue; particularly out of a house with the *tiqanal* to step over.

Rowo-matag-goro, to rise and look out in fear of enemies.

Rowo-mavamava, to move heavily.

Rowomot, [*rowo* 3.] of money ceasing to come in.

Rowomotmot, to leap, move so as to break one's *rotig; rowo* 2.

Rowo-negneg, to hop about squatting, like birds, as in the *mago*.

Rowo-neremot, of taste, half good.

Rowo-nurnur, a yam not running with the vine so much as making tuber downwards, *nur*.

Rowopalag, to rush about, getting in one another's way; *palag*.

Rowopata, to enter a house; see *rowolue; rowo* 2.

Rowo-piai, to get into a condition like *piai*, said of *lot* when it is well pounded and tenacious, *magaegae*.

Rowopilolo, to come out into curled leaves in æstivation as some crotons do.

Rowopute, to jump and sit; of birds to settle after flight.

Rowoputput, to leap about stamping in defiance, or in starting a *sawai; put*.

Rowo-qasqasvat, to pass over stepping-stones, jump from the top of one stone to another; *qasqasevat*.

Rowoqet, [*rowo* 3.] to be lost and gone, of money spent or wasted; or of property.

Roworaka, to rise up generally; also with the various meanings of *rowo* 2.; particularly of the sun.

Roworeag, 1. [*rowo* 3.] to be lost, gone away, as money, property.
2. generally, to go off, away.

Rowo-susraveg, to fly skimming along the ground; met. of a loan, a debt owed by a man who can be depended on will come quickly in.

Rowotaqa, to move forward and fall on the face, to prostrate oneself; *taqa*.

Rowo-tasotaso, to trip on tip-toe.

Rowo-teqateqa, to go about from one thing to another; *teqa* 1.

Rowo-tete, to dash along; *ura rowotete,* very small sea crawfish; *tete*.

Rowotetete, to go with the exceedingly short rapid steps in the *qat*.

Rowotira, to take a firm stand; make an advance and take up a position.

Rowotuwale, [*rowo* 4.] a single thing, an only child, a friendless man; met. from vine with single shoot.

Rowo-ukauka, to advance with bow drawn; *uka*.

Rowo-valgoro, to run across the line of shooting and be hit: *val* 1.

Rowo-vaskir, to continually change or break off work; *ra sakir; tama we anumay o sinaga.*

Rowovatira, M. same as *rowovotur.*

Rowoviro, to slip out of joint; *riro.*

Rowovisa, how many, in counting vines of creeping plants used as lines; *gae rowovisa? ta rowotol*, how many vines? let there be three; *rowo* 4. *visa.*

Rowovotur, V. to jump up and down without changing place, jumping and standing; as a man in a rage, a crowd in excitement; *rowovotur goro*, to jump up and down in front so as to stop, defy, provoke.

Rowoag, [*rowo*] to stretch out, as a line, *rowoag o tal, o gae; rowoag nu maea*, said of a yam that grows along the surface, in the open *maea*, not down into the hole.

rowoag-tal-kole, a man who is to *kole* goes about telling people the day before with a view to their aiding him with gifts. Hence the recent word *rowoag-tal-som.*

Rowoasu, a large *rowo* 5. fish, which makes the sea smoke, *asu*, as it springs, *rowo* 2.

Rowog, tr. [*rowo* 2.] to make to send fly, off in flight; *varowog.*

Rowosag, to cry out in pain.

Rowo-ti-aqo, met. of one who is very quick to go to work, fight, &c. *ni we rowo ti aqo.*

Rowov, tr. *rowo* 2. to advance upon a person, startle.

Rowovag, *rowo* 2. tr. determ. to serve, work for, minister to.

rowrowovag, 1. v. to do service. 2. n. a servant, one who works for another.

Rowovagis, *rowovag gis* as *rowo gis*; to serve actively with reference to some one.

Rowou, a bonito, fish.

Rua, numeral, two.

ruarua, two and two, by twos, double.

Ruav, *rue, av;* to come in abundantly, excessively; *o rue ti ruav ma* of the tide; *av* 1. hot, excessive.

Ruavsis, abundance; met. from *ruav, sis* 4.

Rue, flow of tide, flood-tide, high tide.

rue lava, flood at spring tides.

rue makira, flood at neap tides.

rue sis M. high tide, full; *rue sus* V.

rue sus lava, sis lava flow of spring tides.

Ruka, tree, gardenia.

Rukruk, a sweet-smelling plant, a sage.

Rumane, a sea anemone; Sam. *lumane.*

Rumeg, to shake to and fro; active.

Rumrumuga, adj. fat, of man or pig.

Runa, very weak.

Rupe, butterfly, moth; *gamo rupe*, two canoes sailing together, looking like a butterfly.

Rupuga, adj. damp, wet.

Ruqa, to bend at an angle without breaking, as a *gaso* bamboo rafter, and the last reed on which yams are trained; see *taur* 3.; *me ruqa veta*, the yam training is over.

Rur, 1. to lop, poll, a tree; *rur*

qatunwa, to lop off the branches leaving the top standing up; see *qatunwa*.

Rur, 2. 1. to blow two or more shell trumpets together; if one only *we tia*. 2. the sound of shell trumpets blown together, *rur tanwe*.

ruruag, to blow many conchs.

Rurqoa, to fall in a mass, as a tree; *me rurqoa goro matesala*.

Rurqonaqona, a game; a boy hides; if not seen he jumps up and counts pigs against the others; *ti tiu gara o qoe*.¹

Ruruag, [*rur* 2.] to blow a great number of shell trumpets at once.

Ruruga, to bury for a time yams meant for planting, when ground enough is not ready.

Руruna, shelter, harbour, from rain, wind.

Ruruntap, wailing.

Rurur, a fish.

Rurus, 1. v. to draw out; neut. to come out, draw out; *me rurus o qeaqea varu*, the hibiscus rods of the stage in a canoe have been pulled out, or come out of their places by use.

rurus ta Maute, proverbial; *o iwatia te rurus nan o sama, o aka te tapegole ran*, when the yoke pieces of a canoe draw loose from the outrigger and the canoe capsizes.

2. n. a disease believed to draw downwards, rheumatism; *o rurus si o siwosiwo*.

Rurwon, a rank in the *suqe*.

Rusag, to pay for work done, give a person wages.

rusagiva, paying of wages.

Rusai, *rusag*, reward a person, pay for; *na rusai gak malas*.

Rusarusai, redupl. *rusag*, V. *ru-sai*; n. wages, payment for work. *som rusarusag, rusarusai*.

Rusrusvavine, leprosy.

Rusun, to crawl in a sitting posture, as an infant or cripple.

rusunvag, to crawl with, go slowly with.

Rute, 1. to sail slow, to go slowly under sail or paddling, *rurute, rutrute*.

2. n. a slow-moving canoe; *o mala aka ilone, ineia o rute, gate valago gaplot*.

Rutrut, 1. to mumble in eating; *kamam me rutrut matila*. 2. to mumble in speaking; *mamama rutrut*.

S.

S, tr. term. to verbs; *koko, kokos*.

Sa, 1. short for *sara*; 1. what? somewhat; *le sa ma mun nau*, give me something; *ape sa?* what for? *o sa sinaga?* what vegetable food? 2. interr. excl. what! *sa! si*—what if, can it be that—? is it indeed so? Sam. *a*.

Sa, 2. a prefix apparently meaning downwards.

Sa, 3. adj. term. *vulasa*.

Sa, 4. an addition to the suff. pron. *k; napaneksa, kikiksa;* with no ascertained meaning.

Sag, 1. to hang round the neck as an ornament or nosegay; same as *roan;* V. L. word.

2. a nosegay of scented leaves, &c. same as *ita, uta*.

Sag, 3. tr. determ. suffix to verbs; often signifies numerous objects: Fij. *caka;* Sol. Islands, *sagi;* Sam. *sa'i*.

Saga, stem of the following word.
Sagarag, to view steadily, gaze, gaze at.
Sagaraka, to snatch up a person's property in his absence; *ko we map o sara, isei we sea we la kalo gaplot*.
Sagaro, to clear away, pull or cut away.
Sagatavalrua, a woman who marries into both *vere; o tarine tuwale ti lag soyoi, ti lag o tavalaima*.
Sage, 1. to settle down, sink downwards; same word as Motlav, *hag* to sit.
sager, to settle down upon.
Sage, 2. adv. of direction, upwards, inland; of time, future.
3. v. to go inland towards the inner upper part of the country, particularly to go to the gardens, to work; generally to rise.
4. descriptive prefix with numerals and *visa*, when men on board a canoe are numbered. Mao. *ake*; Sam. *a'e*; Tong. *hake*; Fij. *cake*; St. Crist. *ta'e*; Tagal. *sakai*; Saw. *ha'e*.
Sage-ketekete, to rise, as a ship on the horizon, or an island; *sage* 3. *kete*.
Sagelanalana, [*sage* 1.] to sit, stand, unsteadily, as anything unevenly resting on the ground; to be unsteady, uncertain; *lana*.
Sagelukluk, [*sage* 1.] to sit with legs drawn up, *luk*; met. to be idle, stay-at-home.
Sage-mar-siwo, [*sage* 1.] to subside, sink down; *mar*.
Sagemaran, work all night; *sage* 3.
Sage-mot, [*sage* 3.] to go a little way and stop; to step aside; *sage* without particular direction.

Sagenug, [*sage* 1.] to sit and get up again, be restless, never sitting still; *tete pute nev lai, tama si o nug alo putena*.
Sagepute, [*sage* 1.] to settle down in a mass, as the starch in making sago.
Sage-roqoroqo, [*sage* 1.] to sit, as a bird, with rough feathers and outstretched wings; *roqo* 3.
Sagesal, [*sage* 3.] to go to the garden with someone, passing over, *sal*, one's father, or other with whom one ought to go.
Sagesaru, [*sage* 1.] to sink down and pass away; transient.
Sage-uqauqa, [*sage* 3.] to rise, and raise up, *uqa*, the earth, as yams do when they grow large.
Sagevisa, so many on board; *sage* 4.
Sagevule, [*sage* 1.] impersonal, to weary, distress; *o virtig me sagevulea; vule*.
Sagevutvut, [*sage* 3.] to rise up in a heap, *vutvut*; as earth over a growing *tomago* tuber.
Sager, tr. *sage* 1, to settle down upon, press upon; *o ganawono me sager nina*, distress was upon us.
Sagera, perch, roosting-place of birds, flying-foxes; *sage* 1.
Sagerai, (k) constr. e. the parts of a house which rest upon the ground, the butts of *tursana, pete*, and the *paparis*.
Sageraqai, a tree.
Sageremaleg, a plant; the perch of the *maleg*.
Sagereqaratu, a tree on which flying-foxes hang; their roosting place, *sagera*.
Sageretiwia, a stone on the beach on which *tiwia* sit; *o vat maeto a lau*.
Sageretoa, the rail on the top of

a fence, *yeara mun*, on which fowls roost.

Sagerewose, the man who sits behind the steerer; *ni we sager o wose*.

Sagiai, 1. (k) the peculiar smell of things which hangs about them and remains on the hands of those that touch and handle them; *pun sagsagie gopae*, the smell of the odour of a sick person.

Sagiai, 2. (k) [*sag* 1.] festal decorations, ornaments, of a man or a place; *sagie tavusmele*, the ornaments of a man of high rank.

sagie vagalo, the ornaments which a man puts on when going into battle, amulets, &c.

Sagietavus, *sagie tavusmele* as above.

Sagig, a few cocoa-nuts left on a tree; *me ramo sagig veta*.

Sagilo, 1. [*say* 1.] to decorate a place with leaves and flowers.
2. n. a bunch of flowers or leaves, the mark of a *tamate* society.

Sak, 1. to hang, as a thing hangs over a line, a part on each side, as two yams or *palasa* across a pole, one on one side, one on the other, tied together at the crown.

sak gona, to hitch and hang, as a fish-hook does when caught in a tree, *gona*.

2. act. to catch, hang on a line; *sak kalo* catch a thing, under it, as it falls; hang up on a line.

Saka, 1. to stand up stiffly, like bristles, fins, leaves of thriving plants; *o vanua we saka*, the village is up in excitement; to have the bristles up; *sakasaka*, the hair on end; *saka goro*, to protect, defend, like an enraged boar with bristles up.

Saka, 2. the name of a *tamate* society.

Saka, 3. to be let go from the hand; *me takuk ti, qara ul o panei, we saka*.

sakarag, tr. to cast, by letting go from the hand.

Sakalo, to catch hold of a thing lest it fall, *sakalo goro*.

Sakar, to shoot with a forked arrow, *kara* or *qatiysar*.

Sakarag, [*saka* 3.] to cast, let go from the hand.

Sakariu, (k) a prickle, thorn; probably *saka* 1.

Sakaru, the rough, *saksakara*, coral stones on the *warelau* between the surf and beach.

Sakasaka, redupl. *saka*, up on end.

Sakau, to catch in the hands.

Sakerewaka, hastily, heedlessly; *au saksakerewaka*, to go along not regarding injuries, &c. *mawui sakerewaka*, to work briskly.

Sakir, to break off, snap; *o gae we sakir mot*.
sakir latelate, to be brittle.

Sako, to pay in compensation, make up in default; *kamam we sako ineia me mate*, we pay for him who is dead; *ko te sako ape suqena*, to pay the introducer for a friend's *suqe*; *te sako o qoe* when pigs are exchanged, and money is given with one to make up the value.

Saksakara, [*sakariu*] prickly, thorny.

Sal, 1. v. to cut, with slashing cut. Sam. *sele*; Mao. *here*.
sal late, to sever with slashing cut; *sal mot*, cut short off with same motion; *gasal*, a knife.

saliag, tr. determ. to cut off.
Sal, 2. v. to snare, take fowls or fish with a line, *gasalsal;* te sal o iga. Sam. *sele; sal tapare* when how many men have caught fish and lay them in a row, *tapare tuwale.*
Sal, 3. adv. higher than, above; over and above, in addition to the rest; used also as v. *me sal ma; tano salsal, la salsal,* see *salsal.*
Sal, 4. v. to assist; *alo vagalo tasina te sal avunan tasina.*
Sal, 5. to be clean and smooth in breakage, contrary to *sipa* jagged; a *naeru* will eat a cocoa-nut broken by its fall if it be *sal,* if *sipa* he will not.
Sala, 1. (k) path, road; in *matesala, manursala,* &c.
  Fij. *sala;* Fl. *hala;* Mao. *ara;* Sam. *ala;* Mal. *jalan;* Jav. *dalan;* Motu N.G. *dala;* Malag. *lala;* Marsh. *ial;* N. H. *sala, hala;* Sol. Islands, *tala, tara.*
Sala, 2. a messenger.
Sala, 3. n. a tree, euphorbia, its leaves used in dyeing.
Sala, 4. 1. to boil; with hot stones in a wooden bowl, *wumeto,* or cocoa-nut shell *vinlasa;* or in the bark of a tree, *vin palako,* or a leaf, or in *vinlasa* over embers or a torch of leaves.
  virsala, to cook squeezed cocoanut juice in *vinlasa* on embers; *sala sun,* to try out oil by stone boiling.
  2. to prepare dye, and dye in the preparation; as men dye *wetapup* with *gar laqe,* and women *pari* with *no sea,* boiled, *sala,* with water.
  3. to prepare poison and charms by boiling; *sala o garata; we sala o mino,* to poison fish in a rock-pool on the beach with *vin wotaga me pusa mun o vat qara sala.*
  4. met. *sala naapena,* to put one to shame by disclosing the truth.
salag, tr. to cook with hot stones.
Salagaraqa, [*sala* 1.] a fresh arrival, new-comer.
Salamate, 1. [*sala* 1.] ready prepared, for a journey, or generally; *mate* 2.
Salamate, 2. [*sala* 4.] to cook a charm; *mate* 1.
Salananare, [*sala* 1.] long in coming home; one waited for, *nare.*
Salanawono, [*sala* 1.] one who goes aimlessly, *gap, nawono.*
Salaparaus, [*sala* 1.] one who comes from a distance, *paraus.*
Salaras, [*sala* 1.] one who has come a long way; *ras* 1.
Salasun, [*sala* 4.] to cook cocoanut with hot stones in a bowl, *wumeto,* for oil; *o ligiu te sun lue.*
Sala-tamate-gaviga, [*sala* 4.] to cook strong-smelling leaves, *sav,* &c. and hold a madman over the steam so as to make him call the name of the ghost that possesses him.
Sala-ta-tagir, M. [*sala* 1.] one who came last and will go first.
Sala-ta-tawur, V. the same.
Salatawurgape, [*sala* 1.] one who is always late.
Sala-te-mule, [*sala* 1.] going in the future; said to one who delays, *iniko o sala te mule.*
Salatoga, [*sala* 1.] one who has come to stay.
Salatowo, [*sala* 1.] one who comes for the first time, *totowo.*

Salavano, [*sala* 1.] a traveller arrived.

Salag, 1. tr. *sala* 4. to cook with stone boiling; *salag o toape* by putting hot stones upon it in the *um*.

Salag, 2. to lay flat, hold out open hand; *te salag o no-retal ape loko;* to lay flat as a snare, *we salag o gae ape takele tangae.*

Salagau, to cross over; probably contracted from *sale lagau.*

Salagoro, the lodge of the *tamate liwoa* club.

Salasala, redupl. *sala* 4. to poison fish with *vin wotaga* and other such things.

Salava, [*sao* 1.] same as *sao lava,* principal landing-place; not Mota form, but used in names, *Losalav.*

Salavasisia, [*sala* 4.] to cook food for a woman who has just had a child; *vasis.*

Salavatuga, [*sala* 4.] food cooked with hot stones, but with no *pig,* so *vatuga.*

Sale, 1. constr. of *sala* 1. path, road, in compound words.

Sale, 2. v. l. to float, drift, soar with open wings; 2. from floating in the sea on the back, to lie back.

sale gatavag, to lean sideways as if looking through beside the door.

sale gomgom, of fish when they float panting on the surface when poisoned; of men lying back floating, with water running into their mouths.

sale kokopei, to soar and float so still that water would not run off the wings; said of birds, and of kites, *rea.*

salepapan, to float beside, drift along the coast, of canoes.

sale rua tasi, said of fish that live both in sea and fresh water.

sale taragiate, to lie on the back, looking upwards, *ate,* as in floating in the sea.

sale tingoro, to lie, lean back, listening, with attention.

*sale wariria*g, to soar like a man-of-war hawk, *mantoganae,* with stiff wings boring its way against the wind; *warir.*

sale wawae, said of an empty *tapera;* it lies on its back with nothing in it.

salewawana, to lean back open-mouthed in astonishment.

salewolo, to lean back with head turned aside, *wolowolo,* and look hard at a person.

sale wotwot, to float on the surface, of fish; with head out of the water, of men.

salevag, to float with.

Sale, 3. to flow, run with water; to run when melted, and so to melt.

salevag, to run with; *salevag pei,* to run with water as anything thoroughly soaked.

Sale, 4. to leap; *sale sur,* jump down; *sale lagau,* jump across.

Sale, 5. things of all sorts and kinds; *o sale manu* birds of all kinds, *o val sale manu* birds in all their various kinds.

sale pulai, property of all kinds, from various sources.

Salea, a creek in the coral of a reef through which canoes are brought through to shore.

Saleaka, [*sale* 1.] a way of passage for canoes, through the reef, or down the beach.

Salegasuwe, the rat's path, the wall-plate of house or *gamal.*

Salegeara, [*sale* 1.] the place for a fence to go, its course.

Salemala, term of reproach for

one who goes about the village like a sow, *mala.*
Salemara, [*sale* 1.] the run of ground doves.
Salemaran, [*sale* 1.] forerunner of morning; *i Woqas me mamata alo vula salemaran,* woke when the moon was shining before daylight.
Salemoa, the first in the path, lead.
Salena, scattered abroad.
Salepulai, 1. [*sale* 1.] (k) source of wealth; *urivtag me ge tagea nasalepulamam* by withholding payment. 2. *sale* 5. (k) property of all kinds.
Salesale, a kind of *tomago.*
Salesasasaravag, [*sale* 1.] to dash along the path hastily, carelessly; *sasar; o mot te lamasia tamaine.*
Salesava, [*sale* 1.] coming for what; *o salesava?* what has he come for ?
Salevag, 1. [*sale* 2.] to float, &c., with.
Salevag, 2. [*sale* 3.] to flow with.
Salewol, [*sale* 1.] one coming to trade; *ineia o salewol.*
Saliag, tr. determ. *sal* 1. to slash off, as a damaged banana leaf.
Salilina, the beach between high and low water-mark; ashore, from the point of view of the sea.
Salit, v. to sprout, shoot out from branch or trunk of trees; *sasalit.*
salitiu, n. sprouts, shoots from branches or trunk of a tree.
Salite, a deciduous tree with eatable leaves and nuts; catappa terminalis: also *salte.*
Salmit, [*sal* 1.] to cut to a point.
Salnamename, to hang down, name.

Salo, 1. to lay at length; *we salo o qatsnmai,* lay the ridge-pole of a house in its place; *we salo o toto ape paparis gamal,* poisoned arrows in course of preparation are laid lengthways on the wall-plate. 2. to lay a corpse in a cave, or in a food-chest, unburied. *salo vatitnai,* to be laid at length with the middle on the ground and the two ends not touching it, like a long log balanced on its middle; hence to be balanced on the middle.
Saloi, 1. a high thing; *o saloi tanun,* a tall man; *salo ima,* a lofty house; *salo tanwe,* a high hill; *salo maave,* very tall. 2. the middle finger.
Salona, the decorations of a *salagoro.*
Salpepeten, [*sale* 1.] to float near a rock as fishes do without moving; met. to hang about people as children do; *peten.*
Salqat, to bring shares; *salqat lito,* each man brings his quota of firewood to the common fire.
Salroperope, [*sale* 1.] to float as fish do flapping their fins, swaying their bodies.
Salsal, 1. [*sal* 2.] to snare a fowl with a string; fish with rod and line; *gasalsal,* the line.
Salsal, 2. [*sal* 3.] adv. 1. above the head, *tete tano salsal lai ape qatun o tanun liwoa,* must not take anything from above the head of a man of rank; *o qaliga neia, tete tano salsalia,* he is a relation by marriage, must not touch anything above his head; 2. thence, insolently; *vara salsal,* speak insolently; *tete na salsalia* must not take

anything over his head, or step over his legs rudely.
salsal gor kereva, when food is divided out, but one says *inau o salsale goro kerekere!* no food is allotted to him, but each man gives him a portion, so that he gets the largest share; the practice when food is insufficient of each giving to make up; *o tanun nitol, o sinaga nirua, isei te la isei te la.*

Salsal wowot, same as *sale wotwot* above, *sale* 2., float with head out of the water; *gate tul nanagona.*

Salsale, [*sale* 2.] set afloat; *salsale aka.*

Saltaroaroa, swift.

Salte, same as *salite*, catappa.

Saltekau, a small species of *salite* with hooked thorns; *kau.*

Salworag, to pour out, *sal liworag.*

Sama, 1. the outrigger of a canoe; 2. to tack, lie on the other tack. Pol. *hama, ama*; Fij. *cama*; Mortlock Island, *tam.*

Samagalao, the outrigger on the left; met. one who uses both right and left hands.

Samai, (k) constr. *e;* useless remains, refuse, as of *tou, gire, gea*, vine with fibres taken out for use.
  samaga, like refuse, not fit to eat, stringy; *ga* 5.
  saman, tr. to champ, as a stringy *tomago.*

Samal, *un* word for rain, wet.

Samaluag, to put out of the mouth, *luag*, the *samai* of what has been chewed, as *gea.*

Saman, to champ, eat, what is soft and juicy and has *samai* fibres in it; pigs *saman* leaves, &c. Motlav people are said to *saman* their food because *tomago* is stringy.

Samanola, 1. to smack the lips in eating, like a pig champing food. 2. to make a smacking noise as in beating water with the flat of the hand.

Samar, to fall after setting, drop before ripe, of fruit; met. to die young, when just grown up.
  samariu, (k) a fruit that falls unripe, wind-fall.

Samasama, to deceive, same as *sansana.*

Samate, [*sao* 1.] the lee side of an island, a sheltered place for a *sao; mate* of surf as in *tasmate.*

Samerumeru, [*sa* 2. *meru*] branch or tree bent down with the weight of fruit; *samerner.*

Samesus, the last pig of a litter, youngest child of a family; *samai* of the *sus;* *samsamesus.*

Samrere, to get a little wet in rain; *samure.*

Samsam, *wena samsam* drizzle, *samai* of rain.

Samsamaga, [*ga* 5.] like refuse, such as would be put out of the mouth as fibrous refuse, *samai;* stringy, of meat, wood, *tomago*, &c.

Samsamuga, ragged, see next word; *ga* 5.

Samui, fringe, as on a *tana.*
  samuga, fringed, with ragged edges or ends.

Samure, to be rather wet, as in *wena samsam*, damp.

San, to deceive.

Sana, spotted, panther, cowry.

Sanakae, an abscess, bad sore.

Sanasana, [*san*] to deceive, same as *samasama.*

Saneg, 1. to put in a crotch, hitch, to set a snare; *we saneg o gae avune tangae qara tut o manu nia.*
2. said of a vessel that stops on her way, hitches up, *neira me*

saneg a Maewo qara taso ma i Mota.

masaneg, hitched up.

Saniere, spiky like *sani ere*, the spikes of a pandanus; *we saka tam o ere.*

Saniu, (k) a prickle, spike; *sani ere,* above.

saniga, prickly, spiky; *ga* 5.

Sano, to hitch in a loop, hold or fasten with a line passed twice round; to carry a few sticks in a loop, to carry the hand in a sling, with the thumb hitched into a loop.

Sanoqaro, to put an arm in a sling while the wound is fresh, *qaro;* met. to do a thing quickly.

Sansaniga, prickly, *saniu.*

San, to spoil, destroy.

sanrag, tr. determ. to spoil.

Sana, a fork, crotch, forked stick or post: Fij. *saga;* *tursana,* the main post of a house forked to receive the *qatsuna.*

Sanasana,

Sanavul, numeral, ten. Mal. *sa puloh;* Malag. *folo;* Mao. *ngahuru;* Sam. *gafulu;* Tong. *hongofulu;* Bks. Islands, *sanovul, sanwul, sanwil, samol, henawol;* N. H. *sanavulu, hanvulu, sanwulu, sanaul;* Sol. Islands, *sanavulu, hanavulu, tanahulu, tanahuru, naguru.*

sansanavul, by tens, ten at a time.

Sanavuliu, M. *sanavului* V. tenth.

Sanene, small.

Sanerenere, thin, shrunken, small with sickness.

Saniani, [*san*] impersonal, *me saniania,* he is in bad condition, said of man, pig, bird.

Sanita, weep, cry out with grief.

Sanrag, tr. determ. *san,* to do heavy damage to, ravage, much distress.

Sansan, n. the rotten inner part of a tree, perished wood; redupl. *san.*

Sansanavul, ten at a time, by tens.

Sansansawava, [*san*] destroying trees, killing pigs, fowls, &c. as part of a *kolekole*, after a *sawai.*

Sao, 1. n. a place on the shore without breaking surf, a landing-place for canoes; *tursao, wesao, salava.*

Sao, 2. v. to take up fish in a net, *we sao o gape, o iga;* to take up by some contrivance as fruit from a tree. Pol. *hao, sao.*

saova, 1. a contrivance for gathering fruit, a leaf *noarvau* pinned, *rino,* into a cup, and tied to bamboo stick; *te sao o gaviga mun o saova.*

Saova, 2. to skim with a *saova* 1. *we saova we golo,* to skim off the scum.

Sapalo, to carry on the palms of the hands; *te sapalo o igot me sura o lot avunana.*

Sapan, [*sa* 2.] to lead by the hand or arm, *panei.*

Saproro, *un* word for *mate,* to die.

Sapur, bad, indifferent to goodness; *iniko sapur!* you don't know what is good; *kamiu sapuri, o ima we tatas,* satisfied with a bad house; *linasapur.*

Saqat, to guard the fingers against anything hot or dirty with a leaf, *nosaqsaqat.*

Saqeka, a shrub with very light wood: *tansaqeka.*

Saqereta, shallow; *o mino, o namo, we saqereta* can be forded; *o tapera we saqereta,* shallow dish.

Saqo, to burn with heat, act. and

neut.; *me saqo gina!* that has stung! when something sharp has been said; *o malatutun gate nit, gate as, we saqo,* said of the bite of ants; *nalolona we saqo,* he is hot with anger.

saqora, to scorch.

Sar, 1. to be opposite, equal to, to make equal, match, suit, be suitable; thence, to avenge, punish; *we sar taniniga,* to be exactly opposite to; *te sar mun o tavalalea ape nau,* to avenge me of my adversary, to make it equal to him on my behalf; *te sar munia ape pugana,* punish him for his fault, make an equal return to him.

sarig, tr. to make equivalent.
sasarita, equal.
sarsar, n. punishment.

Sar, 2. same word as *sar* 1. in special sense as to money payment in the *suqe; inau we ye o suqe mun A., ineira we vene mun nau; nau te sar o som muneira; A. te qara guratapug;* to make a return for a small present of money given to the candidate.

Sar, 3. to shine, neut. act.; *sar anoano,* to shine with yellow light, of sun or moon; *sari toworay,* shine after rain; *sar mate,* to kill with heat, *o loa me sar mate o tanun ta Opa nitol.*

sariu, shining.

Sar, 4. to pierce, stab.
sarig, tr. to pierce something.
isar, a stabber, spear.

Sar, 5. to pour out, act. and neut.; *sar vano,* pour away, throw out in a mass, as rubbish out of a basket; *o totoe vetal te sar lue,* banana juice spurts out, pours downwards; *saru.*

sargag, tr. determ. throw.

Sar, 6. to start growing again; *o ga-paka ta mot te sar mulan,* if the aerial root of a banyan be cut or broken off it will grow again.

Sar, 7. same as *saru,* to put round.

Sar, 8. n. an echinus, or cidaris, blue, with needle-spines; put on bunches of banana fruit to frighten away *matika.*

Sar-nagoi, an expression of modesty, or, ironically, of impudence; *nanagok gate sar iniko,* I am not able to address you as an equal, have not the face; *sar nanagona!* like his impudence!

Sara 1. (k) court, open space; the lodge of *tamate* society, *sare tamate; sare av,* the place where the *suqe* fires are; *tinesara,* the open space in the midst of a village, *vanua.* Mal. Jav. *salang.*

Sara, 2. v. to pass, draw along, sweep, move with drawing motion, be swept away; *o tanun we qoqo we sara ma, we sara ae,* a crowd draws together, men come in a crowd, for nothing; *o iya we sara ma ilo gape; na avuana me sara,* the scales of a butterfly's wings have been brushed away; *sara tagea,* to pass away, draw off; *o viniu we sara ulul,* the skin is peeling off; *sara ma,* come hither; *we sara ut,* to go out in a body; *sara olorag,* to stoop and pass under. Mao. *hara mai.*

sarag, tr. to wipe away.
sarav, tr. to rub, move away, make to pass away.
saravag, tr. determ. to brush.
sarasara, to come or go in a body together.

saratuwale, adv. together.
Sara, 3. v. to gather, bring together; *te sara o sisipe*.
sargag, tr. determ. to assemble, contribute.
Saragao, [*sara* 2.] to make level, *tama we ninin we sasarita*, to cover over something level *sin gao*.
mawui saragao, to clear gardens so that they shall join on in one clearing, with no uncleared parts between.
Saragete, the second leaf of a cocoa-nut, which begins to break into frondlets.
Saragogogo, [*sara* 2.] to wither, shrink; *gogo*.
Sarakamot, same as *sagaraka mot*, to snatch up at once.
Saramao, mildew; same as *punmao*.
Saraninin, [*sara* 2.] to draw together round; *sara ninin goro o vanua*, surround a village, besiege; *nin*.
Saraparana, to be hard, full-grown, of edible leaves, so as not to be fit to eat.
Sarapun, [*sara* 2.] to wipe away and destroy utterly; *pun* 1. *vus sarapun*, kill and wipe out.
Sarasara, 1. v. redupl. *sara* 1. to assemble and go together, *we sarasara ma tama we gogorag ma*.
Sarasara, 2. a plant, malvaceous, with strong fibre; Big Jack in Norfolk I.
Sarasara, 3. a fish.
Saratawurgape, one who comes too late.
Saratuwale, [*sara* 2.] adv. together, meeting in one; *nom saratuwale*, combine, agree, in purpose, opinion.
Sarav, tr. *sara* 2. 1. to sweep over, pass over with drawing motion, sweep, wipe, away; in native doctoring to stroke the painful part and remove the pain.
2. in songs, to join in with chorus after a single singer has begun; *sarav goro*.
Saravqote, the name of the evening star; because when it is up men rise to go to bed, and brush with their hands, *sarav*, the part of the person, *qote*, on which they have been sitting.
Sarava, 1. to daub; as *palako* logs with red earth, *mea*; same as *sarav*.
Sarava, 2. n. a man with whom nothing remains of his money and property, *me sara qet vetu nania*.
Saravag, [*sara* 2.] to brush, as in passing.
Sara-vasinot, [*sara* 2.] to bring fire together, pushing the firesticks end to end; *sino*.
Saravatu, to put a hot stone into a wrap of food in a *qaranis*.
Sarawag, to go without fear of consequences or danger; as a man violates a *soloi* to get cocoa-nuts; *way*.
Sara-walulpea, [*sara* 2.] to come together in great numbers to work, make a bee, congregate round a feast, *we pute waliog o sinaga; walul*.
Sarawia, a shrub.
Sare, to tear; *sare o ritata*, to loosen the lacing of a sail.
  masare, torn.
Sarere, 1. when the reed of an arrow splits as it is shot, it cannot fly, *ti sarere gap*. 2. met. a cracked voice in singing.
Saresare, adv. with a tearing

M

noise; *o manu ti vara saresare* of very loud thunder.

Saretamate, [*sara* 1.] the lodge of *tamate* society.

Saretana, a charm to produce the birth of pigs, putting a bag of *nai* above a sow's head.

Saretapug, [*sara* 1.] a division in the *gamal* appropriated to a rank in the *suqe*.

Sarevagalo, [*sara* 1.] a fighting place.

Sarevnata, [*sara* 1.] customary place for shooting, *rene*, fighting.

Sarevugvug, customary place, *sara* 1., of assembly; *vug*.

Sarewolwol, market-place, a recent word.

Sargaela, cocoa-nut with tough stalk, *o sariu we gaela;* can't be pulled in the usual way, *tete takar lai, te galolo ran,* must be twisted off.

Sargag, 1. to bring together, contribute, *sara* 3.; met. *sargag qalo,* to succeed in convincing by adding argument to argument.

Sargag, 2. [*sar* 5.] to throw, dash down; *sargag siwo,* throw from a height, *sargag valiliug,* throw head over heels; *te sargag siwo o matetipatipag ilo tanona,* to thrust down the door, shutter, into its place. 3. *sargag o nin,* to fix a fence.

Sargovgov, [*sar* 3.] to dazzle; *o loa we sar govgov namatak,* the sun dazzles my eyes.

Sarig, 1. [*sar* 1.] tr. to make equal; *sarig-nov; vasarig*.

Sarig, 2. [*sar* 4.] tr. to pierce, prick.

Sarignov, [*sarig* 1.] to make exactly equal; *nov; gana sarignov.*

Saritagiu, [*sar* 1.] likeness, equality, in place or quality;

tama we sasarita gegese; o saritagiu, it is all the same.

Sariu 1. [*sar* 3.] (k) shining.

Sariu, 2. (k) a handle, stalk; *sar wose,* handle of a paddle.

Sarlano, [*sar* 7.] a *kolekole* for wearing the *lano* hat.

Sarmatekaova, [*sar* 3.] to shine, as the sun, through a narrow opening in the clouds, like egret's eye.

Sarmeme, [*sar* 6.] to grow hanging down as a creeper.

Sarnai, 1. a fish. 2. a kind of *tomago*.

Saro, 1. v. to draw into. *saro tul,* to enter and sink, act. and neut. *we saro tul o gape; we saro tul ilo wowor.* sarova, meeting. sarovag, saromag, to enter. 2. n. a string of cocoa-nut fronds used in shooting fish.

Sarog, M. *saroi* V. to go without permission into a place that has been made *tapu,* to violate a *tap*.

Saromag, tr. *saro,* to sheathe.

Sarora, hide and seek.

Sarov, to fill to repletion; *me sarovia; saro* 1.

Sarova, verbal n. *saro* 1. meeting, drawing together, of clouds, of ants in a path.

Sarovarua, a net with two entrances, places to *saro* in, to take both small and large fish; *tuara iga te saro alo takele gape, tuara alo takelei.*

Sarovag, [*saro* 1.] to enter, draw into.

Sarsar, 1. [*sar* 1.] punishment, payment.

Sarsar, 2. [*sar* 5.] spouting out; *riawo sarsar.*

Sarsaravatut, of the hair standing high above the head.

Sarsarawuqa, [*sara* 2.] to take away the *wuqa;* which see.

Sarsaretou,

Sarsarina, adj. [*sar* 1.] equal, same as *sasarita.*

Sarsaru woganase, [*saru* 2.] same as *lul woganase.*

Sartamate, very straight; *tamate* 5.

Sartavene, perfectly level, as if a straight shot.

Sartaworag, [*sar* 3.] to shine fully as sun in noon-day, moon high in heavens; *taworag.*

Sartuka, disused word for wire, taken to be, or called, stalks, *sariu* 2., of the sky; compare *gartuka.*

Saru, 1. to put on or off what is drawn round the body or a limb in one piece; such as *tamate* hat, *pane* bracelet, *lala* armlet, *malosaru* the dancing-dress put over the head; *saru goro qatui mun o tamate*, to put a hat on the head, surround with a hat; *saru savrag*, take off, draw from around; cannot *saru* a *malo* or a *vioviog. saru gona,* see *vasaru* 3.

Mal. *sarong;* Dy. *salui;* Malag. *sarona;* Tagal. *salong.*

sarun, tr. to draw down.

Saru, 2. to pour out in a mass.

Saru, 3. to pass away; *o gopae gate saru mantag tiqa; saru viviviv*, to pass away like mist *vivir; o no-paka ti nun saru*, banyan leaves are shed.

Saru, 4. to begin a song with many voices together.

Saru, 5. to complete what is necessary for attaining a rank; *val sale suqe ni saru qet, gate toga ti si tuwale.*

Sarun, tr. *saru* 1. to draw down from around; *sarun vartig*, when a line tied round a stick cannot be undone, draw it down, still round the stick, into a mass, then unravel it.

Sarusaru, [*saru* 2.] 1. a shoot of water spouting out from a bamboo for bathing, &c. *viawo sarusaru;* 2. adj. flowing, of hair; *i Marawa nauluna we sarusaru.*

Sarwirwirig, [*sar* 3.] sunshine following rain; *wirig; wena moa, o loa tagir.*

Sarvenevene, [*sar* 1.] straight as a shot.

Sasa, 1. n. the croton, in many varieties; the leaves used as the mark of *tamate* societies.

Sasa, 2. to carry by two or more on a stick, or by hand; *sasa ta Maute*, to cut the ends of a heavy object in carrying it.

sasan, tr. to carry.

Sasa, 3. to overtake, collide with.

Sasa, 4. prefix redupl. *sa* 2.

Sasae, V. adj. different, M. *sea.*

Sasagatur, hair standing on end, with fright.

Sasagav, to level the surface in adzing, to adze down; *we tara o tangae, we sasagav sur we vutvut*, cut down projecting pieces.

Sasai, (k) constr. e. name. Fl. *aha;* Fij. *yaca;* Pon. *ata;* N.B. *ya.*

Sasakarewaka, hasty and reckless in work, &c.; *sakarewaka.*

Sasakariga, vehement, strong, eager to work, in good sense; in bad sense violent, headstrong.

Sasakirkir, redupl. *sakir,* brittle, snapping short off.

Sasala, a flowering shrub, eranthemum; varieties, *sasala mataplea, susala pita.*

Sasaleniga [*sale* 2.] running with fluid, as eyes with tears, ripe fruit with juice, mouth watering with appetite.

Sasalev, to crowd round a person to see him.

Sasalit, redupl. *salit*, to shoot out from trunk or branch of tree.

Sasalo, to carry a big fish, by one man alone.

Sasalovega, *malawo.*

Sasamalea, said to one who continues to call one's name, *iniko sasamalea.*

Sasamaliga, having thin hair, the *samai* of a good head.

Sasamanau, adv. amiss; *vasogo sasamanau*, count incorrectly, *gaganag sasamanau*, give a wrong account, *ni me vet si naakanina, nava tagai.*

Sasamanman, [*sasa* 4.] to sail, float, close to shore or rocks.

Sasamrag, begin to rain a little, *samsam.*

Sasamtega, quick in doing things; of well or ill.

Sasan, determ. *sasa*, to carry something; of two or more men.

Sasapanpan, to sail, or swim, along close to shore or rocks; *sasa* 4. *panpan*, beside.

Sasapirpir, 1. thin from hunger. 2. ashamed, bashful.

Sasaqanau, to pretend, boast, say that one has seen what he has not.

Sasaqo, [*saqo*] *un* word for *loa*, sun.

Sasar, 1. to pull, tear, apart, strip as leaves from a branch; *gare sasar ma o us*, to pull the bow with a tug; *ni*t *sasar*, bite and pull; *o makaru te sasar o pea*, the flying-fish will tear the bait.
2. to lower the *gapan*, mast and sail.

Sasara, redupl. *sara* 2. to go about in company, of men; to straggle away, of fowls; to rush out altogether, as pigs.

Sasarag, [*sara* 2.] to wipe away.

Sasargava, steep, precipitous.

Sasariaeae, to fall, be thrown down, an empty space, not falling against anything; *ae*.

Sasarita, adj. [*sar* 1.] equal, level, right.

Sasaroro, 1. [*sasa* 4.] to slip down, out, *roro* 2.; as sticks out of a bundle.

Sasaroro, 2. the eggs of bluebottle flies, &c., *ti ris ulo nia, ti ris lano nia;* also the pupa, the change of the maggot not being observed.

Sasarur, to hang weakly down, be feeble.

Sasasawa, to run, trickle, down a surface, as water down the trunk of a tree in rain, down a split *pue; sawa* 1.

Sasav, to make one feel full with little eating; *o matig me sasav inau.*

Sasaviara, thin from hunger.

Sasavurvur, redupl. *savur*, falling, flying, in dust; *sasarurur.*

Sasawa, [*sawa* 1.] to run as a fluid; met. to go on without stopping, of a vessel passing along a coast, a party passing through a village.

Sasawaiga, to throb, beat, as the breast after running.

Sasawe, 1. n. a sunflower.

Sasawe, 2. v. *sasawe mala*, to put grated cocoa-nut on a sow's back, a charm to promote birth of pigs.

Sasawilil, to roll down, over and over; *wil.*

Sasawilwil, to assemble, crowd round ; *wil*.

Sasawuara, profitless, one who does no good ; *nu gate maros we mule sasawuara vag gap o gagapalag, nu gate vet lue munsei apena*.

Sasawui, steam ; *we sawu kalo nan o qaranis*.

Sasawuluga, adj. bad in a high degree.

Sastarama, from *sasai* and *taram*; a man must not mention the name of another because it is the name of one who is related to him by marriage, *qaliga*; he therefore calls him *Sastarama*.

Sau, 1. v. to lift up.
2. to dance round in a *kolekole* holding something for show ; *sau o pane qoe*.

Sau, 3. a way of cooking *toape*, edible hibiscus leaves, in wrappers with hot stones ; *we rereg o novao, we salag, we map o toape, we pala o vat alolona, we mona goro, qara vapteg vune av*.

Sau, 4. far ; *asan*, afar. N.H. and Sol. Ids. *hau*.

Saua, a mess of food cooked as *sau* 3. ; *saue patau*, breadfruit with *nai*; *saue loko*.

Sauma, a fish.

Sausau, food cooked as *sau* 3.

Sav, 1. a shrub, panax, with strong-smelling leaves, *ita*.

Sav, 2. v. to pluck, pull out hair or feathers.

savrag, to throw with quick action.
qalo savsav, to hit a bird and make the feathers fly ; *savi esuesu*, to pluck a living bird.

Sava, 1. n. something ; interr. pron. what? in short form *sa*. Mao. *aha*; Sam. *a*; Mal. *apa*; Marsh. *ta*; Fij. *cava*; Mel. *sava, hava, sav, hav, sa, ha, taha, tava, ta, safu, naha, neva*; N.G. *saha, tava, daha*; N.B. *ava*.
2. with personal art. *i sava? iro sava?* referring not to the person, but to the name of the thing which has been taken as the name of the person, what is his, her, name? compare *gene*.
3. of a kind, what kind? any kind whatever ; *o tol sava manu?* the egg of what kind of bird is it? *ta kalo pata ilo sava ima*, into whatever house, into any sort of house, one may enter.

savai, n. (k) 1. corresponding to interr. *sava?* a thing of what sort? in what condition? *ko we savai nake?* how are you now? what are you like?
2. corresponding to indef. *sava*, something of indefinite character ; *natoqak me savai gai*, my feelings were something indescribable. 3. what? of any part of a man ; what? of any relation of a man ; *ni me masu vavo tangae me rosag nasavana?* what part of him was hurt? *nasavama? i tamak nan qa*, what is he to you? my father to be sure.

savasava, everything, all sorts of things.

Savag, 1. to annoy, worry.

Savag, 2. to throw up earth, level for house-site or path.

Save, to strip, tear off, not breaking ; as a shoot from a tree, leaflet from a cycas, by the base, or banana from bunch.

Savir, to pull, tear off with finger and thumb, as a single leaf. Mal. *sapit*.

Savrag, [*sav* 2.] to throw quickly away, with the motion of *sav*.

Savret, to pluck at the edge, *sav*, *ret*, and so startle ; *savret kal*.

Savsavai, something or other, of some character or other; *savai*.

Savsavawora, [*wora* 3.] a mere something, thing of no consequence, common ; *we ge sarsavawora*, treat as a common thing.

Savta, [*sav* 2.] draw quickly, as fish going off with a line *we savta lue o gae*; probably *savtag*.

Savula, to wash the hands, *sarsavula*.

Savur, 1. to scatter, sprinkle ; redupl. *sasavurvur, sasavuvur; vur* as in *matavuvur*.
2. excl. on seeing many things ; *savur!* what a lot !

Saw, v. same as *sawu*, to blow. *saw malav*, blow cool ; *saw mot*, cease blowing.
Mao. *hau*, wind ; Mangarewa, *hau*, to blow.

Sawa, 1. v. to run on, as a fluid advances, and cocoa-nut juice runs up the arms ; see *sawarasu; sasawa*.

Sawa, 2. v. to dance by a drum ; singing with shuffling steps, not *lakalaka; te sawa goro o sawai*, dance according to the tune on the drum.

  sawai, 1. the tune on the drum, or song to which men *sawa;* the dance with the song and drumming ; *we map o sawai*, to end the song and dance, after the shouting and leaping of *lul woganase; sawai puterua*, two dancings and drummings going on together.

Sawag, 1. to twist yarn with the fingers for *tali* cord.

Sawag, 2. to dandle a child.

Sawai, 2. a tree ; *we tara mun o aka*.

Sawalagiu, (k) same as *sawaliu*.

Sawaliu, (k.) the first fruit of a season on a tree ; *sawal taqai*, the first fruit of a tree, of its first bearing.

Sawan, to flog, as with *woqat* in *valval lamas*.

Sawano, a kind of *qauro*, wild yam.

Sawan, same as *sawag*, so pronounced by some.

Sawarasu, [*sawa* 1.] to run as fluid ; if too much water is used to *woro*, for squeezing out the juice from grated cocoa-nut, the *woro we sawaras nan o toape*, runs off the hibiscus leaves, and also will *sawa*, run up the arm of the one who squeezes.

Sawarirvas, a kind of *sawai*, of Gaua.

Sawasawa, [*sawa* 2.] to go with a trotting motion ; *valago sawasawa*, to trot.

Sawe, to mix *nai* almonds with bread-fruit.

Sawewe, to shine brilliantly ; *o vula we sar mantag, was o vula we sawewe*.

Sawov, impers. v. 1. to go wrong, ill, with; *we sawovia* all goes wrong, ill, with him. 2. to show that one is wrong, doing wrong, like *norov*.

Sawsawemala, [*sasawe* 2.] 1. a charm when a sow is about farrowing for the first time ; putting grated cocoa-nut on her back. 2. said of people who snatch or scramble for food.

Sawsawui, [*sawu*] steam as it escapes, *we sawu kalo;* met. *la o sawsawui*, give an imperfect account of anything, the steam, not the food, of an oven.

Sawu, 1. to blow, of wind, to puff forth, burst out, of steam. *sawu ae*, to escape, of steam; met. of few men in large house; of zeal, energy; *sawu malav*, blow cool, *o lan we saw malav kel;* said also of an oven when the stones are not hot, *o av ti saw malav;* met. to grow cool about anything; *sawu kule maligo*, wind after a cloud; *sawu mot*, to cease blowing; *saw tutun*, said of water not very hot but gives off steam. Mak. Bug. *sau;* Sawu I. *habu*, steam.

sawsawui, steam.

vasawu, steaming, burning with a blast.

Sawu, 2. said of a person sick, chilled by the wind, his hair on end, his skin gooseflesh, *ni we sawu apena.*

Se, verbal particle used in songs. Fij. *sa.*

Sea, 1. M. adj. apart, different; *ra ta Uta we log sea*, call it differently.

searag, tr. divide.

2. v. to move the hot stones of an oven into place before the food is put on them.

Sea, 3. a plant the leaves of which, *no-sea*, make a red dye.

Seanig, adv. in small pieces, *sare seanig*, tear to bits; *sea* 1. probably and *nigiu.*

Searag, tr. *sea* 1. to put aside, divide.

adv. severally; *rug searag.*

gao searag, of fire which having consumed the fuel in the middle burns on at the extremities.

Segao, continually, a word taken from songs; *se* v. p. *gao*, to spread on.

Segere, excl. of surprise; *tama we mamakei.*

Sei, 1. interr. and indef. pron. who? some, any one; with or without pers. art., *isei, irosei, irasei, irarosei.* Fl. *hei;* Bugotu, *hai;* Mao. *wai;* Sam. *ai;* Motu N.G. *sai;* Mel. *se, he, tei, ti, di, si, ai, oi;* Fij. *cei;* Amboyna, *sei;* Bat. *ise;* Sangir, *isai;* Sawu, *he;* N.G. *tai, dai.*

Sei, 2. adj. V. same as *sea*, apart, different.

3. remove out of the way, as *noota* from old roof.

4. move about, arrange, stones in an oven with *ipala.*

sesei, redupl. substitute, remove.

Seke, stem of m*asekeseke.*

Selselvag, to glance off, as a blunt axe in hewing wood.

Sem, 1. redupl. *semsem*, stuck with matter, as the eyes.

Sem, 2. to scold; Sam Fletcher has left in this form of his name a memorial of himself.

Sene, 1. to move swiftly and continuously, as a vessel moves; *sua sene mot goro*, to paddle quickly and cut off the course of another.

sene ut, to go straight out into the bush; *ut sene uwa; man seneuwa*, said of a torn net, or a house full of holes.

Sene, 2. to strain liquid; to strain sago, *ota*, through *tapera gae;* to clear from dregs by passing liquid from one cup, *vinlasa*, to another.

Sene, 3. a mimosa.

Sepere, a place in V.L. to which certain Mota families trace their origin; *ira ta lo Sepere.*

Sere, to move swiftly; to blow hard and steady, as the trade wind, *lan sere;* to make a sudden appearance, *sere lue* like an apparition.
sere maniy, to dive straight into the water.
sere mot, to cease blowing strongly, *o lan· sere ti sere mot.*
sere nala, to run on steadily though panting.
sere nononono, to go through the bush.
sere wana, to run with mouth open.
sereag, tr. to blow hard against; *o lan ti sereag nau.*
sereg, tr. to blow hard against; *o lan me sereg nau.*
Serlawalawa, to flame strongly; *gao serlawalawa,* burn with strong flaming.
Sersernowo, a bird.
Sertaqataqa, to be much bent down, *taqa; ser* as in *serlawalawa.*
Sese, 1. to take apart, pull to pieces.
sese makomako, to take apart the garland, a part of the ceremony of admission into the *suqe.*
sese rauraun, to empty a bag by taking things out one by one.
sese saru, to drop out, be left behind.
sese wora, take to pieces.
seserag, tr. determ. to take apart.
sesevag, tr. determ. pull asunder.
Sese, 2. a smooth shell, turris; in which the *gatou* lives.
Sesei, 1. v. redupl. *sei* 3. to remove; also *seseg.*
  2. n. (k) thing or person in place of another, substitute; *we la seseina,* take another in his place.
  3. adj. different, same as *sea* M. *sasai* V. used at Gatava.
Seserag, [*sese*] tr. determ. to take away the several parts; *me seserag o rene, o aka qara mataketake,* the canoe was lightened by throwing out the cargo.
Sesere, a bush.
Seserenau, of a stone that misses a bird and hits leaves.
Sesevag, tr. determ. *sese* 1. to remove; *o tanun te sesevag o nam,* when there are many tubers on one root; *we sesevag sur siwo,* to level down by removing what stands too high.
Seva, to breathe faintly; *maserasera.*
Sewao, a tree.
Sewara, hard and uneatable, as leaves of *palako, pulva,* too old, or too long gathered.
Sewere, to make a feast, *kole,* on setting a stone before a *gamal.*
Si, 1. conj. disjunctive, or; *iloke si ilone,* this or that.
  2. conj. alternative, either; *si iloke si ilone,* either this or that.
  3. conj. conditional, if, whether; *sin qe wena,* if there should be rain; *si ta taro si ta nawo,* whether there be calm or surf.
  4. conj. illative, that, in order that; *ni me siwo veta ilau si ni sugsug,* he has gone down to the sea that he may bathe, in order that he may bathe; *si a sugsug,* to bathe.
  5. conj. declarative, that; *neira me gaganag ape neia si ni me*

siwo i lau, they told of him that he was gone down to the beach.

6. conj. narrative, that ; as if a clause were understood before it ; *i Qat iloke ni gate toga ran ma, nava si rarerena apena*, this Qat was not without a beginning, (but the story is) that he had a mother. An idiomatic use of *si* is of this character ; *ira tatasina we maros we la naakan Qat mun akara, wa irasoana si mun rasoara*, his brothers wanted to take his canoe to be their own, and his wife (they wanted to take) for theirs.

7. conj. of quotation, used with the sign of quotation *wa*, when there is not a direct narrative or declaration, but a reference to what has been said ; *neira me vet wa si ni me mate veta*, they said that he was dead, *i. e.* they said, this is what they said, that he was dead. The quotation is indirect. It is incorrect to use *si* in a direct quotation, or *wa si* where there is no quotation.

wa si often becomes *was.*

si 1. is used in suspense, breaking off before the alternative clause, as if asking a question ; *we tano si—?* beautiful, or is it not ? *o tanun me mate qet si?* the people would all have died—would they not ?

si qa ilo, a civil way of saying look ! also *si ka ilo.*

In the following sentence *si* is not narrative, but rather illative ; *o sava o tanun tete gilala apena, si a gilala apena pa tete lai*, something men can't understand, they want to understand but cannot ;

as if it were *neira we ge ilo si a gilala.*

sia is written for *si a*, but the two words are distinct.

Si, 8. excl. to call attention ; *si si!*

Siasiano, to disobey ; a child climbs when he has been forbidden, and falls, *we nun, ape ko me siasiano.*

Sig, to do—perhaps as in *sigsig.*

sig sasamanau, to do half of a thing ; hear part of a story ; *sasamanau.*

Siga, to double a line, or money, generally coiling it over the elbow and between the thumb and fingers, the arm being held up ; *te siga o gae, o som.*

siga motmot, to give out money for *suqe* without regularly measuring it by *siga.*

siga sur, to double a line down to shorten it.

sigag, 1. tr. to stretch the arm up and out, as in *siga ; ti sigag lue napanena.*

2. to stretch, be stretched, stand, straight up ; *o maligo we sigag kalo*, a cloud rises stretching upwards ; *sigag qatuuwa*, to stand straight up like a turtle's head out of water.

Sigerag, impersonal, to startle ; *ti sigeragia*, he is startled ; also *sigrag.*

Sigerai, (k) corner, angle ; *sigere panei*, elbow ; *sigrai.*

Sigiima, one who always stays in his house ; *sig.*

Sigirpan, to shrug the shoulder.

Sigmor, *isei we ilo a tanun a matesala, ni we sipa pata, we sigmor alo pei, o nawo.*

Sigo, a kingfisher ; a bird of a sacred character. Sam. *ti'o ;* N.H. *higo.*

pane sigo, the blue flame in fire.

Sigotete, to sail or swim fast, as a kingfisher dashes, *tama o sigo te tete*.

Sigrag, same as *sigerag*, to startle.

Sigrai, (k) corner, angle, same as *sigerai; sugrai* V.

Sigrepanei, the elbow, the outer angle.

Sigsig, 1. to get materials for a *qaranis* of food.

Sigsig, 2. very hot; *o loa we roworowo sigsig*.

Sik, to sound *si! si!* to make a hissing noise, to call attention; *sik varaget*, to stop a man with *si! si!*

Sike, to seek, look for; *sike suar*, find.
sike sasamanau, seek in the wrong place.

Siksik, redupl. *sik*, call attention with *si!* S.

Sil, the root of words meaning dark; *siliga*, &c.

Sila, 1. to stick out in a lump, project; *o pugiu we sila, o pug sila*, a lump on the buttock; *pane sila*, the projecting boom of a sail.

Sila, 2. to raise up, to be raised.
silavag, tr. determ. to erect; set up; *te silavag o mele ape mate wona*, to set up a cycas as a memorial, after it has been carried at a feast or *kolekole*.

Sile, 1. coral stone.

Sile, 2. the inner fat of a pig.

Sile, 3. a kind of yam.

Silgon, to entangle in a string; *silig, gona*.

Silig, to string, attach to a string; *sisilig matig*, to attach cocoanuts to a string.

Siliga, 1. adj. [*sil, ga* 5.] dark, black; 2. n. darkness, the dark, blackness; *silsiliga*.

Silmatoga, very dark; *sil* and perhaps *maeto*.

Silor, to poke off fruit with a stick.

Silsil, redupl. *sil*, dark, to be dark; *o qon silsil*.

Silsilig, redupl. *silig; silsilig kor*, bunch of dried bread-fruit in string; met. a bunch of flying-foxes hanging together.

Silwala,

Sim, 1, to sip, sup, up; *sim liwu*, the sound of lips supping, (Gaua word) to express refusal; *gana simpei*, to sip water while eating, as in sickness, eat and drink at once like Europeans.

Sim, 2. to dry gradually up; *me sisim qega*, has been quite dried up.

Simliw, to express refusal, reluctance, as above *sim* 1.

Simsim, 1. redupl. *sim* 1. to make the sound of sipping with the lips, see *sumsum*.

Simsim, 2. a tree.

Sin, conj. *si* with *n* 2. for *ni* pron.; same as *si ni*.

Sina, a tree, mimosa; *walsina*, the gum of it.

Sinaga, solid vegetable food, food generally, if vegetable, particularly yams.
Mtlav, *hinag*; Sesake, *vinaga*; D.Y. *winaga*.
sinaga gana valea, inferior food such as those eat who *valval* in mourning, e.g. *o nam o vanerasiu apena*, scaly yams.

Sinai, (k) the midrib of leaves, of the frondlets of palms, *sine ota* of sago; not of all leaves, but of those which have a stiff midrib.

Sinpea, same as *si nipea*, that it be not; *pea* 1.

Sin, 1. to burn, act. and neut.

2. n. a torch ; v. *sin*, to go with torches ; *sin goro*, to go after with torches. Fij. *cina.*
3. v. to fish with torches, *we sin o iga*.

sin tamate, *sin* 1., to be very hot, *o loa sin tamate*, a blazing hot sun ; compare *sar tamate*; see *tamate* 5.

Sina, to shine. Fij. *siga*, day, sun ; Mal. *sinar*; O.J. *sinang*; Mak. *singara*.

sinar, tr. to throw light upon, make to shine with reflected light.

sinarag, tr. determ. to enlighten, illuminate, *o pul we sinarag o ima*.

sinai, (k) shining.

Sinasinai, (k) redupl. *sinai*; n. shine, shining ; *o sinesine loa*, the shining of the sun, sunshine ; *o loa ti rasinar o marama mun nasinasinana*.

Sinerei, in moderation, sparely ; *we gana sinerei*.

Sino, to thrust forward the snout, as a pig smelling at food ; met. of a canoe, *we sino suar o lan*, meets a wind dead ahead.

sinov, tr. to set the snout, nose, to ; *pute sinov*, to sit nose to nose, heads close together.

vasnot, *va-sinot*, put end to end.

Sinoi, the antennæ of beetles, crawfish, &c. ; lines radiating from a point, rays, beams as of the sun, *o sinosino loa*; *o sinosino ura*, *susmawo*; *sinosinoi*.

Sinsin-nopatau, 1. to burn bread-fruit leaves in a garden, on a place prepared for a snare ; 2. a saying for not having worked.

Sio, sneeze.

Siola, M. to move along the ground, glide.

Siolo, V. same as *siola*; *sisiolo*.

Siopa, cloth ; said to be so called from the dress of Tonga visitors to Qakea, with metathesis of vowels from *siapo*. Mao. *hiapo*; Sam. *siapo*.

Sipa, 1. to turn aside ; *sipa nan*, turn aside from, err, go wrong. Mao. *hipa*; Sam. *sipa*; Mal. *simpang*; Malag. *simpan dalana*.

2. to be jagged, irregular. Mao. *hipa*, to exceed in length. Sam. *sipa*, to be awry.

Sipa, 3. slice, pare ; *sipa worawora*, slice into pieces, cut up, as a pumpkin.

matesipa, the tortoise-shell knife used for paring bread-fruit.

Sipala, the projecting ends of bamboo purlins, *varat*, of a house, sliced to a point, *sipa*, as a distinction ; an occasion for *kolekole*.

Siparnawo, a fish.

Sipe, to take off, out, pick with finger and thumb, or with toes, or in the same manner with a stick.

siperag, tr. determ. to pick off.

masipe, picked out.

Sipela, a hollow in the side of fruit.

Sipelei, a bread-fruit developed only on one side, the *uloi* showing on the other ; a cocoa-nut developed only on one side, as when something has bitten the young fruit.

Siperag, [*sipe*] to pick out, with finger, toe, stick.

Siplag, to hang up, against something, the thing hanging does not hang clear.

Sir, 1. v. to shave, cut close ; *te sir nawununa mun o mavin*;

we sir o tui, shave off the bark of an euphorbia for poisoning fish.

sirvag, tr. determ. to cut close, pare.

Sir, 2. M. to draw along, through, follów along; same as V. *sur* 1. *sirpan*, to go quite close along, *gamo sirpan*, or *sua*, sail or paddle along the shore; *sir sala*, one who follows a path; *sir vanua*, to pass successively through . villages; *sir we nana*, to go through the country drawing people from village after village into company; *sirsir navaisa, tuqei*, to go along by the cliff slope, gardens.

Sir, 3. M. prep. of motion to a person, not place; V. *sur* 9.; it has a use also of general reference, as Maewo *suri*, &c.; *ravevema wa gol amen kamam siriko*, lest your mother be angry with us on your account; *ni we tantan sir inau*, cries for me, thinking of me.

Sir, 4. M. adv. down, downwards; V. *sur* 6.

Sirgawug, mad, said of one supposed to have gone on a *gawug* where graves are; also *sirgawuw* V.

Siriam, [*sir* 1.] to nibble, *am*, the shavings of cocoa-nut.

Sirig, to move to another place of abode.

Siriga, to refuse, disobey, be disobedient.

Sirigavtag, *siriga vitag*, refuse and leave.

Siriv, a waterfall; *siriv roworua*, a double waterfall.

Sirnog, [*sir* 1.] to scrape *wo-us*, hog-plum, with a shell, *vingar*, for want of teeth; *o liwopas we na*.

Sirqae, [*sir* 1.] to make a crackling noise, *qae* 2., when shaved; *o tarape tanun gate menmen we sirqae*.

Sirsir, redupl. *sir* 1 and 2. *sirsir lovana*, a proverbial expression when food has been sold; *me tuvag qet sinaga naniko, o sirsirlovana ineira ilone me tuvag ti*.

Sirvag, tr. *sir* 1. to cut close, pare; *we sirvag o tano*, pare the surface of the ground; *sirvag valis*, cut grass close.

Sis, 1. M.V. to pierce; *sis o manui*, pierce the nose; *sis o qoroi*, pierce the lobe of the ear; *sis vinvin*, to pierce the surface; also V. *sus* 1. Mak. *sisi*; Mal. *sisip*; Malag. *sisika*.

sisgag, tr. determ. to run a point into.

Sis, 2. M.V. to point a finger, with a finger; *we sis o vanua*, point out a place; *sisvanua*, the index finger; to push the finger into; *sis o qoroi*, put the finger in the ear.

sisgag, tr. determ. to fix an accusation on a person.

Sis, 3. M.V. to rub or knock off skin or bark, flay. *me sis napaneua, napisuna*, said of the produce of a man's own work, he has rubbed off the skin of his hands and fingers at it; *na me sis napisuk apena*, I have worked at it myself; to remove the rind or bark from a large fibrous plant, *ti sis o gavar, ti vir o tal*, pulls off the fibrous bark; *me sis sisco, tagai o wiai*, tried by stripping off the outer part, no good inside.

tawasis, rubbed.

Sis, 4. M.V. 1. to swell, to be distended, increase in bulk. 2.

we sis, to be too large; when e. g. an armlet, *pane*, is too small, fits too tight, they say in Mota *we sis*, in English it is 'too small'; but *sis* refers to the arm not to the armlet, too large, not too small.

sis laqelaqe, to rise in a blister.

sis laqolaqo, to rise in a blister.

sis loqo, to swell up in a lump, as after a blow.

sis wora, be distended to bursting, swell asunder.

natoqak me sis reta, I have had enough to eat.

Sis, 5. M. same as V. *sus* 3. to shrink, to decrease in bulk, to crouch down; to cease flowing; to hide.

sis, or *sisi*, *epeepe*, to cower down below a slight shelter; *rasei ta siwo ilau, pa o wena we poa, neira te sis epeepe alo lia gate poa*.

sis malukluk, crouch with bended knees.

sisnara, money given to stop flow of blood.

sispara, to avoid by turning aside and crouching.

sisvitag, to get out of someone's way by crouching down, shrink away from.

sisig, to crowd close, shrink together.

Sis, 6. M.V. to slip.

sispalag, or *palai*, to catch the foot and slip.

sis rawarawa, to slip down a steep place, as down a cocoa-nut, or other tree trunk, as earth slips back into the hole from which it has been cast up. 7. n. landslip.

Sis, 8. M. 1. the breast, nipple. 2. to suck.

Sisepeepe, *sis* 5. slight shelter; *we log ape ima we mosiu o pei we qoqo alolona, pa o tanun we togu alolona*.

Sisgag, 1. [*sis* 1.] to stick a point into, to fasten on a point, to take up on a point, on a stick; *te sisgag lue o matig*, pierce through the eye of a cocoa-nut.

2. [*sis* 2.] put it on a person as an accusation, by pointing the finger at him.

Sisgaliwoi, [*sis* 1.] 1. what sticks into the teeth, as underdone food; 2. a small bit of food such as will get between the teeth, a toothful; *sisiga* 2.

Sisgarov, [*sis* 1.] *manoga sisgarov*, underdone, as if the hard inside can be felt by piercing; *garov*.

Sisgon, [*sis* 4.] to close firmly against, fit tight to, as the jaw of a gaff against the mast; *gona*.

Sisi, the sound made to call attention; *sik*.

Sisia, matter in the eyes, as after sleep or after inflammation; *o matai te semsem nia*.

Sisig, to shoot and glance off.

Sisiga, 1. a shrub.

Sisiga, 2. adj. [*ga* 5.] shrinking, crouching, *tama we sis* 5. *siwo*.

Sisigaliwoi, same as *sisgaliwoi*.

Sisim, to dry up, decrease as fluid, *sisim qega*; *sim* 2.

Sisiolo, n. a toboggan, a cocoa-nut rachis, *lape matig*; v. to slide down a steep place on one; *siolo*.

Sisioloolo, same as *sisiolo*, a toboggan, to toboggan.

Sisipe, a sea-snail, winkle, nerita; *we vasvas sisipe*.

Sisirat, to slip on a smooth tree, or hill.

Sisire, n. and v. looseness of

bowels, diarrhœa; *sisire nara*, in recent use, dysentery.

Sisirig, redupl. *sirig*; *o savasava we vile we qoqo*.

Sisirvag, redupl. *sirvag, olo sisirvag*, to come ashore shaving a rock.

Sisis, to cut down the trees of a dead man.

Sisisiro, to dig *qauro* on the mountain.

Sisiu, M. (k) 1. the breast, nipple; 2. breast as projecting part; the outer corner of the wall-plate of a house, *sisi ima*; boss on a rock, *o vat o sisiu apena*.
sisiu Ro Lakar, a proverbial expression referring to a woman with remarkably small breasts; *o vavae tenegag ta Luwai ape gene mantagai*.

Sisiva, mushroom coral.

Sislapa, [*sisiu*] a woman with large breasts; *nasisina we lapalapa*.

Sisnara, [*sis* 5.] money given to a man one has injured to stop the quarrel and revenge, to stop the flow of blood; *o nara tama te sis apena*.

Sispalag, [*sis* 6.] to catch the foot and slip; *palag, palai*.

Sispara, [*sis* 5.] to avoid by crouching aside; *para*.

Sisqoa, [*sis* 4.] to swell in cooking.

Sisvinvin, [*sis* 1.] to prick on the surface only, as in sewing when the needle does not go deep.

Sisvitag, [*sis* 5.] crouch down out of the way, avoid by shrinking; *vitag*.

Sito, the cry in the *mago* to mark the change in the song which the dancers are singing to themselves; the only word in which s sounds z.

Siu, 1. gall, the gall-bladder.

Siu, 2. a lump of curled hair; *we pipisiag o siu*.

Siusiu, same as *siu* 1. gall.

Sivsiv, to blow sparks of fire on a man; same as *gorgoriav*; *sivsiv ta Roua*.

Sivui, 1. the operculum of an univalve shell.
2. (k) constr. *siv*; a seed, from the shape of *sivui* 1.
o siv sava? what is it the seed of?

Sivure, a parrot.

Siwil, to crowd round; *siwil goro*.

Siwo, 1. adv. down, of direction towards the sea, West.
Mao. *iho*; Sam. *ifo*; Tong. *hifo*; Motu N.G. *diho*.
2. n. a squall, coming down; *siwosiwo*.
3. v. to come, go, down, descend.

siworag, tr. determ. to descend upon.
siwo nona kala, to descend head foremost, like a *kala* lizard.

Siwo-nur, to go deep, *nur*, down, *siwo*, into the earth, as a yam with tuber, or tree with root.

Siwo-revereve, [*reve*] to come down low, as a *tapera* with long strings on the back of the man who carries it, *veverag*.

Siwo-tano, look down to the ground; *si ta vava munsei ape sava, pa ni we ate sur gese ilo tano*.

Siwo-tuwale, a recently made word, assembly.

Siwon, lame, of hand or foot.

Siwor, 1. to rub hard and quick, as in *sososo av*.

Siwor, 2. to pelt people when they land from a new canoe at a *tursao* not their own; a joke, to be bought off.

siwor ta Gasega, a place in V.L.
3. to attack, *o vui we tatas ti siwor o tanun*, and makes him ill.

Siworag, 1. tr. determ. *siwo*, to come down upon, catch; *o siwo me siworagia*, he was caught in a squall.

Siworag, 2. to plant a second time; *siworag kel*, to plant a yam back for a second growth in order to get a very large one.

Siwosiwo, 1. same as *siwo* 2. a squall, descending gust.

Siwosiwo, 2. rheumatism, thought to go down, *siwo*.

So, an auxiliary verb, which cannot be translated without an object; to do, move. Mao. *ho*.

Soa, things used in making a *nule* image, and such works of native art; *mea*, &c.

Soae, [*so*] to go without meeting anyone or anything, *ae*.

Soai, (k) constr. *soe;* member, component part of an organic whole; *soasoai*. Mao. *hoa;* Sam. *soa*.
soe aka, met. people on board a canoe which sinks, *nina me soe aka.*

Soarua,

Soasoa, an amulet, of stone, worn round the neck, &c.

Soasoai, (k) constr. *soesoe*, members, parts of a composite whole, body, tree, canoe, house, &c. *soai*.

Soasoat, a bird, *pilage*, that cries *soat soat*.

Soat, [*so*] to proceed, go; *at*.

Soeteete, [*so*] to turn up the face; *ete* for *ate*; met. of a hoe.

Sogae, *un* word for *qoe*, pig.

Soganawono, [*so*] to be stunned by a fall, or by sorrow.

Sogavag, to crawl like an infant.

Sogo, 1. to give, bring, contribute, distribute.
sogon, tr. to stow.
sogov, tr. to make a gift.

Sogo, 2. to measure money, a measure of money; *sogo siwo*.

Sogo, 3. descriptive prefix to numerals, of things together in a bunch, such as cocoanuts; *gaviga sogorua, sogo visa*.

Sogoi, (k) n. one of the same *reve*, family division; v. to be one of the same. Fl. *hogo*, brother.

Sogon, tr. *sogo* 1. to bring together, pack, stow.

Sogoro, [*so*] to go against, meet; *goro; ni me sogoro gap*, a stone thrown at another hit this man, he came in the way of it; *sogoro numatana*, to go against the wind, meet it after starting; *ni me sogoro nanagona mun o vavae*, scolded him to his face.

Sogosanavul, [*sogo* 3.] ten in a bunch; name of a *tomago;* and of a very double hibiscus, *qagala sogosanavul*.

Sogosiwo, [*sogo* 2.] a short length, scanty measure, of money; met. *lologagara sogosiwo*, short temper.

Sogosogo, a variety of cocoa-nut, fruit small and abundant.

Sogot, tr. *sogo* 1. in *vasgot, vasogot, sosogot*.

Sogov, tr. *sogo* 1. to give freely, gratis; a free gift.

Sogovisa, [*sogo* 3.] how many? so many, in a bunch.

Soilo, [*so*] to divine, inquire about loss, death, recovery, &c.; by lifting the hands over the head and rubbing them together with a call to a ghost; the answer being given by cracking of the joints; *ilo*, to see, learn.

Sokalmagrua, M. double; *we ge sokalmagrua o gae.*

Sokalmalate, V. double, of a line; *we na sokalmalate o gae.*

Soke, 1. to seek idly for a thing, as firewood; *soke ae,* to seek and not find; *sosoke.*

Soke, 2. sweet in smell.

Sokelkeleag, [*so*] to move the eyes about.

Sokesoke, redupl. *soke* 1. sweet of smell, pungent, what is agreeable in smell to natives; *puna sokesoke.*

Soketag, and *soketai* V. untidy, careless of appearance; *ni we na soketai gap neia,* he takes no care of himself; *soke* 1.

Soko, to heap out of the way, as rubbish in making gardens, &c.; *te soko ape qeteg tangae,* throw up in a heap against a tree.

sokoi, tr. to heap up; *sokoi goro matesala,* to stop a road with trees, &c., *o ranua sin gona,* done by enemies or *tamate; sokoi goro,* heap up rubbish against or over something so as to hide it; hence met. to be hypocritical, disguise truth.

masoko, rubbish heap.

Sokom, [*so*] to stuff the mouth with large pieces of food; *komkom.*

Sokorai, constr. *sokore;* a bad, inferior, thing or person; ill-favoured, ugly; *sokore tanun,* &c.

Sokoregatava, [*sokorai*] people coming by night and besetting the door of a house, *gatava.*

Sol, to be or do beforehand; *sol goro,* anticipate.

Sola, 1. to pass away down; *o gopae me rap, me rap kalo, me rap lue, me sola sur,* the progress of a disease; see *solasola.*

Sola, 2. n. a grub.

Solalape, [*so*] to draw the bow, *ukag.*

Solanalana, [*so*] to turn on edge, as when wind blows the trees to one side above a cliff; to be blown to one side; *lanalana.*

Solasola, redupl. *sola* 1. to pour forth in a thick stream, as matter from an abscess; met. of fluent speech.

Soleas, [*so*] to alter course; *ni me soleas naranona,* turned his foot instead, *leas,* another way.

Solil, [*so*] to go beside the way, turn out of the way, *lil.*

Soloi, 1. a mark set up as a warning that something is reserved, forbidden. 2. to set such a mark; *we soloi goro o salagoro.*

Solorag, to be general in a place; *o gopae solorag,* an epidemic disease; *we mena solorag,* fruits ripen all together, same as *we mena nol.*

Solqelate, [*so*] to hang on both sides over a line; *so-luqelate.*

Solsol, [*sol*] adv. beforehand, prematurely, too soon.

Solsoloi, redupl. *soloi,* a place or thing with mark of reserve.

Som, 1. a univalve cone shell used for making money. 2. native money; made of *som* 1.; *som ta Roua,* fine and valuable *som* worn as necklace; *manmanosom,* very small, not used as money but for ornament.

som raravaragoro, money paid to secure effect of charms; see *raravara.*

Soma, to gobble, eat like a pig.

Somalarowo, [so] to give a start, startle; malarowo.

Soman, [so] to put the nose to, smell; manui.

Somantag, [so] to take good care; mantag; ko we so mantagiko nan wa tara wora napanema.

So-matamot, [so] to give the last thing.

So-mate, [so] be quiet properly; mate 2.

So-matemate-lea, to follow a new phrase, take up a new word, as the sul does in any place.

So-mavmav, [so] to tire, make one tired of a thing; mav; as of food so as to sicken him, or a beating that he may not come again.

So-mot, [so] to take a short route, turn off from the main road, or from the road hitherto followed.

Somotag, tr. somot, to do work badly, scamp work, not go on straight with work.

Somtak, [so mataka] to put oneself forward, presume.

Son, to take a deep breath.
sonnag, tr. breathe deep in preparation.

Sonago, [so] to turn the face, with hatred, distrust; also without composition, ni we so nanagona.

Sonatrena, a ripe wotaga, yellow, rena.

Sonenenene, [so] to pant, with heaving breast; navarana we sonenenene apesa? nene.

Sonnag, [son] to take a deep breath and bang the drum in starting a sawai; we sonnag o kore, o lakalaka, to start; met. sonnag o vagalo, to begin a fight with a dash.

Sonun, to go off with report; so nun; o tamate we sonun.

Son, to deceive.

Sonarnarag, [so] to go about hawking things for sale; narag.

Sonerag, to shake, as one shakes water in a cup, or a sleeper.

Sonon, a mispronunciation of sogon, but good Mota.

Sonorag, to stretch out the legs, sit or lie with outstretched legs.

Sonus, [so] to put out the lips, nusnui, a sign of hatred, to show hate, to hate; also, ni we so nanusnua.

Sopata, [so] to enter, turn into a house; pata.

Sope, to mark with leaf or flower, the sign of something reserved or forbidden; we rou sope, according to tamate or rank in suqe.

Sopesur, to shoot at a long distance.

Sopuga, large, swelling, as the calf of the leg.

Sopun, [so] utterly, completely; pun 1.; gana sopun, to eat completely up.

Soqantela, sudden, unexpected.

Soqo, abundant, in excess.
soqosoqo, adv. excessively, without restraint.
soqosoqoga, adj. [ga 5.] excessive.

Soqoron, [so] to expose to hard weather; qoron.

Sor, 1. to be close, firm; soru.

Sor, 2. to turn colour in getting ripe; soroga, asor; sor qaro, turn while unripe, met. of one who appears unexpectedly.

Sor, 3. n. a plant, amomum, used in charms; sor iga, a variety; o sor me arutia.

Sora, to plan, arrange for; sora

N

o ganagana, arrange for a feast; *sora ninag*, to put off what has been arranged for; *sorasora vannag o vanoga*, to keep on putting off a start; *sora rusag*, to arrange for payment, agree about wages.

sorav, tr. to plan against, for, a person.

Soraka, [*so*] to pay a party for dancing.

Sorako, at a time, prefixed to number, *sorako visa?* how many at once? *sorako tol*, three at a shot; *ni me gana sorasorako o avrik wa o qatagiav*.

So-ranoi, to go, move the foot; not a compound word, *ni me so naranona*.

Sorarai, *sorarag*; to point, aim, an arrow; *te sorarai avunansei o qatia*; probably *sora*.

Sorasora vannag, to keep putting off; *sora*.

Sorav, tr. *sora*, to make plans, plot, against a person, *me soraria*; in good sense to settle for, *we sorav o ganagana*.

Soro, to take a long breath with a sound; to make a droning noise like a *puna* tree-cricket; *soro kalo*, to draw deep breath with noise; *we soro*, to be at the last gasp.

sorov, tr. make a snorting noise at.

Soroga, [*sor* 2.] red, colour of *pes nai* when ripe. *sorsoroga*, dark red.

Sororo, [*so*] 1. to set about a report, *roroi*, start news. 2. to make a sound as an omen, as *sigo* and certain birds do; *sororo matua*, to cry on the right a favourable, *galao* on the left an unfavourable, omen; *o man me sororo matua, galao*.

3. *me sororo galgalao ape neia*, said of one who boasts and fails; *sororo poroporo*, a mocking omen.

sororog, tr. to set afoot a report, to make known, proclaim.

Sorov, to grunt, snort, at; tr. *soro; o mala me sorovia*, the sow made an angry noise in her throat at him.

Sosor, 1. adv. *o rigariga we riga aneane apensei we log si we riga sorsor*; probably from colour.

Sorsor, 2. n. cinnamon, *vin sorsor* cinnamon bark; *sor* 2.

Sorsoroga, [*sor* 2.] dark red, colour of ripe *pes nai*, of very ripe *gaviga*, dark crimson.

Sorsororo, [*sororo*] *lea sorsororo*, a rumour.

Soru, same as [*sor* 1.] to be close and firm, as a string drawn close, a hole in which a thing fits tight.

soru, or *sor*, *netenete* quite fast and tight.

soruga, adj. [*ga* 5.] fast and firm, as a big tree.

Sosalamate, [*so*] to be ready for a start, *salamate*.

Soso, 1. to rub backwards and forwards, as a stick in a groove, or in a hole; *we sososo av*, make fire with stick and groove.

sososo o vini uwa, a strip of bamboo with the fibres pinched from the edge is twisted in a screw and used for sawing tortoise-shell in making the hook for taking flying-fish.

Soso, 2. to stuff, pack, be stuffed; *me soso goro*, stuffed so as to prevent passage; *nalinak we soso*, my voice is stuffed, I am too hoarse to speak; *soso ura*, to pack full; to prepare a charm by stuffing a bamboo with various magical ingredients.

sosomag, tr. determ. to stuff something.

vasosov, to push on, as by shoving into a pack.

Sosogongon, 1. difficult, *gona*, to pack more, because full; *soso* 2.

Sosogongon, 2. [*so*] deep hollow in shape, *gonogono*, said of a pool, *qilo a lau*.

Sosogot, redupl. *sogot; maran sosogot*, a fruitful season; *vene sosogot*, to shoot by accident.

Sosoke, redupl. *soke*, to go carelessly after and fetch things; *ape sa ko me sosoke ma o matig we puna?* what do you mean by bringing me stinking cocoanuts? *ni we taka o suava, we sosoke alele ima*, going on a voyage he fetches food, money, &c. from the house.

Sosolea, to tempt to leave husband or wife.

Sosoleag, to spoil food, tumbling it in the dirt.

Sosomag, 1. tr. determ. *soso*, to stuff, pack, a thing; 2. to let down the hook into the sea in fishing with a line.

Soso makomako, filling the garland in the reception of a member of the *suqe; sese makomako*.

Soso-nam-ta-Qakea, to sit down at one end of the *gamal;* the Qakea people stow away yams at the one end of the house.

Sosope, a wrap of *loko* in *toape* leaves.

Sosoporapora, a charm to make wind; *pora*.

Sosopunpun, word used in charming.

Sosoromiga, very hot, causing people to pant, *soro; o tine liwomaran sosoromiga*, gasping hot at noon.

Sososor, to make a present of money to visitors in the way of a loan, *we tawe*, which they have to repay.

Sosotana, to bring food to sell, as people from other villages do on a death; *soso tana*, fill the bag.

Sosovanirnir, to crowd into a place; *nir*.

Sosovaqirqir, to crowd into a place; *qir*.

Sosovunvun, a word used as a charm, like *sosopunpun*.

Sosur, [*so*] 1. to give, *so sur ma*, as *la sur ma*, give me some; *sur* 5. 2. to cut off low down.

Sot, probably tr. *so; sot mot*, cut short.

Sotal, [*so*] 1. to make a round out of the way, a détour, same as *van tal;* 2. to set oneself up, boast, *ni we sotal kelua*.

sotaliva, pride, boasting; verbal noun.

Sotaplag, [*so*] make to fall end over end; *tapulag*.

Sotaqa, [*so*] said of many working well together; *taqa*.

Sotaso, [*so*] to go straight on, *taso*.

Sotmot, [*sot*] to cut off short, as a long line in the middle.

Sotoga, [*so*] to subside, quiet down; *natoqana gate sotoga lai; toga*, to sit.

Sou, 1. a large-leaved prickly solanum.

Sou, 2. v. 1. to lengthen by addition, by joining on, splicing on; *malawo sou* of a *qeta* starting to grow afresh; 2. to graft, as they graft crotons, *sasa;* 3. met. to set oneself up, be proud, *sou kelua*.

soua, a joint, joining; a joint of the body, a joining of boards, of ataps of thatch.

Souleas, a plant the shoots of which can be transferred and grafted, *sou*, one into the place of the other, *leas*.

Sov, probably tr. *so;* to rest on, lean against; met. trust on and in; *apesov*, with easy mind; *ni we sov naapena*, he leans himself on what supports him, he is confident, at ease.

Sova, 1. to draw breath with difficulty; to have asthma; *sova wora*, just draw difficult breath, *i. e.* be expiring; *sova mot* 1. to draw the last breath; *sova mot* 2. to breathe with difficulty because of rage, so to forbid, threaten. 2. n. asthma.

Sovake, to hold the breath, in astonishment, or listening.

Sovanovano, [*so*] to do quietly, before others.

Sowag, [*so*] to go without thought of danger, *wag; sowag lue*.

Sowo, excl. in approbation, satisfaction.

Sowot, [*so*] to come out, stand forth, *wot; i gene iloke me sowot lue;* rather a Gaua word.

Sowotawota, [*so*] to stand up, stick up, *wota*, as a thing buried sticks up out of the ground.

Sowotwot, [*so*] to cut off a tree high up; *sosur* 2.

Sua, to paddle; make a canoe voyage.
  suava, a paddling, canoe voyage; *we taka o suava*, to start on a voyage.
  sua goro o aka ta Gaua, proverbial, to paddle after a Gaua canoe, to anticipate without cause; it will come soon enough without going after it.

Suaqea, to lean; *o ima we garaqa we tira, ti naru ti sua qea, rigrig ti masu.*

Suar, 1. v. to present itself, appear, as a vision; impersonal; 2. adv. so as to attain to, coming to hand; *ilo suar*, to find by looking; *tano suar*, feel for and find, find by touch; *sike suar*, find, seek and attain; *taur suar*, meet with and hold; *o maran suar*, a fruitful season, when fruits present themselves.

Suava, paddling, verbal n. *sua*, a canoe voyage made by paddling not sailing.

Sueg, to pass over, give over; *ukeg mamasa.*

Suei, a wedge of *lot; tuaniu we nolo nol; we sura mun o igot.*

Sug, 1. to wash; neut. to get into water; *sugsug*, to bathe.
  vasug, to wash, tr.
  sug tatano, to feel about for *sisipe* and other shell-fish while in the water; *tano.*

Sug, 2. to dig up, transplant; *sugleas*, take up and transplant. Mao. *huke.*

Sug, 3. 1. to grow up in a quantity, of plants. 2. to stand up on end.
  1. *sug lanar*, to grow up, as seedlings, in abundance, *lanar; sug raka*, begin to grow up.
  2. *sugsug raka*, of the hair in fright, *naqatik ti sugraka; naapena ti sugraka*, he is recovering his spirits; *apei.*

Suga, M. same as *suwa* V. to move backwards stooping.
  suga pelu, to move backwards and in a round.

suga qote, to back with the head low; *masu suga qote*, fall backwards on one's seat.

sugasuga, met. to loathe, *sugasuga nan*.

Sugrai, (k) V. same as *sigerai* M. an angle, corner.

Sugsug, 1. redupl. *sug* 1., to bathe; *sugsug nol*, to bathe the whole person; *sugsug matika*, as the bird washes in *qilos tangae*, to wash a little; *sugsug non o pilage*, scanty washing, as of that bird.

sugsug sese, to dive, or to go into the water, for *sese* a shell-fish.

Sugsug, 2. redupl. *sug* 3., to stand on end with fright; *naqatina ti sugsug raka.*

Sugsug, 3. *un* word for a charm, *takamatai.*

Suke, to make a noise in driving away fowls; to drive away fowls with that noise, *we suke o toa.*

Sul, 1. n. a number of people together, crowd, the people of a place; 2. all, in the mass, of people only; *o tanun sul*, all men; 3. v. to meet, come together in a crowd, *we sul ma.*

Sula, to shovel.

susula, to root in the earth, of pigs.

sulatag, tr. to shovel up.

Sulasula, a small black larva in dung.

Sulataramoa, a centipede. Mao. *hura.*

Sulatag, tr. determ. *sula*, to shovel up with the snout, as pigs do in rooting.

Sulate, a worm; Mal. *ulat*; Bat. *hulat*; Malag. *olitra*; Tag. *bulati.*

Sulavagarua, double kernel, cocoa-nut with two developed carpels.

Sule, a bivalve, cockle; the Maori *pipi.*

Sulet, to shove up; *we suletia*, give one a shove up a tree.

Suleverua, two cocoa-nuts in one husk, the partition between not hard; two *vara*, two trees will grow up; rare; *sulavagarua.*

Suliu, M. a sucker from roots, shoot from tubers; see *sului* V.

Sulitotou, the growth from yams remaining in the ground not harvested; *o sulsuliu we totou.*

Sulsul, redupl. *sul*, assemble in numbers; *o lou we titkeliga, gate sulsul tiqa*, the sun is too hot for people to come together in their parties.

Sului, V. same as *sulin*; 1. sucker, *o sului ti ana lue ma nan o tano*; 2. met. children, offspring.

3. *un* word for *qeta*, caladium. Sam. *suli.*

Sulvetal, name of a fish; banana sucker.

Sum, the noise made to call pigs. *sumsum*, to call pigs to their food.

Sumut, a fish; if one has been killed the blood, &c. will attract others, *ta ge mate, pa o tuaniu me toa, te kel ma*; hence proverbial expression, *we ronronotag o nare sumut*, when men in succession go to a village and are killed.

Sun, to trickle out, as in trying out cocoa-nuts for oil, *o ligiu we sun lue, alo we sala sun*; to drip, weep like stones.

sunur, tr. trickle.

Sunpei, to trickle with water; said of wet firewood, also of drinking while eating.

Sunsun, to swell with fluid; *naranona we sunsun,* before death.

Sunur, tr. *sun;* 1. to be full of water which trickles out, as a rotten log; 2. to trickle along; *sunur rorono,* as water creeps through grass.

Suna, same as *nuna,* to look out for something one desires, such as a loan.

suna mot goro, to seek an opportunity to do harm to a person; *ni we suna mot goroko; ko ta mule ma te ge iniko.*

sunasuna, seek for a loan of money, be a borrower.

Sunur, to stupefy, make one heavy; *o ganagana soqosoqo te sunur isei; ni te gana sunuria.*

Suqe, 1. the club, society, a conspicuous feature of native life; 2. to join the club; *suqe veto,* one who does not join, *gate suqesuqe.*

Sur, 1. v. V. to draw along, through, follow along; same as *sir* 2.; see *sur lau, surpei, sursala.*

2. with same root meaning, *susur,* to sew.

3. to sing; *we sur o as,* to sing a song, *i. e.* to follow the tune through its successive parts; thence generally to sing.

Sur, 4. V. to shave; same as M. *sir* 1.

Sur, 5. impers. v. to tire; *me sur nau o tautaur ima,* I am tired of house-building; *me gis val goro nol, gate sur sei nan,* all went to work, not one got tired and left off.

6. to do, go for a while; *nina sur wora galtag iake a Masevono,* let us stop short here for a while, not being able to reach Gaua further on; *map sur namona,* desist; *toga sur,* desist; probably also from this *vasur goro,* to prevent.

Sur, 7. adv. down, downwards; M. *sir* 4.

8. v. to put down; *we sur o gape,* to lay a net, begin to set.

Sur, 9. V. prep. motion to a person, not place; *sir* 3.

Sur, 10. excl. M. indeed! is it not so? V. *tasur.*

Sur, 11. constr. *suriu,* bone.

Sura, 1. v. 1. to push in lengthways, introduce, as into an opening or narrow space; *sura lue,* to poke a hole through; *tape sura,* to enter a house, by the narrow entrance; 2. to push the *igot* knife under the wedge, *suei,* of *lot.*

surag, tr. to poke a thing.

suravag, tr. determ. to push a thing in.

vasurat, to push forward.

Sura, 2. a narrow entrance, as into which one must *sura* 1. particularly the entrances into *Panoi,* Hades, in several places, of various character; *sure lumagav, sure tupa.*

Surag, 1. tr. *sura* 1. to poke off fruit with a stick introduced between branches, &c.

Surag, 2. to bow, throw oneself forward on the face; *ti suragia;* probably also *sura* 1. in the sense of throwing oneself forward at length.

Surata, mid-day; *liwo-surata, tine liwosurata.*

Suravag, 1. tr. *sura* 1.; to thrust in lengthways; as an arrow into grass to hide it.

2. adv. completely; *vus suravag,* to kill every one, *gana suravag,* eat everything.

Surere, 1. a scitamineous plant; *nosurere,* used for closing thatch on ridge of houses.

Surere, 2. a place more distant than *Panoi; a Surere.*

Surere, 3. see *sur-rere.*

Suriu, M. (k) constr. *sur;* bone. met. strength, *ineia mun nasurina.* A common word in Mel. Mafoor *kur;* Fl. *huli,* body ; N.B. *ur;* N.G. *uri, kuri, turia.*

suriga, bony.

Surgolo, trembling of the bones, in fear or anxiety ; *nipea nasurima we gologolo;* redupl. *surgologolo; nan we rave alo surgolo o aka me nina veta ma,* I am anxious not to miss the chance of writing.

Surlau, [*sur* 1.] to follow the beach.

Surlava, *sura* 2., *lava* 2. a mountain in V.L.

Surmake, a small thing.

Surmarea, lycopodium squarrosum, eel's backbone.

Surmata, (k) tears ; *o surmata we tapitu.*

Surpei, [*sur* 1.] follow stream of water.

Surpupuima, [*sur* 1.] to go round by the back of the houses, *pup,* not coming into the *tinesara* from shyness.

Sur-rere, [*rere*] trembling of the bones, *suriu;* fear, apprehension; *nasurina we rerere;* incorrectly *surere* 3.

Sursala, [*sur* 1.] one who keeps in the road. M. *sirsala.*

Sursuriga, [*ga* 5.] bony ; *suriga.*

Surtagtageag, [*sur* 7.] to make of no account, despise ; *tagea.*

Surtamate, 1. an arrow with head of dead man's bone, *sur tamate.*
2. a tree.

Surtatas, [*sur* 8.] to pay beforehand for work.

Surun, to blow the nose ; *surun nav,* expel mucus from nose.

Surunqote, full-grown, come to full size ; *qote.*

Surut, collection of rain-water in hollow of stones on beach.

Survitag, adv. *vava survitag,* to tell openly of something wrong done.

Surwotmalai, a man makes a present by way of acknowledgment, *malai,* to his *reregae* who comes upon him, *wot,* as he goes along, *sur* 1., and finds him working in his garden.

Sus, 1. V. same as *sis* 1. to pierce; run through ; *o gatava o lape ota me sus,* the door is made of sago stalks run through with a stick.

susgag, same as *sisgag* 1.

Sus, 2. V. 1. the breast ; *we tiu o sus,* give the breast ; teats of pigs, &c. 2. to suck : same as *sis* 8. See *susiu.*

Sus, 3. V. same as *sis* 5. to shrink, crouch down, sink ; see compound words ; *neira me sus qet; o loa si o vula we sus,* if it goes down behind mountains, *we tul* in the sea. *o loloi we sus,* the heart sinks, spirits fail ; to be dismayed ; *risa sus,* lie down and hide.

susrag, tr. push down, force under.

4. to sweal, melt away in burning, as a *pul,* native candle.

Sus, 5. V. same as *sis* 6. to slip.

Sus, 6. a kind of yam.

Sus, 7. a tree the leaves of which are used to poison fish. Motu N.G. *duha.*

Susgag, tr. *sus* 1. same as *sisgag* 1.

Susgalete, [*sus* 3.] to shrink with

a curl like a *wosoisoi*, to warp like wood, or underdone food in oven.

Susganere, [*sus* 3.] same meaning as *susgalete*.

Susgoro, [*sus* 3.] to crouch, squat down, with a gesture of contempt or derision against someone; *tama avawo tas;* hence to assert with that gesture.

Susiu, (k) constr. *susi*, the breast, paps, dugs of animals; the projecting boss of a rock, the outer corner of wall-plate of house, *susi ima;* same as *sisiu; sus* 2. Mao. *u;* Sam. *susu;* Fij. *sucu;* Mal. *susu;* Dy. Tag. *suso.*

Suslelo, an annelid in holes in coral, covered with poisonous *qaligiu* hairs.

Susletou, a millepede in rocks by the sea.

Susmalukluk, [*sus* 3.] to crouch with bending knees in fear or hiding; *maluk.*

Susmawo, the native cockroach; now the common cockroach.

Suspata, [*sus* 3.] to crouch down and hide; *pata.*

Susrag, tr. *sus* 3. to make to *sus*, to go down, push down, force under; *te susray o av alo tarowo, si a ge mate, sin sus; susrag tayea*, get rid of by pushing down.

Susramalue, to dive through a hole in the rocks.

Susravag, redupl. *susuravag, suravag* to lay at length; met. of an industrious man.

Susrene, [*sus* 3.] to crawl; *susrenerene*, to crawl under a small shelter.

Sustaqa, [*sus* 3.] to duck the head, dodging a missile; *taqa.*

Susug, [*sus* 5.] also *susuw*, to slip out.

Susuga, redupl. *suga.*

Susugnat, a fish.

Susui, V. (k) constr. *susu;* same as *sisiu* and *susiu*, from *sus* 2. breast, dugs, nipple; boss of stone, corner of house.

Susula, redupl. *sula,* v. and n.; *tano susula, susule qoe*, rooting place of pigs.

Susuletou, same as *susletou.*

Susuluaga, [*ga* 5.] of the skin, having a creeping feeling, goose-flesh.

Susunur, redupl. *sunur,* inert, heavy.

Susur, redupl. *sur* 2. to sew. In sewing mats for a sail a needle is used, a ray's sting, *togo var,* or sharp piece of tree-fern wood, *o qatia o qasai apena,* with a head to which the string, *gavaru,* is tied. In sewing on thatch the *qatia* is used as a pricker, and the fern-line, *gaqir,* follows in the holes, *we sus mun o qatia, qara arovag tataga.*

Susurut, [*sur* 1.] to draw forward, advance.

Susus, V. redupl. *sus* 1. to stick on points, branches or twigs, as certain fruits are put up as marks.

Sususu, redupl. *sus* 5. to slip away downwards as rotten stuff comes to pieces in the hands.

Sususug, redupl. *susug,* to slip and fall, as out of the hands, or out of a bundle.

Sususuw, V. redupl. *susuw,* same word with *sususug.*

Susuwui, a kind of *qeta,* caladium esculentum.

Suswona, a certain *Vui.*

Sutarara, a young cocoa-nut with

shell just formed, and *ligiu* fluid within not yet fit to drink, *tam o nawo, we pei nia; sus tarara.*
Sutavun, to make a false accusation or imputation against a person; *kamiu we sutavun inau.*
Suwa, V. same as *suga* M. to step back bending forward, to bow down and draw back.
 suwa ae, to move backwards and fall; *suwa mule*, said of a stone which rebounds and strikes, *o vat suwamule; suwa qote*, to step back with head very much down; *suwa tatu*, to bump against when stepping back; *suwa pata*, to back into hiding; *suwa valiliug*, to go over backwards.
suwav, tr. to lay an egg; see *varsuwavrua*.
Suware, to send, send for, with *at* or *ma*, to call by voice or messenger, to fetch.

T.

T, 1. tr. suffix to verbs; *wono* close adj. *wonot* to make close.
T, 2. euphonic, sometimes inserted between vowels; as *rakatia* for *raka-ia*.
Ta, 1. prep. of, belonging to, in relation to place; *o tanun ta Mota, o ravae ta Mota;* with the same sense in compound prep. *tape, talo, tamen, tavune,* &c., also with adv. *ta iake, ta vunana.* Some compounds, such as *pun-ta-lig-as, lesles-tagasuwe* show a general sense of relation, as in Fl., Bugotu, *ta;* Northern N.H. *ta.*
Ta, 2. v. p. modal, potential, optative, commonly with view to future.
Ta, 3. prefix of condition with verbs, sometimes with nouns; by which something like a participle is obtained; not so much passive as middle; see *taavaava, takorkor, tanasenase,* &c. Common in Bks. Ids. and Northern N.H. *ta, t-, 'a, da;* Fiji, *ta;* Sol. Ids., Fl., Bugotu, *ta;* D.Y. *ta;* Mao. *ta.*
Ta, 4. n. (k) companion, mate, person with one; *tak! eke tak!* friend! mate! With suff. pron. comes to be translated 'and'; *tak i tasik*, I and my brother, *i.e.* my brother was my companion, the person with me on the occasion; *taksei?* who will go with me? who my companion? *tamasei?* who was with you? who your companion? *kara tak tamak*, I and my father, *i. e.* we two, my father being the person with me; *tana tamana,* he and his father, *i. e.* there was he, and his companion in the affair his father. So through every person and number. The use is not restricted to, though appropriate with, persons; *o tuka tan o tano*, heaven and earth. Probably this *ta* is originally the same with *ta* 1.
Ta, 5. n. man, human being. Mtlv. *et;* Volow, *ta;* Motu N.G. Celebes, *tau;* Rotuma, *fa;* the stem in Fiji *tamata,* N.H. *tamoli, tanaloe, tatua, takata;* Mao. *tangata;* Mota, *ta-nun* real man, living, *ta-mate* dead man, *ta-vine* woman, female human being; see *tamaragai, tamatua, ta-maur, tavus.*

Ta, 6. adjectival term.; *sasarita* from *sar, taperata* from *tapera;* Fiji, *ta, dregadregata* gluey, *drega* glue; Maewo, *sa*.
Ta, 7. constr. of *tae*, dung.
Taaloalo, [*ta* 3., *alo* 2.] leaning forward; *rereg taaloalo*.
Taam, [*ta* 7., *am*] 1. when grating almonds one nibbles the bits on the grater, *we am o nai nan o vai; o taam;* hence 2. v. impersonal, to be very nice to a person; *we gana o sinaga we neremot, we vet si we taamiam inau*.
Taavaava, [*ta* 3., *ava* 1.] tottering, as if missing footing, *ava*, as under a heavy load.
Tae, n. (k) constr. *ta;* 1. excrement, dung; *gak taema*, an expression of admiration. 2. bits, remnants, inferior parts; *taam, taus, taetaeai*.
Mao. Pol. *tae, kae;* Macassar, *tai;* Malag. *tay;* Mal. *tahi;* Bat. *ta, tahe;* Motu N.G. *tage;* Pon. *jak,* to defæcate.
Taera, a shrub.
Taereere, [*ta* 3. *ere*] slender.
Taetaeai, [*tae*] n. part of a thing not so good as the rest, as fruit near the rind; *taetae aka*, a poor kind of canoe.
Tag, 1. n. neighbourhood, land round a village; *a tag ta Tasmate*, near Tasmate.
Tag, 2. constr. of *tagiu*.
Tag, 3. tr. determ. suff. to v.; *rono* to be in a state of feeling, *ronotag* to feel something; *al* to go about, move, *altag* to go about looking after something. Bks. Ids. *tag, teg, tea, te;* N.H. *tag, tagi, tai, ta;* Fiji, *taka;* D.Y. *tai;* Sam. *ta'i*.
Tagagaro, [*ta* 7., *garo* 1.] such as can only be scooped up, of water, cannot be dipped into; *kamam me gagagaro o tagagaro*.
Tagai, 1. n. nothing, naught; 2. v. to be nothing, come to naught, not to be; *me tagai;* 3. negative, not, no. Not the negative with verbs, see *gate, tete*. With *i* 5. *itagai*.
Tagaragara, [*ta* 3., *gara* 2.] open, gaping, *o wo-make we tagaragara*, a chestnut that is coming open; *tira tagaragara*, stand with legs apart.
Tagarawae, [*ta* 3., *gara* 1.] *me kota mot*.
Tagarir, a mantis with brown-yellow wings, in dead trees; *pan-tagarir*.
Tagataga, 1. n. rim of stones on edge round the mouth of an oven, *o tagataga ape pagig um;* 2. adv. on edge, *map tagataga, wil tagataga*, set, raise, on edge; *matir tagataga*, sleep lying on the shoulder; *av-tagataga*.
Tagea, to be lost, be gone.
tageag, tr. redupl. *tagtageag,* make of no account.
Tagege, [*ta* 3.] fall sick again after apparent recovery, to have a relapse; of an old wound breaking out again.
Tagelegele, [*ta* 3.] straight.
Tagere, 1. a bird, flycatcher.
Tagere, 2. an amulet, of coral stone.
Tagir, M. 1. n. (k) back, back parts, *a tagirik* at my back, behind me; 2. adv. behind; V. *tawur*.
Tagir-mera, younger child.
Tagiu, (k) constr. *tag, tagi;* owner, proprietor, employer, master; *i tag nona* the owner of it, *arivtag o ima i tag nona me ratnorag o gene ti aia* near

the house the owner of which had hid the thing there ; *tag pug, tag mon pug* a creditor, lender.
tagiaka, owner of a canoe, of whom there may be many, *qat-tagiaka* the captain among them, *we gilala o turwose;* *tagiima*, householder ; *tagvanua*, a joint owner in a village; *tagtuqei*, the man whose garden it is.
Tagogoi, [*ta* 3.] happening quickly, quickly ; *gogoi.*
Tagole, [*ta* 3.] rolling, move rolling from side to side, *gole;* *tagole lue* said of big pig or heavy man.
Tagologolo, [*ta* 3.] straight ; not from *golo.*
Tagor, to cook grated dry almonds, ne *kor*, by themselves.
Tagora, 1. n. the inside of yam scooped out, *wawarir*, before planting; probably *ta* 7. and *gora* in *goras.*
Tagora, 2. to rush headlong, roll, bundle out ; *ta* 3., *gora* 1. ; *tagora sasariaeae, o qoe qe valago a navaisa.*
tagorai, such a thing as will roll ; *o gene we taptapapa.*
Tagtageag, redupl. *tageag;* of no account ; *nom tagtageag*, think nothing of, despise.
Tagut, to be startled ; a pig when roused *we tagut;* from stem of *matagut*, which see.
Tagvanua, 1. an owner of house, house site, &c., in a village, *tagiu.* 2. (k) neighbour ; the suff. pron. belonging to *vanua; tag-vanuak*, one who has a house in my village, my neighbour.
Tak, 1. v. to convey, hither or thither with *ma* and *at*, take, bring.

Tak, 2. expl. excl. *eke tak!* but *ta* 4. with suff. pron. *k.*
Taka, 1. to undertake, set about, attend to ; *ni gate taka* does not stir ; *gate taka ran* refuses ; *taka o vanoga, o snawi*, to undertake, begin, a journey, a voyage, *na gate taka ran ineira* would not consent to them.
Taka, 2. to attach, be attached, as with fingers over a string.
takar, tr. 1. to take between fingers and pull, as in gathering cocoa-nuts ; *o matig we sargaela tete takar lai*, a cocoa-nut with a tough stalk cannot be gathered so, it will not come away when pulled with the stalk between the fingers. 2. met. of the feelings, attachment, yearning ; *nalolok we takar ape neia, suria.*
Taka, 3. to do violence, same meaning as *kesa.*
takas, tr. to do violence to, attack ; *o tamate te taktakas o matawonowono*, a member of a ghost society chases and beats the uninitiated.
Takarakara, dry, parched ; *o nene takarakara alo marou.*
Takarkar, redupl. *takar*, to have a longing ; *o valai we takarkar* said of one who has a longing to eat meat or fish.
Takataka, redupl. *taka* 1. to be quick, active, up and about, to do quickly and well.
Takau, to catch hold, attach ; *o palao me takau*, convulsive twitching has seized him ; *taka* 2. ; *vatakau.*
Takaura, a kind of yam.
Takavakava, [*ta* 3.] of the toes, wide apart.
Take, stem of *mataketake.*
Takelaiwa, 1. to carry a thing on a stick over the shoulder, *iwa*,

the burden being at the end; 2. to balance a burden at one end of a stick with a weight at the other; in either case it is *takele iwa*, not a complete *iwa* carrying.

Takela-rua-au, a bamboo strip that cuts on both sides; proverbial expression; see *nig* 2.

Takelei, (k) a part, piece; *a takelei*, partly; *a takelei a takelei*, bit by bit.

takelei is also a *sogoi*, as a part of the *veve*; *takele rua*, a man and his *sogoi*, both sides complete. The two preceding words show *takela* for *takele* constr.

Takir, to be lazy, careless about one's own business; *ni me takir gap, gate gagapalag nagana.*

Tako, to hang by some attachment, neut., as fruit by a stalk, bat by its claws; a child *we tako sage* clings to, hangs on, the back of one who *pepe* it; *tako ususur.*

Takoakoa, [*ta* 3.] to stagger, with a weight; *koa.*

Takolate, 1. v. to hang, *tako*, and break, *late*, like a fruit that does not develop but falls off; 2. adv.: short off, prematurely; *rave takolate*, to pull and the thing breaks; *vava takolate*, to break off in a story.

●**Takolo**, 1. a wading bird.

Takolo, 2. a. volute shell, olive; used in charms.

Takolokolo, [*ta* 3.] shallow, shrunk, of water dried up by the sun, of low tide.

Takor, [*ta* 3., *kor*] 1. black, dark; 2. a black crab; *iniko takor*, you are as black as a *takor* crab.

Takorkor, [*ta* 3., *kor*] not redupl.

of preceding, but of same composition; dry, dried up.

Takoromag, to crackle in the mouth in eating.

Taktakar-ga-vara, to make angry, as plucking, *takar*, at the heart, or liver, strings.

Taktakas, 1. redupl. *takas,* attack, fight; 2. with *goro*, resist, contend with; *taktakas goro matila*, withstand in vain.

Takuk, to grasp in closed hand; *me takuk ti, qara ul o panei, we saka.*

Takul, to catch hold of, grasp, constrain.

Takura, to fasten down with stones; *te takura o loko alo um sin manoga* stones are put on *loko* in the oven, that it may cook well; *we takura o vilog a lau, qara kor*, the leaf of an umbrella palm is spread on the beach and kept down in place with stones, so as to dry in shape.

Tal, 1. n. same as *tali*, a line, rope.

Tal, 2. v. to go round; act. neut.; *we tal o vanua*, go round about in a place; *o iga we tal o gape*, fish to go round and round in a net; same as *tale.*

taliag, tr. to turn round.

talig, tr. to make circuit.

taliog, tr. to surround.

3. to lay out money, *we tal o som,* not in a coil, but in loops backwards and forwards.

4. n. a turn from one stick round the other and back, when they *siga o som;* a double length.

5. descriptive term, from 4., in counting money, *tal visa* so many turns, *tal sanavul* ten turns, double lengths.

6. adv. round about, around; *mule tal*, go round.

Tala, 1. to turn round the head;

tala ris, turn round so as to look the other way; *nanagomu we tala*, your face is turned away. 2. to refuse to recognize, from the motion of turning away; to disclaim, deny that one knows; fail to see.
tatalag, tr. to turn the head with reference to persons.
tatalaiga, adj. ignoring, careless.
ti-tatala, forget.
Tala, 2. *we gaw o tala tano* in preparing for planting a garden, gather up in hands rubbish, small bits of wood, &c., and put in baskets.
Tala-gavug, to move very fast; so as not to be distinctly seen; as if *tala* fail to see, and *gavug* from the motion of a fan before the eyes; *we poa talagavug*, to grow exceedingly.
Talai, 1. the giant clam, tridacna gigas; *vin talai*, a clam shell; 2. a tool, adze, made of clam shell; 3. in recent use, iron.
Talai-tur, a dance; two men stand up, *tur*, like the shells of the clam, *talai*.
Talalanana, [ta 1.] belonging to the under side, *lanai*; underneath.
Talalane, [ta 1. *lanai*] comp. prep. under, from under; belonging to the under side of, *talalane ima*.
Talamatai, a charm; a bundle of various things tied together, *vil*, with a magic song, *mana*, and laid in a path; to prepare it is to *vil o talamatai*, to bind it.
Talamaur, one who eats or has eaten part of a corpse to obtain magic power; one whose soul goes out to eat the soul of a dead person.

Talao, Portuguese man-of-war, physalia.
Talasa, a feast when a newly-made member of a *tamate* society is freed from attendance, *goto*, in the *sara*.
Talasag, adv. for a short time; *pute talasag*, to sit down but not settle down to talk; probably *talasag*, tr. determ. *tala* 2. the person disregarding those he joins.
Talatlat, the larva of the mosquito and similar insects.
Talau, cobweb, either single line or web; *o marawa ti tia o talau* forms its web with its claws, not spins it with its spinnerets.
Talava, a term of contempt; *tae lava*.
Talavag, 1. tr. determ. *tala* 1. to let out carelessly something confided in secrecy; 2. adv. *o roro sava te gao talavag*, because some one has let out the secret.
Talavano, added to *arisa*, the day after to-morrow.
Talavivis, to move so quickly as not to be seen; *tala* 1., *vivis*.
Talawai, by metathesis for *tawalai*, i. e. *tawalag*.
Talawelawe, [ta 3.] long-shaped, like the fish; *tam o lawe alo qilo gap*.
Tale, same as *tal* 2. to go in a round, take a turn in a walk, with no particular business, so, quietly, slowly.
tatale, tatatale, to take a walk; *tale nounou*, to go about gently.
taleag, to turn; *taleag ris*, turn in another direction.
taleva, v. n. keeping quiet.
talevag, tr. determ. to go round with.

tale galon, to go empty-handed.
tale goro, to go round about for something.
tale ure, to go round visiting each village.
Talegagaviga, a kind of clam, *talai*, the fish blue in colour.
Talepu, a black man or pig.
Taleva, 1. [*tale*] a going slowly round, doing nothing, quietness.
Taleva, 2. cry in a hurricane, *lan taleva!*
Talevaleva, keeping quiet for fear of stone or arrow, when enemies are about.
Talevanovano, a very large clam shell, *talai*.
Talewasa, to come out, forth, V.L. word for *rowolue ma.*
Tali, a rope, cord, made of plaited or twisted lines; *we vir*, plaited with three lines, *gae*, twisted on the thigh, *galo*; *we saway* twisted with two *gae me galo*. Mao. *tari;* Fiji, *tali,* to plait; Mal. *tali;* Malag. *tady,* rope; Tagal. *dalin,* bind; Bis. *talika;* S. Cape N.G. *tari;* Ponap. *jal.*
talig, tr. to flog with a rope.
Taliag, see *taleag*, but if tr. v. from *tal* 3. 6. it is *taliag;* both forms are written; *ti taliag ris*, he turns round to go in another direction.
Talianago, to turn face about, *tal* 2. *nagoi.*
Taliaqat, to tie a band round the head; *tal* 2.
Taliaso, to miss by going round about; *tal* 2. *aso.*
Talig, 1. tr. *tal* 2. to make a circuit; *valago talig kel*, to run back making a round.
Talig, 2. tr. v. *tali*, to flog with a cord.
Taligarap, a cord to climb cocoanut trees with; *tali, ga* 3., *rap;* also *taligrap.*
Taligira, a mollusc, chiton, on rocks in the sea.
Taliog, tr. *tal* 2. to surround.
Talkov, dark, dim, all round or over; *tal* 2. *kov;* with *goro.*
Talmagae, long.
Talo, comp. prep. *ta* 1. and *lo;* of or belonging to; *o tangae talo mot*, a forest tree.
Taloi, v. to seek.
Talova, to sweep with a branch or bunch of leaves; *mun o no-tangae gap*, not *werasa.*
Talo-vatitnai, (k) constr. *talovatitne*, belonging to the midst, from its place in the midst; *we tavea nan? talovatitnai*, where is its place? it belongs to the middle; *we talovatitne vanua*, belongs to the middle of the country.
Talpane, guy, *tali*, to the boom, *pane*, of a canoe.
Taltal, the strings, *tali*, of a *gete* basket.
Taltalimata, a children's game, holding hands and twirling round.
Taltalimatea, to go, *tal* 2., and catch a disease, or get killed by the enemy.
Taltaloai, (k) very small quantity, crumbs; same as *vaivainiu.*
Taltaloi, redupl. *taloi*, to seek, look for.
Taltalorai, (k) same as *taltaloai.*
Talule, 1. to be always doing the same thing, incessantly crying, or talking always on the same subject. 2. n. one who so does.
Talvava, [*tali*] 1. a sling; 2. to sling a stone; 3. to carry over the shoulder with a string (doubtful); *te naliog o talvava*, to whirl a sling round.

Talvei, (k) brains.
Talvisa, [*tal* 5.] how many ? so many, in counting strings of money.
Talvun, to crowd as spectators to see the man who figures in a *kolekole;* come round, *tal*, in a bunch, *vun.*
Talwur, to go away without one's knowing it, in one's absence.
Tam, 1. same as *tama* 1. adv. as, like; *tam o sava?*
Tam, 2. same as *tama* 2., *ta* 4. and suff. pron. m.
Tama, 1. adv. as, like; *tamaike* thus, *tamaine* so.
Tama, 2. [*ta* 4.] person with thee, suff. pron. *ma* 5.; *tama sei?* you and who with you ? who was with you ?
Tama, 3. v. impers. to come awkwardly, be confusing, overpowering; *me tama munia*, he was confused, did not know what to do; 2. left-handed.
Tama, 4. *tika* numeral for four.
Tama, 5. prefix signifying spontaneity; Lepers' I. *tuma.*
Tamai, (k) father, in relation to individuals; *o retamai*, those who have children in the place, the fathers of the village as a class; *i tamana, tamara* his, their, father; redupl. *tamtamai.*
 Sam. Fij. Fl. D.Y. Motu N.G. *tama;* Celebes, *jama, ama;* Amboyna, Ceram, *ama;* Gilb. *tama;* Pon. *jam.*
Tamaia, [*ta* 1.] belonging to him, her, having its place with him, *maia.*
Tamaike, thus, *tama* 1. *ike* this.
Tamaiko, [*ta* 1.] belonging to thee; see *tamaia.*
Tamaine, so, like that, *tama* 1. *ine.*
Tamaira, [*ta* 1.] belonging to them; see *tamaia.*

Tamala, a flowering shrub, eranthemum; like *goyor*, and *sasala.*
Tamalaso, [*tama* 5.] to slip out, down; as a fish out of the hand.
Tamalera, [*tama* 3.] impers. to confuse so that one wanders, *lera; me tamalera munia*, he did not know what he was about, in delirium, e. g.
Tamaniu, (k) something with which a man's life is intimately connected, animate or not; Maewo *tamani* is used as equivalent for "soul."
Tamaragai, [*ta* 5.] an old man, who shakes, *maragai; tanotamaragai*, man's old age.
Tamarere, [*tama* 5.] to flow back, *rere*, as the water in a small channel or pool with the ebb; *o nawo ti kalo, ti tamarere kel.*
Tamarurus, V. [*tama* 5.] to unravel of itself, draw out, of string &c.; *rurus.*
Tamasuria, a rank in the *suqe.*
Tamat, see *tamate.*
Tamata, peace.
Tamatan, something like a hair, *ul tamatan*, in bad ulcers.
Tamate, 1. [*ta* 5.] a dead man; *mate;* a corpse; referring to the body.
 2. a ghost, a dead man in separation from his body.
 3. a society in which men are supposed to associate with ghosts; very numerous; each member is called a *tamate;* *we tiro o tamate*, to become a member.
 4. the hat, head-dress, belonging to each *tamate* society; in recent use any hat.
 5. adv. superlative, *sar tamate, sin tamate.*
Tamate, 6. *rave o tamate*, to reef the native sail.

Tamate av, ashes of a fire carried into the air by the wind ; as if the ghost of the fire.

Tamatei, 1. (k) a corpse, *tamate* 1., regarded as that of some particular person ; *na tamatena*, his dead body.

Tamatei, 2. (k) something black, not eaten, in a crab, *gave*.

Tamate-gangan, a magic stone, long in shape, in which is the power of a ghost, *tamate* 2. which will eat, *gan*, the life of a man whose shadow falls on it.

Tamate-garugaru, a waterspout, as if a wading ghost.

Tamate-ginitia, ghost-nipped, said of a bitter m*ake; si qe gana o* m*ake we gogona we vet si we tamateginitia, wa si o tamate me gin*.

Tamate-kurkur, a ghost, *tamate* 2., that devours, *kur*.

Tamate-liwoa, the Great *Tamate* 3.; the chief society.

Tamate-qasa, one of the *tamate* 3.

Tamate-qatia, a very dark man is so called, as a ghost, *tamate* 2., the colour of a tree-fern trunk, *qatia*.

Tamate-ronopal, an eavesdropper, as if a ghost listening secretly.

Tamate-takau, a ghost that joins one on the road ; *takau*.

Tamate-tiag, a ghost that looks like a shining snare ; *tiag*.

Tamate-tiqa, a ghost-shooter ; a tube of bamboo stuffed with magic and shot off, *tiqa*, against the person whom it is desired to injure ; to prepare one, *we soso o talamatai;* in recent use a gun.

Tamate-tirapata, a man who mixes scented herbs, leaves, &c., and stands out of sight, *tira pata*, that others may smell, *rono puna*, and think it is a ghost.

Tamate-wasawasa, a harmless *tamate* 3., does not beat and chase.

Tamate-woroworo, an image of a dead man carved in a tree-fern stem ; or the same figure in tattoo.

Tamat-lelera, a wandering ghost, *tamate* 2., supposed to possess a man and make him mad ; a man so possessed also so called.

Tamat-memegel, a dance.

Tamat-ronopun, a fish.

Tamatua, [*ta* 5.] a full-grown person, *matua ; o retavine tamatua*.

Tamatug, [*tama* 5.] elastic, giving when pressed ; *tug, matugtug*.

Tamat-viroviro, a *tamate* 3. that goes about, turning out of the way.

Tamaur, [*ta* 5.] a man alive, *maur*, as opposed to a man dead, *tamate*.

Tamavea, [*tam* 1.] adv. how ? 1. in what manner ? 2. of what sort ? *ko we maros tam avea?* how will you have it ? or which do you like ? see *avea*.

Tame, comp. prep. *ta* 1. and *me* 2. with, from, having place with.

Tamelea, [*ta* 3.] tasteless.

Tamen, comp. prep. *ta* 1. and *men* 1. same as *tame; tamenina*, having place with us.

Tames, to go against the teaching, wishes, commands of one in authority.

Tamoa, [*ta* 1.] belonging to what was before, *moa*.

Tamon, comp. prep. *ta* 1. and *mon* 2. belonging to some one's doing; *tamonsei?* of whose doing was it ?

Tamtamelea, redupl. *tamelea;* tasteless, without any nice taste, mawkish.

Tamtametuga, [*tama* 3., *ga* 5.] awkward, *e. g.* in dancing.

Tamunmun, [*ta* 3.] chubby, stumpy; of a pig or man, short-legged, thick-bodied.

Tamur, a grub.

Tamurmur, [*ta* 3.] fat and large.

Tan, 1. same as *tana;* *ta* 4.

Tan, 2. the trunk, stem, of a tree; not used alone; *tan-mol,* the native orange tree, as opposed to the fruit, *womol;* *tangae,* a tree, is no doubt *tan-gae.*

Tana, *ta* 4. with suff. pron. *na;* see *ta* 4.; must often be translated 'and,' but cannot be a conjunction.

Tananora, [*ta* 1.] belonging to yesterday, *nanora.*

Tanaqarig, [*ta* 1.] belonging to past part of to-day, *naqarig.*

Tanarisa, [*ta* 1.] belonging to the day before yesterday, *narisa.*

Tanasenase, [*ta* 3.] dry so as to rustle; *nase.*

Tanavaluna, [*ta* 4.] it and its fellow, *un* for *rua* two.

Tangae, 1. [*tan* 2.] 1. a tree; *gae* not the same with *gae* a creeping plant, but Mal. *kayu,* Batak, *hayu,* Malag. *hazo;* Fiji, *kau;* Mao. *kau* in *rakau;* Gaua, *gai* in *regai;* N.H. *kau, gau, gai, cai;* Sol. Ids. *gazu, gai, hai;* Motu N.G. *au.* 2. wood, wooden.

Tangae, 2. shrouds, *tali* ropes that support the mast, *turgae,* of a canoe.

Tangemarmaros, a tree, *tangae,* planted for common use or pleasure, *maros; isei qe maros we la o woai o tawagasiu.*

Tangesar, a sharp bit, splinter, of wood, *tangae, sar* 4.

Tangetavine, the cross piece of wood, *tangae,* at the foot of a net, to which it is fastened.

Tangil, [*tan* 2.] a digging stick; *tangil vutvut; gil* 1.

Taniav, (k) the piece of wood in which the pointed stick, *mategerare,* rubs a groove in making fire, *soso av*; met. *nataniavina,* a fire to warm him. *taniav-soso,* the same.

Taninene, straight.

Taniniga, straight, right.

Tano, earth, ground; takes poss. *ga* 1. *gak o tano,* the ground belonging to me; *anatano,* on the ground.

tanoavuava, loam.

tano-gao, an even stretch, *gao* 1. of land unbroken by ravines, as at Luwai; conf. *vatgao.*

tano garo, hard clay; *garo.*

tanolava, mound of earth to plant yams in.

tanomaran, infertile ground; see *maran.*

tanomasa dry ground, *mamasa.*

tano-meameaga, red earth, with *mea* about it.

tano we pipisiag, clay.

tano pul, or *pulut,* red, black, volcanic earth which sticks, used in building *wona* at Gaua.

tano qaro, a yam ground which has not been burnt off according to the Mota practice.

tano sin, burnt earth, brick, in recent use.

Mal. *tanah;* Bat. *tano;* Macas. *tana;* Malag. *tany;* Gilbert, *tano;* N.G. *tano, hano.*

Tanoag, to smooth the soil, as after planting, or as a turtle after laying her eggs.

Tanoi, (k) place of or for something; receptacle; time of or for.

tano-alal, [*al* 1.] a place to walk about in.

o

tano-ararovag, 1. n. the hole above the door of a house, through which the cord, *tal*, is put for tying up the door; 2. adv. *a tanoararovag*, end foremost, in the way of inserting lengthways; *arovag*.

tano-aruaru, a place where *aru*, casuarina, trees are, therefore awful, sacred.

tano-ateatev, a look-out place; *atev*.

tanoepa, (k) bed place, where the mat, *epa*, is spread; *tanoepe gopae*, sick man's bed.

tano ireire, a woman who asks for food.

tano-garagara, place to take a bite, where a bite has been taken, *gara*.

tano-giginpis, place to pinch the ground with the toes, *ginpis*, to take off for a jump or attack.

tano-ima, house site, town land.

tano-lalamera, time of childbearing.

tano-lavlav-natmera, the same.

tano-ligoligog, trysting-place, for keeping an appointment, *ligog*.

tano-lumagav, young man's lifetime.

tano-magatea, old age of woman.

tano-malamala, girlhood.

tano-mapsag-ae, place below the ribs, in a man's wind.

tano-mas-ne kala, place where the *kala* lizard has fallen; proverbial expression when a thing is quite lost, as a bad debt; *o som me van ape tano mas ne kala*.

tano-maturu, sleeping-place.

tano-nolonolo, the gullet; *nolo*.

tano-oloolo, the place where a man offers, *oloolo*, for another; the object, stone, &c., in regard to which he makes the offering, *we oloolo apena*.

tanopane, the place where the bracelet goes, on the arm.

tano-panei, where one's hand has been, handiwork.

tano-pei, receptacle for water.

tano-poa-mot, the time when growth stops, *we poa mot*, so full growth.

tano-pul, place where a gum torch is set, *pul* 2.

tano-pute, or *putepute*, seat, sitting-place.

tano-ravrav, 1. place for dragging down canoes; 2. met. sum of money given by the borrower to the lender to make payment of the debt run easily; see *lano goro*.

tano-ravravlue, place where things are dragged, *rave*, out of the wood into the *vanua*.

tano-rea a clear place where there are no trees; *rea* 1.

tano-reremera, childhood, boyhood.

tano-rono, holy place, sacred ground; not *tano*.

tano-rotrotig, the place where the girdle, *rotig*, goes, the waist.

tano-rowo-ne-loa, the place where the sun rises, sun-rising.

tano-sasa-ne-lea, place from which commands are carried; i.e. a chief man; *o tanun liwoa, neira we sasa ma o lea amaia*.

tano-sina, a place where the *sina* grows, where no large trees grow, as at Veverau.

tano-sisgag-ne-lea, the place where regulations are made, *sisgag*; i.e. a chief man, *tanun liwoa*; as above *tano-sasa-ne-lea*.

tano-tamaragai, the old age of a man.

tano-tilatila, one on whom all faults are laid.

tano-tultul, the same ; see *tila, tul.*
tano-tul-ne-loa, place of sun-setting.
tano-ververesag, place to tread, steps in a steep place.
tano-vetvet, place of command, *i. e.* a chief man who can command ; *inau o tano vetvet ?* am I a chief ?
tano vilewora, place of parting, where roads cross and travellers separate.
tano-viraviras, place of showing off, *i. e.* a man who talks as if everything were his own ; *viras.*
tano-rivispanei, the place where the guard for the bow hand is bound round, the wrist.
tano-wora, opening in a reef.
Tanorenore, [*ta* 3.] utterly dried up, of water.
Tanovag, beat down, destroy utterly ; compare *tanoag.*
Tansag, lay even, spread level ; *tama we vava munsei qe wosalag tatas, " tansag, we loqo."*
Tansaqeka, [*tan* 2.] the wood of the *saqeka*, very light.
Tantanoga, dirty, as by falling on the ground, *tano.*
Tanu, 1. to bury with earth ; *tanu goro*, to come down and bury like a landslip or falling cliff.
Mao. Pol. *tanu;* Mal. *tanam;* Tagal. *tanim.*
2. a landslip.
Tanun, [*ta* 5.] man, human being ; *ta-nun* real man not *ta-mate;* *ni te tanun ?* will he live ? *nina me tanun qet si tagai ?* are we all saved ? from shipwreck.
Tanuvag, to slip down with, as falling earth ; separable *vag* 2.; *me tama avea qa, ni me vara taso, si o tano me tanuvagia ?* whether his foot slipped or the earth gave way with him.
Tan, to weep, same as *tani*, which see.
Tana, (k) a bag, deep basket. Sam. Fij. *taga.*
Tanamanana, a lucky bag ; a man who has much money coming in puts it into such a bag.
Tananoi, [*ta* 3.] utterly gone out, of fire.
Tanarnai, fine ashes ; *we tiu o av, ti gao, o naenaeai ti mas.*
Tanaro, a morsel of food or drop of kava, *tanaro sinaga, tanaro gea*, thrown or poured for a ghost, with a *tataro*, *"gam o tanaro sinaga ; mam o tanaro gea."*
tanaro wia, if some small thing happens to fall, or suddenly appears on such a morsel, it is a good sign, a man will attain his desire ; it is a *tanarowia.*
Tanaroa, name given to certain stones, carried or hung up in a bag, possessed of magic powers as the abode of a *vui;* or to a shark, or other creature, in or with which a *vui* is present ; *we oloolo munsei, te vava ape pagoa sin kel ma.*
Tanaroi, (k) a thing belonging to a person which, as *tanaro* or *tanaroa*, has magic power.
Tanasama, a bag, *tana*, with some bark, leaves, &c., *samai*, which have power with *mana*, and generally a stone amulet ; worn round the neck.
Tanavisaga,
Tanawonowono, a bag with no opening, *wono;* met. a thing that cannot be made out ; as when a man is ill, and the

cause is *garata*, but what cannot be discovered ; *o sava o tanun tete gilala apena ; si a gilala apena, pa tete lai*.

Tanegana, the womb of a sow ; *tana, gana*, as if the stomach.

Tanerenere, [*ta* 3.] same as *tawatwat ; nere* 2.

Tani, 1. to weep, cry, with reference both to tears and sounds ; 2. to cry, of birds, animals ; sound, of musical instruments ; 3. to weep, as a tree when chopped ; often *tan*.

tanis, tr. to cry for ; *vartanis*.

taniva, v. n. crying, grief. Very common ; Mal. Day, Tagal. *tangis* ; Jav. *nangis* ; Mao. *tangi* ; Pol. *tagi, tai, kani* ; Fij. *tagi* ; N.B. *tangi* ; Motu N.G. *tai* ; N.H. *tani* commonly ; Lepers' I. tr. *tanihi* ; Sol. Ids. *tani, 'ani, tanihi, 'anisi* ; Gilb. *tan* ; Marsh. *jon* ; N.B. *tagi*.

Tano, 1. to touch, with the hand ; *tano vano ape, tano ape*, to touch tr.

tanov, tr. to lay hand upon.

tanovtag, remove the hand which has been touching.

tatatano, redupl. grope, feel the way. Mao. *tango* ; Sam. *tago*. Connexion, Mal. Jav. *tangan*, Malag. *tanana*, hand.

Tano, 2. adj. nice, beautiful.

Tanoanoa, [*ta* 3.] quite gone out, extinct, of fire ; *noa*.

Tanoavuai, (k) tomentum, fluff, *avuai*, fallen from leaves, &c. when touched, *tano*.

Tano-goro-nagolagia, to make a return on the part of the bride's family for what is given by the bridegroom's family to secure the bride, *la goro o tavine* ; in lesser quantity.

Tanolinoli, [*ta* 3.] very small, short ; *nol*.

Tanos, embers, of fire still alight or burnt out, *tanosiav*.

tanosnos, reduced to embers, a fire burnt out.

Tanosalsal, to take a thing above the head of a superior or connexion by marriage; *salsal*.

Tanosanosa, [*ta* 3.] panting ; *nosa*.

Tano-ukag, hold and let go ; *i. e.* release in shooting.

Tanov, tr. *tano*, to apply the hand, to lay on with the hand, as in native treatment with water on the sick.

Tanovtag, to remove the hand from something, *tano vitag*.

Tanowut, to search for *wut* in the head.

Tantan, 1. redupl. *tan*, weep, cry, sound.

Tantan, 2. a fish.

Tantanaro, to curse, *rivnag*, by a *tanaro* ; e. g. " *Tataro—gam o tanarosinaga, neira me vusiko ti, me wuroko ti—taur ape panera ravravera at i Panoi, ni tamate*." *Alo me ronotag si ni me mas, ti vet wa, 'Eke ! nok o gan vivinag me mana ineia, me mate.*'

Tantut, to cry till one can cry no further ; *tut* 6.

Tao, a kind of canarium ; ne *tao*, see nai.

Taoraora, [*ta* 3.] rough, of wind and sea.

Taowoowo, [*ta* 3.] exceedingly dry.

Tap, 1. a quiet day, for death, or by order of *tamate* 3., no drumming, singing, playing ; *tapu*.

Tap, 2. same as *tapa* 2.

Tapa, 1. (k) a board, slab of wood flat and thin ; a surf-board ;

met. *ni me lin sur natapana*, he has brought his surf-board down over the breakers, he is safe.

Tapa, 2. prefix to v. signifying spontaneity; probably another form of *tava*; Fl. *tapa*.

Tapaasas, [*tapa* 2.] to come down sharply, in drops that pierce, as; *o pei ti tapaasas* from a waterfall.

Tapai, constr. *tape*; a small quantity or number, few; *o tape ului*, a single hair.

Tapagalagala, [*tapa* 2.] to be near giving birth; of pigs.

Tapagoara, [*tapa* 2.] unsteady, not stiff, as a canoe with parts not properly bound tight, *gate vilit mantag*.

Tapagole, [*tapa* 2.] rocking from side to side; *gole*.

Tapalava, [*tapa* 1.] a broad board; met. a broad man.

Tapalinrag, [*tapa* 2.] to overflow, *linrag*.

Tapaliwoliwo, [*tapa* 2.] to run over and down, *liwo* 2.; *me tapaliwoliwo o surmata*.

Tapaliworag, the same; *liworag*.

Tapalworag, same as *tapaliworag*; overflow.

Tapan, to carry, holding on the palm of one hand.

Tapantuwale, a large, very large, thing.

Tapana, yellow.

tapanaiga, [*ga* 5.] thoroughly ripe and yellow; met. of a man in good condition, *we wenewene, we tapanaiga, tama o vetal we mena*.

Tapanau, 1. a mat of cocoa-nut leaves, large, coarsely woven.

Tapanau 2., a fish.

Tapare, 1. v. to put one thing after another, as disk after disk in threading *som*; thence, in recent use, to thread a needle.
2. adv. in succession, one after another; *sususur tapare o noota*, to sew the ataps of thatch one after the other on to the purlins; *ronotag tapare nia*, hear what has come from one person to another; *gaganag tapare at*, pass information on from one to another.

tapareg, tr. to put in a row; also *taparei*.

taparegarega, [*ga* 5.] adj. in a row.

Tapariu, [*tapa* 2.] to move on a course, *riu*; of the sun declining, *o loa we tira tapariu*, has moved on.

Taparua, [*tapa* 2.] with one side higher than the other; *o aka we sale taparua*.

Tapas, slab, flat stone; *tapa* 1.

Tapasiu, broad and thin, slab-like; *o laqe wose we tapasiu*.

Tapatapa, cocoa-nut fronds platted to go on the ridge of a house in thatching.

Tapatiu, 1. leaning to one side, as a ship or sleepy man.

Tapatiu, 2. thin, thin legs, like *patuai*.

Tapatue, [*tapa* 2.] to swing of itself, *tue*.

Tapatug, [*tapa* 2.] same as *tamatug*, elastic, giving; *tug*.

Tapatui, V. same as *tapatiu* 2.

Tape, 1. comp. prep. *ta* 1. *pe*; belonging to.

Tape, 2. v. 1. to love, feel affection for; 2. propitiate with a gift; *tape goro* a person who has offended, or his fault, so as to save him from punishment; also *tape goro* the offended person to appease him.

- **tapeag**, tr. to agree with.
tapeva, v. n. love, propitiation.
Tape, 3. v. to set up on end, hoist, erect; *we tape o epa*, set the sail; *tape o paito*, put up a shed; *tape kalo naranona*, gather up his legs; *tape raka*, set up straight.
4. to raise the voice higher in singing.
tape-ae, to strike in out of tune; *isei me ret ti, pa ni we tape ae*, some one has started the song, and he follows on *ae*, missing the place.
tape-siwo, to sing out of tune; ought to *tape* but goes down, *siwo; lalaptape*.
5. to tilt up, tip up or over.
tape ilo, to tilt up a vessel, *pue*, &c., to see if there is water in it.
tape ir, to swing round a projection.
tape wawanag, to tip up a *pue* with the mouth open for the water, *wawana*.
Tapeag, tr. *tape*, to agree with a person, consent to; we *tape-agia*.
Tapeapea, [*ta* 3.] hollowed in, as the bottom of a bottle.
Tapegoro, to propitiate, appease, defend with a gift; see *tape* 2.
Tapeir, to swing oneself round a projection; as the *rat-taptapeir* at Mota, or on the top of a cocoa-nut palm; raising oneself up, *tape* 3., with drawing away of the shoulder, *ir*.
met. *tapeir matua, galao*, to the right or left; *si ko qe tapeir matua*, if you live; *si qe galao*, if you die.
Tapelagau, to step over the doorsill, *tape* 5. and *lagau*.
Tapelin, to lean far over, *tape* 5., *lin*; *wil tapelin*, to turn over; *taptapelin*, to roll as a ship.
tapelinrag, tr. determ. *linrag*, to tip up and make pour, as a *pue*, bamboo water-carrier.
Tapen, [*tape* 1.] of, belonging to; *tapen kamam*, &c., see *apen*.
Tapena, [*tape* 1.] of it, belonging to it; see *apena*.
Tapenon, a small plaited cocoa-nut leaf mat; *tapai, non*.
Tapera, 1. [*ta* 1.] appertaining to them, *pe, ra* 2.; see *apera*.
Tapera, 2. a woven open bag, basket, platter.
tapera gae, a shallow basket woven of twigs.
tapera ganarawe, one of a superior make, with rim and hollow.
tapera golopilug, one with rim curled like pig's tail.
tapera kakenwa, one with some resemblance to a certain crab.
tapera non Qat, fungia coral.
tapera pilu, a woven dish with a curled rim.
tapera wol, one deep and hollow, *we gonogono*.
taperata, [*ta* 6.] shallow, like a *tapera*.
Taperiris, to turn over and over, to set up, *tape* 3. and turn over, *ris*.
Tapesopeso, [*ta* 3.] leaning, in uneasy attitude; *we matur tapesopeso tam alo toretore*.
Tapesura, to stoop and rise again, *tape* 5. in going into a house, *sura*.
tapesuravag, to duck the head in going under a branch, creeping under a tree, &c.
Tapetape, n. propitiation.
Tapeto, a quiet, peaceable, harmless man; *tape* 2.
Tape-ului, a single hair, *tapai*.

Tapeva, v. n. of *tape* 2. 1. love, affection; 2. token of love; 3. propitiation, gift to appease.

Tapewun, to touch another's beard with the hand.

Tapia, a wide flat wooden platter.
tapia non Qat, round fungia coral.
tapiapia, broad, like a *tapia,* of a man's back.

Tapiai, a little.

Tapilita, said of one who does not take care of the fragments of his food; *isei o garata tapilita me map nagaratana iake?* also *tapilta;* see *garata*.

Tapirpir, [*ta* 3.] thin from hunger.

Tapisqoe, [*ta* 3.] cut on one side and brought to a point in the shape of a pig's toe, *pis qoe,* as the digging stick, *tangil,* is shaped.

Tapit, [*ta* 3.] *tapitu,* to roll over, fall or flow with rolling motion; as falling cocoa-nut; as tears gather and roll, *surmata we tapit,* either with grief, or at seeing something beautiful, or with delight; *ko we ge nau tama o surmata tapit; o surmata we tapit!* how beautiful! see *mapit.*
tapitvag, to roll over with, *o vat me tapitvagia.*

Taplagolago, [*tapa* 2., *lago*] a toy; *we tuwur o noota mun o gaqir, o puto gaqir; we wulug;* a hoop of sago frond set rolling by children, who cried *taplagolago!* Thence a wheel; and further, any wheeled machine; in recent use.

Taplolos, [*tap* 2.] to writhe, wallow, as in pain on one's mat; *lolosa.*

Tapogopogo, [*ta* 3.] round like a cask, bulging equally all round.

Tapraras, [*tap* 2.] to fall slap down, or with a smack; *ni we tapraras avune lama,* in jumping into the sea; *o sava ti masu siwo ti maworawora, wa si we tapraras.*

Taptapapa, redupl. *tapa* 1. flat like a board.

Taptapui, racing in play, *valago taptapui;* one after another.

Taptapup-sul, people crowding on one another, like a *tapupui.*

Taptapemalol, [*tape* 2.] one loved in vain, as an adopted child who is disobedient; *malol.*

Tapu, taboo, unapproachable, not to be touched, under a prohibition with the sanction of some *mana* belonging to men; so distinct from *rono;* a very common word.
vatapu, to render *tapu.*

Tapua, a thing or place made *tapu;* a mark or sign set up, *tura,* as a memorial of *suqe* and other rank attained; *nan ti rig non o palako, ti turatura non o tapua; nan neira wa, pa si o tap sa nane? nan neia wa, o tap suqe nan iloke na me gana ti wa na me sar ti.*

Tapug, to make, or made, *tapu;* a mark of *tapu;* so anything belonging to the *suqe* society; *av-tapug,* the fire belonging to each rank; *gana tapug,* to make the meals necessary for taking a step in rank, *ime tapug* the *gamal; tapu.*

Tapul, to throw a stick end over end; also *tapule.*
tapulag, tr. to throw end over end; *sotaplag.*
tapulgag, tr. determ. to throw lightly, toss, end over end; *gate vivir, gate virtig.*

tapulgay mot, said of an arrow breaking and turning over when it has hit the object.

tapulepule, adv. turning end over end, *we masu tapulepule*.

Tapulsama, to capsize with the outrigger, *sama*, of the canoe turning upwards; *tapul*.

Tapupui, a dress of overlapping leaves, &c., worn by *tamate* 3.

Tapur, [*ta* 3.] to cover over, *pur*, stop up; with *goro*; *we tapur wonowono goro kule ima*, to cover over and hide the roof of a house, as a creeper will.

Tapusapusa, [*ta* 3.] like the down of feathers; *o nawo ti tapusapusa ape nago aku*.

Taqa, 1. v. to lie forward, lean forward, be prone.
  o ima we taqa, a house is not said to stand, *we taqa olovag*, leans over forward, and turns up, *taqa gagao*, has a depressed gable; *taqa late*, to stop short and turn back, as in climbing a tree, or, met., in fighting; *taqa rorono*, hang the head in silence.
  o maligo we taqa goro o nago vanua, a cloud lies over the face of the country.
  2. to lie flat and stick, as a limpet on a rock.
  3. adv. lying flat, on the face, *matur taqa*, so as to oversleep. a seine net, *gape taqataqa, we taqa goro o iga*.
  4. descriptive prefix to numerals when houses are numbered; *o ima taqavisa? taqa vat*, four; or flying foxes hanging together.

taqava, v. n. covering.

taqai, tr. V. for *taqag* to lay flat.

taqar, tr. to lie forward upon.

taqav, tr. in *vataqav*, to lie upon.

Taqaasas, to stay in one place and work.

Taqagato, 1. a fish easy to shoot; 2. met. a man who cannot dodge or ward off an arrow.

Taqai, 1. v to lay flat down, to lay; *taqa* 1.; especially to put wood on the fire, *we taqai avune av; we taqai o av*, to make up a fire, laying on chips, small wood, sticks, &c. *taqai valaqat*, to lay one thing on another so as to cover it.
  2. adv. 1. in addition, one on another; so, 2. making a beginning, a new start; *we matur, we gana, taqai alo ima qara taur ti*, to sleep, or eat, for the first time in a newly built house; *sawal taqai*, the first fruit of a tree.

Taqalate, to stop short, *late*, and turn down or back, *taqa*, in climbing or fighting.

Taqale, a fish; *taqale qoe*, one of a larger size; *taqale kilakilau*, another kind.

Taqalil, to bend, *taqa*, with fruit, till the leaves turn over, *lil*, said of a tree.

Taqalon, to bow down; *taqa*.

Taqalsai, (k) the back of the head and neck, nape.

Taqalse, a man who keeps by himself, not joining with others.

Taqalsemate, a bald patch on the *taqalsai*, back of the head.

Taqaniu, (k) 1. side of a thing; *taqani-aka*, the side of a vessel; *taqan-panei*, or *paniu*, the shoulder; *taqan tauve*, the side, shoulder, of a hill. 2. the outline, outside, of a figure, general outline and shape without regard to parts; so, something seen without features, an apparition of ghost or *vui*.

Taqar, tr. *taqa*, to bend forward upon, overlie; with *goro; o toa we taqar goro nanatina*, a hen broods over her nestlings, *goro natolina*, sits on her eggs; *te taqar goro o sul mun o panei*, to quiet a crowd with downward motion of the hand.

taqar tano, met. of one who is a bad runner.

Taqarasag, to bend, *taqa*, so as to brush, *rasag*, the ground, said of low growing tree.

Taqarvat, to lean upon a rock, said of rock-growing plants.

Taqarur, to lean, *taqa*, half falling, like a ruinous house, or trees after a gale; *gate masu nev ran, we taqarur*.

Taqas, 1. an arrow armed with a reed, with a circular edge; used for shooting birds, and in sham fights.

Taqas, 2. native oven, *qaranis; taqtaqas*, a Gaua word.

Taqasilsil, to lean, *taqa*, in the dark, *sil;* said of one who is ill and sits indoors.

Taqasrag, a hole in the ground covered with a *patue tangae*, a slab made of the thin buttress of a tree, used as a drum, beaten with a rammer; *taqas* 2.

Taqataqa, redulp. *taqa;* 1. lowering as sky, or countenance, threatening; *o vanua we taqataqa, o wena wun.* 2. *o gape taqataqa*, a seine net, *te taqa goro iga*.

Taqatut, to ascend, not directly, but leaning over; said of smoke; *taqa* and *tut* 7.

Taqava, 1. v. n. of *taqa;* the covering of the fore and after parts of a canoe, *aka paspasau*, decking.

Taqava, 2. a climbing plant, a *gae.*

Taqavara, a trap to catch rats; *we rare*.

Taqeaqea, [*ta* 3.] flattened in shape; *qea*.

Taqei, to assist, second; *we taqei goro*, when giving a second coat of paint.

Taqel, to descend, go down hill, connected with *taqa*.

Taqelava, a pepper, piper methysticum, but not the true *gea* of which kava is made.

Taqelea, one who will not attend to what is said to him; *lea;* should be probably *taqel*, as next word.

Taqel-lineline, one who misunderstands, bungles; a name of *Tanaro loloqo*n.

Taqeraqera, [*ta* 3.] wide and shallow; said of a low forked and spreading tree.

Taqes, an adze; a new word; *ti taqa*.

Taqesa, [*ta* 3.] to go upon a creeper, such as *gataqava*, not a branch, when up a tree; to alight as a *qaratu* does, on leaves and pass on to a branch; *qesa*.

taqesaga, [*ga* 5.] bending down, as a tree with its crop.

Taqesala, one who adds himself to a party; *sala* 1.

Taqesara, a dance.

Taqesgag, to leave a strip to tie with, as when husking cocoa-nuts *te goso taqesvag*.

Taqitqit, [*ta* 3.] very white.

Taqonag, also *taqonai* V. a cuttle-fish, sepia.

Taqosoqoso, [*ta* 3.] short and fat; *qoso*.

Taqoteqote, [*ta* 3.] short and thick; as a fruit shaped like a peach, like one kind of *natu;* of a man with short body and thick legs; lumpish, *qote;* ni *gate pute, ni we tur we ate taqalon, we tur qoqote.*

Taqtaqar, redupl. *taqar;* 1. *taqtaqar goro mun o panei,* to make a sign for quiet, silence ; 2. *taqtaqar soko,* to cover oneself with rubbish to frighten children, in sport ; *soko.*

Taqtaqau, a game like prisoner's base; each party has its *um* in which it is safe; if caught outside players are counted dead.

Tar, 1. v. to lay, as a net.
tarnag, tr. determ. to lay, set.

Tar, 2. adj. 1. very many, of indefinite number ; *tar mataqelaqela, tar valenalena,* bewildering in number, countless.
2. as a numeral, thousand; *tar tuwale,* one thousand ; *o vetal me tar vagavat,* there were four thousand bananas. Esp. Sto. *tar,* a hundred.

Tara, 1. v. to hew, chop, cut, as with a *lakae.* Mao. *tarai.*
tara ningoro, to cut a flange.
taragag, tr. determ. to chop trees, &c.
taravag, tr. determ. to chop.

Tara, 2. v. 1. to mention a living person, or part of his name, in telling an old story ; or in conversation ; 2. to introduce a person's name in a song, make a story about one ; 3. to make part or whole of a person's name, as some common noun may ; *ape sasansei we tara o av we un,* if the word, *av,* fire, makes part of a man's name, the custom is to use another word, to *un,* when speaking of fire ; as in this case would say *tawene* for *av.*
vava tara, to happen on a word in speaking which is a man's name, *we tara* (1.) *ineia.*

Tara, 3. *ta* 4. with pron. suff. *ra*
3. sometimes to be translated 'and'; *taragai, tarasei, tara ragai, tara rasei.*

Taraga, a fish.

Taragag, tr. *tara* 1. to hew, cut down, chop ; *we taragag o parapara ape qeteg tangae,* to chop an axe into a tree ; *taragag qaro,* to cut down trees and clear for a garden, but to plant *qeta* among the stuff without burning off ; as if *qaro,* uncooked.
taragag vagarua, said of an arrow which breaks when it strikes, and strikes a second time.

Taragiate, adv. on the back with the face upwards; *matur taragiate,* sleep lying on the back ; *sale taragiate,* to float, as in swimming, on the back ; thence to fall or lean backwards ; *ate.*

Taraka, [*ta* 3., *raka* 1.] to come out again after seclusion ; *we vet ape tanun me vene ti, ti goto, wa o qon tavelima ti kalo lue.*

Tarako, to chirp as a tree cricket ; *o puna we tarako* when it makes a short cry, *we soro* when it drones.

Tarakrak, [*ta* 3.] big but thin ; of man or pig.

Taraluqeag, to cut down, *tara,* trees one upon another, *luqe,* without cutting off the branches of the one first felled.

Taram, to suit, be becoming to, match ; *na usuna gate taramia,* his bow does not suit his stature, too long or too short; *gate taramia* is not becoming, as a black hat on a black person; *me malakalaka apena, was we taram nagolona,* the fantail bird rewarded with a fan-palm-leaf said it matched her tail.

Tarama, to answer a call.
  taramag, to answer another; *ko we vava, nan we valui, aia, aia.*

Taramal, shade moving onwards, shadows of evening lengthening, beginning to lengthen; *malumalu.*

Tara*n*, v. to go, form, in ranks; *tar 1.*
  taranag, see *tarnag*, to arrange in ranks.
  tara*n*iu, n. (k) a rank, a generation.

Tarapei, (k) body, shape, colour, appearance.

Tarapul, to work altogether, *pul 5.*, to make a bee.

Tarapupur, to fell, *tara*, trees, &c. so as to stop, *pur*, a path.

Tarara, 1. a shrub with white square flowers.

Tarara, 2. adj. that has not had young.
  tararai, n. a sow, grown, that has not yet had young; *o mala me tararai veta.*

Tararaveag, to fell, *tara*, trees and drag them, *rave*, at once out of the garden.

Tararu, to coo like a dove.

Tarasa, to yearn, long, desiderate; with *ape; ni we tarasa ape tasina.*

Taratara, redupl. *tara 1.* n. a hoe; new word.

Taratarasa, sand for rubbing money.

Taravag, tr. determ. *tara* 1. to chop; *taravag vagarua*, to chop twice because the first stroke fails.

Tarave, adj. unripe, not yet fit to gather; of fruit; *tano tarave*, to handle fruit not yet ripe.

Tarekrek, [*ta* 3.] dry, as cut grass.

Tarerere, [*ta* 3.] unsteady, not standing stiff, staggering; as a man under a heavy load, supple tree in the wind; *rerere.*

Tari*n*a, to set a net; to arrange cocoa-nuts; form of *tarnag*, *tar 1.*

Taritrit, [*ta* 3.] M. hanging back, reluctant; as a sulky wife follows her husband; a jibbing horse *we ge taritrit.*

Tar-mataqelaqela, numerous beyond counting; *tar 2.*, see *mataqela.*

Tar*n*ag, 1. to set in due place, *tar 1.*, *we tarnag o gape ape kere rerea*, to set a net so as to meet the back flow of a channel in the reef; 2. to arrange in a row, *o iga nan we tarnag nanagora* fish swim together with a level front, heads in a row; *te tarnag o matig*, arrange cocoa-nuts in a row; *pute tarnag*, to sit in good order. See *tarina* and *taran*; probably two stems *tar 1.* and *tara*n produce *tarnag* and *taranag*, which coalesce.

Taro, calm, a calm; *taro popo*, a dead calm, solid, *popo; taro matamal*, a dead calm with glare that hurts the eyes; *taro tul*, very calm.

Taroa, a kind of pigeon; *we gana o no-toape.*

Taroamate, adv. like a *taroa*, quite still; *we pute taroamate.*

Taroaroa, [*ta* 3.] thin, small; *we asu taroaroa*, smoke losing volume; conf. *maroaroa.*

Taroi, constr. *taro;* a trifle, small thing; *o taroi nane!* a trifle, never mind; *iniko taroi;* commonly used ironically, *o* *taro tanun, o taro ima?* is the man, house, so good as all that?

Taroroae, a hole from which the surf cannot flow back.

Tarowasa, adj. clear, unencumbered ; *wasawasa.*

Tarowo, ashes, white ashes of burnt out wood.
tarowo tanpaka, said in ridicule to a dirty man.

Tartaragogona, bitter or sour, *gogona,* but not much.

Tartaramalu, redupl. *taramal;* shadow thrown from above.

Tartaroga, striped, ringed black and yellow like a *mai.*

Tartaru, adv. out of time or step; *vara tartaru.*

Taru, to cook with a slow fire ; either 1. when a large quantity of food is to be ready the next day, *we taru we qaro, te like a maran;* or 2. warming up food already cooked, *we ganagana matila, we taru kel.*

taruva, v. n. recooking food.

Tarunlea, a magic stone swung about in an invaded place to take away the courage of the invaders.

Tarutrut, V. same as *taritrit,* to do unwillingly, reluctantly.

Tarvalenalena, great abundance, great riches : *tar* 2. multitude, *valena* bewildering.

Tarwuwua, with dusty, scurfy, body ; like an old man or one who has skin disease ; *natarapena we wuwuaga.*

Tas, 1. sea, salt-water, as in the name Tasmate, and the word *tasig.*
2. the name of the lake at Gaua, so called because the water of it is not *pei,* simple water, but *tas,* brackish.
3. the retiring place, cleft in a rock, &c., used as a cloaca, and retaining in its name the remembrance of the practice of going into the sea.

A very common word in Ocean languages in the two senses of sea and of salt. Mal. Day. *tasik,* lake ; Tagal. *tasik,* seawater; Amboyna, Ceram, *tasi;* Matabello, *tahi;* Celebes, *sasi, asing;* Kawi, *tasik;* Malag. *tasy,* lake ; Fiji, *taci;* Mao. Pol. *tai;* Motu N.G. *tadi;* Sol. Ids., *tahi, tasi, 'asi.*

Tas, 4. slippery ; in *tasgala; o matesala we ge ne tas; a pan qarana me ge ne tas,* it is slippery there, *ne,* on the road, beside the gully.

Tasgala, [*tas* 4.] slippery ; conf. *masisgala.*

Tasig, [*tas* 1.] to pour the saltwater into the *qaranis;* the water poured *gatasig;* used as *un* word for *pei* 2.

Tasior, to usurp another's place or property ; with *goro;* connected with next word.

Tasis, 1. a bird, the female of the *qatman* though taken by the natives for one of another species ; *o tasis we suwa goro natolin o qatman* and cannot be driven away ; hence, met. one who sticks to another, won't leave him; *iniko o tasis.*
2. v. to take a place where another should be, usurp ; *tasis goro* same as *tasior goro.*

Tasiu, (k) younger brother or sister, according to the sex of a person to whom he or she is related, being of the same sex; in recent use not so strictly confined to younger brother and sister ; it is applied to all *sogoi* where no special relation exists, and widely to all friends.

ro tasiu is used by a woman instead of the name of another to whom she is connected by marriage. *tur tasiu*, brother or sister by same father or mother. Pol. *tehi, tei*; Motu N.G. *tadi*; Fij. *taci*.

Taslana, [*tas* 4.] to slip, be slippery; *o tanun we rara kalo, we van alo we taslana, we vara taslana; we rara taslana kel*, to step and slip back; the sole of the foot *ti lana* in slipping.

Tasmatagaraqa, the next after the first-born, younger brother or sister, *tasiu*.

Tasmate, a district of Mota to leeward where the sea is quiet or dead; generally the lee side of an island; *tas* 1.

Tasmaur, the weather side where the sea is lively, *maur*; answering to *tasmate*; both used in N.H. and Sol. Ids.; in Madagascar Taimoro.

Taso, 1. v. to dash, with quick course; *o til ti tasotaso sasagav* leaps dashing through the water; *neira me valago qatvanua si a taso goro kaman*, they ran through to cut us off; to glance off as an arrow, *gate qalo nev we taso gap at*.
2. to cut with dashing strokes, cut to a point with an adze; generally cut with an adze, the stroke glancing on; *taso vasartag*, to adze smooth.
3. adv. going right on, continually; *tira taso*, to stand on, continue the course.

tason, tr. to adze.

tasovag, tr. to dash against.

Tasoal, *taso, al* 1., see *tastasoal*.

Tasogoro, to cut across and meet at an angle, as in sailing or with parties going through the country; *taso*.

Tason, tr. *taso*, to adze to the size desired.

Tasosa, to lead an infant by both hands, holding it up and letting its feet touch the ground, and singing *ta-so-sa*.

Tasosama, to go off and follow on at an angle, as a canoe when it has tacked, *sama*, or as stuff sometimes tears; adv. obliquely; *taso*.

Tasovag, 1. tr. determ. *taso*, dash, as one's foot against a root or stone, *ape qeteg tangae si o vat*.

Tasovag, 2. *taso* with separable *vag*, dash on with; *mule tasovag*, go continuously on with.

Tasovule, all along, with long continuance; *taso, vule*; *pulan o av alo gamal, ti tasovule*, light fires in every rank all through the *gamal*.

Tasroe, a fabled bird with red head.

Tastasilum, a game.

Tastasoal, 1. to move, *al*, with a dash *taso*, irregularly about. 2. a busybody; 3. used in V. when M. say *tasosama*.

Tasur, excl. indeed! really! is it not so? V.

Tasusus, [*ta* 3., *sus* 3.] shrinking, drawing in length; as a trepang when touched; become at the same time shorter and thicker.

Tasvat, very hard, brother to a stone, *tasin o vat*.

Taswamule, 1. to rebound; *ko we vivir o vat, pa ti qalo o tangae; o vat te kel ma suriko, we taswamule ma.* 2. met. to walk, or go in canoe, to two places, and the farthest first.

Tata, 1. vocative to *maraui*; *nan ti vet mun marauna wa Tata*.

Tata, 2. redupl. *ta* 3.

Tata, 3. to lace together, connect with string along a line, bind with a running string ; *we tata o togo*, fasten upright reeds with a running line to a horizontal rod in making a screen; *we tata o pugoro*, lacing the sides and lid of the food-chest ; *tata wurvag o gape, o epa*, mend a net, a mat ; *we tata o vilog*, lace round the edge of a palm leaf for an umbrella ; *ritata*.

tatag, to run a line round a few sticks of firewood and carry them ; to carry over the shoulder with a line.

tatagiu, a bundle of sticks with a line round them.

tatal, to bind round with running line.

Tataga, 1. v. to follow ; *tataga sur sei*, to attend to.
2. adv. accordingly, following.

Tataga-av, to follow fire as a bird does at night ; met. to follow one about, stick to him.

Tatagalete, [*ta* 3.] to bend with a curve in the length, with a kink ; as a branch, a log that will not lie straight ; *lete, galete*.

Tatagapelu, crooked, following a bend ; *pelu*.

Tatagarete, [*ta* 3.] crooked, curving ; *garete*.

Tatagasuwe, a tree.

Tatageregere, [*ta* 3.] loud giggling, long laughing, *o retavine gese*.

Tatagiu, a bundle, as of firewood, run round with a line for carrying ; *o tatag lito ; tata* 3.

Tatagora, [*ta* 3.] to run, roll, about ; *o nat qoe te tatagora goro*, at play ; *maur e! tatagoragora mae!* said when an infant sneezes, as if its soul were being drawn away.

Tatagoras, a bird, glyciphila.

Tatakala, [*ta* 3.] *we tira tatakala* stand with legs apart, like a *kala* lizard.

Tatakau, redupl. *takau;* move catching hold with the hands, as in a tree ; *tatakau goro ape tangae*, to catch hold and prevent a fall ; *takakau ae*, miss hold.

Tatakor, a child always carried, *takor*.

Tatakrega, [*ga* 5.] adj. said of one who stirs himself to action when out of sorts.

Tatal, to bind round with a running line, *tata*, as in *geara venegag*, fastening horizontal bamboos to upright stakes.

Tatalai, V. [*tala* 1.] to turn the head and look at ; *nipea tatalai kelkel*, don't be looking about.

Tatalaiga, [*ga* 5.] heedless, wanton ; *ni me ilo tatalaiga ineia*, he did not recognize him, saw him carelessly; *nom tatalaiga*, insolent ; *vus tatalaiga o qoe, o tanun*, not caring, mischievously; *tala* 1. as in *titatala*.

Tatalanago, to act insolently to show off ; *tala, nago;* like *tatalaiga*.

Tatalaora, [*ta* 3.] said of eyes stuck with *sisia* in the morning ; *namatak te qale tatalaora ti*, my eyes are gummed, as a man says when he does not want to get up.

Tataleg, [*tale*] to keep about at home; *lag tataleg*, to marry in one's own village ; *pal tataleg*, steal one's neighbour's things only.

Tataliora, same as *tatalaora*.

Tatalgaso, [*tal* 2.] one who keeps

at home, goes no further than the rafters' ends, *gaso;* we *mule kelkel gese alo vanua, gate irasu.*

Tatalo, in making a fence to put a bamboo lengthways on both sides of the top of stakes and bind over, *tata,* with *gatogo;* in making a stage, *qeaqea,* to fasten the rods with lines passing under and over.

Tatalovag, to take the very last.

Tatalviro, to keep to oneself; *ni we toga tatalviro; ni we tal viro gese* when he walks, *tal,* he turns away, *viro.*

Tatamera, coleus, Moreton Bay nettle.

Tatametoga, adv. awkwardly, clumsily; v. impers. *we tatametoga ineia,* it is awkward to him; *ni we ge tatametoga,* he does it awkwardly; *tama* 3.

Tatano, thick, said of smoke so thick that nothing can be seen; *o asui we tatano;* said also of a fat sleek pig.

Tatapaga, [*ga* 5.] flat and hard; said of a boil with edge defined; *tapu,* a board.

Tatapuga, [*ga* 5.] unhurt, untouched, entire; *tapu.*

Tataqarqar, redupl. *taqar;* to tumble headlong in eagerness; *o sul we rowo avune gene tuwale.*

Tatar, 1. v. to cover the head with palm-leaf umbrella, *vilog;* 2. n. *un* word for *vilog.*

Tataram, to make known a secret; a person *te tataram munsei,* and he tells it publicly.

Tatarepa, to crow in the dusk; *o kok ti kokorako alo matarav, ti tatarepa.*

Tatarmot, 1. to tear apart the fastening of a bag; *tana;* 2. neut. to tear away as a hook does from the jaw, *palasai,* of a fish; *gate tavalaso.*

Tatarnun, to make a loud report, *nun; tatar* in this and preceding word plainly means to rend.

Tataro, 1. to pray, prayer; *i. e.* invocation of a dead person, and of *vui* Qat and Marawa, with a form of words beginning with *tataro;* used in danger, sickness, the opening of an oven, making a libation of *gea.* San Crist. *'ataro,* a powerful ghost; Sam. *tatalo;* Hawa. *kalokalo,* prayer; Gilb. *tataro.*

2. to pay for what is done with a form, spell, of words; *tataro pei,* to pay a person for magic medicine, *pei mana; tataro laso qoe,* to pay for gelding pigs.

3. when a thing is taken back which was supposed to be given, *ko me tataro͂ inau mun o gene ilone.*

Tataroaga, [*ga* 5.] adj. iridescent; *we rave o tanun we ilo.*

Tatarowoga, [*ga* 5.] adj. ashy, dusty, mouldy; *tarowo.*

Tatarua, both; probably *ta* 2.; see *tutatol.*

Tatarur, the cooing of doves.

Tatarwasa, to come out safe, *wasawasa; tatar* as in *tatarnun.*

Tatas, bad. Bks. Ids. *tes, set, sasat, het;* N.H. Maewo, *seseta,* Eromanga, *sat,* Anaiteum, *has;* Mal. *jahat;* Matabello, *rahat;* Malag. *ratsi.*

tatasvag, v. to be bad with, go bad with; of a wrecked vessel *o aka me tatasvagia* he was wrecked.

Tatataui, remains of a crop of fruit, one here, one there.

Tatatol, all three ; and so with other numerals ; *tatarua*.

Tataturag, stutter ; *taturag*.

Tatave, to defecate ; Fij. *dave*; Pol. *tahe*, to flow ; Fl. *tare toto*, dysentery.

Tatavnar, 1. [*ta* 3.] adv. indistinctly, *we vava tatarnar* ; 2. said of a ripe bread-fruit; *vinar*.

Tatavrega, [*ga* 5.] adj. mealy.

Tatavun, redupl. *tavun*, to disappear.

Tatawakal, [*ta* 3.] to unfold, open as a butterfly its wings ; *o wis vetal ti ul tatawakal; waka*.

Tatawalsom, description of *maniga* when a child has it before the proper time, fatal.

Tatawerawera, laid flat out ; *we pute tatawerawera ; wera, tawera*.

Tatawilwil, [*ta* 3.] rolling over and over, *wil ; o vat we tatawilwil siwo ma*.

Tatawora, [*ta* 3.] to come apart, *wora*, become divided.

Tataworag, redupl. *tawo ;* to pluck in quantities, excessively, carelessly; *rag* 2.

Tatawras, breaking, of rain, *o wena sin mamasa ; tatawura*.

Tatawura, of rain stopping, *we vava ape wena ni mamasa*.

Tatietie, [*ta* 3.] to stagger ; *tie* same as *tue*.

Tatige, to start, wince.

Tatiotio, [*ta* 3.] to sway about, *tiotio*, as a tree heavy laden with fruit in a wind.

Tatoape, a small fish in pools, sphyrænid.

Tatu, to meet, encounter ; *tatu goro*, to come up suddenly against.

 taturag, tr. *rag* 2. ; to bound, bump, frequently on or against.

vava taturag, tataturag, to stutter in speech.

vatatu, to meet, encounter, in the way.

Tau, 1. n. season, either of planting, or of the maturity of what is planted ; *o tau nam* the season of planting yams, *o tau patau* the season when bread-fruit comes in ; *o vetal, o matig, o tau tagai*, because there is no season for planting cocoa-nuts or bananas, or for their fruiting.

tau gogona, a bad planting season.

tau matua, the season when yams are fit to dig.

Mao. Pol. *tau ;* Jav. *tahun ;* Tagala, *taon ;* Malag. *taona ;* N.B. *taun ;* Pon. *jau*.

Tau, 2. v. to set in place so as to catch or intercept ; *we tau o wowor*, to fasten down with stones a fish-trap, lobster-pot, &c. ; Fiji, *tau-ca*.

tau namu, n. a mosquito net ; a recent expression founded on a story of Ro Lei who covered her face with a net.

Tau, 3. n. a nest of ants in the ground ; *tau niniu, tau gan, tau malatutun*.

Taum, to swarm, crowd thick, as flies, *lano, telepue*, round a dying man : also *teum*.

Taur, 1. v. to hold ; to carry holding in the hand ; *taur goro*, to lay hold on ; *tautaur*, to handle ; *taur viroag*, keep back what ought to be given up.

2. to build, a native house only.

3. to train the vines of yams, *we taur o tue nam, o nam*. In training yams *we viawo, we qeteg taur, we la kalo o tuei avune toyo*, the reed being first

stuck upright; as the vine grows *we latey o togo*, break and bend down the reed to pass the vine on to the next; when the vine ceases to run *we ruqa*, bend down the end of the last, perhaps tenth, reed into the ground.
4. said of fish, *we taur o iqa*, when many are caught with the hook.

Taure, n. construct. of *taura*; collection, used as plural; *taure ima* a number of houses together, *taure niniu* a swarm of ants, *taure tamun* a lot of men. V. L. *'aur, 'au'aur, tare, tore.*

Taurmate, ready, perfect; *mate* 2.; *matemate, gis mamate.*

Taus, a wild kind of yam.
tausgae, 1. a kind of *taus*; 2. met. long-continued crying, like the long vine, *gae*, of the yam.

Tausuus, a soft cocoa-nut, *matig we maqisqis*.

Tautaur, 1. what is carried in the hand, bundle, tools, &c. *taur* 1.
2. the training of yam vines; *me makarag o tautaur o tue nam; taur* 3.
3. house-building, *me sur nau o tautaur ima; taur* 2.

Tauwe, 1. (k) a hill, mountain; *qase tauwe* hill-top; *taqan tauwe*, hill-side; *tauwe gamal qaratu*, a hill where flying-foxes resort, have their *gamal*; *tauwe qoe, som*, place where there are heaps of pigs, money; *tauwe tano*, a mound of earth in which yams are planted.
2. a shell, conch, cassis; *tauwe malum*, a triton shell. Pon. *jaui*.
3. a conch shell used as a trumpet; *we tia si we rur o tauwe*, to wind conchs singly or together.

Tav, 1. v. to dip and take up water in a vessel; *tav pei ma*, dip and bring water; *tav ura*, fill a vessel with dipping.

Tav, 2. prefix, same as *tava*.

Tava, prefix of spontaneity. N.H. Bks. I. *tava, tav, 'av;* Sol. I. *'ara, tapa;* Malag. *tafa.*

Tavaaso, to come out of joint, as rafters which break at the ridge and get out of place; *na qatagpanena me tavaaso*, his shoulder was put out; *aso*.

Tavais, [*tava*] to come off a peg; *is* 3.; as a thing hung up slips off of itself, comes unhitched.

Tavala, constr. *tavalai;* becomes adv.; beyond, the other side of; *tavala pei*, the other side of the water, across the stream; *tavala maran*, next morning, after light; *tavala qon tavelima*, after five days.

Tavalagamal, the other side of the *gamal*.

Tavalai, (k) a side, one of two parts; *tavaliu.*

Tavalaiga, a flat fish, as if only half a fish; it swims on edge.

Tavalaima, the other side of the house; members of the other *veve*, with whom alone marriage is allowed.

Tavalala, to come asunder of itself; *tava, lala; tavalala wora*.

Tavalalan, wind divided by a point of land, along the two sides of which it blows, having a *ruruna* between.

Tavalalea, those who are on one side or the other in a quarrel, enemy or ally; usually those who are of the contrary part, the enemy; see *tavala-us*.

P

Tavalanusui, (k) a lip, upper or nether, one part or other of the *nusui*.

Tavalapanei, (k) the other hand; met. a wife; *natavalapanek itagai*, I am single-handed.

Tavalasasai, (k) namesake; the other side of one's name, *i. e.* a person's name which is the same with one's own.

Tavalaso, to come out, come loose, of itself, *tava; o gau me tatarmot nan o palase iya, gate tavalaso*, the hook was torn out from the fish's jaw, did not come out of itself; same as *tamalaso*.

Tavalavagalo, one on the other side in a fight, *tavalai*; the enemy.

Tavala-us, (k) the other side of the bow, *i. e.* one who shoots as enemy; also one who belonging to one side helps the other, shoots at private enemies.

Tavaliu-ui, (k) constr. *tavalu, tavali, taval*; another form of *tavalai*; 1. a side or part, where there are two, the one or the other; the party on one side or the other; *ira tantavalina*, the people on his side. *a tavalina* M. *tavaluna* V. on the other side of it, on the one side, or the other. 2. to be on one side or the other; *te tavaliu amenau* will be on my side; *te tavaliu mun nau*, will be on the side against me; thus the compounds.

Tavalrua, on both sides, *tavaliu, rua; qalo tavalrua*, hit on both sides, in a fight; V. *tavalirua*.

Tavaltuwale, on one side, one-sided; *qalo tavaltuwale*, when one side only in a fight is hit.

Tavalvasei, lop-sided, uneven, side not answering to side; *vava tavalvasei*, to tell half the story.

Tavamasu, to fall of itself, *tava, masu*.

Tavanana, to come off, out, of itself, *nana*, draw off.

Tavanavana, [*ta* 3.] shining, luminous, as the *matawenewene*.

Tavanas, said at Gatava for *tavamas*, by change of *m* to *n*; fall of itself.

Tavaraka, to rise of itself, arise; *tava, raka* 1.

Tavarasu, to slip of itself; *gavir tavarasu*, to hold and let slip from grasp.

Tavareag, to make departure, *reag*.

Tavaroro, to hang down, sink, go under; *o vat nan we tavaroro*, when the tide rises; *tava*.

Tavasese, to come apart, spontaneously, as an ill-tied bundle letting things out, *sese*.

Tavasuqe, 1. a grade in the *suqe; tavasuqe lava*, the next rank above.

Tavasuqe, 2. a kind of yam.

Tavasur, to sink down, *sur* 7., fall away of itself; *o ganawono qara tavasur nan kamam, kamam qara sora o ganagana vovo*, when the pinch of distress had passed we arranged for a feast.

Tavasvas, [*ta* 3.] of fingers with flesh worked from the sides of the nails and gathered; *pis tavasvas*.

Tavatmonon, a V. L. fish.

Tavatuqe, 1. to break off, *tuqe*, and move spontaneously, *ta-*

va; o tanwe me tavabuqe, there has been a landslip on the hill. 2. met. to move all together, of a crowd.

Tavaul, to come undone, *ul*, of itself, *tara*; come loose, unravel.

Tavauwe, [*tava*] to fall through, out of, a rotten *gete*.

Tavawo, [*ta* 1.] belonging to above, *vawo*; *iniko tavawo tuka*, you belong to the region above the sky.

Tavea, [*ta* 1.] belonging to where, *rea* 1.; *iniko we tavea?* where do you belong to?

Tavelima, five, *lima*.

tavelimai, fifth.

Tavenoveno, [*ta* 3.] *ta rasa o nam gate maremare, pa we aqaga, tete vet ape we manoga.*

Taveris, to turn, alter; *ris*, neuter.

Taveta, a piece of yam with an eye that has shot, whether for planting or already planted.

Tavgaga, [*tav* 2.] become torn, ragged, *gaga*, of itself.

Tavgagata, sounding like tearing, as a sail, or a falling tree.

Tavig, to bury; *tavig goro*, cover over with earth. Mao. *tapuke*; Sam. *tapu'e*.

Taviolo, to burst or run out, as *loko* bursting through the leaves it is wrapped in; to slip out as an infant from *epa pepepe*.

Tavine, M. [*ta* 5.] female, woman; used also of animals and birds; *vine*, feminine; Mao. *wahine*, *hine*; Mal. *bini*; Jav. *winih*; Malag. *ravy*; Yap, *papine*; Motu N.G. *haine*. See *vavine*.

Taviro, [*ta* 3.] to turn, *viro*, out of sight, round something.

Tavirvir, [*ta* 3.] thin from hunger; *vir*.

Tavisoviso, a tree.

Tavkoran, [*ta* 2.] to break off short of itself, *koran*; *o wot tangae me tarkoran malarowo gap ineia*.

Tavlesag, to carry a story, telltale.

Tavnanar, [*tav* 2.] to fall apart, as a ripe *vun gire* falling separates into the *woai*.

Tavnornor, to beat a drum out of time.

Tavret, [*tav* 2. *ret*] set on the edge of what has a deep hollow; *tama we pute retret, gate roro*.

Tavsare, [*tav* 2.] to become torn, *sare*.

Tavsoga, adv. taking off the outside; *sipa tavsoga*, to slice, *tara tavsoga*, to chop, the outside.

Tavsovso, same as *tavisoviso*.

Tavteqona, the *nai* nut ejected by the pigeon; met. a generous man, *we ukeg gaplot*.

Tavtete, [*tav* 2.] to fly off, as sparks from a fire stick, when struck or in the wind; *tete* 3.

Tavtoro, [*tav* 2.] to turn, of the high tide; *toro*.

Tavun, 1. to bury, conceal; 2. met. be lost to sight; another form of *tarig*; *tuaniu we vet si tavun, tuaniu si tavig*; *marawatavun*. Motu N.G. *tahuni*.

Tavunana, belonging to the region above; heavenly.

Tavune, [*ta* 1.] belonging to the upper part of something, *tavune tuka*.

Tavunavuna, [*ta* 3.] wide, of a canoe or house.

Tavus, used for *tavusmele*; *sagie tavus*.

Tavusmele, [*ta* 5.] a man who has reached high rank in the *suqe*, such as m*ele*, by killing, *vus*, pigs for feasts; Motlav, *etvuh*m*el*; a man of great influence, a chief.

Tavusrawe, [*ta* 5.] a man arrived at rank and power, by killing *rawe* pigs at feasts.

Tavutmagav, to pain, *magav*, for a long time, *tavut*; *me tavutmagavia*, he has long suffered.

Tavutiu, (k) an old companion; *ko we titatala tam avea o tanun iloke? o tavutui nake*, how can you forget one with whom you have lived so long? *o tavut ita*, a nosegay long used and discarded.

Taw, 1. prefix, same as *tawa* 3.
Taw, 2. a bird.
Tawa, 1. v. to ooze smoothly out; *o pei ti tawatawa lue ma alo vat*, water oozes out of the rock, *mate tawatawa*.
Tawa, 2. n. a woman; a Gaua word; *tawa irir*, a woman who will not obey her husband.
Tawa, 3. prefix of spontaneity, as *tava*.
Tawa, 4. a bird, *eops altera*.
Tawaga, [*ta* 3.] to open out; of flowers, plants, to blossom; of morning light, *o maran ti tawaga lue*, opening dawn; part and make an opening, as when planks warp and shrink; *waga*.
  tawagasiu, (k) the opened flower; *o qoqoe tangae ti tawaga ul, o tawagas tangae nake; tawas vagalo*.
Tawakewake, [*ta* 3.] dried up as with the sun; *o loa ti sar wakewake, o pei ti tawakewake apena; o meat tawakewake*, a very low tide, leaving the surface dry in the sun; *wake*.

Tawala, [*ta* 3.] wide open; *wala*.
  tawalag, 1. tr. v. to open wide; *rara tawalag*, go and leave the door open; *ni me tira tawalagia*, he stood with (the child) between his open legs; 2. adv. with open legs, as a man sitting across a log, or on horseback.
Tawlaka, [*ta* 3.] to gape open; *walaka*.
Tawalaka, same as *tawlaka*.
Tawalaso, [*tawa* 3.] to get loose and fall; same as *tamalaso*; *arlasolaso*.
Tawaleale, lingering, long; *nipea va tawaleale*, don't go and stay late, or long.
Tawalikelike, [*tawa* 3.] to burst and come open, as skins or husks of cooked m*ake*, &c.
Tawaluka, [*tawa* 3.] to peel off, neut., to open and come off; met. to go out of sight.
Tawalwal, [*ta* 3.] very dry, as the throat in thirst or fever; *o meat we tawalwal*, very low and dry ebb; *we mamasa tawalwal*, exceedingly dry; *wal* 3.
Tawan, a fruit tree; Fiji, *dawa*; a kind of lichi, nephelium pinnatum.
Tawanalnalwora, [*tawa* 3.] a young unmarried person, who goes freely about, *nal wora*, in the village; of either sex; when married he or she will *toga nev*.
Tawarasu, [*tawa* 3.] to slip off, not stay on; as *woro matig*, sauce made with too much water, will not stay on the *lot*.
Tawarawara, [*ta* 3.] wide, as a canoe or house; *warawara*.
Tawarig, *tawa* 2., *rig* 2. a daughter-in-law is so called by her father or mother-in-law.

Tawasa, [*ta* 3.] clear, of sight and voice; *wasa*.
tawasawasa, redupl. *maran tawasawasa*, clear morning.
Tawasis, [*tawa* 3.] chafed, broken, of skin; *sis* 3.; *gagan tawasis*, bruise, scrape, so as to break the skin.
Tawasole, [*tawa* 3.] to turn clean out of husk, as a very ripe fruit of *tawan*.
Tawasvagalo, the beginning, opening out, *tawagasiu*, of a fight, *vagalo*. When children play at fighting the elders stop them, *rigrig wun o tur vagalo*; see *tawagasiu*.
Tawatawa, redupl. *tawa* 1.; clear smooth, as water oozes out over a rock; *o pei ti tawatawa alo apena* is said of a man very smooth, *niniaga*, in skin; ne *tawatawa*, a kind of canarium, *nai*.
Tawatoatoa, [*tawa* 2.] a woman who runs away from home; *toa* 2.
Tawatwat, [*ta* 3.] to be choking, wheezing, as in coughing incessantly, or laughing and speaking at once.
Tawe, to lend money to, make a man debtor; *we tawe isei mun o som*.
Tawela, wide in extent.
Tawene, a live coal, a single live ember, a spark that does not fly, as in *tuwus*; used *un* for *av*, fire.
Tawena, said of a child lying uncared for on an *epa*.
Tawerai, (k) the palm of hand or sole of foot; *wera*.
  vatawerai, spread open the palm.
Taweraga, burning slowly with dull embers; *o av ti gao taweraga*; *taweris*.

Taweris, dull black embers; *gartaweris*.
Tawes, [*ta* 3.] to break off, neut., as a knob or round end, as *qat nam* the head of a yam; so of a broken hip-joint.
Tawesa, [*ta* 3.] shelving, of a beach or shore, giving easy access; *wesuo*.
Tawesawesa, said of unripe *tawan* fruit.
Tawisraga, to recover health and strength; of a child.
Tawiuwiu, one who goes afar, *wiuwiu*.
Tawles, [*taw* 1.] turning over backwards; *les* 1.; *we mas tawles*.
Tawlaka, [*ta* 3.] to come open, *walaka*; *o maran we wia qarig, o loa we tawlaka*.
Tawluka, [*taw* 1.] same as *tawaluka*.
Tawo, to pluck, pull, as fruit, flowers, &c.
  tawor, tr. determ. to pluck; *we tawor o nai*, pull the almonds off the bunch on the tree.
Tawonwon, [*ta* 3.] quite dry; *o lito we tawonwon*, firewood quite fit for burning.
Tawora, a tree.
Taworag, [*ta* 3.] 1. to spread out level, as water *ti taworag goro*; as *nai* spread out, not heaped up; *taworawora*.
2. the floor of a *pugoro*, the rods laid over the *wopugoro*.
Taworau, to begin to make *kor*, dried bread-fruit.
Taworawora, [*ta* 3.] well spread out level, as a *no-ganagana*; well set, as a sail; *taworag*, *wora*.
Tawosa, [*ta* 3.] coming open, apart; a ripe bread-fruit falls and squashes, *ti tawosa*; a hen *ti tere tawosawosa nato-*

lina, a hen pecks her eggs to make them open.

Tawowose, to luff up to the wind.

Tawrakae, [*taw* 1.] to rise and scream, *kae*, as birds do, or flying-foxes.

Tawtawao, a kind of wild yam, *qauro*.

Tawtawilis, [*ta* 3. *wil*] to be rolling from side to side; see *gan-tawtawilis*.

Tawtawui, (k) the upper layers, as in a heap of firewood; in recent use *tawtaw ima*, upper storey of a house.

Tawtawurua, a level place fit for a garden below the cliff, with descent again to the sea; *tawtawui nirua*.

Tawu, (k) a man away from his own place or country, a stranger in a foreign place, a guest; *ni me lavia mun tawuna*, made him his guest.

Tawunwun, very dry; *tawonwon*.

Tawur, V. same as *tagir* M. (k) behind, the hinder place or part, back; *a tawur*, behind; *a tawuruna*, at his back, behind him.

Tawure, met. from a place near Valuga, said of a man who does mischief when set to some task.

Tawurmera, younger or youngest child; *tawur*.

Tawurpea, to treat as of no consequence, *pea* 1., by turning the back, *tawur*, have nothing to do with; thence adv. with the back turned; *we pute tawurpea*.

Tawusag, to begin making a net; *we qeteg o gape, we tawusag o gape mun o gae we sea*.

Te, 1. v. p. generally future; to some extent signifying certainty or continuance, particularly when followed by *ti*; *o manu te rorowo ti*, birds keep flying off.

Te, 2. neg. particle, combined with *ga* 4. present, and *te* 1. future, *gate, tete*, is not, does not, will not; the neg. part. *te* follows the verb in Bks. Ids. Motlav, V.L.; in N.H. *tea* in Maewo, Opa; also Bks. Ids. *ta, tia*; Mao. Pol. *te*.

Te, 3. the phrase *van te vanua, mule te vanua*, to go to another place, is not explained.

Tea, 1. in *laveatea*, six, *tea* is numeral, one; Torres, *jia*; N.H. *tea, tewa*; Sta. Cr. *ja*; Sol. Ids. *ta, tai*; Mal. *sa*; Malag. *isa*; Mao. *tahi*.
2. indef. pron. anything at all, something, anything, whatever; *la mu tea*, give me some; *o sava tea*, anything whatever; *na gate lav mok tea*, I have not received anything at all; *apena tea?* is there any? Fate, *tea*, some one, any one.
3. adverbial, at all; *si ta lai tea*, if it be at all possible; *si na ilo tea*, that I may have a sight of him.

Tegteg, on tiptoe; *autegteg*.

Teketeke, high; by metath. for *ketekete*.

Telepue, a neuropterous insect like a bee; *we turturuga natarapena, ti vasus o ulo we esu ran*; met. *o telepue ti ruvuv*, when a man does not speak out, buzzes.

Temtemer, a dance.

Tenegag, to liken; *ni we tenegag apena*, he makes something like it; *vava tenegag*, to make a proverbial comparison; *vavae tenegag*, a proverb.

Tepere, with twisted toes.
Teqa, 1. v. to come against, meet an obstacle ; *rara me varteqa*, they ran one against the other. 2. shallow, to be shallow, to get low, of liquids. 3. unmarried.
Tere, to peck, pick at ; *o toa ti tere kalo o vain sinaga*, fowls pick up crumbs ; *o toa ti tere tawosawosa natolina*, a hen hatches her eggs ; *o nat toa te teretere lue*, the young birds will peck their way out of the egg ; *o iga ti teretere ape pea*, fish pick at the bait ; *tere qalo*, to hit with the bill. N.B. *telek ;* Fij. *diri*.
Terelawa, brilliant in colour ; *lawa* 2.
Terep, to drip, shed water in drops, as when trees after rain are shaken by the wind.
Teresusuli, an annelid on trees, with stinging hairs.
Teretere, gray in colour.
Terevanutnut, to mutter with protruding lips, *tere ; vanut*.
Terit, an urchin fish.
Tertere-mataqelava, swelling in lumps ; the leaves of *taqelava* have lumps on them.
Tete, 1. an infant ; *i tete*, Baby, a personal name.
Tete, 2. neg. part. future ; *te* 1. and *te* 2. will not, shall not.
Tète, 3. to dash along with quick motion, to fly off as sparks or chaff in wind ; *tete rovrov*, to dash throwing up water, as a fish or swift canoe ; *tavtete*.
 teteag, tr. to dash about, as one struggles in water.
 teten, tr. determ. to dash at, make a dash in attack ; *o sigo ti teten o qoe*, the kingfisher dashes at a pig ; *o toa ti teten goro nanatuna*, a hen dashes at one who comes near in defence of her chicks.
Tetea, redupl. *tea* 3. *na ilo tetea ineia*, that I may just see him anyhow.
Tetemavuru, a month in which fragments from seeded reeds fly off, *tete*, in the strong wind.
Teteqa, redupl. *teqa* 1. to go stumbling forwards, to go feeling the way as a blind man.
nom-teqateqa, to have hesitating, doubtful, mind.
Teter, to stretch, pull, out ; *we nit teter*, to bite and pull ; *teterpan*.
 teterag, tr. determ. to stretch, pull straight ; *te rave teterag o siopa we pilpilita ; we teterag o epa*, stretch out, shake with hands outstretched, a mat ; *o manu ti teterag nauluna*, a bird preens its feathers, pulling, straightening ; *o tanun mulan te teterag nauluna*.
Teterpan, with outstretched arms ; *teter, panei*.
Tetete, redupl. *tete* 3. *o lan ti vus tetete o togo*, the wind beats and scatters ; *tetemavuru*.
Teteteram, to solicit ; of either sex.
Tetevei, peaked, as if cut sharp, *teve ; o nagoi ti tetevei*, in sickness.
Tetrawarawa, [*tete* 3.] to fly apart ; *rawarawa*.
Tetug, M. 1. a grade in *suqe*. 2. a kind of yam.
Tetuw, V. same as *tetug*.
Teum, to swarm, crowd together ; as *gatou* on *same gire ;* same as *taum*.
Tevag,
Teve, 1. v. to cut with a drawing motion.

teve matekuova, cut with an opening like an egret's eye, said of clouds. Pol. *tefe*; Malag. *tevy*.

teveteve, n. a knife; *un* word. Fij. *teve*; Pol. *tehe*, used of circumcision.

Teve, 2. adv. 1. equivalent to *kere* 2. before v. without v. p. only, just, nothing but; *ni we tan apesa? tagai, na teve tut qap neia*, what is he crying for? nothing, I only just hit him with my fist. 2. negative, *teve palpal*; *ragai, kamiu me ronotag si teve ge tamaine*, do not steal, you have heard that you are not to do so; 3. combining 1. and 2. *ni teve gogoroi*, if he had not forbidden I should have done it.

Ti, 1. v. p. of continuity, succession; so in narrative with no temporal force.

Ti, 2. particle, following the verb; throws back time, making pluperfect.

Ti, 3. particle, following v. moderating directness; *van ma ti*, just come here.

Ti, 4. adv. still remaining; *o kereai ti*, there is still some remaining at the bottom; *mantagai ti*, a little still; *mantagai ti e o aka me tul*, the canoe was within a little of sinking.

5. follows v. gives sense of an incompleteness, continuance; *ti tiratira ti*, he keeps standing about; *o manu te rorowo ti*, the birds fly off one after another.

Ti, 6. v. to set, makes comp. v. as *tikula*; *ni me ti nanagona ape vanuana*, he set his face towards his own place, *me ti maremare nanagona*; *me ti naqorona*, turned his ear.

Tia, 1. to catch and put to something else; so of a spider to weave, *ti tia o talau*, makes its web taking and attaching with a claw the line it spins; *o ulo*, maggots, *we tiatia*; hence to make a net, *we tia o gape*; to weave an armlet of *som* or beads, *we tia o pane*; to make the beginning of a platted mat, *we tia o epa, qara vau*; see *vau*.

2. with the same notion to take additional food and add it to one's portion, *we tia ape gana alo we maros nagana we qoqo*; and in the same way to add to the price in selling, *we tia ape som*, tries to get more money.

3. from the above, to make equal portions in dividing food, taking from and adding to; hence in recent use to weigh, in the first instance with steelyard, adding, or taking away, to make the balance.

4. see *tialovelove*.

tiag, to catch in a snare.

tiarag, to tease.

tias, to tease.

tiav, to lay a plot.

Tia, 5. to wind a shell trumpet, *we tia o tauwe*.

tiava, v. n. the winding, sounding of a trumpet.

Tiag, tr. *tia* 1. to catch in trap or snare, snap up; *qat tiatiag*, a trap.

Tialo, a red kind of crayfish, in mud in fresh-water, not good to eat.

Tialovelove, to approach quickly, *o sul we qoqo alo matesala we mule ma*; *o aka we tialovelove ma*.

Tiamui, the cry of the pigeon *qona*; *tia* 4; *mui* represents the sound.

Tiana, to be pregnant; probably from *tia*, belly, as in Esp. Sto., Ysabel; Tagal, *tian*.

Tiar, to take a clam, *talai*, by putting a stick into it; see *tua* 4.; probably parallel with *tiag*.

Tiarag, tr. determ. *tia* 1. to pluck at, tease; a child *ti tiatiarag i tamana, ti tiatiarag ape neia*, when it wants to go with him.

Tias, tr. *tia* 1. 2. to tease, as *tiarag*, ask persistently.

Tiatia, 1. to set out equal portions of food, *tia* 2., *we tiatia ape ganagana*.
2. in recent use to weigh; *qat tiatia*, a balance.

Tiatiaqo, 1. to go quickly about something; *o tanun we mule gaplot ape sava*; see *tialovelove*; 2. to urge to do something and a disaster follows; *ni me tiatiaqo kamam*.

Tiav, tr. *tia* 1. to lay a plot for or against a person; *we tiav sei*.

Tiava, v. n. *tia* 5. blowing, sounding, of a conch trumpet; *tiava toqal tauwe*, when a man slept away from home, in the morning *te tia o tauwe si o varowog o uqu*.

Tiavgao, to set fire to; *ni me tiavgao natuqena*; *ti* 6., *av, gav*.

Tie, M. same as *tue* V. to lean.

tieg, tr. as in *vatieg*.

Tig, 1. M. same as *tug* V. to loosen, untie; *ti tig o mateima*, undoes the fastenings of the door; *tig o qoe*, untie the line from the stake to which the pig has been fastened, so as to lead it away.

Tig, 2. M. V. to finish off the platting of a mat; *we tig o epa*.

Tig, 3. to swallow; a Gaua word; *o puepuei nipea tigtig*.

tignag, tr. determ. swallow.

Tiga, 1. to set up on end, as a stick or prop.
tiga goro, to set a prop against, to prop up; *we tiga goro o noota*, prop up ataps of thatch to make a shelter.
2. to gag, with a short stick, *qat-tigatiga*, set upright in a pig's mouth, to prevent biting.

Tiga, 3. to come out into sight, as a vessel from behind a point of land, *we tiga lue*.

Tigarapita, a tree-trunk set up, *tiga* 1., by which to climb up, *rap*; as to mount to a *gamal*; in recent use a ladder.

Tigawun, propping, *tiga* 1., the chin, *wuniu*, on the knees; *we pute tigawun*.

Tignag, tr. determ, *tig* 3.; 1. to swallow down something; 2. *un* word for *ima* to drink.

Tigo, to go leaning on a stick, use a walking-stick, *qat-tigotigo*; *ni we tigotigo wia*, he can only go about with a stick.

tigonag, tr. to push with a stick, &c.; to push off a canoe, to punt, with paddle or oar.

Tigoro, [*ti* 6.] to ward off, defend against, *goro*, shield; in recent use a shield.
met. to stand between a man and his creditor, by lending him money to pay a debt.

Tigotigoi, (k)

Tika, 1. to glance off; *o qatia me tika taso*, the arrow glanced off and flew on.
2. n. 1. the game, played with reeds which glance off the ground; 2. the reed used in the game; 3. v. to play the game, *we tikatika*. Sam. *ti'a*; Fij. *tiqa*; Tonga, *jika*.

tikarag, tr. *tika;* 1. to shove off from the shore with the hand, not as *tigonag,* making the canoe pass on ; 2. met. to send off on a voyage ; to start on a voyage.

Tike, to poke, push a way through; *o pei ti tike lue o vin,* water works its way through a dam ; *tike sau,* to lift and open thatch.

tiketike, adv. *we ge tiketike,* to disturb.

Tiketikegape, a fish that makes its way, *tike,* through a net, *gape.*

Tiketkev, *tiketikev* tr. of *tike ;* to disturb ; *ni gate tiketkev,* said of a man who eats some of his yams and leaves the others untouched ; said of a wind which damages part only of a garden.

Tiko, to stir; as in *matikotiko.*

tikol, tr. to stir ; *tano tikoi,* to touch so as to stir.

tikotiko, adj. disturbed, with disturbance.

Tiktik, adj. small ; a word at one time in very common use, but doubtfully Mota ; a V.L. word.

Tikula, [*ti* 6.] to turn the back, *kulai;* to turn the back upon ; *ni me tikula navanuana.*

Til, 1. a large garfish : *o vale til,* ends of bamboo purlins shaped like the mouth of this fish in the front of a house as an ornament, put up with a feast, *we kole.*

Til, 2. a volute shell ; used as a chisel ; a chisel made of the shell.

Til, 3. to wind a fishing-line lengthways, on bamboo, reed, or stick.

Tila, to bring a charge against, accuse, charge with a fault ; *tila galegale, tila nun,* falsely or with truth.

Tili, same as *til* 1. and 2.

Tiltil, a mitre shell.

Tilue, [*ti* 6.] custom in the *suqe ; ape gana o tapug, we toga rorono gese, paso nan ti lama o kore.*

Timalas, [*ti* 6.] to hang up, preserve, uneaten food, *malas.*

Timena, [*ti* 6.] to approach ripeness ; *ti timena.*

Tin, 1. M. same as *tun* V. to roast on or over embers.
2. dried bread-fruit.
tintin, a roasted yam.

Tinaeai, (k) entrails, bowels.

Tinagoi, [*ti* 6.] to set the face.

Tinai, 1. (k) entrails, bowels ; *ratinai.* N.G. *sinai.*
2. middle, midst ; *alo vatitnai,* in the middle, *vatitinai ;* see *tinesara,* &c.

Tinanai, go-between, mediator.

Tinawono, barren, of animals ; *o tinai we wono.*

Tinegaro, strength, energy ; *we la o tinegaro,* to exert oneself ; met. from *tinai, garo* 2.

Tineliwomaran, high noon ; *tinai.*

Tineqatui, (k) the crown of the head ; *tinai.*

Tineqon, midnight ; *tinai.*

Tinesara, the open space, *sara,* in the midst, *tinai,* of a village.

Tinetanun, a man in middle life ; *tinai.*

Tintin, 1. a roasted yam, *tin* 1.
2. redupl. as *titin ; we ge tintin naapena,* to restore confidence ; *naapena te tintin amaira.*

Tin, 1. to make, create.
tiniva, making, creation.

Tin, 2. to set a bound ; *tin goro o ranua,* mark the boundary of a district, *tin goro o tuqei,* lay

MOTA DICTIONARY

trees on the ground to mark property in a garden.
3. to dam up water; *tintin pei*, to dam back water to make enough to dip.
4. to become deep when dammed up, or prevented from flowing away; *o nawo ti kalo, ti tamarere*, the sea-water rises in an enclosed pool, *qilo*, with the tide, *ti tin* as the tide backs it up, *we ura kalo sage, gate malate lai*, full and still.

tinvag, separable *vag*, is full, rises full, with, *we tinvag wun o tangae si o lum, o vat nan we tavaroro*.

Tin, 5. a palm.

Tinerei, residue of water, a very little liquid left, in a *wetov*.

Tingoro, 1. [*tin* 2.] to set a boundary; [*tin* 3.] to block against, block back.
2. stones set to mark boundary, as *e. g.* of Luwai; *tingoro vanua*.

Tiniu, M. const. *tin*; a "hand" of banana fruit.

Tiniva, v. n. *tin* 1. creation, making.

Tinlop, to pop a leaf over the half-closed fist.

Tinqilos, a pool in coral, a small *mino, qilosiu*, in which the water is backed up, *tin* 4.

Tinqoro, to lend an ear, listen; *tin* 2. *qoroi*.

Tintin matawono, a boar full grown, but with tusks not yet grown long; *o liwo tagai tiqa*.

Tintiniav, a division in the *gamal* between the *um* belonging to the several ranks of *suqe*; *we tin* (2.) *goro av nia*.

Tinvag, *tin* 4. with separable *vag*.

Tio, a fish, with barbules, like mullet.

Tiotio, to sway, as a tree heavy with fruit in the wind; *tatiotio*.

Tipa, to knock, strike downwards, beat one stone on another, knock roughly, *popolotag*; a very swift canoe is said to *tipa o rep*, split the waves; *tipanala, tipawowo*.

tipag, tr. to strike downwards; thence M. to put the shutter into its place in the doorway of a house.

tipag goro o mateima, to shut the door, *i. e.* to close the way with the shutter; *te sargag siwo o matetipatipag ilo tanowa, we vil, me tipag reta*; see *gatava*.

Tipanala, met. of very swift canoe; *we tipa o rep*.

Tipara, a crab.

Tiparapara, have sidelong direction; *ti* 6., *parapara*; *namatana we tiparapara*.

Tipasau, to knock and take up.

Tipawaka, to knock open; *te tipa o vat sin tawalaka*.

Tipawowo, met. of a swift canoe; strikes and notches the waves; *wowo*.

Tiqa, 1. to shoot, not in fighting.
2. n. a blunt arrow, bird arrow, inverted cone-shaped wooden head, or a shell, such as *nurnuriaka*.

tiqan, tr. to shoot and hit.

tiqarag, tr. intens. shoot about.

Tiqa, 3. to flow swiftly out, spurt, gush out, as water; *me tiqa ran sage ape matai*.

tiqar, tr. to spurt.

Tiqa, 4. adv. yet, by and by.
5. excl. presently! wait a bit!

Tiqalano, 1. a kind of yam; 2. a kind of *tomago*.

Tiqale, to say one thing and mean another; *tiqale goro*, to give a deceptive answer.

Tiqamasmas, said of a man who gives as soon as he is asked; shoot, *tiqa*, and the bird falls, *mas*.

Tiqa-mate-wakole, to shoot and kill a loud-voiced bird; met. of one who loudly denies a charge, but when it is brought home to him he is silent.

Tiqamule, a Vui who takes charge of *tomago*.

Tiqanun, to beat the surface of the water when bathing and playing; *nun*.

Tiqanur, 1. a needle shell; 2. an arrowhead, *tiqa* 2., made of a *nurnuriaka* shell.

Tiqan, tr. *tiqa* 1. to shoot at and hit.

Tiqanal, the raised threshold at the door of a house, consisting of two parallel bamboos, or pieces of banyan wood, between which the shutter, *gatava* or *matetipatipay*, is thrust down when the door is shut.

Tiqanwono, a high rank in the *suqe*.

Tiqar, tr. *tiqa* 3. to spurt out, as water.

Tiqarag, tr. *tiqa* 1. to shoot all about, *tiqa kelkel*.

Tiqataso, the steering horn of a canoe.

Tiqatiqa, adj. spotted.

Tiqatiqasausau, [*tiqa* 1.] a shooting match, two sides, count pigs on success, *we tiu o qoe apena*.

Tiqatiqasus, said of pandanus fruit, *gire*, ripe and sunk together; of hand or foot swollen and looking short; *sus* 4.

Tiqoe, to give another something as a sign that you have been somewhere, a stone, a leaf; he makes some return present; *ko te tiqoe munia, wa o tuara ilone te rapa apena; ti* 6.

Tiqoman, said of two men, or two parties, when the latter succeeds in what the former has failed in.

Tir, 1. to drop, drip, as water. Mal. *tiris*; Dyak, *tirit*; Tagal. *tilis*; Jav. *turuh*; Tong. *tulu*.

tir manirnir, drop and make holes.

Tir, 2. a form of *tira*, whence *tiriaga*.

Tira, 1. M. 1. to stand; 2. to stand good; to be sufficient, adequate, to prevail; to be a duty; 3. to take a place, go on.

tirag, tr. to assign what is due, give share.

2. descriptive prefix to numerals, *tira visa*, of arrows, and sailing canoes.

Tira-gilgil, to persuade, entice; *gil* 2.

Tiragoro, to withstand; *tira goro sala*, to oppose in the road.

Tiralate, to break off in the course, journey; to stand, stop short; *late*.

Tiralue, stand forth, come out and stand.

Tiramoai, to precede, take place in front, be leader; *moai*.

Tirapalag, to stand close to a person, across him; *palag*.

Tirapatarag, to stand and spy.

Tirasalamoa, to go first, take the lead; *sala* 1.

Tirataso, to go straight on without stopping.

Tira-tatakala, to stand with legs apart.

Tira-tawalag, to stand with a child, or something, between one's legs.

Tira-vavagovgov, said of the sun setting, hanging on the horizon, with dazzling train of reflection; *govgov*.

Tiravitag, to stand off, of a vessel; *ti tira vitag ti*, continues to stand away from.

Tirag, [*tira* 1.] to give due portion, to distribute properly.

Tiratoto, to drive away an accused person from a village.

Tiravag, to stand with, *rag* 2.; to take the blame, *tiravag o lea*, to be responsible, as if one's companion is shot he has to make it up to the relations; *na te tiravag purei*, I will take the risk.

Tiravisa, how many, so many, of arrows shot, and canoes under sail; *tira* 2.

Tiren, reflective v. to be startled; *me tiren nan*.

Tiriaga, [*tir* 2.] to stand fast; *tiriaga goro*, stand firm against, steady under.

Tiriv, the seeds in bread-fruit.

Tiro, 1. to be initiated, become a member of a *tamate* club; *we tiro o tamate*; probably Mao. *tiro*, to see.

Tiro, 2. clear; Mao. *tiro*, to see.

Tironin, 1. a little pool of water used as a mirror; either natural, or made in *qilos vat, qilos tangae*. 2. in recent use a looking-glass, and thence any glass. 3. to look in a pool or mirror; *alo isei me gapalag qet o savasava, qara tironin si we wia*; *nin* 3.

Tirotiroga, clear, pure; *ga* 5.; *tiro* 2. as in *tironin*.

Tis, tr. *ti* 6, to set, turn; seen in *titis*.

Tit, to split, strike off splinters, flakes; to shape by striking pieces off; *me tipa wia o vat ape* nolmeat; *me nunvag sage ma, qara tit ran*, the stones which were roughly knocked into shape on the reef, were chiselled square after they had been brought inland.

Titatala, [*ti* 6.] to forget; *tala*.

Titawala, [*ti* 6.] to turn open; *ni me ti tawala naqorona*, he turned an open ear.

Titgon, redupl. *tigo*, with tr. *n*; *titigon*.

Titi, redupl. *ti* 1.; see *titiqon, tititau*.

Titiarag, redupl. *tiarag*, to ask persistently, bother; to follow persistently.

Titiganame, n. contrivance for hanging up uneaten food; *ga* 3. *name*; same as *titmalas*.

Titin, M. hot; *tin* 1.; met. *nom titin*, to be earnest.

Titiole, to laugh uproariously.

Titiqan, to be short, of breath; *o mapsagiu ti titiqa*n.

Titiqon, from day to day; on days after days with regular successive intervals; every other day.

Titiriaga, redupl. *tiriaga*.

Titis, redupl. *tis*; *titis vitag*, to reject.

Tititau, every other year; recent expression corresponding to *titiqon*.

Tititipa, to seek and get shellfish, &c., *vanona*, by knocking them off rocks, breaking stones to get at them; *tipa*.

Tititiro, a game, throwing at a tree and counting pigs, *we tiu o qoe*.

Tititrog, redupl. *tiro* 2. in tr. form *tirog;* to make clear, visible; to chew cocoa-nut and spurt it out on the surface of the water so as to make it smooth and clear, that shellfish, &c. may be seen at the

bottom : comp. *tironin;* see *titrog.*
Titkeliga, hot ; heat ; met. of haste ; *we ronotag titkeliga,* to be impatient; *o vanoga we titkeliga,* the going off is hastened, hasty.
Titlop, to rebound, as an arrow from hard substance ; conf. *maloplop.*
Titmalas, redupl. *timalas;* 1. to hang up food cooked and uneaten, *malas,* to keep it from rats ; 2. n. a hooked stick, stick with several crooks, on which a *tapera* of *malas* is hung up.
Titol, a fresh-water shrimp.
Titpa, same as *tititipa.*
Titpei, the cross sticks on which bamboo water-carriers, *pue,* rest ; conf. *titmalas.*
Titrog, [*tiro* 2.] redupl. in trans. form ; to make smooth and clear ; see *tititrog; we gat o matig, we pupsag ilo nawo, ti ninroa apena.*
Titrovrov, redupl. *tiro* 2. with trans. term. *v,* to make clear and smooth ; same at *titrog.*
Tiu, 1. same as *viog.*
Tiu, 2. v. 1. to apply, set ; 2. give a name ; 3. make a start ; 4. count in games.
1. *tiu o av,* apply fire, set fire to ; thence *tiu o pul,* in recent use, light a candle.
tiu o sus, give the breast, give suck.
tiu o qatia, to fix an arrow in the ground, so as to prick thieves or intruders ; whence
tiu werasa, to stick a besom in the *tinesara* in middle of village, to show that no one is there ; met. no one at home.
2. *tiu o sasai,* to give a name ;

tiu leas, give a new name in place of another.
tiu vawot sasa, to name a child after a deceased father.
3. *tiu o tuqei,* to start a garden with a few seed-yams to begin with ; met from *tiu* 1.
tiu perperir, to set wrongly about a thing.
4. *tiu o qoe,* to count pigs in games to mark advantage gained ; *tiu nagara o qoe,* count pigs against the other party, pigs they are supposed to pay.
tiu o as, to pay for one's song.
5. *tiu tatas o tanun,* to forbid a man to do something, as by authority of *tamate* society.
tiutiu, 1. v. [*tiu* 5.] when a man tells his boy not to do something, such as shooting at cocoa-nuts, with a certain sanction, such as reservation for *mawo* 2.
tiutiu, 2. adv. 1. by degrees, from time to time. 2. adj. *maniga tiutiu,* ulcers which spread here and there, *we gan popolotag o turie tanun; wena tiutiu,* showers, rain from time to time.
tiutiu, 3. v. to bring food on the death of a *sogoi;* n. the food for each *um* in a *gamal* on the fifth day after death of a relation.
Tium, same as *teum,* to swarm.
Tiutiug, same as *tiutiu* 2.
Tive, a shell, used as a chisel ; *mativetive.*
Tivitag, [*ti* 6.] to turn away, give up, reject, leave off from ; *vitag; me ti vitag naqorona.*
Tivtag, same as *tivitag.*
Tivitivi, a fish, chætodon.
Tivui, to pour water on anything ; *we tivui o qaranis.*

Tiwa, to make an opening; *tiwa lue*, to make a hole through, *tama we as lue*.

Tiwanau, to pop a leaf in half-closed hand ; *tiwa*.

Tiwe-ae, to fall clear down ; *ilogoroko nan wa tiweae a matenua*.

Tiwe-lama, to be in middle sea.

Tiwe-pei, of mouth watering, either with nausea or appetite ; *tiwetiwepei, tiwtiwepei*, insipid, like *toape* without salt.

Tiwia, a wading bird, like a smaller *takolo*.

Tiwil, V. to roll over; *wil*.

Tiwila, M. same as *tiwil*.

To, a tree, excœvaria agallocha ; see *toto*.

Toa, 1. n. the native domestic fowl.

Toa, 2. v. to go away, flee. in causative form *vatoa, vatoav*.

Toale, a fern, with narrow fructifying fronds.

Toape, an herbaceous hibiscus the leaves of which are eaten.

Toavag, [*toa* 2.] to go off with ; separable *vag*.

Toavtag, same as *toa vitag*, to go off and leave.

Toga, to abide, dwell, endure, live, behave, be ; in origin to sit, as in Motlav, Lepers' I., &c. Sam. *to'a*.
toga mantag, to live properly, behave well.
toga matapuna, to be one's own master.
toga tanotano, to behave nicely, well.
toga wurvag, to behave well.

togag, tr. to settle in, take up abode in ; *togag ima, vanua*.

togara, v. n. way of life, behaviour, conduct ; *we toga tama avea*.

togava, v. n. position ; *we toga avea*.

Togalau, a N.W. wind, over Ureparapara ; *o tine togalau ti tur ma alo Rona* ; see *wasovaluga*.
Mao. *tokerau;* Sam. *to'elau;* Fiji, *tokalau*.

Togaras, [*ras* 1.] one who lives, *toga*, at a distance.

Tagawora, to be easy, not entangled or confused, lying apart, *we toga wora, gate gona*.

Togo, 1. a mollusc, top shell.

Togo, 2. a reed ; see *towo, vatogo*.

Togoi, (k) constr. *togo;* point, pointed projection, vertebra ; serrated edge or ridge ; *togo pagoa*, the dorsal fin of the shark, *togo var*, the sting of a ray ; *gatogoi*.

Togoqisa, heavy, said of an arrow of which the head or foreshaft is too heavy for the reedshaft and will crush it, *te qisan o togo*.

Togosiu, (k) 1. edge, rim, as of a leaf ; 2. met. anything very thin and small.

Togtogagoropeka, one who acts as if he were alone, *we toga goro peka ; tama si neia magesena, tete nonom ape sul*.

Togtogewia, the fourth finger ; the idle one, *we toga wia*.

Togtogoa, 1. adj. stiff, hard, tight, not slack ; 2. adv. quickly, without delay, slackness ; *totowo*.

Togtogvis, a bird, V.L.

Toi, 1. a species of euphorbia ; used to poison fish.

Toi, 2. a spot, dot, as in tattoo; to make a dot.

Toke, to make a clashing noise, as in beating a drum, to champ the teeth ; *o laso ti toketoke ape mala ; o nawo we toktoke* *ilo aka,* the sea dashes with heavy noise into the vessel.

Tokos, to feed, nourish, bring up supplying food.

Toktokmemea, a bird, the Norfolk I. robin.

Tol, 1. same as *tolu,* the numeral three ; often with *ni* 2., *nitol,* and other v. p. *me tol, te tol, ta tol ; nitoltol,* three at a time ; *vatoliu,* third ; see *tolu ; ratol, pultol.*
2. before v. imperative 2d person, addressed to three or a few persons ; *tol van at ; tolpea.*

Tol, 3. constr. *toliu,* egg.

Tole, adj. long, tall ; *toletole* v. to grow long, lengthen, neut.

tolevag, lengthen with ; separable *vag.*

tolevtag, to lengthen and leave behind, *vitag ;* get too long for, grow out of.

Tolgan, 1. the egg of the ant, *gan ;* 2. met. from the shape, a long oval, said of a young *wotaga* fruit ; see *tol-puaso.*

Tolig, a single fruit ; *tolig moa,* the first single fruit on a tree ; *tolig tagir,* a single fruit at the end of the season, *we uwa tugtug tuwatuwale.*

Toliu, (k) constr. *tol ;* egg ; *tol manu,* bird's egg ; *tol rupe,* cocoon, and chrysalis, of moth or butterfly; *tolman,* testicle. Mal. *tulor ;* Gil. *toli ;* Malag. *tody, toly ;* Fl. *tolu.*

Tolo, to make a noise in the throat, belch ; *o natmera ti tolo kalo o sinaga,* a child who cannot swallow will throw its food up with noises in the throat. Bis. *tolon,* Tagal. *ti-lin ;* Malag. *telina.*

tolov, tr. to gulp at with open mouth and noise, go at as if to bite, as an angry pig.

tolovag, 1. tr. determ. to gulp, swallow with noise and difficulty, *ti tolovag o sinaga,* is swallowing food with choking noise.

tolovag, 2. separable *vag ;* is choking with food, *i. e.* swallowing with noise and open mouth.

Toloqloq, [*tou* 2. *loqu*] growing lush ; *vule toloqloq,* the spring month when things grow again after the summer heat.

Tolpea, [*tol* 2.] neg. imper. addressed to three, or a few, persons, don't ; *pea* 1.

Tolpuaso, [*tol* 3.] 1. egg of the lizard *puaso ;* 2. met. from the shape, oval, not so long as *tolgan ;* the *wowotaga* as it grows larger and shorter, *amoa o tolgan, pa ti tolpuaso.*

Tolrupe, [*tol* 3.] a chrysalis, or cocoon.

Tolu, numeral, three, same as *tol.* Pol. *toru, tolu, tou ;* Mel. *tolu, dolu, tel, tal, sul, 'olu, 'oru ;* Jav. *talu ;* Cel. *toro ;* Ceram. *tolo, tol ;* Matabello *tolu ;* Malag. *telo.*

Tomago, a yam with prickly vine. *tomagolava, tomagomotmot, tomagoqauga,* varieties.

Tomava, to pay for work with food.

Tomo, to press down *lot* of *nai* almonds with *qat-gelot.*

Tomule, [*tou* 2.] yams left to grow for next year.

Tona, in recent use a foreign country ; *tanun ta Tona,* foreigner, *vava ta Tona,* foreign speech.

Topa, to fall from a tree, as a ripe fruit, or windfall, as a leaf. Sam. *topala.*

topai, a fallen fruit.

Topetope, the ends of the floor

of a *pugoro* which appear outside.

Topulano, a kind of yam.

Topur, to plug; *we topur o materuas*, plug the holes where a canoe is sewn.

Toqa, a basket, pottle, to keep *nai* or *wotaga* nuts in; so called from its shape.

Toqai, (k) constr. *toqe*; 1. belly; 2. seat of the affections; 3. condition of pregnancy, *o toqai apena, natoqana apena. toqai we vaseisei*, difference in opinion.

Toqal, to crack, sound with cracking report, bang.

Toqamena, to be near childbirth; *o toqai we mena*.

Toqaro, [*tou* 2.] a new garden, planted for the first time; *qaro*.

Toqasir, 1. a rough cocoanut tree, which scrapes, shaves, *sir*, the *toqai* of the climber; 2. a man who often climbs and so *we sir natoqana*.

Toqelawe, (k) the calf of the leg, from the shape like the *toqe lawe*, blenny fish.

Toqo, 1. to have the belly, *toqai*, full; *o epa we toqo*, the sail is full; met. to be ready to bear fruit, *o patau we toqo*.

toqoa, adj. full.

toqosag, tr. to be full of.

toqovag, separable *vag*, be full with.

Toqo, 2. to weave plainly; *we vau toqo; we toqo. ae*, to weave without a pattern.

Toqogale, name of a bread-fruit; *tama we toqo, pa gate maul we malinsala kel*, deceives one *we gale*.

Toqon, *un* word for *tana* basket; *toqo* 1.

Toqosag, to be full of something,

tr. determ. *toqo* 1.; met. of feelings, *we toqosag o lologagara*.

Toqovag, *toqo* 1. separable *vag*, to be full with; *o epa we toqovag o lan*, a sail bellies with the wind.

Tora, a timber tree.

Torag, M. *torai* V. to set a mark to warn, prevent access or touch; *isei we torag goro o matesala* when he throws down leaves or a branch where roads fork to warn one following not to go one way; *te torai goro o patau mun o sasa* to warn off from eating; less serious than *tapu*.

Torako, a shrub.

Toratora, comb or crest on head of bird.

Toratorai, (k) comb of cock or hen, standing stiff; *vatoraga*.

Toratorasa, browned, as *lot* which has been rebaked.

Tore, to give over, making a speech; *tore goro*.

toretore, to make a speech when something is given, thence to make a speech generally; *toretore goro*.

toreg, tr. to hand over, with a speech, as a pig or money in the *suqe; we toreg o som ape suqe; toreg mol*, to give up a man to close a quarrel, *ul vagalo*, making even the loss and success on both sides.

torevag, separable *vag;* to carry about speechifying, as in a *kolekole* or other feast; *we torevag o som alo tana we roan, alo tapera; we torevag o paluko*.

Toro, deep; *o rue we qeteq meat kel we toro*.

Toroas, to belch; *toromasa*.

Toroi, a small mash cooked with

few almonds, *o nai gate purat alo pipis*.

Toromasa, to clear the throat with noise, make the noise of clearing the throat ; *toroas*.

Toron, to desire, be eager after.
  toroniva, v. n. desire, eagerness for something.

Toroperope, a fish.

Torotoro, adj. excessive ; *wena torotoro*, very heavy rain; *toro*.

Torou, caterpillar.

Torovalau, to ask over and over again ; Tasmate word ; *valau*.

Torow, a dove, at V.L.

Tos, to encounter, come against or across ; *tos goro; rowo tos goro*, to run, fly, and receive what was meant for some one, something, else, arrow, stone, &c.

Tosmot, to cut short, *tos; isei me rowo tosmot goroa*, somebody ran across him, cut him off.

Tot, 1. a bird that sits alone.

Tot, 2. constr. *totiu; tot we tuai*, old stump of much-used *lakae*.

Totgir, *tou* 2. *tagir*, yams, &c., planted late in the season.

Totiu, (k) constr. *tot;* a stump, stumpy thing ; *tot magarui*, a little old man or woman ; *tot parapara*, an axe worn to a stump ; *tot qetegiu*, the stump of a tree-trunk.

Toto, 1. to be diminishing ; connected with *totiu; toto rirtig*, pain ceasing, decreasing ; *nuranok me toto virtig*, my leg is easy ; *o talamatai me toto*, the effects of a *talamatai* charm are over ; *totomatava*.
  totos, tr. to diminish pain, make it cease.

Toto, 2. to cut with light chopping strokes, chop, chip, beat ; *we toto o iya ilo gape*, drive fish into a net by beating the surface of the water with a stick.
  totogag, tr. determ. chop into.

Toto, 3. an arrow prepared with the juice of the *to, noto*, excœvaria, poisoned arrow.

Totoai, (k) juice of tree, thick fluid in bark ; *totoe tangae*. Pol. *toto*, blood.

Totoanu, to strike, cut, *toto* 2., with an edge ; *we gar o tanun mun o gasal wa o parapara, we rus mun o talai, gate mun o qatkere*.

Totoepe, upright, to rise upright.

Totogag, *toto* 2. tr. determ. to chop into, to strike an axe into a tree and fix it.

Totogale, a carved image, chopped, *toto* 2., in imitation, *gale;* in recent use a picture ; *we toto o totogale* carve an image, *rave o totogale* draw a picture.

Totogasiosio, a children's play with a rainbow, *gasiogasio;* cut it, *toto*, off and it will not rain ; at Gaua men do it with *qale*, singing.

Totogos, narrow in shape ; *togosui; o tuqei iloke we totogos*.

Totokos, to wake in the middle of sleep, as with hearing rain.

Totolau, by the edge of the sea, *lau; rara totolau*.

Totomatava, early morning.

Totomot, chop short ; *rave totomot*, to draw away the hand as if for fear of its being chopped off.

Totoqoa, [*toqo* 1.] adj. redupl. *toqoa*, filled, distended, as a bladder blown out.

Totor, to stretch out the arms, lifting clasped hands above the head, when tired or yawning.

Totora, a kind of *tomago*.

Totorako, by change for *kokorako*, to crow.

Totoroi, mash with scanty almonds or cocoanut ; *qe lotu si qe loko, pa o nai si o matig tete purat.*

Totoromiga, [*totor*] stretching, as a hook stretches, or a man stretches himself.

Totorousa, [*totor*] stretched, drawn up, as plants too close together, or tall thin man.

Totos, to squeeze, so as wring out moisture, to draw a wound close, bring wounded flesh together ; *o tavine te totosi*, a woman will rub, squeeze, as in massage, to ease pain ; *o gismana te totos, te vamleg o gopae*, a native doctor will rub and squeeze with leaves to charm away pain; *toto* 1.

Totou, redupl. *tou* 1. to grow, spring up ; of vegetation, hair, &c., not of bodily growth.

Totovasiwo, [*tou* 2.] a garden of *tomago* growing for the second year, the small tubers gathered, leaving the main tuber to grow further down, *vasiwo*.

Totovivtig, [*toto* 1.] to cease from pain, become easy.

Totowo, 1. v. to stand up, rise up, straight ; *o aru ti totowo*, the casuarina tree grows straight up ; *towo* same as *togo* in *togtogoa*.

Totowo 2. V. v. to do for the first time; adv. for the first time.
  totoworag, M. same meaning, v. and adv.

Totpul, [*totiu*] stump of a gum torch, *pul* 2.

Totqetegiu, [*totiu*] stump of felled or broken tree.

Totvanua, the double teeth.

Tou, 1. to spring up, grow ; *tou mule*, sprout fresh ; redupl. *totou*; of vegetation.

2. growth, in composition *to; toqaro*, &c.
  Tagal. *tubu* ; Bali, *tou*; Jav. *tuwu*; Timor, *tuvu*.

Tou, 3. sugar-cane ; *we koe tou*, to pull sugar-cane ; with poss. *ma* 1. *mak o tou*, cane for my chewing.
  Pol. *to, ko*; Fl. *tovu*; Mal. Jav. *tebu* ; Dyak, *tewu*; Tag. Bis. *tobu*; Ceram, *tohu*; N.G. *tohu, tou*; Mefoor, *kob*; N.B. *tup.*

Toumule, [*tou* 2.] yams left in the ground to grow for next year ; *tomule.*

Tov, 1. v. to begin cutting a canoe into shape.

Tov, 2. spring below high-water mark, the brackish water of such a spring.

Tove, to hire for money, as a house, or canoe for common voyage ; see *wono wose.*

Towo, 1. to measure with a rod, measure.

2. to measure, compose, a song ; *towo o as.*

3. n. (k) a composition, song ; *natowona*, a song of his composition.

towo probably same word as *togo.*

Towoil, to arrange the pattern for tattoo, *il.*

Towola, 1. to plunge, dive, roll ; *o ririgo ti towola*, a porpoise goes plunging along ; *o rep ti totowola*, the waves roll one over another ; *o wirita ti towtowola mun nakarkaruna*, an octopus rolls itself along with its tentacles.

towola talig kel, to dive forward and return ; met. of a canoe going to a place and returning the same day.

2. a measure ; the distance one dives under the water.

Towolag, same as *totowo* 2.; for the first time, do for the first time.

Toworag, M. 1. to do, use, for the first time; *nau we totoworag mok ape purin,* the first time of my eating pudding. 2. adv. for the first time.

Towos, to flog, with stick or cord.

Towosur, vertebra; *towo* same as *togoi, suriu.*

Towtowoas, songmaker, poet; *towo* 2.

Towtowowis, a bird, pachycephala.

Tua, 1. (k) fellow, companion, assistant; *tuak!* my friend; *tutua.*
2. n. (k) making indef. pr. *i tuamiu sei,* one of you; the stem of *tuaniu;* see *tuara.*

Tua, 3. a creeping plant used to poison fish.

Tua, 4. v. to take a clam, *talai,* by diving, see *tiar;* dive and put a stick into the open clam, dive again and hammer it in, then draw up the fish.

Tua, 5. to burst, *tua wora.*

Tuaga, 1. elder brother or sister, acccording to the sex of the younger. Sam. *tua'a;* Mao. *tuakana;* Fiji, *tuaka;* Fl. *tuga.*

Tuaga, 2. v. to snap something tender, break off.

Tuai, adj. of long duration, past or future, so old, lasting onwards; *we tuai ran ma,* since ever so long ago; *ti tuai,* for ever. Pol. *tua;* Sam. *tuai;* Jav. *tuwa;* Dyak, *tua;* Malag. *toa.*

Tuan, v. to add, help; *tua* 1.

Tuaniu, (k) n. const. *tuan,* some; making equivalent to indef. pr.; *tuanimiu* some of you, *ra tuanina* some of those with him; *o tuan tanun* some men, *o tuan qon* some days.

Tuapaka, the last man in shooting, in *parparat.*

Tuaqata, to crush, come smashing, crashing on; as falling bread-fruit smashes, thunder or heavy surf crashes.

Tuara, 1. indef. pr. some, some one, *o tuara tanun, o tuara sei,* some man, somebody; 2. n. the other, another; *alo tuara tau,* the other year, past or to come; *tuara qon,* the other day; *o tamate ti kur o tuara gariga, ti la mun o tanun o tuara,* the ghost eats one fruit and gives the other to the man; see *tua* 2. *tuaniu.*

Tuatuae, to swing on a *tuetue.*

Tuawora, to burst asunder; *tua* 5.

Tue, to lean, incline, swing to one side; see *tie, tieg.*

tuetue, redupl. to swing backwards and forwards.

tueg, tr. to swing.

tuevag, tr. determ. to walk with a swing.

Tuei, a tendril or terminal shoot; *vakalov o tue nam,* to train yams.

Tuetamate, [*tua* 1.] one who is a friend of a ghost, *tamate; si tuan o tamate, o tanun we mule alo qon, gate gogolo tamate.*

Tuetue, 1. v. to swing; 2. n. a swing, aërial roots of banyan trees.

Tuevag, to walk with a swing to one side; *tue.*

Tug, V. to loosen, slacken, untie; M. *tig;* Pol., Fiji, *tuku.*

Tugrave, to become small, as the face in sickness.

Tugraveag, said of quick motion; *o aka si o iya si o tanun we valago, wa o tangae qe tole sal.*

Tugtug, redupl. *tug;* to be slack, slow in movement or action, to be late; 2. adv. late, behindhand.

Tugtug-rere, to be carried away by the current, *rere; ineira we tugtugrere;* also *tuwtuw.*

Tugtug-tanun, to break off a friendship.

Tuk, to dip something into a fluid; *me tuk mot o kor qara mana.*

Tuka, the sky, viewed as a covering over the earth; *tuka kor,* clear, cloudless sky; *tuka oloolo,* anything that hinders one from carrying out a fixed plan.

Tukatukai, (k) a circular brim, disk; *o tamate kamiu we sarusaru o tukutukai apena.*

tuketuke nua perhaps from this.

Tuketuke-nua, surf leaping up when the reflex wave meets an incoming wave; said to be *tiketike nua.*

Tul, 1. to sink, act. and neut.; to be drowned. Mal. *turun.*

tul o vat, to anchor; *tul ilo,* take soundings, new; *saro tul,* fish get into a net and sink it down; *sogon tul,* to load a canoe till it sinks; *mate tul,* to die outright; the sun and moon *tul* when setting in the sea.

Tul, 2. to beckon, nod the head, mark time with the hand; *tul goro mun o panei,* sign to be quiet.

3. *tul o kore,* to beat a drum with a dash at starting; *tul siwo,* to dash down the drumsticks; *tul vitag,* go off with a dash.

Tul, 4. to place stones as on firewood to be heated for a native oven, or take them out in preparation; *me tul arune lito ape qaranis;* to cover with stones, *we tul o av mun o vat;* *me tul goro o mate qarana mun o vat; tul lue,* make a way through a stone fence by removing stones.

Tul, 5. V. same as *tila* M. to accuse, lay blame; *ni me tul goro ape nawo,* he laid the blame on the surf.

tul goro, to excuse, by laying blame elsewhere; *ko we tul goroko,* you make excuses for yourself; *we tul goro mun o vavae,* to make excuse; *tul reag,* to get off with an excuse.

tul lue to indicate a person, *tama we map lue ineia.*

Tul, 6. with regard to money; one who borrows money from a person, and then lends what he has borrowed to another, is said to *tul* the first lender.

Tul, 7. n. wax in the ear. Fij. *tulu;* Mal. Jav. *tuli;* Tagal, *tutuli.*

Tulag, 1. to buy back a father's garden (by his sons) from his *sogoi,* to whom by right it should revert; *ni me tulag pulana mun o qoe; me tulag i sogon i tamana.*

2. to give money to quiet a person who claims on account of a death; a man's brother or *maraui* has died away from home, he goes and demands compensation; the people of the place give money and *tulag savragia;* see *vatulag.*

3. to scold a man who is away from home and takes liberties, so as to send him off; *neira we golgol amaia, ko gate tagvanua, kel rowo at.*

Tulgona, [*tul* 4.] a way of making a fence.

Tulgoro, 1. [*tul* 2.] to make signs with the hand for silence, &c.

2. [*tul* 5.] to make excuse.

Tulreag, [*tul* 5.] to get off with an excuse.

Tultul, a yam purple inside, *o nam tultul*.

Tulvitag, [*tul* 3.] to begin drumming by dashing down the drumsticks.

Tum, 1. to nibble at ; *o iga ti teretere tumtum o pea*.
2. heavy drops before a storm *we tumtum*.

Tumui, a dot, small spot.

Tun, 1. to buy at a great price, as when one desires a thing and asks for it; not by way of compensation ; *tunkel* in recent use, to redeem at great price.

Tun, 2. V. same as *tin* 1. to roast on embers, toast. Mal. Jav. Phil. *tunu;* Motu N.G. *tunua;* N.B. *tun*.

tun taniniga, to straighten by laying over a fire, as a bamboo for a fishing-rod.

Tunsaganai, the windfalls of *gaviga*, &c.

Tuntun, V. *tun* 2. a roasted, toasted, yam.

Tunusa, a skin disease.

Tun, V. same as *tiniu* M. a hand of bananas.

Tunlava, juicy, of fruit ; possibly *tun*, Lak., water.

Tunraga, juicy.

Tuntuntaqagata, a fish.

Tup, adj. sharp ; *wena tup, pei tup* when rain or water springs up in points.

Tupa, silly, foolish, imbecile person.

Tupleas, one who takes another *tupui*, grandfather, instead, *leas*, of his own, which may be by taking another father ; conf. *mamaleas*.

Tuplera, an adopted child takes an adoptive *tupui* by error, *lera*, who really is not his own.

Tupui, (k) one of the second generation in the ascending or descending line, so grandparent or grand-child, or great uncle or aunt, great nephew or niece, generally ancestor or descendants. Pol. *tupuna*.

Tuqa, V. same as *tiqa* 5. excl. forbidding.

Tuqe, to break something not hard, as a *tuntun* yam.

Tuqei, (k) a garden, cultivation : *kere tuqei* the lower part, *qat tuqei* the upper end, *paris tuqei* the side.

Tuqerag, to shove, thrust ; perhaps *tuqe*.

Tur, 1. same as *tira* 1. to stand ; and *tira* 2. of arrows. Malag. *joro;* Mal. *diri;* Fiji, *tura*.

Tur, 2. imp. particle, 2. pers. pl. before verb.

Tur, 3. stem of *turiai;* the real, main, thing, very, undoubted ; *o tur ineia*, his very self, the very thing; *tur tamana*, his real, true, father; *na turiakana*, the canoe of which he is the real owner; *o tur gene*, the real thing.

Tur, 4. *tur o sala*, to send one to solicit a woman.

Tura, 1. a leg, prop, as of a *qea*, platform, or *pugoro*, foodchest ; *ture gape*, the handle of the *gape saosao*.
2. v. to make the *turatura* of a house, close in ends.
3. to set up a *tapua* as a sign of feast given, rank gained.
4. *tura goro*, to prop up with a stick, *tiga goro*.

turag, tr. also *turai* V. to set a mark to warn off ; *we turag goro o matig mun o no-palako*, stick a branch in the ground before the tree.

Turana, the double supports of

geara mun; support of a very tall sugar-cane.

Turateate, [*tur* 3.] the evening before a *kolekole* when people go to view, *ate,* the man who has been in seclusion, *goto,* and give presents; the real view as opposed to *atepalu.*

Turatura, the closing in with upright bamboos of the ends of a house on either side of the door.

Ture, stem of *matureture.*

Turerea, the surf rushing back, as in a *masasa; o matesale rere.*

Turgae, the mast of a canoe, *aka.*

Turgaputo, [*tur* 3.] a real relation, *ape tanun tur sogona; ga-puto,* navel string; as in the proverbial saying, *ko ta rave naputona, naputok te maymagoa apena,* pluck his navel and mine will vibrate.

Turgoro, V. same as *tiragoro,* to withstand.

Turia, a kind of yam.

Turiai, (k) const. *turie;* from stem *tur* 3.; body, trunk, hull, mass.

Turiavarovaro, a kind of yam.

Turlei, to go in the rain.

Turmana, really, very, full of *mana* 1.

Turpea, [*tur* 2.] imp. 2nd pl. negative with *pea* 1. forbidding, do not.

Turqon, one who keeps late hours; *o tanun ti kelkel gese ma alo qon.*

Tursala, [*tur* 3.] the true road, *sala.*

Tursalemoa, V. *tirasalemoa* M. to be first in the path, to lead the way; *tur* 1., *sala, moai.*

Tursana, [*tur* 3.] the middle posts of a house or *gamal* in the fork, *sana,* of which the ridge-pole, *gatsuna,* lies.

Tursao, [*tur* 3.] good, principal, landing-place, *sao* 1., where there is no surf.

Turtur, [*tur* 1.] 1. wild, as of bananas with fruit stalks which stand upright; 2. met. wild, of animals.

Turturuaga, same as *tuturuaga,* blue or green.

Turturuga, blue or green, if clear and bright, with regard to brightness rather than colour.

Turturuva, to get leaves for cooking, as of *palako, no-sasala,* &c., to *sau* them; redupl. *turuva.*

Turturva, same as *turturuva.*

Turuva, to gather leaves for *qaranis,* &c.

Turvaloriag, to gather various leaves for cooking, *turuva loriag.*

Turvara, [*tur* 3.] the two first, entire, *wono,* leaves of a growing cocoanut; *o matig we mas, paso nan o noliu ti sigag kalo, o qoqoe vara; paso nan o naui nirua we wono, o turvara nake.*

Turvisa, how many, so many, arrows shot, or canoes under sail; *tira* 2.

Turwia, [*tur* 3.] thoroughly good.

Turwol, to go about in the rain dressed up, to get food; *tuture.*

Turwose, [*tur* 3.] the steering paddle, *wose.*

Tut, 1. to beat with fist, thump; *tagai, gate rus; me tut wia neia.*

2. to break off with blows of the fist; *te tut o lape matig;* climb a tree and *tut savrag* the fruit.

3. to take down the sail.

tutgag, tr. determ. to bump, thump, upon.

tutuag, tr. to ram.
Tut, 4. to draw a snare; *we tut o manu, tut o gae.*
Tut, 5. to come to an end, short; *tutut.*
6. to turn short back; *tut kel* same as *nug kel.*
Tut, 7. to lift; *we tut kalo o av,* so as to be seen and show the way; see *taqatut.*
Tutgag, tr. *tut* 1. to thump, beat hard, upon; *o aka te tutgag avune malo.*
Tutkol, *tut* 1., *kulai;* to thump the back; children pull up a grub from a hole in the ground with a straw, and then *tutkol* lest their backs should be humped like the grub.
Tutmana, thick through; *tama o lot si o loko we wono we malumlum, gate marinvin.*
Tutnunun, [*tut* 2.] to lop the branches of a tree; *nun* 1.
Tutnunnun, [*tut* 1.] to beat the devil's tattoo.
Tutnai, sloping face, or side, precipice; *tutne tanwe; tutne tano,* steep bank of earth; *tutne qatui,* the neck where it joins the shoulder; *tutunai.*
Tutpilage; or *pilage;* to stamp, *tut* 1., with the foot, as when one sneezes, saying, *vara sursur o lea nan nan, ni masur, nira vetvet wora, nira sorsora wora;* from the action of the bird *pilage.*
Tutras, [*tut* 5.] exceedingly, quite; *we wia tutras; me mate tutras; ras* 1.
Tutuag, 1. [*tut* 1.] tr. determ. to ram into the ground, as a stake, *palako,* &c.
Tutuag, 2. to stumble; probably *tut* 1. with the foot.
Tutuai, (k) brother or sister, according to sex of relative, brother to female, sister to male; *tua* 1.
Tutuga, to dry almonds, or breadfruit, in a food-chest, over a fire; *we pulan o av alalane pugoro, we tutuga o nai si o koru.*
Tutumiu, *o gene we tup, si ko we mule alo matesala we wotwotora.*
Tutun, V. hot; *tun* 2.; met. *pulsalak we tutun,* my dear friend.
tutunsag, tr. to cause heat; *o gopae tutunsag,* or *titinsag* M., a fever.
Tutunai, same as *tutnai; tutunetano,* steep bank.
Tutup, adj. fat, as the meat of fish or bird, not of pig, the fat does not harden.
Tuture, to go in the rain without shelter.
Tuturuaga, blue or green, with regard to brightness, not colour; *turturuga.*
Tutut, redupl, *tut* 5. to an end, a short bit or time; *ti gan tutut o siopa,* the wick of a lamp is consumed to a short end.
Tututul, to turn over stones, looking for *gave,* &c.; *tul* 4.
Tutvulage, [*tut* 1.] to stamp with the heel, *vulagei.*
Tuvag, 1. to buy or sell, with or for money. 2. money; *turag talo tana.*
Tuvagsak, mutual discharge of debt, and mutual loan, a loan and repayment made between two men, for the sake of display; *sak,* on both sides.
Tuvag-taso, to buy in succession to some previous buyer.
Tuvag-varea, a pig, as good as money, that stays in the village; *varea.*
Tuw, V. same as *tug;* to give

money to a *gismana* to get back the fragment of food, &c., *garata*, by which he is going to work; see *rarawara*.

Tuwale, 1. numeral, one; 2. adj. single; 3. adv. together.
  tuwalei, (k) a single one; redupl. *tuwatuwalei*.
  tuwatuwale, one by one.

Tuwales, to fall backward; *lesu*.

Tuwapaka, to shoot after another.

Tuwtuw, 1. same as *tugtug*; slack, late, behind time. 2. *tuwtuw rere*, to allow oneself to be carried by current.

Tuwur, 1. to bind on *noota* thatch; to thatch; *we tuwur o noota mun o gaqir*.
  tuwur patu, to bind the atap, *noota*, close up and firm to the rafters, *gaso*.
  tuwur raon, to bind the ataps, *noota*, close one up to another, making a thick thatch.
  tuwur rasnug, to put on the thatch loosely, gaping, so that the pins, *nug*, can be plucked out, *ras*.
  For thatching the atap, *noota*, is made; *late o togo* break off the reeds, *towo we sasarita*, measure them equal; *ras o nug ape ota*, pull out the prickles at the base of sago fronds; *save o no ota nan o lapai*, pull off the frondlets from the frond stems of the sago; *late sarrag o sinai*, break away the midribs of the frondlets; *luqe goro o togo* bend the frondlets over the reeds, *qara rino mun o nug* pin them with the prickles; the whole thus made is a *noota*. A scaffold is put up tied to the *tursana* for thatching. For binding on, *tuwur*, the thatch, *we niy o uto gaqir* pinch out the heart of the ligodia fern; the first row of ataps is tied on, *mamalu*, to the bamboo next the *paparis*, beginning the eaves; above these *we sususwr tapare*, sew in succession, with the *gaqir* and sharp bits of bamboo for needles. Many work for wages. The thatch does not come quite up the *qatsuna*, ridge-pole. To finish the ridge, *tut o lape matig* knock off cocoanut fronds, and *van o tapatapa* plait them into mats, and lay them over the ridge-pole; *no vele*, leaves of a barringtonia are also used; then soften in an oven, *qaranis o no surere*, the leaves of a scitamineous plant, and close in above the *tapatapa*; fasten this with longitudinal bamboos tied to the rafters; lay over this *no eri* leaves of a pandanus, bent over the ridge, *we ruqa*, in quantities, and secure with bamboos as before; the whole process is *vus* or *pusa goro o qati ima*, to thatch the ridge.

Tuwur, 2. another name for *tika*.

Tuwus, 1. the accumulation of ashes in a fire-place; *alo av tapug ti taqai taqtaqai, o tuwus we poa aneane*; 2. to accumulate.

U.

U, introduced for euphony before *a* 1. suff. pron. after v. and adv. *mapua, ranua*; perhaps also in const. nouns *ulu qoe, qatu qoe*.

Ug, M. to blow, act. and neut.; of mouth, and wind.

Uk, to clasp with the arms; *variukiuk, varukuk*, to wrestle.

Uka, to draw the bow; *tete uka lai o us.*

ukag, tr. put out of the hand, let go; to let fly, release the arrow; *te ukag o qatia; ti ukag vitag siwo o lasa wa o gea*, puts down; *tano ukag*, to let an arrow go from one's hold.

Ukeg, to let loose, give, allow.

Ul, 1. V. same as *il* M. to smear, paint, draw figures on *tamate* hat.

Ul, 2. to loose, unravel, unfold, untwine; *te ul o panei me takuk ti*, to open a doubled fist.

ul savrag, unloose and remove; *ul wora*, unravel, untwine strings, e. g. which are *gona.*

ul kel, untwist, as yam vines that have run.

ulsag, tr. determ. to loosen.

3. met. 1. to narrate, explain; *ul weswes*, let a thing be known right out.

met. 2. *si na ul napanek*, let me unwind the string from my hand, let me tell my story, deliver my message.

met. 3. proverb, *ul paka mule wora*, said by one who wishes to know what is concealed.

4. to set free, as the complications of fighting or prohibitions which make places and things *gona; ul vagalo*, to make peace by loosing the cause of quarrel; when a place has been *tapu*, a man may go after payment, *neira we ul munia mun o som, qara mule lai;* see *saroi;* to make payment in compensation for an injury, as when a man has carried off a woman; *i tamana ti rile o qoe ti ul mun natuna*, a man brings a pig and makes atonement for what his son has done.

5. to change the skin, shell, to cast the slough; so, met. to go on living and not die, as when men shed their skins before death began; *ul ta marama*, eternal, continued, life of things.

Ul, 6. const. *uliu*, hair; *ul qoe, ul tatas.*

Uliu, M. (k) hair, *naulina;* constr. *ul;* see *ului.*

Ulo, 1. n. a maggot. Jav. *uler;* Motu N.G. *uloulo;* Sam. *ilo.*

ulosa, maggotty.

Ulo, 2. the male flower of breadfruit; see *uloi.*

Ulo, 3. v. to howl, cry; *woulo*, a single cry.

ulog, tr. to cry to, at.

Uloi, (k) 1. the male flower of bread-fruit; *o uloi ti laviulo.*

2. the core, or placenta, of the bread-fruit to which the seeds are attached; *te goa o ulo patau mun o matesipa*, in making *kor.*

Ulosa, [*sa* 3.] maggotty, full of maggots; *pup we ulosa.*

Uloulog, redupl. *ulog*, to howl at, challenge.

Ulsag, tr. determ. *ul* 2. to effect reconciliation, to make payment for, settle.

Ului, V. (k) constr. *ulu, ul;* hair, feathers; *o tape ului*, a single hair.

ul ganamena, the down on a young bird.

ul gavaru, hair soft and loose like *gavaru; naulun Oror nan.*

ul-man, a feather; met. *o vavae o ulman*, a report that has spread rapidly.

ul mausa, white hair, the colour of *mausa*.
ul mesmes, reddish hair; *mes* 1.
ul tamatan, something like a white hair in bad ulcers.
ul talas, hair that does not curl properly, straight or wavy.
ulvaruei, (k) second hairs, grey hair; *na ulvarueik*.
ulvat, hair close curled. Mao. *huru*; Mal. *bulu*; Jav. *wulu*; Malag. *volo*; Fiji, *vulu*; Fl. *ulu*.

Uluna, V. same as *ilina*, a pillow, to pillow; *me uluna naqatuna*. Mao. *urunga*; Sam. *aluga*; Pol. *uluna*, *uruga*, *uru'a*; Ponap. *wulinga*.

Ulusiu, M. *ulusui* V. (k) constr. *ulus*; an end, extremity; *o ulusui wegowego*, the uttermost end; *ulus ge lama*, the branches of a cocoanut tree which are beaten in getting off the nuts.

Um, 1. the native oven in which *qaranis* is made; 2. in the *suqe*, the division belonging to the several ranks. Pol. *umu*; Ponap. *um*; N.B. *umbu*; Motu N.G. *amu*.

Uma, to clear away growth from a garden, the first stage in preparation. Bat., Mal. *uma*.

Ume, a large fish with lump on the forehead.

Umpanis, an oven, *um*, lined with leaves not with stones, *o um ta Vanua Lava*.

Un, 1. V. to drink. Mao. Pol. *unu, inu*; Fij. *unuma, gunu*; Fl. *inu*; Mal. *minum*; Tagal. *ominom*; D.Y. *inim*; N.G. *inu*; Mortlock, *unimi*; Ponap. *nim*.
  unuv, tr. to make to drink in.

Un, 2. n. the annelid palolo viridis.
un rig, un goyona, un lara, un werei, the names given to the months, or moons, in which the *un* appears.
un matarav, the *un* taken in the evening, *we suo alo ravrav; un mawiga*, that taken by moonlight, *mawiga*.

Un, 3. to use words in place of those which are the names, or parts of the names, of one's relations by marriage, *qaliga*.

Un, 4. to finish, end.

Untai, (k) hair on the body.
untaga, (*ga* 5.) adj. hairy with *untai*.

Unun, [*un* 4.] adv. finally, at the finish; *vau unun*, weave to the finish, a *tapera* or *wowor*.

Ununtai, *matig ununtai*, little fellow with much *untai; matig* 3.

Unuv, tr. *un* 1. to sink in, be absorbed, of a fluid.

Uqa, 1. v. to prise up; *we uqa o tano mun o tangil*.
  uqatag, tr. to rise up as a bird, or a canoe on the top of a wave, as if prised up; *we vet ape gene we purat, ape manu, si o qoe we roworaka sin toa*.

Uqa, 2. also *wuqa*; (k), an injurious influence proceeding from a man, which strikes another at night; *wowuqa*.

Uqava, a tree.

Ur, 1. v. to stay in one place; *ur qon*, stay at home all day.

Ur, 2. v. to cook in hot ashes; *ur tarowo, we tavig o sinaga alo tarowo we tutun, qara manoga*; see *uru*. Jav. *urub*; Malag. *oro*; N.B. *ur*.

Ur, 3. M. same as *us*, spondias dulcis; *wour*, the fruit.

Ura, 1. v. to be full, abound; *lin ura*, to pour and fill; *ura liwat*, be quite full, of liquid.

uravag, be full with, abound with; sep. *vag.*

Ura, 2. 2d pers. dual imperative sign; also *wura; ura pea,* do not, addressed to two persons.

Ura, 3. n. crawfish; *ura talo pei, ura pei,* fresh-water crawfish.

ura gan Qat, a sea crawfish, red.

ura gato, a very large species.

ura marasam, a large and light-coloured kind, named after the tree.

ura matawasawasa, large, striped, *kalkalan.*

ura rowotete, very small, *ti rowo tete.*

ura tapana, a yellow kind.

ura ta Panoi, red, with long horns; *we toletole nasinosinona.*

ura tamate, a kind black in colour.

ura we memea, red, but *tete tama o ura sin memea gaplot, we malapusa.*

Mao. *koura;* Sam. *ula;* Fij. *ura;* Motu N.G. *ura;* Mal. *hudang;* Jav. *hurang, urang;* Dyak, *undang;* Malag. *orana;* N. Celebes, *ulang;* Tagal. *ulang;* Pon. *uranna.*

Urai, 1. v. to smear, anoint, the head.
2. n. 1. decoration of the hair by colouring, anointing, &c.; *urai non Qat,* a colouring of the hair with red, a distinction to be gained by a dance and feast. 2. the stuff used in this decoration.

Urai, 3. a kind of yam.

Urasa, adj. ripe, of bread-fruit only.

Uravag, [*ura* 1.] separable *vag,* to be full of, abound with; *uravag vitag,* to be full and leave over.

Ure, 1. a place full of something; probably constr. of *ura* 1.; an assemblage of things, where there is nothing but these things; *o ure tawu,* only strangers in the place. Thus the sea names of the Banks' Islands; *Ure gave* place full of crabs, Merig, *Ure kere* of clubs, Meralava; *Ure kor,* of dried bread-fruit, Mota; *Ure marete,* of sea-slug, Ravena; *Ure pug,* of money, debt, Qakea; *Ure quuro,* of wild yams, Vanua Lava; *Ure tigalano,* of certain yams, Sta. Maria; *Ure us,* of bows, Ure-parapara, which also is full of slopes; *Ure wari,* full of certain yams, Saddle I.

Ure, 2. n. the open; *tale ure,* to go through the country; *ureure.*

Uresaga, adj. bubbling with foam, white with foam.

Uretaqa, [*ure* 1.] said of an island, like Qakea, without a hill, *ti taqa wia.*

Ureure, [*ure* 2.] clear; *o tuka ti ureure* on a starlight night, *o maran ti ureure* in early morning.

Uro, to be empty, hungry; *uro mate,* to die of hunger.

uroiva, v. n. emptiness, hunger, famine, getting thin.

Uroi, (k) the empty shell or slough of mollusc or crab.

Urouroga, blear-eyed.

Uru, same as *ur* 2., to cook in hot ashes.

uruvag, tr. determ. met. *ti uruvag natarapena alo tarowo,* of a man sitting in ashes.

Us, 1. V. v. same as *is* 2.

Us, 2. V. excl. same as *is* 3., dissatisfaction, enough of this! *us! na mule; us! tavun.*

Us, 3. V. same as *isa* 1. to chew sugar-cane, &c.

Us, 4. a bow; N.H. *usu, vuhu, vus, ihu, hisu*; Bks. Ids. *ih, wuh, vus*; Fij. *vucu*; Amboyna, *husul, husur, apusu*; Amblaw, *busu*; Saparua, *husu*; Gilolo, *pusi*.
us mamar, prov. a man slack about fighting.

Us, 5. V. same as *ur* 3., spondias dulcis; *wous*, the fruit.

Us, 6. adv. of direction, outwards, upwards; *laus, ragaus*.

Usa, 1. to foam at the mouth; 2. foaming at the mouth.
o palao me rave aneanea, wa o usa me lavia.

Usgave, a shrub.

Usur, 1. v. to pass on, relate.
usurag, tr. to pass on.
2. prep. according to, in pursuance of.
3. adv. in continuance, going on; *we gayanag usur ma*, told by tradition; *tako ususur*, to hang on in succession.
4. to make the first advance to the *tamate* Society by giving a *rawe* pig.
5. n. (k) a stepfather, or one in a corresponding relation; a man's father's sister's husband is *usurina*.
usur gae, one who stands in that connexion; see *veve gae*.

Usurag, 1. v. tr. *usur* 1. to pass on, hand on, relate.
2. adv. by succession, by tradition.

Ususur, redupl. *usur* 1. v. and adv.
ususur ga-matawasia, met. to tell a long story; *matawasia*, a very long *gae* creeper.

Ut, 1. to cut or break across; *te ut o marea*, chop an eel into short bits; *ut tole*, to cut into lengths, into long pieces.

we ut o wotaga mun o rat, break *wotaga* nuts with a blow; *ut wora*, to divide a string of money.

Ut, 2. a fish, a sphyrænid, baracouta.

Ut, 3. adv. of motion, quick not lasting; *sene ut, sara ut; le ut pei ma*.

Uta, 1. the bush, forest, unoccupied land; the inland country. Pol. *uta*; Mel. very commonly, *utu*; Mal. *utang*.

Uta, 2. V. same as *itu*; sweet-smelling leaves and fruits, a nosegay; a tree or plant used as *uta*.

Utag, (k) land planted, used for gardens and fruit-trees, held in ownership; *utagina*.
utag toga, an *utag* every one may not go to.

Ute, to urge as in questioning; *vagante*.

Uto, 1. to come above the surface in water.
2. *uto nawo*, surf on the surface of the sea; *o nawo taso, ta malate amoa, pa tagir lego o uto nawo*; met. *uto nawo we gavelate*, very white, *we vet ape gene we agaga aneane*.

Utoi, (k) pith; the inner part, if hard, within the bark; *we tuwur o noota mun o ga-qir, o uto gaqir, we nig savrag o riniu nan o utoi*.
Mal. Tag. *utak*; Dyak, *untek*; Jav. *utek*; N. Cel. *utok*.

Utu, a large, long fish, with very sharp teeth, small scales; *ut* 2.

Utut, *utuut*, to surround and drive fish into holes to catch them.

Uw, V. same as *ug*, to blow, with the mouth, or of wind; neut. and act. *uw savrag*, blow away. N.B. *vu*; Mal. *umbus*.

Uwa, 1. to bear fruit.
Uwa, 2. to bubble, be globular; *uwauwa, uwalava*.
Uwa, 3. a turtle.
  uwa iga, the leathery turtle; *uwa gan Tariaka*, very large turtle, fathom long; *uwa kalo*, the hawk-billed turtle.
  met. *inau o uwa?* do you think I can't feel?
Uwalava, [*uwa* 2.] very large, globular; *wena uwalava*, rain with large drops; *qagala uwalava*, an hibiscus with large double flowers.
Uwarowo, [*uwa* 1.] a tree past bearing, as an old cocoanut.
Uwauwa, [*uwa* 2.] to come into bubbles, as in fast boiling, or liquor curdling.
Uwauwalog, to lift the voice in weeping.
Uwauwalon, said by some for *uwauwalog*.
Uwe, 1. excl. of assent, affirmation, yes; *we* 2.
  2. v. to affirm, assert, lay it upon a person as true; *uwe weswes*, to affirm publicly, constantly.
uwesag, tr. determ. to make a statement in dispute, fixing a fault on some one.

V.

V, tr. suff. to verbs; *tanov, vanov, vatagav*.
Va, 1. v. M. to go or come.
  2. the same used as auxiliary with the notion of going on, but not easy to distinguish from the causative *va*; *i Bishop* (Patteson) *gate matmatur, we va mamamata* does not sleep, is always awake; *ape manara we tutun, a lau we va mamarir* where the hot springs are it is hot, on the beach it is always cool.
Va, 3. causative prefix, same as *vaga*, which see. N.H. Bks. I. Sta. Cr. Sol. I. *va, fa, v-* ; Loy. *a*; D.Y. *wa*; Fiji, *va*; prefixed to Ordinals and Multiplicatives.
Va, 4. expletive; *iloke va!* here it is; *iloke veta va* here all the while; *o sava va!*
Va, 5. term. of verbal nouns, *tapeva, galeva*.
Vaasaasa, [*va* 2.] to fight furiously; *asa* to rub.
Vaatev, M. [*va* 2.] to go and view, *atev*; visit.
Vaesu, 1. [*va* 3.] to make live, well, to save; *esu*.
  2. n. (k) one who saves; *i vaesuna* his preserver.
  3. v. to dodge an arrow, &c., *na me vaesu vagaqoqo*.
vaesuva, [*va* 5.] v. n. saving, preservation, salvation.
Vag, 1. tr. term. of verbs; *sir* to shave, *sirvag* to cut something close. Fl. *vagi*; Fiji, *vaka*.
Vag, 2. term. of verbs, but, unlike *vag* 1. a separable suffix, equivalent in meaning to 'with'; *ni we togavag naranona* he is laid up with his leg; *mule* to go, *mulevag* to go with; *we mulevag o tapera* go with a dish, *mule raveaglue o tinesara vag o tapera* go through the open space with a dish; in fact, as in Fiji, the compound *mule-raveaglue-o-tinesara-vag* becomes one word in verbal form.
Vaga, 1. causative prefix, but rarely prefixed to verbs; *vagaqoqo* to multiply.
  2. pref. to Ordinals and Multiplicatives; *vagarua* twice, *va-*

garuei second; also with *qoqo, visa, maul, purat.*
Mao. *whaku;* Sam. *fa'a;* Pol. *faka, aka, hau;* Fij. *vaka;* N.H. Sesake, Fate, *vaka, baka;* Sol. Ids. *faga, haa;* Malag. *faha;* Batak, *paha.*

Vagae, 1. to tie, with a knot; probably *va* 3. *gae; vagae maslag* to tie with running knot, *vagae pup* to tie with a firm knot; *vagae mereata* to tie a reef knot, *vagae tavine* a granny.
2. adv. always, often.
3. to stir round stiff *lot.*

vagaegae, adv. in lines, regularly; *o nawo nun ti malate ragaegae.*

Vagalateg, to dispute, argue, with.

Vagalavearua, [*vaga* 2.] seven times.

Vagalaveruai, seventh time.

Vagalaveatea, six times.

Vagalaveteai, sixth time.

Vagalaveatol, eight times.

Vagalavetoliu, eighth time.

Vagalaveavat, nine times.

Vagalavevatiu, ninth time.

Vagalo, to fight, a fight.

Vagaloa, a sword-fish.

Vagaluwe, to be successful, lucky, in taking; *ni we vagaluwe o iga.*

Vagamate, to sew on both sides, as a sail is sewn.

Vagamaul, [*vaga* 2.] for a long time; *maul.*

Vagamele, a fish.

Vagamelnol, a hundred times.

Vagamena, to be clever at doing things.

Vaganai, to dance with rapid short steps; *alo vara qat tuwale te rorowo tetete, we vet si we vaganai.*

Vagangan, 1. [*va* 2.] to go on eating; *gan* 1.

Vagangan, 2. to be beautified, adorned.

Vaganun, to talk in a low voice.

Vagaov, [*va* 3—*gao*—*v.*] 1. to pass on, circulate, a report; *vagaov o varae;* 2. to take, or bring, and leave; as to ferry a person from V.L. to Qakea in canoe and go back.

Vagapurat, [*vaga* 2.] often, often enough; *purat.*

Vagaqaro,

Vagaqero, to give money the day after a feast to the leader of the *sawai, i gene we put raka,* who gives to the party that danced.

Vagaqone, to try a man with a question.

Vagaqoqo, 1. [*vaga* 1.] to multiply, make many, *qoqo.*
2. [*vaga* 2.] oftentimes.

Vagaragara, 1. [*va* 3., *gara* 1.] to bite.

Vagaragara, 2. [*va* 2., *gara* 3.] to spread along in sound, as when many *rigo* or *wegore* are heard; *o line vigo ti vagaragara ti.*

Vagarat, 1. [*va* 3.] to make the ends of firebrands, *gartanasul,* meet, *gara* 1., so as to keep the fire in; *ti la ma o lito we poa aneane, we vagarat o av apena,* arranges the logs so as to keep in the fire. So of smouldering fire; *t* tr. term.
2. to bring close together, as stones in a *wona,* compact.

Vagarat, 3. [*va* 3., *gara-t.*] to make to eat; *we vagarat o sinaga mun o som,* a man who refrains from certain food, *we naro,* gives money to some one and then eats as before; *o som vagarat.*

Vagarere, to do in haste, without completion.

Vagarir, to shake, tremble, as in cold, or in *soso av*; *rir* 1.

Vagariv, [*vaga* 1.] to set a charm in planting a garden, *riv*; *vagariv tuqei*, charm a garden; see *vagvagasa*.

Vagarua, [*vaga* 2.] twice.

Vagaruei, second; a second time.

Vagasag, to gather, pluck, for the first time in a garden; *vagvagasa*.

Vagasanavul, [*vaga* 2.] ten times.

Vagasanavuliu-lui, tenth time.

Vagatar, a thousand times; exceedingly often.

Vagatavelima, five times.

Vagatavelimai, fifth time.

Vagatet, [*vaga* 1.] to perform the swift steps of the Qat, *o sul we vara, ineia te tetete*; see *vuganai*.

Vagatol, [*vaga* 2.] three times.

Vagatoliu, M.—lui V. third; third time.

Vagatuwale, once.

Vagaus, [*us* 6.] to pass on from one to the other, a piece of news.

Vagaute, [*vaga* 1.] adv. persistently, vehemently; *ute*.

Vagavat, [*vaga* 2.] four times.

Vagavatiu, fourth; fourth time.

Vagavisa, how many times, so many times.

Vagingin, [*va* 3.] pricking, shooting, of pain; *gin*.

Vagis, inaccessible, from above or below, difficult to understand, mysterious; *namatevura woke we vagis*.

Vagisgis, [*va* 2.] to go about work, *gis* 1., with industry, success; rather in another's business than one's own.

Vagita, a stone with *mana*.

Vaglala, n. a sign, proof, mark; adv. clearly, plainly; probably *va* 3. *gilala*.

Vagoar, adv. constantly, abidingly; *va* 3. *goara*.

Vagogoi, M. [*va* 2.] to make haste, *gogoi*; adv. hastily.

Vagogonag, [*va* 3.] to make *tapu*, *gogona*, forbid approach, engage under supernatural sanction; tr. of *vagona*.

Vagoloi, [*va* 3.] to make to shake; *golo* 1.; *nipea vagvagoloi nasurima* don't be afraid; *vus vagoloi* to strike so as to frighten, weaken, not to kill.

Vagona, 1. [*va* 2.] M. to go in difficulty, danger, as when the country is closed, *gona*, by war. &c.; V. *van gona*.

Vagona, 2. [*va* 3.] to tie in a knot, entangle, make *gona*.

3. to make a place *gona*, closed to common access, as by enemies, or *tamate* societies; to forbid access under a curse.

Vagoras, [*va* 3.] to pare off the inner rind of a yam, *sir savrag o vanarasin; goras*.

Vagorgor, [*va* 3.] adv. hastily, hurried; *au vagorgor* to take short quick steps; *nipea vava vagorgor* don't speak too quickly.

Vagoro, to heap up; *me vagoro vitag* left in a heap.
vagorogoro; *isei we gaganag vagorogoro goro mun nau* some one who has damaged my property comes and tells me that some one else has done it.

Vagosogoso, [*va* 3.] to prick, job in, *goso*; met. *o vanua we vagosogoso* the place is in disturbance.

Vagotgot, [*va* 3.] to run in, stick into, *got*; as lumpy ground into a person lying down, or rough burden into the back,

Vagovgov, [*va* 3.] to dazzle, bewilder, *gorgor* 1.; *o lamu ti ragorgor o matai.*

Vagtesurmalate, to make one's back break; met. to weary one by destroying good things.

Vagvagalu, to ask over and over again.

Vagvagalul, [*vaga* 1.] dancing motion; 1. *o loa ti vagvagalul* when it shines hot and strong, making the air dance; *ragovgov*; 2. *o lan ti ragvagalul* with a catspaw, when the ripples don't break, *we lul* 1. *gate malatelate.*

Vagvagasa, trees planted over the *mana* stones set in a garden; *ragariv tuqei;* such as *karia, qayalu, sasa.*

Vagvagol, a charm, or *tapug*, placed against a tree.

Vai, M. a rasp, grater, for *nai*; made of *qatia;* V. *vea.*

Vailo, [*va* 2.] to go and see, visit.

Vainiu, constr. *vain;* fragment, crumbs, chips, &c.; *vain sinaga.*

Vaka, to have strength, energy; *ni gate raku goroa lai*, he had not strength to do anything; *vavaka.*

Vakalas, metath. for *valakas.*

Vakalit, [*va* 3.] to tease, annoy; *kalit.*

Vakalov, to tie so as to keep upright, keep up with a stick, train to run up; *va* 3., *kalo* 2. *v* trans.

Vakasai, (k) haste, hurry, self-assertion, strength; *navakasana sin taur lai o gene nan we qoqo*, to show off his strengh.

Vakasalai, (k) effect, success, in undertakings; *navakasalana apena*, he has success, his gardens thrive, &c.

Vakasalava, great strength, energy, speed; *vakasai, lava.*

Vakasolsol, too soon, too quickly; *neira me ge vakasolsol inau; o aka gate maul lai, na tete rave tole.*

Vakaukau, [*va* 3.] caught, entangled, as with hooked thorns, *kau.*

Vake, expletive, here, anyhow; *iloke vake!* here it is at any rate, when a thing has been found; *na van vake*, I shall go anyhow, when one has waited in vain for another; probably *va* 4. and *ke* 1.

Vakel, [*va* 3.] to take, turn, back; *gate wia si a vakel ragai alo matesala me taka veta o vanoga*, not right to turn those back on the road who have begun their journey.

Vaketeag, [*va* 3.] to set up, make proud; *kete, ag* tr.

Vakikina, [*va* 3.] to terrify; terrible; *kikina.*

Vakiksag, [*va* 3.] v. to go beside, be alongside of; *kikiu*, with tr. term. *sag* 3.
adv. by the side of, beside; *wil vakiksag*, to turn over beside another thing, so as not to touch.

Vakiskislag, [*va* 2.] to behave ill, bad conduct; *kiskislag.*

Vakokot, [*va* 3.] to close in, keep close; to shorten; reef sail; *kokot.*

Vakolesag, [*va* 3.] to roll one about to wake him; to tease, plague; *sag* 3.

Vakolosiu, [*va* 3.] having a narrow opening; as a hole with small mouth and big below; *koloi.*

Vakome, [*va* 3.] met. to fight, so as to break, *kome*, the fingers.

Vakotakota, [*va* 2.] go on chattering, keep up a chatter; *kota.*

R

Vakotokoto, very nice in smell, as *ruka*, gardenia.

Vakovako, insensible, as in heavy sleep.

Vakteg, to charm for a good crop.

Val, 1. v. to refrain from certain food as a sign of mourning; same as *naro*.

Val, 2. v. to put force into; *val o suara*, put strength into paddling; *val gai!* make haste, don't be slack about it.

Val, 3. v. to match, to set one against another; *un*, to count. 4. *un* word for one, *tuwale*.

Val, 5. adv. in all places, to every one; *val vanua* in every island, in every village; every; *val sale sinaga*, every kind of food; *tiray val tanun*, give share to every one.
valtau, every year; other years as they come.

Vala, thin stones set on edge round the rim of the native oven, *um*.

Valago, to run; probably *va* 3. and *lago*, same as Fiji *lako*, San Cris. *rago*.
valago ninaninag, to run jumping as when one carries another upon his back.
valago sawasawa, to trot, with the movement of *sawa* dancing.
o valago goro tapia, proverbial saying, *we poroporo isei gate valago aneane*.

valagorag, tr. determ. to run after.

Valagogona, the mouth *gogona*, bitter, sour, for want of *pigpig*.

Valagoquloqulo, a shrub.

Valagorag, tr. determ. *valago*, to run with reference to some person or thing, run after.

Valagotiravag, to run slowly, as if standing still with it.

Valai, 1. (k) constr. *vale*; a mouth, mouthlike opening; *o an o valai apena*, a bamboo with notched end; *o rale pagoa*, the shark's mouth, the opening of the *nin* enclosure for the Qat, where ends of fence overlap.
Bks. Ids. *velegi, velei, valan, vala*; Wano, San Cris. *hara*; Ulawa, *wala*, to speak.
2. v. to cut in the shape of a mouth; *we valai o tursana ape qatsuna*, a notch is cut in the top of the main posts to receive the ridge-pole.

Valailai, [*ra* 3.] to fight, strive for mastery; *lai*.

Valakas, [*ra* 3.] to decorate, beautify, adorn.

Valaklak, 1. hard and tough as a piece of firewood that will not break.
2. to smack one hard on the face.

Valakorag, to put things confusedly.

Valakorai, adv. in a mess, ill-arranged; same word.

Valala, to dry kernels of *make* chestnuts, cooked in an *um*; open the cooked chestnuts, *lanon* the kernels on *qat lanon*.

Valalava, loud-voiced, big-mouthed; *valai, lava*.

Valamalea, one who does not tire of eating the same thing; *navalana we malea*.

Valanov, to pile firewood in order; *va* 3.—*lano* 2.—*v* tr.

Valapaere, to beg.

Valaqan, [*ra* 3.] to cook in a leaf wrapper on embers; *laqan*.

Valaqar, [*ra* 3.] to break something that springs; *laqar*; *valaqar o au*.

Valaqat, [*va* 3.] to flatten, so as to make *laqa*, *t* tr.; *vara valaqat*, to stamp and take up quickly the foot, *te laqa kalo; ilo valaqat*, to see an object as if flat before another and so making part of it; *toga valaqat*, to be close up to.

Valaqon, to cook on dull embers without much wrapper, *o tarapei te qale wia*.

Valasaola, a beggar.

Valaslas, [*va* 3.] branched like coral *las;* as trees; *o mot we ralaslas tete mule lai*.

Valaslaso, *nipea lenalena valaslaso goro*.

Valatelate, [*va* 3. *late*] met. to fight, breaking fingers.

Valau, to ask over and over again.

Valavala, loud indistinct talking, mouthing; *valai*.

Valavlav, [*va* 3.] to do strongly.

Valawar, [*va* 3.] to shine upon, enlighten; *lawa, r* 2. tr.; n. a shining light.

Valea, [*val* 1.] refraining from good food in mourning; *sinaga gana valea, o nam o vanerasiu apena, gate wia*.

Valeag, 1. to persevere; *te qale raleag sin lai ran*.

Valeag, 2. *raleai;* to dissipate the bitterness of *qauro* or *rava* by washing; perhaps the same word.

Valearoaro, an arrow with two points made of reed only, to play with; *valai*.

Valeasag, 1. [*va* 2.] to dispute, *leasag;* 2. [*va* 3.] to cause dispute.

Valeg, to hand from one to another; one after another takes up a knife, at last *me valeg tagea*.

Valeleas, 1. [*va* 3.] changing in colour, brilliant, variegated; *leas;* 2. *mai valeleas*, the changeling snake, which takes human form.

Valenai, 1. [*va* 3., *lena* 1.] to put out of sight, lose; *ni me valenai nok o gasal*, has taken and lost.

Valenai, 2. heart-burn.

Valenalena, [*va* 3., *lena* 1.] 1. bewildering, confusing to the sight; 2. so abundance; *tar valenalena*, number beyond counting; *saru valenalena*, putting on all the ornaments of rank.

Valepagoa, shark's mouth; the entrance of the enclosure, *nin*, of the *Qat* 2., where the fence overlaps so that *matawonowono* cannot look in.

Valeqas, [*va* 3., *leqa* 2., *s* tr. suf.] to put to hasty flight.

Valera, [*va* 3.] to cause to go wrong, *lera*.

Valerag-rai, to confuse, bother; *valera, g* tr. suff.

Valesam, to imitate, mock, especially in speech; as in the dances *tamatmemegel, temtemer, sawa-rir-vas*.

Valete, to exchange.

Valevale, a shrub.

Valgoro, 1. to meet, come, one thing against another, *val* 3.; as when a man goes by a tree which another is throwing at, and gets hit; or runs against a tree he does not see. 2. to stand up against all round, as mountains, clouds; *goro*, prep.

Valgoro, 3. [*val* 2.] to put out strength to meet, against, to be strong enough for a thing.

Valigtag, to despise, reject with contempt.

Valigoligo,

Valil, [*va* 3., *lil*] to do things wrongly, foolishly; adv. wrongly; *valvalil*.

valiliug, tr. 1. turn over, head

over heels, headlong; 2. met. wrong end first; to turn away from what is right, wrongly. *nar valiliug*, barbed, with spikes reversed.

Valipe, [*va* 2.] to quarrel; see *vanlipetag*.

Valis, a tall coarse grass; in recent use grass generally, and onions; *oro valis*, straw.

Valmasale, deficient, *masale*, short of a match, *val* 3.; single-handed, *valuna tagai*, *tasina tagai*; opposite to *valvalwia*.

Valoa, same meaning as *vasoal*; an open-handed man; *o tanun alena*, *gate gogoroi o savasara*.

Valol, [*va* 3.] to pay no attention to reproof; *lol*.

Valoloae, [*va* 2.] to stay away, without attending; *loloae*.

Valorlor, [*va* 3.] to mix, be mixed; *lor*.

Valot, [*va* 2.] to fight at close quarters, smash, *lot*; *valot ta Qakea*, people of one village fighting among themselves.

Valov, a way of weaving, platting; *we vau*, *gate maremare*.

Valqei, [*va* 3. *luqeg*] to make to bend over; *malate valqei*, *o tangae me masu amoa*, *tuara ti mas valagatia*.

Valqon, [*val* 5.] every day or night, always.

Valreag, [*val* 3.] to put away, *reag*, the odd thing, so as to make even.

Valsei, [*val* 5.] each, every, one; *sei* 1.

Valtei, [*va* 3.] to stick out one's stomach; *lelete*, *g* tr. suff.

Valu, 1. same as *val* 3.; to match, one against another, two and two; to stand opposite; *o tauwe nan we valu kalo a Vanua Lava*. Mal. *balas*; Bug. *wala*; Malag. *raly*.

valu ava, to come short of the match.

2. same as *val* 5., each, every; *valuima*, each house.

valug, tr. to set in pairs, one against another, in order.

valui, n. match, fellow.

3. same as *val* 4.; *un* for *tuwale*, one of a pair.

Valu, 4. same as *val* 2. to put strength into, hasten; *valu o suava*, paddle with full strength; *valu!* bestir yourself! make haste.

Valuava, [*valu* 1.] 1. to fall short of even number, in pairing or counting; to come short, fail.

2. *un* word for *tolu*, three, the odd number.

Valug, tr. *valu* 1. to put things in pairs; generally to arrange in order.

Valuga, M. part of Saddle I. opposite M. side of Mota.

Valui, 1. v. to answer; same word as *valug*.

2. (k) a fellow, match, mate; *valuna tagai*, he has no one to help him, is single-handed.

Valulug, [*va* 3.] to make increase, numerous, *lul* 1., overspread.

Valumasale, same as *valmasale*; *o wotuwale*.

Valum, [*va* 2.] to shoot at close quarters, *lum* 1.

valum saru, to close the fight; *me valum saru veta*.

Valuwa, V. same as *Valuga* M.

Valuwia, one that has a pair, *valu*; hence one who has a mate, friend, brother, *valuna*, *tasina apena*.

Valval, 1. to refrain from certain food in mourning; *val* 1.

Valval, 2. adj. everywhere; to each one; *val* 5.

Valvalai, 1. v. to cut the end of a

bamboo purlin, *rarat*, into a mouth ; 2. a purlin, or other bamboo, so cut ; *te kole o valralai*.

Valvalama, *valval lama*, general disturbance, noise.

Valval-lamas, a practice in *kolekole*, flogging men with *woqat* to get money from the maker of the feast.

Valvalua, [*valu* 1.] to lie in steps ; *o taqan nua we valvalua*.

Valvaluava, odd, out of match.

Valvalug, adv. in order, in an orderly way ; *valug*.

Valvalul, to cry complaining.

Valvaluwia, even, matched in pairs, all in couples ; belonging to a pair ; *valu* 1.

Valvalwia, even ; *un* for *nivat*, four.

Vamamarir, [*va* 2.] to be cool ; *a lau we va mamarir*.

Vamauka, [*va* 2.] to ease the bowels ; *mauka*.

Vamerag, to spoil, destroy.

Vamleg, 1. [*va* 3., *mule* 2. *g* tr. suff.] to refresh, recover ; *o gismana te totos vamleg o gopae*, the doctor will rub with leaves and charm away the disease ; *vara vamleg*, to tread as just recovered ; met. feeble-minded.

Vamleg, 2. [*va* 3., *mule* 1.] to return, tr.; *vamlei* (V.) *kel o vavae*, to return an answer.

Vamormor, [*va* 2.] to come or be in numbers ; *gate sul we va mormor ti!* the crowd will never cease coming ; *mormor*.

Vamot, [*va* 2.] to advance in rank, as one for whom a *kolekole* has been made ; *mot* 2.

Vamotmatelea, when one *vamot*, the person who makes the *kole we vene o qoe apena*.

Vamumuag, to sit on the bare ground.

Van, V. to come or go, *van ma, van at*.
van mot, motmot, to go in parties.
van tak, to carry, go with.
van wotwot, to come out into the open.

Vana, a pandanus, uneatable kind of *gire*.

Vanagona, a *tamate* 3. *na* 4.

Vanamalue, a *tamate* 3. ; *na* 4.

Vanameag, [*name*] waste, useless ; *vanua vanameag*, waste land ; *lama vanameag*, sea clear of the land ; *mot vanameag*, forest untouched ; *wota vanameag*, to be born a bastard.

Vanameg, [*va* 3. *name*, *g* tr. suff.] to hang, suspend.

Vananae, [*va* 3.] to make slippery with wet ; *nanae* ; as when children dabble in puddles.

Vananoi, (k) a man's sister's child.

Vanatev, V. to visit, same as *vaatev* ; *ni me van atev inau*.

Vanau, a tree.

Vanenes, [*va* 3.] to crackle, as a *wotaga* in eating ; *nenes*.

Vanerenere, [*va* 3.] to make a scratching sound, as a rat.

Vangona, V. to go in danger, difficulty ; *vagona* 1.

Vanin, to do a little at a time ; *vanin motmot*, to go in parties; *vanin werwer*, the same, *o sul gate mule saratuwale*.

vaninis, tr. to take up all the water in a *pue*, so that the next comer has to wait for a new supply to collect.

Vaninin, redupl. *vanin*, said when there is very little water in a *qaran pei*.

Vanin, to pour, stow, liquid in a close vessel.

Vanina, [va 2.] to meet, go and meet, *nina*.

Vanlipetag, to fall over another's legs; *van-lipe-tag*.

Vanmaroasag, to go, *van*, and work; *na van maroasag amen kamiu apesa? o som tagai*.

Vannag, *va ninag* M. *van ninai* V. to cause delay, put off doing; *neira we taka si a mule; i gene we pute kel, we vannai*.

Vano, 1. V. to go or come, *at* or *ma*.

  vanoga, v. n. going or coming.
  vanogag, tr. determ. to convey.

Vano, 2. adv. of direction; not definite in regard to compass.

Vanoa, the white ant; *o vanoa varvar-rowo* when they have wings.

Vanoga, a journey, coming, going; n. v. *vano* 1.

Vanogag, V. tr. determ. *vano* 1. to convey, carry.

Vanonom, [va 2.] to go thinking, *nonom*.

Vanoranora, [va 2.] to go along rattling, *nora* 4., as when carrying a bunch of *palasa*.

Vanornor, adv. in confusion.

Vanotoga, to go and stay, remain, *toga*, where one has come, *vano*; *o vanua vanotoga*, place of abode after a move.

Vanov, to make to lie down, lay down.

Vanov-toqai, people of her *veve* give money, *vene* 2. about a woman in her first pregnancy, and receive a return, *we sar muneira*.

Vanovara, to tread under foot.

Vanovtag, *vano* 1. *vitag*, to go away from, leave.

Vanqagasuwe, to hop on one foot, as when sore on the other; *van-qaui-gasuwe*.

Vanreag, to go away and leave.

Vansarqaqa, to meet one in the path and turn back with him; met. from sugar-cane which stops short in growing, *qaqa*.

Vantagasur, to go as a man with one leg shorter than the other.

Vantak, to fetch, come or go carrying; *van tak*.

Vantapekere, to carry a man or thing away without telling any one.

Vantatu, V. to encounter, come up against; *van tatu*.

Vantig, a late, slack, comer, *we van tugtug ma*.

Vanua, (k) land, island, village, place.

  vanua gona, the country occupied by enemy or *tamate* 3.; *o tavalalea we mule gona ma, o vanua we gona mun kamam apena*.

  vanua mot, a piece of land lying separate; *vanua rig*, a small village.

  vanua wot, a small island, such as *Merig, Roua, Qakea*; *o vanua we wot ma*, an island rises into view.

  Mao. *whenua*; Sam. *fanua*; Malay, *benua*; Bugis, *wanua*; Bisaya, *banua*; D.Y. *wanua*; N.G. *vanua, hanua, vanuga*.

Vanun, to keep the fire in by putting the logs together; *we vanun o av ape lito sin ona galara*.

Vanvanoron-sur, [va 2. *noron*] to go rattling bones, *suriu*.

Van, 1. the first bud of cocoanut, *wovan*.

Van, 2. to abuse, scold harshly.

Vana, 1. n. a *wowor* trap to catch bats; *we vau mun o ga-malmalagauro*.
  2. adj. shallow.

Vanae, [va 3.] to cause to whine, cry, *nae*.

Vanan, 1. to feed. Mao. *whangai;* Sam. *fafaga;* Fl. *vana* food. 2. a yam.

Vanan-pal, to put something secretly, *pal*, in food to do harm; by magic, and so by poison.

Vananqoroi, to put an ornament in the ear, *qoroi;* an ear ornament.

Vanansinasina, to put in the ear a shining ornament, *sina; we vanan o qoroi mun o no sara we aqaga.*

Vanaranara, [*va* 2.] to chatter, *kakakae gap.*

Vanarasiu, the inner rind of yams; *we waga o vanaras nam, we wil o viniu.*

Vanerasiu, M. (k) scales on fish.

Vaninis, to pick the top leaves of *toupe.*

Vanir, [*va* 2., *nir* 1.] to go with apprehension, fear; *vanir goro.*

Vanirnir, [*va* 2.] to be crowded, in a press.

Vanitnit, [*va* 3.] a creature that bites, *nit.*

Vanona, 1. to catch fish with a line, to get shell-fish, &c., for a relish, on the reef or in canoe. 2. things got to eat with vegetable food, on the reef or by fishing.

vanonas, tr. to supply with *vanona* 2.

Vanusag, [*va* 3.] to blunt by use or rough usage; *nusa.*

Vanut, [*va* 3.] to speak in a low voice; *tere vanutnut.*

Vanvanov, to waken.

Vanvanona, 1. the practice of fishing, getting molluscs on reef, &c.; 2. the relish for food, fish, shell-fish, &c. *vanvanona ta Qarnin,* when each man takes what he can.

Vao, a heliconium, same as *mata* 2.; *no-vao.*

Vaon, at short intervals, close; *au qalo vaon,* a bamboo *au* 1. with short lengths between knots; *au qalo vaon,* to take short steps, *au* 2.; *pute vaon,* sit close; *tuwur vaon,* to put on the thatch thick.

Vapeas, [*va* 2.] to lead the way; *ni we peasira* entices them to follow.

Vapego, to give orders to one's superior, to be impertinent.

Vapewu, to make weak with a charm; *was o tanun we sea we vapewu isei ni wa mawmawut aneane.*

Vapipin, [*va* 2., or 3.] to crowd, crush, in going along, or pressing others.

Vapitpit, delicious; *ko we gana ilo, pa tama we ar navarama; va* 3., *pit.*

Vapoa, [*va* 3.] to enlarge.

Vapteg, [*va* 3. *puteg*] to seat, make to sit.

Vapulut, [*va* 3.] to stick together, act., make to stick, *pulut.*

Vapunas, [*va* 3. *puna, s* tr. suff.] to cause a smell to diffuse itself, to give a smell to a person; *o punai te vapunas nina nia.*

Vapunus, as *vapunas,* from *pun* V.

Vaputeg, [*va* 3.] see *vapteg.*

Vaputput, [*va* 3.] to stamp as in rage, provoking to fight; *put.*

Vaqer, to persist in doing what is disliked; *vaqer goro.*

Vaqilas, [*va* 3.] to cover over with a number of things; *me vaqilas goro mun o vat.*

Vaqirqir, [*va* 3.] to crowd together, *qir,* confusedly; *o nawo we malate vaqirqir,* surf breaks irregularly.

Vaqisa, [va 2.] to smash together. qisa ; met. to fight furiously.

Vaqoqo, [va 3.] to make many, much, qoqo, increase, multiply ; *iro Som we pute alele ima pa ti vaqvaqoqo maremare o som*, sits in the house hard at work multiplying the money.

Vaqoqoi, 1. to invite to an insufficient meal ; 2. met. to repeat a tale ; *isei we gaganag mun o tuara, ni we vaqoqoi gap avunansei we sea*, saying that it was he.

Vaqoriag, [va 3.] to mix, *qoriag*.

Var, 1. *vari*, a fish, the ray, sting ray ; *var* ma*la*, a b*la*ck ray white on breast ; *var pagoa*, a very large kind. Mal. *pari* a skate.

Var, 2. to do secretly.

Var, 3. prefix, 1. of reciprocity 2. of plurality ; *o reremera we var raraog*, children crying all together ; *o qoe we varvar rarao*; see *varmatir*. N.B. *wara* reciprocal with verbs, and with n. when things are duplicated.

Var, 4. hibiscus, *varu*.

Vara, 1. to tread, stamp, walk ; to strike as a hawk its prey, and lightning ; *vara kalo*, go up hill; *vara qat*, dance in Qat. 2. to measure by feet ; *we vara o uwa*.
varas, tr. to trample.

Vara, 3. to hide ; *vara goro ; vara lana* to lift up, *lana*, the edge of a mat and put something under.

Vara, 4. to contribute, distribute ; *tur vara o sinaga ape matea ; neira me vara o malas*, assigned portions of cooked food.

Vara, 5. n. 1. the shoot, plumule, of the cocoanut, as it forms first within the nut, afterwards when it shoots outside, and finally as growing up from the radicle.
2. a cocoanut in which the *vara* is forming or from which it has shot ; *vin vara*, the husk of such a cocoanut.
qoqoe vara, the shoot of growing cocoanut, both plumule and radicle.
tur vara, the two first leaves, *we wono*.
3. the top, crown, of the caladium, *qeta*, the top of sugar-cane, *tou*, which are planted.

Vara, 6. adv. qualifying, rather ; *vara poa*, rather large, larger.

Vara, 7. constr. of *varai*.

Varaae, no standing-place ; *alo lama o varae-ae ; te vara ae alo lama*.

Varaanan, to tread, *vara*, into mud, *o matesala we vara anan ; an ; vara anian* the same.

Varaasaasa, to rub with the feet ; *vara* 1. *asa*.

Varagai, to strengthen, support, brace up ; *gamo varagaia*, to sail with tightened ropes ; *varagai savrag ilo sama*.

Varaget, 1. to stand strong, firm ; *vara, get*. 2. adv. firmly : *sik varaget*, bring a man to a standstill with *sik ; taur varaget*, catch and hold firm.

Varagetnam, a tree, like castanospermum.

Varagogolo, to go in fear ; *vara* 1.

Varai, (k) constr. *vare ;* 1. the breast, the liver.
2. the *vara*, head, crown of *qeta*, forming shoot in cocoanut.
vara, in composition, feeling, state of mind.

Varakalkal, to hesitate, be in two minds, *isei ta ilo o sava, sin ge, sin la, pa gate lai; was me varakalkal apena.*

Varakat, [*va* 3., *raka* 1. *t* tr. suf.] to renew, do afresh; *me ava ti, we ge mulan.*

Varake, a tree; the shells of the fruit tied on the ankles as rattles in dances.

Varakekete, to walk on the toes as in crossing a muddy place; *vara* 1.

Varalana, to make known a secret, disclose; *nipea varvaralana pulan narua o qeta; vara* 3.

Varalava, one who is easily frightened, makes much of nothing; *o sava o mantagai ta ge, te ge poa apena, ineia o varalava.*

Varalil, [*vara* 6.] discoloured.

Varaloloqon, to lose sense and memory; men ate the *varai*, liver, of a corpse in order to get *mana* for courage and strength, *vavakae*; the liver made them forget everything, be *loloqon*.

Varaloqoloqo, [*varai*] pigeon-breasted; *loqo.*

Varaluqeag, [*vara* 1.] to tread upon and crush flat; *luqe.*

Varamalumlum, to become easy, light, of disease; *kamam me ronotag si we mano varamalumlum nania.*

Varamamatuaga, [*vara* 6.] flourishing.

Varamatapalpal, a fish.

Varamomogo, to tread cautiously, with dread; *momogo.*

Varamoramo, [*va* 3.] to seize things for oneself; *ramo.*

Varamot, n. [*vara* 7.] something that much distresses, a great sorrow; *me ge o varamot munia.*

Varanasenase, to tread so as to make a crackling noise; *nase.*

Varapa, twin children, a twin. *varapatol*, three at a birth.

Varaparapa, said of two canoes sailing close together, *we gamo rupe; varapa.*

Varapoa, [*vara* 6.] comparatively large.

Varapuna, [*vara* 6.] rather smelling.

Varapura, *varapra goro*, to forbid anything to be given to another.

Varaqages, [*vara* 1.] to walk lame; *qages.*

Varaqeqet, [*vara* 1.] to stamp upon, *qeqet*, as a sign of scorn, rejection.

Varaqonag, [*vara* 1.] to go in fear, *qonag.*

Vararerea, to go in fear; *rere* 1.

Vararerere, [*vara* 7.] to be in fear, with trembling breast; *rere* 1.

Vararoma, [*vara* 6.] rather stale or rank; *roma.*

Varas, tr. *vara* 1. to stamp for something, to trample on; to trample to death as intruders in a *gamal.*

Varasaka, a feeling of sickness; *o varai tama we saka.*

Varasama, to tack, in sailing a canoe; *sama.*

Varasamai, *o sinaga we qoqo, o som gate purat;* but see *varavarasamai.*

Varasorako, [*vara* 1.] said of a cloud coming in a mass over the sea, *ti varasorako ma; sorako.*

Varasqoe, to stamp, dance, with reference to a pig given at a feast; *vat varasqoe*, a stone set up by *wona* for *varasqoe.*

Varasurlea, a stone with power, *mana*, to daunt enemies; *we sonnag alo vagalo.*

Varasuwasuwa, to step, *vara* 1., backwards, bending down, *suwa*.

Varat, the purlin of a house.

Varataso, to strike the foot, *taso* 1., in treading, and miss footing.

Varatawaga, [*vara* 6.] to clear up a little, clouds opening, *tawaga*, as on a wet day.

Varaton, [*ra* 3.] to warm up cold vegetable food, *raton*.

Varatoperag, [*vara* 1.] when many *tope nai* or *salite* have fallen one says, *gate tope salte ti varatoperag ti!*

Varatotolau, the bush by the edge of the water.

Varavara goro, term applied to money given to a wizard that he may not relax his charm; *nau we tuw mun* T. *o som ape garatan* N.; *paso nan* M. *we la mun* T. *o som varavara goro,* I give money to T. the *gismana,* to get back from him the *garata* with which he is bewitching N., lest N. should die; M. knows it and gives *som varavara goro*.

Varavarasamai, to be in doubt as to what to do.

Varavravesus, to draw back crouching, *sus,* out of sight.

Varawel, to wrench, twist, ankle or foot; *rara* 1. *wel*.

Varaweretag, to stamp upon, crush, spoil, kill, some soft thing.

Varea, a village, place of a village settlement; *un* for *vanua*.
 a varea, out of doors, outside the house; *ta varea,* belonging to the village precincts.

Vareag, [*va* 1.] to go away from, *reag*.

Vareai, (k) the outside of anything; *talo vareai,* outer, belonging to the outside.

Varean, to praise, thank.

Vareg, [*ra* 3.] to make a sign with the head, *reg;* thence to give direction, order, command; *me vareg munia*.

varegiva, v. n. giving orders, direction.

Varematikawia, a dark rain-bearing cloud.

Varenasiu, V. metath. for *ranerasiu,* scale.

Varepagoa, a red *kalato* tree.

Varerere, [*va* 2.] to stagger, hesitate, as one who is in fear; *rere* 1.

Vargapa, [*var* 2.] to give money or food secretly as a sign from a woman to a man; *gapa* 1.

Varginit, [*var* 3.] to plan together, agree; *ginit*.

Vargol, [*var* 3.] to quarrel, scold one another in anger; *neira we vargol amenau; gol*.

Vargon, to send, order; Gaua word; *un* for *vatran*.

Vari, [*var* 1.] the sting ray; *togo vari,* the spike, used as a needle.

Variara, [*var* 3.] chase one another, race; *ara* 1.

Variaso, [*var* 3.] to overlap, to pass one beside the other, get out of joint; *aso*.

Variava, [*var* 3.] to miss meeting, go wrong on both sides; met. of mistakes, misdeeds; *ava* 1.

Varir, [*ra* 3.] to crowd together, push; *rir* 2.; *varirir*.

Varirgala, adv., in a crowd; *ilo varirgala,* to distinguish, *ko gate ilo varirgala wun inau, wa na me tira goro nanagoma,* you did not recognize me in the crowd, although I was standing before you.

Varis, M. same as *varus,* to ask, inquire; *varis saro,* to ask a thing back.

MOTA DICTIONARY

Varisar, M. to ask after a person; *ko we varisar ineia ape sara?*

Varisaro, same as *raris saro*.

Variukuk, [*var* 3.] to wrestle together, *uk; varinkiuk*.

Varkaut, [*var* 3.] to pluck, twitch, so as to call attention; *kaut*.

Varkes, to rebake *kor*, dried bread-fruit, the second day.

Varlai, [*var* 3.] to try strength one against another, to contend; *lai*.

Varle, [*var* 3.] V. to contend, compete.

Varleas, [*var* 3.] to interchange, to change in many things.

Varleasag, [*var* 3.] to argue, contradict one another, quarrel; *leasag*.

Varligoligo, [*var* 3.] to chase or follow.

Varmatir, [*var* 3.] to sleep together in a number.

Varnalia, [*var* 3.] to go about in excitement; *nalia*.

Varnanau, to give death-bed directions; *ratavata varvarnanau*, arrangement about succession to property.

Varnina, 1. [*var* 3.] to meet one another; *nina* 1.

Varnina, 2. to knock one against another; *nina* 3.

Varnit, [*var* 3.] to join close one to another; *nit*.

Varoiroi, white hair.

Varono, [*va* 3.] to make holy; a new word, see *rono* 2.

   varonova, v. n. consecration, making holy, being made holy.

Varoro, [*va* 3.] to let down, *roro* 2. *tamate varvaroro*, a palmer worm that lives in *virot paka*, and when the banyan sheds its leaves lets itself down by a line into the earth.

Varoroag, in abundance, see *war*, and next word.

Varoroasa, [*var* 3.] adj. crowding one another, very many; same stem in *orosaga*.

Varovaro, a tree.

Varowo, [*va* 2.] to make progress in a certain direction, *rowo*.

Varowog, [*va* 3. *rowog*] 1. to cause to fly, send flying away; *te varowog o sor we avut o sul nia*, by blowing a conch. 2. to put off with a sort of curse, *vawo aru! vawo wonawona! melwotrow!* sending off to places where ghosts are; same meaning as *norag*; one perceives another doing wrong, or wanting to do him wrong, and *we varowogia*.

Varowot, *we vile alo matava, we togotoga avune nol meat*.

Varpis, [*var* 3.] salute by pinching fingers, *pisui*.

Varqisai, trodden down, as a place where a party has been playing or fighting; *qisa*.

Varsar, [*var* 3.] to make mutual recompense, make up to one another; *sar* 1.

Varsaru, [*var* 3. *saru*] adv. *lag varsaru*, when two men marry each the other's sister.

Varseseg, [*var* 3.] to take in turns; *sesei*.

Varsoro, [*var* 3.] to cry, *soro*, in a number together; children or flying foxes.

Varsuwav-rua, [*var* 3.] 1. of two birds laying their eggs together in one nest; *suwav*; 2. met. of two pieces of food in one wrapper.

Vartawo, [*var* 3.] of numbers gathering together; *tawo*.

Vartela, [*var* 3.] to strike together, as two *nine* in the game.

Vartike, [*var* 3.] to stir up one

another to quarrel; to quarrel; *tike.*
Vartikula, [*var* 3.] to turn the back one upon another, to go opposite ways from the same point; *tikula.*
Varturtur, [*var* 2.] to act as pander, as a woman is *saka* for a man who steals a woman; *we varturtur toto, o vavine we varturtur o sala.*
Varu, hibiscus tiliaceus; *var* 4. Mal. *baru;* Jav. Bug. *waru;* Malag. *varo.*
Varuarua, [*va* 3.] by twos, in two directions; *nom varuarua,* to doubt.
Varuei, [*va* 3.] (k) second; *rua;* constr. *varue; ul varuei,* gray hair.
varue sasai, other name, when a man has two.
Varug, to prevent, protect.
vat varug, as at Tasmate, when knocked on the ground will prevent enemies from coming.
Varurmag, to press down; *we vara varurmag o wetov ilo pei,* press down a bottle into water with the foot.
Varus, V. to ask, enquire, enquire for.
Varusar, V. same as *varisar.*
Varvaramake, a tree, like a *make* chestnut.
Varvaramate, said of firewood which burns out very quickly.
Varvaramatika, a kite that preys on the *matika; vara* 1.
Varvaratet, a game played with *nai* almonds, hide-and-seek, *varvaratet qalo.*
Varvaravatpuna, a fish that feeds on madrepore coral.
Varvaresauma, a fish.
Varvargapa, to give food or money secretly; *vargapa.*
Varvariara, to race; *variara.*

Varvaririsag, to lie in numbers together; *var* 3. *varir, sag* term. of number.
Varvug, [*var* 3.] to assemble together.
Varwenir, [*var* 3.] many make a noise at play together; *wenir.*
Varwora, [*var* 3.] two persons part and go different ways; *wora* 1.; *ni me mule varwora nan tuana.*
Varwota, 1. [*var* 3.] to knock, *wota* 3., one against another.
Varwota, 2. [*var* 3. *wota* 1.] to be born to match.
Varwotawota, things in pairs or together, big and little, as things are born in pairs male and female; *varwota* 2.; *we vile varwotawota.*
Vas, to pick off, take up with the fingers, such things as *qero, sisipe, nug.*
Vasageg, [*va* 3.] to bring up, *sageg* tr. *sage* 3., people to fight, hiring them.
Vasager, [*va* 3.] to set up, *sager* tr. *sage* 1., place upon, as bread-fruit on fire, things on a *qea; we vasager o patau alo av,* in making *kor; vasager o pei,* &c., in recent use to boil water, by setting it on the fire.
Vasakar, [*va* 3.] to make to stick up, *sakar* tr. *saka; te vasakar o pisui.*
vasakar sis mala, a charm for the first litter of a sow, *we savur o tawagas wotaga ape sis mala we tiana matagaraqa.*
Vasale 1. [*va* 3.] to make to melt, to melt, act., *sale* 3.
2. to make to float, to launch; *sale* 3.
Vasaleag, [*va* 3.] to drive, cause to drift; *saleag* tr. *sale* 2.
Vasaleg, [*va* 3.] 1. to irrigate, to

make water *sale, y* tr. suff. ; 2. n. an irrigated place.

Vasaliag, to rush, as a *tamate* after a man who shouts, *ulo; saliag*.

Vasaloloi, to pass sideways through a fence.

Vasaloloia, the tallest of a clump of trees ; *va* 3. *saloi*.

Vasamai, same meaning as *valenai*.

Vasaqo, [*va* 3.] to burn, inflame, *saqo*.

Vasaqoi, a small thing in many wrappings, a large *qaranis* and little food, a few things put loosely into a bag or box so as to make it look full ; said in joke from *vasaqo* above.

Vasar, [*va* 3.] to change money on to a new *gararu* string, make it *saru* 1. ; *vasaru*.

Vasaram, to do again what was failed in before, try again ; *na gate valgoro lai, ka vasaram,* I am not strong enough, you try.

Vasarawag, [*va* 2.] to go without fear, *sarawag*.

Vasarig, [*va* 3.] 1. to put together in due place, *sarig* 1., to fit, contrive, plan ; *nom vasarig*, to think out a plan, design. 2. adv. orderly, corresponding.

Vasarorov, with prep. *goro*, to plant one thing in place of another.

Vasarsar, making equal, *va* 3. *sar* 1.; adv. *vara vasarsar*, to agree in what is said.

Vasartag, [*va* 3.] even, level; *sar* 1. with tr. suff. *tag*.

Vasaru, [*va* 3.] 1. to put on round something, *saru* 1., or to put off; as a *lala* bracelet, *vasaru sage* to put it on, *vasaru lue* draw it off.

2. *vasaru gona,* to put on a round lid that passes closely over ; *tama ira ta i siwo we saru gona goro o laim mun o pue*.

3. *vasaru som*, to deal out money ; see *vasar*.

Vasasa, a wonder.

Vasasai, to shift a thing in place, lifting it a little from the ground, as a *pugoro*.

Vasasaravag, [*va* 2.] to go brushing the bush, *i. e.* to be idle ; *o tanun gate mawmawui, ni we mule mamasa gap.*

Vasaug, [*va* 3.] to rouse, drive out with a charm what may make a sow with young savage ; *we qasis o notangae, we savur goro, o mala wa kita.*

Vasawu, [*va* 3.] to burn strong with a rush of air, *sawu*. *vasawu av,* roaring fire.

vasawuw-ug, tr. to let out a blast of steam ; *we lana vasawuw, we lana o wogae, we like si a ilo*, to lift up a leafmat, letting out steam, to see whether the food in the oven is done.

Vaseisei, [*va* 3. *sei* 2.] irregular ; said of native pan-pipes, *vigo*, when the intervals are not correct.

Vasgag, same as *vasugag*, to rebound ; *o vat me qalo ape tangae, me vasgag kel, qara qalo ineia.*

Vasgot, [*va* 3. *sogot*] v. to receive hospitably, to be kind, peaceable ; *we lavia sin toga nev amaia, we vasogotia;* adv. quietly, peaceably, without quarrels ; *we toga vasgot; we lav vasgot.*

Vasigig, to crowd in.

Vasigsig, [*va* 3.] hot, heat ; *sigsig*.

Vasigtag, to despise, treat contemptuously.

vasiksik, [*va* 3.] to be hissing hot, making the noise *sik*.

Vasiliag, [*va* 3.] to darken, *sil* with tr. suff. *ag*; met. *me vasiliag nau*, I forgot, *nalolok me qon*.

Vasimqatu, a custom in the Qat, to give money and then take it back; *ni me vasimqat nau mun o som*.

Vasinar, [*va* 3.] to enlighten, make light, throw light upon; *sinar*.

Vasipa, 1. [*va* 2.] to turn aside, neut. *sipa* 1.
2. [*va* 3.] to turn aside, divert, act.; *sipa* 1.

Vasir, to reproach, rate, curse.

Vasis, M. to give birth, *va* 3. *sis* 8.
vasisgag, tr. determ. cause to bring forth, beget.

Vasisgona, difficult birth, a child still-born; a woman dead in child-birth.

Vasisig, [*va* 3.] v. to sit touching, close together; *sisig*; n. the small *wogire ape pilei*, the topmost in the compound fruit of the pandanus, which is crowded.

Vasiwo, [*va* 3.] to make to go down; *gav vasiwo*, to loosen the earth with the fingers, *gav*, about a young yam so as to let it grow down; *toto vasiwo*, to make a new tuber downwards, as a *tomago* part left in a hole; *vasiwo gil nam*, to paddle deep with upright paddle, as if digging.

Vasliag, same as *vasiliag*; *rigrig ko te loloqon gaplot, me vasliagiko*.

Vasnug, leaving the *nug* pins in the thatch so that they can easily be picked out, *vas*; bad thatching, *tuwur vasnug*.

Vasnot, 1. [*va* 3., *sino, t* tr. suff.] to set, push, the ends of firebrands together to make them burn.

Vasnot, 2. said by some for *vasgot*, as some say *sonon* for *sogon*.

Vasoal, to give freely; n., a liberal man.

Vasogo, [*va* 3. *sogo*] to put together, to count; in recent use, to read.

Vasogot, tr. to bring together.

Vasosogot, [*va* 2.] to meet, come against, *sosogot*.

Vasososo, [*va* 3.] to crowd, stuff close, *soso*; said of fruit growing close together.

Vasosov, [*va* 3.] to push, poke, as in stuffing things into a pack, *soso* 2.; met. to push on, stir up, encourage.

Vasperag, [*va* 3. *siperag*] to pick out; *vano vasperag*, to go along picking things out of the way with the toes.

Vaspit, to add to a complaint; if one has eaten what is bad for his cough, *me vaspitia*.

Vasuar, [*va* 2.] to go and meet, find.

Vasug, [*va* 3. *sug* 1.] to wash, bathe; act., to water plants.

Vasugag, [*va* 3. *suga, g* tr. suff.] to make to go backwards; to change course, as a canoe; to restrain; to rebound; *o lito ti vasugag kalo*, when chopped; *isei we mule ape non o sava, o tuara we vasugagia, nipea, ni kel ma*; *vasgay*.

Vasuqe, to thrust the upper mandible of a bird through the lower, so that it cannot bite.

Vasur, V. same as *vasir*.

Vasurat, [*va* 3. *sura* 1. *t* tr.] to push forward, send forth.

Vasus, V. same as *rasis*, to give birth, said of both sexes; *vasus qulo*, to become a mother very young.

Vasusmag, [*ra* 3. *sus* 3. *mag* tr. suff.] to jam down, cram, as a post into a hole; *me gana vasusmagia*, he crammed himself with eating; *o tangae me malate vasusmag goro*, a tree broken and crushing down others.

Vasusnag, probably *ra* 3. *sus* 3. with tr. suff. *nag; pute vasusnag*, to sit up after illness and pain returns.

Vasusun, [*ra* 3. *sus* 3. *n* tr. suff.] to squeeze together, drive down as a stick into the ground; met. to stir up to fight.

Vasusus, to work to the end, *we mawmawui gai paso*.

Vasvas, 1. redupl. *vas;* small fish pick off the bait from a hook, *we vasvas o pea nan o gau;* met. *o vasvaspea*, a man who picks a little food.
2. from the same, to depreciate, minimize; *vasvas goro*, to deny that one has a thing when one has it; *manvas*.

Vasvasager-qat-gamal, to heap up, as children in play jump on the top of one another, or yams grow one on the top of another; *vasager*.

Vat, 1. numeral four, *vati;* Mao. *wha;* Sam. *fa;* Pol. *ha, a;* Mal. *ampat;* Jav. *papat;* Bouro, *pa;* Malag. *efatra;* Tagal. *apat;* Formosa, *hipat;* D.Y. *wat*.

Vat, 2. same as *vatu*, a stone.

Vat, 3. constr. *vatiu; vat tangae, vat tanun*.

Vatae, [*ra* 3.] to call by dirty names, as mothers scold children; *tae*.

Vatagoloi, [*va* 3.] to spin, roll, revolve, as a fat child beginning to walk; *vatagoloi o nine*, to spin the shell in a game.

Vatakau, [*va* 3.] to hang up, act., by some attachment; *takau*.

Vatamaea, [*va* 2.] to have space, *maea*, go freely.

Vatanau, to learn, to teach, by practice.

Vatap, [*va* 3.] to make a *tap*, a time in which certain things may not be done; *vataptap*.

Vatapar, to ask, enquire.

Vatapare, [*va* 3.] in succession; *tapare*.

Vatapu, [*va* 3.] to make *tapu*, set apart, reserve, prohibit, under sanction of *vui* and *mana*.

Vataqav, [*va* 3. *taqa*, *v* tr. suff.] to turn over, down, to shut; *vataqav namatamiu*, shut your eyes; *vataqav goro*, cover; *matur, risa, vataqar*, to sleep, lie, on the face; *ligo vataqav o qoe*, to tie a pig with a line so that its head is bent down; *we vara vataqav o aka*, to turn over a canoe with the feet.

Vataqov, said by some V. and M. for *vataqav*.

Vataran, [*va* 3.] to put in order, in rows, *taran*.

Vataroroi, to take a bad taste out of the mouth; *me gana paso o sara we sea, qara gana goro we neremot*.

Vatatu, [*ra* 2.] to go and meet, *tatu*, come against.

Vatauweg, adv., to steal when people are about, but unseen, *we pal vatauweg, we pal alo sul, isei gate gilala apena*.

Vatavata, to make agreement between two parties, covenant; *vatavata varvarnanau*, the arrangement made before death for succession to the property of the dying person.

Vatawala, [*va* 3.] to open, act., throw wide open; *tawalag; waka vatalaway*, to open wide.

Vatawaleale, to be a long time about a thing, because not attending to it alone; *nipea vatawaleale*, don't stay long and late.

Vatawasag, [*va* 3.] clear, open; *tawasa* with *g* tr. suff.; of voice, space; *sai* V. for *sag*.

Vatawerag, [*va* 3.] 1. to spread open the palm, *tawerai; g* tr. suff.; *vatawerai* V.; 2. adv. with open hand.

Vatawilgag, [*va* 3.] to make revolve, twirl, set rolling; *ko we vatawilgag o vat, ti tatawilwil*, when a stone is thrown with a twist it revolves as it flies; *gag* tr. suff.

Vatetei, V. *vateteg, va* 3. *tete* 3. *g* tr. suff.; to make a dash; *sike vatetei*, to make hasty search.

Vatgalgalolo, a grindstone; new word, the stone that is turned round and round; not *vului*.

Vatgao, [*vat* 2.] stone in its bed, rock, as opposed to boulders; continuous, *gao* 1.; in recent use *ima vatgao*, a house built of hewn stone.

Vatgaviga, a way of fastening the *lakae* shell adze; *pasau vatgaviga*, the shell mounted on a separate piece of wood, and that hafted.

Vat-ge-lot, [*vat* 3.] a pestle for *lot*.

Vat-ge-uro, [*vat* 3.] a small drum, of a length, *vatiu*, of bamboo; held by one and tapped by another, used for *sawai*.

Vatgen, [*va* 3.] to balance on end; *tiga*.

Vatieg, [*va* 3. *tieg*] 1. to bring one thing against another, as fire-sticks to kindle; to bring the bow of a canoe to shore; *vatieg qat gape*, to put a net into a shallow place *o navo ti liliv wa ti tamarere kel aia*; to lean, repose upon, *ni we vatieg naqauna*, he kneels; *na me vatieg siwo naqatuk ilo tano*.
2. to consider, think out.
3. to bargain, chaffer.

Vatieqau, to kneel; *vatieg qau*. to lean the knee upon the ground, *we vatieg o qaui*.

Vatike, see *vatiu* 1. this place.

Vatinai, [*va* 3.] to disembowel; *tinai*.

Vatine, see *vatiu* 1. that place.

Vatipatipa, said of men high in the *suqe*, and very large pigs; *we vug vatipatipa vires*.

Vatira, M. [*va* 3. *tira*] to make to stand, set up, establish; *vatira wono*, establish completely.

Vatiriv, same as *vatriv*.

Vatitnai, (k) [*va* 3.] the middle, centre; redupl. *tinai, vatitinai; alo vatitnai*, midway, among.

Vatiu, 1. M. a place, spot; *alo vatike* here, in this place; *alo vatine* in that place, with directive particles, *ke* and *ne*.

Vatiu, 2. M. the space between knots in bamboo, sugar-cane, &c., and between the branches of a tree; including the knots; *vat tangae*, a log, *vat tanun*, a short thick-set man; constr. *vat* 3.; *vatvat*. Malag. *vatana*; Mal. *badan*; Jav. *watang*; Jagal. *batang*, body.

Vatiutiu, [*va* 2.] to come or go from time to time, with intervals; *tiutiu*.

Vatlag, same as *vatulag; vava*

vatlag, to bid farewell ; *nau gate ilo vatlag iniko*, I did not see you to say good-bye.

Vatleag, [*va* 3. *taleag*] to pass on from one to another, rejecting in turn. Vatleag in a story was rejected as a son by two women.

Vatligo, a stone, *vat* 2., to which a canoe is attached, *ligo;* an anchor.

Vatligoligopisu, a rock on the *vat-aleale* at Mota.

Vatliwogasuwe, a stone, *vat* 2., of *maeto*, volcanic, with holes in it, as if made by rats' teeth.

Vatloa, a round stone used to make sunshine, *loa*.

Vatmaeto, the black volcanic stone in boulders ; *maeto*.

Vatman, 1. [*vat* 3.] a toggle in a bird-snare.
2. met. said of a canoe straight on with a point of land.

Vatnoro, [*vat* 3.] the smallest bamboo drum, used in the Qat, carried and tapped by a dancer; *noro*.

Vatnorowawao, [*vat* 3.] a short *pue* water-carrier, made of a length, *vatiu*, of bamboo, with opening at the end ; *noro, wawao*.

Vatnorag, to hide, conceal.

Vato, a white grub in dead trees, eaten.

Vatoa, [*va* 2. *toa* 2.] to escape ; *ko me vatoa lai,* you got away.

Vatoav, [*va* 3.] to drive away, send away ; *toa* 2. *v* tr. suff. *ko me vatoavia,* you sent him away.

Vatoga, [*va* 3.] to stop, stay ; act. and neut. ; *toga; na we toga vatoga gese alo tanoi tuwale,* I stay permanently in one place.
vatoga nara, a charm to assist the birth of first litter of pigs, *we la o taqelawa we memea we vus o kule mala nia*.
gava vatoga, to hover.

Vatogar, [*va* 3. *toga, r* tr. suff.] to stay, strengthen.

Vatogo, [*va* 3.] 1. to fit the *qatia* head of an arrow into the reed, *togo*.
2. met. to teach.
vatogoa, v. n. teaching.

Vatoliu, [*va* 3.] third ; *tol*.

Vatopoi, to pour on too much sauce ; *woro mun o lig matig we goqo aneane*.

Vatoqal, [*va* 3.] to crack, with a noise, *toqal; we woso o nai ti toqal*.

Vatora, [*va* 3.] to cut short, making what is cut to stand up like *tora; we vit latelate*.

vatoraga, [*ga* 5.] adj. short, strong ; a short strong man.

vavatoraga, [*va* 3.] to cut short, *we vit qatqatutui*.

Vatoto, pins which fasten the yoke-pieces, *iwatia*, to the outrigger, *sama*, of a canoe are *pis vatoto;* see *aka*.

Vatowo, [*va* 3.] same in meaning with *vatogo* 2., but from *towo*, which again is another form of *togo*.

Vatowoline, [*va* 3.] to reprove, speaking with hard words which will *qalo;* from *towo*, stem of *towos*.

Vatowos, [*va* 3.] to lash, *towos; o wena ti vatvatowos*.

Vatpetin, [*vat* 2.] a stone used to shore up, e. g. a canoe in course of making.

Vatpuna, [*vat* 2.] madrepore, brain coral ; *puna* 2.

Vatqalon, [*vat* 3.] a water-vessel, *pue*, of one or two lengths of bamboo, with a hole in the end ; *we goro late mun o vin-*

s

gar si o sava, we as lue o qaloi, cut from the bamboo with a shell, the diaphragms in the knots knocked through with a rod.

Vatqoa, a small thing in large parcel; *vatoqoa, toqo.*

Vatran, to command, order; probably *vataran.*

Vatrei, shallow; in planting *gate riv roro*; in shooting *we log mulan ape we vene mun o us, o qatia gate roro.*

Vatrewao, short; an unusual word.

Vatrig, adv. *ratiu* 1. *rig* 2. in the place; all at once; *o qoe wota vatrig.*

Vatriv, [*va* 3.] to make a stand, stand; *vatriv goro*, to withstand, oppose.

Vatrororo, loose stones, *vat* 2. on a slope which roll down under one's feet, *roro.*

Vatsirsir, a stone to shave with, *sir* 1., *i. e.* obsidian flake.

Vat-tangae, [*vat* 3.] a log of wood, the trunk between branches.

Vat-tanun, [*vat* 3.] a stumpy man, big, heavy.

Vatu, a stone, rock. Mao. *whatu*; Sam. *fatu*; Mal. Tagal. *batu*; Malag. *vato*; N.G. *vatu, vau*; Mel. very common.

vatuga, [*ga* 5.] adj. stony.

Vatuatualate, very quickly; *we gaplot aneane.*

Vatuevag, [*va* 2.] to go with a stoop; *tuevag.*

Vatuga, [*vatu*] stony; *lot vatuga*, mash with no *nai* almonds.

Vatui, 1. V. same as *vatiu* 1. a place, spot.

Vatui, 2. V. same as *vatiu* 2. the space between knots, or whorls of branches.

Vatuke, V. *vatui* 1. this place, here; same as *vatike.*

Vatulag, [*va* 3.] to send away, with farewell words, giving last directions; *tulag; vatlag.*

Vatultul, [*va* 3.] to motion with the hand; *tul* 2.; *vatultul meimei*, to obtain quiet by motion of the hand.

Vatune, V. *vatui* 1. that place, there; same as *vatine.*

Vatunus, [*va* 3.] to comfort a sick person with warm food; *tun* 2., with tr. suff. *s.*

Vatur, V. [*va* 3.] to make to stand, set up, establish; *tur* 1.

Vatura, the splintered shaft of an arrow, the shaft broken from the head; *o vatura ti rowo, o surtamate qale toga alo turiai.*

Vatut, [*va* 3. *tut*] on end, set, held, lengthways up; *we tira vatut, we taur vatut.*

Vatutgag, same as *vatutuag; tutgag.*

Vatutuag, [*va* 3.] to order about so as to weary a person; *tutuag.*

Vatuwale, [*va* 3.] once; *vatuwale ran*, once for all.

Vatvat, [*vat* 3.] with many *vatiu*, with short intervals of trunk between the branches; *malawowatvat.*

Vatvataligo, to engage, betroth; with *goro; vatavata, ligog.*

Vatvuv, a stone with bare round top, *vuv* 2.; near the shore, *we pute alo nawo.*

Vatwesawesar, [*vat* 2.] a stone for breaking *nai; wesar.*

Vatwosoputon, a stone used to drive the *puton* of a house into the ground.

Vatwosowoso, a stone for hammering, *woso*, for breaking *nai.*

Vatwot, [*vat* 3.] a water-carrier made of a single length, *vatiu*, of bamboo, with a hole at the side.

Vatwotaga, a big *wotaga;* a term of reproach.

Vau, 1. n. a pandanus.

Vau, 2. v. to mat, plait, weave as mats and baskets are made; the spider that makes a cross in the midst of its web *ti tiatia o talan pa ti vau ilone; te vau o non, o wowor, o epa, o tapera; rau unun*, to finish the weaving of *tapera*, &c., *un* 4.

Vauwuw, [*va* 3.] to make to blow, *uw;* same meaning with *vasawu*, cause a blast, of wind or fire.

Vava, 1. redupl. *va* 1. M. to come or go; *isei we vakel isei we sea me rara nu ti siria.*

rava ta vureg, to go and frighten something that another man is after.

rava talaway, or *talawai*, to go and leave the door open.

Vava, 2. to speak, say. Probably Malag. *rava;* Bat. Bis. *baba;* Mao. *waha*, mouth; see *wawan.*

rava nawono, to speak without due consideration or respect.

rava pulasag lea, to speak with deceit, as when one asks for a thing as if he had it not, when he has it.

rava tapisqoe, to speak crooked, like a pig's foot, *pis qoe*, met. not straightforward.

rava taveris, to say what makes a man change his purpose; *taveris;* or shows a change.

rava viro, to avoid the use of a word which it is not right to say, and use another; as in *qaliga, un;* e. g. in saying *o parou me ar* for *o nawo we malate.*

vavae, word, speech.

vavag, tr. to speak at, against a person.

vavat, tr. to speak against.

Vavag, 1. M. to go with; *va* 1.; separable *vag;* convey.

Vavag, 2. to speak against, talk at; *rava* 2. tr.

Vavagaile, to worry, annoy.

Vavaka, redupl. *raka*, to be strong.

vavakae, n. strength, self-assertion, valour.

la o vavakae goro, to play the strong man with people, bully, threaten.

Vavalil, redupl. *valil*, 1. to fade; 2. adv. erroneously.

Vavalul, redupl. *va* 3. *lul* 1. to make increase.

Vavanov, to waken, rouse from sleep; Fiji, *vagona.*

Vavapa, a kind of crawfish.

Vavarav, to use an expression to a person which has a serious effect, *o vavae we mava*, either to protect or obtain protection; a word of affection or humiliation, or cry for mercy; *te vavarav mun o vavae iloke 'gak taema';* a *tanun liwoa*, chief, will stop a quarrel with such a word; when a chief *me vararav sei*, others will not hurt him.

Vavasus, to speak so as to frighten, make *sus* 3.

Vavat, tr. *vava* 2. to speak at, against; *ravat qalo.*

Vavatak, to speak harshly to; same as *vavavag.*

Vavatavureg, see *vava* 1.

Vavatawalai, see *rava* 1.

Vavatiu, fourth, fourth time.

Vavatoraga, 1. [*va* 3.] to cut short, *vit qatului; vatoraga.*

Vavatoraga, 2. redupl. *vatoraga*, short, stumpy, of man or tree.

Vavaul, to explain, unfold a tale; *vava* 2. *ul* 2.

Vavava, redupl. of *vava* 2. and of *va* 1.

Vavavag, redupl. *vavag*, to speak harshly to.

Vavine, V. woman, female; Mao. *wahine;* Sam. *fafine;* Mal. *bini;* Malag. *vavy;* Tagal. *binibini;* Yap, *papine;* common in Malay Archipelago, Melanesia; N.G. *vavine, haine.*

Vavinir, [*va* 3.] to pull out, remove, making open; *vinir; vavinir kalokalo* or *rakaraka,* to pull up, *e. g.* bananas too closely planted, so as to make room.

Vavnun, redupl. *vanun,* a log of some size, such as they would *vanun,* put together to keep in fire.

Vavrai, [*va* 3.] staring eyes; *namatana we vura kalo.*

Vavtig, adv. in, into, a heap, crowd, in heaps, sets; *vile vavtiy,* bring together in heaps, sets.

Vavtigiu (k) constr. *vavtig;* assemblage, crowd, heap, flock, set.

Vavus, [*va* 2.] to fight; *vus.*

Vaweneg, [*va* 3.] to scrape clean and white; *wene* in *wenewene,* with tr. suff. *g.*

Vawerei, to turn up the eyeballs; *me vawerei namatana.*

Vawia, [*va* 3.] to make things well, *wia,* for a person, to bless.

Vawilis, 1. [*va* 3.] to roll; *wil* 1. with tr. suff. *s; vawvawilis mata,* to roll the eyes.
2. to cook, *sau, qeta* in *toape.*

Vawinur, to bring small things only; *winur.*

Vawlig, adv. collectively, in an assemblage.

Vawo, adv. upon; *vawo aru! vawo mele! vawo qoga! vawo wonawona,* forms of *varowog: vawo aka,* on board ship.

vawoi, to heap on the top, add to a heap; *vawog.*

Vawonot, [*va* 3.] 1. to complete, fill up void, close in solid; 2. *un* for *sanavul,* completing the ten of the fingers; *wonot.*

Vaworai, to stuff full; *vaworag.*

Vawosag-sai, V. [*va* 3.] to throw soft things, such as squash, *tawosa.*

Vawota, [*va* 3.] to bring to birth, beget; *wota* 1.

Vawotag, [*va* 3.] to take possession of a seedling or sucker, *wotai,* of a fruit tree.

Vawuwuw, to crowd or crush together.

Vea, 1. n. the place where; with article *o vea; o vea ilone? what place is that? ko me nina ape vea?* to what place have you reached? with prep. *a vea, i vea* adv. *avea, ivea;* with adv. *ma* comp. adv. *mavea.* Mao. *hea;* N.B. *ve, wai;* Sol. Is. *hei, vei.*

Vea, 2. M. a grater for *nai,* &c.; *o lape qatia.*

Vean, V. 1. to spread on the ground; *vean goro,* to lay a rough mat, &c., as a guard against dirt, &c.
2. V. to put the leaves of tree fern, *no-qatia,* or *toape,* into wraps, *mona,* of fish to cook together.

Vear, M. same as *vean* 1. but both words are V. and M.; *vear goro,* to line.

wora vear, to bear fruit for the first time.

Vearag, M. same meaning as *vean* 2.

Veasag, to press flat with cocoa-

nut shell in making *lot patau; ti qusa mun o vatgelot, ti vesag mun o vin matig.*
Vega, M. to climb, with the use of the arms and legs.
  vegarag, tr. determ. to climb often.
  vegatag, tr. determ. climb for one, go up tree to get food for one; *isei te vegatag inau?* who will now climb for my cocoanuts ?
Vele, a tree, barringtonia edulis.
Vene, 1. to shoot with a pointed arrow; not *tiqa.*
  venegag, tr. determ. shoot with effect on something.
Vene, 2. to give a short bit of money as a preliminary in *ganatapug* in *suqe*, or in *tiro tamate*, in those societies; *inau we ge o suqe mun Ar; ineira we vene munau; nau te sar muneira; i Ar qara garatapug; te vene mun o som ape tamate.*
Venegag, 1. tr. determ. *rene* 1. to shoot with pointed arrow with effect on some one or something; *me venegag tagea o qatia*, have shot away and lost an arrow.
Venegag, 2. name of one kind of fence, *geara venegag;* see *geara.*
Venemakea, the dance, *lakalaka*, of the man who makes a *kolekole*, before he shoots the pig; *we nun o sawai mun i gene ni venemakea.*
Venevene, n. *vene* 1.; a shooter; *un* for *us*, a bow.
Veravera, a millepore, used to polish in making *igot, vatgelot*, &c.
Vereg, to lift up, stretch out, the hand; in offering something; as when looking for something a man holds up his hand as a sign that he has found it.
Veresag, to mount by steps as on a steep ascent, to climb with the legs only; *te veresag mun o ranoi.*
  tano ververesag, a stepping-place to mount up.
Veria, a fish, chilodactylus.
Verig, a man gives this word for his name, instead of it, not being willing to name himself.
Veris, to ask, inquire for; same as *varus.*
Vero, to begin to grow, as the tuber of a yam, becoming unfit for food.
Veru, to screw up the face, as for crying; to pout.
Vet, 1. to say, speak, give the word; *na me vet nalinak*, I have said my say, in the way of command, opinion, determination.
  tano vetvet, met. a man of consequence, with whom it rests to give the word.
Vet, 2. to start, lead off; *we vet o as*, begin a song.
Veta, adv. already, past and over, used with v. when past tense is emphatically given; by a use not common, *nina we sua veta naké*, after long waiting, now after all we are off.
Vetal, a banana; *vetal tiratira* or *turtur*, the wild or half-wild banana, with standing fruit-stalk; the bunch of fruit is *o gaei;* to get the fruit, *we ramo si we rare o gaei.*
  vetal mena, proverbial expression for a long time about a thing, as a long voyage from Mota to Gaua, time enough for bananas to get ripe.
Veve, 1. division of the people for

marriage purposes, of which there are two.
2. less exactly, a family; *veve tut*, a family that has always caused quarrels.
3. (k) mother, aunt, female *sogoi* of the *veve* 1. of the parents' generation; in plural form *raveve*, my mother *raverek*; *o reveve*, the mothers of the village, as a body.

revegae, one's father's sister, therefore not *sogoi*, not really *veve*.

veve vusvus rawe, one who is called mother only after a *rawe* has been killed for her; not *sogoi*, treated with respect; see *keleva*.
4. v. to call mother; *isei me veve inau?* who called *veve!* to me?

Veveg, 1. to distinguish, divide, thence judge, condemn; from the stem *reve* with tr. *g*.
2. adv. exactly coinciding; *na me gopa reveg o paka me rasu ma*, I fell ill exactly at the time the vessel arrived.

Vevegarag, redupl. *vegarag*, tr. *vega*, to climb often or after much fruit.

Vevera, red-hot, as stones for the oven; *o vat we revera me tul avune lito ape qaranis*. Mao. *wera*; Sam. *revela*.

revera mule, beginning to cool, no longer red with heat.

Veverag, to carry with a stick over the shoulder; *te tatag o lito qara reverag*; met. *we reverag o rarae*, to carry word.

Veverau, a district of Mota, set of villages.

Via, 1. the giant caladium. Malag. *via*.

Via, 2. the crocodile; *we rasus alo puaka a Qakea*; met. a voracious eater; *we gana guplot aneane we log si o ria*. Malag. *roay*; Mal. *buaya*.

Viavia, a fish.

Viawo, 1. n. a water-pipe; *o viawo pei o sarusaru ape sugsug*.

Viawo, 2. to train yams when the vine begins to climb; *we viawo, we qeteg taur, we la kalo o tuei avune togo*.

Viga, nine, in *tika* counting.

Vigo, native pan-pipes.

Vil, to bind round, tie strongly. *ima vil*, a strongly-built, tied, house; *vil raririr*, to bind things close together; *vil qat*, to bind the head with ornamental band; *vil wot*, to bind round high up.

In making charms things are bound round with the magic song; hence *we vil o talamatai*; *o loa vil*, long-continued sunshine, as if by reason of a charm; *vil o taro*, to cause calm weather by a charm.

vilit, tr. to bind firm.

Vila, 1. lightning; *vila we memea*, summer lightning. Fl. *vivira* (thunder); Fiji, *lira*; Mao. *uira*; Sam. *uila*; Mal. *kilat*; Malag. *hilatra*; Bugis, *bila*.

Vila, 2. pearl-oyster; *wovila*, the bivalve complete; *vin vila*, a single shell.

Vilavila, a tree; *vilavila memea*, a red species; *vilavila we memea, we tenegay ape gene we rono, tama o masaoi we rono*.

Vile, to bring, give, convey, distribute, contribute.

vile matagesegese, to take one's own things only.

vile mataperper, to twinkle, as a star, blink.

vile pulai, to make return, by the person taking a step in the *suqe*, for what his introducer

has distributed for him to the members.
vile qoriag, to give out confusedly.
vile taptapui, to take one's own things only.
vilevile wotuaru, much the same as *varowog*.
vilerag, to bring together.
Vileqat, to duck the head, avoiding a missile.
Vilerag, tr. *vile* with suff. *rag* of number, many contributing; many birds singing together, all in their own way, *vilevilerag*.
Vileris, to change, be changed, *ris*; *nanagonsei qe gopa we vileris*; *natoqana we vileris*, his feelings changed, from good to bad, to anger.
Viletuwale, to bring together, unite.
Vilevarau, to produce in great numbers, like the fruit of the *rau*; *va* 3.; said of a prolific sow.
Vilevarwotwota, to bring in pairs; *varwota*.
Vilevile-mate-veve, when two of the same *veve* fight no one interferes, and there is no *rapa*; it is an affair of the family, *mate veve*.
Vilevilerag, combine in numbers, as when birds sing together each its own song.
Vilewora, bring, take, apart, separate.
Vilewotuaru, to bear witness, or call to witness, with a kind of oath; conf. *varowog*; the top, *wotui*, of the casuarina, *aru*, being *rono* as a seat of ghosts.
Vilget, to bind and hold; *get*; conf. *varaget*.
Vilit, tr. determ. *vil*; to bind firm, strengthen with binding, serve round.

Viloag, to mumble, in eating or speaking.
Vilog, 1. an umbrella palm; 2. a frond of that palm used as an umbrella.
Vilvilnir, to bind, *vil*, round the leg, in the *salagoro*, a leaf of *garne gae*, heated and scraped white.
Vilvilqat, to bind, *vil*, round the head a festive ornament, *garilvilqat*.
Vilvil-wotakolo, a way of snaring birds, with *takolo* shell.
Vilvilwot, to bind round high up; *isei ta rot o 'gae, we rot eleele, was we vil wot*.
Vin, 1. to throb; redupl. *vinvin*.
vinrag, tr. determ. to gush out in throbs.
Vin, 2. constr. of *viniu*, skin, bark, husk; particularly of cocoanut.
Vinai, 1. (k) the thigh, shank.
Vinai, 2. v. to mix leaves with flesh in cooking; *we vinai o qoe mun o toape, o imal, o noqatia*.
Vinar, same as *vinir*; rather V. than M.
Vinaroaro, [*vin* 2.] a shell.
Vinewer, thin shanks, a man with thighs, *vinai*, like the shanks of a *weru*.
Vingar, [*vin* 2.] a cockle-shell, with which cocoanuts are scraped out, *goras*.
Viniaro, [*vin* 2.] the shell of a mactria bivalve.
Viniga, [*ga* 5.] with the husk on; *we savrag o vin matig nan o wuei, pa si, o viniu qale toga apena we log was we viniga*.
Vinikere, [*vin* 2.] the tail of a plucked fowl.
Vinir, to come out of a close place into the open, as out of a bush into a path, as tall trees rising

through and above the wood; *vinir mot*, to come out breaking through vines; *ravinir*.

Vinit, 1. to add more *garine gae* to a mat, *epa*, in course of weaving, and so make a seam; *kamam me artag wa kamiu me vinit*; 2. the middle seam of an *epa*.

Vinitiu, (k) same as *viniu*; skin, bark, husk, rind, shell.

vinit-manaronaro, a yam with skin like the bark of the *manaro*, rotten outside.

vinit matai, the eyelid.

Viniu, (k) skin, bark, husk, rind, shell; constr. *vin* 2. D.Y. *pin*.

viniga, adj. with the husk on.

Vinlasa, 1. a cup, *lasa*, made of a cocoanut shell, *vin* 2.
2. the knee-cap; from its shape.

Vinleilei, an oyster shell.

Vinmalu, the husk of a young cocoanut.

Vinman, a cocoanut husk used to wipe with; *man*.

Vinnornai, stuff in the salt water like the inner skin, *noriu*, of *nai*, almonds; used to whiten *toto* arrows.

Vino, to fasten with pins, fold over and pin; as *no-via*, to hold water, *no-ota*, for thatch; *te vino goro o noota me luqe mun o nug*.

Vinosiu, the inner skin of the kernel of *nai*; *we pes sarrag o vinos nai*.

Vinostagai, a kind of *tomago* with no *vinosiu*.

Vinparpar, [*vin* 2.] chips made in chopping out the inside of a canoe; *par*.

Vinpatau, a kind of madrepore like the rind of bread-fruit.

Vinpeapea, the shell that holds tinder for use in rubbing fire, *soso av*.

Vinqoe, in recent use leather.

Vinrag, tr. determ. *vin* 1. to spurt, gush out in throbs; *o nara me vinvinrag lue ma*.

Vinsorsor, [*vin* 2.] cinnamon bark.

Vintaratara, chips made in hewing wood; *tara*.

Vinvara, [*vin* 2.] the husk of a growing cocoanut, *vara*.

Viṇvin, 1. redupl. *vin* 1. to throb, beat in throbs; *naqatvarana ti vinvin ti*, when he is out of breath; *vinvinrag*, redupl.

Vinvin, 2. a crustacean on the shore; *ti vinvin mun naliwona, we malarowo*, one can hear the noise of it, and it hits hard.

Vinvin, 3. a tree.

Vinwovila, a pearl shell, single valve.

Vin, 1. to tip up; *vin kalo*, support by putting something under;
2. to lay along as support or protection, as logs before the door, *we vin goro o mateima*; or on a slope to keep up the earth of gardens; to dam back water.
3. n. a dam; *o pei te tike lue o vin*.

Vinai, (k) the armpit; whence *avnag; vivinai*.

Vinasa, [*vinai*] an abscess under the arm, *virnasa*; *ti riga, ti logo, ti niniaga, ti malue*.

Vinvin, [*vin* 1.] to be stuck up, go about in pride.

Viog, 1. to throw a mat, *epa*, round the body; *viog goro*, to protect from sun, wind, cold, as an infant.
2. met. to plant food for a person expected, *we viog nagana*.

Vioviog, n. a mat used to *viog* with.

Vir, to twist, wring, squeeze with a twist; *we vir o tal*, plait a cord ; *we gat o gea qara vir*, chew the pepper root and wring out the liquor; *we vir o nau*, for poisoning fish; *we pusa o ganau te run o iga nia qara rir; rir goro*, to wring out over; met. *matavir*, a stingy man.

virgag, tr. determ. throw with a twist.

virsag, tr. determ. to wring out.

vivir, redupl. to throw with a twist given to the stone.
Mao. *whiri*; Sam. *fili*.

Viras, to boast, make boastful professions ; *te vet ape tanun we vara si ni te na mate sei, pa gate nun, we vara gap*.

Vires, adv. only, merely.
lav vires isei, to be partial.

Virgag, tr. determ. *vir*, to throw away with a twist, whirl away ; *we virgag o rat*.

Virig, to pull oneself together to endure; *rono virig*, to endure pain with courage.

Viris, stem of *viviris*, hardly.

Virisa, same as *virsa*, stem *vir*.

Viro, 1. plexus at the base of the fronds of sago and other palms, *ape qeteg lape ota*.

Viro, 2. to turn, go round, change, turn out of the way ; Motu N.G. *giro; alo tan we viro*, at the turn of the season ; *we vara viro*, to change words so as to disguise meaning, same as *vava pata; o lan we viro*, the wind goes round ; *o qaui we viro*, twisted knee.
viro gologae, to go round a bad place in a road, by the tips, *goloi*, of the creepers, *gae*.
viro goro, a term in money lending, to divert payment ; *nau we tawe i Sava mun o som tal sanavul; ni we lano goro nau mun nivat; nau we viro goro muniko mun laveatol; ni we wono nau mun sanavul rua*.

virog, tr. to put aside.

viroag, tr. turn away round ; *we viroag o taure*, turn round the flank of a hill.

virot, tr. turn away.

Viroag, tr. *viro* 2.; to turn away round or behind ; *naakara we viroag nina*, their vessel sails round us.

Virog, tr. *viro* 2.; 1. to set apart, as yams for seed ; 2. to put out of sight ; *gate virog*, there is nothing underhand.

Virogoro, see *viro* 2.

Virokor, to become dry inside, as *make* and *wotaga* very ripe, *o virotiu me kor*.

Virot, 1. tr. *viro* 2. to turn away from some one ; *virot goro*, turn aside, turn back upon.

Virot, 2. constr. of *virotiu; virot paka*, the covering of young banyan leaves.

Virotiu, (k) the involucre of leaves or flowers ; *virot togo, virot ton, virot paka, virot gaas*.

Virovirot, the caps of *toto* arrows, put on to protect the points.

Virsa, same as *virsag*.

Virsag, tr. determ. *vir*, to wring out, particularly *lig matig*, cocoanut sauce ; used M. as V. *woro*.

Virsala, to wring out, *vir*, cocoanut juice into *vinlasa* or *wumeto*, and boil it with hot stones, *sala* 4.

Virsig, [*vir*] to strain the *samai* of *pewu, rava*, in bags of *gavnegae;* not sago.

Virvir, n. redupl. *vir;* the wringing out of the *gea*.

Visa, how many? so many; *vaga-visa*, how many times; with v. p. *ni, me, te, ta.* Like a numeral, *visa* is preceded by words describing more or less the things or circumstances, viz. *pul* 9., *raka* 3., *rowo* 4., *sage* 4., *sogo* 3., *sorako, tal* 5., *taqa* 3., *tira* 2., *tur* 5. Mao. *hia*; Sam. *fia*; Tong. *fiha*; Motu N.G. *hida*.

Visaga,

Visarag, to break, smash, throw down hard and break.

Viso, 1. v. to break off small pieces of food; *viso raka*, break off and take up.

Viso, 2. n. a reed, arundo, with edible flower heads. Sam. *fiso*; Motu N.G. *hido*.

Visogoi, (k) flesh. Fiji, *viciko*; Motu N.G. *hidio*.

Vit, 1. chop short, in lengths; *vit mot*, cut off in a length, *vit latelate*, chop into lengths; also *vitu*.

Vit, 2. same as *vitu*, a star. *vit ni wowor*, children in the evening choose a clear space in the sky and watch for stars to appear in it, crying *titit pulak vit ni wowor!* let my stars come out in plenty.

Vitag, adv. away from, when something is left; *map vitag*, put away from other things, mislay; *i* often left out, *gevtag, toavtag; rave vitag o aka*, drag up and leave.

Viteg, same word with *vitag*, away.

Vitig, impers. v. to pain; *we vitig nau*; redupl. *vivitig, virtig*.

Vitu, 1. same as *vit* 1.

Vitu, 2. a star; *vitu asuasu*, a comet. Mao. *whetu*; Sam. *fetu*; Mal. *bintang*; Malag. *kintana*;

Tagal, *bitoing*; Bug. *witueng*; Day. *betuch*; Sol. Ids., *veitugu, he'u*; N.H. *ritui, risiu*; Bks. Ids., *vitig, viti, veji, vit, vi'*; Pon. *uju*; Motu N.G. *hisiu*.

Viu, to whirr, whizz; of the sound of pigeons' wings; of a bullroarer, *o nanamatea ti viu*; of a thrown stone, *we vivir mun o vat we marinviu, o vat ilone ti viuviu*.

Viv, 1. M. to buzz, hum, whizz, as a thrown stone *ti viv ma alo qoroma*; come with the whizz of wings, *ni we ronotag o tamate we viv ma tama o manu*; same as *vuv* V.

Viv, 2. to stick to a person; *ni we viv amaia*; conf. *pip*.

Viv, 3. to bind round; *we viv o kor.*
vivis, tr. to wind round, bind.

Vivinai, (k) redupl. *vinai*, the breast; *na me tantan ape vivinama.*

Vivir, tr. *vir*, to throw, giving a twist, twirling motion, as to a stone; *we vivir o vat*, throw a stone; *we vivir o tanun mun o vat*, throw at a man with a stone.

vivirgag, tr. determ. to throw with violence, *vivirgag o vat; virgag*; met. to blow a shell trumpet loudly.

Viviris, adv. barely, grudgingly, against the grain; *we es viviris*, to be barely in health.

Vivis, tr. *viv* 3. to tie, bind, round and round.
vivis mot, adv. quickly; probably from the quick movement of *vivis*.

Vivisarag, to throw things about in a rage; redupl. *visarag.*

Viviv, mist lying horizontally, a line of mist lying close; *viv* 2.

Vivnag, to utter, work upon with, a spell, charm, curse ; see *taturo;* when on opening the oven a mallow leaf was thrown with a *taturo* to a ghost, desiring evil to those who might have done mischief to the dead person, it was *gan rivnag;* if anything happened, *ni me mas wun, nan neia wa, Eke! nok o gan rivinag me nana ineia, ni me mate.*

Vivnasa, redupl. *rinasa*, an abscess in the armpit.

Vivrog, redupl. *virog;* to set apart, as yams for seed.

Vivsailima, to walk with hands behind the back ; *vivsag*, from *viv* 3., *lima*.

Vivsara, to move away *kor*, dried bread-fruit, from the *um*, for binding, *viv* 3., *sara* 2.

Vivtig, redupl. *vitig;* v. to pain, *we rivtig nan;* to feel pain, *te vara lai si nau we rivtig;* n. pain, *we ronotag o rivtig*, to feel pain ; *o vivtig we rakut*, pain causes suffering.

Vono, 1. to whisper, consult in whispers, thence to consult, agree about something.

  vonog, tr. to consult with regard to some one, settle what he is to do or to be done to.

Vonvono, redupl. *vono; vonvono matea munsei*, settle that a man shall be killed, in whispers.

Vovono, redupl. *vono;* to whisper.

Vorotai, (k) refuse of food, of bird or rat.

Voson, [*son*] to flatter ; *o tanun we vavava sonson isei.*

Votur, adv. on end, upstanding, *tur* 1.; *rowovotur*, to leap up, as men in excitement, *rowovotrotur*, waves dancing ; *qatsakavotur*, hair on end ; see *rowotur.*

Vovo, to commemorate escape, recovery ; *na me vovo gak,* I have made my feast after my illness ; *o ganawono qara tavasur nan kamam, kamam qara sora o ganagana vovo.*

Vug, to assemble, meet together.

Vuge, a fern.

Vui, 1. a spirit ; used, perhaps recently, of the human spirit, *alo vuik.*

2. any big thing ; *me vui gai!* of a boy much grown ; *vui lama*, exceedingly large : *lama* 2.

Vul, see *vului* 2.

Vula, 1. the moon.
  Mal. *bulan ;* Malag. *volana;* Bks. Ids., *vul, rol, wol;* N.H. *vula, wula, ola;* Sol. Ids., *vula, hula.*

2. a month, season marked by moon ; (k) when a person's time is measured by months, *navulana nirat reta*, he is four months old, or has been here four months ; constr. *vule; vule vutvut, vule wotgoro, vule vusiaru, vule tete mavuru, vule lamasag noronoro*, working seasons, &c., according to months.

3. white ; *make vula* a white-leaved *make;* Fiji, *vulavula;* Fl. *pura ;* Gilolo, *wulan;* Molucca, *bulam ;* Rotti, *fula;* Solor, *burang.*
  Phases of the moon ; *o vula ti wot ma*, becomes visible ; *we qulo*, young ; *ti tavisa*, is in her first quarter ; *ti matua, ti sogon wono*, at the full ; *ti maturvag no-ranorano,* or *maturvag mera*, when rises after children are gone to bed ; *ti tavisa kel*, in the third quarter; *ti e mantagai*, wanes ; *ti e tagea*, disappears ; *vula sale-*

maran, when there is moonshine before the morning. *O vula ti rowo raka*, rises ; *ti e kalo*, mounts upwards ; *ti waga kalo*, rises clear of trees, &c.; *ti sus*, sinks behind trees, hills ; *ti tul*, sets in the sea.
vulasa, adj. term. *sa* 3. fair.
Vulagei, (k) the heel.
Vulaqulo, girl with first menses ; *qulo*.
Vulasa, [*vula* 3.] fair, in complexion.
Vulavulasa, redupl. white, unripe, of a yam.
Vule, imp. v. to tire, weary, trouble one ; *me vule veta inau we toga iake*, I am tired of being here ; *gate vule isei*, no one made a trouble of it ; *me un vulera*, they were tired of drinking, had enough ; *sage vule*, to distress ; *taso vule*.
Vuleai, (k) the tail of a crawfish, *we log o golo ura si o vuleai*.
Vulesinaga, [*vula* 2.] a season when food ought to come in, is abundant.
Vuletokor, [*vula* 2.] season of the scarcity of food, when yams are planted ; *tou* 2., *kor* 1.
Vul-lava, [*vului* 2.] *ilo vul lava*, prov. expression, when a man is big and appears strong.
Vulua, the stem of a tree-fern carved with a face of *tamate*, and set up for a *kolekole*.
Vului, 1. to whet, sharpen on a stone ; *vat-vulvului*, a stone on which shell adzes were sharpened.
Vului, 2. (k) constr. *vul* ; the hair of the body ; perhaps another form of *ului*. Mal. *bulu* ; Malag. *volo*.
Vulvulgasuwe, rat's fur ; met. *tama isei we sirsir ineia, pa ni gate sir mantag*.

Vun, 1. to poison fish, with leaves, fruits, bark, rubbed, *asan*, in the hands ; with *ganau, gatuwa*, if big fish, with *vin wotaga, wornt, wosus*, if small.
Vun, 2. n. something which causes plants to wither, dry up, die ; not seen.
vunuga, (*ga* 5.) affected with *vun*.
Vun, 3. to deceive ; *vuvun* 2. ; *gavun*. Motu N.G. *huni* ; Malag. *vuny*, hide.
Vun, 4. to be last, at the end.
Vuna, to be sore, of the head; a sore head.
Vunai, (k) the upper side or part ; *a vunak*, above me ; with prep. makes compound prep. *arune, ivune*, and adv. *avunana, ivunana*. Malag. *vovona*.
Vunalolo, an ulceration, *maniga*, of a child's head.
Vunana, *vunai* with suff. *na* 3. the upper part, top of something, the region above, heaven.
Vunue, a tree.
Vunuga, [*vun* 2.] said of food, old and dry in the ground.
Vunur, a yam.
Vuvun, [*vun* 3.] to deceive ; *vuvun goro*, same meaning as *gale goro*.
Vunvun, adv. [*vun* 4.] at the close of all, finally.
Vunvunanai, [*vun* 4.] the last of a set or series, final ; *anai*.
Vun, a bunch of fruit, cocoanuts, *nai* almonds, (not bananas or pandanus, *ga-vital, ga-gire*). Mal. *bongkus* ; Bug. *bungkus* ; Malag. *vongo*, bundle.
Vunan, a kind of yam.
Vur, 1. same as *vuru*, cough.
Vur, 2. to be full.
Vura, to spring forth, rise up, as water ; Dyak, *pura*.

vuras, to come forth, as out of house, or into the open ; *vuras lue.*

vuratag, to spring forth forcibly ; *o nawo we vuratag kalo,* from a blow-hole.

Vuravura, v. to bubble, spring up ; n. a spring of water.

Vure, to drive.

Vurenam, a shrub.

Vuretaqas, an oven lined with leaves of *varu; me vear goro o sasawui.*

Vuro, a volcanic vent, hot spring.

Vurovuroro, to eat a great deal, *we gana o sinaga we poa.*

Vuru, 1. cough ; disease causing coughing ; 2. a charm causing the disease.

Vus, 1. to strike, beat ; to kill by blows.
vus nawono, murder, kill wantonly.
vus pal, to kill stealthily, murder.
vus vagoloi, to wound by blows, not kill.

vusrag, to strike hard ; *rag,* intensitive.

2. to tattoo, *vus o pul,* making strokes, *vus,* with an instrument, *mategas,* and rubbing in soot of nai gum, *pul.*
vus kakalatoga, tattoo out of the pattern.

Vus, 3. to finish the thatch of the ridge of a house ; put on *novele,* woven *no-matig, no-eri,* and bind on bamboos longitudinally ; *we vus goro qatiima.*

Vus, 4. to plait flattened bamboo ; *me vus o au ape lago we sogsogon o nam alolona,* done also for the front of a house.

Vusa, a green cocoanut, such as are drunk ; *vusa gorgor,* the meat, *wuei,* formed enough to scrape, *gor ; vusa maremare,* the meat, *wuei,* hard ;

vusa sisis, can be scraped, *sis o wuei,* with the thumb-nail.

Vusage, contracted for *vut sage.*

Vusiag, to turn round; *vusiag kel,* turn back.

Vusiaru, a month or season of wind which beats the casuarina trees ; *we vus o aru,* a hurricane month.

Vusmaru, to blow hard and then become calm, *o lan me vus ti, qara maru.*

Vusmena, a full-grown man, adult.

Vusoko, a rubbish heap ; *soko ; vu* for *vut.*

Vusrag, tr. intens. *vus* 1. to strike forcibly.

Vus-sororo, giving notice, *sororo,* of the death of a chief ; *isei tama liwoa qe mate, we lama o kore, we tia tawwe, we rarao.*

Vustape,

Vustavun, same as *sutavun,* to bring a false accusation, find fault without cause.

Vusvusuqa, money, *som vusvusuqa,* paid when one's *uqa* is supposed to have attacked, *vus,* some other.

Vut, 1. to dig, heaving up the soil as with digging-stick, *tangil vutvut,* making holes for yams.
vut nol, dig up whole.
vutuag, tr. to dig up, remove.
2. v. same as *avut,* to move.
3. v. to stand up, *vutvut kalo.*
vutrag, to project.
vutuag, to plant high.

Vut, 4. barringtonia, *vutu.*

Vutei, (k) the buttocks ; *o nug qa alo vutena; ti vutvut.* Malag. *vody;* Bat. *pudi.*

Vutgaqaleg, to loosen the earth only and plant on the surface ; *vut* 1.

Vutmamasa, a hump, *vut* 3., of earth without anything planted

or buried in it; *we vut mamasa kalo.*
Vutnol, to dig up, or remove, whole; *vut* 1. or 2.
Vutrag, *vut* 3., to stand out; *o sis malamala qara qeteg.*
Vutrai, constr. *vutre;* a small garden, village, wood; *vutre tuqei, vutre vanua, vutre* mot.
Vutu, the barringtonia speciosa; *wovutu, wovut,* the fruit.
Vutuag, 1. [*vut* 1.] to dig up, remove.
Vutuag, 2. [*vut* 3.] to plant yams in a shallow hole, so that they stand high out, as is done with some kinds of short yams.
Vutug, to put a string to a bow, *we vutug o us mun o ga-paka.*
Vutuqaleg, same as *vutgaqaleg.*
Vut-uqauqa, dig, prising up the earth; *vut* 1., *uqa* 1. *we uqa o tano mun o tangil.*
Vutvut, redupl. *vut* 3., 1. to stand up high; 2. n. a hillock, heap; 3. adj. hilly.
vutvut sal, to stand higher than others.
Vutvut-matai, the upper eyelid over the eyeball.
Vutvuturmea, the newly-formed *tawan* fruit.
Vutwora, 1. to dig the yam-holes in a garden so as to leave a path in the middle; *vut* 1. *wora* 3.
2. to smash a yam in digging.
Vuv, 1. to hum, whizz; same as *riv* 1.
Vuv, 2. v. to smooth, remove inequalities; adj. smooth.
Vuvlasoga, smooth, of men or fruit.
Vuvras, redupl. *ruras,* to be full to overflowing.
Vuvui, to pour water upon, cool with water; redupl. *rui,* as in *tirui; we tirui o qaranis, we ruvui mate o av.*
ruvui sawsaw, to cook in leaves with a hot stone, pouring water to make steam; *sawsaw.*
Vuvun, 1. redupl. *vun* 1., to poison fish; *i Qat me vuvun,* said of fish killed by the heat in shallows.
Vuvun, 2. redupl. *vun* 3., to deceive, hide; *map pata nansei, gale goro sei.*
Vuvur, [*vur* 2.] to be over-full, *o som we vuvur goro o mate tana,* a bag over-full of money.
Vuvusiag, to turn back, *vusiag,* as yam vines turn back and twine over themselves.
Vuvusrag, redupl. to strike often, forcibly; *rag,* intens.
Vuvutur, *we vet ape matai tama o one alolona.*
Vuvuv, 1. redupl. *vuv* 1. to hum, buzz; *o telepue ti vuvuv;* met. to mumble, not speaking out; *vuvuv goro,* to make a humming sound, as a stone falling from above before one; *o lan te vuvuv goro o nago aka.*
vuvuvus, to make a noise as a number of birds; *sin ronotag rowo o man ti vuvuvus.*
Vuvuv, 2. redupl. *vuv* 2., *qat vuvuv,* a head with hair cropped close to an even length.

W.

Wa, 1. conj. copulative, and.
Wa, 2. conj. lest; *ilogoro ko wa masu,* take care lest you fall.
3. word of warning, ware! *wa iniko!* take care of yourself; *wa iniko nan o vat,* get out of the way of the stone. Motu N.G. *va.*

Wa, 4. excl. that's it!

Wa, 5. sign of quotation; *nan neia wa,* then (said) he as follows; in direct quotation; if indirect *wa si, was,* conj. *si* 7. A message when delivered will begin *was,* as if 'I was to say that—.'

Wa, 6. expl. to be sure, or drawing attention; *na me gaganag reta ne wa.*

Wa, 7. excl. of pain, grief, fatigue, *a wa!*

Wag, v. to go without thought of danger; *sarawag; wagwag,* adv. openly.

Waga, 1. to be open, not touching, leaving a space; *we waga lue alo geara,* get clear through a gap; *gavir waga,* grasp with the fingers not meeting, *gate gavir nina; o vula me waga kalo,* risen clear above trees, hills, &c. *o tika we waga gap, gate qalo ape tano, tete vasogo.*

Waga, 2. to peel off the inner rind, *vanarasiu,* of a yam, as *we wil* the outer *viniu.*

Wageloa, *o tanun gate poapoa.*

Wagwag, adv. openly, imprudently; *alo maea; wag.*

Wai, to take up in closed hand or fingers, to handle earth, &c., to take up grated yam for *waiwai.*

  waig, 1. tr. to clench the fist, *ko te waig napanema,* to clench the fingers upon something, *ko te waig o tano mun napanema.*

  2. n. a small lump or heap, conical or round.

  3. adv. in a lump, heap; *we pute waig, risa, matur, waig* to sit, lie, sleep, nose and knees together, huddled up as in chill.

Waiwai, yam grated, taken up by handfuls, *wai,* and lapped in *toape* leaves to cook.

Waka, to open; act. and neut.

Wakae, to scold, be angry with.

Wakar, a very large pepper; like *gea,* piper methysticum.

Wakei, to dry up; *o meat me wakei, gate ilo o qilo; wakewake, tawakewake.*

Wakele, to pull out with finger thrust in; *kele.*

Wakewake, adv. very dry, *wakei; o loa we sar wakewake,* the sun is so hot as to dry up the mino pools and kill the fish; *me meat wakewake,* the tide has ebbed so far as to leave everything quite dry.

Waklei, a small child with a loud voice; met. from the bird *wakole.*

Wakole, a bird, glyciphila, which sings loud; in V.L.

Wakore, to eat out the inside of fruit, as a rat or bird does.

Wal, 1. to leap.

Wal, 2. to form in lumps, rise in lumps; thence 1. to boil as water, surf, &c., bubble up as fat in cooking. 2. to harden in lumps as gum on trees; *o malasina me wal.* 3. burn ill as fire, in which the fuel cakes. 4. *o qoe, o tanun, ti wal,* when there is no proper growth, something inside the pig is seen to have formed in hard lumps. 5. to rust, in recent use, from the lumps of rust on iron.

  waliai, (k) 1. gum hardened upon trees, *o walie malasina,* the gum of an acacia.

  2. the lumpy formation seen inside pigs which *wal; we ilo vires waliai, o garake tagai.*

  3. rust, in iron, in recent use.

Wala, to open; neut.; *tawala*.

Walaka, to lift, open up; *walaka savrag*, take up and throw away, as one pinches off the corner of a piece of paper.

Walaso, to loose a line; *ti rega sage ti walaso o gue nan o rano man*; to take out the hook from a fish's mouth, *me valago sage ti walaso*.

Walasoi, (k) 1. the sting, ovipositor, of an insect; *o walaso manlope*; a part of a crustacean, *walaso gare, naeru*. 2. the end of the *iwasola*, foundation of a food-chest; *walaso pugoro*.

Walaua, to collect things for a voyage.

Walawalau, to paddle all together; *neira we walawalau tuwale alo taro popo*.

Wales, 1. to pinch, nip off; 2. met. to argue against, oppose; conf. *ginita*; *o tuara manu te wales goro o tuara*, sing in rivalry, scream down another. 3. to contradict, disobey. *wales goro o mate toape*, a proverbial expression, to take the word out of one's mouth, to stop one from saying what he was just going to say right; met. from nipping off the top shoot of the plant and so spoiling it.

Waliai, (k) [*wal* 2.] constr. *wal, walie*; 1. gum formed in lumps on a tree, *walie malasina*; 2. lumps in flesh.

Walietuka, a small kind of flying fox; so called because it flies very high, near the *tuka*, and has *waliai, gate tutup*.

Waliog, 1. adj. round; 2. adv. round about, with *goro*; *wawaliog*.

Waliogiu, a small garden.

Walsina, 1. the gum, *waliai*, of the *sina* acacia; 2. greenish in colour, like the gum.

Walu, brother-in-law, sister-in-law; men call their sister-in-law *ro walu*. Malag. *valy*; D.Y. *wari*.

Walui, (k) the same in relation to some one; one's brother or sister-in-law.

Walul, to shout, same meaning as *rorov*; *sarawalulpea*.

Walwaliav, said of a yam that will not cook; see *wal* 2.

Wane, to bring in profit, as a canoe let out to hire.

wanea, gain, profit; money, as *un* for *som*.

Waneneag, to scold, urge, speak hard words to.

Wana, 1. to open the mouth, gape, gasp.

wanai, a gaping, opening like a mouth; *wanwanai*, gills of fish. Mao. *whanga*, bay; Tong. *faga*, mouth of a basket; N.B. *pagaga*.

Wana, 2. lightning, as in *gapilwana*; used to *un* for *rila*.

Wanana, to pull out, as a tooth; pull off, as a bracelet.

Wanara, to fork, branch, as a tree or road, to be forked; *wana* 1. **wanarai**, (k) a fork; branch. **wanaraga**, adj. [*ga* 5.] forked, branching.

Wanawana, to gasp, to breathe with gills like fish.

Wanepei, a thirsty man, who gapes, *wana*, for water.

Wanewaneloa, gaping on account of the heat of the sun; *wana* 1. *loa*.

Wanwanai, redupl. *wanai*; 1. gills; 2. *matig wanwanai*, loud-voiced, wide-mouthed.

Wao, to cry out, *ulo*, as in a *kolekole*.

War, 1. to twist, screw, curl over; come with a curl; *o liwo qoe ti war lue alo wopawurana,* boar's tusks come out with a curl from his jaw.
  warir, to bore; *r* tr. term.
  waririag, exactly.
  2. to have curled tusks; *o qoe we war.*

Wara, the cry of an owl, *manwara;* to cry in that way.

Waralava, a loud talker; *ti warawara.*

Waratagai, shameless, impudent; no forehead, *nawareana tagai,* no sense of shame.

Warawara, 1. redupl. *wara; o wis ti warawara,* the owl hoots.

Warawara, 2. metath. from *rawarawa,* as in *tawarawara.*

Wareai, (k) constr. *ware, wara;* front, brow, forehead; regarded as the seat of shame, in *waratagai.*

Warei, v. to be getting ripe, said of *nai* almonds when the kernel begins to turn brown, *me warei veta.*

Warelalav, beside the oven, on the brow, edge, of the fire; *wareai, kalaviai; we pute warelalav.*

Warelau, the margin, *wareai,* of the beach, *lau;* the space between *nolmeat* and *salilina,* between high and low water; *o sakaru aia.*

Wareloa, a place where there is always sun; *o loa we toga vagae aia, ape wareloa;* met. from analogy of *warelau,* &c.

Warevat, the brow of a rock or stone; *wareai.*

Warevutvut, the brow of a hill, or hillock, place where there are such.

Wareware, a large bare forehead; *wareai.*

Warget, to stick fast, *get,* in a hole into which the thing has been (more or less) screwed; *war* 1.

Wari, a kind of yam.

Warir, to bore, scrape out, scoop, with circular motion, *war; te warir lue o nam mun o matewarwarir.*
  waririag, adv. in a penetrating way, as if by boring, *sike waririag,* seek persistently, searchingly, exactly.

Waru, 1. to push money, *som,* along the string, *gavaru.*
  2. met to remain as a debt unpaid.

Warur, mash, *lot,* of *wotaga.*

Warwar, redupl. *war;* 1. adj. curled over, crooked; *piswarwar.*
  2. vehement, returning again and again; *we tila warwar,* to accuse vehemently; *o pei, o sul, we lil warwar ma,* water pours out abundantly, curling out, a crowd pours together, conglomerates.

Warwartagai, adv. shamelessly, impudently; *me sis warwartagai avunana, pa me qalo; neira me tila warwartagai avunak; waratagai.*

Was, 1. to drive a hole, make a hole by hammering in some tool; *we was lue o irav mun o nurnuriaka, qara vil,* to drive holes through the plank side-pieces of a canoe, with a shell tool, and lash them to the hull.
  2. met. to beat against the wind in sailing, *we waswas goro o mate lan.*

Was, 3. same as *wos,* to whistle; *was varaget,* to whistle and stop a man.

Was, 4. same as *wa si,* in indirect quotation; and so at the be-

T

ginning of a message; *was*—I am to say—; used also in explanation; *o nogire pa o wisiu, was o wis-nogire*, a pandanus leaf but not expanded, what is called a *wisnogire*.

Wasa, the stem of *tawasa, gariawasa, wasawasa*, with the sense of clearness; not used alone.

Wasaniu, a narrow space or interval between.

Wasawasa, safe; as from a fight in which a man may not have been untouched; free, clear.

Wasia, 1. a bird, merula.

Wasia, 2. a red *qeta*, caladium.

Wasisig, to sit, lie, stand, close together.

Waslava, [*was* 3.] little whistler and great noise.

Wasmata, barefaced, shameless, open; *matai* with perhaps *was* 4.; *o matev wasmata*, disposition to oppose openly, obstinately; *gol wasmata*, to scold, abuse with outspoken words, *gate vava pata*.

Wasovaluga, a wind; *wa ilone we log was o wasovaluga, o Togalau nan qa, pa ni we tur malate rua ran goro o Motalava, o tavala lan ti saw tal ma alo Roua, wa o tavala lan ti saw tal ma alo Nortorona*.

Wasvat, 1. hard as stone, *wa si vat; was* 4.; obstinate, stubborn.
2. a tree.

Waswas, 1. redupl. *was* 1., to hammer, drive holes, *waswas lue*; met. to beat in sailing, *waswas goro o mate lan*, beat against the eye of the wind.

Waswas, 2. redupl. *was* 3. to whistle; *waswas loglog*, to whistle a person's name, call him by whistling his name.

3. a myrmecodia in which ants live, hung up in a village to give warning of the approach of enemies by a whistling noise.

Wata, to be windbound; first a very long, should perhaps be *waata*.

Watia, a yoke, yoke-piece; same as *qatiiwa; iwatia*.

Wawa, a kind of eel; met. a greedy man.

Wawae, 1. adj. empty, with nothing in it; without fat, lean with sickness; *gate tutup, we wawae; o tanun we gopu, ti mar, ti gogo, ti wawae*.
2. adv. in vain.

wawaeg, adv. only; *ni me la wawaeg*, he gave to some only.

Wawalig, tr. warm up *toope*, &c., with hot stones.

Wawaliog, adv. round about; *wawaliog goro*.

Wawalul, redupl. *walul*, to shout in a crowd.

Wawana, wide and flat, as a *vinlasa* for *gea; we gamo alo lama wawana*, a long distant sail. Malag. *fafana*; Mal. Tag. Dyak, *papan*; plank.

Wawanraga, open, bare, of space.

Wawan, to speak out boldly, plainly; *wana* 1.

Wawana, redupl. *wana*, to open wide the mouth.

wawanag, tr. determ. to open the mouth for, upon; *tape wawanag*, to tilt up a *pue*, or *wetov*, so as to pour the water into the open mouth.

Wawao, open, with orifice; as a bottle, a fence with holes in it; as a turned-up nose showing open nostrils; *vatnorowawao*.

We, 1. v. p. with no temporal

force, belongs to a word used as verb.

We, 2. affirmative; yes.

We, 3. form of *wo* 3., a Gaua form.

Wegoa, [*we* 3.] 1. the paper nautilus. 2. a dolium, harp-shell.

Wegore, native pipe, flageolet.

Wegowego, adj. empty; as of a bag, fruit, seed, without the due contents.

Wein, one who will not be refused; not used to one of opposite sex.

Wel, to turn over, twist; *vara wel*, to twist, turn over, the ankle.

Wele, the leach of a sail; *lil o wele* when no wind.

Welesu, to twist off the head of a *wirita* octopus, properly *wel lesu*.

Welewele, a small dug-out canoe, no boards or mast.

Welgan, a high rank in the *suqe*.

Welil, [*we* 3.] a shell with a large white operculum; when a diver takes this he hides the operculum with his hand lest a shark should see it.

Wemeteloa, [*we* 3.] the man in the sun; a high rank in the *suqe*; the image representing it; *womateloa*.

Wena, rain; to rain.
wena gilgil, heavy lasting rain which digs the earth with streams.
wena manin, light rain, dripping, tapping.
wena para, rain that falls elsewhere, squall.
wena samsam, drizzle; same *wena*.
wena torotoro, heavy rain.
wena uwalava, heavy rain, in large drops.
wena tiutiu, intermittent rain.

Wenewene, clean, bright.

Wenwen, adv. near, close up; *kalo wenwen*, creep close.

Wenereqoe, [*nere* 1.] one who wears a pig's tail in commemoration of a *kolekole* he has made; *we* 3.

Wenir, to be noisy at play.

Weqetkeria, [*we* 3.] the name of a man in a story who never missed in shooting; proverb, a good shot.

Wera, 1. to flow shallow and swift, of water; met. to pass quickly as a crowd; to carry water in a lead or trench, same meaning as *leqa* 1.

Wera, 2. to step in, or touch, dirt.

Wera, 3. stem of *tawerai*; flat, the flat of the hand. Ambr. *vera*; Mallicolo, *fera*, hand; Fl. *pera ni lima*; Malag. *fela tanana*.

Werasa, to sweep with *sine ota*; 2. a besom of *sine ota*, midribs of sago frondlets.

Werasniuniura,

Were, 1. v. to be loose, of the bowels, diarrhœa.

Were, 2. to whine, cry; *tamate werewere*, one of the *tamate* societies.

Werei, (k) 1. the small of the back, loins.
2. met. inferior remainder, rump; *un werei*, the last poor month of the palolo; *were vetal*, the small fruit at the end of the bunch, *gaei*, of bananas.

Werimaga, large.

Weru, 1. a bird, eulabeornis, a rail; *weru pita*, a light-coloured variety.
2. met. a man who catches no fish, shoots no birds.

Werwerei, redupl. *werei*; the small bananas at the end of a bunch; the youngest born.

Wes, 1. same as *wesu* 1. to come, arrive, of time.

Wes, 2. stem in *mawes, tawes*, break off ; *wesu* 2.

Wes, 3. v. to show off other people's things as one's own ; n. one who so shows off.

Wesao, to afford a good landing ; *sao*.

Wesar, to husk with a stone ; *we wesar o nai, o wotaga*; to knock off the shell of a crab, *we wesar o gave*.

Wesemena, one who takes other people's food and things ; same as *qoa gap* ; *wes* 3.

Wesevir, one who boasts of things he has not done ; *wes* 3.

Wesewesu, to pluck off ; *wesewesu no-al* ; *wes* 2.

Wesinita, a fish.

Wesiu, constr. *wes*; same as *wisui*; a bud, leaf bud or shoot ; *o wes matig*.

met. used ironically as praise, *iniko o wesiu gai!*

Weslawe, name of a shrub on the beach ; same as *lislawe*.

Wesu, 1. to arrive, come near in time, time has come.

Wesu, 2. to break off, remove ; *we wesu kalo o naui nau o sariu*.

Wesu, 3. ten, in counting *tika*; from *wesu* 1.

Wesukut, a high rank in the *suqe*.

Wesula, a fish.

Weswes, 1. adv. redupl. *wes* 1. correctly, exactly ; *ni me gaganag wesiwes*, he said it would be so, and as the time came, *wesu*, it was so.

Weswes, 2. a kind of yam.

Wet, a game, begin a tune, sing a little, begin to dance.

Wetae, a game, to catch a person, who then has to catch.

Wetagor, a mess of almonds ; *o pipis ne kor vires*.

Wetamaragai, a ferntree figure, image of a man, *tamaragai*, set up as a memorial in a *marana*.

Wetapup, [*we* 3.] a braid of fowl's feathers, white or stained crimson, worn round the neck or ankle, a mark of having made a *kolekole*.

Wetaur-o-maligo, [*we* 3.] a high rank in the *suqe*.

Wetawetae, a game of catching ; *wetae*.

Wetegeregere, a bird, flycatcher. Gaua name for *tagere*.

Wetenia, a mess, *loko*, of rasped cocoanut.

Wetewil, [*we* 3.] a shell-fish.

Wetogor, a word used in scolding children ; not before women.

Wetov, [*we* 3.] a cocoanut shell water-bottle.

Wetovut, [*we* 3.] 1. a fish ; 2. met. an old woman who always stays in the place.

Wetuka, [*we* 3.] title given to a man in the highest rank of the *suqe* ; *tuka*.

Wetwetiga, having a large stomach.

Wetwetoqoe, a badly laid up rope or string, one of the strands crossing over another.

Wewe, [*we* 3.] 1. a shell, bulla ; 2. met. the white gristle on the bone of the thigh-joint.

Wewen, to take a thing close at hand instead of at a distance ; *wewen wora*.

Weweneriga, extremely white ; *wenewene*.

Wewenoga, adj. from *wewen*; *wa ko we ge wewenoga mun neira, neira we ge o sava?*

Weweruaga, opening wide like a single flower.

Wia, 1. adj. good, of the right sort, without anything un-

MOTA DICTIONARY

usual; *o tanun we wia gai, gate tanun ta Qauro*, he is all right, one of us, not of foreign parts; redupl. *wiawia*.
2. adv. merely, only.

Wiai, M. the inner part, as opposed to shell, rind, skin, so kernel, fish in the shell, wood in a vine; constr. *wie*; same as *wuai* V. and more remotely the same as *woai*.

Wie, constr. of *wiai*; *wie pal*, one who steals much. often.

Wievavae, to speak favourably of, express good wishes for; to bless in that sense; *wia, vava;* should probably be *wievavai* from *vava*.

Wil, 1. to turn over, turn on axis; *namatana me wil*, his eyeballs turned, either in death or sleep, *me wil kel*, in awaking; *te wil gole*, to turn round horizontally; to peel, turning the fruit over in peeling; *we wil savrag o viniu; we wil siwo o qeta*.
wil ris, turn round so as present another side.
wil reag, turn round away from and leave.
wil tagataga, turn over and set up on end.
wil tapelin, to turn over and upset.
wil vataqar, turn upside down, as a canoe which loses its outrigger.

wilit, tr. determ. to turn over so as to do something to the thing turned; *e. g.* to peel a fruit.

wilrag, tr. determ. to turn a thing round.

tatawilwil, rolling over of itself.

Comparisons with Pol. *wiri, whiri*, may suit *vir* as well as *wil*; but Mal. Dyak, Tagal, *giling*.

Wil, 2. a tree, eatable fruit.

Wile, a creeping mimosa, abrus precatorius; the seeds crabs'-eyes.

Wilit, tr. determ. *wil* 1. to peel off, turning the thing peeled; *te wilit o purusa nan o maniga*.

Wilrag, tr. determ. *wil* 1. as in *ratawilrag*, make to turn round.

Wilreag, turn over and away, roll away; *wil* 1. *reag*.

Wilris, to turn, roll, over so as to bring over the other side; *wil* 1. *ris*.

Win, to turn red, rusty, with mildew; *o malas me win*.

Winrag, to tease, bother.

Winwinur, to remove small weeds, therefore slowly.

Wir, 1. a mess of *loko* without *nai*, made for women after childbirth.

Wir, 2. a bird.

Wir, 3. V. same as *gir* in *gir vasosov*, to urge on, stir up; at Tasmate the small *wogire*, at the top of the pandanus bunch of fruit is the *wir*; it ripens first, and thence ripeness spreads.

wiris, tr. to hasten.

Wirig, 1. v. to neglect, leave uncared for, as when a man does not gather his fruit, &c., or have his hair trimmed; *ni we wirig nauluna*.
2. adj. inferior, as food left till last, *sinaga wirig*.

Wiriga, black, dark; a Gaua word used in Mota, rather as a nickname for a dark man, black pig.

Wiris, to make haste about, *wiris taurmate*, to make ready, *wir* 3. tr.

Wirita, an octopus. Malag. *hurita;* N.B. Motu N.G. *urita*.

Wirnatnat,

Wis, 1. an owl.

Wis, 2. constr. *wisiu*, leaf bud, flower-shoot.
   wisiga, adj. coming into leaf.

Wisir, to be out of the way, get out of the way; *i tag tuqei me wisir tagea sin tatawo matig.*

Wisiu, constr. *wis*; a flower-shoot, a leaf-bud, unopened leaf, not yet uncurled; used ironically, as *wesiu*; *iniko o wisiu*, you are a fine fellow. Malag. *fizio*;

Wismata, the unopened leaf, *wis*, of the heliconium, *mata* 2. *we sawa mun o wismata*, a man who makes *suqe* for another puts *wismata* with money rolled round them about the *tinesara*, they *sawa* for the *wismata* and are paid with the money.

Wisnogire, the leaf-bud, *wis* 2. of the *gire*, pandanus; *o nogire pa o wisiu, was o wisnogire.*

Wisparapara, a tomahawk; a small axe, a *wisiu* as compared to a full-sized one; recent word.

Wisparou, [*wis* 2.] 1. the flower-shoot of the male pandanus, *parou*, bearing no fruit.
   2. met. a man vainly pretentious.

Wistail, [*wis* 1.] to look about, *tail*, like an owl.

Wistapana, [*wis* 2.] a kind of piper methysticum with yellow leaf-shoots; *tapana.*

Wisvao, [*wis* 2.] the unopened leaves of the *vao*; same as *wismata.*

Wiswisiroa, a cuckoo.

Wiswisiga, [*ga* 5.] coming into bud; *wis* 2.; *wisiga.*

Wiswisis, singing in the ears; *wiuwiu.*

Wiswisiu, redupl. *wisiu,* young leaves not yet unfolded; *o wisiu we qoqo.*

Wiu, to buzz, make singing sound; *tawiuwiu, qorowiuwiu; naqorona te wiuwiu.*

Wo, 1. constr. *woai*; fruit, tuber, shell; *wo-mol,* the fruit of the native orange; *wovila,* pearl shell.
   2. prefixed to the shortened forms of personal names of men; Wogale for Galepasoqoe; also with names of individual pigs.
   3. a prefix properly descriptive of form, *woai*, a round object, to some extent corresponding to a numeral co-efficient; common in Gaua, rare in Mota; *woxat,* a stone; *woiras,* a baler.
   4. *wo ta Luwai,* the Luwai fruit, the *nari.*

Wo, 5. a white stone or hardened earth, ground down in water. *te pupus avune qatiu,* puffed over the hair for decoration in dances.

Woai, (k) constr. *wo*; 1. a globular object.
   2. a fruit, bulb, tuber, shell. Mal. *buwah*; Dyak, *bua*; Malag. *voa*; Gilb. Mort. Pon. *ua*; N.B. *vuai*; Mao. *hua*; Pol. *hua, fua*; N.G. *vua, bua, huahua.*

Woalag, to throw a rod with a finger at the end.

Woana, the drinking of the *gea,* piper methysticum.

Woapei, [*wo* 3.] (k) the *apei* of a man; *na woapena!* said in surprise at a person's impudence, what a man it is! *ineia o waratagai.*

Wog, 1. to whistle, as in climbing a hill.

Wog, 2. to change, in character or colour.

Woga, 1. to trouble, give pain to ; *ni we ge tamaine me wowoga i maramua.*
2. to be troubled, annoyed ; *o iga gate wota ma, o tanun te woga apena.*
3. to do a thing that gives trouble ; *ko qara woga,* do it yourself.
wogas, tr. to affect with pain.
wogarag, tr. to put trouble into a thing or a person.
wogat, tr. to give pain.
Wogae, [*wo* 3.] a trap, like a *wowor,* for fresh-water crawfish, woven with creepers, *gae* ; the main body of the trap is the *rere,* and the small receptacle at the side of it the *natui.*
Woganase, [*wo* 3.] the fish *ganase,* in *lul* and *sarsaru woganase.*
Wogarag, tr. determ. *woga* ; to trouble, give work to ; *we anumag ape sarasara.*
Wogas, tr. *woga* ; to affect with pain ; *ti wogas o qatui.*
Wogat, tr. *woga* ; to affect with pain, suffer pain ; particularly used with regard to arrow wounds ; *si ta vene isei ti, pa o palao ta qaloa, ni we wogat.*
wogatvag, separable *vag,* suffer with ; *ni we wogatrag o qatia, we rarakut.*
Wogata, [*woga*] labour, trouble ; *non o wogata me roro vanameag,* all his labour and trouble, in bringing up his child, have been in vain.
Wogetegete, [*wo* 3.] a Gaua basket ; *o tapera nomatig ; gete.*
Wogire, [*wo* 1.] a single fruit of the bunch, *vun,* of the pandanus, *gire.*
Woi, a white winkle shell, *sisipe.*
Woiras, [*wo* 3.] a baler, *iras* 1.; *o tangae, we tara o loloi apenai, qara ras o pei nia nan o aka.*
Woiv, [*wo* 3.] the dug out part of a canoe before the side planks are sewn on.
Woke, an albino, applied to both sexes ; see *lul* 1. and *manawo* ; used as proper name *Woke.* Esp. Sto. *voke,* white.
Wol, to barter, buy or sell by exchange ; *wol ma,* get by exchange, buy ; *wol reag,* barter away, sell ; not properly of money passing. In the *suqe* to enter or advance *we wol tapug* ; particularly to repay to the introducer what he has advanced ; see *vene, sar, vile pulai* ; *o qoe amenau, i vananok me wol nau nia,* the pig is mine, my nephew has given it me in return for my help in his *suqe.*
Mal. *beli* ; Dyak, Tagal, *bili* ; Malag. *vily, vidy.*
Wola, the calamus palm, cane ; *gawola* ; without hooks.
wola kalato, a calamus that breaks like *kalato.*
wola kaukau, calamus with hooks ; *kau.*
Sam. *lofa.*
Wolakaukaut, tr. v. to catch and hold like a *wolakaukau* ; *t* tr. suff.
Wolalak, [*wo* 1.] Adam's apple in the throat ; the fruit of the *lalak.*
Wolalate, v. to cross ; adv. crossways, one across another, *we risa wolalate goro.*
Wolamotmot, a brittle calamus.
Wolano, knots in a bow ; make it strong.
Wolas, to tie on, attach, with a double hitch ; to fasten the hook on to a fishing-line ; *gawolawolas.*

Wolipelipe, [*wo* 1.] a land snail with shell.

Wolo, stem of the following words, *woloi, wolowolo, wolos.* N.B. *bolo.*

Woloi, a large junk of wood laid across, *wolowolo goro,* the upper layer of firewood for a *qaranis* in the *um.*

Wolowolo, 1. adv. crossways; *ilo wolowolo,* to look askance at, with envy; *qat wolowolo,* the head full faced.
2. n. a crosspiece.

Wolos, to cut across; *wolos late-late,* to cut, chop, in lengths; from *wolo* stem of *wolowolo,* with *s* tr. suff.

Wolreve, to exchange, barter, at a distance, *rere,* as Roua men take fish far away to get yams, &c.

Woltapug, to buy the *suqe; tapug.*

Wolwolul, to glisten as a white reed, *togo.*

Womakemake, kidney, from likeness to nut, *woai,* of the *make,* Tahitian chestnut.

Womalopusa, one who works well and is not tired.

Womaraqaraqa, [*wo* 1.] the scarlet fruit of the *maraqaraqa; we sisgag ape salagoro, si ape qale rara,* stuck about as *soloi.*

Womatanamo, [*wo* 1.] a univalve with handsome operculum.

Womatig, [*wo* 1.] nut of cocoanut palm, *matig;* name *nomatig,* to hang in a bunch like the nuts of the *matig.*

Womel, same as *rawo* m*ele!* to put off, *rarowog.*

Womera, [*wo* 2.] the dark part of the eye, iris and pupil.

Wometeloa, same as *wemeteloa,* rank in the *suqe,* and image belonging to it.

Womotar, [*wo* 1.] the orange cowry shell.

Womresinaga, [*wo* 2.] one fond of eating, *mansinaga; meresinaga; mere.*

Womrematig, [*wo* 2.] the thumb; *merematig,* from the use of the thumb to scoop out the meat when the cocoanut has been drunk.

Wona, 1. a stone platform, raised for *suqe* feast, as an object to *kole;* generally close to the *gamal,* part of the assemblage of a *marana; o wona ne, o mele ne—* to build a platform *we woso o wona* or *wonawona; we woso o vat apena.*
2. a fish-fence, wall to confine fish; *we av o wona iloke,* pile loose stones.

Wonaenae, [*wo* 1.] a cone shell with points.

Wonaga, a tree.

Wonane, a perfectly round object.

Wonarasiu, (k) the shin.

Wonatnat, the heart, from likeness to the fruit, *woai,* of the *natu.*

Wonau, [*wo* 1.] the fruit of the *nau;* a bitter thing.

Wonawona, redupl. *wona,* stone platform, burial-place of great men, close to *gamal.*

Wono, 1. v. to close, fill up, make solid, oppress; *lolowono,* sorrow; *na lolok we wono,* I am sorry. -
2. to pay a debt; *wono pug,* close the transaction; *wono inau,* pay me.
wono ar, to finish all payments and dues for advance in the *suqe; av* 2.
wono late, to pay an instalment of a debt; *late.*
wono mal, to pay for a *malu*

made *mana* as medicine in sickness.

wono nagara, if a man dies out of a party of travellers or visitors he is said to do thus; *kamam me ret si ko te wono naganina, pa tagai, nina me esu qet.*

wono naranona, to pay a man for going on an errand, pay for his legs.

wono pug, close a loan, pay a debt; *wono pug ta Maewo*, said of a man who shoots one of another village, and afterwards goes to that village and is killed.

wono qon, to pay for rain-making; *ape si sei qe ret munsei was ni na o wena; paso nan o wena ti wena, i gene ilone qara le o som munia apena.*

wono sursur, to pay, but not in full measure; *sur* below what it ought to be.

wono wose, pay one or a party for paddling, for fetching pigs, payment with a pig, or pig and money.

3. adj. solid, close, filled up, entire as leaves.

wonoi, n. something that closes, fills up.

wonot, tr. v. to close something, compress.

wonoga, adj. become hard, close. Mao. *hono*; Sam. *fono*; Fl. *pono*; Malag. *fono*.

Wonoga, adj. [*ga* 5.] solid, close; of an egg addled, of food *gate tatas, gate pun, we maremare gap, tama we wono.*

Wonoi, [*wono*] 1. a place wanting mending, as in a fence; 2. a mended place, a filling up.

Wonolate, to pay an instalment of a debt.

Wonon, to throw stones, pelt; *we vivir rasei mun o vat.*

Wonoronoro, [*wo* 3.] a toy rattle, *ti noro.*

Wonot, tr. *wono* 1.; to make solid, oppress; 2. met. to distress; *o ganawono me wonot.*

Wonowono, redupl. *wono;* 1. a thick overgrown place, close, shut in.

2. a mended canoe.

3. complete, brought to a close in numbers; *sanavul rua wonowono*, twenty complete; in full numbers, *kamam nol qale toga wonowono.*

Wonwonoqaliga, to pay for going too near a relative by marriage; *we la o som ape me ra rirtag o qaliga.*

Wonana, [*wo* 3.] food chewed, *nana*, to feed children with.

Woota, [*wo* 1.] 1. the nut of the sago palm, *pta;* imbricated.

2. adv. met. with ripples, movements up and down, as of things floating; *o taro woota*, a calm in which the ripples are regular like the imbrications on the sago nut.

Wopanas, [*wo* 3.] the first bud of the cocoanut; *we togo tam o togo ti wot;* same as *roiroi, wovan.*

Wopawura, (k)[*wo* 3.] 1. the place in the jaw whence the boar's tusk starts, a rounded part, *pawura; o qoe we war alo wopawurana.*

2. the ankle-bone.

Wopeas, [*wo* 3.] a pet, tame creature; *peas.*

Wopolopolo, [*wo* 3.] a temporary basket made in the bush; *we sare o nomatig, we rau tam o tapera, qara vir tuwale,* tear the frondlets apart, weave the two sides, and then plait the ends together.

Wopugoro, the short pieces of wood laid across the *iwasola*, the foundation of a food-chest, *pugoro*.

Wopulagao, [*wo* 2.] one who goes on without ceasing; *ni tete mapsag tagogoi*, is in no hurry to rest.

Woqage, [*wo* 1.] the poached egg cowry.

Woqat, [*wo* 3.] a bunch, stalk of a heliconium, *qatu* 2., with which men are flogged in *sawan woqat, valval lamas*.

Wor, to dry in the sun, spread to dry.

Wora, 1. v. to divide, cleave asunder, split; act. neut. *wora taso*, to break off in splitting.
2. to come through, go forth, pass between; *o aka we wora lue ape tursao; neira me wora-wora sage ma*, came through the reef to land; *o tanun te wora goro utag*, makes his way out; to spring forth as water; come forth as *wo patau*.
3. n. a cleft, in a rock or coral reef.
4. n. a spring of water.
5. adv. asunder, apart; *toga wora*, to lie unentangled, therefore easy.
6. adv. only, merely, in vain, in a trifling way; *we meromero wora*, does nothing but sulk.

worag, tr. make to come through.

woras, tr. to push way through.

mawora, broken, come apart.

Worag, tr. *wora* 2. to make a person come, compelling him with a charm; *we sur o mana ape nol tangae si ni mule ma*.

Worageara, a fence broken with trees growing through it, *o tano geara vat we tuai, pu we ilo vaglala ape vat si o tangae me maur ti ape geara*.

Woragoro-lo-utag, a scout, *wora* 2.

Woramata, a saying, or answer, made when a thing is not possible; *o nonomia nirua apena*; 1. *si qe paere o sava nansei pa si tagai, ni te vet tamaine*; 2. *si ko qe vatransei we mageregere ni ge o sava, te vet tamaine*.

Woraqat, to break a head; *wora* 1.

Woras, tr. *wora* 2.; to go through a *wora* 3., as a canoe *te woras lue*.

Woratap, [*wora* 2.] to bring food into a *salayoro* for sale, thus breaking through a *tap*.

Woravear, to bear fruit for the first time; met. from *wora* 2. and *vear*.

Worawerawe, [*wo* 1.] a cowry shell, long and dark.

Worawora, 1. redupl. *wora* 5. adv. in pieces, all apart.

Worawora, 2. redupl. *wora* 6. adv. of no consequence, *tanun worawora*, one of no account.

Worepes, [*wo* 3.] a debt, *repes*.

Woriu, small things, rubbish, weeds.

Wornenegea, *o gene we wia*.

Woro, to squeeze, wring out, juice of herbs, liquor of fruits, over food, and things prepared for charms; to add cocoanut sauce to *loko*, &c.

woro garata, to prepare charm with fragments of food, &c.

woro qaro, to add uncooked cocoanut sauce.

Woroaroan, [*wo* 3.] an ornament hung on a string from the neck; *roan*.

Wororoi, (k)[*wo* 3.]same as *roroi*; *nawororona*, the fame of him.

Worosiu, small things crowding together ; *woros vat*, small stones, pebbles, collected about a big stone.

Woros, v. to collect, as small things together, maggots, &c.

Worotoga, one who stays in the *vanua*.

Worworsai, the small tubers about the *tur nam*, large yam.

Worworuai, a collection of small things, all small together, *o worworuai gese; woros*.

Worworur, to fall and sink into the sea.

Wos, to whistle ; same as *was* 2. *wos galegale*, to hide a word by pronouncing it without vocal sound.

Wosa, 1. n. a boil.

Wosa, 2. v. to slap, smack, clap. *we wosa o qoe alo kolekole*, to deliver over a pig with a smack on the back; *wosawosa panei*, to clap the hands ; *wosa lapalapa*, to flap the wings like a cock crowing.

Wosa, 3. stem of *tawosa, wosalag, vawosag*; open.

Wosag, 1. to snatch away, carry forcibly off.
2. n. a charm to take disease away.
wosagiva, v. n. carrying off, capture.

Wosalag, to spread a mat, *wosalag o epa*; to lay out *som me siga veta: wosa* 3.

Wosar, to season with salt-water, as *toape*.

Wosarave, *we taur o epa we savrag o tano nan o tapanau, paso nan qara wosalag o epa*.

Wosawosa, redupl. *wosa* 2. to move the hands in the way of quieting a disturbance.

Wose, a paddle.
wosega, adj. paddle-shaped.

Mao. *hoe*; Sam. *foe*; Fiji, *voce*; Sol. Ids. *vose, hote*; Motu N.G. *hode*; Sund. *boseh*; N. Cel. *bite*; Bug. *wise*, Sumb. *busi*; Malag. *voy*, to paddle.

Woso, 1. to beat, hammer.
wosorag, to beat hard.
2. to build with stones ; *we woso o wona, we woso o vat ape wona; woso goro mun o vat*, make a partition with a stone wall, or lay down stones as pavement.

Woso, 3. to pain, be in pain ; same as *virtig*.
wosoag, tr. to give pain, tire, weary ; as with work, or being sent about.

Wosoisoi, [*wo* 3.] a kind of trepang, bêche la mer ; *o wosoisoi ti susgalete, o marete ti mantagai*.

Wosolagia, the feast made on the last payment for the bride ; *we woso o mateqatia ape som*; the wedding feast ; *lag*.

Wosoleqaleqa, to hammer temporarily, put in pegs to mark out a house site ; *o ima me towo paso, qara woso o tangae nitol si nivat, tavala ima wa tavala ima, qara rot o au apena, o vaglala si te taur nake*.

Wosomaimai, a catamaran, raft.

Wosorag, tr. determ. *woso* 1. to beat hard, often ; *rag* intens.

Wosowoso, redupl. to champ the teeth ; *o qoe ti wosowoso naliwona*.

Wosvotot, very short.

Woswosega, paddle-shaped ; *wose*.

Wot, to rise up, stand up, appear, shoot up ; Sam. *fotu*; Fiji, *votu*.

o vanua me wot ma, land came

in sight, was raised; *o vanua wot*, a small island.

o aka me wot ma, a ship rose above the horizon.

o vula we wot ma, a new moon appears.

In the *suqe*, one who rises to the highest rank *ti wot*, emerges; *ni gai wot, ni gai gana qet ran o suqe*.

wot goro nolin, fruit appearing at the top shoot.

we toqo tam o togo ti wot, swells as a shooting reed.

wotlag, tr. to lift up, raise.

Wota, 1. to be born, come into being.

wota qulolava, to come quickly into full size, met. of a breadfruit.

wota usur, one who follows the ways of his father.

wota vanameag, to be born without a known father.

o qoe wota vatrig, a pig born in the place, so stays about the village.

wotai, a sapling, young plant.

wotava, v. n. birth.

wotavag, sep. *vag.*; to be born with.

Wota, 2. to take the bait, of fish; probably same word.

Wota, 3. to knock, break by knocking. Motu, N.G. *botai;* Malag. *boka*.

o qaui we varwota, knees knock one against the other; *wota o lito*, break up firewood, knocking one piece on another, or the ground; *we wota wora o matig mun o vat*.

4. to castrate; done by bruising with stone or stick.

Wota, 5. to plait in, as *som* into a belt; *o gaprono o som we wota alolona*.

Wotaanai, suckers, groundlings, growing from roots; *wotai, anai*.

Wotaga, 1. a barringtonia, the nut eaten; the bark used to poison, *vun*, small fish.

2. *wotaga pei*, name given to the early dug *qauro* wild yams; *ape qauro gese, we gil taqai*.

3. *wotaga*, used as a kind of superlative, the nut being choice eating; *wotaga wia*, very nice to eat; only used of food.

Wotai, 1. constr. *wote;* [*wota* 1.] a young plant, seedling, sapling, rod.

wote raverave, a fishing-rod.

wote tangae, a stick, rod.

2. a short cocoanut that fruits.

Wotano, 1. weeds; as if *wo* 1. of the earth, *tano*,

Wotano, 2. [*wo* 3.] a swelling in the groin.

Wotanokov, a yellow earth, used for colouring *tamate* hats.

Wotanlas, [*wo* 1.] a curious fruit, at V.L. and in the New Hebrides.

Wotapatapa, [*wo* 3.] a cocoanut frond plaited to play with.

Wotapeapea, a kind of yam.

Wotarara, [*wo* 1.] a club with the head in the shape of a *tarara* fruit.

Wotarevrev, small, wizened.

Wotarewrew, same as *wotarevrev*.

Wotava, v. n. *wota* 1. birth, being born.

Wotavae, [*wo* 1.] a kind of gourd, eaten.

Wotavag, to be born with; *wota* 1. separable *vag*.

Wotepispis, a bird, *merula*.

Wotet, [*wo* 1.] the nut of the *tet*, Sol. I. *tita*, used as cement; a V.L. tree.

Wotgoro, the name of a month or season, *vule wotgoro*, the time when the *togo* reeds shoot up into flower; *wot*.

Wotiu, M. same as *wotui*, top shoot, bough.

Wotiva, [*wo* 1.] the chambered nautilus.

Wotlag, tr. *wot;* to raise, lift up the voice, in singing.

Wotoi, to scold.

Wotora, adv. *gara wotora*, to bite upon something hard in food; see next word.

Wotorai, [*wo* 3.] a bit, small part of hard food; *wotore sinaga; tora*.

Wotovara, [*wo* 3.] charcoal, *gartaweris;* a Gaua word.

Wotpatau, a fish.

Wotuai, (k) top; *wotue tangae*, tree-top; *wotue qatui*, top of the head.

wotue ima, a house with a top running up to a high point; *we kole o ima, o wotue ima, ape ima kole*.

Wotuaru, V. *wotiaru* M. the top, tips of branches, *wotui* or *wotiu*, of casuarina trees, *aru*, the haunt of ghosts; hence *vilevile wotuaru*, to adjure.

Wotui, V. *wotiu* M. the tip of a tree or branch, bough.

Wotutgag, the spine; *tapare wotutgag*.

Wotutge, [*wo* 1.] the hollow down the backbone.

Wotuwale, [*wo* 3.] adj. only; n. 1. an only child, single piece of property, pig, &c. 2. a person who is alone, without helper; *valuna tagai*.

Wotwot, redupl. *wot;* to be set up, elated.

2. adv. in high place, conspicuous, aloft, so as to be seen; *pute wotwot*, to sit above the common level; *van wotwot*, to come out of the bush into the open; *rene wotwot*, shoot an arrow skywards; *vatira wotwot*, set up conspicuously.

3. n. a sign, pole, or other conspicuous thing, set up on a hill when people first ascend; *pa kara me nina alo qase tauwe, nau me riv o kariu, o vaglalu si na qara nina totowo aia*.

Wotwotora, adj. [*ra* 4.] rough, lumpy, *we wotwot; o matesala we wotwotora*.

Wou, 1. to cry out in the *mago* dance.

Wou, 2. to be desolate, deserted, empty of people.

Woulo, [*wo* 3.] a single cry, *ulo* 2.

Wouromao, [*wo* 3.] a lump of pumice; *uroi, mao* 1.

Wouto, [*wo* 3.] a float, anything that floats on the surface, such as a *wovut*.

Wovagoro, [*wo* 3.] food heaped up, *vagoro*, by a house for a feast.

Wovan, [*wo* 1.] the bud of a cocoanut in its earliest stage; same as *roiroi, wopanas*.

Wovat, [*wo* 3.] a small, roundish, stone, *vat*.

Wovila, [*wo* 1.] the pearl oyster *vila*, either 1. the bivalve, more correctly, or 2. a single pearl, *wo* 3.

Wovile, 1. a small familiar bird.

2. met. one who chatters, *vava vagorgor;* or, a small person.

Wovoroa, a slang word for *tatas*.

Wovut, [*wo* 1.] the fruit of the barringtonia *vutu;* used to poison, *vun*, small fish.

Wovutei, (k) [*wo* 3.] also *wovtei*, the *vutei*, posteriors.

Wowaiaga, [*ga* 5.] cylindrical.

Wowo, 1. v. to chip, *wowo sarrag o viniu nan o matig*.

2. a notch, jag; *we manilenile, o wowo apena*.

Wowoai, (k) [*wowo*] a crevice ; *o wowoe gasuwe*, a rat's hole.
Wowoga, 1. [*ga* 5.] white, whitish ; *wo* 5.
Wowoga, 2. redupl. *woga*, to work continuously.
Wowolakalaka, a shelled cocoanut for *lot wetene*.
Wowolavlav, to cause thirst ; *isei ge gana o sinaga we mamasaiga, pa o marou ti ge neia apena*.
Wowonara, [*wo* 3.] drops of blood.
Wowonorag, to grope about amongst dirt.
Wowor, 1. a round fish-trap (not long like a *wogae*) ; *we tau o wowor*.
Wowor, 2. to weed, gather weeds, rubbish, from ; *we wowor nan*.
woworiu, weeds, things gathered up from gardens.
Wowor, 3. to scatter, sprinkle.
Woworo, to scatter, be scattered ; *wowor* 3.
Woworosiu, (k) redupl. *worosiu*; met. a man's properties accumulated around him.
Woworsai, *woworosai*, the small yams about the main tuber, the *tur nam*.
Wowosa, a kind of yam.
Wowosag, to turn over dry brushwood.
Wowosega, [*ga* 5.] paddle-shaped, of an ill-formed leg ; *wose*.
Wowot, redupl. *wot*; to stand up as a rock out of the water, *o vat we wowot alo qilo*.
Wowotag, redupl. *wota* 3. with tr. suff. *g*, to knock, run the head against something.
Wowotaga, 1. [*wo* 1.] the hind leg, ham, of a pig, from its shape. 2. a fish, from its shape.
Wowotoriga, [*ga* 5.] adj. with something hard inside, *o wotore sava*.
Wowotuaga, [*ga* 5.] adj. lumpy, part hard, part soft ; *we wotwot ; tama o kor qa we tuk, we mana o takelei*.
Wowuqa, (k) [*wo* 3.] same as *wuqa*.
Wowut, [*wo* 3.] one who is liked, admired.
Wuai, (k) V. same as *wiai* M. and *woai*. Mao. *hua*; see *woai*.
Wuawua, same as *wuwua*, with derivatives.
Wuei, V. the meat of the cocoanut, &c.; same as *wiai* M.
Wukai, V. i. e. *wukag* for *ukag*, to let fly, arrow, stones ; *wukai ritag*.
Wul, a tree.
Wula, 1. underdone, of food.
Wula, 2. adj. said of a garden made too large for the plants put in it ; *i tag tuqei me maran nan*.
Wulagaleg, a fish ; also *wulagalei*.
Wulano, n. noise, disorder ; v. to be noisy, disorderly.
Wulapeg, to bend, act. and neut.; to fail, give way.
Wulug, to close over; *we tuwur o noota mun o gaqir, we wulug*, for a *taplagolago*; next word.
Wulun, bend close, shut up.
Wulus, a man's brother-in-law.
Wumeto, a wooden bowl, used for stone-boiling. Fiji, *kumete*; Sam. *'umete*.
Wun, probably, as one supposes ; *wun!* most likely.
Wunana, bent in a curve.
Wune, to conceive, to become aware of conception ; Fiji, *kune*, to find, experience, *kunekune*, to conceive in the womb.
Wunuka, excl. on hitting the mark.
Wuniu, (k) 1. the beard ; 2. the chin. Mao. *kumikumi*.

Wu*n*revereve, a long beard; *reve*.
Wu*n*wetewil, a beard like *wetewil*, very long in the middle of the chin; *o wuniu we roro*.
Wuqa, 1. (k) n. same as *uqa* 2., *wowuqa*.
Wuqa, 2. v. same word as *uqa* 1., to begin digging yam-holes, mark the holes by lifting earth with the digging-stick.
Wur, 1. with *raroroag*, to be very abundant; *o kau we qoqo apena? eke! we wur varoroag ti*.
Wur, 2. to brush, sweep; V.L. word, stem of *wurvag*.
  wurvag, tr. to clean, set to rights.
Wura, 1. to spring forth, throw up, jet forth, of water; *o matepei we wura savrag o pei; o pei we wura lue alo matepei*. Probably same word with *vura*.
  2. to jut out, project; *matawura*, a lizard with projecting eyes; *mawurawura*, with projecting heels.
Wura, 3. V. same as *ura*, imper. 2d dual.
Wura, 4. numeral used in counting *tika*, for *rua* 2.
Wura, 5. a plant.
Wurare, to make a confused noise; a noisy person.
Wuras, to feed up an animal, same as *peas*.
Wuraveg, to take things one by one.
Wurawura, redupl. *wura* 1. to spurt upwards.
Wure, to make inarticulate sounds, as babies; *wurewure*, to chatter like parrots, children, *ni we wurewure goro gese;* buzz like bees.
Wuro, 1. to prepare a *garata*

charm, *woro; me wuro mate neia*.
Wuro, 2. to cease work, neglect; *wuro vitag*, to leave a garden half cultivated, *gate mawmawui get, o takelei me pea*.
Wurqasa, bare, like a bald head, *qasai*, or stone standing out of water.
Wuruga, scurfy; *qat wuruga; tama o tarowo apena*.
Wuru*n*, to crawl in a sitting posture; same as *rasun*.
Wurvag, 1. v. [*wur* 2.] to clean, put to rights, repair; *wurvag lesu*, to set perfectly to rights.
  2. adv. perfectly well, very well; *toga wurvag, gilala wurvag*.
Wurwasa, same as *wurqasa*.
Wurwurpilage, a fish.
Wurwuruone, a fish.
Wut, same as *wutu*, louse.
Wutiu, M. same as *wutui*.
Wutmata, a pig-louse or tick.
Wutmule, a great number.
Wutoto, to grumble, be discontented.
Wutowuto, a balloon fish, sunfish, tetrodon.
Wutu, a louse.
  Mao. *kutu;* Sam. *'utu;* Mal. *kutu;* Tagal, *kuto;* Marsh. Ids. *kid;* Motu N.G. *utu;* Bks. Ids. *wut, uru, gut, git;* N.H. *wutu, gutu, gut, cet;* Sol. Ids., *gutu, u'u, u;* Gilb. *uti;* N.B. *ut*.
Wutuai, the top shoot of a tree, ornamental finial of a *gamal kole* or house; *wotuai*.
Wutui, the seed-tuft of sugarcane, reeds, &c., panicle, flower; constr. *wut*.
  wutqeta, wutvia, flower of caladium; *wutvalis*, panicle of arundo.
Wutulum, a small cuttle-fish, *wutu, lum* 2.
Wutu*n*, to bend down and break

the soft no*liu* of a plant, as of *toape* to make it leafy; *wutui*.

Wutwutua, [*wut*] an unwashed person.

Wuwua, dust.

   wuwuaga, [*ga* 5.] dusty, white with dust, rough with dirt.

Wuwuai, redupl. *wuai*, lump, small bit, particle; *wuwue tano* dust, *wuwue nawo* spray, dried by the sun.

Wuwuaga, dusty, white with dust.

Wuwur, to get, bring, what is bad, filthy; *o tanun we wuwur*, dirties himself; *wuwur ma ivea?* whence bring together a bad, nasty, lot of things? *wur* l., *gawur*.

Wuwutui, to appear; *o tamate we wuwutui munsei*, a ghost appears to a man.

INDEX

A

a, o, tuwale
abandon, toavtag
abhor, vasigtag
abide, toga, goara, gogae
able, lai
aboard, vawo aka, sage
abode, tano-togatoga
abound, asoa, gir 3., lolona, qoqo, rowo sal, ura 1.
about, ape, kelkel, tal, wawaliog
above, avuue, avunana, sal 3.
abreast, tarnag
abroad, avarea, salena
abscess, maniga, vivnasa, wosa, wotano
absorb, unuv
abstain, ora, sur 5.
abundant, asoa, soqo
abuse, linasapur, vasir
accident, mateawota
acclivity, kalokalo, taqaniu, tutnai
accomplish, lai, qalo
according, sar, sasarita, tataga
accumulate, av, vawlig, vile vavtig
accurate, nurnur, mantag
accuse, sutavun, tila, tul 5.
accustom, avu
ache, vivtig
acid, namisa
across, pala, wolalate, wolowolo
act, gapalag, ge, na
active, gis, rowogis
add, makei, taqai, tuan
admire, arike, mamakei
adopt, ramo
adoption, ramova
adorn, valakas
adrift, sale
advance, susurut
adversary, tavalalea
adult, tamatua
adultery, pakapaka

adze, lakae, taqes ; *v.* taso
afar, aras, asau
afflicted, lopsag
affright, kikina, matagtag
afloat, sale
afoot, ranoi
afraid, gogolo, matagtag
afresh, mulan, qara
after, kulai, tagir, tataga
afterwards, tagir
again, kel, mulan
against, ape, goro 1.
age, tanoi
ago, paso, veta
agree, pul, saratuwale
aground, pute
ague, masag
aid, *v.* pirin, tuan ; *n.* piriniva
aim, sorarai
air, maea, mapsagiu
akin, sogo
alarm, malarowo
albino, woke
alight, *v.* rowo pute
alight, *adj.* ona
alike, sasarita
alive, esu, tamaur
all, gese, lolog, nol, qet
alligator, via
allot, aseg
allow, ukeg
almost, arivtag, mantagai ti e
aloft, avunana, wotwot
alone, magesei, tuwale
along, pan, taso
alongside, vakiksag
aloof, asau
aloud, poa
already, veta
also, mulan
alter, leas, map sea, ris, taveris
altercate, varleasag
alternate, varleas

U

altogether, qet, ran, tuwale
always, vagae, valqon
amidst, alo, vatitnai
amiss, ava, sasamanau
among, alo, vatitnai
amulet, ava, masile, qatag, soasoa
ancestor, tupui
anchor, vat-ligo
and, wa, ta 4.
anew, kel, mulan
anger, lologagara, mero ; gol
angle, noriu, sigerai
ankle-bone, pawurai
annoy, anumag, ge-risris, kalit
anoint, nonon, ram, urai
answer, valui, sar, tarama
ant, gan 4, niniu, malatutun
antenna, karui, sinoi
anticipate, sol goro
anxious, surgolo
any, sei, tea
apart, gara 2., masal, sea, wora
apiece, valval
apparition, taqaniu
appear, nana, rowo lue, suar, wot
appease, tape 2.
apply, tiu 2.
appoint, sora, veveg, vonog
apportion, aseg, tirag
approach, nina, peten, rasu 2., rivtag
argue, leasag, wales
arm, panei, paniu
armlet, pane
armpit, vinai
around, goro 1., wawaliog
arrange, map, sora, tarina, valug
arrive, nina 1., rasu 2., wesu 1.
arrow, qatia, qatigsar, tiqa, toto 3.
as, tama
ascend, kalo
ashamed, apegalo, apekiria, apemaragai
ashes, tarowo, tuwus
aside, lil 3., para 1., sipa 1.
ask, paere, varus
assault, kos
assemble, sul, vug
assent, mawui
assert, uwe
assign, tirag
assist, pirin, tuan
asthma, sova

astride, tawalag
asunder, wora
at, a 2., lo, pe ; *at all*, ilo 2.
atone, tape
attach, taka, wolas
attack, takas
attain, suar, qalo
attend, taka 2., tinqoro
aunt, veve
avenge, rapa, sar 1.
avoid, irvitag, vakiksag
awake, mamata
away, reag, vitag
awe, momogo
awhile, galean, galtag
awkward, tama 3., tatametoga
axe, parapara

B

babble, wure
baby, pipio, tete
back, *n.* kulai, pup, tagir, taqalsai ;
    v. qora, suwa ; *adv.* kel, taragiate
backbone, gatogoi
backwards, kel, suwa
bad, mala 2., malkeke, sapur, sokorai, tatas
bag, tana, tapera
bait, nunur, pea 2.
bake, laqan, ranai
bald, qasa
bale, malqei ; *v.* ras
baler, iras
ball, woai
bamboo, au 1., pue
banana, vetal
band, gae, gavivis
bandage, gaqoas
bang, toqal
bank, matai, pagigin, tutnai
bare, mamasa
barefaced, wasmata
barely, viviris
bargain, qil
bark, viniu
barren, kelo, maran, tinawono
barter, wol
bashful, apemaragai
bask, masil
basket, gete, tapera
bat, gapa 2., gapgaperu
bathe, sugsug, vasug

INDEX 291

bawl, awo
be, toga
beach, salilina
beak, manui
bear, taur, veverag ; uwa 1., vasus
board, wunui
beat, lama, nam, ninag, vus, was 1.
beating, vusiva
beautiful, lulum, tano 2.
because, apo 1., manigiu
beckon, alovag, tul 2.
become, qeteg ; taram
beetle, manu
before, amoa, moai, nagoi
beforehand, gis 1., sol
beg, paero
beget, vasisgag, vawota
begin, qeteg ; *adv.* qara, raka
beginning, qetegiu
beguile, gale, nule
behave, toga
behaviour, togara
behind, kulai, tagir
belch, tolo
believe, nomtup
belly, toqai
belong, anai, pulai, ta 1.
below, alalane, siwo
bell, rotig
bend, galete, luk, luqe, malulpeg, ruqa, wulapeg, wulun
beneath, alalane, alalanana, siwo
bent, maluk, tatagalete, tatagapelu
beside, pagig, pan, vakiksag
besiege, sarauinin
besom, werasa
betel, matavgao
betray, manirin
betroth, vatvataligo
between, masaoi, vatitnai
beware, ilo goro, wa
bewilder, lena 2., mataqelaqela, qalena, valenalena
bewitch, gagalesag
beyond, tavala
bicker, govgov
bid, vatran, vet
big, liwoa, poa
bill, manui
bind, qoas, rot, tatal, vil, vilit, viv 3.
bird, manu
birth, vasus, wotava

bit, manci, wotorai
bite, gara 1., nau, nit
bitter, garamisa, gogona, namisa, naunauga
black, silsiliga, wiriga
bladder, meme
blade, laqai, matai
blame, map
blast, lalav, vasawu
blaze, lawa
bleed, nara
bless, vawia, wievavac
blind, matanena, matapei
blink, mataperu
blister, laqolaqe
block, vatiu ; tin, vin
blood, nara
bloody, manaranara
blossom, tawaga, tawagasiu
blow, v. tawaga ; garaug, sawu, sere, ug ; *n.* vusiva
blue, gesagesaga, manurlama, turturuga
blunt, les 2., lol, nono, qanusa
blush, galgaluanara
boar, qoe, nuru
board, irav, tapa
boast, sotal, sou, valalava, viras
body, tarapei, turiai
boil, goqo, sala 4. ; *n.* wosa 1.
bond, gae, garotrot, gavivis
bone, suriu
boom, pano
border, pagigiu
bore, warir
born, wota 1.
borrow, avu 1.
bosom, varai
both, tatarua
bottle, wetov
bottom, kerei
bough, wanarai, wotiu
bound, taturag ; tin 2.
boundary, tingoro
bounty, alena
bow, n. us 4.
bow, v. matueg, surag 2., taqulon
bowels, tinai
bowl, wumeto
boy, mera, reremera
boyhood, tanoreremera
brace, varagai

brackish, malean, tov 2.
brain, talvei
branch, wanarai
breadfruit, patau
break, aqo 2., gape 2., kome, koran, late, mot 2., nere, nile, ninag, nove, tawes, tuqe, visarag, wora, wota 3.
breast, sus 2., varai
breath, mapsagiu
breathe, mapsag, son, sova
breed, vasus
bride, lag
bridegroom, lag
bridge, pelagolago
bright, marmararan, wenewene
brilliant, lenas, peru, terelawa, valeleas
brim, matai, tukatukai
brimstone, malau-gan-Qat
bring, nunvag, tak, vile
brink, matai
bristle, saka 1.
brittle, sakirlatelate
broad, tapiapia, tawala
broil, gavtun, ranai
broken, mawora
brood, taqar
broom, werasa
brother, tasiu, tuaga, tutuai
brother-in-law, walu, wulus
brow, warcai
bruise, malot, pepemera, puapuaga
brush, lamas
bubble, goqo, uwa 2., wal
bud, qoqoi, wisiu ; *v.* awisiga, qoqo
build, *native house*, taur ; *with wood*, pasau ; *with stone*, woso
bulge, loqo
bump, ninag
bunch, gaei, in, qatagiu, vun
bundle, galaqot, lakitiu, laqotiu, mona, rotiu, tatagiu
burden, rene
burn, gao, gan 2., gargarat, lawalawa, saqo, sin
burrow, livun
burst, malue, mawora, tua 5., wora
bury, livun, tanu, tavig, tavun
bush, mot 1., uta 1.
busy, gis 1., lalalano
but, pa, nava, panava
butterfly, pepe 2., rupe

buttock, qote, vutei
buy, girei, tulag, tun, tuvag, wol
buzz, viv 1., vuv
by, mun, nia ; pan, pe

C

cackle, kokoko
calf of leg, toqelawe
call, log, suware
calm, taro
can, lai
cane, wola
canoe, aka, welewele
capsize, tapulsama
careful, matanur, nurnur
careless, ganawono
cargo, rene
carry, alig, avnag, iwa, iwasasa, pepe 1., rig 1., rorot, sapalo, sasa 2., tapan, tatag, veverag
carve, tit, toto
cast, sakarag, savrag
castrate, wota 4.
catch, kau, sakau, takau, tia 1.
caterpillar, torou
catspaw, garululu, lul
cave, lia
caulk, pul goro
cause, manigiu, qetegiu
cease, mot 2., paso
centipede, sulataramoa
chafe, sis, tawasis
challenge, uloulog
champ, nau, saman, toke, woso
change; leas, ris, viloris, wog 2.
channel, garere, salea
charcoal, gartaweris
charge, altag
charm, garata, malov, mana, talamatai, tamatetiqa ; *v.* gagaleg, woro
chase, ara
chatter, kota
cheat, gale
check, palasai
cheer, masekeseke, maskara
chest, pugoro
chew, gat, isa, nana 2., nau
chief, tavusmele
child, mera, natiu, natmera
childbearing, lalamera
chin, wuniu
chink, wowoai

INDEX

chip, *n.* vainiu, viuiu; *v.* nile, wowo
chirp, tarako
choke, gis 2., gisir
choose, aris, iloraka
chop, gar, nir 3., qaia, tara 2., toto, ut, vit
chrysalis, toliu
cinnamon, viusorsor
circuit, tal
clam, gima, talai
clap, wosa 2.
clash, toke
clasp, gavir, uk
clatter, nona
claw, gave, mariu, pisui
clay, tano
clean, weneweno
cleanse, awosa, wurvag
clear, kor 3., *m*alete, melumelu, tarowasa, tawasa, tiro 2., ureure, vatawasai; *v.* gir 1., sagaro, u*m*a; *adv.* ae
cleave, tara wora
cleft, wora
clench, gara 1., *n*i*n*in, waig
clever, menaro
cliff, nua 1.
climb, garav, kakarau, kalo, laget, rap, vega, veresag
cling, kata, takau
clip, pala
close, gara 1., *m*os, qir 2., rir 2., soru, vakokot, vaon, wono
cloth, siopa
cloud, maligo
clouded, gagavu
cloy, lanar
club, kere
clubfoot, qale, qelu
clump, mo 2.
clutch, gagaro
coal, tawene
coarse, no-lava
coast, pan-vanua
cobweb, talau
cockle, gar
cockroach, susmawo
cocoanut, matig, vusa
coil, kalmag, pora 1., qalu, qal*n*ag, siga.
cold, malaso, mamarir
collect, vawlig, woros

colour, tarapei
comb, nugras; toratorai
combine, pul 6., qat 5.
come, mule, nug 2., rasu, va, van, vano
come out, avu 2.
comet, vitu-asuasu
command, vatra*n*
common, purei, pul, savsavawora
compact, qolo, vagarat 1.
companion, pulsala, ta 4., tua
company, sul, vavtigiu
compassion, magarosa
compensate, avtogo, sako
complete, mawia, nov, qet, vun, wono
conceal, tavun, vat*n*orag
conceive, wune
concerning, ape
condition, matevui
conch, tauwe
condemn, veveg
conduct, *v.* tak; *n.* togara
confident, apesov
confused, kakalatoga, popolotag, valakorag, valerag
conspicuous, ma*n*a*n*a, wotwot
constantly, vagae, vagoar
consult, vono
contend, varlai
continue, taso, vagae
contort, pilotag
contract, kolo, sis 5.
contradict, leasag
contribute, sargag 1., sogo
convey, mulevag, tak, vanogag, vantak, vile
cook, laqan, qaranis, san 2., taru, ur 2.
cooked, manoga
cool, molemole
copy, makala, makaliu
coral, las, puna, sile 1.
cord, tali
core, uloi, wiai
corner, sigerai
corpse, tamate
correct, weswes
cough, vuru
count, liwun, vasogo, tiu 2.
country, vanua
court, sara
covenant, vatavata
cover, lil, luqai, qava, tapur, taqava, vataqav

covet, arike
cower, sus 3.
cowry, womotar, woqage, worawerawe
crab, garuwe, gatou, gave
crack, gaga, toqal
crackle, laklak, nase, qae 2.
crafty, nurnurug
cram, soso, vasusmag
crash, toqal
crawfish, ura 3.
crawl, kalo 3., rusun
creak, gior, nir 2., ori
crease, pilita
create, tin
creditor, tag-pug
creek, salea
creep, kalo 3., magun
creeper, gae
cripple, mawea
crocodile, via 2.
crook, qale 2., qelu
crooked, gaqale, kekeluag, perir
crop, n. gavut ; v. nol
cross, lagau, levegao, pala, wolowolo
crouch, sis 5.
crow, kokorako
crowd, n. sul, vavtigiu ; maliqo, sasalev ; v. vaqir, varir
crown, vara 5.
cruel, matawovat
crumb, vainiu
crumple, kukulmatag
crush, manoa, ninag, qisan
cry, areare, awo, nere 2., rarao, tani
cuckoo, wiswisiroa
cull, gin, vas
cunning, nunurug
cup, lasa, vinlasa
curdle, golo 3., putoa, uwauwa
curl, lete 2., pilolo, pilu, pipisiag, war
current, ar 1., gar 5., rere 2.
curse, varowog, vasir, vivnag
curve, pelu
cut, ari, goro, got, naras, pari 1., sal 1., tara, teve, toto 2., ut 1.
cuttlefish, taqonag
cylinder, wowaiaga

D

daily, valqon
dam, vin, tin 3.
damage, kas, sanrag
damp, nene, nima
dance, lakalaka, lena; vagalul
danger, gona, vagona 1.
dare, nom-mot
dark, qon, siliga, talkov
darken, garasilsil, kov, vasiliag
dash, a 3., lekir, taso, tete 3.
daub, poi, sarava
daughter, natui tavine
daughter-in-law, qaliga, tawarig
dawn, nera
day, maran, qon
dazzle, govgov
dead, mate
deadly, matemate
deaf, qorowono
deal, tirag ; wol
dear, meratape
dearth, maro, raravea
death, matea
debt, pug
decay, naru
deceit, galeva
deceive, gale, meregale, nule, pula, son, vun 3.
deck, v. sagilo
deck, n. qeaqea, taqava
declare, gaganag, manasag
decorate, sagilo, valakas
deep, piroro, roro 2., vagis
defecate, tatave
defend, tigoro
deficient, masale
defy, put, uloulon
degrees, tintiu
delay, maul, vaninag
delirious, gato, lera
dense, wonowono
deny, leasag, tala 1.
descend, siwo, taqel
descendant, tupui
deserve, sar
desert, vanameag, wou 2.; toavtag
desire, maros, toron
desist, sur 5.
desolate, mamagese, wou 2.
despise, sur-tagtageag, valigtag, vasigtag
destroy, tagea
dew, mewu
diarrhœa, sisire, were

die, mate
differ, sasae, sea
difficult, gona
dig, gil, nur, sug 2., vut
diligent, ma*n*as, matanur
dim, maravrav
diminish, mantagai, toto 1.
din, qorogatagata
dip, manig, tav, tuk
dirt, gawur, lepa, pulua
dirtiness, lepava
dirty, lepa, pulua
dish, tapera, tapia
disk, masoe
disobey, leasag, lol, siriga, tames, wales
disorder, popolotag
disposition, matevui
dispute, leasag, vagalateg
distant, aras, asau
distinguish, varirgala, veveg
distress, ganawono, sagevule
distribute, aseg, tirag
disturb, anu*m*ag, gagaqor, ge-risris, lakosa, tiko
dive, manig, towola
diverge, vasipa 1.
divert, vasipa 2.
divide, aseg, palala, searag, wora
divine, soilo
divulge, nir 1.
dizzy, maaniani
do, gapalag, ge, na 4.
docile, mamaru
dodge, vaesu
dog, kurut
door, gatava, matei*m*a, matetipatipag
dot, toi 2., tumui
double, luqe, pala, qolo
doubt, lolovaruarua, nomvaruarua
dove, mantap, mara, qona
down, siwo, sur
down, *n*. avuai, pusa 2.
drag, ramo, rave
dragonfly, roropei
draw, nana, ramo, rave, rurus, sara 2. saro, sir 2. ; uka
dread, kikina
dream, qore
dregs, samai
drift, rerevag, sale 2.
drill, warir

drink, inna 2., un
drip, terep, tir 1.
drive, ara, poarag, vatoav, vure
drizzle, samsam
droop, manol
drop, sakarag, samar, tavamasu, tir 1.
dropsy, pura
drown, tul
drowsy, maloaloa, matmatuav
drum, *n*. kore, vatgeuro, vatnoro ; *v*. atu 2., avut 3., pala 4.
drumstick, gavetlamalama, gavettultul, qatavuvut
dry, kor, mamasa, rano, rara 2., sim 2., takorkor, tarekrek, tawu*n*wu*n*, wakewake, wor
duck, qage
duck, *v*. tapesura
dull, qatwono
dumb, luto, pona
dun, gagapiag
dung, tae
duration, tuai
dusk, muluuav, rav
dust, gagasiu, wuwuai
dwarf, ganae
dwell, toga
dwindle, mar
dye, sala 4.

E

each, val
eager, lolotutun, matakalava
ear, qoroi
ear-ornament, vananqoroi
early, nunuuwa
earth, tano
earthquake, rir
east, mateloa, rowo
easy, masur, togawora
eat, gan, gara, kur, nalo, pig
eaves, goloi
ebb, meat
echo, nanare
eclipse, mate
edge, matai, ret, tagataga, togosiu
eel, marea
egg, toliu
elastic, tamatug
elbow, maluk, sigrai
eloquent, lineul
elsewhere, avea we sea

embark, rap, vega
ember, tanos, tawene, taweris
embrace, garovag, goro 3.
emerge, uto, vinir
employ, gis 1.
employer, tagiu
empty, gariawasa, qega, uro, wawae, wegowego
enclose, kokor, kokos, nin, ninin
encounter, varnina, vatatu, tos
encourage, vasosov
end, *n.* ulusui; *v.* mot 2., paso, vunvun; *on end*, vatut, votur
endeavour, galoi
endure, toga, virig
enemy, tavalalea, tavalavagalo
energy, tiuegaro
engage, gona, ligog
enlighten, sinar, valawar
enlightenment, lolomaran
enough, purat, sasarita
enquire, varus
entangle, gona
enter, pata, saro, sopata
entice, awo 2., pea
entire, tatapuga, wono
entrails, tinaeai, tinai
entreat, tias
envelope, lolos
envy, matawolowolo
equal, sar 1., sasarita
err, ava, lera, sipa 1.
error, lerava, lilil
establish, vatira
even, sasarita, valuwia, vasartag
evening, ravrav
ever, galava, tuai, vagae
every, val 5.
everything, savasava
everywhere, valval 2.
evil, mala, tatas
exact, namalag, waririag
exaggerate, gawo 1., puso
example, makaliu
exceedingly, aneane, ras 1., tutras
excessive, munqoro
exchange, valete
excite, iraka, mataka; vasosov
excrement, tae
excuse, tul 5.
expire, mapsag mot
explain, vavaul

extended, paparau
eye, matai; *v.* matag
eyebrow, kilsai

F

face, nagoi
fade, golo
faggot, tatagiu
fail, ae 1., ava, masale 1.
faint, malewa, mate
fair, lul, manawo, pita, vulasa
faith, nomtup
fall, masu
false, galegale
falsehood, galeva
fame, roroi
family, veve 2.
famine, maro, raravea, uroiva
famish, uro
famous, ronoga
fan, gavug, qit, rivriv
far, aqit, gavig, ras 1., sau
farewell, vatlag
fast, maremare, netenete, warget gaplot; *v.* gargara mamasa, matir wora, val 1.
fat, garake, masopsop, tutup
father, mama, tama
fathom, rova
fatigue, nala
fault, pug, pugai
favour, ilo mana
favourite, wowut
fear, gogolo, mataglag
feast, ganagana, kolekole
feather, ului
feeble, galo 2., mageregero
feed, pugas, tokos, vanan, wuras
feel, rono 3.
feign, gale
fellow, valui, tua
female, tavine, vavine
fence, geara, nin; av 5.
ferment, goqo
fern, gaqir, puget, qatia, toale, vuge
fester, maniga
fetch, tak
fever, tutunsag
few, tapai
fibre, gae
fierce, kita
fight, vagalo, varvus

figure, tarapei
fill, ura, vawonot
film, pesiu
filth, lepa
filthy, pulsama, pulua
fin, pagpagoai, panei
final, paspasoanai, vunvunanai
find, suar
finger, pisui, 1st, sis vanua ; 2nd, malawosal ; 3rd, togtogewia ; little, pisuarig, gogoragvalis
finial, wutuai
finish, paso, un 4.
fire, av 1.
firebrand, gartanasul
firefly, muleqleq
firewood, lito
firm, netenete, nev, pup 2., sor 1., tiriaga, varaget
first, amoa, moai
firstborn, matagaraqa, moemera
firstfruit, sawaliu
first-time, qara, raka, taqai, totowo 2.
fish, iga ; *v.* rave, vanona
fish-fence, wona
fish-trap, wowor 1.
fist, waig
fit, *adj.* sasarita ; *v.* gara 1. vasarig ; *n.* mateawot
flake, av 4.
flame, *n.* garameav ; malawo ; *v.* lawa, lolowo
flank, kikiu, pagigiu
flap, gava, lapa, rope
flare, lolowo, peperoworowo
flash, gapilwana
flat, paloloi, taptapapa, taqeaqea, wawana ; *n.* rata
flatten, qean, qearag, valaqat
flatter, son
flay, sis 3.
flea, qoe ta Maori
flee, toa
flesh, visogoi
flinch, tatige
fling, savrag, vivir
float, sale 2., uto ; *n.* wouto
flock, vavtigiu
flog, loas, towos
flow, sale 3., rue, wera 1.
flower, tawaga ; *n.* tawagasiu, wutui
fluid, ligligira ; ligiu, pei
fluff, avuai

flutter, gava
fly, *n.* lano
fly, *v.* a 3., gava, leqa, rowo, sale, tavtete
foam, muromurosa, usa
fold, kokorou, les 2., luqe
follow, sir 2., tataga
food, sinaga
fool, qaqae, tupa
foot, malekai, ranoi
footprint, malekai
forbid, gatogoro
forefather, tupui
forefinger, sis-vanua
forehead, wareai
foreign, Tona
forerun, sala, tursalemoa
forest, mot 1., uta 1.
forget, loloqon, qalena, titatala
forgive, nomvitag
fork, sana, wanarai
form, tarapei
former, moai
formerly, amoa, tuai
fornication, pakapaka, petepete
forsake, toavtag
forth, at, lue
fortieth, sanavul vavatiu
forty, sanavul vat
forward, at, taso, vasurat
foster, tokos
fount, matepei
four, vat 1.
fourth, vavatiu
fowl, kokok, toa 1.
fragment, garatai, vainiu
free, wasawasa ; *v.* ul
freely, sogov
freight, rene
frequent, vagaqoqo
fresh, qaro, qolo
friend, pul, pulsala
frighten, kikina
fringe, samui
from, a 2., ma 2. 3., nan
front, nagoi
froth, moromorosa
frown, manitnit
fruit, woai ; *v.* uwa
fuel, lito
full, liwat, toqo 1., ura 1.
fullgrown, matua, tamatua
fungus, qero

furl, lil
further, taso

G

gag, tiga
gain, wane
gall, siu 1.
gap, masaoi
gape, gara, mamaova, nira 2., wana 1.
garden, tuqei, utag
garland, makomako
garment, malo, siopa
gasp, nosa, soro, wana
gate, mategeara
gather, gogorag, lolona, nene, sara 3.
gaze, sagarag
general, solorag
gentle, malumlum
ghost, tamate
giddy, maaniani
gift, tapeva
gills, wanwanai
gird, rot
girdle, rotig
girl, malamala
girlhood, tanomalamala
give, la, le, sogo 1., sueg, vile, ukeg; *up*, makarag
glad, malakalaka
glance, tika
glide, siolo
glisten, wolwolul
globe, woai
glue, pulut, gapulut
glutinous, gagapiaga
gnaw, kur, nau, roto
go, mule, nun 2., soat, va, van, vano
go-between, tinanai
good, matai 2., wia
gourd, wotavai
graft, sou 2.
grandchild, tupui
grandparent, tupui
grant, ukeg, vasoal
grasp, gavir, pulun, takuk, takul
grass, magoto, valis
grasshopper, paut
grater, vai, vea 2.
gratis, mamasa, sogov
grave, qarana
grease, nimiu
great, lava, liwoa, poa

green, gesagesaga, turturuga, wa qaro
grey, teretere
grey hair, mausa, ul-varuci
grief, lolowono
grin, ninisa
grip, gintag
groan, momoro, mur, ririnitiga
grope, tatatano
grove, mo 2.
ground, tano
grow, poa, rip, sug 3., totou;
grudge, gogoroi, nor 2.
grumble, wutoto
grunt, nora, soro
guard, ilogoro, kokomag, saqat,
guest, tawu
guide, ave, tursalemoa
gullet, puepuei, tano-nolonolo
gully, qarana
gulp, garapul, tolov
gum, manaroi; pul, waliai
gush, solasola

H

habit, avu 2.
hack, toto
Hades, Panoi
hair, ului, untai, vului
hairy, untaga
half, tavaliu
ham, wowotaga
hammer, was 1., woso
hand, lima, panei, paniu
handfull, gawu
handiwork, tanopanei
handle, pale, sariu 2.
handsome, lulum, pula
hang, name, sak, siplag, tako kau
hanker, ararike
happen, qalo
happy, malakalaka
harass, anumag
harbour, ruruna
hard, garo 1, lulaktera, mai togtogoa
hardly, viviris
harmless, tapeto
haste, titkeliga, vagogoi, va val 2.
hat, tamate
hatch, tere

hatchet, lakae, parapara
hate, loloanu, lolotatas, *n*ustup, sonago, so*n*us
have, amen, taur
hawk, mala ; *v. n*arag
haze, marav
he, ineia
head, qatiu
headlong, valiliug
heal, koko, lulus, mawo
heap, *v.* av 5., avtag, soko, vagoro, vawoi ; *n.* polotai, vavtigiu
hear, ro*n*otag
hearken, tinqoro
heart, wonatuat
heat, laviai, titkeliga
heaven, tuka, vunana
heavy, mava, qatwono
heedless, linalina, *n*ompurei, sakerewaka, tatalaiga
heel, vulagei
heir, lelesiu
help, piri*n*, tuan
helpless, gagalo
hence, iake at
her, ineia, a 1.; poss. ga 1., ma 1., *m*o 1., no, pula
here, iake, iloke, ke, nake
hesitate, varakalkal, varerere
hew, tara 1.
hibiscus, qagala, toape, varu
hide, gavug, li*n*arag, suspata, vara 3., vat*n*orag
high, eleele, kekete, saloi, tole
hill, tauwe, vutvut
hillock, raketea, vutvut
him, ineia, a 1.
hinder, *adj.*, tagir
hinderpart, kulai, pup, tagir
hip, pugiu
hire, qil, tomava, tove
his, ga 1. ; ma 1., *m*o 1., no, pula
hiss, is 2.
hit, qalo, tiqa*n*, tut, vus ; map
hitch, saneg, sano
hither, ma 3.
hoarse, arosa
hoary, mausa
hog, qoe
hoist, tape 3.
hold, pul 7., takau, takul, taur
hole, koloi, matemalue, qara*n*a, qarasiu, wowoai ; maluelue

hollow, loloi, qilosiu
holy, ro*n*o, tapu
hook, gau, qale ; *v.* kau
hoot, wara
hop, get 2., negneg, ninit
hope, maros-nerei
hospitable, vasgot
hot, titin, titkeliga, vevera
house, ima
householder, tagiima, tagvanua
hover, vatoga
how, gasavai, gasei ; ta*m*a
how many, visa
howl, ulo 3.
huddle, waig
hug, gorovag
hum, mum, vuv
humble, aperig, pepewu
hump, kula, qote
hundred, melnol
hundredth, melnolanai
hunger, malinsala, uro
hurry, gasuware, lavlavat, vasosov
hurt, rosag, vivtig ; manaras
husband, rasoai
husk, viniu ; *v.* goso 1., wesar
hut, paito

I

I, inau, nau, na
idle, mara*n*
ignorant, loloqo*n*, lineline, qure
ill, gopa, mala 2., tatas
illness, gopae
image, totogale, nule, liwautamate, wetamaragai
imitate, makala
impudent, pugete, waratagai
in, lo 2., lele 2.
inaccessible, vagis
inarticulate, wure
incline, lin
increase, poa, qoqo
indistinct, malol
inert, rono
infant, meomeo, pipio, tete
inferior, parasiu, purei
inhabit, togag
inherit, leles
initiate, tiro 1.
injure, kas
inland, sage 2.
inlet, reve

insect, manu
insensible, vakovako
insert, arovag, gaslag, gasomag
inside, lele, lolo
insipid, tamtamelea
interchange, varleas
interest, rowo 3.
interval, masal, masaoi
intervene, tinanai
intricate, gona
introduce, sura 1.
involucre, virotiu
inward, loloi
irregular, kakalotoga, popolotag, vaqirqir, vaseisei
irrigate, vasaleg
irritate, anumag
island, vanua, vanua-mot
islet, nat-vanua
it, ineia, a 1.
itch, gagara, gagarat

J

jagged, sipa 2., wowo
jaw, palasai
jealous, qonag
jeer, apes
jest, pula 1.
job, goso
join, pasau, sou 2., viletuwale
joint, qaloi, soua
joke, poro
journey, muleva, vauoga
joy, malakalaka
judge, veveg
juice, ligiu
jump, rowo, wal

K

keep, koko
keep off, ara
kernel, wiai
kick, vara
kidney, womakemake
kill, mate
kin, sogoi
kind, matevui, sale 5. ; lolotape, lolowia
kindle, ona
kindred, sogoi, veve
kinsman, sogoi, tasiu
kite, mala, rea 2.
knee, qaui

kneel, vatieqau
knife, gasal, igot
knob, qat 3.
knock, nene, nene, nina 3., tipa, wota 3.
knot, v. gona, vagae; n. kasavui, nanoi, qaloi 1., qogorai
know, gilala, ilo 1., lolomaran
knuckle, qaloi

L

lace, ritata, tata 3.
ladder, tigarapita
lagoon, namo
lame, qages
land, vanua
landing-place, salava, sao 1., tursao
large, lava, liwoa, poa
lash, gatowos
last, lego, paspasoanai, vunvunanai
lasting, galava
late, tugtug
latrina, tas
laugh, marae
laughter, maraeva
launch, vasale 2.
lay, lano 2., map, salag, salo, taqai, tar 1., vanov
layer, tawtawui
law, lea
lazy, maran
lead, sapalo, sapan, tiramoai, tursalemoa ; *water* leqa 1.
leaf, naui, nosiu, wisiu
leafy, ropa
lean, lin, matueg, pesenag, sov, tapatiu, tapelin, tapesopeso, taqa, tue, vatieg
leap, rowo, sale 4., wal 1.
leave, mapvitag, toavtag, tivitag, vanovtag, vitag
left, galao, tama
leg, ranoi, tura
lend, galtag, tawe
lengthen, sou
lengthways, ararovag, vatut
let, mamasug, maukeg, ukeg, varoro
level, rata, saragao, sasagav, sasarita, tansag, vasartag
liberal, alena, vasoal
lick, namis
lid, matai
lie, risa 1., taqa

lie, gale, galeva
life, esuva
lift, lana, raka, sau 1., tut 7., vereg, wotlag
light, *n*. maran
light, *adj*. maaeae, mataketake; malagesa, pita
lightning, vila 1., wana 2.
like, sar, sasarita; *adv*. tama
like, *v*. maros
liken, tenegag
limb, soai
line, gae, garatigiu, matesala; *v*. vear
linger, maul
lintel, qatmateima
lip, nusui
liquid, *n*. ligiu, pei; *adj*. ligligira
listen, tinqoro
listless, rono
little, mantagai, rig, tapai, tapiai, tiktik
live, esu, maur, toga
liver, varai
load, rene
loathe, loloanu, suwa
locust, paut, puna 1.
lofty, eleele, ketekete
log, vatiu 2.
loin, werei
lone, magasei
long, paparau, malowo, reve, tole; *v*. taka, tarasa
look, ate, ilo, matag, patarag, sagarag
loom, ani
loop, maslag
loose, *v*. koe, tig 1., ukeg, ul 2., walaso; *adj*. makoekoe, malagolago, masug
lop, rur 1.
lopsided, tavalvasei
lose, tagea, valenai
loud, poa
louse, wut
love, tape 2., tapeva
low, pepewu, roro 2., teqa
lower, *v*. varoro
lower, taqa
lump, qote, sila 1., wai, wal 2., woai
lumpy, vagotgot
lungs, anus
luxuriant, tuloqloq

M

mad, lera, tamat-lelera

madrepore, puna 2.
maggot, ulo 1.
maimed, mut
make, ge, na 4., tin 1.
male, ata, mereata; *flower*, parou
malice, lologona, nor 2.
man, ta 5., tamaur, tanun
manifest, nana 1.
manner, linai
many, purat, qoqo, visa, vaga; pepe 3., pul 9., raka 3., rowo 4., sage 4., sogo 3., sorako, tal 5., taqa 4., tira 2.
mark, vaglala
marry, lag
mash, lot
mask, tamate
mast, turgae
mat, epa, non, tapanau, tapenon; *v*. vau 2.
match, sar, val 3.
mate, ta, tua
matter, pus, nana, sisia
mature, matua
mawkish, tamtamelea
me, inau
measure, towo, vara 2.
mediator, tinanai
medicine, pei-mana
meek, lolo-pepewu
meet, sogoro, tatu, teqa, valgoro, vanina, varnina, vatatu, vug
melt, sale, vasale 1.
member, soai
memorial, ilo-nagoi, manvetvet
mend, mon, wono, wurvag
merciful, magarosa
mercy, magarosa
mere, vires, wia, wora
mesh, ava 3., masaoi
messenger, sala 2.
middle, tinai, vatitnai
midrib, sinai
meteor, mao
midnight, tineqon
mildew, mao 1., punmao, win
mind, nonom, nonomia
mingle, lor
mirror, tironin
mischief, ganor, kiskislag
miserable, lopsag, magarosa
mislead, nule, valeri
miss, aso, ava, taliaso, variava

mist, marav, viviv
mistake, ava
mix, lor, loriag
mock, porosag, valesam
molest, ge
money, som
month, vula
moon, vula
moreover, mula*n*
morning, maran, matava
morrow, maran
morsel, wotorai
mosquito, namu
moss, lumuta
mossy, lumtaga
mote, naenaeai
moth, rupe
mother, veve
mould, tano ; punmao
mountain, tauwe
mourn, naro, ruru*n*tap, val 1.
mouth, valai
move, al, nua 2., sere, tapariu, *tr.* vut
much, aneane
mucus, nav, *n*or
mud, mormor
muddy, gagavu, puaka
multiply, vaqoqo
multitude, sul
mumble, rut
murder, nawono
murmur, wutoto
mutter, va*n*ut
my, ga 1., ma 1., *m*o 1., no, pula
mysterious, vagis

N

nail, pismaremare ; pis Marawa
naked, mamasa
name, sasai ; geue, sava
namesake, tavalasasai
nape, taqalsai
narrow, kokota
nature, matevui
nautilus, wegoa, wotiva
navel, putoi
neap, makira
near, noga 1., pete*n*, rasu, rivtag, wenwen
neck, nenei
neglect, wirig, wuro
neighbour, tagvanua

nephew, vana*n*oi
nest, nigiu
net, gape
new, garaqa
newcomer, salagaraqa
news, roroi
nibble, ani, tum
nice, neremot, ta*n*o 2.
night, qon
nine, laveavat
ninth, lavevatiu
nip, ganig, gin, koto, *n*ol, wales
no, tagai
nod, mawui
noise, qaloi
noisy, wulano
none, tagai
noon, liwomaran
nose, manui
nosegay, ita
nostril, qara*n* manui
not, gate, tagai, pea 1., te 2., tete 2.
notch, nar, wowo
nothing, pea 1., tagai
nourish, tokos
now, iake, iloke, nake
numb, matewonowono
number, vasogo
nutmeg, naraga

O

obedient, meremanas
obey, manas, mawui
oblique, tasosama
obscure, kov
obstinate, qatwono, waswat
obstruct, pur
occupy, goua
occur, tatu
odd, valuava
often, vagae, vagapurat, vagaqoqo
oil, ligiu, nimiu ; *v.* men
old, tuai, tavutiu ; magatea, tamaragai
on, alo 1., avune, ivune, vawo
once, vatuwale
one, tuwale
only, gap, gese, nu*n*us, tuwale, vires, wora
ooze, tawa 1.
open, lala 1., lik, like, maea, malue, tawaga, tawala, vatawerai, waga 1., waka, wawao

INDEX 303

opening, gaplei, matai
openly, maea, wag
oppose, wales
opposite, sar 1.
oppress, wonot
order, vareg, vatran ; tarnag
orifice, matai, qarasiu
ornament, sagiai 2., sagilo
orphan, manua
other, tuara
our, ga, ma 1., mo 2., no 1., pula
out, lue, avarea
outline, taqaniu
outrigger, sama
outside, avarea, vareai
outward, at
oval, tolgan, tolpuasa
oven, qaranis, um
over, goro, lagau, makei, sal, tavala
overcast, malakoukou
overflow, tapalinrag
overgrow, malakoukou, malalolou, mot
overlap, variaso
overlie, taqar
owe, pug
owl, manwara, wis
owner, tagiu

P

pack, sogon, soso 2.
paddle, *n.* wose ; *v.* sua
pain, magav, rakut, vivtig, woso 3.
paint, gapulut ; lamas
pair, valu 1.
palate, mamaroi
pale, malagesa
palm, metigtig ; tawerai
palpitate, vin
palsy, mawea
panicle, wutui
panpipe, vigo
pant, nala, nosa, sova
pap, qis 1.
pare, sipa 2., sirvag
part, takelei, tavaliu ; *v.* sese ; makarag ; nin 1.
particle, nacnaeai
partition, nin 1.
pass, goro 4., sara 2., saru 3., sola, sneg, usurag
patch, mon, wono
path, matesala, manursala, sala 1.

patient, malumuaga, rono
pattern, makaliu
pay, rusag, tomava, wono
peace, tamata
peaceable, tapeto, vasgot
peaked, tetevei
pearl, vila 2.
peck, tere
peel, *n.* viniu; *v.* lil, tawaluka, wil, waga 2.
peer, patarag
pelt, patun, siwor
people, sul
pepper, gea, matavgae
perceive, gilala, ilo
perch, sagera
perfect, taurmate
perhaps, wun
perish, tagea
permit, ukeg
perpetual, galava
persuade, pes
persist, kat, waririag
pestle, vatgelot
pet, peas
pick, pit, sipe, terc, vas
picture, totogale
piece, takelei
pierce, as 1., sar 4., sis 1.
pig, karwae, qoe
pigeon, mara, qona
pile, av 5.
pillow, ilina
pin, vino
pinch, gin, ginit, nere, wales
pipe, viawo 1., wegore
pistil, putoi
pit, qarana
pith, utoi
pitiful, magarosa
pitiless, matagaro
pity, magarosa
place, masaoi, tanoi, vatiu 1.; *v.* map, vapteg, vatira
plain, *n.* rata
plainly, vaglala
plait, vau 2., vir, wota 5.
plan, sora, vasarig
planet, masoe
plank, irav
plant, *v.* riv 1.
platform, qea, wona
platter, tapera, tapia

play, oraora
pleasant, pula 2.
plenty, linlin, purat
plot, sora
pluck, pit, sav 2., save, savir, tawo
plug, topur
plunge, manig, towola
poet, towtowo-as
point, matai, nere 1., nusui, togoi
point, v. sis 2.
poison, vanan pal, vun
poke, gis 2., sura, tike
pool, mino, qilo
poor, magarosa, masara
porpoise, ririgo
portent, rono 2.
position, tanoi, togava
post, pete, tursana, vatira
pottle, pora 2.
pour, lin, liwo, sar 2., tivui, vanin, vuvui
pout, veru
power, mana
practice, vatanau
praise, varean
pray, tataro
precious, matavires
precipice, lalaviai, malnai, tutnai
prefer, ilo-sur
pregnant, tiana
prepare, gismamate
presently, rigrig, tiqa 4.
preserve, vaesu
press, aue, pipin, qeret, qisan
presume, somtak
pretty, lulum
prick, as 1., sarig
prickle, qaligiu, sakariu, saniu
prickly, saksakara
principal, moai, tur
print, qisan
prise, lipe, uqa 1.
probably, wun
proclaim, sororo
prod, got
profit, rowo, waue
profitless, sasawuara
prohibit, tapu
project, sila 1., vut 3., wura
promise, ligog, vatavata
prone, taqa, vataqav
proof, vaglala
prop, rapai, tiga ; *n.* tura

property, pulai
propitiate, tape
prophesy, ligog
prosper, vagisgis
prostrate, rowotaqa, surag
protect, tigoro, varug
protrude, lete
proud, vaketeag, vinvin
prove, sargag 1.
proverb, tenegag
provoke, uloulog
public, maea
pucker, pilita
puff, pup 3.
pull, koe, lue, ramo, rave, savir, sese, teter, wanana
pumice, wouromao
punish, sar 1.
pupil, pulei, womera
pure, matartoga
purlin, gawolowolo, varat
pus, nana
push, sura 1., tigonag, tuqerag, varir, vasosov, vasurat
put, map ; *put on, off*, saru 1.; *put out*, pun

Q

quarrel, kesa, vargol, varleasag, vartike
quench, vuvui
quick, gaplot, tagogoi, vivis-mot
quicken, vasosov
quiet, ape 3., nae, rorono, tapeto
quit, toavtag
quite, qet, tutras
quiver, *n.* qatmona
quiver, *v.* govgov

R

race, variara
radiant, lenas
raft, wosomaimai
rafter, gaso
rage, saqo, sova
rain, samal, wena
rainbow, gasiosio
raise, lalanag, sau, tape 3.
rake, gagar
range, lanon, tarnag
rank, taran
rank, *adj.* roma
rap, nini

rasp, vai, vea 2.
rasp, rasa
rat, gasuwe
rather, mano, vara 6.
rattle, nora 3., noro ; wouorouoro
ravage, sanrag
raw, gele, gira, qaro
ray, sinoi
ray, var 1.
reach, kaka, nina 1., reret
ready, salamate, taurmate
real, tur 3.
reason, manigiu ; nonomia
rebound, taswamule, titlop, vasugag
receive, lav, taur
receptacle, tanoi
reciprocal, var 3.
reckless, garviteg, nawono
reckon, vasogo
recoil, titlop, vasugag
recollect, nomkel, nomsuar
reconcile, ulsag
recover, esu, mauka, *na*narag 2., rip, vamleg 1.
red, memea, mera, soroga ; mal
redeem, wol kel, tun kel
reed, togo, viso
reef, *n*olmeat
reek, asu
reel, tatiotio
reflection, niniai ; rara*n*
refresh, mule 2.
refuge, ruru*n*a
refuse, gogoroi, irvitag, siriga
refuse, *n*. *m*asoko, sa*m*ai
regard, ronom
regular, vagaegae
reject, gevtag, isvitag, titis, tivtag
rejoice, lakalaka, qara 2.
relapse, tagege
relate, gaganag, kakakae, usur
reluctant, ir, taritrit
remain, toga
remember, nomkel, ilo nagoi
remnant, garatai, malisiu
remove, kearag, sagaro, sei 2., sese, sirig
rend, gape, sare
renown, ronoga
repair, mon, wurvag
repine, arike
report, roro 1., vagaov
reproach, vasir

reprove, *n*orov, vatowo
reserve, soloi
resist, tames
resolve, nom-*m*ot 1.
resound, nu*n*
responsible, tiravag
rest, mapsag, sov
restrain, ora
return, kel, keluva, nug kel, vamleg 2., vusiag
revenge, rapa
revive, esu
revolve, galolo, gole, vatawilgag
reward, sar 1.
rheumatism, rurus, siwosiwo
rib, lalai
rich, *m*eresavasava, *m*eresom
ridge, tegoi ; qatii*m*a
ridge-pole, qatsuna
right, matua ; taniniga
rim, togosiu
rind, vanarasiu, viniu
ringlet, qoleqole
ripe, matua, mena, umsa
ripple, lul 3.
rise, get, kalo, kekete, raka, rowo, tavaraka, wot
road, matesala, sala 1.
roar, murmur
roast, *r*anai, tin
rock, vat, vatgao
rock, *v.* gole
rod, wotai
roe, niwiai
roll, mapitu, tagole, tapeli*n*, tapit, tatawilwil, wil
roller, ilano
roof, kulei*m*a
room, masaoi, nin; vatamaea
root, gariu
rope, tali
rot, naru
rough, taoraora, wotwotora
round, sotal, tal 2.; *adj.* tapogopogo, waliog
rouse, gir 2., vasosov, vava*n*ov
row, garatigiu, tapare
rub, asa, pun, rasa, sis 3., soso 1.
rubbish, *m*asoko, oroi, woriu
rudder, turwose
ruddy, galgalamemea
ruin, mosiu, oroi
rule, riga 1.

x

rump, werei
run, valago ; sale
run against, teqa
rush, tagora
rust, waliai
rustle, mama, nase

S

sacred, rono 2., tapu
sacrifice, oloolo
safe, sarawag, wasawasa
safety, esuva
sago, ota
sail, n. epa, gapaue ; *v.* ga*m*o
sake, manigiu
saliva, ninisa
salt, gatasig, nawo, tas 1.
salute, varpis
same, ran
sand, one 2.
sandstone, rotava
sap, piai, totoai
sapling, wotai
sauce, woro
save, vaesu
say, gaganag, vava 2., vet
scab, purusa
scale, vanerasiu
scalp, garov, viu-qatiu
scarcity, gan rowo, maro, raravea
scare, kikina
scatter, salena, savur, wowor 3.
scent, punai
scoff, aresag, *m*araesag
scold, gol
scoop, warir
scorch, lalav
scorpion, golowa*n*ara
scrape, gagarag, gar, gor, ras, rasa, rasag
scratch, gagata, kakarmag, karu
scream, qara 2.
screen, no*n* 1., qarqar
screw, war
scum, morosai
sea, lama 1., tas 1.
scam, vinit
search, sike
seaside, lau
season, tau 1.
seat, v. vapteg ; *n.* putei, tanopute
second, varuei
secret, palu, pata, puel

see, ilo, matarag, patarag
seed, sivui
seedling, wotai
seek, sike, soke 1.
seize, takul, wosag
select, ilo-raka
self, magesei ; kel
sell, girei, *n*arag, tuvag, wol
send, suware, vatra*n*
sensation, rono 3.
sense, ronovia
separate, adj. sea ; *v.* ase, vilewora
serve, lapasag, rowogis, rowovag
set, map, saneg, tape 2., tar*n*ag, tai 2., tiu, vapteg, vatira
settle, rowopute, sage 1., togag
sever, worn 1.
sew, susur
shade, malumalu ; *v.* giskov
shadow, niniai
shady, malakoukou, malalolou
shake, act. gagamail, *m*agoa, nene nag, no*n*erag, rino, ru*m*eg ; *neut* gogolo, so*n*erag
shallow, saqareta, teqa, vana, vatrei
shame, apemaragai
shameless, waratagai, wasmata
shape, n. tarapei ; *v.* tit
share, aseg, ti*n*ag
shark, pagoa
sharp, tup
sharpen, vului
shave, sir 1., sirvag
shawl, viog
sheathe, saromag
shed, paito
shed, v. nun 1
shell, pi*n*ai, viniu
shelter, ruruna
shield, tigoro
shin, wo*n*arasiu
shine, lawa, sar 3., si*n*a, valawar
*shoal, m*alo ; vavtigiu
shoot, tiqa 1., vene 1.
shoot, salitiu, *v.* salit, wisiu
shore; lau, panpanlau, salilina
*short, m*ot 2., qan, qatua, qatutui, tu 5., valuava
shorten, vakokot
shoulder, qat-panei, qatag-panei
shout, rorov, walul
shove, sulet, tikarag, tuqerag
shovel, sula

show, gaganag
shower, tiutiu 2.
shred, masarei
shriek, qara 2.
shrink, galete, gogo, ir, kik, kiksag, kiria, kora, sis 5., tasusus
shrivel, gogo, mimir
shrug, gagapior, ir
shudder, rere 1.
shuffle, riu
shut, tipag, vataqav
shutter, gatava
shy, apekiria, apemaragai, qonag
sick, gopa
sickness, gopae
side, kikiu, pagigiu, taqaniu, tavalai, tavaliu
sideways, para 1.
sift, sene
sight, ilova
sign, tul 2., vaglala, vareg
silence, roronoa
silent, uaenae, rorono
silly, tupa
simple, qae
sinew, gapalao
sing, aleg, raw, sur
single, tolig, tuwale
sink, mar, mawowo, roro 2., tavaroro, tavasur, tul 1.
sinnet, gaun
sip, nim, sim 1.
sister, tasiu, tuaga 1., tutuai
sister-in-law, walu
sit, pute
size, tarapei
skeleton, qalqalosur
skilful, menaro, matagis, mawu
skim, saova 2.
skin, viniu, vinitiu
skinny, viniga
skirt, goloi
sky, tuka
slab, irav, tapa 1.
slack, matugtug
slander, goso 2.
slap, wosa 2.
sleek, masopsop
sleep, v. matur ; n. maturiva
sleepiness, matamaragai
slender, maretret, rereosa
slice, sipa 2.
slime, nimsai

sling, talvava
slip, masisgala, sasaroro 1., sis 6., susug, tamalaso, tanu, tasgala, taslana, tavarasu, tavaul
slippery, genetas, tas 4., tasgala
slope, malnai, tutnai, navaisa, parapara
slough, maului, nl 5., uroi
slow, malapusa, rute
slumber, matuav
small, mauoa, mantagai, natiu, rig 2., vutrai
smart, mamarisa
smash, munrag, pura, rosag, visarag
smear, il, non 1.
smell, puna, ronotag, somau ; n. sagiai 1.
smile, marae
smoke, asu
smooth, malmaluga, nimtoto, ninin, pasiu ; tanoag, vuv 2.
smoulder, vagarat 1.
snail, wolipelipe
snake, mai, mata, matmatantas
snap, koto, sakir
snare, sal 2., tiag
snatch, wosag
sneeze, matia
snore, nora
snort, nora
snout, nere 1., norin, nusiu
snuff, pupun
soak, nunur 2., tuk
soar, sale 2.
sob, masorsor
soft, garamama, magavgav, magisgis, magorgor, maloplop, malumlum
soften, mana 5., noga 2.
soil, tano
sole, malekai, tawerai ; lele
solid, popo, wono
solitary, magesei, puel
some, tea, tuaniu, tuara ; one sei 1.
something, sava
son, natiu
song, as 4., towo
soon, rigrig
soothe, mei
sore, gagan, gov, livit, maniga, vuna
sorrow, lolowono
sort, matevui, sale 5.
soul, atai
sound, n. linai, maaviu, qaloi 2., roroi ; v. tani

sour, gogona, namisa
source, matai, qetegiu
sow, mala
space, maea, masaoi, vatamaea
spare, gogoroi
spark, peperoworowo, tawene
speak, gato, vava 2., vet, wawan
spear, isar
speckled, tiqatiqa
speech, gato, vavae ; alan, tore
spicules, aliaga
spider, marawu
spike, nug, saniu
spin, tia, vatagoloi
spine, gatogoi, wotutgag
spirit, vui
spit, anus
splice, roa, sou 2.
splinter, tangesar
split, garawora, nig, tit, wora
spoil, sanrag
sponge, manman-pul
spontaneous, matapui, tava
sport, oraora
spot, malaqo, tiqatiqa, toi 2., tumui
spout, sarsar, viawo
spray, gagas-nawo, garusa, nawo
spread, gan 2., gno, gara 3. kcke, lil, lolo, tansag, taworag, vear, wor, wosalag
spring, n. matepei, matevura ; v. ana, laqa, rowo, vura, wura
springy, lalapcag
sprinkle, savur, wowor 3.
sprout, salit
spurt, tiqa 3., vinrag
squall, siwo 2.
squash, tawosa
squat, luk, sus 3.
squeak, nere 2.
squeeze, gavir, qeqe, totos
stab, as 1., sar 4.
stage, qea
stagger, tarerere, tatietic
stain, sala 4.
stake, gatipa
stalk, sariu 2.
stammer, tataturag
stamp, ane 2., put, qisan, vara 1.
stand, tira, tur
star, masoe, vitu
stare, sagarag
start, gisraka, tatige, vet 2.

startle, malarowo, sigerag, tagut
starve, uro
stay, goara, gogae, toga, ur ; rapai, roa, vatoga
steal, palu
steam, gagas-pei, sasawui
steep, kalokalo, sasargava
steer, alo 3., ave
stem, qetegiu, sariu
step, au 2., lago, vara ; n. tano-ververesag
stern, kerei
stick, nariu, qat 3., wotai ; *walk with*, tigo ; v. kata, pul, pulut ; mao 2. ; sisgag
sticky, gavetaga
stiff, gagao 2., gatig, get 1., lova, togtogoa
stifle, maumau
still, adv. gale, ti ; adj. rorono
sting, walaso
stingy, matamotmot, nis
stir, anor, kal, tiko, vasosov ; nalia
stomach, toqai, gavut
stone, vat
stoop, kaltatau
stop, gis goro, mot 2., vatoga ; qiroso
store, sogon
storm, lan-vus
story, kakakae
stow, sogon
straight, gagao, tagologolo, taninene, taniniga, totowo
strain, sene 2., virsig
strait, masorowolue
strange, sea
stranger, salavano, tawu
stray, lelena, lera
strength, tinegaro, vavakae
strengthen, varagai, vatogar, vilit
stretch, kaka, lalaus, rereg, rova, rowoag, sigag, teter, totor
strike, qalo, sipa, vus ; av 4.
string, gae ; vutug
stringy, gaela, magaegae
strip, v. ar 2., nig 2., sasar, save
striped, kalan, ravraveag, resa
strive, varlai
stroke, vusiva ; v. sarav
stroll, nal
strong, maremare, vaka, vakasai
stubborn, mastag, wasvat
stuff, soso 2.

stumble, tutuag
stump, totiu
stumpy, tamunmun
stunt, gora 3.
stupid, lol, loloqon
stutter, gatpoa, nanora, taturag
subside, mar, qega, sotoga
substitute, sesei
subtract, lareag
succeed, lai, qalo, vagisgis, vakalasai
succession, tapare, usurag
succulent, quio
such, tama
suck, sus 2., riv 2.
sucker, suliu
suckle, sus 2.
sudden, malarowo
suffer, rono, ronotag
suffice, tira
sugarcane, tou 3.
suit, sar 1., taram
sulky, mero
sulphur, malau-gan-Qat
summer, magoto
sun, loa
sunder, wora
sunrising, tano-rowo-ne-loa
sup, riv 2., sim 1.
supine, taragiate
support, rapai
sure, sov
surf, nawo
surfboard, tapa.
surface, nagoi
surge, rep
surround, pue 2., taliog
swallow, nolo, tignag ; *n.* gapagapa
swamp, puaka
swarm, gara 3., taum
sway, tatiotio
sweat, susrag
swear, vagogonag
sweat, lalais
sweep, gora 1., sara 2., talova, werasa
sweet, neremot, soke 2.
swell, riga 2., sis 4.
swift, gaplot, piro, sene 1.
swim, gagao 1., gan 3., garu, sale, towola
swing, tape 2., tapeir, tue
swoon, mate-mule

T

tack, sama
tackle, renren
tail, goloi
take, la, lav, le ; sao 2., sau
tale, kakakae
talk, gato, kae, vava
tall, eleele, malawo, tole
tame, mamaru, peas
tap, nene 2., noro
taste, nam 4., nim ilo, ronotag, *n.* linai
tasteless, malea, tamtamelea
tattoo, pul, vus
teach, vatogo
tear, v. gagaro, gape 2., sare
tear, n. surmata
tease, kalit, tiarag, tias, vakolesag
tedious, vule
tell, gaganag, kakae, vet
temper, matevui
temperate, ora
tempest, lan-vus
temple, paririu
tempt, gale, ge ilo, meregale
temptation, galea
tenacious, gapapiaga, pulut
tendon, gapalao
tendril, qoroi, tuei
tentacle, karui
terrible, kikina, matawutiana
terrify, vakikina
tetanus, palao
tether, ligo
than, nan
thank, varean
that, ilone, ine, ne
thatch, n. noota ; *v.* patu, tuwur, vus 3.
their, ga 1., ma 1., mo 1., no, pula
theft, palpal
them, ineira, ra ; *dual* rara, *trial* ratol
then, alo ine, ilone, qara 1.
thence, ma aia
there, aia, iane, ne ; apena
thereby, nia
therefore, manigiu
therein, alolona
thereupon, qara
these, iake, iloke
they, ineira
thick, matoltol, qatmatau
thicket, mogaegae
thieve, pal

thigh, vinai
thin, mavinvin, tapatiu 2.
thing, gene, sava
think, nonom
third, vatoliu
thirst, marou
this, ia, iake, ike, iloke
thither, at aia
thorn, sakariu
thorny, saksakara
thoroughly, mou, ran
those, iane, ilone, ragai
thou, iniko, ko
thought, nonomia
thousand, tar 2.
thread, gae, *v.* tapare
threaten, gagar
three, tol
threshold, tiqanal
thrice, vagatol
throat, nenei, puepuei
throb, vin
through, lue, raveaglue
throw, sargag 2., savrag, tapul, vivir
thrust, sura, tuqerag
thumb, pislava, womrematig
thump, tut
thunder, manu 3.
thus, tamaike
thwart, wolowolo
thy, ga 1., ma 1., mo 1., no, pula
tickle, magalgal, magirit
tide, meat, rere, rue
tie, ligo, nit, rot, vagae, vil; *n.* garotrot
tight, netenete, rait, togtogoa
till, gai 3.
tilt, tape 5.
time, masaoi, tanoi
time-to-time, titi, tiutiu
tinder, vinpeapea
tip, pilei, ulusui; *v.* tape 2., vin
tiptoe, autegteg, ninit, varaketekete
tire, nala, pugapuga, sur 5., vule
to, a 2., i 1., sur 9.
to-day, qarig, anaqarig
toe, pis-ranoi
together, pulpul, saratuwale, tuwale
to-morrow, maran
tongs, ipala
tongue, garameai
too, mulan
tool, ren

tooth, liwoi, patiu
toothless, liwopas
top, qasai, wotnai
torch, nosin, pul, sin
toss, avtag, namalag
totter, taavaava
touch, tano 1.
tough, gaela, magaegae, valaklak
track, malekai, lelevai
train, taur, vakalov
trample, ane, varas
transient, sagesaru
transplant, sug 2.
traveller, salavano
trap, qat-tiatiag
tread, vara 1.
tree, tangae
tree-fern, qatia
tremble, gogolo, maragai, rere 1., vagarir
trepang, wosoisoi
trick, gale, pulapula
trickle, lona, sasawa, sun
trifle, gewora, taroi
trot, sawasawa
trouble, matikotiko, woga
true, nun 3.
trumpet, tauwe
trunk, tan 2., turiai
trust, matueg, sov.
try, galoi, ge-ilo, vasaram
tuber, woai
tuft, wutui
turmeric, ano
turn, ate, galolo, gole, kerevag, kilau, lana, olo 1., sipa, soleas, solil, somot, tala 1., taliag, tikula, vakel, viro 2., vusiag, wil
turn, ris, sor 2., wog
turns, varleas, varsesci
turtle, uwā 3.
tusk, liwoi, patiu
twice, vagarua
twilight, malurav
twin, varapa
twine, galo 1., galomtag
twirl, naliog
twist, galoag, gaqoag, gawo 2., gawoag, pipis, qes, sawag, vir, war, wel
twitch, kan, numeg

U

ulcer, maniga

INDEX 311

umbrella, vilog
unbind, ul
uncle, maraui
under, alalane, ilalane, sur siwo
underside, lanai
understand, gilala, lolomaran
undertake, taka
undo, tig, ul 2.
unequal, valuava
uneven, vaseisei
unfasten, tig, ul 2.
unfeeling, matagaro, matmetir
unfold, lil, lik, tatawakal, ul 2.
unfurl, lil
unite, pultuwate, viletuwale
unhitch, is 3.
unhurt, tatapuga
unless, ta tagai
unmarried, qilowar
unmerciful, matagaro
unpack, sese
unravel, ul 2.
unripe, qaro, tarave
unskilful, qure
unsteady, lana, malesles, tarerere
untie, tig 1., ul 2.
until, gai
unwilling, viviris
unwind, ul 2.
up, kalo, raka, rowo, sage
uphill, sage
upon, vawo, vunai
upper, vunai
upright, totoepe, vatut, votur
uproar, gorogoro 3.
upward, lan 2., raka
urge, ute
urgent, gagarakae
urine, meme
us, inina, ikamam
useless, vanameag
usurp, tasior
utterly, ran, sopun

V

vagabond, ranoal
vain, ae, matila, wawae
valiant, vavaka
valley, qarana
valour, vavakae
variegated, valeleas
various, seasea
vast, lama 2.

vehement, sasakariga, warwar
vein, gapalao
verandah, malmaluima
very, aneane, ras, tur 3.
vex, anumag
vibrate, magmagon
victorious, lalakete
vie, varlai
village, vanua, varea
vision, iloilo, ilova
visit, atev, vailo
voice, linai
volcano, vuro
vomit, lua
voyage, gamova, suava

W

wade, garu
wages, rusai
wail, ruruntap
waist, tano-rotrotig
wait, nare, nerei
wake, mamata, vavanov
walk, mule, tale
walking-stick, qat-tigo
wall, geara, paparis, wona
wallow, lolosa
wander, lera, nonono
wane, mantagai
want, maros
wanton, nawono, tatalaiga
ward, tigoro
warm, tutun
warn, nir, norag, torag, turag
warp, lete
wash, aqo, savula, sug 1., vasug
waste, gariawasa, manamana 2., one, vanameag
watch, mamata
water, pei ; v. tivui, tiwe, vuvui
watercourse, masalepei
waterfall, siriv
waterhole, rewu
waterspout, tamate garugaru
wattle, palag
wattles, nannanai
wave, rep
wave, v. avtag
waver, nom-varuarua
wax, tul 7.
way, matesala
we, ikamam, inina
weak, mageregere malawo, malewa

weapon, renren
wear, saru
weary, apemot, vulo
weatherbeaten, nagomasansan
weave, tia 1, vau 2.
wedding, wosolagia
weed, *n.* wotano ; *v.* nowo, wowor 2.
weep, rarao, sanita, tani, uwauwalog
weigh, mava, tia
west, siwo
wet, nima
whale, kio
what, sava
wheel, taplagolago
when, naisa, anaisa, ananaisa
whence, mavea
where, vea 1.
whet, vului 1.
which, avea
while, alo 2.
whine, nere 2., were 2.
whip, gatowos, qat-towos ; *v.* towos
whirl, naliog, qoriag
whirlwind, lan-ta-Panoi
whirr, viu, viv 1.
whisper, vono
whistle, galaviv, milos, was 2., wog 1., wos
white, aqaga, owo, wenewene, wowoga
whither, ivea
who, sava, sei 1.
whole, nol, wono
why, ape sava, apesa
wicked, ganganor
wide, one 1., tawala, tawela
widow, naro
wife, rasoai
wild, kita, pulemot, turtur
wilful, mastag, qatwono
will, maros
wince, nir, tatige
wind, gavgavui, lan
wind, tia 5., til 3., vivis
windbound, wata
windfall, topa
wing, panei
wink, mataperu
winnow, gavug
winter, rara

wipe, man, sarav
wisdom, gilaglala, lolomaran
wish, maros
witchcraft, gaqaleva
with, ama 2., amen, ma, me 2., mun nia
wither, gogo, golo 2.
withhold, gogoroi
within, lele
without, varea
withstand, tiragoro, vatriv
wizard, gismana
wizen, qaqa
woman, tavine, vavine
womb, tanegana, toqai
wonder, *v.* mamakei ; *n.* vasasa
wood, tangae
word, vavae
work, mawmawui ; manasia
world, marama
worm, sulate
worn, mosiu
worry, anumag, vavagaile
wound, mataqa
wrap, mona
wreath, mako
wrestle, variukuk
wring, galolo, gavir, vir, woro
wrinkle, mimir, pilita
wrist, tano-vivis-panei
write, rave
writhe, gagao, lolosa, pilosag
wrong, valil

Y

yam, nam
yawn, mamaova
year, tau 1.
yearn, tarasa
yellow, anoano, pepega, tapana
yesterday, ananora ; *day before*, ani risa, risa
yet, qale, tiqa 4.
yoke, iwa
yolk, rerena
young, qolo, tawurmera
you, kamiu, *dual*, kamurua, *tria* kamtol
your, ga 1., ma 1., mo 1., no, pula
youth, lumagav

R. Clay & Sons, Ltd., London & Bungay.

www.ingramcontent.com/pod-product-compliance
Lightning Source LLC
Chambersburg PA
CBHW021154230426
43667CB00006B/388